ADULT LIFE

Second Edition

ADULT LIFE

Developmental Processes

Judith Stevens-Long

California State University, Los Angeles

 **MAYFIELD PUBLISHING COMPANY**

Library of Congress Catalog Card Number: 83-062836
International Standard Book Number: 0-87484-577-7

Manufactured in the United States of America
10   9   8   7   6   5   4

Mayfield Publishing Company, 285 Hamilton Avenue, Palo Alto, California 94301

Sponsoring editor: Franklin C. Graham / *Manuscript editor:* Joy Dickinson / *Managing
editor:* Pat Herbst / *Art director:* Nancy Sears / *Photo researcher:* Lindsay Kefauver /
Interior and cover designer: Sharon Smith / *Illustrator:* Irene Imfeld / *Production managers:*
Ron Newcomer & Associates and Cathy Willkie / *Compositor:* Computer Typesetting
Services, Inc. / *Printer and binder:* R. R. Donnelley

Text Credits

PAGE 117 J. L. Horn, G. Donaldson, and R. Engstrom, "Apprehension, Memory, and Fluid Intel-
ligence in Adulthood," *Research on Aging*, 3, 1981, pp. 33–84. Copyright © 1981 by *Research on
Aging.* Reprinted by permission of Sage Publications, Inc.
PAGES 146–49 "Love Scale Questionnaire" from *Styles of Loving* by Marcia Lasswell and Nor-
man M. Lobsenz. Copyright © 1980 by Marcia Lasswell and Norman M. Lobsenz. Reprinted
by permission of Doubleday & Co., Inc.
PAGE 275 From *Midpoint and Other Poems* by John Updike. Copyright © 1969 by Alfred A.
Knopf, Inc. Reprinted by permission of the publisher.
PAGE 284 Nancy Wadsworth Denney, "Aging and Cognitive Change" in *Handbook of Develop-
mental Psychology*, edited by Benjamin B. Wolman, © 1982, p. 819. Reprinted by permission
of Prentice-Hall, Inc., Englewood Cliffs, N.J.
PAGE 306 Reprinted by permission of the publisher, from Michael P. Farrell and Stanley D.
Rosenberg, *Men at Midlife* (Boston: Auburn House Publishing Company, 1981).
PAGE 338 From *Little Treasury of Modern Poetry: English & American*, edited by Oscar Wil-
liams, 1946. Published by Charles Scribner's Sons.
PAGE 472 From "When I'm Sixty-Four" (John Lennon and Paul McCartney). Copyright © 1967,
Northern Songs Limited. All rights for the U.S.A., Mexico, and the Philippines controlled by
Maclen Music, Inc., c/o ATV Music Corp., 6255 Sunset Blvd., Los Angeles, California 90028.
Used by permission. All rights reserved.
PAGE 512 From *Without Feathers* by Woody Allen. Copyright © 1975 by Random House, Inc.
Reprinted by permission of the publisher.

TO MY FRIENDS

Contents

Preface

In the years between the first and second editions of this book, trips to the library became emotionally charged experiences. As I walked toward the shelves, I was always both excited and dismayed. What new ideas would I find? Would I have time to get them into the new text before the presses rolled? The literature has been growing so quickly that nearly every chapter needed to be rewritten and hundreds of new references added.

In particular, the chapters on love and marriage in early adulthood and on family at midlife have been restructured in light of new developments. As a more interactive view of human development takes hold, it is not surprising that one of the first areas to benefit is research on coupling and parenting. Our understanding of fathering has been enormously expanded, and the role of children in the shaping of their parents' lives has finally been acknowledged if not extensively researched.

The idea that human development is multicausal and multidirectional has profoundly influenced thinking about intellectual performance in adulthood as well as every aspect of personality research. Thus I scrapped the treatments of intelligence, learning, memory, cognition, personality traits, and midlife crisis that I wrote in 1979 and began again. New information from longitudinal and sequential research studies has appeared nearly every month, and you will find it scattered through nearly every chapter, but especially those on middle age.

New thoughts on retirement, work, leisure, and the physical environment in later life contributed mightily to the revision of Chapters 10 and 11, and the changing attitudes of the whole society toward the subject of aging cast these chapters in an entirely different light. I think you will find them much more positive and upbeat than their predecessors in the earlier book.

Probably the chapter least altered by the passing years is the last. While there is evidence that attitudes toward death and dying have changed somewhat, especially among people in the health care services, new theoretical concepts and complex research schemes have not emerged. Perhaps in a society where the life span continues to increase, most of us still hope we will never have to deal with those issues.

The organization of the second edition is much like that of the first, using chronology as a clothesline from which to hang the many topic areas of interest in the study of adult life. The placement of a particular topic is always at issue in this approach, but the device is appealing and stimulating for students. It simplifies the task of filing and retrieving information and allows the teacher a natural, logical progression through the course materials.

The organization within each chronological section moves from the inner context of development to the personal context to the extended context. Topics like biology and sensation, perception and cognition, are included in the chapters on the inner context. Research in personality and the development of intimate relationships fills the chapters on the personal context. Literature about family, work, and the social and physical environment is the focus of material on the extended context. Again, the placement of a topic may be debatable, but the debate can serve as a stimulus for class discussion.

The first two chapters are devoted to a discussion of theory and methodology. These subjects are sometimes perceived as difficult by students, but the progress that has been made in the study of adult development in the past few years is so obvious and so intriguing that students feel rewarded when given an opportunity to examine even the most sophisticated analyses. These chapters also give the instructor an opportunity to show that the study of human development can be as fulfilling to the scientifically oriented student as it is to the student interested in its application to everyday life.

Finally, in this edition you will find four sections called "Perspectives." The objective of these pages was twofold. First, they allowed me to talk to the reader in a more personal way. Second, they provided an arena in which I felt comfortable speculating about both the future of the research and the future of aging itself. I hope these new additions lead to entertaining discussions and an occasional flight of fantasy. Thinking about the future of aging is, after all, thinking about our personal futures, and what is more fascinating than that?

Judith Stevens-Long

Acknowledgments

If there is a more interactive, transactional, dialectic process than writing a new edition, I know it not. Unlike a child, a book can be changed and there is no doubt at all that it changes the writer. I am indebted to all the researchers and thinkers who have interacted with me and my book through their work and often through their personal input. These include, of course, professional reviewers, among whom I am especially grateful to Elaine Blakemore of the University of Wisconsin at Eau Claire, Margaret P. Isaac of Central State University, Eugene L. McGarry of California State University at Fullerton, and Clara C. Pratt of Oregon State University.

The staff at Mayfield has, as usual, done a wonderful job. Their attention is always personal and their product is always professional. Thanks, everyone—but this time especially to Pat Herbst and Frank Graham, who phoned me what seemed to be nearly every day as the deadlines approached. Also, honorable mention to Joy Dickinson, who did a terrific job of copyediting despite the birth pangs of a new career in design. It never ceases to amaze me that no matter how many drafts you write or how many books you finish, there is always something more to learn from a good editor.

As always, I want to acknowledge my friends Richard Lavender and Sandy Rader, Nancy Cobb and Mike Wapner, Joyce and David Bock, Pat Hodges, Valerie Israel, Deirdre Platt, Tom and Cindy Gray, Kathy and Rick Neumeyer, Stuart Fischoff, Harold Gottlieb, Nina Colwill, Tom Graham, Jim Laughrun, and all the others who read and commented and helped. With their support, *Adult Life* is definitely better the second time around.

JS-L

ADULT LIFE

I

Foundations of Adult Development and Aging

Introduction:

The Study of
Adult Life

The longer I live
The more beautiful life becomes.

FRANK LLOYD WRIGHT

This book is about the last two-thirds of the human life course as seen by developmental scientists—the psychologists, sociologists, and biologists who have begun to study the life span as a whole. *Development*, in all its aspects, refers to the series of changes that individuals characteristically experience as they progress in time toward maturity and through adulthood into old age (Birren, 1964). It follows that the study of human development over the *life span* includes every phase, every period, and every aspect of age-related change, from the moment of conception to the moment of death.

Until sometime in the 1960s, the study of human development focused almost exclusively on the first few years of the life span. Driven by tremendous social and economic forces such as the spread of compulsory education and the exclusion of children from the labor force, the demand for information on learning and maturation in children and adolescents grew steadily through the first half of the twentieth century. As teachers, parents, and researchers began to appreciate the complexity of childhood and adolescence, these periods were increasingly perceived as distinctive, each holding important mysteries of its own. Today, we speak of infancy and toddlerhood, the preschool child, middle childhood, early and late adolescence; there is evidence, moreover, that adolescence will soon be viewed in terms of early, middle, and late phases (Stevens-Long and Cobb, 1983).

For some reason, however, the richness and variety of research about childhood and adolescence did little to stimulate interest in adult life as a distinct period or group of periods in the life span. Most often, adulthood has been viewed, somewhat negatively, as at most a two-stage period, first, of stability (if not stagnation) without noticeable change, followed by an inevitable second stage of degeneration or regression. Perhaps, like physicians in need of healing themselves, developmental researchers did not see their own adulthood as appropriate subject matter. Perhaps the study of adult life awaited social and economic forces similar to those that focused attention on childhood. In any event, this book is touched by the irony that the study of adult development is still in its infancy compared with the relatively mature state of knowledge about childhood and adolescence.

In the United States through the mid-twentieth century, adulthood has rarely been studied at all as a period of life, although some attention has been given to the problems of the elderly in terms of poverty, housing, and the delivery of medical services. During World War I, interest in the psychology of adults was foreshadowed by a heated public debate over the use of intelligence tests to screen army recruits, and even now, issues of intelligence often dominate the research about adulthood. Certainly, however, notions such as the assets of maturity or the possibility of development after adolescence were given short shrift for decades even after the study of childhood began in earnest. (Although some brilliant life-span developmentalists were publishing in Germany around the turn of the century, their sophisticated insights did not have much impact on subsequent research and writing until very recently [Reinert, 1979; Baltes, 1979]).

It has been largely since the 1950s that researchers have come to recognize the importance of understanding the biological, psychological, and social realities of adulthood. As a large number of healthy, active people begin to live longer and longer lives, it has become increasingly apparent that we will need much more detailed and accurate information if our society is truly to grow old gracefully.

THE GRAYING OF AMERICA

In the fifteen years between 1959 and 1975, some 50,000 articles on aging and gerontology appeared in scholarly books and journals, outstripping the total for all the previous years of this century. Between 1969 and 1975, the number of doctoral dissertations on aging increased by 50 percent the total number of dissertations on the topic since the turn of the century (Birren, 1980). One obvious reason for such rapidly growing interest lies in another set of expanding figures: census data for the years since World War II indicate that there are many more adults than there used to be, and they are living longer than ever before in history.

Some of the numbers from the Census Bureau are startling. During the past hundred years, the elderly population in the United States has increased seventeen fold, three times the rate of the general population, with the age group over 75 the fastest growing segment. In 1900, people over 65 represented just 4 percent of the population. Today, this group includes over 10 percent of the population; by the year 2030, the number will double again, representing as much as 16 to 17 percent of the population (Decker, 1980; Cox, 1978; U.S. Department of Commerce, 1981; Butler and Lewis, 1977). Figure I.1 presents census figures on the growth of the older population in the United States for the twentieth century.

This unprecedented increase in the number of people over 65 years old is a product of two kinds of population trends. First, over the past 70 to 80 years, death rates for older people have consistently declined. Around the turn of the century, the average life span for American males was

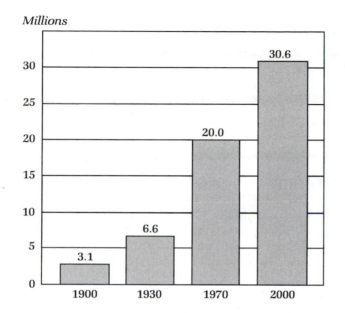

Millions

FIGURE I.1
Growth of the older population in the twentieth century

SOURCE: U.S. Department of Health, Education, and Welfare, Facts About Older Americans, 1976 (Washington, D.C.: U.S. Government Printing Office, 1976).

Year	Total	Men	Women	Ratio Women/Men
1900	3,080,000	1,555,000	1,525,000	98/100
1930	6,634,000	3,325,000	3,309,000	100/100
1970	19,972,000	8,367,000	11,605,000	139/100
1975	22,400,000	9,172,000	13,228,000	144/100
2000	30,600,000	12,041,000	18,558,000	154/100

about 45, and the death rate for both sexes stood at about 20 per thousand. Today, the average life span has increased to 67 for males (75 for females), and the death rate has declined to 8.9 deaths per thousand. Moreover, there are more than one million people over age 85 and at least 106,000 who have survived beyond the age of 100 (U.S. Department of Commerce, 1981; 1973; U.S. Department of Health, Education and Welfare, 1976a; Butler and Lewis, 1977). The *Los Angeles Times* recently reported (June 2, 1983) the Department of Agriculture now estimates that by the year 2000, the average life span for American males will be over 75 years, and for American females, over 86 years.

Anticipated medical advances in the next few years may very likely extend the life span of many by another substantial period. It has been estimated, for instance, that control of the major cardiovascular and renal diseases would grant the average person an additional ten years (Decker, 1980).

The second major trend in the "graying of America" is the declining birth rate. As data for the 1980 census reveal, females aged 18 to 24 are having fewer babies than the government considers necessary to maintain the population at its current size (U.S. Department of Commerce, 1981). This means a larger and larger part of the population consists of adults rather than children or adolescents. As a result, the median age in the United States has been increasing for at least 150 years, from 16.7 in 1820 to 25.3 in 1920, and finally to age 30 in 1980. The *median age* divides the population into two equal age groups. That is, in 1980 one-half of the population was older than 30 and one-half was younger.

The age distribution of the population is of interest to us in many ways. Current U.S. census data show that the age distribution as it stands is very different from the classic population "pyramid" that characterized most of history. Look, for example, at the first graph in Figure I.2, which shows age groupings for the United States in 1900. As you can see, the number of people in each age group declined steadily from birth to death, resulting in a pyramid-shaped representation of the total population (the bar at the top is slightly bigger than the one below only because it represents a wider age range, 65–100+).

Now examine the next two graphs (see Figures I.2 and I.3), which show age distributions for 1940 and 1970. Notice the slight ballooning of the 1940 graph for the 40–54 age range. A second, more intriguing bulge occurs in the 1970 graph for the age range 5–24. These two pronounced bubbles are the two baby booms that followed both World War I and World War II. They have been a source of interest and speculation for psychologists and sociologists since the dimensions of the second baby boom became apparent in the late 1950s (Wheeler, 1974; Decker, 1980).

THE BABY BOOMS

There is little doubt that, as one author put it, "the sudden 'dumping' of an extraordinarily large number of people of a specific age on society necessarily results in certain upheavals in that society's institutions" (Bowmer, 1980, p. 29). Some have suggested that the much-discussed "generation gap" of the 1960s was spawned by these two population bubbles, since many of the parents of the second, post–World War II boom were themselves products of the post–World War I birth explosion.

Certainly, American businesses discovered the buying power of adolescents as the first members of the second baby boom became teenagers. As they become adults, their power continues to be apparent. Automobile makers are busy producing small, economical family cars designed for the

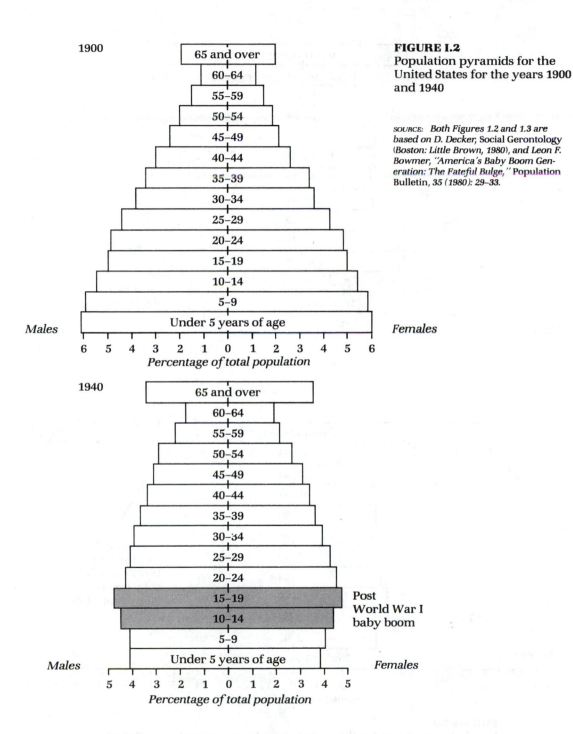

1900

65 and over
60–64
55–59
50–54
45–49
40–44
35–39
30–34
25–29
20–24
15–19
10–14
5–9
Under 5 years of age

Males
Females

6 5 4 3 2 1 0 1 2 3 4 5 6
Percentage of total population

1940

65 and over
60–64
55–59
50–54
45–49
40–44
35–39
30–34
25–29
20–24
15–19
10–14
5–9
Under 5 years of age

Post
World War I
baby boom

Males
Females

5 4 3 2 1 0 1 2 3 4 5
Percentage of total population

FIGURE I.2
Population pyramids for the
United States for the years 1900
and 1940

SOURCE: *Both Figures 1.2 and 1.3 are
based on D. Decker, Social Gerontology
(Boston: Little Brown, 1980), and Leon F.
Bowmer, "America's Baby Boom Gen-
eration: The Fateful Bulge," Population
Bulletin, 35 (1980): 29–33.*

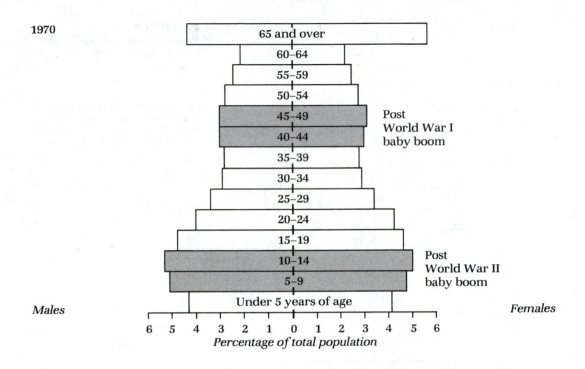

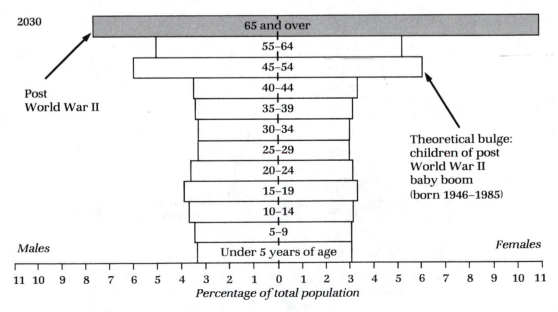

FIGURE I.3
Population pyramids for the United States for the years 1970 and 2030

People who share the same historical period, even the same family, do so only in a limited sense, for the accumulating record of life events affects the interpretation and meaning of all experience.

small, energy-conscious families of today's adults. Demand for single-family dwellings has risen so intensely since the post–World War II baby boom came of age that owning a house may be a bygone part of the American dream.

Especially as the members of the baby-boom generation pass thirty, the whole culture seems much more concerned with maturity and aging. Moisturizer has been added to the makeup that used to cover pimples. Pop psychology books on adult life and aging are consistently on the best-seller list. Descriptions of how to achieve healthy longevity proliferate, meeting the demands of what has been called the "command generation," the moving bubble of the post-war years.

It is not simply their sheer numbers, however, that explain the tremendous impact this generation has had on the social fabric. The numbers alone do not adequately describe today's adults. The changes are qualitative as well as quantitative.

THE NEW ADULT

Today's adults not only live longer, but are also richer, more vigorous, and, therefore, more powerful than ever. Even the most senior groups are socially active and politically savvy. The emergence of the Gray Panthers is eloquent testimony to the growing involvement of older Americans, and the panthers do not stalk the political jungles alone. Such organizations as the National Association of Retired Persons and the National Council of Senior Citizens are becoming major political interest groups (Uhlenberg, 1979).

Today's older adults are more financially secure and better educated than ever before. For example, the number of elderly living below the poverty level dropped from 37.2 percent in 1959 to 15.7 percent in 1974 (Uhlenberg, 1979). If we compare the average educational level of those turning sixty-five in 1975 (10.5 years) with those who died (8.9 years), the difference is quite impressive. By the year 2030, when almost all the second baby-boom generation will be over sixty-five, the level of education is expected to rise to 11.9. Some have predicted that the modal (most common) educational level of the elderly in the twenty-first century will include some college experience. And this crop of college students from the late 1970s "can probably expect to live almost as long after retirement age as they did before it" (Cox, 1978, p. 1).

How will these more educated, more sophisticated people respond to the changes of aging? It already seems apparent that they will demand more attention and more information from political, social, and economic institutions. The children of the sixties will grow old, but they seem unlikely to do so silently. This generation also seems more completely aware of the enormity and pace of social change than any before it and may be more interested in the need to control and direct the future. As Alvin Toffler has argued in *The Third Wave* (1980), adults seem to be consciously choosing to lead lives that make more emotional and social sense than their predecessors'.

Toffler also reminds us that people can make such choices only when they have some idea what to expect. All of us can expect to age. Further study of adulthood and aging should help us all to make the wise, sensible decisions Toffler believes will lead to a better future. A definition of the normal expectable life cycle, for example, could help people forecast their personal future, plan ahead for major turning points, and create islands of stability during unstable times. Such possibilities provide special impetus for new work on maturing, aging, and death (Neugarten, 1969).

THE STUDY OF ADULT DEVELOPMENT

George Bernard Shaw once said that "everything happens to everybody sooner or later if there is enough time." Part of both the excitement and the frustration of studying adult development is that it does, indeed, encompass everything: all the events that adults typically experience, as well as their physical and emotional impact.

Faced with this wealth of material, researchers and writers are continually attempting to define the study of adult development in a more comprehensive, meaningful way. James Birren (1980), from whom we shall hear much more, has outlined at least two basic approaches to organizing research and theory. He sees it, first, as the attempt to understand the evolution and genetic limits of longevity and behavior and, second, as the exploration of how such limits might be modified. Birren tends to be rather biological in his orientation. Other seminal researchers, such as Paul Baltes, believe that approaches like Birren's may focus undue attention on what is universal and irreversible about aging. Baltes believes that our definitions must remain open to new discoveries and to changes in the field of life-span development.

In his own work, Baltes has offered a continuously evolving series of definitions, starting in 1970 with the suggestion that the study of development over the life span is the study of (1) changes within a person, (2) the development of integrated ways of conceptualizing those changes, and (3) the discovery of which observations about one age group apply to other age groups and which observations suggest cause-effect relationships (Baltes and Goulet, 1970). In 1977, Baltes added the study of the modification, or optimization, of change to his earlier definition, and then in 1979 he completely revised his original ideas by calling for the study of the larger context as well as of the individual (Baltes and Willis, 1977; Baltes, 1979). According to Baltes, three significant classes of events must be understood if we are to account for the complexity of life-span development:

1. The biological and environmental events that are strongly associated with chronological age (*normative age-graded influences*). These factors are the ones usually considered in the study of development, like the process of maturation or the analysis of how we acquire age-appropriate behaviors and abilities.

2. The general social and historical background of a particular group of people, born into a culture at the same time (*normative history-graded influences*).

3. Environmental and biological events that do not occur for everyone or occur in regular patterns (*nonnormative influences*). Nonnormative influences include such events as marriage, parenthood, occupational career, health, and so on.

This increased emphasis on the importance of *biocultural context* in human development is associated with a general shift among both psychologists and sociologists from the study of *age-related* change to the study of *time-related* change (Lerner and Ryff, 1978). Richard Lerner and Carol Ryff point out that "one of the first benefits derived from the life-span attention to explanation is the clarification of the age variable as being *noncausal* and inevitably in need of further explanation" (p. 10). In other words, life-span researchers are making it clear that chronological age is only a marker or an index of development, and not an explanation in itself.

The shift from age-related change to time-related change makes it possible to study developmental markers other than chronological age. We may find that life experiences or historical events are useful signposts of individual development as well as development over generations. It is possible, for example, that parenthood precipitates a particular phase of development regardless of the chronological age at which it arrives (Lerner and Ryff, 1978).

In general, the role of context is emphasized more in the study of adult development than it is in the study of childhood and adolescence. In fact, many believe that the interdependence between the person and the environment increases with age, although this does not mean that internal or biological events can be ignored in adults (Birren, 1980).

Finally, as we have noted, some of the recent literature addresses the definition of optimizing, or modifying, age- and time-related changes. What does it mean to grow old gracefully? What are the psychological characteristics that accompany an optimal adjustment to age and aging?

Offering one kind of response to these questions, Birren (1980) has contended that mental health is found in the self-awareness that allows one to maximize pleasure or reward and to avoid pain and discomfort, usually increasing the probability of survival. He believes that beneficial changes in self-evaluation occur as a result of one's attempt to integrate life experiences. Such benefits—derived from the experience of mastery in the emotionally and intellectually demanding situations of adulthood—can help produce what Birren calls the "elite aged": older adults who are "strong yet flexible, feeling yet controlled, living in the present yet planning for tomorrow, feeling less need to justify their past views and behavior, which brings them into the present with pride and strength" (p. 43).

In the rest of this book, we will examine all of these issues of adult development, emphasizing particularly the importance of context as well as biological events in changes over the life course. In spite of the recent growth of research on adult life, we will see that much of the life span—especially the years from twenty to sixty-five—remains in large part unexplored. So that we can most fully understand what has been accomplished, we will begin, in the rest of Part One with a review of the research methodologies and theories that have shaped the study of adult life. In Chapter 1 we will look at what questions are being asked about adult development, what methodologies have been developed to answer them, and how the results are being evaluated. In Chapter 2 we will outline the major models and theories that have both followed from and shaped the process of definition we began to examine in this Introduction.

Our initiation into developmental practice and theory complete, we will proceed to the remaining three parts of the book. There the ordinary course of adult life becomes a structural line for presentation of topics on which information is currently available. This organization, however, is not meant to imply the existence of particular, well-defined stages of adulthood, but rather simply to provide a straightforward, commonsense approach to the material. Thus, marriage, for example, is covered principally in the chapters on early adulthood, not because early adulthood is the best time to marry, but because it is the time when most of us who marry do so for the first time.

The three chronological parts—on early adulthood, middle age, and later life—consist of chapters that examine the biological, psychological, and social events typically associated with that period of the life course. The first chapter in each set outlines the personal context of development: biological and cognitive function, the development of sensory, perceptual, and psychomotor skills as well as health and sexuality. The second chapter in each set is devoted to the interpersonal context—to such topics as attachment, marriage, parenthood, and friendship—and to research on personality. The final chapter in each section covers the social context from work and leisure to the impact of the physical environment, housing, and financial circumstances. The book concludes with a chapter on death and dying as a final context for human development.

At the end of each of the major divisions of the book, you will find a short essay introduced by the title "Perspectives." These sections provide an opportunity for us to examine some of the more speculative ideas and issues that may affect the study of adult development in the future. For example, the biological foundations of aging may be much better understood in the foreseeable future, exerting considerable impact on the study of developmental psychology and sociology. Some of the current, intriguing biological theories are explored in the first Perspectives essay on developmental theories. The other three Perspectives sections deal with the particular biological, social, or psychological forces that might reasonably be expected to affect young adulthood, middle age, and later life.

Chapter 1

The Context of Observation: Problems of Definition and Research in the Study of Adulthood

Sit down before fact as a little child,
be prepared to give up every preconceived notion,
follow humbly wherever and to whatever abyss nature leads,
or you shall learn nothing.

THOMAS HUXLEY

We will now look more closely at some of the most important problems of definition and research that provide a backdrop for understanding both theory and information throughout the rest of this book. In this chapter we will address questions of methodology—questions about what form research ought to take, from matters of research design and data collection to interpretation of information about adult development.

FORMULATING THE QUESTIONS

To begin with the most elementary question, we might simply ask whether it is reasonable to assume that people do indeed change or develop significantly during the course of adulthood. Unfortunately, we won't find an undisputed, definitive answer even at this basic level.

Do Adults Develop?

It has been argued, on the one hand, that the changes of adult life are not of sufficient magnitude, when compared to those of childhood and adolescence, to warrant the label "developmental" (Flavell, 1970), and, certainly, there is evidence that some aspects of experience do not change very dramatically over the years between 20 and 70. For instance, general levels of adjustment, integration, and competence do not change much with age (Newman, 1982; Thomae, 1979; Neugarten, Havighurst and Tobin, 1968). Patterns of social interaction also seem to evolve slowly, if at all, through much of the adult life course. Measures of mood and self-reported happiness do not fluctuate radically between age groups in the adult years; excellent evidence also suggests continuity in intellectual function (Cameron, 1975; Schaie, 1977; 1979).

On the other hand, biographical material and clinical interviews have repeatedly suggested that adults experience many important, if subtle, changes. In one such study, the autobiographies of 180 men and women born around the turn of the century were analyzed in 1965 and then again in 1972 (Thomae, 1979). The average person reported about 17 major changes or turning points over the life course as they had lived it.

Alterations in the subjective aspects of experience are consistently reported by adult subjects. For example, self-esteem and one's attitudes about mastery of the environment or how people deal with their own impulses and how aware they are of their own ideas, attitudes, beliefs, and behavior are all perceived as changing over the years. Adults also report changes in how time seems to pass. Middle-aged males appear to experience the passage of time most quickly, whereas young people describe its passage in less hurried terms (Gould, 1980). These subjective aspects of experience have been called the *executive processes* or *intrapsychic phenomena*. Such changes must be psychological, of course, for the earth rotates on its axis at a steady rate, the seasons change, and the years come and go consistently. In other words, the objective definition of an hour or a week or a month is the same throughout life, but something about the subjective experience of time changes.

Over twenty years ago the social gerontologist Bernice Neugarten wrote that such changes reflect the accumulation of our experience: that people become more complex with time (Neugarten, 1964). She believed that a person's life history, with its growing record of adaptation to biological and social events, results in a continually changing basis within the individual for perceiving and responding to events. In 1979, Han Thomae reiterated this theme in terms of a "continuous sequence of gradual changes" that constitutes the "normal pattern of development throughout the life span" (p. 304).

Of course, the presence of negative change in adult life has always been accepted. Most people, including most developmental researchers, have usually conceptualized the changes of adulthood almost exclusively in terms of decline. The *irreversible decrement model* of aging was supported by the bulk of traditional psychological and social research for several reasons. First, since the larger culture strongly supported (and still largely supports) the stereotype of decrement with advancing age, it is not surprising that American researchers have found evidence of decline in function with age. Researchers are likely, for instance, to look at the functions that probably deteriorate, since there was little common wisdom about areas of improvement or increased maturity. Second, American scientists almost always assume that a person's performance can only increase, decrease, or remain stable. They have rarely considered the possibility that some processes are exceedingly complex and must be treated as an array of functions, some declining with age, some remaining stable or improving, and some even undergoing transformation with the years (Schaie and Hertzog, 1982; Horn, 1982).

Such simple assumptions and simple research approaches are inadequate. As John Nesselroade (1977) put it, "Behavioral change over the life span is a complex, multifaceted phenomenon whose proper study requires the researcher to utilize methodological tools which are sufficiently complex to match and, if necessary, even 'overpower' the data" (p. 59). Just as the irreversible decrement model falls short, so does the notion that people become more mature, complex, discriminating, or intelligent with age. As Richard Lerner and Carol Ryff (1978) have pointed out, a "conceptual and empirical pluralism" is required. In other words, we must be open to many ways of thinking about and looking at the changes that we observe over the life course.

If we as developmental thinkers and researchers are open to the idea that anything can happen—that developmental change can be expansive or decremental or both or even transformational—we will then require some sophisticated research tools. If we add the idea that change may be gradual or fairly rapid, the demands on our research designs are increased because people must be observed over long periods of the life course and at many different times during that span. Even the ways in which we define adulthood may have to vary, depending on the matter being studied.

Dividing Up the Life Course

If we are to observe changes during the life span, it is obvious that we must make comparisons between the behaviors and attitudes characteristic of people at one age and those of people at another age (or, the same people may be compared at different points in the life span). Meaningful differences have been found between age groups separated by twenty or more years, and by as little as a few months (Baltes and Reinert, 1969). Table 1.1 presents a few of the many ways the life span has been divided for the purposes of theory and research.

Any attempt to identify characteristic stages of adulthood is influenced by the strong cultural assumptions that most of us share about how the course of adult life should run—about the supposedly "normal" timing for the major social and psychological events of life. In one study, for example, 84 percent of the people surveyed felt one ought to finish school before twenty-five. Of these same respondents, 70 percent thought a man should choose a career by his mid-twenties, and nearly 90 percent believed a woman should marry between nineteen and twenty-four. There was also general consensus about the appropriate age for grandparenthood, retirement, and a host of other milestones (Neugarten, Moore, and Lowe, 1965).

Although such studies have shown remarkable cultural agreement, consistent class differences in attitudes about the life course have been

TABLE 1.1
Dividing up the life course

Bromley (1974)		Levinson et al. (1974)		Gould (1972)		Havighurst (1972) and Neugarten (1974a)	
Juvenile Phase							
0–11	Childhood					0–6	Early childhood
						6–12	Middle childhood
11–16	Adolescence	16–20	Leaving home	16–18	Ambivalence	13–18	Adolescence
16–20	Transition	20–29	Getting into the world	18–22	Leaving home	18–35	Early adulthood
				22–28	Establishment		
Adult Phase							
20–25	Transition			29–32	Thirties transition		
25–40	Middle adulthood	30–34	Settling down	33–40	Adulthood		
		35–39	BOOM[a]	40–43	Midlife transition	35–60	Middle adulthood
40–60	Late adulthood	40–42	Midlife transition	43–50	Midlife		
		43–50	Restabilization	51–60	Flowering		
60–65	Preretirement					60+	Later maturity
65–70	Retirement					55–75	Young-old
70+	Old age					75+	Old-old
	Terminal stage						

[a]Becoming one's own person

demonstrated as well. For instance, Bernice Neugarten has found that middle-aged, middle-class people usually divide the adult life course at thirty, forty, fifty, and sixty-five, with forty considered the prime of life, fifty labeled middle-age, and seventy seen as old age. In contrast, working-class people view forty as the beginning of middle-age and tend to say that old age begins at sixty (Neugarten, 1968a). Of course, any of these notions can be affected by the work of psychologists and sociologists, especially as it is translated and distributed by the mass media. Books like Daniel Levinson's *Seasons of a Man's Life* (1978), popularized paperbacks on male menopause, or handbooks for retirement planning not only flow from the reality they describe, they also shape that reality. Research has social implications, and the actions of researchers can eventually have an impact on the social system (Meacham, 1980), a notion we shall discuss again later in the chapter.

  In the end, researchers will divide up the life span and choose the segments to be studied on the basis of the subject matter they are investigating. That is, if we were interested in investigating learning and memory, it would be reasonable to compare performance at widely separated points in the life span (e.g., at forty, sixty, and eighty). Political issues, however, may produce meaningful differences over much smaller age spans. Consider how attitudes toward an issue like the military draft can be influenced by rapid social changes. Today, people in their teens, twenties, thirties, forties, and fifties have had very different experiences with the draft and with military service in general.

The last point brings up a critical issue of methodology in developmental psychology. Although there are many differences between people of different ages, and although the same person may be very different from one time to another over the life span, only some of these differences are related to the passage of time in an individual life. Others are far more strongly related to historical time, in several ways. First, the historical period in which the individual grows up, matures, and grows old produces certain behaviors and attitudes. Second, the historical period during which the individual is being observed and measured affects behaviors and attitudes as the researcher sees them. The recognition of historical context as an important determinant of how people age has served as a well-spring for work in research design, statistical analysis, and theory, producing some exciting new resources for developmental scientists.

CONDUCTING THE RESEARCH

Once researchers have determined the issues of life-span development to be investigated, they must grapple with problems of methodology. *Methodology* refers to the principles and strategies involved in the pursuit of knowledge about any scientific subject. In the study of human development, it has been defined as "the principles and strategies involved in the pursuit of knowledge about the way individuals change with time" (Baltes, Reese, and Nesselroade, 1977, p. 14). Methodology includes rules for making observations, for analyzing them, for drawing conclusions, and for generalizing and integrating generalizations in the explanation of a particular phenomenon. Methodology doesn't produce research ideas, but it does provide both rules for translating ideas into testable statements and guidelines for determining the scientific validity, or accuracy, of the statement.

The Validity of Research Designs

To be valid means to be sound and well-founded; to have force, weight, or cogency; to be authoritative. In scientific research, the term *validity* refers to "how accurately a procedure measures what it is supposed to measure" (Achenbach, 1978, p. 78). Validity may characterize the conclusions a researcher draws, whether or not they are someday proved false. In other words, valid conclusions are not necessarily true; they are logically related to the relevant observations. Conclusions may demonstrate two kinds of validity: *internal validity,* the degree to which a particular piece of research allows one to make unambiguous statements about the relationships observed in the data, and *external validity,* the degree to which these conclusions can be generalized to other subjects and conditions (Schaie and Hertzog, 1982; Campbell and Stanley, 1967).

Although most developmental research offers problems of both internal and external validity, the study of aging offers some special obstacles to internal validity because people do not age in a vacuum; they age in a larger social and historical context. Suppose, for example, that we are interested in whether there is developmental change in the degree of self-awareness adults of different ages experience. In other words, suppose we want to know whether self-awareness increases, decreases, or remains steady with age. To research this question, we might compare a group of twenty year olds with a group of thirty years olds and a group of forty year olds. If, after administering our cleverly designed measure of self-awareness, we find that the twenty year olds are the most self-aware and the forty year olds the least, can we conclude that self-awareness diminishes with age? Would such a conclusion have internal validity?

In most developmental research, and certainly in the research described here, such a conclusion is only one of several tentative explanations for any observed differences. All that we would know at this point is that our three age groups exhibit age differences in self-awareness. *Age differences* imply that people of different ages behave differently. We would have no idea why, however. Typically, there are three possible alternative explanations: the differences may be the result of age changes, cohort changes, or a variety of factors peculiar to the time of measurement (Schaie, 1967, 1973, 1979; Schaie and Hertzog, 1982).

Many researchers studying adulthood are only interested in phenomena that they feel constitute true age changes: predictable, age-related changes in biology or experience that can be considered universal. Age changes ought to emerge in any cultural or historical setting. For instance, we might find that people everywhere show slower motor response after the age of thirty-five, or that hearing for high-pitched tones declines after adolescence.

Although age differences may indicate the presence of age changes, they may also reflect certain cultural and historical influences that are not universal. Because of historical changes, people who are all born at the same point in historical time (called a *cohort*) may age rather differently than people born at another point. Researchers define a cohort in the way that best suits their particular research problem. Thus, all people born in 1945 may constitute a cohort in one study, whereas everyone born between 1940 and 1950 may be treated as a single cohort in another piece of

Rapid decline in the birth rate over the last decade may change the meaning of our most sacred institutions, especially those that define family life.

research. Obviously, people born in 1945 have had very different cultural and historical experiences from people born in 1925 or 1965.

People born in 1945 grew up in the United States of the post–World War II period. They had no personal experience of the Great Depression or World War II, but they were probably much affected by the social and political upheaval of the 1960s and the conflict in Viet Nam. One might expect their attitudes toward war and peace and world politics to be very different from those of the birth cohort of 1925. People born in 1965, on the other hand, have had no personal experience of war at all. They grew up with television, feminism, environmentalism, and micro-chip technology; and their attitudes, behavior, thoughts, feelings, and perhaps even their physical development will reflect such historical forces.

Historical context can also produce certain age differences as a function of another force we mentioned—the *time of measurement*. Let's say that we carry out a study on memory over the life span. If we were to do the study today, we would need to consider that most people, including both the subjects in the study and the experimenters, believe that memory begins to fail with age. Such attitudes may shape the behavior of people in different age groups and also influence the way in which their behavior is perceived. Thus, age differences may simply reflect the biases or stereo-typed expectations of the researchers, the subjects, and the culture at a particular moment in time.

Returning to our hypothetical study of self-awareness, we could ana-lyze our data according to each of the three explanations of age differ-ences, as follows.

1. *Age change.* As people accumulate experience or undergo matura-tional changes (or some combination of the two) self-awareness may be heightened in young adulthood. If so, evidence of similar phenomena should appear among people in Namibia or Ecuador, and we should expect that any future birth cohorts will also show intense self-awareness during this period. Similarly, we assume that the older people in our study were more self-aware as young adults.

2. *Cohort differences.* The heightened self-awareness of the twenty year olds may be unique to people born twenty years ago. Perhaps growing cultural emphasis on personal emotional growth over the past two decades has produced an exceptionally self-aware cohort. If so, then these individuals may have always been and may al-ways be preoccupied with their inner experience. People born in other historical periods or in other social settings might well not appear so self-aware at twenty.

3. *Time of measurement.* We may see age differences in self-aware-ness because we expect to. If we believe that young adults are more self-aware than middle-aged or elderly people, we may even construct a measure that reflects that bias. For example, if the test items we thought would measure self-awareness ("I spend several minutes meditating every day") use language or examples that ap-peal to young people but not to the middle-aged or elderly, then the age differences observed in the study may well be a time of measurement effect.

How can we determine which of these explanations best accounts for the age differences we observed? Part of the answer lies in choosing a research design that permits us to decide—that has internal validity. Part of the answer involves the careful construction of the measures to be used, and, ultimately, part lies in how we interpret the results. To understand how these conditions are met, we turn to the specifics of research and design and measurement.

Observational Research Designs

Unfortunately, many developmental researchers stumble at the starting gate, choosing a design that will not allow them to draw unambiguous conclusions. In fact, the most common developmental research design—the *cross-sectional design*—is also the most difficult to interpret. In a cross-sectional research design, two or more groups of people born in different years (two or more cohorts) are selected to represent different age groups. All the research is carried out at one time of measurement. In the simple cross-sectional design shown in Figure 1.1, for example, the investigator has selected a group of people born in 1950 as representative of all twenty year olds, a group born in 1955 as representative of all fifteen year olds, and a group born in 1960 as representative of all ten year olds. (The time of measurement was 1970.) In this design, different age groups are represented by people from different cohorts, and everyone is observed at the same time of measurement.

If we collected our hypothetical self-awareness data in a cross-section, it would be impossible to explain any age differences that emerged. Age changes and cohort differences are confounded; that is, they cannot be sorted out, because people of different cohorts also represent different age groups. Moreover, because there is only one time of measurement, we would not be able to say whether current attitudes and beliefs about aging or psychology produced the results.

Cohort by year of birth

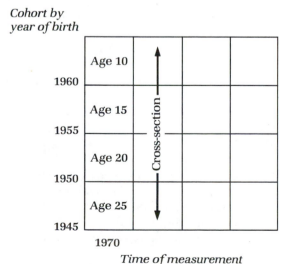

Time of measurement

FIGURE 1.1
Cross-sectional design

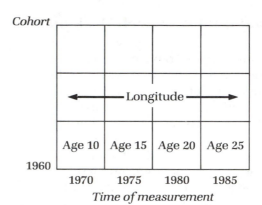

FIGURE 1.2
Longitudinal design

Because it is so difficult to interpret evidence collected in a cross-section, many developmental researchers consider a *longitudinal design* superior. In longitudinal research, the investigator observes the same people over and over again; thus, there are several times of measurement and several ages observed, as the same people get older. (See Figure 1.2, a typical longitudinal approach to the same age groups represented in Figure 1.1.) Age differences found in a longitudinal study may reflect age changes or changes in cultural expectations (time-of-measurement differences), but they cannot be a product of cohort differences, because there is only one cohort. Longitudinal research presents significant problems of external validity, however, since the researcher cannot know whether data from one cohort can be applied to any other cohort.

Longitudinal research is also plagued by the special curses that are the side effects of observing the same people again and again, over time. Participants may become more proficient at some tests over the years (the *practice effect*); they may become bored; they may even become hostile or annoyed. Repetition alters the behavior of subjects, the meaning of measures, and the perceptions of the experimenters as well. These potential *test-retest effects* in a longitudinal study are many, varied, and difficult to foresee (Baltes, Nesselroade and Reese, 1977; Schaie and Hertzog, 1982; Nesselroade and Baltes, 1974).

In addition, a second set of more obvious difficulties arise when subjects are required to keep in touch with experimenters over the years. Some move away; some lose interest; some decide they don't like the experiment; some may even die. The available evidence suggests that these problems of *experimental mortality* (failure to return to the study) are more likely to occur among less intelligent, more rigid, less healthy subjects.

Those who disappear also seem to be from lower socioeconomic classes and to show lower self-esteem and less frequent social interaction than those who return (Atchley, 1969; Maddox, 1962; Riegel, Riegel, and Meyer, 1967; Rusin and Siegler, 1975; Siegler, 1975).

If our research on self-awareness were longitudinal, our observation that self-awareness declines after twenty might well be the result of the most self-aware subjects having dropped out of the study. This might well occur if self-awareness were related to mobility, for example. Obviously, it is difficult to be confident that the differences observed in either longitudinal or cross-sectional research are age changes. And yet, until recently, these two designs were the only two variations to be found in developmental research. In the last few years, however, researchers have made progress by combining and extending these designs to reap the advantages of both. Probably the most important result of the effort so far is the sequential research design.

A *sequential design* involves the use of at least two simple cross-sections or two longitudinal analyses (see Figure 1.3). Any sequential design involves at least two cohorts, at least two age groups, and at least two times of measurement. Having two estimates of each factor means that the researcher can subtract. As simple as it seems, subtraction is actually the heart of much of statistical analysis. Subtraction gives us a number representing the differences between two values, and statistical analysis allows us to determine if that difference is significant. If we were to use a sequential design for our self-awareness study, we would be able to estimate the difference between at least two cohorts, two age groups, and two times of measurement; we could then apply a statistical analysis to clarify whether any of these differences is significant.

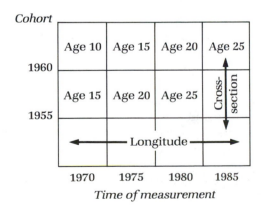

FIGURE 1.3
Sequential design

The most sophisticated sequential design, or what K. Werner Schaie has called the "most efficient design," calls for both cross-sectional and longitudinal sequences (Schaie, 1982). At each time of measurement, new subjects in each age group are selected and tested, and subjects tested before are tested again. By comparing the behavior of new subjects with subjects tested before, researchers can begin to estimate the influence of practice or other test-retest effects. They can also decide whether experimental mortality is affecting the data in an important way (Baltes and Schaie, 1977).

Although a sequential design is clearly a powerful strategy for the collection of data, developmental researchers have debated about whether or not this design, especially when combined with certain statistical analysis, can explain anything. If one is willing to assume that all age changes are a product of an inevitable maturational process, it is possible that one need go no further. Often, those who hold that the important mechanisms of development are internal and maturational feel satisfied with observation alone. C. P. Snow once said that "science is the refusal to believe on the basis of hope." For those who contend that life events and the social structure play an important role in development, it is also the refusal to believe on the basis of observation alone. Unless one can control as well as observe, it has been argued, no real understanding exists. The search must continue, they assert, for the external events or conditions that generate, or at the very least affect, age changes.

It has also been argued that the statistical tool most often used with sequential designs (the ANOVA, or analysis of variance), is inappropriate for analyzing the data. Some researchers believe the use of ANOVA overestimates the importance of cohort differences. As we shall see, when sequential designs are employed and ANOVA is used, cohort effects usually do overwhelm any evidence of age change (Nunnally, 1982; Buss, 1980).

One possible solution to both the issues of explanation and the statistical problems of sequential design is the use of multiple regression. Because this statistical technique allows researchers to test causal hypotheses, it is particularly useful for analyzing observations beset by co-unfounded influences.

MULTIPLE REGRESSION TECHNIQUES.   Research designs and statistical techniques usually reflect current attitudes about causation in any area of science. Thus, the use of multiple regression techniques by most developmental scientists is evidence of their belief that observed age differences are caused by many different biological, psychological, and social forces interacting in the development of the individual. We will be examining the concept of interaction at great length in the next chapter; but for now, it is important to note that the use of both sequential research designs and multiple regression suggests that human development must be seen as an extremely complex, multifaceted interaction.

To put it simply, *multiple regression* is a statistical technique that allows researchers to say, for example, how much of a particular age difference is related to factor *A*, how much to factor *B*, and how much is dependent on the presence of both factors. Basically, multiple regression yields a set of correlations, statistics that indicate how often two phenomena are found together. To be concrete, let's assume a research team determines that occupational aspirations can be predicted by educational achievement and I.Q.; that is, the researchers note that I.Q., educational achievement, and occupational aspirations are correlated. If the researchers go on to determine how well each of the two factors (educational achievement and I.Q.) predict occupational aspirations when considered alone, they can then assign to each predictor a weight that reflects its relative usefulness. Let's say that educational achievement is twice as effective in predicting occupational aspiration than is I.Q. (although both taken together are better than either alone). The researchers would then assign educational achievement twice as much weight as I.Q. in their statistical analysis. A multiple regression analysis would thus be achieved.

Once the weights have been determined, it is possible to go even further, using multiple regression to develop a path analysis. *Path analysis* suggests which of the factors in the multiple regression act through other factors. For instance, perhaps I.Q. predicts occupational aspiration only because it is an important determinant of educational achievement. Path analysis permits researchers to state that although I.Q. does not determine occupational aspirations directly, it does determine educational achievement, which, in turn, determines occupational aspirations (Achenbach, 1978). According to Allen Buss (1980), path analysis is the method "par excellence for getting at direct and indirect effects of variables assumed to be affecting each other" (p. 138).

Note, however, that path analysis does not permit one to say that I.Q. *causes* educational achievement or that educational achievement *causes* one to have high aspirations. It only points to this hypothesis as a best guess for particular data. In other data, those with high occupational aspirations may later become the strong educational achievers. It is also possible that some factor the researchers have overlooked, like socioeconomic class, determines all the other relationships. Path analysis suggests that a particular hypothesis is a good guess, but it does not rule out other possibilities.

In part because path analysis and other sophisticated techniques for analyzing observed data can be inconclusive, many researchers believe that a really convincing demonstration must be carried out in the laboratory; that is, the experimenter should attempt to induce age changes through the manipulation of the forces thought responsible for change. We cannot change a person's biology or environment in such a way that age can be randomly assigned, however. Often, we cannot even assign people to the conditions we believe cause age change. Such experimental work might be either impossible or unethical (or both).

For these reasons, it has been said that developmental research in the laboratory is only semi-experimental (Underwood and Shaughnessy, 1975). That does not mean, however, that it cannot be scientific. There are other sciences—astronomy, for example—in which the conditions of interest (the gravitational pull of Saturn) cannot be reproduced in the laboratory. Although the conditions can only be simulated, such simulations permit astronomers to construct explanations and to apply what they discover to the everyday world. By the same token, laboratory researchers in the developmental sciences believe they can not only test theories and hypotheses but also discover how to understand the aging process, perhaps even how to modify it (Birren and Renner, 1977; Birren, 1980).

Experimental Research Designs

In the developmental sciences, the most common form of experimental research is called *age simulation*. Like an engineer who uses a wind tunnel and a model airplane to simulate flight conditions, the developmental researcher tries to create conditions in the lab that are analogous to conditions in the real world.

AGE SIMULATION.   The most extensive age-simulation research is described in the literature on cognition and memory, particularly in the attempt to improve the learning and memory performances of elderly people. One researcher, for example, offered older subjects practice in the use of *mnemonics*—a technique for improving the memory through the use of codes to help store and recall information. (For example, children might learn to repeat the names of the presidents of the United States by taking the first initials of their last names and forming a sentence from words beginning with the same letters.) Younger people are more familiar with this technique than are older people, because they are often taught a variety of mnemonic devices in school. On the other hand, older people often learned to recite things in school through simple rote memorization, a cornerstone of the North American educational system before World War II. Once they are given practice in the use of mnemonics, their performance improves on both tasks of learning and tasks of memory (Arenberg and Robertson-Tchabo, 1977).

Operant-conditioning research offers another technology for the simulation of age. *Operant learning* refers to changes in behavior produced by environmental consequences, that is, by punishment and reward. Using one or two subjects at a time, B. F. Skinner has repeatedly demonstrated the power of operant learning. (You may have read Skinner's Ping-Pong-playing pigeons in your introductory course in psychology.) Some of Skinner's students believe that operant research designs may prove invaluable in the study of human development (Baer, 1973). There is little doubt that elderly people respond readily to positive reinforcement, sometimes even in cases where extensive biological damage is suspected (Hultsch and Pentz, 1980).

Whether an age-simulation experiment is based on operant analysis and reinforcement or on simple guidance and information, critics of experimental research usually attack its external validity. To what degree, they ask, is it possible to generalize from experiments conducted in the laboratory or procedures that have a therapeutic effect to the causes of ordinary development?

EXPERIMENTAL DESIGNS AND EXTERNAL VALIDITY.   If we knew whether laboratory research re-created events similar, or at least analogous, to the events of ordinary development, we could evaluate external validity. But often laboratory interventions are very different from what we might suppose are normal developmental processes. Just because a particular procedure, like teaching mnemonics, improves performance does not necessarily mean anything about the process that shaped performance in the first place. (It might, of course, but we cannot say for sure.) There may be no *homology,* or likeness in structure, between developmental processes and laboratory interventions. It is possible, for instance, that older people remember less well because of some kind of biological deterioration and mneumonics simply permits them to overcome the biological problem (Birren and Renner, 1977; Baltes, Reese and Nesselroade, 1977).

Often the biggest problem of homology for the developmental researcher is the necessity for *time compression* in the simulation of age. Processes that may require months or even years to unfold in normal development must be simulated in weeks, hours, or even minutes in the laboratory. If we tried to create aged performance in young people, for example, by repeatedly exposing them to situations that may produce a particular age change, we would probably have to carry out the whole process in much less time than is the case outside the lab. The subjects might become bored or overstimulated and therefore behave differently, but the process could be very different than the one responsible in everyday life.

It must be apparent at this juncture that developmental methodology has become a focal point of today's research. As you wipe your brow after pondering the problems of sequential research or the issue of homology, it may seem that we have lost sight of the proverbial forest in favor of the trees. Don't feel alone. Others suspect as much too. In fact, you are in rather good company if you feel vaguely concerned about the ramifications of our increasingly complex research technology.

Drawbacks of Laboratory Research

Despite great sophistication, some important conditions of human existence (for example, privacy) simply cannot be reproduced as long as researchers observe current ethical standards. Beyond ethical considerations, laboratory research is limited by the need for control. When a situation is controlled to aid observation, the environment may lack critical interactions that determine development outside the laboratory. For example, researchers often report huge declines in hearing beginning in early adulthood. Outside the lab, however, subjects rarely experience any hearing deficits until very late in life. All sorts of environmental cues like lip movement and the use of gesture and facial expression provide information about the meaning of sounds. Daily behavior remains essentially unaffected by hearing losses that seem substantial to the scientific observer.

Some writers have charged that current methodology emphasizes formalism and science at the expense of the usefulness of the material (Riegel, 1977). Others contend that because the conditions determining human development change continuously, laboratory research, no matter how exacting, can never produce complete understanding and explanation. Kenneth Gergen (1980), for example, has argued that since causal conditions are probably always in a state of flux, the true role of the researcher is not verification, but merely *vivification*. By this he means that observation and experimentation can sensitize us and motivate us to question our assumptions but that we cannot expect predictive value from laboratory research and statistical analysis.

Concern about the significance and validity of developmental research does not end with criticisms of design or statistics or homology. There are also important issues to be raised about how subjects are selected, how measures are constructed, and how results are interpreted. Nicholas Butler, a great American educator, once said that "art and science have their meeting point in method," and certainly a credible methodology requires not only knowledge and wisdom but also sensitivity and intuition. One must be able to make good guesses and question the commonly accepted ways of doing and interpreting things.

All the sights and sounds and subtle interactions that profoundly influence people's behavior in the real world cannot be replicated and examined in any controlled environment.

SUBJECTS AND MEASURES

Subject Selection

A *sample* is a group of people chosen for a particular experiment. For a social scientist, the ideal subject sample is one that can be said to represent a much larger population of individuals. If the sample is representative of a population of interest, one would expect no significant differences between the two in a variety of important characteristics: education, age, income, and so forth. Basically, there should be no reason to believe the population would behave differently from the sample.

A representative sample is usually chosen by *random sampling*, a procedure designed to select subjects on the basis of chance alone. Random sampling minimizes the chance that the sample will differ in a consistent way from the larger population that is being studied. Unfortunately, people of different ages are not equally easy to sample. Whereas young adults are readily available in colleges and groups of elderly can be found in senior-citizen centers or retirement communities, it is quite difficult to sample older middle-aged people. They do not have children in school, and although they are moving out of occupational life and into retirement, they are not yet members of identifiable groups or communities of retirees.

Even if we could choose people at random from different age groups, it is not clear that random sampling actually yields the best results for the study of human development. Randomization may place too much emphasis on cohort differences, because it produces samples that reflect all of the characteristics that we know to be cohort-related (education, socioeconomic status, health, and so on). Perhaps the best procedure would be to match age groups according to important characteristics; that is, for example, to select only those older people who are similar to younger people in such characteristics as health and level of education. Unfortunately, however, this tactic usually identifies an elite group of older people and an average group of younger people. Most younger people have at least high school educations and are healthy, but among the elderly, only the most advantaged are well educated and in good health, especially in the oldest age groups.

There may be no really satisfactory way to sample for developmental research. Instead, we may have to rely on careful description of the people we are able to study. K. Ernst Schaie, the author of sequential design, has suggested that only by accurate, complete description of the subjects in a study will we be able to limit our generalization of the results to the appropriate group in the population (Schaie, 1977).

Accurate description will contribute to validity, like choosing the proper design. At each step in the organization of a developmental study, researchers make decisions that affect both internal and external validity. Everything counts. Now the choice of tests and measures becomes crucial. We must make sure that the instruments we have selected are actually measuring the attitudes or abilities we believe them to measure. We must also determine that the attitudes or abilities measured are equally important in each of the age groups observed.

Instrumentation and Measurement

Age equivalence means that a measure or test reflects the same set of abilities or attributes for all ages observed. It also implies that this set of abilities is equally important in each group (Eckensburger, 1973).

Members of different generations differ not only in age and experience and health, but in thousands of ways defined by the unique history of any cohort and by the attitudes all of us have toward that history.

In the traditional task of measuring intelligence, for example, in which most testing instruments are designed to measure a hypothetical capacity called problem solving or learning, the same test that is appropriate for ten or eleven year olds would not be suitable for preschoolers. Rather than reflecting intelligence in the preschoolers, the test used for ten year olds would probably reflect the younger children's ability to understand verbal instructions or their inclination to sit still. Among the oldest age groups, the same standard intelligence test might reflect health status or motivation. In other words, the same test could not measure the same thing in all three age groups: it is not age equivalent.

Let us assume, however, that we knew we were measuring exactly the same abilities in all three groups. We still might not be able to predict the behavior of all three groups in a typical problem-solving or learning situation. The problems of a preschooler (e.g., how to get a cookie from Mommie before lunch) are very different from those of a ten year old (how to sort baseball cards into the fifteen available shoeboxes) or an elderly person (how to get to the dentist making only two transfers on the bus). The factors that predict problem solving may differ greatly over the life course since the problems people face are very different.

One approach to the problem of age equivalence involves multivariate techniques and makes some of the same assumptions as multiple regression. Rather than use a single measure, we could employ a set of measures. Thus, from the multivariate perspective, the concept of intelligence can be defined as a profile or pattern of abilities on a set of measures that changes over the life course. Multivariate techniques permit us to discover general patterns of stability in performance despite changes over time in scores on different measures (Nesselroade, 1977).

Clearly, the issue of valid instrumentation and measurement is as complex as any we have discussed so far. One prominent researcher recently declared that the worst problems in the area of developmental research are problems of measurement construction (Nunnally, 1982). In addition to the matter of age equivalence, special problems arise, for example, if we are testing the same subjects over and over again, in a longitudinal study. Then we must compensate for the distortions of the practice effect and the fact that some of the test items become dated over time.

Research design, sample selection, test construction, and the application of statistics all influence the results of a study. Ultimately, however, it is the direct effect of the experimenter on the experiment that is most influential. At every turn, the researcher's beliefs, expectations, attitudes, and decisions are decisive.

Interpretation

Every project begins with a hypothesis, at the very least, and the researcher usually has some idea how the data will look before the first piece is collected. Such expectations can and do influence how evidence is collected, recorded, and interpreted. Experimenter bias is both subtle and powerful. It has determined the outcome of behavioral studies involving adult subjects, school children, and even white rats (Rosenthal, 1966; Achenbach, 1978).

In a set of classic experiments in psychology, Robert Rosenthal clearly demonstrated well the spectacular effects that the expectations and biases of investigators may have on the behavior of their subjects. Rosenthal designed a scale from −10 to +10 (extremely unsuccessful to extremely successful) and recruited a number of students to act as experimenters. Their charge would be to ask subjects to rate photographs of people according to the degree of success the pictured person appeared to have achieved in life (Rosenthal, 1969).

One group of experimenters was told that they could expect a mean rating of −5 from the subjects they would observe, while a second group was led to expect a mean rating of +5. Subjects were then randomly assigned to the experimental groups, and all experimenters read exactly the same instructions to their subjects.

Combining results from three such studies, Rosenthal demonstrated that the experimenters indeed found just what they were looking for. The lowest mean rating of any experimenter expecting high ratings was higher than the highest rating obtained by any of those who expected low ratings!

Similar effects have been achieved using animals as subjects where one group of experimenters is led to expect a particular kind of performance (like fast running) and another is led to expect the opposite from randomly assigned groups of animals. Although the causes for such results may differ from one experiment to another, the effects of the experimenters' expectations are surprisingly consistent and disconcertingly substantial almost every time.

As John Meacham (1980) has pointed out, while experimenters think of research as a monologue or one-way interrogation of subjects, the reality is much closer to a dialogue in which subjects both sense and respond to a variety of unstated and unexamined beliefs and expectations in the experimenters. Subjects can reinforce some ideas that researchers have and disabuse them of others. In turn, the results researchers report influence people's ideas, attitudes, and behaviors. Meacham believes scientists ought to be more aware of how their own historical time and their personal developmental histories influence their research. Do we study topics that have caused problems in our own lives?

Pitifully few precautions are taken to control the expectations of either the researcher or the subject in most social or psychological research. We need more studies, for example, that systematically examine the effect of age (of the experimenter and the subject) on the outcome of experimental results. Studies of the impact of sex and race on research provide a model for students of development and document the importance of social bias and stereotypy (Sistrunk and McDavid, 1971; Jung, 1971; Rosenthal, 1969).

James Birren (1980) has offered some valuable suggestions about the evaluation of research, and his thoughts on the critical examination of a researcher's conclusions are especially helpful. He poses nine questions that researchers ought to ask before accepting the conclusions any study presents:

1. Are the author's conclusions pertinent to the problem as originally posed?

2. Are the conclusions clearly supported by the results?

3. Are the limitations of the study clearly stated?

4. Are results generalized to the population? If so, is that generalization valid?

5. Have unexpected results been rejected merely because they do not match the experimenter's expectations or because they really conflict with common sense?

6. Are statistically nonsignificant tests evaluated or are they interpreted as meaningless?

7. Will the study generate new questions or hypotheses?

8. What is the potential importance of the results and what scientific or practical benefit may follow?

9. What contributions have been made to the theory of the subject?

The information in this chapter should enable you to begin to analyze a developmental researcher's conclusions, with the exception of the last area raised by Birren's last question: What contributions have been made to the theory of the subject? In the next chapter, you will begin to develop the background you will need to assess a piece of research in the light of current theory.

SUMMARY

At the most elementary level of observation in a study of adult development, one might simply ask whether it is reasonable to assume that there are significant changes during the course of adult life. Although some theoreticians have argued that the changes of adulthood are too gradual and too dependent on social context to be considered developmental, the empirical evidence is inconclusive. Measures of socioadaptive processes, including adjustment, mood, and life satisfaction, do not show much change over the years, but biographical materials and clinical interviews consistently suggest important changes in the way people perceive themselves and their experiences.

One approach to the study of development merely seeks to establish whether or not there are reliable changes in psychological function with age. However, even the researcher who simply sets out to discover whether there is change must make some important decisions about what is meant by the term *developmental change* and how long such change can reasonably be expected to take.

Simple models of developmental change, including the irreversible decrement model or even the notion that people mature or improve with age, are too simple to reflect the multifaceted behavioral changes we might expect to accompany age. We can expect anything, and we might well expect anything to happen at any time. It is quite unlikely that whatever changes take place in adult life happen in any single universal time frame. Some changes will be more gradual than others; some will show more variation in time from one person to the next. Some changes are more heavily influenced by the social and historical times than others are.

Even the matter of defining characteristic stages of adult life turns out to be a fairly complicated problem. Various writers and researchers have adopted very different approaches, in part as a function of the questions they wish to study but also because historical and social forces affect the attitudes and behaviors both of the people participating in developmentalists' studies and the approaches researchers take. The tremendous impact of these forces on human beings as they age has led some investigators to question the soundness or validity of the research designs and statistical analyses that have been traditional in the area of developmental psychology.

Developmental research, especially when it focuses on adulthood, presents special problems of external and internal validity. In order to achieve internal validity, investigators must be able to determine whether the age differences that may appear in a developmental study actually indicate age changes, or whether they are instead the results of differences between cohorts or time-of-measurement effects.

Age changes are developmental or time-related changes; cohort differences, in contrast, are attributable to the effects of the historical period and social climate in which people of particular ages grew up, matured, and began to age. Time-of-measurement effects reflect the social and cultural influences at the time of an experiment as well as the preconceptions of the researcher and the sophistication of available theory and methodology.

Traditional cross-sectional research designs do not allow experimenters to discriminate between these three major explanations for observed age differences, and do not allow one to generalize to other points in historical time. Although longitudinal designs eliminate the effects of cohort differences, they still do not allow researchers to determine whether time-of-measurement effects or age changes are producing any age differences observed over time. Moreover, longitudinal research is confounded by the presence of test-retest effects and experimental mortality.

A sequential research design involves the use of at least two cohorts, two age groups, and two times of measurement. Therefore, the procedure allows researchers to estimate the impact of age change, cohort factors, and time of measurement. Moreover, test-retest effects can be estimated and experimental mortality examined if both new and old subjects are interviewed or tested at each time of measurement. Some researchers believe, however, that sequential designs must be applied along with a multiple regression statistical analysis in order to approach the level of sophistication necessary to make causal statements. By using multiple regression analysis, researchers can examine the relationships between a variety of causal factors and one outcome. Once the multiple regression is complete, path analysis may even permit them to test whether or not a particular order of causes and effects is the best explanation of multiple regression data.

Still other researchers believe that causal analysis ultimately depends on the development of experimental research designs in which the forces thought to be causing age changes are manipulated and the effects of such manipulation observed and recorded. Age-simulation experiments represent one kind of experimental design, while the technology of operant conditioning offers another approach. Unfortunately, we cannot be absolutely sure that the induction or modification of age changes in the laboratory is homologous with age changes in the outside world. Because we can create or control something by means of a particular intervention does not mean that we have discovered the process by which the phenomenon developed in the first place.

Clearly, a multifaceted approach to developmental research is required for the study of adulthood and aging. But obstacles to internal and external validity do not end with the choice of research design and the use of statistical analysis. Developmental research also presents challenges of subject selection and measurement construction that have drawn much recent attention.

It is often difficult to select a random sample of an adult population, because all members of that population are usually not equally available for selection. Even if they were, random selection might maximize cohort differences. Attempts to match older and younger subjects on cohort characteristics, however, might well lead researchers to select a relatively elite group of elderly people while choosing a fairly average sample of the young. For these reasons, the most sensible sampling procedures involve the detailed description of both the sample obtained and the method of selection.

Validity is also affected by the researcher's selection or construction of tests and measures. It is difficult to be sure that the same set of abilities or attributes is tapped in each age group observed and that the abilities and attributes measured are equally important in each group. These problems of age equivalence are more likely to be at issue when researchers plan to examine a large age range.

Ultimately, the validity of any piece of research depends on the caution and judiciousness of the investigator. At every stage of planning and execution, the expectations and biases of the researcher can affect the outcome of the study, not only through indirect channels (as in the selection of research design or statistical procedures) but also through directly influencing the behavior of subjects called into the experimental situation. Because research is actually a dialogue between subject and experimenter, we must develop an acute appreciation of how research is influenced by the developmental histories of both experimenters and subjects, as well as by the times in which they live.

Chapter 2

The Context of Discovery: Models and Theories of Human Development

In formal logic, a contradiction is the sign of defeat; but in the evolution of real knowledge it marks the first step in progress toward victory.

ALFRED NORTH WHITEHEAD

To this point, we have looked at the reasons why researchers have become more interested in the study of adult life and have also examined the practical problems they must overcome in order to pursue that interest.

In this chapter, we will be looking at some of the explicit assumptions and theories that have been offered by the developmental scientists who are working from a life-span perspective, and, in particular, by those who are studying adult life.

It is possible, of course, to pursue the study of adulthood completely at the level of research and observation, never attempting to construct a more general hypothesis or a more comprehensive explanation than is necessary in order to understand a specific set of results from a particular study. Some researchers have even argued that the search for age changes is best carried out at a purely *empirical* level: that it is not possible for developmentalists to talk about the construction of a general theory until they have compiled an adequate data base.

On the other hand, there are those who believe that the pursuit of data without theory is likely to be painfully slow at best, fruitless or wandering at worst. From this point of view, all research is guided by theory in any case—at least by some set of assumptions—and the best way to proceed is to make those implicit theoretical ideas explicit so they may be amended and may serve to guide the efforts of others in an efficient, effective way.

Sometimes researchers' underlying assumptions constitute a general framework or belief system, a set of ideas that address the most important issues of development without providing a set of testable hypotheses. These more general frameworks, which we will call *models*, generally offer a researcher a set of ideas about the role of maturation and the environment in human development, the nature of developmental change, and the prospects for intervention in that change. In the first part of this chapter we will examine the two major models that have dominated research in human development since the turn of the century, the mechanistic model and the organismic model; we will look at how each system has addressed the major issues of development and will also discuss recent attempts to synthesize mechanistic and organismic thought in one superordinate model, sometimes called the dialectical view.

Models may serve to guide the work of some researchers, but others prefer the more concrete frameworks provided by a specific set of assumptions: a theory of development. At the same time, the work of theoreticians is usually guided by one or the other of the general models, and so, in the second part of the chapter, our discussion of specific theories will be organized in terms of the models associated with each one. The ideas of the behaviorists, for example, are associated with the mechanistic model, whereas the theory proposed by Jean Piaget follows from an organismic point of view. In this part of the chapter, we will see how the general framework of a model can eventually lead to a very specific hypothesis, such as the notion that there is a special kind of change in the nature of intellectual thought between the ages of eleven and thirteen. Finally, we will consider current criticisms of contemporary theory and look at how the attempt to synthesize competing models is proceeding.

The information in this chapter will give you a framework for organizing, interpreting, and evaluating what follows in later chapters. Theories may ultimately be rejected or upheld. They may be popular or unpopular. But understanding theory will help you to organize and remember information. It is easier to remember what someone did when you understand why it was done, or what someone was trying to prove (or disprove). As you add this information to the ideas presented in Chapter 1, you should be able to say not only why a particular developmental study was done, but also why it was done in a particular way. Knowing why and how information about adult life was obtained will help you to evaluate that information: Is it important, and how does it fit in with the things you already know?

MODELS AND THEORIES IN THE STUDY OF ADULT DEVELOPMENT

The great French dramatist Caron de Beaumarchais once said, "It is not necessary to understand things in order to argue about them." Often, in fact, the most hotly contested ideas are the least well understood. A model provides tentative answers for the unanswered and perhaps unanswerable questions of human nature. What makes people tick? A *model* offers an analogy or metaphor, often an idea that has been developed in one field and is then applied to another, usually less well-developed field. The model embodies a basic set of beliefs or assumptions about how something works. It may imply that behavior is predictable and can be controlled, for instance. Or it may suggest that all behavior is guided by biological imperatives. To illustrate, early in the history of information processing, it was popular to use a telephone switchboard as a simple model for the nervous system. Lately, the computer has more often served as the best analogy or model.

The telephone switchboard and the computer are models for rather specific areas of study. The models that have served those interested in human development are more general, but they serve the same function. They offer general principles that guide description, explanation (including theory construction), and the development of evidence. Unfortunately, there is not much agreement among developmentalists about what general principles can reasonably be assumed. The central issues are as old as psychology itself: the nature/nurture controversy, the role of an organism in its own development, and the nature of change. Each of the major models embodies a set of beliefs about these issues that are essentially untestable. They are general ways of understanding the universe, not specific testable hypotheses.

The major developmental issues can be phrased as simple questions. The *nature/nurture controversy* boils down to this: How much of human behavior is determined by external, environmental forces and how much by internal, maturational factors? Is the human organism basically passive and receptive, or does it play a more active part in the construction of its environment and the direction of its own growth? Questions about the part played by an organism in its own development are strongly related to the nature/nurture controversy since a belief in the importance of external, environmental forces tends to limit the role of the organism. Finally, is the nature of developmental change qualitative or quantitative? In other words, is it regular and predictable and cumulative, or are there great leaps and unexpected events? In the history of Western thought, two sets of answers to all these questions have long existed in apparent opposition: the mechanistic and organismic views (Reese and Overton, 1970; Reese and Nesselroade, 1977; Reese, 1976; Miller, 1983).

The Mechanical Model

The idea that people can be understood as though they behaved like sophisticated machines has certain implications for research and theory. From the mechanistic point of view, events that take place in the environment are input; behavior is output; and the role of the developmental scientist is to discover how the two are related. Organisms, from amoebas to presidents, are viewed as receptive rather than active, and all behavior is perceived as the predictable product of thousands (or millions or billions) of lawful associations between simple events.

The stand of the mechanist on each of the major issues of developmental psychology follows in a rather straightforward way from the model. The core notion of the mechanistic perspective is that people grow to be what they are because of their environments. The organism does not construct the environment; the environment constructs the organism, psychosocially at least.

Since the mechanist believes that change flows from the environment in a predictable, observable way, the nature of that change is assumed to be cumulative, quantitative, and continuous. We learn to behave like adults bit by bit, piece by piece, response by response. Complex behaviors are really chains of simpler responses. The mechanist's model also stresses the idea that human behavior is plastic, that it changes from one situation to the next and that the potential for growth is unlimited. As this relates to adult life, the mechanist view of aging is really a rather optimistic one: if we could discover those events that cause people to age in unfortunate ways, we could prevent or slow or even reverse the process through the control of the environment.

The assumptions of the mechanist's model also lead to a search for lucid definitions, rigor, and testability in theory. For example, the timing of positive reinforcement and punishment has been studied in great detail, and a variety of schedules of reinforcement have been described, along with their particular effects on the frequency and timing of behavior. In this way, experimenters have established that a continuous schedule of reinforcement (the rewarding of a response every time it occurs) is the most effective way to teach a new response, but an intermittent schedule (on which responses are rewarded only now and then) is the most effective way to maintain performance once a response is learned. The analysis of complex behaviors into chains of simple events requires clarity and specificity (Baldwin, 1980).

The Organismic Model

For the organismic theorist, the inner processes of the organism rather than any environment events are the primary forces behind development. The organismic view suggests that social and psychological development are analogous to physical development, especially the physical development of the embryo. Embryonic growth occurs in stages, each qualitatively different from the others. Every organism starts out as a single cell; the cell reproduces and there are two, then four, then eight, then sixteen, and so on. In this first stage, however, no matter how many cells, they are all alike. But, at some point in the process, *differentiation* occurs. In human beings, a primitive eye emerges, then a spinal cord, then an ear, and so on.

The cells that form eyes are different from the cells that form ears: the reorganization that has taken place in their structure or function indicates a qualitative change. In terms of human development, a qualitative change means a distinctive change in the nature of behavior—not just more of the same, or better, but completely different (Reese and Overton, 1970; Diamond, 1982). Thus, a child who possesses verbal behavior may think in a way that is completely different from a child who does not speak.

According to the organismic viewpoint, people grow to be what they are because of the forces within them; that is, the reorganization of internal structures occurs because the organism is always active. It may even seek change or stimulation, and it is always interpreting and structuring its own experience.

Organismic theorists generally agree that environmental events play a facilitating or modifying role in development, not a causal one. They argue that the environmentalists gravely exaggerate the role of external events and that understanding human development means understanding the internal structures and processes of the human organism. These processes are thought to be general and to occur in invariant sequences in all human beings.

If a process is general, it must prescribe changes in performance in a wide variety of tasks, not just in one or two behaviors. For example, if an elderly person suddenly finds it difficult to remember phone numbers, an organismic theorist would not assume that a stage of "intellectual decline" had been reached. Only a change in a general process—in many aspects of memory, learning, and problem solving—would qualify as representing a life stage or be thought to reflect a universal trend (Crain, 1980).

Over the past twenty years, as the work of Jean Piaget has become increasingly popular in the United States, the organismic position has gained many advocates. Probably the most appealing aspect of the organismic view is the notion that people are constantly engaged in the interpretation and construction of their own reality. Yet, interestingly, the least popular tenet of the organismic view seems to be its assumption that external environmental events are not important determinants of behavior. Americans have a deeply rooted belief in the benefits of teaching and education as well as a reverence for individual differences (Riegel, 1977).

Attempts to reconcile the notion that human beings are active in their own development with the tenet that environmental influences such as education indeed make a difference have produced a strong movement toward the integration of the mechanistic and organismic views. This integrated perspective, sometimes called the transactional or dialectical model, is particularly useful in discussing the behavior of adults. It is difficult to describe and explain the development of people past puberty without referring to their social circumstances and life experience. According to the dialectical model, the organism is active and constructive, while developing in the context of continually changing social and historical forces.

The Dialectical Model

The term *dialectics* refers to any method of argument or exposition that systematically weighs contradictory facts or ideas with a view to the resolution of their real or apparent contradictions. In other words, dialectics describes a system or theory that emphasizes the importance of conflict. Dialectical thinking usually speaks of conflict in terms of change. Conflict produces change, and change, in turn, produces conflict.

In the study of human development, dialectics suggests that conflict is necessary for social and personal evolution. The metaphor offered by the dialectical model is that of speaker and listener. (The speaker is also a listener, and the listener is also a speaker.) As a speaker, one is changed by what is said by others as well as by the things one says oneself. Likewise, the individual is changed by the external, environmental conditions and, at the same time, participates in his or her own development by changing those conditions (Riegel, 1975, 1977; Buss, 1979). This may sound like a paradox at first, but it is not unlike the commonsense notion that although people are affected by the circumstances in which they find themselves, they can change those circumstances in order to grow and develop in more beneficial ways. In a sense, what this means is that the mechanistic and organismic views need not be seen as competing views, but are, to some extent, complementary (Labouvie, 1982).

The dialectical model posits a state of constant change both within and outside the organism; thus it also encourages a search for the causes of development in events that occur both inside the organism and in the world around it. The model considers interactions among the organism, the environment, and social and cultural history, as well as interactions within each of these spheres. Thus, development occurs through interactions between a changing system in the organism and a changing world, as a response to some disharmony: a changing individual and a changing world interact; interaction produces tension or conflict; new growth occurs. New development will both create harmony and, at the same time, make possible new discrepancies, and growth again.

Dialectics does seem to include important ideas found in both the mechanistic and the organismic models. In fact, it has been called a superordinate model (Reese, 1976). However, it is somewhat difficult to illustrate the specific ways in which dialectics might synthesize mechanistic and organismic thought because it is a relatively new set of ideas in this country and has just begun to generate research and concrete analysis. Nonetheless, within each of these three models there exists the potential for many more specific explanations, or theories, about development. *Theories* offer concrete hypotheses within the framework of assumptions offered by a model.

Models and Theories

A model offers a set of untestable assumptions. It provides answers to very general questions about life, the universe—everything. For example, we cannot really design an experiment that will prove whether nature or nurture is more important. A *theory*, in contrast, is basically an attempt to explain something. Theories generate the kinds of hypotheses that can be tested.

Like an ordinary explanation, a theory shows how something we do not understand relates to the things we do understand or believe to be true. For example, if I walk out one evening and sight a huge cigar-shaped light in the sky, I might call the police and ask if there had been an explosion or if some special test was going on in the area and if other people were calling with similar reports. If no one else saw it, I might shrug it off or I might call an optometrist (or maybe a psychotherapist). If there had been an explosion or a rocket test, I would feel I had a satisfactory explanation of my sighting. I would have developed a theory of the light in the sky beginning with my model about how the universe works and ending with a testable hypothesis. If I had immediately called the Air Force and reported a UFO, I would be working from quite a different model.

Theories about human development, like theories in physics or chemistry or astronomy, are attempts to explain certain phenomena (like the behavior of middle-aged people) in terms of general principles (such as principles of maturation or learning) that one already assumes to be true. Unfortunately, however, current developmental theories are not comprehensive, rigorous explanations of human behavior like the theories offered by chemistry and physics to explain the behavior of the physical universe. Explanation implies the application of logic and the presence of truth. Certainly, we are a long way from explaining human development.

Nevertheless, even rudimentary theories generate enlightening discussion as well as healthy doubt. Systematic theory also may guide observation and discovery (Guthrie, 1950). Theories may prove wrong and be discarded, but even wrong theories may, as Francis Bacon said, be better than chaos.

Theory is, then, a tool as well as a goal. It can organize and integrate existing knowledge. In fact, at this stage, the best criterion for the importance or excellence of a theory may be how useful it is, rather than how thoroughly it explains human development. A theory may prove to have little relation to the facts as they are known and still be useful. It may provide just the necessary raw material to produce a new and better idea (Marx, 1964; Zigler, 1964; Achenbach, 1978; Baldwin, 1980).

All three models—the mechanistic, the organismic, and the dialectical—have produced useful theories of both child and adult development. Although it is sometimes difficult to show how each aspect of the parent model is reflected in every theory, the following review of theoretical families will help to clarify the basic ways in which members of one theoretical family rely on common assumptions.

THEORETICAL FAMILIES

Mechanist Theories

Theories spawned by the mechanist point of view tend to focus on the differences among people and differences in the behavior of the same individual from one situation to another. For this reason, such theories stress *nonnormative influences.* As we learned in Chapter 1, nonnormative events are those that do not occur for all individuals in a regular sequence or pattern, such as marriage, parenthood, and occupational career events (Baltes, 1979). They also stress the ways in which important differences in behavior can evolve from the slightest variations in the timing and nature of environmental events.

People often seem to change radically with only minor alterations in experience. They discriminate among and respond to minute differences in stimulation. In fact, according to Walter Mischel, a well-known proponent of the mechanical model, the only thing that is really consistent about human behavior is the fact that people perceive themselves as consistent. Mischel has argued that the human mind functions like a reducing valve, making unified wholes out of almost anything. He contends that people perceive a good deal more consistency in their own behavior than actually exists. For example, people tend to see themselves as generally honest and sympathetic even though they may lie and be insensitive at times (Mischel, 1969).

Psychological and sociological theory must, according to the mechanist, account for the fact that behavior varies considerably from one cir-

Perhaps we are attracted to people who look and think and act as we do because they are unlikely to demand big changes in the way we live our lives.

cumstance or society or historical period to another. Research demonstrates that complex discrimination or differentiation characterizes adult behavior and cannot be explained if one focuses exclusively on what is universal in human development. Why does a person engage in sophisticated moral reasoning in one situation and think like a hedonist in another? Why are sex differences so much more salient in one culture than another? These are the kinds of questions that intrigue the mechanist (Labouvie, 1982).

The mechanist position is also illustrated by researchers who are trying to analyze the important events of adult life in terms of the opportunities they offer for learning new behavior. For example, Inge Ahammer (1973) assumes that adults develop and change throughout the life span because they are constantly confronted with fresh settings and relationships that constitute new sources of behavioral demand. New skills are learned, new attitudes emerge, and new motives and cognitive as well as emotional patterns are formed when people find themselves in new circumstances. In fact, Ahammer argues, as long as the situations or persons in the environment continue to change, development will continue.

Ahammer also acknowledges, however, that change is slower in adult life than in childhood because adults avoid situations that require change. Because, Ahammer believes, adults experience the demands for change as aversive, they are attracted to other people and to environmental settings that are familiar (birds of a feather . . .). Children are forced to face new situations by both law (compulsory education) and convention (parental control). Ahammer also thinks it is possible that children do not experience change as aversive since they respond better to physical stresses.

Ahammer's approach suggests that researchers might profitably break down the large, changing, complex events of life, such as marriage and parenthood, into simple connections between new stimuli and new behaviors. Thus, she has tried to describe the objective dimensions of life events and then categorize them in terms of their behavioral effects. In her analysis, however, she tends to concentrate on one event at a time (such as marriage), and discuss the myriad ways in which that particular milestone is likely to cause developmental change. Another type of approach, illustrated by the work of Orville Brim, Jr., and Carol Ryff, involves the development of a typology of events: a grouping together of events that are likely to have similar effects.

A TYPOLOGY OF EVENTS.   Brim and Ryff (1980) have distinguished three major types of life events: (1) biological events, such as hormonal changes, disease, and growth; (2) social events of both the customary type (marriage, work, and parenthood) and the noncustomary type (criminal involvement, accidents, and adultery); and (3) physical events, such as earthquakes, natural cycles of time, body function, and weather. All three types of events—biological, social, and physical—may be described in terms of their effects on personality development, the perceptions people have of them, and their objective properties.

Among the many objective properties events may have, one of the most important is distribution. By *distribution*, Brim and Ryff are referring

TABLE 2.1
Life events typology

Correlation with age	Experienced by many		Experienced by few	
	High probability of occurrence	Low probability of occurrence	High probability of occurrence	Low probability of occurrence
Strong	**1** Marriage Starting to work Retirement Woman giving birth to first child Bar Mitzvah First walking Heart attack Birth of sibling	**3** Military service draft Polio epidemic	**5** Heirs coming into a large estate Accession to empty throne at 18	**7** Spinal bifida First class of women at Yale Pro football injury Child's failure at school Teenage unpopularity
Weak	**2** Death of a father Death of a husband Male testosterone decline "Topping out" in work career Children's marriages Accidental pregnancy	**4** War Great Depression Plague Earthquake Migration from South	**6** Son succeeding father in family business	**8** Loss of limb in auto accident Death of daughter Being raped Winning a lottery Embezzlement First black woman lawyer in South Blacklisted in Hollywood in 1940s Work disability Being fired Cured of alcoholism Changing occupations

SOURCE: O. G. Brim, Jr. and C. Ryff. On the properties of life events. In P. B. Baltes and O. G. Brim, Jr. (Eds.) *Life-Span Development and Behavior*, Vol. III, N.Y.: Academic Press, 1980.

to whether many people experience the same event, whether the event is age-related, and whether it is likely to occur in the life of a particular person. Table 2.1 presents the kinds of events that might fall into each of the categories Brim and Ryff have created.

Too often, Brim and Ryff believe, people try to explain behavior in terms of extremely vivid or recent events; for example, John may explain his erratic record at work in terms of the recent death of his father, who

The war in Viet Nam may have affected the development of one whole generation not so much because it was vivid, but because no one was prepared to fight in an unpopular, losing war.

was only fifty-two, or Elaine may say that she is having trouble sleeping since she was separated from her husband of thirty years. According to Brim and Ryff, it is the distribution of an event rather than its nature or even its vividness that is most important. If the event is a common occurrence—if it takes place at the time in the life span when others experience the same sort of event or if the individual has always known that this event was likely to occur in his or her life—anticipatory socialization occurs. *Anticipatory socialization* is the process by which people are rehearsed and prepared for an event by the social delivery of information and training. People are socialized for common, age-related events and for those uncommon events they are sure to experience. It is not the death of John's father that is as important as the fact that he was unprepared. Elaine might not be sleepless if she knew a number of women who had been through divorce in late middle-age.

THE PERCEPTION OF EVENTS.   Another kind of mechanistic analysis is illustrated by David Chiriboga and Loraine Cutler (1980), researchers who are interested in how events that are perceived as stressful affect a person's behavior. This type of approach has been called cognitive-behaviorism because it often emphasizes the importance of how people perceive an event as well as the nature of the event itself.

As long as it is possible to objectify and measure an internal process such as perception, a mechanist may refer to an event that is basically unobservable. Thus, in keeping with the ideas of the mechanical model, Chiriboga and Cutler believe it is important to objectify and measure such concepts as stress. They have devoted much of their research to this problem, beginning with an analysis of the Holmes and Rahe Social Readjustment Scale (1967). Table 2.2 presents the Social Readjustment Scale in a form often used to evaluate a person's experience during any six-month to one-year period. The points assigned to events are added for the events occurring in the previous six months (or year), and the total number of points is used to predict the probability, for example, of major stress-related disease in the following year.

Chiriboga and Cutler's refinement of this scale makes it an even better predictor of personality and behavior. To begin with, they added a number of important events, including some that were most appropriate for older people. (For instance, an event like losing one's driver's license might be especially stressful for an older person with little hope of getting it back again.) Second, Chiriboga and Cutler allowed their subjects to assign point values to events on an individual basis and to discriminate between positive and negative stressors. The birth of a long-desired baby, for example, might be rated very differently on the scale than would the birth of an unplanned, fourth child in a family living on the edge of poverty.

By implementing these refinements, Chiriboga and Cutler found that their subjects fell into one of four major groups with regard to the stress responses: those who avoid stress, those who are "lucky" (who are able to increase the amount of positive stress in their lives without increasing the negative stress), those who are "overwhelmed" because there is so much negative stress in their lives, and those who are stress-prone (reporting high levels of both negative and positive stress).

The studies of Chiriboga and Cutler illustrate the mechanists' propensity for finer and finer analysis of events and their relationship to behavior. Such analyses always demonstrate a strong empirical quality. An

TABLE 2.2
Social readjustment rating scale

Life event	Mean value
1. Death of spouse	100
2. Divorce	73
3. Marital separation	65
4. Jail term	63
5. Death of close family member	63
6. Personal injury or illness	53
7. Marriage	50
8. Fired at work	47
9. Marital reconciliation	45
10. Retirement	45
11. Change in health of family member	44
12. Pregnancy	40
13. Sex difficulties	39
14. Gain of new family member	39
15. Business readjustment	39
16. Change in financial state	38
17. Death of close friend	37
18. Change to different line of work	36
19. Change in number of arguments with spouse	35
20. Mortgage over $10,000	31
21. Foreclosure of mortgage or loan	30
22. Change in responsibilities at work	29
23. Son or daughter leaving home	29
24. Trouble with in-laws	29
25. Outstanding personal achievement	28
26. Wife begin or stop work	26
27. Begin or end school	26
28. Change in living conditions	25
29. Revision of personal habits	24
30. Trouble with boss	23
31. Change in work hours or conditions	20
32. Change in residence	20
33. Change in schools	20
34. Change in recreation	19
35. Change in church activities	19
36. Change in social activities	18
37. Mortgage or loan less than $10,000	17
38. Change in sleeping habits	16
39. Change in number of family get-togethers	15
40. Change in eating habits	15
41. Vacation	13
42. Christmas	12
43. Minor violations of the law	11

SOURCE: T. H. Holmes and R. H. Rahe, "The Social Readjustment Scale," *Journal of Psychosomatic Research*, 11 (1967): 216.

empiricist is a scientist who prefers to observe and experiment with few preconceived ideas about the direction results might take. Accordingly, mechanists do not deal in concepts like optimal development or maturity; they do not suggest the existence of any natural goals or an ideal personality (Hogan, 1974). The organismic position, in contrast, tends to be much less empiricist. Although it may not be demanded by the organismic model, most organismic theories do assume some natural goal of development, even if the goal is something as basic as adaptation. In fact, since most of the popular organismic theories, such as Jean Piaget's, are stage theories, they tend to be quite explicit about the nature of optimal behavior and personality development (Craine, 1980).

Organismic Theories

"If you are not beautiful by 20, strong by 30, rich by 40, and wise by 50, you never will be," says Mother Goose, a stage theorist herself. In line with the assumptions of the organismic model, organismic stage theories propose that development over the life course cannot be adequately conceptualized as the simple accumulation of experience or associations. Completely different achievements emerge at different stages in the life cycle. For example, Jean Piaget believes that the mental abilities a person demonstrates as a toddler are qualitatively different from those demonstrated in infancy because language makes possible a completely new set of skills.

STAGE THEORIES.   Piaget's theory is the most elegant and elaborate of the current organismic theories. Devoted to the description of intellectual development, Piaget's work has given us a stunning example of the organismic model in action. His stages of intellectual development reflect strict adherence to the assumptions of the model: human beings are seen as active organisms, continuously constructing their own reality through interaction with their environment. As people pass through various stages, their reality changes because new skills and abilities become available. For example, a child who can talk sees the universe differently from one who cannot. In turn, talking allows the child to interact with the environment in new ways, eventually leading to the next stage of social and intellectual development.

Table 2.3 presents an overview of the course of intellectual development according to Piaget. Since this framework ends in adolescence, a number of writers have offered versions of a fifth, adult stage of cognitive development (Riegel, 1973b; Arlin, 1975, 1977; Commons and Richards, 1978; Commons, 1982). In the next chapter, we will discuss several of these

TABLE 2.3
Piaget's stages of cognitive development

Stage	Age (approximate)	Description
Sensorimotor	Birth to 2 years	Behavior suggests child lacks language and does not use symbols or mental representations of objects in the environment. Intentional behavior begins, such as learning to seek objects and to make interesting sights last.
Preoperational	2 to 7 years	Child begins to represent world mentally, but is unaware that others do not see the world in the same way. Child is unable to focus on two aspects of a situation at the same time.
Concrete operational Operational	7 to 12 years	Child can adopt viewpoint of others, can classify objects in a series (longer, shorter) or as subordinate and superordinate (a dog is an animal), but cannot systematically formulate and test alternative solutions to a problem.
Formal operational	12 years and above	Mature, adult thought emerges characterized by deductive logic and the consideration of various possibilities prior to solving a problem. The ability to abstract and to form and test hypotheses systematically appears.

SOURCE: Based on S. Rathus, *Psychology* (New York: Rinehart and Winston, 1981), p. 386.

hypotheses, but here, the work of Michael Commons and Francis Richards (1978; 1982) is of special interest because they have been careful to outline and preserve the assumptions of Piaget's original formulation.

Commons and Richards point out that organismic stage theories make several critical assumptions about the nature of stages and the nature of developmental sequences. First, the new abilities that define a particular stage must be general or *content free;* that is, they must be applicable to a number of content areas. For example, the ability to classify can be applied to almost any area of knowledge. Second, stages must follow one another in an invariant sequence. In other words, all individuals must go through all stages in the same order; neither skipping stages nor regression is permitted in classical stage theories. Finally, the elements of each stage must form a logically necessary basis for the next stage. Each new stage is built upon and includes the elements of the one before it (Commons and Richards, 1982; Richards and Commons, 1982; Flavell, 1963; Miller, 1983).

Commons and Richards's *structural analytic stage* of cognitive development was generated both by Piaget's general assumptions about stages and by the specific elements of his stage of formal operations. *Formal operations* permit people to understand and consider the variability of all the elements in a situation and to make hypotheses about how the changing elements of a problem are related. Formal operators know how to systematically test a hypothesis, holding some elements constant and manipulating other aspects of the problem one at a time. For instance, different combinations of blue, green, and white paint change both the hue and the intensity of a pot of turquoise. With some thought, the formal operator will be able to determine the exact proportion of blue to white and green necessary to match a particular shade of turquoise. The only way this can be accomplished in an orderly fashion (rather than by luck) is to hold the amount of color 1 (e.g., blue) and color 2 (e.g., white) constant while adding progressively more of color 3 (green). If at first you don't succeed, then hold 2 and 3 constant while increasing the amount of 1; then hold 1 and 3 constant while increasing the amount of 2.

Commons and Richards propose that once people are able to figure out the relationships among the elements in a problem that require formal operations, they can proceed to the *structural analytic stage* of cognitive development. Whereas a formal operator makes statements about the relationships between elements in a problem, a structural analytic thinker makes statements about the relationships between relationships in different problems. For example, when we analyze how the stages in Piaget's theory are related to one another, we are using formal operations. When we compare a model of human development (which outlines a set of relationships) with another model, we are discussing the relationships between relationships. The study of models and their corresponding frameworks and their relationship to theory is permitted by structural analytic thought (Commons and Richards, 1978; Commons, 1982).

Not all organismic theories define stages in the way Commons and Richards or Piaget do. It is not necessary that formal stages exist for qualitative change to occur over the life course, guiding development toward some natural goal or optimal form. One of the more important nonstage organismic theories of adult life is called *disengagement theory* (Looft, 1973).

DISENGAGEMENT THEORY.   One way to describe disengagement is to say that as people age they deal with events more abstractly. They exhibit increasing interiority; that is, they tend to be concerned with their own ideas and experience rather than with the opinions of others or with current environmental circumstances and events. Disengagement theory suggests that there is a mutual withdrawal between older people and the social system. This phenomenon is thought to be accompanied by a reduction in the energy available to older people for investment in the external

"Growing old is no more than a bad habit which a busy man has no time to form."
André Maurois

environment (Cumming and Henry, 1961; Henry, 1965; Cumming, Dean, Newel, and McCaffrey, 1960).

Disengagement has been described as a satisfactory, even an optimal, adjustment to growing old. It is assumed to be universal and to reverse the engaged, active, social participation that characterizes young adulthood. Through disengagement, older people are supposed to experience a release from the sense of importance that young people tend to attribute to external events (Henry, 1965).

After years of critical examination and empirical investigation, it appears that disengagement may describe the adjustment of some individuals and may provide high levels of life satisfaction for those who choose it freely, but that not all well adjusted older people are disengaged. Although there is evidence that some decreased commitment to external events characterizes the behavior of older people, high levels of life satisfaction are also associated with active social participation and emotional involvement among the elderly (Lemon, Bengston and Peterson, 1972; Havighurst, Neugarten and Tobin, 1968; Maddox, 1968).

Nonetheless, the concept of disengagement is useful in the description of some individuals. What is more, the adjustment of most elderly people depends on the freedom to disengage or withdraw in certain areas while remaining committed in others (Havighurst, 1968). For example, an elderly person may want very much to retire from the labor force, but may choose continued deep involvement with the friends made over a lifetime of work.

As critics are quick to point out, the description of an ideal or fully mature state of adulthood has been problematic in the development of organismic theory. Disengagement theory has been unpopular among those who felt that the withdrawal of the elderly was all too often forced by a society eager to be rid of its older citizens. Piaget has been criticized because his stage theory seems to end abruptly in adolescence, never fully capturing intellectual maturity. It has also been suggested that Piaget's theory is ethnocentric—that it exhibits a certain cultural bias, especially in the description of formal operations, for they do not appear uniformly outside of Western, industrialized countries (Buck-Morss, 1979). *Ethnocentrism* is the tendency to see the behaviors that are valued in one's own culture as universally optimal or mature.

MATURITY: A CULTURE-FREE DEFINITION? Susan Buck-Morss (1979) has pointed out that the great cultural variability apparent even in intellectual maturation threatens a general stage theory of cognition (or perhaps a general stage theory of development). Buck-Morss believes that formal operations appear regularly only in those economic systems that deal with commodities in an abstract way. (For example, Americans value skills, like management and marketing, and the learning of principles, like the rules of scientific methodology, that can be applied to many different commodities and subjects.) Thus, Western capitalism both reflects and determines formal operations, since they represent an abstract, content-free kind of thought. If Buck-Morss is correct, structural analytic thought would also arise only in industrialized, Western nations, since formal operations are prerequisite. Buck-Morss warns against the tendency to equate the behaviors of so-called successful people with maturity.

On the other side of the fence, one dedicated cross-cultural researcher believes it is possible for a Western psychologist to construct a culture-free definition of maturity. In a series of "dogged and imaginative studies of Haverford College students who had been judged by their peers and faculty mentors to be notably mature or immature" (Smith, 1977), Douglas Heath developed and tested a definition of personal psychological maturity (Heath, 1965; 1977). Defining maturity as a life-span process that involves drawing on experience in the process of adapting to new demands, Heath has described five dimensions of maturity—symbolization, allocentrism, integration, stability, and autonomy.

HEATH'S DIMENSIONS OF MATURITY. Heath uses the term *symbolization* for the degree to which a person's values are accessible to awareness; that is, the degree to which a person can represent feelings and ideas in words. Well-symbolized cognition is reflective, imaginative, and relatively free of repression. Symbolization not only allows us to accurately assess our self-concept, personal values, and motives, but also to be objective in our evaluation and to understand the limitations, possibilities, and anxieties we possess.

Heath's second dimension, *allocentrism*, means to take on multiple perspectives, to put oneself in someone else's shoes. Allocentric people are able to make realistic judgments, to test reality appropriately, and to understand how others see them. They are able to predict the views of others, to show tolerance and respect for differences in values or motives, and to express social feeling, warmth, compassion, and empathy.

Integration implies a coherent system of values, motives, personality traits, and beliefs. It depends on distinguishing and organizing life events in a meaningful way. Such skills are critical in problem solving and deductive, flexible thinking. They also allow the coordination of thought and feeling about the self and the organization of one's values into a workable life philosophy. Finally, the integrated person is discriminating in relationships, yet trusting, open, and self-disclosing.

Stability and *autonomy* are inseparable in discussing maturity, according to Heath. Stability provides the necessary base for autonomous behavior. Stability and autonomy allow us to think independently of the particulars of a situation, and they free cognitive processes from emotional bias. A stable, autonomous self-concept permits certainty about our strengths and weaknesses and allows us to evaluate the ideas of others objectively. With stability and autonomy, less dependent, freer, and more enduring relationships are possible.

Heath believes that these five dimensions define the core traits of the adaptively effective or *competent* person. He equates adaptability not with adjustment, but with the ability to master things on one's own terms. It means responding to the environment in an optimal way and still retaining the ability to meet our own needs for integration.

To test whether or not his ideas had any transcultural validity, Heath did a series of studies in such diverse areas as Italy, Sicily, and Turkey. After asking local psychologists to pick groups of men they considered especially mature and immature, Heath was able to confirm his hypothesis that the most mature men met the same criteria he had developed using his Haverford sample. Many of Heath's ideas about the importance and the nature of the self-concept and cognition were strongly confirmed in all five samples. He had more difficulty with hypotheses about interpersonal relationships and autonomy, perhaps because his measures were not effective or because he was interviewing males during late adolescence when autonomy and intimacy may not be clearly established. It is also possible that Heath's concepts of autonomy and intimacy in personal relationships did not translate well into other cultural milieus.

It is, in part, the magnitude of social, individual, and historical differences in psychological development as well as the idea that we may be defining adaptation in terms of conformity that has led to the search for a broader theoretical framework. There have been a number of attempts to synthesize the organismic and mechanistic views. Various suggestions have been labeled "interactional" or "transactional" or "contextual." None has yet produced a mature or general theory. Here we will use the term *dialectical* because it has been closely associated with some of the longstanding theoretical ideas offered by psychoanalytic thinkers such as Erik Erikson.

Dialectical Theory

In the first volume of the book *Life-Span Development and Behavior,* Hugh Urban (1978) wrote that the search for a synthesis of developmental approaches has been prompted by the desire for explanation of multilevel, multidirectional, and multiply-caused change. In particular, researchers are looking for theories that permit transactional change. *Transactional changes* are not active in the organismic sense or reactive as the mechanical model suggests. They are not even interactive. In an interaction, an effect is achieved if, and only if, two or more elements are present (e.g., element 1 could be some aspect of one's heredity while element 2 could be some external environmental event). Neither element by itself can produce the effect; and, although the effect cannot be described as a simple addition of the effects of the two necessary elements, the elements themselves remain unchanged. In a *transaction,* the elements themselves are changed. There is an exchange of influence in a transaction, and each element is affected by the presence of the other.

To make this abstract idea more accessible, let's assume that the evaluation of a person's physical appearance by society constitutes an interaction that affects the personality development of the individual. We have evidence, for example, that a man who possesses an athletic body type is likely to develop confidence and self-esteem. The development of self-esteem is not *caused* by one's body type, however. Both the body type and the positive social evaluation of that type are required; there is an interaction. If men were to begin an active campaign to make people more aware of the damage that is done by the judgments we make about people because of their body types, and if, eventually, they were able to create a more positive social attitude about diversity in admired body types, the society would have changed as well as the individual. The genetic pool might even change in the end, if the athletic body type were no longer considered much more desirable than any other type. In a transaction, there is an exchange of influence; both elements are affected.

People are changing systems living in a changing environment. They change their reality and are affected by that reality as well. Both the social system and the individual develop. Whereas the organismic view of development tends to underrate the effects of the social system and the mechanist's viewpoint ignores the role the individual plays in the creation of social reality, dialectics allows for the possibility that the mature person can change the social and physical world, eventually changing the definition of maturity itself. Thus, maturity is a relative idea in a dialectical framework. A mature person may question the social and political realities of his or her own world, entering into a transaction that changes both the world and the person. The concept of adaptation is inadequate if it is possible for the individual to change the system.

THE DIALECTICS OF ERIKSON.   Although no coherent psychological theory has yet been developed using the dialectical model, it has been suggested that the groundwork laid by Erik Erikson might serve as a good starting point for a dialectical theory because Erikson emphasized the importance of mutual influences in the biological, personal, cultural, and even historical factors that affect individual development (Riegel, 1975a; 1975b; 1977). Erikson's theory is based on the notion that people move through a series of universal stages governed by a genetic ground plan, or epigenetic principle, that determines the timing of individual development (Erikson, 1963; 1968a; 1982). *Epigenesis,* a term borrowed from developmental biology where it is used to describe the forces behind the growth of the fetus from one stage of development to another, is used here to describe the internal drive or force assumed to produce qualitative changes or stages of growth

TABLE 2.4
Erikson's eight stages of life

Conflict at each stage	Emerging value	Period of life
Basic trust versus mistrust Consistency, continuity, and comfort produce a feeling of security and predictability.	Hope	Infancy
Autonomy versus shame and doubt Parental firmness allows for the experience of demand fulfillment with limits that produce self-control.	Will	Early childhood
Initiative versus guilt The development of the superego and cooperation with others support the growth of planning and a sense of responsibility.	Purpose	Play age
Industry versus inferiority Working and learning with others produces skill and the ability in using tools, and weapons, and method, as well as feelings of self-esteem.	Competence	School age
Identity versus role confusion The physical changes of adolescence arouse a new search for sameness and continuity and the need for a coherent sense of self.	Fidelity	Adolescence
Intimacy versus isolation A new ability to tolerate the threat of ego loss permits the establishment of mature relationships involving the fusion and counterpointing of identity.	Love	Young adulthood
Generativity versus stagnation The adult need to care for children and to guide the next generation produces the desire to leave something of substance as a legacy.	Care	Maturity
Integrity versus despair An accrued sense of order and meaning allows one to defend one's own life cycle as a contribution to the maintenance of the human world.	Wisdom	Old age

(Kitchener, 1978). A second important dialectical aspect of Erikson's theory is its emphasis on the importance of conflict in human development. Proposing that all growth proceeds from conflict, Erikson has cast each of his stages of development in terms of a unique crisis (see Table 2.4).

Erikson also believes, however, that societies as well as individuals reflect and support the stages he outlined. For example, societies are age-graded: new challenges and demands arise as the person ages. According to Erikson, age-grading reflects the interaction between epigenesis and the social structure (Erikson, 1963; Lerner, 1976; Riegel, 1977). Erikson's interest in cross-cultural research convinced him that every society sets up institutions designed to cope with the biologically based changes that occur during development (Miller, 1983).

Profoundly influenced by the work of the great cultural anthropologists, Erikson also concluded that the nature of the specific behaviors and arrangements at each stage of development must vary immensely from one culture to another, just as they must have varied radically over the course of history. Human development changes the structure of social institutions, just as social institutions influence development. For example, the institutions that govern adult heterosexual development will either promote or prevent the development of intimacy, which, when it does develop, will support certain institutions and not others. In Erikson's opinion, monogamous marriage is the institution most likely to promote the development of mature, intimate relationships, and the development of intimacy will, in turn, continue to support the institution of monogamous marriage as an important social structure.

Erikson's beliefs about marriage, and many other of the specific hypotheses he presents in the description of his theory, have been a basis for debate and criticism. Erikson sees his own theory in terms of its historical context; he even understands his own interest in adolescent ego development as a response to living in a highly technological society. Nonetheless, he has been criticized as ethnocentric, in part because he seems exceptionally positive about the social institutions around him, especially the American family. He never seems to consider the notion that the nuclear family may promote social isolation or be emotionally oppressive. The virtues he admires seem conforming at times, and it has been argued that he gives too little thought to the importance of rebellion and doubt. For example, Allan Buss (1979) has contended that Erikson's definition of integrity as the acceptance of one's life tends to stress the importance of acceptance at the expense of continuing development. Buss does not agree that acceptance is the capstone of personal growth.

It has also been pointed out that Erikson leaves the mechanisms of conflict substantially unexamined. Although he describes his stages in terms of conflict, he does not discuss the role of conflict or the process of resolution in any detail. Instead, he describes the content and outcome of each crisis, from infancy through old age, and explains the factors that influence movement through a particular stage (for example, parental attitudes and beliefs, cultural opportunities); he does not, however, specify the

Erikson believes that values like love, hope, faith, and charity are universal because they express the developmental rudiments of human strength.

mechanism by which we acquire particular behaviors. If development is, at least in part, dependent on external environmental events, how do these events make their mark? Is conditioning important? Modeling? Observation? We are not given the answers to these kinds of questions. In fact, the lack of such detail led Patricia Miller (1983) to write that "Erikson presents his theory as would a novelist or an artist rather than a scientist. At most, the theory is a loosely connected set of ideas and observations that could not, strictly speaking, be called a . . . theory" (p. 173).

In his own defense, Erikson argues that most of the terms he uses to explain development are everyday words found in the "living languages" and that as such "they express both what is universally human and what is culturally specific" in human values (1982, p. 58). Therefore, terms such as hope, faith, charity, and love must harbor some relation to the developmental rudiments of human strength; if we try to define them in simple, objective ways, we may well miss the most important aspects of their meaning. Erikson believes that his system embodies a developmental logic that reflects universal values, although the precise expression of those values may differ from one social system to another.

LOGIC AS DEFINITION.   Although he has not presented exacting definitions, he has detailed the logic of his stages in terms of the meaning of developments at each stage. According to Erikson, the strengths and virtues of earlier stages are necessary for development at each new stage. If growth falters at any of the eight stages, all further development is jeopardized. For example, the development of integrity in the last stage of life depends on the growth of generativity in the middle years of adulthood. The definition of the term "integrity," therefore, demands the inclusion of the qualities developed at the previous stage.

To illustrate, Erikson (1982) argues that *integrity,* in its simplest form, is a sense of coherence and wholeness that integrates the biological, psychological, and social aspects of one's life. He believes it is reflected in the wisdom of old age, which he defines as a "shared proclivity for understanding or for 'hearing' those who do understand, the integrative ways of human life" (1982, p. 65). In order to develop such understanding, one must care for people and for ideas, and caring is the central contribution of the middle adult stage of generativity. *Generativity,* which encompasses productivity and creativity, produces a widening commitment to *take care of* the persons and the ideas one has learned *to care for.* Thus, in middle age, "all the strengths arising from earlier developments . . ., from infancy to young adulthood (hope and will, purpose and skill, fidelity and love)," are "essential for the generational task of cultivating strength in the next generation" (1982, p. 67). Moreover, only when we have "taken care of things and people," and adapted to the "triumphs and disappointments" of the normal life cycle, do we possess an accurate sense of order and meaning—a sense that our own life cycle is a meaningful contribution to the maintenance of the human world (Erikson, 1963). In Erikson's theory, the last stage of life brings us full circle, for the development of trust in infancy is said to depend on the growth of integrity in the older generation.

Erikson also argues that the biological, psychological, and social aspects of development interact to produce each of the conflicts described in Table 2.4. For instance, children develop because they experience biological growth, which confers new psychological status and a new sense of mastery. Growth also influences how people react to the developing child. The entire environment is transformed by biological growth; at the same time, the environment is an important predictor of the extent and timing of such physical development. Growth in a changing environment produces a succession of imbalances within the child and between the child and the outside world. As the child tries to adjust the imbalance, personality structure changes. The child begins to interact with the environment differently, expressing adaptation and sowing the seeds of new conflict. Erikson calls this constant balance and imbalance the individual/society dialectic—the mutual exchange of influence (Langer, 1969; Riegel, 1977; Buss, 1979; Erikson, 1982).

Erikson also argues, however, that an individual who has too much conflict is unlikely to experience optimal development. He believes that a balance must be struck in the amount of conflict as well as the resolution of it. Perhaps for this reason, Erikson has always rejected radical change and argued that current institutions, including monogamous marriage and traditional parenthood, are necessary for mature development in adulthood. His critics disagree. For example, as Allan Buss (1979) asks, isn't it possible that confusion, doubt, or shame are in fact healthy psychological responses in a society that is oppressive or inhumane? It has also been suggested that Erikson's concept of identity achievement in adolescence is a particularly masculine, Western sort of solution to the definition of self (see Stevens-Long and Cobb, 1983, for a more extensive discussion of this issue). Perhaps *identity diffusion*, a less definite sense of identity, is more appropriate in a rapidly changing social structure. Moreover, in an oppressive or inhumane society, it may be healthier if individuals do not develop integrity—do not passively accept their lives as they have been lived—but continue to question and rebel to the very end.

Looking back on his life, the man called Zorba the Greek felt that although he had lived life to its fullest, he still had not done enough. "Men like me," he said, "ought to live a thousand years." Does mature development always depend on the acceptance of one's life as it has been lived and on the ability to encounter death without regret? That seems one kind of resolution, but it may not always be the bravest and the best. Mature developmental resolutions may be various and dependent on the social and historical atmosphere.

Generally, the same issues arise for any organismic or dialectical theory that offers a description of stages or optimal development: Are such descriptions muddied or even invalidated by the theoretician's own unconscious ideology? Even when a goal as simple as adaptation is proposed, we must consider it carefully. Is it always most mature to adapt? Are there times when survival or adaptation must be sacrificed for some abstract value? What of Patrick Henry's "Give me liberty or give me death!" Was he speaking and behaving in a mature way? Was his behavior adaptive?

Attempts at Synthesis and Criticism

Patricia Miller (1983) has written that the current theories available to developmental researchers fail to consider all relevant sources of influence on development and lack adequate descriptions of the mechanisms of development. It does seem to be true that no current theory offers much of a basis for synthesis, but current theoretical work does at least underline the problems and point up the need for a solution. In the past decade, the rational discussion of theory has occurred more often than the heated but often unenlightening debates that were aroused by the popularity of behaviorism or the growing influence of Jean Piaget through the late 1960s and early 1970s.

Ultimately, the problem of describing the causes and defining the mechanisms of development is the problem of resolving the nature/nurture controversy. That is what Miller means when she refers to the failure to consider all relevant sources of development. How shall we integrate the regular and seemingly universal appearance of some developments, like the acquisition of certain aspects of language, the impact of hormonal events or the importance of genetic directives, with the evidence that critical events, from infancy through old age, guide development in exceedingly complex and significant ways?

Some writers have proposed that development may be truly discontinuous (Birren, 1964; Labouvie-Vief and Chandler, 1978). Perhaps the theories that are useful in understanding childhood and adolescence are different from those that will prove fruitful in the analysis of adult behavior. Adult development may be more situational and less biological than growth in childhood. Although this point of view may underestimate what is universal or even highly probable in adulthood, the great cross-cultural variability that has been observed does not seem adequately explained by organismic theories or universal developmental processes. Indeed it seems shortsighted to describe all development outside of the path proscribed by a particular theory as "immature" or slow. An adequate synthesis must permit development to occur in multilevel, multidirectional ways (Urban, 1978).

In addition to the problem of explaining great individual and cultural differences, organismic theorists are often criticized for using vaguely defined terms, and for a tendency to posit unnecessary causes and processes (e.g., What is epigenesis anyway?). Critics demand operational definitions; that is, they want to know how a process or development is produced. The organismic theoretician, however, does not believe development is produced by environmental operations; therefore, the operations that might define a critical process cannot be specified. In other words, since epigenesis, for example, cannot be changed—since it is an internal, unobservable process—there is no way to define it in terms that a mechanist would accept.

Critics of mechanism, in contrast, argue that environmental analysis ignores both the rich complexity of human behavior and the regularity of development over a wide variety of cultures. Furthermore, they ask, how can the mechanist address topics like curiosity and creativity? If the organism is only capable of reaction to environmental forces, spontaneous or novel behavior is inexplicable.

The dialecticians contend that the environmentalists and the organismic theoreticians are both right and wrong. They argue that both qualitative and quantitative changes occur, that all systems are not only interactive but also transactive, and that the guiding principle of human development is conflict. Although the dialecticians express strong sentiment in favor of a theoretical synthesis, they have yet to offer a concrete general theory. Some dialecticians have even argued that the influence of unsystematic historical events makes concrete theory nearly impossible anyhow.

Where, then, should attempts at a synthesis begin? A. L. Baldwin (1980) has proposed that the most important first step in a true synthesis is the development of a more general language or vocabulary than any current developmental theory or model offers. We must be able to translate terms from one theory to another in order to define areas of overlap and conflict. The primary characteristic of a general language is neutrality: it must offer terms for every kind of phenomenon a researcher or writer might want to mention, whether or not the phenomenon is generally recognized. For instance, we must be able to discuss ghosts (or stimuli, or formal operations) as long as anyone wishes to comment on the subject.

A neutral language must allow for the explanation of both overt behavior and such hypothetical events as thoughts and feelings. It must also permit us to discuss maturation or conflict as well as conditioning, modeling, and observational learning. Motivational concepts like needs must be included as well as the possibility of spontaneous activity.

Moreover, such a language may be critical if the most appropriate explanatory approach is not the same for all the behaviors being studied, or for all stages of the life course, or for all historical periods. The meaning of a multicausal approach has been discussed at some length by Eric Labouvie (1982), who concludes that the task of multicausal theory and research is not so much one of identifying a particular determinant as a cause, but rather specifying the contexts in which a single determinant or a set of determinants is important and whether or not that determinant is sufficient to produce certain behavioral changes in the settings specified. He also points out that any one of several determinants may be sufficient to produce a particular change and yet the presence of any particular one may not be necessary.

Finally, rather than obscuring the one true theory, the multiplicity of theories available may simply permit the variety of analysis that seems required for the emergence of a general synthesis, if there is to be one. If we do not yet have the best idea, then it is very lucky indeed that we have a great number of competing ideas rather than a single inadequate one. It keeps our minds open and our wits sharp. It is certainly better to be wrong in a climate of dissent than to be wrong in a climate of agreement.

SUMMARY

In this chapter, we have examined three different sets of beliefs or assumptions about how human behavior develops: the mechanistic, organismic, and dialectical models. A model is an analogy or metaphor that embodies ideas about the untestable questions that surround human development, including such issues as whether nature or nurture has greater impact on behavior and whether developmental change proceeds in a quantitative, cumulative manner or by stages that represent qualitative change.

The mechanistic view suggests that human behavior may be understood as though it were the output of a very sophisticated machine. All change is seen as quantitative in nature—the result of the accumulation or experience—and is thought to be produced by input from the environment. From this point of view, human behavior is always changing, throughout the life span, but such changes are the predictable result of complex chains of simple events.

For the organismic theorist, the inner processes of the organism itself are the primary source of developmental change, and this change is thought to be characterized by the emergence of behaviors that are qualitatively different through the life span. The environment is usually thought to play a limited role when compared with the general, universal changes that are brought about by reorganization of internal structures through biological, maturational processes.

Finally, the dialectical model represents, to some degree, an attempt to synthesize the mechanistic and organismic views. Dialectics emphasizes the role of conflict in the development of the organismic and admits of change that proceeds both from the environment and from the action of the organism itself. Human beings can only be understood, from this viewpoint, as changing organisms interacting with a constantly changing environment.

Each of these models serves as a wellspring for developmental theory. A theory is a concrete set of hypotheses, an explanation for a particular set of phenomena. Basically, a theory is an attempt to relate something we do not understand to something we already assume to be true. Current developmental theories are not comprehensive, rigorous explanations of human behavior, but may be considered important guides or tools in the future growth of the field.

Mechanistic theories, like social learning theory and behaviorism, focus on the role of nonnormative events, those that do not occur for all individuals in a regular sequence or pattern. Mechanistic theories also stress the great variability of human behavior and the importance of individual differences. Examples include Inge Ahammer's analysis of marriage, parenthood, and other molar events in terms of such concepts as stimulus change, demand for behavioral change, and whether particular changes are experienced as aversive or rewarding.

Other mechanistic approaches, like that of Brim and Ryff, offer typologies of events. Brim and Ryff have demonstrated the utility of classifying events in terms of their objective properties, such as distribution or whether an event is experienced by many people, whether it is age-related, and whether it is likely to occur in the life of a particular person. Other researchers, including Chiriboga and Cutler, have tried to objectify certain important subjective aspects of life events, such as stress. Using an updated version of the Holms and Rahe scale, Chiriboga and Cutler have been able to classify people in terms of the role stress plays in their lives.

Of the organismic theories, the most influential is represented by Jean Piaget's work on intellectual development. His stages reflect all the basic assumptions of the organismic model, including a view of the organism as a constructive, active being, a belief in the universality of change, and the description of change as a qualitative phenomenon. A number of authors have tried to build on Piaget's theory, describing a fifth or adult stage of intellectual development. The most elaborate of these constructions is offered by Michael Commons and Francis Richards in a series of articles on the structural analytic stage.

Two examples of nonstage organismic theories are examined here—disengagement theory and Douglas Heath's study of maturity. Both of these ideas are based on the notion that there is some universal, optimal, or most adaptive form of development, and both have been most severely criticized on this ground. Once a state or stage called maturity is described, it is relatively easy to find examples that challenge the concept as ethnocentric.

The same criticism has been made of Erik Erikson, the one theorist who might be considered an example of dialectical thought. Although no truly representative dialectic theory of general development exists, Erikson's eight stages have served as an example of theory that stresses the importance of conflict and the concept of the changing organism developing in a changing social and historical context. Yet, despite Erikson's acknowledgment of the incredible cultural variety of human society, he is often described as ethnocentric and conforming.

In his own defense, Erikson has pointed out that his key concepts are those that have meaning in most of the living languages of the world. Ideas like integrity, love, fidelity, and trust must contain some part of what is universally human. Yet, there is little doubt that such concepts are difficult to define. In fact, Erikson must define them himself in terms of the logic of the stages he has proposed rather than their objective properties or the operations that might produce them in the real world.

Obviously, each of the theoretical schools has made telling points in addressing the others. Environmentalists are accused of ignoring what is spontaneous and rich and universal in development. Organismic theory appears to relegate the rich variety of human culture to a secondary role and to overlook the importance and power of individual and social differences. In admitting both points of view to some degree, dialectic theory seems to be rather vague about exactly how development proceeds.

What appears most sensible to date is the position that attempts at synthesis should address themselves to the development of a neutral language, one that will allow us to discover points of overlap and conflict between competing theoretical conceptions. Moreover, the encouragement of multiple theoretical and research approaches seems in order, especially of theories that might focus on the interaction between biology, behavior, and environment and emphasize evolutionary and historical change.

Perspectives

The Biological Context of Aging

The search for the biological processes that underlie aging comprises one of the fastest-growing and most fascinating literatures on human development. Since the early Egyptians wrote their medical prescriptions for aging, scientists and adventurers have been looking for the fountain of youth. The theoretical possibility that biological aging can be prevented, reversed, or even slowed has intrigued people in every era and every culture. At last, there appears to be some real, scientific progress toward understanding the critical processes.

A truly comprehensive theory of aging must now explain a variety of well-documented facts about both humans and other living beings. Why, for example, does each species have a characteristic life span varying from a few hours or days for an insect to hundreds of years for certain kinds of plants? And why do certain diseases, like pneumonia and arteriosclerosis, increase with age? Why do people respond less well to stress later in life and become more vulnerable to tissue and organ damage? What accounts for the fact that some tissues transplanted from a dying organism can live longer than the donor organism? How does radiation accelerate aging, and why does fasting appear to prolong the life span of certain animals? What explains the correlation of the life span of a species with the ratio between brain and body weight, and why is it that cells which reproduce through division appear to do so for a limited and specific number of times? Most, if not all, of these diverse observations are probably related and form the present data base for the explanation of biological aging (Brash and Hart, 1978).

Researchers have approached these questions from two general points of view: macroscopic (or extrinsic) theory and microscopic (or intrinsic) theory (Moment, 1978). Macroscopic theories focus on forces that affect the organism as a whole; microscopic theories outline changes in individual cells or in the relationships among cells. Macroscopic theories appear to be the most straightforward explanations for aging, since they represent the commonsense notion that, somehow, we simply die because we wear out.

Macroscopic Theory

WEAR AND TEAR. *The wear-and-tear model of aging stresses the importance of accumulated physical insults over the life span (Timiras, 1972). Organ systems may* simply wear out, or some key part may deteriorate. Alternatively, if different systems of the body age at different rates, a loss of synchrony may eventually occur. Figure P.1 illustrates how aging might proceed under three different sets of assumptions (Harrison, 1978):

1. All systems age at the same rate.

2. Only a key system ages.

3. No key part ages, but the interaction between systems becomes defective.

Disease might be responsible for wear and tear either because of specific effects (e.g., a heart attack) or by producing interactions that are so defective the organism is no longer able to survive. Add the effects of gravity, atmospheric pressure, and temperature, or the effects of radiation, and aging is accelerated. In a temperature-controlled vacuum, weightless and shielded from disease and radiation, some believe people might live to see a seven-hundredth birthday (Sobel, 1965).

In support of wear-and-tear theories, there is evidence that at least ninety deaths in every hundred are partly due to decreases in vitality with age. Wear-and-tear theory cannot account for the consistent differences in the maximum life spans of different species, however. (Table P.1 presents some maximum life-span estimates for various species.)

Why don't human beings live past 120? Despite all the rumors of conclaves of centenarians tucked away in the Caucasus mountains of Russia or in the recesses of the Andes, there is no well-documented evidence that any human being has survived much past one hundred. In fact, the most recent evidence suggests that the people of the Caucasus and Vilcabamba in the Andes are less than a hundred years old (Moment, 1978). What accounts for this "inexorable limitation on life?" (Beaubier, 1980).

ENTROPY. The relationship between the amount of organization in a system and the amount of energy available for useful work is known as entropy. One version of wear-and-tear theory offers formulas that predict maximum life spans based on the assumption that there is some basic life substance that is used up as the organism lives. The use of this substance is reflected, to some extent, in the loss of body heat over the life span, but adjustments must be made for the relationship of brain weight to body weight in order to make very accurate predictions. That is where the concept of entropy, or how efficiently

FIGURE P.1
The Aging Process: Three Possibilities

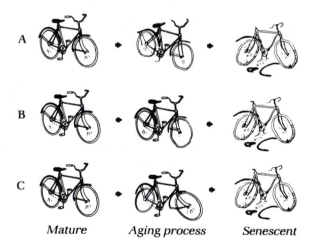

A

B

C

Mature   Aging process   Senescent

These bicycles illustrate three different possible ways aging could be timed on the cell-tissue level. (A) All the parts are intrinsically timed to age at similar rates. (B) Only one key part, the front wheel, is intrinsically timed to age initially. Its malfunction damages the other parts, causing them to age also, although they could have continued to function normally if the front wheel had not aged. (C) No single part ages intrinsically, but the interaction of parts becomes defective. The poorly aligned parts damage each other, causing them to age, although they could have continued to function normally if their interactions had remained correct.

SOURCE: D. Harrison, "Is Cell Proliferation the Clock That Times Aging?" in A. Behnke and C. Finch, eds., *The Biology of Aging* (New York: Plenum, 1980), p. 34.

TABLE P.1
Some typical average and maximum life spans of living things

	Typical life span (years)		Maximum life span (years)	
Trees				
Olive	—		2000	
Douglas fir	—		1000	
Sugar pine	—		600	
White ash	—		300	
Flowering dogwood	—		125	
Coconut	—		40	
Mammals				
Horse	25		62	
Lion	15	(in captivity)	35	
Giraffe	14	(in captivity)	28	
Deer mouse	4	(in captivity)	8	
Black rat	2		4	
Man	70–80		110(?)	
Fish				
Sturgeon	46		152	
Eel	15		55	(in captivity)
Cod	—		16	
Invertebrates				
Atlantic lobster	—		50	
American tarantula	—		20	(in captivity)
Queen ant	—		19	(in captivity)
Earthworm	—		10	(in captivity)
Birds				
Eagle	104		—	
Chicken	20		—	
Goose	50		—	
Owl	—		68	
Mollusca				
Snail	—		18	
Freshwater clam	—		100	(150?)

SOURCE: Based on A. K. Lansing, "General Biology of Senescence," in J. E. Birren, ed., *Handbook of Aging and the Individual* (Chicago: University of Chicago Press, 1959); and L. J. Milne and N. Milne, *The Ages of Life* (New York: Harcourt, Brace, Jovanovich, 1968), p. 313.

the organism uses its energy, becomes important. The greater the cybernetic capacity of the organism—or the greater its ability to adapt to and control the environment—the more the organism is able to acquire and utilize information. In other words, energy is utilized more efficiently, and the organism lives longer.

Entropy theory does a reasonably good job of predicting the maximum life span (Sacher, 1965), but a number of our other questions remain essentially unanswered. Why should radiation accelerate aging? How does entropy account for the fact that cells reproduce only a precisely limited number of times? Why would tissues that are transplanted outlive the donor organism? Most of the questions unanswered by wear-and-tear theories have been handled more effectively at the microscopic level.

Microscopic Theory

Microscopic theories refer to events that take place in the cells themselves or in the processes that occur within and between cells. For instance, each time a cell reproduces, there is a tendency for errors to occur in the new cell. Moreover, with time, the number of highly specialized cells that

do not divide decreases, and waste products build up in cells that are not lost. Taken together, changes in cell function might produce a cascade of degenerative neural, endocrine, and metabolic events (Finch, 1978). These observations form the basis for one very important hypothesis called somatic theory.

SOMATIC THEORY. As you probably remember from high school biology, the nucleus of every cell in the body contains thousands of genes scattered over forty-six chromosomes. A gene is a segment of the complex molecule called desoxyribonucleic acid (DNA), which is composed of two strands of chemical bases wound around one another to form a double helix (Watson and Crick, 1953). Labile cells (cells that consistently reproduce themselves), such as those of the mucosal linings or the red blood cells, undergo constant mitotic activity. That is, they reproduce by a process in which complex nuclear division occurs, usually involving the halving of the chromosomes. During this process, DNA is continually splitting and duplicating itself, creating new cellular material.

Somatic theory is based on the notion that every time a cell is replaced or a segment of DNA is renewed, genetic error or mutation can occur. Mutations will then accumulate with age, curtailing cellular functions (Curtis, 1965). Eventually, the cells become so inefficient that death ensues. In other words, cell death is the result of an error catastrophe (Orgel, 1963). Significant positive relationships do exist between aging and cellular mutation, and it is estimated that by the age of ninety, there is probably one error in every cell in the human body (Curtis, 1965).

Somatic theory does account for species-specific life spans. It also explains the correlation of these spans with heart rate, metabolic rate, and a variety of other phenomena that take place over time, as well as increasing mortality rates after maturity. All of these observations may be a product of the accumulation of damage, especially if there is a threshold past which death results. If the damage threshold or maximum amount of error is genetically determined by, for example, the capacity of the species to repair DNA, then species-specific life spans are explained.

The effects of radiation are predicted by somatic theory, since ultraviolet rays damage the structure of DNA. Moreover, people who age prematurely appear to have a particularly high number of mutant cells for their age. Finally, increased susceptibility to stress with age may result from mutation, because cell redundancy is lost. A large (redundant) number of cells all perform the same task, enabling the body to cope easily with stressful situations. As errors accumulate and cells die, fewer cells perform more of the time, producing fatigue in the remaining healthy cells (Brash and Hart, 1978).

Although the case for somatic theory is fairly convincing, some theorists believe that the rate of mutation in most animals is too slow to account for aging. Other theoretical possibilities, especially the malfunction of the immune system with age, seem to be necessary events in the aging of human systems.

AUTOIMMUNE THEORY. The immune system is very complicated, and several versions of its role in senescence have been proposed. Basically, the immune system produces antibodies that neutralize any foreign agents that enter an organism—for example, viral or bacterial infections. One version of autoimmune theory suggests that as errors accumulate in the cells of the body, the autoimmune system begins attacking these mutant cells. In the end, the body is, in effect, self-destructing (Burch, 1968; Walford, 1965). It has also been added that when mutants, or forbidden clones, as they are sometimes called, are attacked, healthy tissue around the mutant is also damaged (Beaubier, 1980; Burch, 1968).

As the immune system ages, there is also some possibility that it loses the ability to distinguish between self and foreign elements. Healthy tissue may be lost, and protection against infected or cancerous cells may disappear (Adler, 1974; Beaubier, 1980).

Taken alone, autoimmune theory is unsatisfactory, because some organisms that do age do not have immune systems. Most often, autoimmune theory is combined with somatic theory to explain aging within cells. Aging also occurs, however, in the processes that occur between cells.

CROSS-LINKING THEORY. Both the protein that makes up the tissues of the body and the ground substance around all tissues are changed with age. The ground substance dries out as one ages, and tissue proteins, like collagen, become cross-linked or joined to their neighbors. Cross-linking affects tissue the way tanning leather affects cowhide; the tissues become tough, stiff, and leathery. The chemicals that cause cross-linking are continually produced during the normal processes of cell metabolism.

It may even be that cell mutations and the aging of the immune system are produced by the cross-linking of DNA in the cell nucleus. Cross-linking might also impede the diffusion of gases, hormones, and nutrients and the exchange of waste across the membrane.

One of the most intriguing aspects of cross-linking theory, however, is the possibility that aging might be slowed through the control of cross-linking. For instance, overeating produces cross-linking because food products are not properly metabolized. Diets low in fat and intermittent fasting may slow the formation of cross-links. Some also believe vitamins E and C slow the production of cross-linking agents and help eliminate them from the body (Bakerman, 1969; Beaubier, 1980).

One author has even proposed that we will soon learn how to break down cross-linked cells, allowing aging systems to be replaced and rejuvenated (Hershey, 1974). If cross-linked tissues are removed and the growth of new, more elastic protein occurs, the normal life span might be extended by as much as a hundred years! Cross-linking theory is, perhaps, the most optimistic of the microscopic explanations. It can be integrated with another popular concept, free-radical theory, to support many hopeful hypotheses about aging.

FREE-RADICAL THEORY. A free-radical molecule is one that has a smaller- or larger-than-usual number of electrons.

Free-radicals are created during the normal process of cell metabolism. The standard joke is that chemical free-radicals, like their human namesakes, bond with everything in sight.

The bonds formed by free-radicals may account for the cross-linkage of proteins, chromosomal damage, accumulation of waste material in cells, and the deterioration of the cell membrane with age, and they may even provoke the destruction of the immune system. Again, vitamins E and C might help fight the production of free-radicals because they suppress oxidation and slow cell metabolism. American diets often lack not only vitamin E but other essential vitamins and minerals as well. A diet rich in fish, vegetables, wheat germ, eggs, yeast, and fruit might extend the life span (Hershey, 1974; Beaubier, 1980).

The four microscopic theories we have reviewed so far can be integrated, and each offers some cause for optimism in the battle against age. There are those, however, who argue that the data suggest not the hope of increased longevity, but the existence of a genetic mechanism that triggers aging and death. Death-clock theories assume that the death of the individual helps insure the survival of the species.

PROGRAMMED THEORY.   Perhaps the evolution and reproduction of complex organisms is somehow related to the "inherent, progressive, irreversible impairments of function," which "inevitably lead to death" (Sonneborn, 1978, p. 361). Many simple organisms do not age and may be said to die only by accident. In fact, all organisms that have only one chromosome of each kind lack natural aging, whereas all those that, like human beings, have two chromosomes of each kind have natural aging.

Diploid organisms, or those that have two sets of chromosomes, have the potential for recessive genes, making possible the explosive and diversified evolution of complex life. It took about three million years for organisms with only one set of chromosomes to produce an organism with two sets, and only about one-sixth of that time for the rest of evolution to occur.

Tracy Sonnenborn (1978) contends that the elimination of individuals past the reproductive stage is an important part of the process of evolution in complex organisms. Extension of the life span through medicine and technology could slow down the rate of evolution. What effect, he asks, might such slowing have, not only on human beings, but on the entire ecosystem?

Some biologists don't think we need to worry about the answer to Sonneborn's question. Leonard Hayflick (1974) has repeatedly demonstrated that normal human cells reproduce as many as fifty times and then cease to replicate themselves. He has contended that there is a mechanism in the cell, which he calls a death clock, that is responsible for determining the time of death. It may be something like "the end of a tape recording" simply triggering the events that shut off the machine; or death may be a result of the accumulation of error (Hayflick, 1979). If Hayflick is correct, we may be a long way from the technology that will allow us to extend the life span by a great many years.

New Demographic Realities

As Hayflick himself points out, however, "most gerontologists agree that there is probably no single cause of aging" (1979, p. 16). Yet many biologists think that we will understand some of the essential principles and many of the details of aging as early as the year 2000. One writer (Strehler, 1979) has offered the following probabilities: (1) an 80 percent probability of extending the healthy life span by 20 percent; (2) a 40 percent chance of a fifty-to-hundred year extension; and (3) a 5 percent chance of an indefinite extension.

Already, we have reports that the average life span for women has increased to about eight-five years and that most men may see as many as seventy-five years. Undoubtedly, major social and cultural changes will accompany new demographic realities. For instance, retirement age will probably rise at least ten years; there will be increasing difficulty with the Social Security system, and very strict laws against age discrimination may emerge.

Multigenerational families are likely to become commonplace, especially if housing shortages become chronic. Four-generation families could place the care of the youngest and oldest members of the family in the hands of two middle generations rather than one. Intergenerational marriage may become more frequent and women of the 1960s and 1970s may be especially open to new kinds of living arrangements if the men their age continue to die ten to fifteen years before they do (Gordon, 1979; Troll, 1977).

All in all, advances in biology and medicine continue to create strong motives for the study of adult development. The same kind of social and economic forces that set the stage for the study of *childhood and adolescence exist now in the arena of aging. If there are to be millions and millions more elderly people, the social sciences must discover the key to membership in the "elite aged" (Birren, 1980). These special people are "strong yet flexible, feeling yet controlled, living in the present yet planning for tomorrow, feeling less need to justify their past views and behavior, which brings them into the present with pride and strength" (p. 43).*

II

Young Adulthood

Chapter 3

The Inner Context of Development: Biology and Cognition in Young Adulthood

When all the world is young, lad
And all the trees are green;
And every goose a swan, lad,
And every lass a queen;
Then hey, for boot and horse, lad,
And round the world away;
Young blood must have its course, lad,
And every dog his day.

CHARLES KINGSLEY
Song from *Water Babies*

Most dictionaries include among their definitions of age and aging phrases like "to ripen or become mature," and during young adulthood this seems an apt description. In almost every way, the years from twenty to twenty-five are the pinnacle of biological development. Our bones and skin are strong and supple, our muscles are powerful, our senses are keen, our minds are agile, and our teeth are our own. Death seems as remote as Pluto and Neptune.

Ironically, however, even by the age of thirty, physiological decline is measurable in a variety of ways. Some functions—for example, the performance of the heart and the circulatory system—pass the peak of optimal functioning near the end of adolescence. It has been estimated that general bodily functioning may decline at the rate of about 1 percent per year throughout all of adult life (Bierman and Hazzard, 1973). Of course, there are many ways to ensure continuing good health and to slow the negative effects of age, and young adulthood is not too soon to begin.

To start our review, we will look at the level of physical functioning typical of young adult life. It is during this period that most people often experience feelings of peak performance, strength, and prowess. Many systems are functioning maximally; in fact, evidence suggests that skeletal growth continues throughout one's twenties, and as much as one to two centimeters in height are added between nineteen to twenty-eight (Hammar and Owens, 1973). The muscular development characteristic of adolescence continues, and many important signs of sexual maturity appear, from hair on the chest to the maturity of the uterus. At the same time, the data show subtle changes in the functions of organ systems that underline the importance of exercise, good nutrition, and informed health habits throughout adulthood (Fries and Crapo, 1981).

Aging is a multidirectional process; it is accompanied by the benefits of experience, the comforts of a well-established life, and the problems of physical and emotional wear and tear. We will examine both the boons and the burdens here from sensory and perceptual functions to cognition and moral development. Finally, we will look at the social and psychological tasks to which all of these systems and abilities respond in young adulthood.

PHYSICAL FUNCTIONING

Strength

Peak physical strength in the *striped muscles* is achieved between the ages of twenty-three and twenty-seven (Hershey, 1974). (The striped muscles are commonly called the voluntary muscles, like the biceps and triceps.) Thus, the capacity for physical labor and for strenuous athletic endeavors is greatest during one's middle to late twenties. Performance in the most vigorous sports, like tennis and boxing, seems to peak before the age of thirty, while top form in such activities as billiards and golf tends to occur between twenty-nine and thirty-four (Lehman, 1953). Obviously, the sports that require the greatest physical endurance and speed are the ones in which we pass our maximum capacity earliest.

The early effects of aging are also evident in measures like maximum work rate without fatigue or in the ability to climb stairs, run on a treadmill, or crank a wheel (Hershey, 1974). The capacity to work at high temperatures falls off sharply before the age of thirty, a fact reflected in the stamina of coal miners, for instance, who show higher accident rates after thirty under extreme temperature conditions.

Unlike coal miners or professional athletes, however, most of us scarcely notice these kinds of changes in maximum capacity or top performance. Over the years of young adulthood, we learn a variety of strategies designed to maintain vigorous physical condition and satisfactory work performance. We learn to shepherd our strength, carefully expending maximum effort at the precise moment required (Timiras, 1972). Moreover, regular physical recreation and exercise as well as a sensible diet can help ensure many healthy adult years. On the other hand, people who place great value on feelings of physical strength and prowess—professional athletes, for example—may feel older and experience more negative feelings about their age than people who do not assess themselves largely in terms of physical attributes (Bühler, 1972).

Vital Functions and Body Systems

The *vital functions*, which include the performance of the cardiovascular and pulmonary systems, undergo important changes during young adulthood. Evidence indicates noticeable decrease in heart and lung function by the age of forty. Using data collected from the files of the Selective Service during World War II, for example, Goldstein (1951) analyzed records of

Vigorous physical activity doesn't necessarily require expensive equipment, fancy clothes, or tedious hours in the gym.

army physicals with particular attention to tests that measured recovery from the strain of physical activity. Between the ages of twenty and forty, the men being tested showed a substantial increase in the time required for recovery. Moreover, while only 29.3 percent of the eighteen to twenty years olds were rejected for military service, 64.7 percent of those between thirty-eight and forty were deemed unfit for service.

Although Goldstein's study suggests important changes in the heart and circulatory system, it offers no direct evidence such as that derived from tests of *cardiac output,* defined as the quantity of blood ejected each minute by one of the ventricles of the heart. Maximum cardiac output is reached between the ages of twenty and thirty, and slowly declines thereafter (Hershey, 1974). The heart, arteries, and arterioles become less elastic with age; this rigidity may explain both decreases in cardiac output and the increases in blood pressure typical of later life (Ruch and Fulton, 1960). Important changes also take place in maximum breathing capacity. Hershey (1974) estimates that for every ten years or so of adult life, the lungs lose 8 percent of their ability to allow air to pass into the membranes.

Vital capacity—the sum of the *inspiratory* and *expiratory reserves* of the lungs—is one measure of pulmonary function. The difference between the amount of air one takes in during a normal, relaxed breath and the amount one can take in during a maximum breath is called the inspiratory reserve. Similarly, the amount of air one can still exhale after a normal breath is called the expiratory reserve. The sum of these two reserves, the vital capacity of the lungs, decreases sharply between twenty and forty (Bromley, 1974).

Just as the amount of oxygen one can get in a single breath decreases during adulthood, so too does the rate of oxygen consumption, at least in the normal, resting state. The *basal metabolic rate* (BMR), an index of the exchange of energy in the body that reflects the amount of oxygen consumed by a relaxed, well-rested person, is much higher during periods of rapid growth than during adulthood. The normal BMR decreases throughout adult life at a fairly steady rate (Boothby, Berkson, and Dunn, 1936).

Many other direct observations demonstrate that the body is changing throughout early adulthood. The lymphatic system, for example, undergoes atrophy, and some of its components disappear altogether. The thymus gland is replaced by fibroid tissues even before full maturity is achieved (Sinclair, 1969). The output of the adrenal glands declines gradually after the age of twenty-five or so (Bromley, 1974), and at about age thirty, the secretion of gastric juices during normal intestinal functioning declines significantly (Timiras, 1972). Finally, some noticeable alterations take place in the structure and function of the nervous system during the early adult years. The number of cells in the central nervous system actually decreases after puberty (Sinclair, 1969), and the size of the brain decreases. Sinclair (1969) rather wryly summed up much of the evidence when he wrote, "It may even be said that old age begins to make itself felt as soon as maturity is reached."

But just how strongly do we feel these changes? Decreases in muscular strength, vital functions, or gastric secretion do not seriously hamper the day-to-day lives of most adults. The loss of a thymus gland, the attrition of a few nerve cells (even a few thousand), even a general 2 percent decline in the efficiency of body functions goes unmourned by most of us. For all intents and purposes, the physical aspects of early adult life are probably best described as relatively stable. In fact, Lillian Troll (1977) believes that the decline in physical function between twenty and fifty is so gradual that the entire period is most accurately described as a plateau.

Changes in body systems may offer clues to the solutions of theoretical problems to those interested in aging, but they have little meaning for most people, who do not experience them until middle age at the earliest. The one exception—notable not only because of its impact on daily life but also because its optimal functioning is restricted to the period of young adulthood—is the reproductive system.

Reproductive and Sexual Physiology

So much has been written, spoken, sung, and filmed on the subject of sexual behavior in the past fifteen or twenty years that a number of social observers have begun to wonder whether there isn't too much pressure on young people to be sexually active. As Robert Hettlinger (1977) has pointed out, many college students consider it harmful or neurotic to abstain from sexual intercourse. Contending that adolescents learn from adults the message that an active sexual life is an essential characteristic of mental health, Hettlinger notes that popular "sex experts" often sound like salesmen. For example, in the now-classic work of pop sex therapy, *Everything You Always Wanted to Know About Sex (But Were Afraid to Ask)*, David Reuben suggested that "no sex is so stupid it is not even worth considering," certainly a debatable point of view (Rubin, 1969, pp. 107–108).

Considering Americas' recent preoccupation with sexual activity, it is not surprising that in the past generation young adults have changed not only their attitudes but their sexual behavior over the last few decades. This is especially true of young women. Most studies of college-aged females report that about one-half of them have engaged in sexual intercourse by the age of 19 or 20, and in some geographical regions the proportion is much higher (Dreyer, 1975). As recently as the late 1960s, researchers were reporting that only 20 to 25 percent of college-aged females had experienced sexual intercourse (Reiss, 1967).

If we look back even farther, the extent of change in American sexual attitudes and behaviors is more dramatic. One fascinating review of the marriage manuals published during a seventy-year period shows that at the turn of the century, both expert and lay opinion held that normal females did not and should not desire sexual arousal (Gordon and Shankweiler, 1971). Today we are confronted by the concept of multiple orgasm as the definition of "normal" female sexuality. Certainly, there has been a change in the climate of sexual opinion.

As we shall see in Chapter 5, the forces behind this so-called sexual revolution are both direct (women have greater freedom and independence) and indirect (contraception is more readily available; the reduction of infant mortality means the population can grow or be maintained with fewer pregnancies). Perhaps more than any other single effort, the research of William Masters and Virginia Johnson has both reflected and influenced such change (1966; 1970; Masters, Johnson, and Kolodny, 1982). These researchers can recall the prejudice and even outrage that surrounded their early work in the 1950s. At first they were unable to find either the funding or the laboratory space to continue their studies. Yet, just ten years later, their first volume, *Human Sexual Response* (1966), became not only a landmark in the research literature on sexuality but a bestseller as well.

In *Human Sexual Response*, Masters and Johnson outlined the basic physiological responses of both sexes during sexual arousal, describing the sequence of events in terms of four phases or stages and emphasizing the remarkable parallels between the male and female sexual experience. The first two stages, excitement and plateau, are characterized by increasing *vasocongestion* (engorgement of the blood vessels) in the sexual organs of both sexes. In the excitement phase, vasocongestion in the male produces flattening and constriction of the scrotum and elevation of the scrotal sac, along with penile erection. In the female, vasocongestion produces engorgement of the major and minor labia (the lips of the vagina), thus extending the vaginal barrel and forming a kind of orgasmic platform. The third stage, orgasm, is experienced by females over a longer time than the male counterpart. Both male and female orgasm, however, are produced by muscular contractions—contractions of the uterine musculature and the vaginal orgasmic platform in the female and of the musculature in the penis and the scrotal area in the male.

In the final phase, resolution, the vasocongestive responses that characterize the first three phases gradually disappear, and the male experiences a *refractory period* during which he cannot be restimulated to orgasm. Because females do not appear to exhibit a refractory period, they sometimes experience what may have become one of the best-publicized phenomena since the invention of winged flight: multiple orgasm. *Multiple orgasm* refers to the occurrence of several orgasmic phases during one sexual experience; despite its sketchy, vague definition, in the 1970s and 1980s it seems to have become a symbol of female sexual emancipation.

The concept of multiple orgasm has raised multiple unanswered questions. For instance, exactly what is an orgasm? Masters and Johnson (1966) indicated that three to five contractions of the female pelvic musculature constitute an orgasm. Do six to ten contractions then constitute two orgasms? Multiply orgasmic women are said to move back and forth between plateau and orgasm, but what exactly is meant by "back and forth"? How long is the second plateau period? Can resolution (rather than plateau) occur between orgasms? How common is multiple orgasm, and what other kinds of patterns prevail? Nearly twenty years after the publication of *Human Sexual Response*, these questions remained unanswered (Masters, Johnson, and Kolodny, 1982).

And what of male orgasm? Although most American males appear to define orgasm in terms of ejaculation, evidence suggests that erection, ejaculation, and orgasm may be independent processes. Ejaculation can occur without erection, and erection often occurs without ejaculation. Furthermore, some paraplegic and quadraplegic men report the occurrence of ejaculation without orgasm. Others, who can achieve neither erection nor ejaculation still have dreams during which they report that orgasm occurs (McCary and McCary, 1982).

These are only a few of the questions we can raise about even the best research on sexual behavior and physiology. It seems most prudent, then, to regard most of the popular sex manuals and advice columns with a skeptical, questioning eye. The relationships between subjective sexual experience and objective behavior or physiology are not well understood and seem all too easily subject to poorly documented speculation.

Pregnancy and Childbirth as Biological Events

Pregnancy is typically divided into three major stages, called *trimesters*, each three months long. During the first trimester, the uterus enlarges about threefold, but relatively few obvious bodily changes occur. In fact, in the case of first pregnancies many women don't know for some time whether they are really pregnant. The traditional sign is the absence of a menstrual period, since the lining of the uterus is retained after a fertile egg is implanted; however, some slight bleeding or spotting is common even after the egg is implanted in the uterine wall and may be mistaken for a menstrual period.

Other physical symptoms include swelling of the breasts and increased pigmentation of the nipples. Fatigue is also common during the first three months. And as many as two-thirds of all pregnant women experience nausea in the first trimester, especially in the morning, probably as a response to increased hormone production. Another common experience is unusual sweating, which may be caused by increased thyroid production (Insel and Roth, 1982).

Many of the more unpleasant symptoms of pregnancy subside in the second trimester. Throughout pregnancy, some changes become more advanced with every month. For example, the muscles and ligaments around the pelvic area soften and stretch, the cervix (the lower part of the uterus) softens, and the circulatory and respiratory systems become more efficient. Blood plasma, for instance, increases by 50 percent during pregnancy; blood cells increase by 18 percent. Moreover, pregnant women take in about 40 percent more air, a phenomenon permitted by expansion of the rib cage.

Beginning in the second trimester, weight gain proceeds at about one pound per week. Because the skin must stretch to accommodate even moderate increases in weight, small breaks often occur in the lower layers of the skin, which do not stretch easily. These breaks, called stretch marks, appear as narrow streaks on the surface of the skin.

Despite the gains in weight and accompanying changes in body image, many women feel especially well during the second trimester of pregnancy. One of the factors that seems to contribute to this sense of

Despite the need to cope with a radically changed body image, pregnancy can bring bursts of vitality and a heightened sense of well-being.

well-being is the experience of quickening, which ordinarily occurs in the fourth or fifth month. *Quickening* refers to the sensing of fetal movements. It is at this point that many first-time mothers begin to develop an emotional bond with the unborn infant. They can now experience the life they are carrying. Many also feel a great sense of relief, because the greatest danger of miscarriage is over. Most miscarriages occur in the first trimester (Liefer, 1977).

In the final trimester of pregnancy, the demands that the fetus makes on the mother's respiratory, excretory, and circulatory systems become more apparent. Swelling of the legs and general water retention, heartburn, and constipation are common complaints in the last three months. Even women who exhibit no unusual swelling may retain six quarts or more of liquid. In extreme cases, swelling can be a symptom of the *toxemia of pregnancy,* a metabolic disturbance associated with high blood pressure, headaches, blurred vision, and eventually with such dangers as convulsions and coma. Swelling should be reported to the doctor or medical facility, since toxemia can be managed through dietary restrictions and the use of diuretics—chemicals that promote the excretion of urine.

In the final month of pregnancy, the fetus usually drops, or settles, down into the pelvic area. This event is called *lightening*. Although pressure on the pelvic structures increases, lightening is associated with decreasing pressure on the diaphragm, which makes breathing easier.

The uterus, the largest muscle in the human body, is responsible, finally, for labor and, ultimately, birth. Incredibly, the uterus increases to about fifty to sixty times its normal size during childbearing. During labor, the process by which this giant muscular structure expels the fetus, the uterus becomes smaller with each set of contractions. The cervix thins while the upper portion of the uterus contracts and thickens. Labor pains are thought to be a product of the pressure of the fetus on the cervix and the pelvic structure, rather than a result of the contractions of the uterus.

Labor averages fourteen hours for a first birth and eight hours for subsequent births (Insel and Roth, 1982). A normal labor can be divided into at least three stages. The first stage is characterized by contractions that occur every 15 to 20 minutes and last about 25 to 30 seconds each. When the cervix is well dilated, the second stage of labor usually begins. The second stage is defined by the entry of the baby's head into the birth canal; it typically lasts about 30 minutes to two hours for a first birth and 10 to 30 minutes in subsequent ones. Birth itself begins with the *crowning* of the baby's head as it passes through the pelvic outlet and is encircled by the vulva. After the crowning, birth is usually complete in about 2 or 3 minutes. In the final stage of labor, expulsion of the placenta is achieved by continued uterine contractions. This process takes about five minutes.

Following childbirth, the uterus and other sex organs involute, or slowly return to normal size and condition. *Involution* may require six to eight weeks. Evidence demonstrates that the most rapid recovery occurs in the nursing mother.

Pregnancy and Childbirth as Psychological Events

In contrast to most of the biological events and changes of young adulthood, pregnancy and childbirth seem to embody a strong psychological component that should be considered in any discussion of these events. Although research on pregnancy and childbirth as psychological events is not plentiful, a 1977 study by Myra Leifer offers a convincing, in-depth picture of the reactions of twenty first-time mothers. Leifer sees pregnancy as a series of developmental tasks, each of which represents a unique stress or conflict to which the pregnant mother must adapt in order for further maturation to occur.

In her sample of young adults, Leifer found that those women who viewed motherhood as a chance for personal growth rather than as a symbol of security or status were most likely to experience pregnancy as a positive state. She did find, however, that regardless of the degree of satisfaction a woman felt with pregnancy or with her own body image prior to pregnancy, the body changes associated with pregnancy evoked negative feelings. Those with the most positive attitudes toward pregnancy did not feel dissatisfied until the last trimester of childbearing, but eventually all of the women reported some negative feelings.

Many of the women Leifer interviewed were particularly embarrassed by the sexual implications of the changes in their bodies, especially during the first few months after childbirth, when the experience of fetal movements and the extra attention accorded a pregnant woman were no longer available. Leifer found very strong evidence for a general trend toward more negative mood tone after the birth of the child, even in those women who made the best adjustments to pregnancy. Furthermore, she reported that these feelings persisted through at least the first seven months after the child's birth.

Leifer suggests that high maternal anxiety during pregnancy, about the fetus, the self, or both, is a common experience. Contrary to much professional opinion, she argues that such anxiety about the fetus is not neurotic but is a normal part of the development of bonding between the unborn fetus and the mother. Leifer also believes that the bonding process is reflected by the pregnant woman's preoccupation with herself and her pregnancy, by her declining investment in the external world, and by a need to be alone, to withdraw, especially in stressful situations. According to Leifer, disengagement from social life accompanied by increased focus on the fetus is typical of the second trimester of pregnancy.

Leifer's sample also showed increased emotional vulnerability, marked mood swings, tension, and irritability during the last trimester of pregnancy. Yet there were also intensified feelings of well-being at times during the last few months. Immediately after birth, many of the mothers experienced great elation and satisfaction at the birth process itself. Within a few days, however, feelings of depression and anxiety were most common.

For more than two-thirds of the sample, the postpartum period was a very negative one, characterized by irritability and feelings of isolation and depression. In all, the immediate postpartum period seemed to be best characterized as a time of intense emotional stress. After about two months of motherhood, these feelings of depression and anxiety seemed to be replaced by boredom with the routine of child care. Seven months after childbirth, the mood of the women in Leifer's sample was still predominantly negative.

The transition to parenthood, Leifer contends, must be viewed as a period of emotional upheaval that is not necessarily related to emotional growth. Although some of the women in the sample did mature during this period, some did not. While some did indicate an increased sense of completeness as a person, some never became greatly attached to their children or enjoyed motherhood much. (Leifer notes that a positive adaptation to pregnancy seems to presage good mothering behavior, and the degree of affective involvement a woman feels with the fetus by the third month of pregnancy is a relatively reliable predictor of maternal feelings.) Even among those who made the best adjustments, however, feelings of depression, isolation, and increasing dissatisfaction and boredom with child care were common. Furthermore, the majority expressed moderate to high degrees of stress over general changes in their life-styles. They were concerned about lack of household help, curtailment of their personal freedom, and changes in their marital relationships.

We will return to the issues raised by the transition to parenthood in Chapter 5. For now, it seems clear that, even when speaking of those biological changes that would seem most directly related to psychological processes, the nature of such relationships is as yet poorly understood. Another obvious area in which to begin looking for such relationships is in the study of sensation and perception. Because these phenomena are closely tied to the structure and function of sensory systems, they might be expected to reflect any age-related changes in those systems or in the nervous tissues that serve the sensory system.

SENSATION, PERCEPTION, AND PSYCHOMOTOR SKILLS

Sensation

Does an apple taste the same to you whether you are ten or seventy? Do you like the same odors at twelve as at twenty-one? Does the experience of pain decline with age? Changes in what we see and hear and taste and smell are the concerns of those who study sensation and perception over the life span. Sensation involves the degree or nature or intensity of stimulation we experience; perception refers to what we make of it.

Generally, *sensation* is defined as the awareness of simple stimuli and is discussed in terms of the activity of sensory receptors and the coding and transmission of stimulus energy. *Perception*, which involves the recognition of complex stimuli and the interpretation of patterns of sensation, is usually discussed in terms of higher-order processes occurring in the central nervous system (Birren, Kinney, Schaie, and Woodruff, 1980; Corso, 1981). Throughout young adulthood, performance on most tasks designed to measure sensory and perceptual function is stable, despite some reduction in the sensitivity of the sense receptors (which actually can be seen even before young adulthood). This reduction is not apparent in our day-to-day functioning, however (Birren, 1964).

The most impressive evidence for early changes in our sense receptors involves measures of minimal responsiveness—in other words, when stimulation is very brief or of low intensity. (For example, a *threshold* is the lowest intensity of a stimulus that will produce a sensation.) Whether a sensation occurs is a function of the amount of energy absorbed by the sensory receptors, and the amount of energy required to produce sensation increases throughout adult life. Yet, because most stimuli of any importance in the real world occur at magnitudes much greater than threshold values, the sensory systems may show substantially reduced sensitivity before everyday functioning is affected.

Some decline takes place in the ability to see small details (*visual acuity*) after the age of twenty-five, and changes also occur in sensitivity to light as measured in the fully dark-adapted eye. *Dark adaptation* is the accommodation of the eye to darkness. The minimum stimulus noticeable after the eye is completely adapted to darkness is the most sensitive measure of the efficiency of the visual system. Visual efficiency measured in this manner decreases noticeably during young adulthood (Birren, 1964; Corso, 1981).

Several other pieces of evidence indicate that the visual system changes in the years between twenty and forty. After the age of ten, the ability to see clearly objects that are near as well as those that are far decreases (Anderson and Palmore, 1974). You may have noticed that some older people hold a newspaper or photograph at arm's length if they are not wearing glasses. This is because our required viewing distance generally lengthens as the lens of the eye becomes less elastic and more opaque. Also, the eye muscles weaken, and the size of the pupil is reduced (Bromley, 1974). Finally, the data on legal blindness reflect changes in the eye. The rate of legal blindness is twice as high for adults of forty as it is for those of twenty. The incidence of glaucoma also increases dramatically (Anderson and Palmore, 1974).

As for the other senses, research indicates that the ability to hear—especially to hear high-frequency sounds—is probably most acute in late childhood and adolescence. Experimental tests employing high frequencies reveal loss by the age of twenty-five (Birren, 1964). Relatively little research has been done on changes in taste, touch, and olfaction over the life span, but available evidence suggests that these three senses do not change much during the years of early adulthood.

Perception

Perception depends on sensation but also includes the interpretation and analysis of stimulation in terms of the perceiver's prior experience, the demands and expectations of the present, and a variety of individual or situational factors ranging from the health and personality makeup of the perceiver to weather conditions, and the use of glasses. Perception can best be conceptualized as an active, constructive process (Neisser, 1976). Some of the most intriguing examples of the differences between sensation and perception come from the study of childhood. For example, although both children and adults probably see certain things in similar ways, like the blue of the sky, they interpret this information very differently. Children often assume that the sky exists someplace far above their heads; it is impossible to convince them that the sky (or the atmosphere) comes all the way down to the ground (much less that it circles the globe).

Tests of visual perception are many and varied. They include examinations of spatial orientation, visual illusions, part-whole differentiation, perceptual closure, and speed of recognition. Studies of spatial orientation often require such responses as the judgment of verticality for a luminescent rod in a dark room when the subject's body has been tilted to one side. Visual illusions include geometric optical illusions, such as an apparent change in the length of a line when the ends of an arrow point away from a line, as shown in Figure 3.1. Part-whole differentiation involves the separation of an item from its background or context, as in a picture containing hidden figures. Perceptual closure tests focus on the recognition of incomplete forms. Speed of recognition is measured by presenting stimuli for extremely short periods (for example, for .01 second) and measuring the extent to which a subject can accurately describe the materials presented.

Although some evidence suggests that slight changes occur during early adulthood in performance on tasks involving part-whole differentiation (Comalli, 1962, 1965, 1970) and spatial orientation (Comalli, Wapner, and Werner, 1959), peak performance on experimental tests of perception occurs during young adulthood.

Some of the most extensive theorizing on the matter of perceptual change in adulthood is based on research concerning the propensity of people in different age groups to perceive certain of the visual illusions. For example, the effect of the Müller-Lyer illusion, as shown in Figure 3.1, declines throughout childhood and adolescence, plateauing between the ages of twenty and forty. On the other hand, if the Müller-Lyer illusion is presented sequentially (that is, if the line with the arrow pointing away is presented first and the line with the arrows pointing inward is presented alone later on), the effect of the illusion increases during adolescence and young adulthood. One group of researchers believe that the declining effect of certain illusions reflects subtle deterioration in sensitivity to patterned light, whereas the increased effect of sequentially presented illusions depends on our ability to integrate perceptions over time and is a result of increasingly sophisticated intellectual functioning (Pollack and Atkeson, 1978).

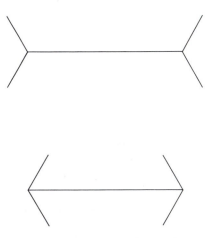

FIGURE 3.1
The Müller-Lyer illusion

Psychomotor Skills

Psychomotor skills require dexterity and agility and are generally believed to improve with practice. They vary from the mundane (running, skipping, dressing) to the sublime (gymnastics, ballet). These skills, which usually involve a pattern of movement, are influenced by the functioning of the central nervous system (Birren, 1964; Birren and Renner, 1977; Birren, Woods, and Williams, 1980). Psychomotor abilities, such as typing or tap dancing, can be automatic, but optimal performance depends on complex sequences of action in which timing is often a critical factor (Welford, 1959). These abilities eventually decline with age, and although the changes are almost imperceptible in young adulthood, some of the simple components of psychomotor abilities, such as speed, do begin to age.

Birren (1964) noted that among the "most reliable facts shown through research on human aging is the trend toward psychomotor slowness." Tests of reaction time in young adulthood foreshadow later psychomotor problems. *Reaction time,* the speed with which a person responds to a stimulus that initiates a response, increases noticeably between the ages of twenty and twenty-five (Sinclair, 1969). Bromley (1974) estimated a 17 percent increase in reaction time occurs between the ages of twenty and forty.

Most of the psychomotor slowness observed in older people is probably a product of increased reaction time, since there are no apparent increases in the time it takes to complete a movement once a subject begins (Birren, 1959; Birren and Renner, 1977). Furthermore, the time required by older subjects to perform psychomotor tasks can be reduced if the subject is warned that the stimulus marking the beginning of a trial is about to appear (Botwinick, 1959, 1981). Such warning signals are known to decrease reaction time.

As with the other documented changes in our physical capacities, the declining sensitivity of the sensory systems and increases in reaction time are seldom important practical considerations until rather late in life. With increasing sophistication and experience, most adults learn to compensate for the gradual decline that accompanies age. "With a little extra effort or attention to particular features of the task, the performance may be maintained or even improved in the presence of physical limitation" (Birren, 1964).

As we get older, we learn to be more careful about the level of illumination when we read. We squint at distant objects or get glasses. We turn our heads slightly more toward the source of a sound. We learn to skip the "one for the road" and to get more rest. No more dancing until dawn followed by a drive up the coast for breakfast and a brisk bout of body surfing. Most of the learning of young adulthood is of a similar sort. We

Finely tuned psychomotor skills enhance the quality of human life greatly by their contributions to the mundane necessities like dressing and driving and by their role in great craftsmanship and art.

pick things up; we learn by doing; we get on-the-job training. Sometimes the things we learn are so subtle that it is difficult to define or express the content, but we learn them nevertheless. It is not unusual to hear an adult wistfully observe that no one ever really teaches us some of the important complex information that we need to run our lives. For example, few of us know the difference between whole and term life insurance until we find we bought the wrong kind. No one teaches us how to run a household, prepare our income taxes, or bring up children, but somehow most of us learn.

LEARNING

Learning can be defined as adaptation. It can also be viewed as a lasting change in behavior. However, experimental studies of learning usually focus on tests of conditioning. *Conditionability* is the speed with which an individual develops a conditioned response. Few studies focus on the performance of young adults, and the same is true of experimental studies of memory. In the data that do exist, comparisons between children and young adults suggest that conditionability in early adulthood is comparable to that of childhood. In fact, a general survey of the literature indicates that the years between twenty and forty are a time of peak performance for a wide variety of tasks, including those that require verbal learning, short-term memory, problem solving, and creativity (Arenberg, 1973; Craik, 1977; Giambra and Arenberg, 1980).

The evidence is clear: young adults are ready to learn. Yet it is also true that the social circumstances of young adult life are simply not conducive to swift, efficient learning. R. J. Havighurst writes of "teachable moments," moments when the organism is ready to learn new skills and abilities. Ironically, of the periods of life, early adulthood seems to be the most full of these teachable moments and the emptiest of efforts to teach (Havighurst, 1972).

Havighurst also describes early adulthood as the most individualistic and the loneliest period of life. During those years one individual, or at the most two, must proceed with a minimum of social attention and assistance to tackle the most important tasks of adult life, from entry into the world of work to marriage and parenthood.

Perhaps because so little institutionalized teaching-learning takes place in young adulthood, little research has been done on the performance of young adults. Most of the available literature reflects the vague, almost incidental nature of learning and socialization in adult life and centers on such matters as how we come to know things we have not been specifically taught and how we are able to solve problems we have never seen.

INTELLIGENCE AND COGNITION

The term *cognition* has been applied to almost all categories of mental activity, including perception, memory, thought, problem solving, and symbolic as well as verbal behavior (Kagan, and Kogan, 1970). We will define it as the process of knowing—a process that involves the inner representation and organization of experience.

Although the study of intelligence usually includes a number of the mental activities listed as possible components of cognition, intelligence is a narrower concept than cognition. *Intelligence* usually refers to the ability to learn, to reason, and to solve problems. Of course, such abilities cannot be measured directly; in order for intelligence to be assessed, someone must solve a problem or exhibit learning. Thus, psychologists have developed a variety of intelligence tests, each reflecting a slightly different conception of the abilities that are the best indirect measures of intelligence.

In general terms, intelligence tests can be categorized as representing two major approaches: quantitative and qualitative (Birren, Kinney, Schaie, and Woodruff, 1980). The qualitative approach is most directly concerned with the structure of cognitive behavior, that is, with what sorts of skills and abilities appear to develop at different stages of life. The quantitative approach emphasizes the number, variety, and speed of responses involved in solving problems of various kinds. Using a quantitative approach, the researcher generally selects or devises a series of tasks that require comprehension, memory, judgment, cleverness, and speed, eventually reporting the performance of subjects in terms of an intelligence quotient (IQ) score.

The Quantitative Approach

Research on changes in intelligence test scores over the life span has generally demonstrated a decline in overall performance after adolescence. The intelligence quotient does not change much over the years because it is a measure of an individual's performance in relationship to all people of the same age. The efficiency quotient (EQ), however, is a measure of an older person's performance relative to that of an average twenty-year-old adult. When this measure has been used, researchers have found a steady decline in performance on omnibus intelligence tests (tests that include a large variety of tasks) over the years of adult life. Bromley (1974) found that about one-third of the overall adult decline in EQ between the ages of twenty and sixty may occur during young adulthood (Bromley, 1974). Bromley further believes that most adults reach maximum intellectual capacity between the ages of sixteen and twenty.

Bromley's opinion is supported by a variety of research studies, particularly by cross-sectional studies of omnibus intelligence measures and by studies of performance on specific individual tasks (such as detecting errors and omissions in pictures, completing jigsaw puzzles, or replicating pictures with the use of real objects). Bromley is not alone in his conclusions; but even he points out that there is conflicting evidence. Some measures of intellectual performance do not show decline with age. For instance, vocabulary, information, and comprehension scores on the Wechsler-Bellvue test do not change throughout most of adulthood. Performance on most tests that emphasize verbal, spatial, or logical reasoning, or the ability to handle numbers, tends to be stable in the adult years (Willis and Baltes, 1980).

Some researchers have argued that most deterioration in test performance with age simply reflects the difficulties people over thirty have on high speed perceptual motor tasks (Birren and Morrison, 1961; Birren, Woods, and Williams, 1980). Decline in the scores of well-educated subjects on intelligence tests can be virtually eliminated when the time limits are removed. Moreover, for a long time researchers have raised a variety of important questions about the meaning of intelligence tests, especially when they are used with middle-aged or elderly subjects. Most of these tests were originally developed to aid educators in predicting the school performance of children and adolescents; it is difficult to say whether they tell us anything about the capacity of adults for absorbing the experiences life has to offer.

Birren and Renner (1977) contend that one must attempt to assess the *social intelligence* of adults—that is, the kinds of performance we expect in adult life. Social intelligence, for example, might predict whether or not a person could file an adequate tax return or find his or her way around a strange city on a bus. The standards that predict school performance often do not predict occupational success, judgment, or the ability to live wisely.

Furthermore, the testing situation itself may be an inappropriate setting for the study of adults, especially older adults, many of whom are basically unfamiliar with the process of taking exams. The standard intelligence tests yield a score that reflects performance at a particular time and place; they do not tell us anything about the range of capacities an adult may possess. As Sherry Willis and Paul Baltes (1980) have noted, "We do not know what aged persons could do. All we know is what they do."

Cohort Differences

Several researchers have taken the position that the experimental evidence demonstrating decline in intellectual performance during adulthood is largely reflective of the differences between cohorts. Almost all of the studies that report substantial declines are cross-sectional in design, and the younger generation is better educated, more actively involved in learning situations, and closer in time to their last years of schooling.

An impressive series of sequential studies by K. Werner Schaie and his colleagues demonstrates convincingly that age cohort is an important predictor of intellectual performance on at least one major standardized intelligence test, the Thurstone test of Primary Mental Abilities (see Schaie, 1979, for an excellent review).

Schaie's data had led Willis and Baltes (1980) to suggest that generalization across cohorts is not possible for current cohorts in the Western world. Instead, they claim that the available longitudinal and sequential data indicate (1) that chronological age accounts for only a modest amount of change in intellectual performance before one's late sixties or early seventies; (2) that the differences between people are large and suggest a variety of patterns characterizing the normal aging of intellectual performance; and (3) that different abilities appear to age differently.

In general, Willis and Baltes (1980) believe that longitudinal and sequential research show the relatively late and limited occurrence of intellectual decline in such healthy, well-educated populations as are represented in longitudinal research. It is important to remember that the people who participate in longitudinal research are likely to perform better on tests of intelligence in the first place than those who fail to participate in the study or leave the study before completion.

Other researchers have suggested that even if intellectual decline characterizes current elderly cohorts, younger cohorts may not show the same kind of change over the life course (Schaie, Labouvie, and Buech, 1973; Schaie and Hertzog, 1982). Younger cohorts are living a life-style in which they are expected to perform at higher levels throughout their lives. Intellectual performance is becoming more central in adulthood, and the decline supposedly evidenced by older people may not be apparent in later generations.

Although these arguments are both convincing and comforting, they are not the only possible explanation for the available data. It is also possible that the cross-sectional evidence reflects some real change that does not appear in the kinds of tests utilized by Schaie and his colleagues. Another group of investigators (Horn, 1982; Horn, Donaldson, and Engstrom, 1981), makes the argument that apparent stability in longitudinal and sequential data may simply be a result of averaging over different kinds of abilities, some of which decline and some of which improve with age.

Fluid and Crystallized Intelligence

Raymond Cattell (1963) has proposed that intelligence tests reflect a number of different abilities, but at least two primary factors: *fluid intelligence* and *crystallized intelligence,* each of which is thought to be measured by different clusters of tests found on the traditional omnibus intelligence scale. A prolific body of research on the matter has been offered by

Cattell's colleague John Horn (1970, 1978, 1982; Horn and Cattell, 1981; Horn, Donaldson and Engstrom, 1981).

Horn believes that intelligence, as measured in the usual ability tests, is a collection of achievements—perhaps as many as eighty different primary factors or abilities. Horn himself has researched a number of these factors or abilities, of which fluid and crystallized intelligence are the best known and most thoroughly described.

Fluid intelligence (Gf) reflects performance on a group of tests involving tasks for which extensive education seems to produce little advantage (perceiving relationships between symbols and objects, formulating concepts, maintaining a variety of factors in immediate awareness, and solving problems). Crystallized intelligence (Gc) in a way involves all the same things, but it shows up in tasks that are affected by education or acculturation (tests of vocabulary, general information, remote associations, and verbal analogies). Some examples of the kinds of tests Horn has developed appear in Figure 3.2.

Horn contends that fluid intelligence declines after the age of fourteen, with the sharpest decline occurring in the years of early adulthood. On the other hand, he reports no fewer than twenty studies, both cross-sectional and longitudinal, that show increased scores throughout adulthood on measures that are assumed to reflect crystallized intelligence. Although both factors seem to be influenced by hereditary and environmental forces, Horn makes the case that crystallized intelligence is most strongly related to the capacity for formal, institutionalized learning and the clearly mandated tasks of society, whereas fluid intelligence reflects a kind of incidental learning of the skills and information one picks up along the way, without much help or any instruction. It might be seen, for instance, in the understandings and skills children develop if they are given the freedom to roam an interesting neighborhood.

Taking another tack, Horn (1982) suggests that fluid intelligence is related to memory, in that the processes involved are those that enable us to organize information and to concentrate intensely on the task at hand. Fluid intelligence may thus be seen as the ability to organize and retain information that is not immediately relevant to the problem at hand. Crystallized intelligence, however, is defined not by initial organization and storage of information but by the restructuring of knowledge to make it more cohesive, correct, and accessible. It allows us to perform well when we are asked for a list of synonyms and connotations or are required to think up new uses for an old object.

Horn's work has shown that fluid intelligence declines first and most dramatically, (three to seven IQ points per decade) between the ages of thirty and sixty. Since 1966 he has replicated this result in a number of

Gf: Fluid intelligence

Matrices: Indicate which figure comes next:

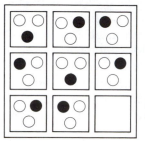

Letter series. Figure out which letter comes next in a series:

ADGJMP?

Topology. Find a figure on right where dot can be placed in the same relation to triangle, squares, and circle as in example on left.

Gc: Crystallized intelligence

Esoteric analogies. Indicate which should go in the space. Socrates is to Aristotle as Sophocles is to _____?

Remote associations. What one word is well associated with bathtub, prizefighting, and wedding?

Judgment. You notice that a fire has just started in a crowded cafe. What should one do to prevent death and injury?

FIGURE 3.2
Examples of tasks used to achieve operational definitions of fluid and crystallized intelligence (Gf and Gc)

studies conducted on eleven different samples; he cannot say, however, whether the decline represents a truly diminished capacity or a growing disinclination to attend to or concentrate on certain kinds of tedious tasks. It also seems, he writes, "that as humans mature they seem to become less intense about 'getting up' for several kinds of activities—e.g., in being challenged by problems" (Horn, Donaldson, and Engstrom, 1982, pp. 74–75). More often though, Horn is inclined to argue that the decrement in fluid intelligence is probably related to small changes in the nervous system, especially those that affect the mental gatekeeping functions such as attention and alertness.

Sar: Short-term acquisition retrieval (Gf)

> After hearing words spoken one after the other in lists of 5 to 13 words, recall as many as possible.
>
> *Serial recall.* This is the sum of the number of words recalled.
>
> *Recency.* This is the sum of the times the last word in the list is recalled.
>
> *Primacy.* This is the sum of the times the first or second word in the list is recalled.
>
> When studying the covariation among these three kinds of memory, entirely different (operationally independent) lists are used to measure each, but when measuring SAR the three kinds of memory are combined.

SD: Sensory detection—visual (Gf)

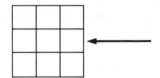

> *Matrix vector recall.* Derived from Sperling (1960). Subject first sees a matrix filled with letters; then sees empty matrix and arrow pointing to a row or column (randomly selected). Task is to fill in letters in designated column or row. Performance indicates that for a second or two a person is aware of more than the 7($\pm$2) that has been said to indicate the human's storage capacity for information processing. Such behavior is said to indicate immediate awareness (IMA) or sensory memory (see Kintsch, 1970; Horn, 1978).

SOURCE: *J. L. Horn, G. Donaldson, and R. Engstrom, "Apprehension, Memory, and Fluid Intelligence in Adulthood,"* Research on Aging, 3 (1981), 33–84.

Neither Schaie (1970, 1979, and Hertzog, 1982) nor Willis and Baltes (1980) find Horn's data compelling. They point out that most of Horn's evidence is cross-sectional and most of his subjects are not of the socially and educationally advantaged class represented in the longitudinal data they prefer. Willis and Baltes contend that the tests Horn has employed are really only appropriate for young adults and that the setting of his research is not likely to evince optimal performances from older subjects. Whatever explanation is finally accepted, it seems clear that thinking about intelligence in terms of both fluid and crystallized abilities has been useful. A multidimensional model of intelligence appears necessary for those who would study intellectual change in adult life. In fact, Willis and Baltes (1980), major critics of Horn's data, emphasize the importance of thinking about intellectual performance over the life course as both multidimensional and multidirectional—that is, as representing the development of a variety of abilities along a variety of different developmental courses.

The Qualitative Approach

If it appears sensible to view intelligence as multidimensional, it is even more obvious that cognition—the process of knowing—is a multidimensional phenomenon. We come to know things in a variety of ways: we think, imagine, create, generate plans and strategies, reason, infer, solve problems, classify, symbolize, fantasize, and dream (Flavell, 1977). Most theories of cognitive development, which focus on how these activities take shape during the years of childhood and adolescence, have been extended to adulthood only by analogy. Of these, the most influential is the framework offered by Jean Piaget (Flavell, 1963; Piaget, 1970).

Piaget has synthesized a lifetime of observations about the problem solving of his own and other children into a series of four stages through which he believes all people move in the development of adaptive intelligence. Piaget's scheme lies within the bounds of the organismic model. He envisions an active organism involved in the construction of knowledge and experience—interpreting, transforming, and reorganizing information from the environment in a way that fits and yet stretches what the organism already knows and allows the organism to achieve an adaptive or equilibrated relationship with the environment. Each stage is thought to be universal, that is, to occur at the same developmental point in the growth of all human beings.

Although Piaget believes that the abilities he outlines are apparent in the development of all people, many other writers have argued that the notion of development inherent in his stages is applicable only to Western, scientific tradition (Riegel, 1973b; Price-Williams, 1981). Clearly, at the final stage, the stage of formal operations, Piaget does address the kind of thinking and reasoning that characterizes the scientific, theoretical, and philosophical endeavors of North American and European thinkers. *Formal operational thought* is described as the most fully abstract and objective form of reasoning, the highest order of cognitive achievement.

According to Piaget, formal operations first emerge in early adolescence and continue to mature throughout early adulthood, allowing the individual a new kind of mental flexibility not previously possible. Conceiving all possible worlds, the adolescent and the adult can see and imagine an infinitely greater number of possibilities than can the child, who is bound to the events and objects of the real world. Children can deal with the things around them: they can label and classify and order and count. They can even deal with concepts like the relationship between the whole and its parts, but they are unable to think rationally and systematically about purely abstract or imaginary situations and ideas. The ability to do so is the primary attribute of formal operations.

The Transition from Childhood to Formal Operations

During early adolescence, cognitive changes occur along at least seven different dimensions—the real versus the possible, empirico-inductive versus hypothetico-deductive, intrapropositional versus interpropositional, combinations and permutations, inversion and compensation, information-processing strategies, and consolidation and solidification (Flavell, 1977).

REAL VERSUS POSSIBLE.   As Flavell puts it, "A theorist the child is not." Children cannot speculate in logical ways about circumstances other than those observed in the situation at hand. Children are tied to concrete realities.

Question: What would the world be like if everyone were deaf?
Child: No one could hear.
Adult: There would be no music or phones, no noise pollution or dancing, no radio.

EMPIRICO-INDUCTIVE VERSUS HYPOTHETICO-DEDUCTIVE.   Adults can hypothesize about the causes of a phenomenon, deduce a prediction, and test it. Such hypotheses are complex objects of thought, not mere representations of concrete situations. Children can deal only with objects or events immediately available to the senses; they are unable to abstract, much less test an abstract proposition.

Question: Why does the sun come up?
Child: The sun comes up because I open my eyes.
Adult: The sun appears to come up because the world turns on its axis.

INTRAPROPOSITIONAL VERSUS INTERPROPOSITIONAL.   The child can propose a single idea or solution and test it against reality; the adult can develop a set of propositions and test them against one another and reality. The adult then is able to use the evidence from one test to evaluate the likelihood of a given outcome in the next test.

Question: How long does it take to bake these cookies?

Child: I think it takes fifteen minutes to bake cookies. I'll wait fifteen minutes and see.

Adult: These cookies probably require fifteen minutes, but I'll check at five. If they are done, I'll take them out. If not, I'll check at ten minutes, and then at fifteen.

COMBINATIONS AND PERMUTATIONS.   Children are unable to think of all the possibilities inherent in a situation and seem to test some possibilities over and over. Mature thinkers can systematically produce and evaluate a series of hypotheses.

Question: What should you do if the cookies burn in fifteen minutes?

Child: Uh oh, the cookies burned. I'll try ten minutes this time.

Adult: !!!! Since the cookies burned, I'll have to try again and check every three minutes, starting at five minutes. If that doesn't work, I'll try a two-minute interval until I get it just right.

INVERSION AND COMPENSATION.   When a relationship changes, there are two possible operations for negating the change: one can reverse change or compensate for it. Children tend to see only one of these possibilities, not both.

Question: How can you make a seesaw work with three people on it?

Child: John and Sue are both on the same end, and Mary is by herself on the other side. John better get off.

Adult: John could get off and solve the problem, or another child could get on Mary's side, or John and Sue could move closer to the middle of the seesaw.

INFORMATION PROCESSING STRATEGIES.   An adult organizes and plans an attack before beginning work on a problem. In addition to generating and systematically testing all the possibilities, an adult tries to order the possible hypotheses in a way that eliminates as many incorrect solutions as possible with each test.

Question: Can you guess how old John is?

Child: Thirty-two? Thirty-three? Thirty-four? Thirty-five?

Adult: Are you over thirty-five? Over thirty? Over thirty-two?

CONSOLIDATION AND SOLIDIFICATION.   Finally, formal operations allow us to consolidate and solidify the useful knowledge of childhood in terms of the more sophisticated logic and understanding of the adolescent and adult.

In Piaget's original scheme, formal operations was described as a universal development. Over the years, however, growing evidence has shown that particular social interests, aptitudes, and circumstances can affect the development of formal operations. Formal operations are probably only partially attained by most individuals in Western cultures. Gifted individuals are far more likely to achieve full formal operations than are adolescents and adults of average intelligence (Dulit, 1972).

Piaget (1972) himself has argued that people will achieve different endpoints of cognitive development according to their aptitudes, experiences, and environments, especially their occupational activities. Formal operations may appear in one domain or area of knowledge and not another. For instance, a writer may exhibit a highly developed ability to reason logically on paper but feel mystified when confronted with two metal rods of the same size, one lead and the other aluminum, that produce equal increases in water level when they are immersed in a beaker. Outside the domain of verbal reasoning, where the writer is formal operational, she may respond like a concrete operational child (the concrete operational stage emerges prior to formal operations) when confronted by phenomenon in the domain of physics.

Not only is it sometimes difficult to demonstrate formal operations in a variety of domains among adults in the Western world, but it has been especially difficult to find evidence for the cross-cultural appearance of formal operations (Greenfield, 1976; Greenfield and Childs, in press). Westernization seems to be a very influential factor in the emergence of formal reasoning, although no one is quite sure whether to attribute this effect to direct training and schooling, to the structure of Western languages, to the sorts of economic transactions available, or to a variety of other possible cultural phenomenon (Price-Williams, 1981).

One of the more interesting explanations suggests that there may be different ideal endpoints in the development of intelligence in different cultures. It is possible that some cultures not only offer little opportunity for the use of formal operations, but may even be structured so that abstract thinking, unrelated to the everyday objects and events of life, may be something of a hindrance (Greenfield, 1976). (Certainly, Piaget's basic definition of intelligence as adaptive behavior might lead to such a conclusion.) On the other hand, some cultural settings may pose challenges that demand a level of reasoning beyond formal operations. Piaget believes that formal reasoning continues to develop in adulthood as it is applied to more and more topics. For example, most adolescents learn fairly early in the development of formal operations that it is possible to change the speed with which a pendulum swings by changing the weights, the length of the cord, and so on. They do not really understand the concept of correlation, however, until later on. In fact, most adults have to constantly remind themselves that just because two things are usually found together (are correlated) does not mean that one of them caused the other (Kuhn, Langer, Kohlberg, and Haan, 1977).

In view of the fact that most of us do not operate at the level of formal operations much of the time (if you don't believe this, go to Las Vegas and watch how people try to buck the laws of probability), it is surprising that there has been much discontent with Piaget's view of adult intellectual development. Nonetheless, the possibility of a fifth and even more sophisticated stage has generated a good deal of interest. A variety of ideas have been offered, although none is nearly as well defined as the concept of formal operations as Piaget presents it.

Beyond Formal Operations

One of the suggestions for a fifth stage of intellectual development concerns a *structural analytic stage* (Commons, in press). In Chapter 2, we discussed the possibility of a structural analytic stage of cognition, a stage that builds directly on formal reasoning. Structural analytic thought allows us to compare assumptions and relationships, as well as models, systems of models, and so on. In our earlier discussion, we saw how the assumptions and implications of different models of human development compared with each other. Such comparative analysis, at its most sophisticated, constitutes structural analytic thought (Commons and Richards, 1982; Richards and Commons, 1982). Michael Commons (Commons and Richards, 1978) sums up the structural analytic stage as follows:

> The properties of relationships found within the system are expressed in terms of assumptions (axioms), definitions and limiting conditions, and their derivable results (theorems, laws and other expressions of systems' properties). In addition, the relationships between various models, systems and finally whole structures and paradigms are determined by seeing what has to be done to transform one system into another by adding or deleting assumptions or by showing that everything that is true in one system is also true in the other.

Another author, Patricia Arlin, has proposed a *problem-finding stage* of cognitive development, focusing on the ability to generate new problems or to raise questions about problems that are ill-defined. In one test for problem-finding thought, a variety of objects are presented to the subject along with the instructions to formulate some interesting questions about them. Each subject's stage of cognition is assessed from the kinds of questions she or he devises (Arlin, 1975, 1977). The questions people formulate are then categorized as problem solving or as problem finding. Questions that request basic information (How many apples are there?) or questions that require classification (Can I group these objects by size, color, or shape?) are the least abstract, most "problem-solving" kinds of questions. Questions about relationships (Is the hole in the washing machine related to the quarter?) or systems (Can you make four triangles at once out of six match sticks?) reflect formal reasoning. Questions about transformations (If you were given this clamp, what could you change it into? What could you make?) and questions about implications (In what ways could you arrange the objects on this table to express how you feel at this moment?) are categorized as problem-finding cognition (Guilford, 1956).

It does appear that formal operations are required before problem-finding behavior emerges and that only some formal operators are capable of problem finding. However, problem finding may already be implied by Piaget's concrete and formal stages and, therefore, may not constitute a separate and more advanced form of cognitive behavior. Moreover, a recent attempt to replicate some of the findings on this version of stage five has been unsuccessful (Commons and Richards, 1978).

A third interesting alternative stage five comes from the dialectician Klaus Riegel (1973b), who is intrigued by how people become aware that the evidence of their senses sometimes contradicts their less mature judgments. Riegel believes the experience of contradiction is central to cognitive growth and eventually forms a basis for stage five. For example, a young child may predict that a heavy object will sink and a light one float, regardless of the sizes of the objects, but the child may be unable to explain how a battleship floats when a small stone sinks quickly to the bottom of the lake. Eventually, children learn to consider density—the relationship between size and weight—and to resolve the apparent contradiction between experience and judgment.

Riegel believed that mature thinkers accept and even invite contradiction, not just as problems to be solved but as a basis for innovative, creative thought. In many ways, his formulation is quite similar to the notion of problem finding. Both ideas emphasize the generation of questions, the role of conflict, the delineation of issues, and the discovery of problems. Both also evoke similar criticisms. Because Riegel does not describe any specific logical operation as being identified with dialectical thought and because there is some evidence that one can see dialectics at earlier stages, it has been charged that contradiction is not a true fifth stage (Commons and Richards, 1978).

Riegel has countered, however, that dialectical thinking may be a different category of cognition rather than a higher form of logical reasoning—that it may develop from *intuition* rather than from formal reasoning. He conceived of intuition as the ability to sense or grasp a relationship without really understanding it fully. Intuition contributes to intellectual growth, as does logical thought, and is indispensable to the emergence of the abilities that Riegel labeled dialectic.

The search for a final, adult stage of cognition has not been limited to the study of intelligence and reasoning. Particularly in the study of moral judgment, a number of researchers and thinkers have explored the direction of adult development. Outstanding among these related ideas is the work of Lawrence Kohlberg on moral judgment.

Adult Moral Reasoning

The study of moral judgment refers to the examination of the reasons adults give for the decisions about right and wrong they make when faced with a moral dilemma. As approached by Lawrence Kohlberg and his associates, moral judgment is studied in subjects' responses to a number of standard moral dilemmas. For instance, subjects are presented with a problem that requires a choice between the right to own property and the right to life. Kohlberg believes that the experiences of adult life play a critical role in the emergence of the most sophisticated forms of judgment. He has argued that maturation directs the growth of the intellect in childhood, but that social and psychological forces are more important after adolescence (Kohlberg, 1973).

Box 3.1 (p. 126) presents an outline of the stages Kohlberg has proposed, beginning in early childhood with preconventional judgment and culminating in postconventional thought during middle age. Kohlberg has based much of his thinking on the results of a small but intensive longitudinal study of Harvard students. His belief in the importance of adult experience is partly based on his findings that not one of the subjects in this investigation appeared to achieve postconventional thought before the age of twenty-three and that, even at age thirty, not one was functioning predominantly at the highest levels (either 5 or 6) (Kohlberg, 1973).

On the basis of such data, Kohlberg concluded that extensive experience of personal moral choice and responsibility must precede the development of postconventional moral reasoning. He found that educational and vicarious experiences of moral problems seemed to encourage developmental advancement through stage 4, but that adult progression demanded "genuine personal challenge" and the experience of long-term consequences. Interestingly, Kohlberg thinks that the critical experiences that produce postconventionality involve conflict between responsibility, as defined by conventional standards, and a larger sense of human principles. This sounds like a rather dialectical point of view.

Despite the fact that so few of his subjects seem to have achieved the highest levels of reasoning outlined in his six stages, Kohlberg has described an even higher stage he calls the *cosmic perspective*. This final concept is reminiscent of Erik Erikson's definition of integrity and involves a religious orientation, although not in a conventional sense. The cosmic perspective, according to Kohlberg, is a feeling of unity with the whole of nature. Paradoxically, Kohlberg argues that this feeling of unity and harmony arises from the experience of despair and meaninglessness. Again, this is a somewhat dialectical point of view, since growth is dependent on the experience of conflict and paradox.

None of the people in Kohlberg's longitudinal study has demonstrated a cosmic perspective. It is not even clear that the cosmic perspective is at all useful in the description of ordinary development. However, Kohlberg contends that it is necessary in order to explain the more abstract and universal moral sense that a few achieve. One can find literary descriptions, from Hermann Hesse's *Siddhartha* to John Lilly's *The Center of the Cyclone*. Consider, for example, the scope of the perspective described by Henry David Thoreau in *Walden Pond*:

> Men frequently say to me, "I should think you would feel lonesome down there and want to be nearer to folks, rainy and snowy days and nights especially." I am tempted to reply to such, "This whole earth which we inhabit is but a point in space. How far apart, think you, dwell the two most distant inhabitants of yonder star? Why should I feel lonely? Is not our planet in the Milky Way?"

Kohlberg's work has evoked a great deal of related research and a fair share of criticism as well. It has not, for example, been demonstrated that postconventional reasoning appears cross-culturally, and evidence for stage 4, law and order morality, is even difficult to find in other cultures (Edwards, 1980). Of course, Kohlberg has argued that formal operations are probably necessary for moral development beyond stage 3 (Kuhn, Langer, Kohlberg, and Haan, 1977); so it is hardly surprising that cross-cultural studies rarely demonstrate postconventional moral reasoning.

Consider also that the transition from stage 4 to stage 5 requires a shift from law-abiding to law-giving. For example, the justice system institutionalizes stage 4 reasoning in North America. The courts do not change the law per se; they simply interpret and reinterpret a set of principles and codes in light of new dilemmas. On the other hand, stage 5 is epitomized by

BOX 3.1
Kohlberg's proposed stages of moral reasoning

PRECONVENTIONAL THOUGHT

At this stage, the individual is responsive to the physical consequences of an action—to punishment and reward or to the exchange of favors.

1. *The punishment and obedience orientation.* Here the child's moral judgments are based on avoidance of punishment and on deference to power. The physical consequences of the act are paramount considerations.

2. *The instrumental-relativist orientation.* Human needs are viewed by the child at this stage in terms of the marketplace. Actions are judged in terms of the degree to which they satisfy one's own needs and occasionally the needs of others.

CONVENTIONAL THOUGHT

At this stage, the individual is responsive to the expectations of the family, the group, or the nation. Conformity and loyalty are paramount considerations.

3. *The interpersonal concordance or "good boy–nice girl" orientation.* The child at this stage judges acts in terms of helping others and gaining their approval. Conformity to the cultural stereotypes is seen as natural and good. Intention is considered, for the first time, in the judgment of an act.

4. *The law and order orientation.* Actions are judged at this level in terms of whether they maintain the social order or conform to the dictates of authority. Duty and respect for authority are paramount considerations.

POSTCONVENTIONAL THOUGHT

At this stage, the individual makes a clear effort, independent of the group or of external authority, to define moral principles.

5. *The social contract orientation.* Actions are judged in terms of the welfare of the majority. Emphasis is placed on the procedures for making and changing rules (for example, due process) rather than on a set of fixed rules. Free agreement and contract are the binding elements of obligation, and there is an understanding that the social order can and sometimes should change in order to serve the greater good.

6. *The universal ethical principle orientation.* Actions are judged in terms of self-chosen ethical principles. Logical comprehensiveness, universality, and consistency are important considerations. There is a sense of justice

BOX 3.1
(continued)

and reciprocity and an understanding that deviation from the conventional idea of goodness can be right if circumstances violate the individual's sense of morality.

SOURCE: Based on L. Kohlberg, "The Development of Children's Orientation Toward a Moral Order: A Sequence in the Development of Moral Thought," *Vita Humana*, 6 (1963): 11–33; and L. Kohlberg, "The Claim to Moral Adequacy of a Highest Stage of Moral Development," *Journal of Philosophy*, 70 (1973): 630–646.

the framing of the U.S. Constitution, for not only does this document suggest certain laws and regulations, it also provides a framework for the orderly development of new laws and even for changes in the original document itself. The framers of the Constitution were law-giving. Edwards (1980) suggests that this transition may not be part of a universal sequence in the development of moral thought, but may reflect a kind of cultural specialization and be mistakenly perceived as optimal or most mature.

Perhaps the emphasis placed upon democracy, conscience, contractual agreement, and individual rights in Western societies creates the context for what Kohlberg calls postconventional thinking. If so, then perhaps the moral judgment of people who live in other cultures, especially in preindustrial settings, is not best described as less mature or less sophisticated, but simply better adapted to differing cultural circumstances.

Kohlberg's work has also been criticized for underestimating the general moral thinking of most people, including children. In one study of preschoolers, 90 percent of the children said they would not hurt someone or steal something even if there were no rules against it (Nucci and Turiel, 1978). In Kohlberg's terms, such a statement is fairly sophisticated. In fact, one researcher believes that the sophisticated reasoning evidenced by preschool children is obscured in middle childhood by a new appreciation for convention and in early adolescence by the need to live up to the standards and expectations of others. The resurgence of abstract morality in late adolescence and early adulthood may then only reflect the final mastery of social norms, according to this view (Hoffman, 1980).

Finally, and perhaps most important, Carol Gilligan (1982) in reporting the results of ten years of systematic research with women subjects, observed that women often found Kohlberg's dilemmas unreal and irrelevant and that they scored consistently lower than men on his scale of moral development despite impressive growth in the articulation and sophistication with which they approached moral dilemmas in thought and real life through the years of early adulthood.

Gilligan believes that the concept of morality as responsibility and caring is absent from most of the current frameworks from which researchers explore moral development. She emphasizes the fact that most theories (psychoanalytic as well as Kohlberg's) are based on the central role of competition and individualism in Western life. She contends that women see what is moral in terms of the integrity of relationships and minimizing hurt, whereas men assume that autonomy and an orderly system for the adjudication of rights defines what is right. For men, what is right is what is just (this would include an eye for an eye, no doubt). For women, it is a matter of choosing to take responsibility for others, not simply because one wishes for approval, but because it is a self-chosen principle that gives integrity and strength of character.

As Elizabeth Douvan (1983) points out, most social researchers in the United States have "a large stake and a long history of investment in constructing development as a unidirectional process of differentiation and separation, in assuming individual achievement in a competitive struggle to be the primary motive for human action, in seeing all relationships as contractual, governed by self-interest and market considerations, and in defining care and connection always in relation to market values or dominance" (p. 262). Douvan believes that the exploration of a system of values based on the activities of care and the bond of attachment will demand great honesty and much hard work, but may be "just what we need to revitalize our field and bring it into a more meaningful alignment with reality."

Both theory and research present some important challenges to the ideas offered by Kohlberg. It seems clear that there is enough negative evidence to demand a major revision, perhaps enough to produce an entirely different perspective. But, Kohlberg's work has also clearly been invaluable in promoting research and thinking in the area of moral development. Theory is, after all, not only a goal but a means. Beyond the utility of a theory, however, there is also the logic and rigor it offers. In some ways, Kohlberg's scheme is very satisfying as it moves rationally from one stage to the next. In other ways it is exasperatingly short of clear definitions and assumptions. These last characteristics are, to some extent, matters of cognitive preference, a subject that has been discussed in the study of adult cognition.

Adult Cognition and Preference

The notion of an additional adult stage of cognition has appeared in yet another area of research. Leland Van den Dale (1975) has been particularly interested in how people come to justify their preferences and has suggested that adults begin to consider the formal or aesthetic properties of ideas rather than simply assessing ideas and theories in terms of whether they fit known facts.

Art has formal properties. If an artist copies life, art may also "fit the facts"; that is, it will look like the subject copied. Formal properties are more abstract. Qualities like beauty, elegance, or the use of space or line in painting are formal properties. Much "modern art" has *only* formal properties. It does not reflect objective reality but relies for effect entirely on the use of space, texture, and color.

Theories have formal properties, too. Some theories, for example, are more complete than others. Some are more internally consistent. Some are more elegant or more parsimonious. Parsimony refers to the simplicity of a theory: the theory that posits the fewest causes or processes is the most parsimonious. Qualities like parsimony may contribute to the beauty of an idea or a system. Buckminster Fuller wrote of formal properties, "When I am working on a problem, I never think about beauty. I think only how to solve the problem. But when I have finished, if the solution is not beautiful, I know it is wrong."

The radical behaviorism of B. F. Skinner (1953) is usually considered very parsimonious. Since all behavior change is attributed to operant learning, the theory has a certain beauty in its simplicity. Some say it is too simple to fit the facts of human behavior, but a system does not have to be true to be aesthetically pleasing.

We have been focusing on stage theories of cognitive development and the qualitative approach. But it is not necessary to adopt a stage-like organismic view to deal with cognition. It is also possible to talk about complex changes in the ways adults think or reason in terms of the accumulation of experience.

Nonstage Conceptions of Cognition in Adulthood

All of the work we have reviewed on cognitive development, even research on possible universal stages, admits of the impact of particular experiences, adult experiences, on the course of development. Research on cross-cultural issues has been of special importance in defining the role of environment and would seem most encouraging to those who approach adulthood from the perspective of social-learning theory. Reflecting the general trend toward a more interactionist view, the social-learning theorists have also tackled some of the organismic and dialectical concepts we have been discussing.

Social-learning theorists have suggested that change and development over the course of adult life might best be conceptualized as adaptation in the face of the conflict created by the ambiguous expectations that surround adult life events. The problems of adult life become crises when they cannot be solved speedily. Both anticipated and unanticipated entrances into complex new roles require adaptations. The nature of these required changes may be ambiguous to the individual on the threshold of a new role. Role transitions may present problems not easily solved, and they are very likely to have significant, long-term social, psychological, and physical consequences (Albrecht and Gift, 1975).

From the point of view of the social-learning theorist, learning—defined as adaptation—can be expected to produce changes in cognition throughout the life span, just as it will produce changes in any other form of behavior. These changes must, however, be considered quantitative rather than qualitative, according to the learning theorist, and they are related to life experience rather than to the inner forces of the organism. Social-learning theorists do not find it surprising that stage theorists are talking about the importance of experience in adult life. This is the basic tenet of learning theory and is thought to apply to the development of both children and adults.

Whether in terms of intellectual performance, moral judgment, or social behavior and concerns, the learning theorist would predict that adult life is characterized by change. Because there is social consensus about what adults should know and do and believe, the learning theorist would also predict that one might find much similarity in development among adults in the same culture.

Learning theorists are quick to point out, however, that organismic theories often lack detailed information about what overt, observable behaviors we ought to be looking for as a consequence of cognitive change. For example, the implications of Kohlberg's stages for individual moral conduct are not at all clear. Prior learning, the differences between situations, and observational learning seem to strongly influence moral conduct as well as group norms, incentive, and the risks in the situation. How does a theory of moral judgment account for the observation that conduct appears to be situationally determined (Seiber, 1980)? These are but a few of the difficult and important questions facing researchers interested in the development of intelligence, cognition, judgment, and values not only in adulthood but throughout the life span.

LOOKING AHEAD: THE TASKS OF YOUNG ADULTHOOD

Young adulthood is not only a time of new optimal biological capacities and intellectual achievements. It is also an important period of social and interpersonal growth. One of the most popular approaches to this interpersonal context involves the description of new developmental demands. For instance, R. J. Havighurst approaches the study of adulthood through the description of *developmental tasks,* which are defined as the prescriptions, obligations, and responsibilities that produce healthy, satisfactory growth in our society. Havighurst describes the developmental tasks as "bio-socio-psychological" in origin and believes that these tasks can be accomplished only at one particular, critical period in the life course. Success at these tasks leads to happiness for the individual as well as to improvement of one's chances for success with later tasks.

Developmental tasks dominate a particular phase of the life cycle, and emerge through the interaction of a biological ground plan, individual psychological forces, and the structure of the social system. Havighurst proposes that the tasks of young adulthood include selecting a mate, learning to live with a marriage partner, starting a family, establishing an occupation, and finding a congenial social group. This description may not apply to many other cultures, but these tasks seem fairly representative of central concerns for most young adults in Western industrialized cultures. The literature on each of these topics will be reviewed in the next two chapters.

Erik Erikson (1968b) offers a more abstract formulation than Havighurst. For example, he writes about the "crisis of intimacy: a counterpointing as well as a fusing of identity." Sexual intimacy is only a part of the general task of intimacy. Intimacy goes beyond sexual relationships and includes all companionship and communion with others, both as individuals and as groups. From Erikson's perspective, intimacy is not exclusive or destructive as relationships in adolescence sometimes are. The growth of identity in adolescence permits mature acceptance of differences among people, eventually heightening one's own sense of identity.

Just as intimacy is the central theme of young adulthood from Erikson's point of view, fidelity is one of the major results. One must find something or someone to be true to. Erikson writes that young adults must test the extremes in order to find a deep commitment, to develop a sense of choice, and to experience loyalty. He argues that the core problem of this stage is discovering how to take care of those to whom one becomes committed upon emerging from the identity period, and to whom one now owes his or her identity.

Some of the same thoughts are echoed and expanded in the work of Robert White (1975). White has focused on young adulthood and believes that the important trends of young adult life continue throughout the life span. Writing of the deepening of interests and the "freeing of personal relationships," White contends that young adults begin to respond to people as individuals, free of much of the egocentrism and anxiety that characterize adolescence. Adults can make allowances. There is room for warmth, respect, and criticism. There is tolerance.

The deepening of interests in early adult life is similar to Erikson's notion of commitment, but White phrases the idea in terms of commitment to something rather than to someone. The deepening of interests always includes wholehearted activity and the progressive mastery of knowledge and skills, according to White. In the last analysis, satisfaction is derived from the activity, not from the social gains that may accompany the activity. Social gains, approval, and attention from others may spark interest, but finally it is the experience of competence that becomes the most important source of reinforcement for a committed individual.

Three other growth trends in early adulthood are suggested by White:

- *Stabilization of identity.* Identity becomes more consistent and freer from transient influence. Judgments arise more often from one's own experience rather than from what others think.

- *Humanization of values.* The young adult becomes increasingly aware of the human meaning of values and their relationship to social purposes. The individual moves from an absolute to a personal system of values based on life experience.

- *Expansion of caring.* The young adult develops a sense of common humanity. There is an extension of the sense of self to the community and a growing dedication to the welfare of others.

White, Erikson, and Havighurst all touch on the same concerns: caring, commitment, and mastery. All of these themes are important throughout adult life. But they seem to be most critical in early adulthood, the period when most people are actively engaged in finding mates, establishing families, developing social circles, and becoming committed to long-term occupations and interests.

SUMMARY

Young adulthood is, in many ways, the pinnacle of biological development. The first clear signs of aging do emerge during these years, however. Biological maturation and decline occur simultaneously in young adulthood. This chapter presents evidence for both trends.

Peak physical strength in the striped muscles is achieved between twenty-three and twenty-seven, when capacity for athletic activities and physical labor is greatest. Ability to perform in vigorous sports begins to decline as early as thirty, and maximum work rate decreases after thirty-

"The sense of self becomes extended when the welfare of another person, a group enterprise, or some other valued object becomes as important as one's own welfare." Robert White

five. Regular physical recreation and exercise appear to be beneficial. Nevertheless, individuals who place great emphasis on physical strength and prowess may feel older and experience more negative feelings about their age earlier than people who place less value on physical attributes.

A noticeable decrease in the efficiency of the cardiovascular and pulmonary systems occurs in young adulthood. Basal metabolic rate (BMR) declines throughout adult life, beginning around age thirty. Although such decreases have little effect on the performance of young adults, changes that occur in body systems even in the thirties raise important questions about the underlying mechanisms of aging and, in particular, focus interest on the biological systems.

The one biological system that has clear psychological implications for adult development is the reproductive system. In this chapter, we reviewed the data provided by Masters and Johnson on the physiological aspects of the human sexual response. Masters and Johnson have divided this response into four stages: excitement, plateau, orgasm, and resolution. Their research has convinced many that the similarities between male and female sexuality have never before been properly appreciated.

In young adulthood, the female reproductive system is optimally functional. Major physical changes occur in a woman's body during each trimester of pregnancy. The childbearing and birth processes have important psychological implications as well. One recent study concluded that, while pregnancy and childbirth sometimes produce a sense of completeness and personal growth on the part of the mother, childbirth is frequently experienced as a time of great emotional stress and is accompanied by feelings of anxiety, depression, boredom, and concern about changes in personal and marital life-style.

On the other hand, a review of the literature concerning most of the biological functions of young adulthood suggests that relationships between biological change and psychological phenomena are elusive and will be difficult to define. This chapter included, for example, a review of the literature on sensation, perception, and cognition in young adulthood. Evidence on sensation suggests some changes in maximal sensitivity of both hearing and vision. However, performance on most tasks involving sensory and perceptual measures is steady despite these changes. Young adulthood can be characterized as a period of peak performance on most common tests of perceptual performance.

Some noticeable increases in reaction time develop between twenty and twenty-five, and these foreshadow one of the major psychomotor changes of adult life. Nevertheless, most adults learn to compensate for these gradual declines and with a little extra effort or attention are able to maintain performance or even to improve.

Cognition is the process of knowing. The study of cognition focuses on intelligence, reasoning, creativity, problem solving, and a variety of related concepts. Much research has been done on the relationship of age to performance on tests of intelligence. There has been much discussion and controversy about what is meant by the term *intelligence* and about how the concept of intelligence relates to performance on a test of intelligence.

Researchers such as John Horn have concluded that evidence suggests some kinds of capacities do begin to decline in early adulthood. The capacities that decline have been labeled fluid intelligence, which is conceptualized as an innate general cognitive capacity and is believed to be manifested in performance on such tasks as memory span and productive relational thinking.

Crystallized intelligence, or intelligence defined as knowledge, is believed to increase throughout most of the adult life course. Some have argued, however, that even where apparent deterioration of fluid intelligence has occurred, the effect may be due to differences in times of measurement or cohort variables rather than to any age-related process.

Interest in the work of Jean Piaget on the growth of formal reasoning throughout childhood and adolescence has led to considerable research in recent years. According to Piaget's original scheme, fully mature reasoning is reached sometime in adolescence with the emergence of formal operations. Formal operations include the ability to speculate about possible versus real circumstances, to hypothesize about the explanation for a phenomenon, to develop a set of propositions and test them in an orderly and efficient way, and to organize and plan an attack on a problem before beginning to work on it.

Cross-cultural evidence provokes questions about the universality of formal operations and suggests that movement from concrete to formal reasoning may be influenced by cultural circumstances and individual abilities, even though specific kinds of training have not been found to be effective in teaching formal operations.

Although many people do not progress much beyond concrete operations, interest in the description of a fifth stage of cognitive development has led to research. The more advanced stages suggested range from the structural-analytic stage described in Chapter 2, to a concept called problem finding that involves the formulation of abstract, general, and novel questions, and to Klaus Riegel's formulation of a dialectical stage of thought involving the seeking and manipulation of contradiction.

Other kinds of adult cognitive changes have been suggested by those interested in moral development and the growth of values. Kohlberg believes that a stage of postconventional moral judgment is achieved only in early adulthood or later. Kohlberg has also posited a yet higher form of postconventional thought in which a cosmic perspective arises, based on feelings of unity with the whole of nature.

Studies of the way in which people come to justify their preferences suggest that adults begin to consider the formal properties of ideas rather than simply assessing ideas in terms of their truth content. Formal properties include such attributes as completeness, elegance, and parsimony.

Some social-learning theorists have addressed the issues raised by the study of cognition in adulthood, but most are concerned only with tests of learning and memory. Early adulthood is considered the time of peak performance in verbal learning, short-term memory, problem solving, creativity, and so on. Nevertheless, most young adults experience little formal preparation or training for many of the critical developmental tasks of the period, including selection of a mate, learning to live with a marriage partner, starting a family, establishing a social group, and beginning an occupation.

Most theorists agree on the central themes of young adult life, emphasizing the importance of intimacy, caring, commitment, attachment, mastery, and the stabilization of identity. This chapter presents the ideas of Havighurst, Erikson, and White on the subject of developmental tasks or challenges, demonstrating a commonality of concern for the growth and progress of the individual embarking upon adult life.

Chapter 4

The Personal Context of Development: Intimacy, Marriage, and Alternatives to Marriage

*Love is the strange bewilderment which overtakes
one person on account of another.*

JAMES THURBER

Psychologists have described the central developments of young adulthood in terms of the achievement of intimacy, commitment, fidelity, and caring. But they have failed to agree upon how we might define, measure, test for, or even observe such phenomena. Because the quantification of such "strange bewilderments" is itself baffling, most researchers focus on more objective matters, like mate selection, marital adjustment, courtship patterns, and the frequency or duration of friendship.

In this chapter, we will be concerned with both the abstract, elusive facets of the emotional bonds between people as well as the more accessible aspects. We will discuss the concepts of intimacy and commitment, attachment, loving and "being in love," as well as the more easily scrutinized topics of courtship, mate selection, and marriage. Types of marriage, satisfaction in marriage, and the particular problems of the "two-paycheck" marriage are also examined.

Like a good many people do, the chapter moves from a consideration of marriage to a discussion of divorce, delineating current trends for marital separation, divorce, and remarriage. The personal problems of responding to and coping with the breakup of an intimate relationship are also considered.

Finally, we will look at some of the emerging literature on alternative life styles, including studies of singlehood, cohabitation, group marriage, and homosexuality.

INTIMACY, ATTACHMENT, AND ROMANTIC LOVE

What do we mean when we say that young adults develop a capacity for intimate relationships with other people? What do we mean by intimacy?

Elements of Intimacy

Several attempts have been made to define the elements of intimacy in relationships between people. As we will see later in this chapter, Erik Erikson and other writers have stressed the importance of commitment in intimate relationships. Reciprocity, similarity, and compatibility have also been called the defining attributes of intimacy (Lowenthal and Weiss, 1976); a third approach has emphasized the concept of attachment (Troll and Smith, 1976; Kalish and Knudtson, 1976); and yet another interpretation stresses the importance of affiliation and dependency (Rubin, 1973).

All intimate relationships are not alike, of course. Moreover, the nature and conduct of such relationships probably change significantly with age (Lerner and Ryff, 1978; Reedy, Birren, and Schaie, 1982). For example, *proximal* or contact behaviors like wandering around holding mother's skirt gradually give way to *distal* behaviors such as eye contact, vocalizations, and the like.

Despite the variety of emotions, motives, and behaviors ascribed to people in intimate relationships, most writers on the subject agree that intimates engage in self-disclosure—that is, they talk to each other, especially about personal matters. In fact, intimacy is often said to exist and develop to the degree that self-disclosure occurs between two people. Self-disclosure must be mutual, of course, and must occur at a comfortable rate (Rubin, 1973). If self-disclosure is one-sided, the relationship resembles a therapist-client situation. If self-disclosure occurs too rapidly, embarrassment and withdrawal follow. We are unlikely to be strongly attracted to strangers who stop us on the street and begin to describe the intimate details of their personal lives.

If we assume that self-disclosure is a defining characteristic of intimacy, we might also expect a fairly strong relationship between intimacy and *identity*. Meaningful self-disclosure requires a strong sense of self. How can you tell someone else about who you are if you don't really know yourself? One research study does indeed report that young adult subjects who possessed a strong sense of identity, or who appeared to be struggling hard with identity issues, were likely to have a variety of intimate relationships with both males and females (Orlofsky, Marcia, and Lesser, 1973). In contrast, subjects who had adopted the identity outlined for them by their parents, and those who had not developed any sense of self at all, were likely to possess only superficial relationships or to develop commitments out of a sense of social convenience rather than mutuality, love, respect, and understanding (Orlofsky, 1976).

The ability to develop intimate relationships in young adulthood has been traced to earlier life as well. The fact that children, in their own way, possess intimacy (or at least its precursor) is of special interest to researchers who take a life-span approach to developmental issues. Concentrating on the importance of the parent-child bond, these researchers are particularly interested in how family relationships differ, if at all, from the intimate relationships of adulthood. The life-span perspective is especially interesting because of its consideration of negative as well as positive interactions in intimate relationships and because of the implication that intimacy may be expressed differently at different points in the life span. Most frequently, authors who are working from a life-span viewpoint use the term *attachment* for relationships characterized by feelings of intimacy and commitment (Troll and Smith, 1976; Kalish and Knudtson, 1976; Lerner and Ryff, 1978).

The Concept of Attachment

Attachment over the life span is thought to proceed from weak, diffuse bonds to closer, more complex ties. Of particular interest is the role of the persistent bond between parent and child. Evidence suggests that children's bonds with their parents are important even in adult life. Troll and Smith (1974) contend, for example, that parent-child bonds may form the basis for all two-person relationships. This is not a particularly radical point of view and has been favored by many psychodynamic theorists. Developmental psychologists, approaching the same idea from a different set of assumptions, suggest that attachment is a function of repeated interaction and that the frequency of parent-child interaction accounts for the strength of the bond (Troll and Smith, 1976).

Another interesting hypothesis suggests that attraction decreases as attachment grows: those to whom we become attached lose their novelty; they are no longer fascinating. Some data have been presented to support this idea, which would seem to have important implications for all long-term relationships and, in particular, for marriage (Troll and Smith, 1976; Taylor, 1968).

Those who study attachment tend to believe that intimacy is relative. Not all intimate relationships are the same. Intimate relationships may differ in intensity and depth, and in degree of self-disclosure or compatibility. A person may have several intimate relationships that are very different from one another, including some that involve little current compatibility or self-disclosure. These kinds of intimate relationships—for example, those between relatives who know each other "all too well"—might best be termed attachments. If we consider attachment to be a form of intimacy, we can extend the definition of intimacy to cover feelings about groups, ideas, and objects. Contending that the only really important characteristic of attachment is strong emotional involvement, authors Richard A. Kalish and F. W. Knudtson (1976) have suggested that attachment develops through the experience of self-produced feedback, which they define as any sensory, cognitive, or affective (emotional) stimulation that follows self-initiated action. Self-produced feedback occurs, for example, when one tickles a baby and it smiles, or when one paints a picture that is pleasing to others or even to oneself.

Attachment may be an important factor in all strong relationships in adulthood. In this chapter, however, we will restrict our attention to adult relationships that are characterized as intimate, and especially to those that are considered love relationships (we will discuss friendship in the next chapter). The idea that love, as well as other intimate relationships, is both relative and based on frequency of interaction has been most strongly developed by the social-learning theorists in a controversial and intriguing interpretation of intimate relationships called *social exchange theory*. Intimacy, they claim, is the product of a reward-cost history in the interaction between two people (Huston and Burgess, 1979; Kelley et al., 1983).

A Search for Equity?

Poets, songwriters, and social exchange theorists remind us that many, if not most, close relationships are riddled with conflict and characterized by negative as well as positive communications. Two people become intimate, not because they experience only positive interactions, but because the total outcome of their interactions exceeds the outcome they usually obtain from a relationship. In other words, we love people who reward us more often and punish us less than we expect (outcome equals rewards minus punishments).

This interpretation realistically admits both negative and postive interactions between intimates. Yet, self-disclosure continues and one's investment in the relationship grows. There is also a growing ability to predict the other person's point of view and a feeling that one's own interests are tied to the quality of the relationship (Huston and Burgess, 1979).

An interesting twist has been added to social exchange theory by Elaine Hatfield, Ellen Berscheid, and others who propose that intimate relationships must not only be rewarding, but they must also be *equitable* (Hatfield, Utne, and Traupmann, 1979; Berscheid, Walster, and Bohrnstedt, 1973; Walster, Walster, and Traupmann, 1978; Huston, 1983). Equity theory predicts that people who find themselves in inequitable relationships will feel distressed whether they are "winning" (getting the most out of the situation) or "losing." Both people in a relationship do not always have the same assets, of course. If Jack is terribly attractive and Jill is quite homely, for example, they may still be in an equitable relationship: Jill may be extremely bright and charming and Jack may be no mental giant. In other words, equity is based on the sum of one person's assets minus the sum of that person's liabilities. Distress occurs if the outcome is not reasonably equitable for both parties. The "winner" in an inequitable relationship feels guilt, dissonance, and fear of retaliation (as well as empathy) for the loser. The loser experiences resentment and anger.

A 1973 survey of *Psychology Today* readers supported the hypothesis that both members of an inequitable relationship report stress, and more recent research on newlyweds and dating couples has produced similar results (Berscheid, Walster, and Bohrnstedt, 1973; Walster et al., 1978; Walster, Walster, and Traupmann, 1978).

Not surprisingly, social exchange theory and equity theory have provoked heated debate. Is there no such thing as unconditional love? Some writers believe that social exchange theory in general, and equity theory in particular, may characterize the first stages of attraction, but they cannot explain the persistence of love in long-term relationships (Douvan, 1977; Rubin, 1973; Murstein et al., 1977). Of course, equity is difficult to calculate over the long term. People's assets and liabilities change over time, and individuals may be willing to put up with periods of inequity if they believe the deficit will eventually disappear. For instance, Jack may support Jill while she completes medical school if he believes she will be successful (and loyal).

It seems unlikely, moreover, that all equitable relationships are alike. If John is a man of few assets but few liabilities, for example, and Frank, who has numerous assets, has terrible liabilities, is Linda likely to feel the same about them? A relationship with someone who is extremely intelligent but very insensitive is quite different from a relationship with someone who is only moderately bright but is also fairly kind.

Neither does equity theory explain why some equitable relationships are passionate while others are not, nor why some inequitable relationships seem passionate as well. Different relationships have different qualities. Many of us enjoy a number of intimate, mutual, and long-term relationships. Some are passionate, and some are not. Some are joyful, some serious, others just comfortable. Yet, which is more valuable? Are some apparently equal relationships more equal than others? Most mysteriously, why do we "love" some people but feel "in love" with others?

Romantic Love

LOVING, LIKING, AND BEING IN LOVE. People who are "in love" express a physical need to be in the presence of another, to touch and be touched, to give as well as to receive (Rubin, 1973). In some ways, the idea of "being in love" involves a reappearance of those proximal behaviors we said characterized the relationships of young children. Lovers express a sense of responsibility and possessiveness that is not characteristic of other close friendships.

Yet "I'm in love" is not a statement that can be verified by counting behaviors or heartbeats. As Kenneth Pope (1980) has perceptively noted, romantic love is a relationship involving the whole person, not just one of his or her roles. "The awful (in the sense of inspiring awe) nature of love is that it brings us up against another person in all her or his offensive, threatening particulars and also that it makes us known the same way . . . without the guiding, reassuring constraints or buffers of limited role interactions" (p. 3).

Pope contends that romantic love is often ridiculed and disparaged because it involves fear and frustration as well as reward—the fear of being known too well, of being "found out," the terror of losing one's sense of identity in union and the fear of pain or loss of control. Pope believes love invites us to reconsider the ideal of independence, leading some to view it as a pathology. For example, one recent popular self-help book entitled *Letting Go* encourages readers to treat a broken heart like an addiction (Wanderer and Cabot, 1979). Grieving lovers are exhorted not only to conjure up mental pictures of garbage each time thoughts of the lost love occur but to make a horrible concoction of eggs, coffee grounds, and other odds and ends while thinking of the lost relationship.

Although deep feelings of reciprocity and mutuality do develop in mature love relationships, it is important to discriminate between love and dependency. Love does not diminish the lover. A truly mature intimate love relationship does not detract from one's sense of identity, but reinforces it instead. A weak sense of self is often associated with loss of identity in close relationships and can create a constant need for adulation and praise, a need that interferes with honest communication and commitment (Rubin, Peplau, and Hill, 1976; Erikson, 1968a, and 1968b; Lowenthal and Weiss, 1976).

Moreover, one must be able not only to retain a strong sense of oneself but also to accept the other person on his or her own terms. Erikson has referred to this phenomenon as the fusing and counterpointing of identity. As another writer puts it, "The capacity to come to satisfactory conflict resolution is the hallmark of a truly adult love relationship, for it is not based on idealization, but on increasing acceptance of the other as he or she really is" (Weiner, 1980, p. 123).

Yet, even as two people say "I love you," they may not always mean exactly the same thing. There may be different types of love and different patterns that dominate various periods of the life cycle. The results of one recent study indicated that passion and sexual intimacy were more important for young adults in satisfying love relationships, whereas affection, emotional security, and loyalty appeared to be of more interest to the older couples in the sample (Reedy, Birren, and Schaie, 1982). Figure 4.1 presents some of the results from this study.

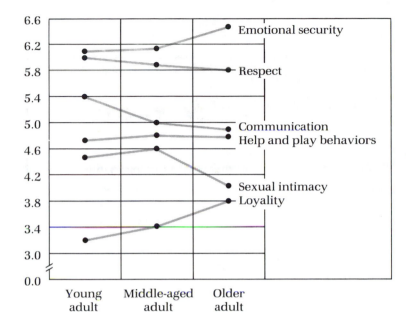

FIGURE 4.1
Mean scores for components of love categories

SOURCE: M. N. Reedy, J. E. Birren, and K. W. Schaie, "Age and Sex Differences in Satisfying Love Relationships Across the Life-Span," Human Development, *24 (1982): 52–66.*

It has also been suggested that romances often begin with a fairly intense phase but are transformed to a less passionate form because what is exciting about romance is the reduction of uncertainty about the other person (Livingston, 1980). When uncertainty approaches zero (when we think we know everything about the other person), our attention drifts to other things. On the other hand, if uncertainty about the other person increases (they seem unpredictable) or persists (we cannot figure them out), the relationship also becomes less attractive. From this point of view, "a romantic affair does battle with the passage of time," and passion will inevitably give way eventually to companionate love (Livingston, 1980; Walster, Walster, and Traupmann, 1978).

Just as love may take various forms at various times, it may also be defined and experienced differently by different types of people. Some may not be terribly attracted by the passionate phase of a relationship. Others may find the companionate period boring. In fact, one researcher, John Lee (1974, 1977) has contended that people exhibit at least six entirely different styles of loving.

STYLES OF LOVING. According to Lee, the six basic styles of loving are *storge*, the love of best friends; *eros*, or romantic love; *ludis*, game-playing love; *pragma*, logical love; *agape*, unselfish love; and *mania*, possessive love (Lasswell and Lobsenz, 1980; Lee, 1977). (Box 4.1 presents a questionnaire

BOX 4.1
The love scale questionnaire

1. I believe that "love at first sight" is possible.
2. I did not realize that I was in love until I actually had been for some time.
3. When things aren't going right for us, my stomach gets upset.
4. From a practical point of view, I must consider what a person is going to become in life before I commit myself to loving him/her.
5. You cannot have love unless you have first had *caring* for a while.
6. It's always a good idea to keep your lover a little uncertain about how committed you are to him/her.
7. The first time we kissed or rubbed cheeks, I felt a definite genital response (lubrication, erection).
8. I still have good friendships with almost everyone with whom I have ever been involved in a love relationship.
9. It makes good sense to plan your life carefully before you choose a lover.
10. When my love affairs break up I get so depressed that I have even thought of suicide.
11. Sometimes I get so excited about being in love that I can't sleep.
12. I try to use my own strength to help my lover through difficult times, even when he/she is behaving foolishly.
13. I would rather suffer myself than let my lover suffer.
14. Part of the fun of being in love is testing one's skill at keeping it going and getting what one wants from it at the same time.
15. As far as my lover goes, what he/she doesn't know about me won't hurt him/her.
16. It is best to love someone with a similar background.
17. We kissed each other soon after we met because we both wanted to.
18. When my lover doesn't pay attention to me I feel sick all over.
19. I cannot be happy unless I place my lover's happiness before my own.
20. Usually the first thing that attracts my attention to a person is his/her pleasing physical appearance.
21. The best kind of love grows out of a long friendship.
22. When I am in love I have trouble concentrating on anything else.
23. At the first touch of his/her hand I knew that love was a real possibility.
24. When I break up with someone I go out of my way to see that he/she is okay.
25. I cannot relax if I suspect that he/she is with someone else.

BOX 4.1
(continued)

26. I have at least once had to plan carefully to keep two of my lovers from finding out about each other.

27. I can get over love affairs pretty easily and quickly.

28. A main consideration in choosing a lover is how he/she reflects on my family.

29. The best part of love is living together, building a home together, and rearing children together.

30. I am usually willing to sacrifice my own wishes to let my lover achieve his/hers.

31. A main consideration in choosing a partner is whether or not he/she will be a good parent.

32. Kissing, cuddling, and sex shouldn't be rushed. They will happen naturally when one's intimacy has grown enough.

33. I enjoy flirting with attractive people.

34. My lover would get upset if he/she knew some of the things I've done with other people.

35. Before I ever fell in love I had a pretty clear physical picture of what my true love would be like.

36. If my lover had a baby by someone else I would want to raise it, love it, and care for it as if it were my own.

37. It is hard to say exactly when we fell in love.

38. I couldn't truly love anyone I would not be willing to marry.

39. Even though I don't want to be jealous I can't help it when my lover pays attention to someone else.

40. I would rather break up with my lover than to stand in his/her way.

41. I like the idea of having the same kinds of clothes, hats, plants, bicycles, cars, etc., as my lover does.

42. I wouldn't date anyone that I wouldn't want to fall in love with.

43. At least once when I thought a love affair was all over, I saw him/her again and the old feelings came surging back.

44. Whatever I own is my lover's to use as he/she chooses.

45. If my lover ignores me for a while I sometimes do really stupid things to try to get his/her attention back.

46. It would be fun to see whether I can get someone to go out with me even if I didn't want to get involved with that person.

47. A main consideration in choosing a partner is how he/she will reflect on one's career.

BOX 4.1
(continued)

48. When my lover doesn't see me or call for a while, I assume he/she has a good reason.

49. Before getting very involved with anyone I try to figure out how compatible his/her hereditary background is with mine in case we ever have children.

50. The best love relationships are the ones that last the longest.

HOW TO SCORE YOUR LOVE SCALE ANSWERS

To score your responses to the questionnaire, the only answers that need to be considered are the "true" responses. The table below shows a heading for each style of love:

Best friends	Unselfish	Logical	Game playing	Romantic	Possessive
2.	12.	4.	3.	1.	6.
5.	13.	9.	10.	7.	14.
8.	19.	16.	11.	17.	15.
21.	24.	28.	18.	20.	26.
29.	30.	31.	22.	23.	27.
32.	36.	38.	25.	35.	33.
37.	40.	42.	39.	41.	34.
50.	44.	47.	43.		46.
	48.	49.	45.		
Total ____	Total ____	Total ____	Total ____	Total ____	Total ____

Put a check by the number of each question that you answered "true." Total the number of check marks in each column. Your test profile will probably show some "true" answers in all the classifications, but with peak scores in two or three of them. For example, you may have answered "true" to four questions of the eight in the Best Friends category and to six questions of the nine in the Logical one. We could then reasonably assume that you are a person who is quite practical in terms of whom you can love and how you love them, but that you also want to make the person you love your closest friend.

Here is another illustration: Say you have answered "true" to four questions of the nine in the Unselfish category and to four of the seven in the Romantic group. It is reasonable to interpret this to mean that you feel a strong physical attraction to a partner at the outset of a relationship; and that you believe that if your love is a true one it will overcome every obstacle, even to the point of giving each other up if that will make you both happier.

Some of you may have scored high (70 percent or more "true" answers) in several or even all of the categories. This does not necessarily mean your definitions of love are confused. It is more apt to be a measure of your

BOX 4.1
(continued)

tendency to agree with a statement even though for you it may be only partially or occasionally true. On the other hand, some of you may have moderate to low scores (50 percent or fewer "true" answers on all of the six scales). This does not mean that you are not a loving person or that your ideas about the meaning of love are hopelessly muddled. What it does mean, most likely, is that you are inclined to be analytical and cautious about your emotional responses and behavior, as well as about deciding how to answer questionnaires such as this one. Thus, if there is any doubt at all in your mind about a statement or your reaction to it, you have probably answered "false." Nevertheless, low scores are just as important a measure of your attitude as high scores are. If you have both some low and some high scores, the low scores can be equally revealing since they tend to reflect what you *do not* believe love to be.

SOURCE: M. Lasswell and N. Lobenz, *Styles of Loving* (Garden City, N.Y.: Doubleday, 1980).

designed to help you assess your primary style.) At least three of these styles—storge, eros, and agape—seem to include most of the characteristics of intimacy and love that we have been discussing, from the presence of self-disclosure and affection to reciprocity and appreciation. The studies conducted by Lee and his colleagues also suggest that several subtypes or mixtures of the basic styles are common (for example, erotic-practical).

A storge, or "best friend," love affair, is characterized by a deep, abiding affection. These lovers enjoy each other's company and are able to be self-disclosing, communicative, and mutually caring. The passionate phase in their relationship (if it occurs) is not considered essential. Often they have known each other for a long time before they discover they are in love, which perhaps explains the less passionate beginning. But an explosive, passionate relationship is also viewed as exhausting and bewildering by the storge lover.

A stereotypical version of eros, the romantic lover, is easy to find in the paperback-book section of any supermarket or drugstore. The protagonists of a gothic romance are erotic lovers, passionate and physical. Yet, they also meet the criteria of self-disclosure, mutuality, and caring. In fact, erotic types may be demanding in such matters, wanting to know everything about the beloved from daily activities to thoughts, desires, and even dreams. Although erotic lovers are eager to establish commitments, the failure rate for this kind of relationship seems to be high, perhaps because extravagant expectations frequently lead to disappointment. The passion of eros seems to promise both great rewards and substantial punishments (from a social exchange point of view), perhaps, but certainly appears as likely to produce intimacy as the storge relationship.

The criteria we have been using for intimacy are also met in *agape*, or unselfish love, which is described as unconditionally caring, nurturing, and compassionate. Difficulties can arise in an agapic relationship, however, when partners find themselves with very different goals. Because unselfish lovers tend to put their partners' needs and desires before their own, communication and self-disclosure can present a greater challenge in this relationship than in a storge or erotic type.

As for Lee's other styles, neither mania (possessive love) nor ludis (game-playing love) seems likely to produce intimacy. The possessive lover, usually a victim of poor self-esteem, suffers what Lee has described as an addiction: a consuming, despairing desire for another, marked by jealousy and fear (1974; 1977). Of course, even an otherwise confident person may experience a manic relationship at one time or another; during a period of low self-esteem, for example, a relationship with a game-playing, ludic partner might produce mania in an otherwise erotic or even storge type.

Nearly the polar opposite of mania, the ludic lover remains essentially unattached. Ludic people appear to be in love with love. Charming and infuriating, they play at love as a game. Ludic lovers shun commitments and are often involved in more than one romantic relationship at the same time.

Equity theorists seem to have described Lee's sixth style of love, pragma, to a tee. Pragma is "love with a shopping list" (Lee, 1974). Believing that a proper relationship is the product of practical compatibility, the pragmatic lover sets out to find and preserve the correct match. It is quite possible, of course, for a pragmatic relationship to become intimate. If self-disclosure and affection grow out of basic compatibility, a pragmatic match may become a storge love affair, for instance. Such developments are common in countries where marriages are prearranged in childhood.

Commitment and Intimacy

So far, we have been discussing love and intimacy in terms of self-disclosure, mutuality, affection, and feelings of desire. Most writers agree, however, that for a relationship to blossom into fully realized intimacy, *commitment* must also exist (Erikson, 1968; Rubin, 1973; Mead, 1970; Pope, 1980; Weiner, 1980; Kelley, 1983). To be committed is to be obligated or bound—pledged to some particular course of action and accepting of the choices that are inherent in committing oneself to someone or something above others.

Sacrifice and investment are characteristic of committed relationships. For example, a study of the nature of commitment in nineteenth-century utopian communities found that the communities lasting the longest, those that fostered commitment, also demanded a good deal from their members (Kanter, 1972). Members often sacrificed such pleasures as smoking, drinking, or dancing and even signed over their properties and other assets to the community. Moreover, many of the most successful communities required members to undergo *mortification*, by publicly disclosing potentially embarrassing information about themselves.

Mortification and self-disclosure foster commitment because they involve risk. When we disclose personal information about ourselves, we risk rejection or embarrassment, and we may consider that risk to be a sign that we trust and love the other person. In other words, it can be argued that we may decide we love someone because we have behaved in a way that we interpret as loving (Rubin, 1973).

Some kinds of social structures, like those exemplified by the utopian communities, seem to facilitate the development of intimacy and commitment, while others make it more difficult. One might argue, for example, that the integration of the sexes in athletic organizations during childhood might help foster greater communication and understanding (and perhaps eventually intimacy) in adulthood, whereas traditional couple dating patterns of adolescents, like those common in the 1950s and 1960s, might ultimately encourage artificial behavior and lack of understanding between the sexes.

Erik Erikson has argued that the social institution of monogamous marriage is the soundest basis for commitment in heterosexual relationships (1968). The institution of marriage developed, Erikson believes, to support the development of truly mature intimate relationships; so-called alternative life-styles, he contends, are unlikely to succeed as well. The growing numbers of adults adopting alternatives to traditional marriage seem unlikely to abate in the near future, however, and controversy about the role of marriage in the development of intimacy continues. Nevertheless, marriage remains the relationship within which most young adults of the Western world attempt to express intimacy, commitment, and fidelity. Certainly marriage is easier to study than either intimacy or love; therefore, the literature on marriage is abundant.

MARRIAGE

"It is better to marry than to burn," noted Saint Paul, the Apostle (which, taken out of context, could be interpreted as a statement of choice between two almost equally distasteful alternatives). What he meant, of course, was that if one wanted to gratify sexual needs, marriage was the only acceptable arrangement (Hunt, 1974). For most of human history, and certainly in Saint Paul's time, marriage was both a business partnership and a reproductive arrangement—not a vehicle for companionship, love, or intimacy. Until the massive changes brought about by the Industrial Revolution, the family existed primarily as a unit of production, rather than as a context for the development of intimacy. Households produced domestic goods and services and provided settings for professional activities and cottage industries. The marital contract set forth specific religious obligations concerning sexual and parental matters, including the training and education of children. Clearly, modern life in the industrialized world has transformed the meaning of marriage. Marriage is no longer considered solely a practical financial arrangement or a framework in which to raise children. It is now viewed as a primary source of emotional gratification and a context for self-actualization (Melville, 1977; Skolnick, 1978).

Formally, traditional marriage may be defined as a "socially legitimate sexual union, begun with a public commitment and undertaken with some idea of permanence" (Stephens, 1963). It includes reciprocal rights and obligations between spouses, which have been dictated by society and may be institutionalized either in statute law or in case law. Such laws may specify who owns the property shared by married partners, who has responsibility for the welfare of children, and even the acceptable emotional and sexual behavior of partners in a marriage (Melville, 1977). Such are the formal aspects of marriage in the Western world.

Informally, however, we often expect a great deal more of marriage. Many sociologists and psychologists have argued, in fact, that marriage as we have known it cannot possibly meet the great number of personal, social, and sexual needs that we have come to expect from it in today's complex, rapidly changing society (Libby, 1977). The institution of marriage, it is argued, evolved to meet social demands that have little in common with needs like intimacy and commitment.

Yet, in spite of our high and diverse expectations, our society also perpetuates a rather long-standing tradition of hostility toward marriage. Arlene Skolnick (1978) has pointed out two strains of ambivalence about marriage. The first is cynical, reflected in the old ball-and-chain school of humor, which pictures marriage as benefiting only the woman: "Every man is plotting seduction and every woman is plotting marriage. No woman ever remains unmarried voluntarily" (Skolnick, 1978). Skolnick believes that such jokes express male resentment of women. (In an alternative interpretation, the ball-and-chain tradition is seen as a harmless form of rebellion that actually protects stable family life from disrupting impulses [Orwell, 1946].)

The second theme of ambivalence also finds its expression in humor, but through more sophisticated channels of social expression. From the

French bedroom farce to magazines like *Esquire* and *Playboy*, "the main source of humor is adultery, and the complications arising from deception and discovery." This brand of humor, Skolnick notes, "reflects the moral order of the Continental upper-middle class, where separation of love and marriage is assumed, love affairs are expected of both spouses, but especially the husband, and conjugal love, particularly of long standing, is perverse" (1978, p. 239).

Despite any ambivalence we may display, however, marriage is one social institution that very few Americans fail to enter. Only about 6 percent of all American men and 4 percent of women choose the single life. Moreover, compared with people in other Western countries, Americans marry young as well as much more often: by their early thirties, over 90 percent have been married. Ira Reiss (1980) points out that, in contrast, as many as 20 percent of all Swedes never marry; although there is a trend in the United States toward singlehood, it seems to be a product of delaying marriage for a few more years rather than rejecting it. Reiss notes, however, that it is too early to be sure. Some people now in their early twenties who are single may choose to remain so despite the past tendency of young Americans to marry before thirty.

For the huge majority who do marry, romantic love will be the most important motivating force. In fact, most Americans claim that love is the only acceptable reason for marriage. Despite this belief in the primacy of love, however, and despite the fact that we are theoretically free to fall in love across social, racial, ethnic, educational, and age boundaries, most Americans tend to marry "the right kind of person"—which usually means someone of similar race, religion, education, and socioeconomic background, one's "own kind." Therefore, it is not surprising that one of the most important predictors of mate selection and marital success is *homogamy*, or the selection of a marital partner similar to oneself in important social and psychological ways.

The Selection of Marriage Partners

Nearly all Americans marry someone of the same racial origin and of similar educational and socioeconomic background. Social homogamy is the rule in the United States, ensured in part by the following important factors:

1. People from the same social class marry each other because they have similar attitudes and values.

2. People of the same social background live near one another (show *residential propinquity*) and are therefore likely to meet.

"As a general thing, people marry most happily with their own kind. The trouble lies in the fact that people usually marry at an age when they do not really know what their own kind is." Robertson Davies

3. Because people of the same racial and ethnic origins marry each other (*ethnic endogamy*), marriage partners are similar in ways associated with particular racial and ethnic backgrounds.

4. Social pressure from one's parents, family, and friends promotes social homogamy.

5. Educational opportunities are most readily available to the middle and upper classes. Because schools and colleges often function informally as matrimonial agencies, marriage is likely to occur between people of the same social class (Eckland, 1973).

No one questions the existence of homogamy for such characteristics as race, religion, age, education, location of residence, and previous marital status. A lively dispute continues, however, over the importance of similarity in such factors as personality traits, attitudes, values, and needs. Is there no truth in the cliche that opposites attract?

SIMILARITY. Bernard Murstein is the leading advocate of the "birds of a feather flock together" school. His research indicates that couples who are involved in serious courtship show significantly more similar value hierarchies and are more alike in physical attractiveness, neuroticism, self-esteem, and degree of sexual desire than individuals who are dating each other less seriously (Murstein, 1982, 1967; 1970–1973).

Murstein believes that people perceive themselves as similar to their chosen marriage partners in a wide variety of dimensions. Often they see their partners as representing not only their ideal mate but also their own ideal images of themselves. One of the most intriguing findings Murstein has reported, however, is that little correlation actually exists between peoples' descriptions of their partners and the partners' descriptions of themselves. Fertile ground for disenchantment (Murstein, 1973)!

According to Murstein, "satisfaction with the partner is largely a projected wish that is uncorrected because of the narrow range of behavior each partner exhibits to the other before marriage." In time, of course, both partners discover that many of the attributes they assigned to the other, including perceived similarity to themselves, are illusory. Murstein concludes that it is not surprising that people often become disillusioned with their partners and marriages in fairly short order.

Murstein's findings fit the evidence generated by the social exchange theorists and the equity theorists discussed earlier in this chapter (Huston and Burgess, 1979; Hatfield, Utne, and Traupmann, 1979; Kelley et al., 1983). Remember that several studies indicated both dating and married couples were happier when the partners' social assets and liabilities were perceived as equal to their own. The similarity hypothesis also explains data showing how the college class system (the prestige of fraternities and sororities) can be used to predict date selection, especially among college students who are courting someone seriously (Reiss, 1980).

On the other hand, Murstein's approach has been criticized on the basis of both contradictory findings and methodological considerations. In one study of over 500 Pennsylvania high school students, for example, researchers found that the students who eventually married were not significantly more alike than acquaintances who did not marry (Snyder, 1973). Since Murstein's subjects were already dating or engaged when he studied them, critics argue, their interactions may have caused them to *become* more alike.

Unfortunately, because the Pennsylvania study was conducted in a small town, all the participants may have been *homogenous* (like one another) before they ever dated. Nonetheless, Murstein himself agrees that selection for similarity may be of primary importance only in the first stages of forming relationships. Later, partners may be motivated by considerations of compatibility or *complementarity* rather than simple similarity.

COMPLEMENTARITY.   One influential hypothesis posits that later stages of mate selection are characterized by attempts to choose a partner who complements oneself, especially in areas where power is an issue. A dominant, nurturant woman, for example, might choose a submissive, receptive man for a partner (Winch, 1974). In one classic series of studies, the most vocal proponent of the "opposites attract" hypothesis, Robert Winch, has delineated four types of marital complementarity:

1. Ibsenian (after the playwright who wrote *A Doll's House*), in which the dominant, nurturant male marries the submissive, receptive female

2. Thurberian (after James Thurber's view of the battle between the sexes), in which the nurturant, submissive male marries the dominant, receptive female

3. Master–servant girl, in which the dominant, receptive male marries the submissive female

4. Mother-son, in which the submissive, receptive male marries the dominant, nurturant female (Winch, 1974)

Winch has also suggested that complementarity of need for achievement may be an important consideration in the formation of marital pairs. Experimental work has indicated, however, that partners who are both highly involved in job-related activities express comparatively low levels of marital satisfaction, whereas marital satisfaction seems to be fairly high among partners who show moderate degrees of job involvement. Clearly, these findings are not completely consonant with the complementarity hypothesis (Ridley, 1973).

The case for complementarity has been attacked with some regularity and with moderate success. Some writers have even argued that most forms of complementarity are really a kind of similarity. A dominant husband and submissive wife both share the same perception of male and female roles. Although their behaviors may be complementary, their attitudes and beliefs are similar. When society dictates that two people in a relationship must play different roles, one is bound to find evidence for complementarity (Friedman, Sears, and Carlsmith, 1981).

Obviously, there is room for a good deal more examination of issues like love and mate selection. Since current research has not yet provided much clarity about what constitutes a good match, it is not surprising to learn that the literature on marriage also fails to agree about what constitutes the basis for a strong, satisfying relationship.

What Is a Good Marriage?

Much of the research on marriage simply reports whether or not people experience their marriages as "satisfactory" or "unsatisfactory," creating an impression that all successful marriages are somewhat alike. But like love, a good marriage does not mean the same thing to everyone, and the most sophisticated, detailed research demonstrates that stable, satisfactory marriage comes in a variety of forms.

TYPES OF MARRIAGE.   In one important study, intensive interviews with over four hundred married men and women from middle-class families not currently in crisis led to the delineation of five types of enduring marriages: the conflict-habituated marriage, the devitalized marriage, the passive-congenial marriage, the vital marriage, and the total marriage (Cuber and Harroff, 1965).

The *conflict-habituated* marriage is characterized by constant arguing, bickering, and nagging. The couple does not see the combat as a reason for breaking up, but find fighting perfectly acceptable. For these two, fighting may even provide a kind of stability.

In the *devitalized* marriage, partners believe they have marital love for one another, but they seem bored or disenchanted, sharing little in their relationship. Still, they perceive the match as a good marriage.

For *passive-congenial* marrieds, life is comfortable and amiable. Marriage is a convenient arrangement, but the partners are not greatly involved with each other. Responsibility is assigned in a way that minimizes conflict.

Vital and *total* marriages, the last two categories, are different from the first three. Whereas conflict-habituated marriage, devitalized marriage, and passive-congenial marriage are considered *institutional* marriages, vital and total matches have been characterized as *companionship marriages.* In a vital marriage, husband and wife are highly involved in all common aspects of family life, including the economic aspects, the emotional concerns, and the recreational, educational, and social activities. People engaged in a total marriage have a sense of profound involvement in every aspect of each other's life, including work, leisure, children, hobbies, moods, thoughts, and even dreams. Such couples are often faced with social disapproval, or at the least are suspected of being a kind of two-person neurosis (Hicks and Platt, 1970).

It has been estimated that as many as 80 percent of all American marriages are institutional relationships in which the emotional bond between the partners is not a primary source of satisfaction. The marital bliss of the couple in an institutional relationship seems to be dependent on

People in a devitalized marriage begin to accept disenchantment and boredom as inevitable parts of married love.

success in the outside world. Until recently, at least, the performance of the male in the traditional role of breadwinner has probably been the most important predictor of marital satisfaction for many conflict-habituated, devitalized, or passive-congenial marriages (Hicks and Platt, 1970; Cuber and Harroff, 1965).

We might extrapolate on the basis of such research that when both spouses are oriented toward success outside the home, an institutional rather than companionate bond is even more likely. This is not necessarily the case, however. Arlene Skolnick, for one, has disputed the notion that the more time people invest outside their marriages, the less they have to give to the marital relationship; and in at least one major study of dual-career marriages, couples reported their relationships were characterized not only by companionship, pride, and role-sharing, but also by feelings of self-expression and growth for the women (Skolnick, 1978; Rapoport and Rapoport, 1969; 1971). Although these marriages could hardly be described as merely institutional, the rewards they bring are also accompanied by special kinds of stress. Nor have considerable stresses been absent, for both partners, in marriages in which women did not work outside the home.

The Stresses of Marriage

In general, the sociological literature on marriage shows that working partners tend to exhibit much satisfaction with their marriages, although they also report unusually high levels of stress (Heckman, Bryson, and Bryson, 1977).

DUAL-CAREER MARRIAGES.   One now classic study of English couples by Rhona and Robert Rapoport described several potential sources of difficulty in the dual-career marriage. Time for shared leisure and social activities usually diminishes as the wife takes on a full career and the husband develops relationships with his children. Limited time and escalating responsibilities produce *role overload*. Women often experience intense conflict between the demands of the wife-and-mother role and the expectations they have developed in a fairly egalitarian educational system. This study suggests that there may be an optimal balance or relationship between the demands in each of the careers and demands at home. The Rapoports refer to this problem of timing as *role-cycling*. If one spouse is forced to delay family concerns because of career events, or to delay peak performance at work because of family responsibilities, dissatisfaction may follow.

In a more recent analysis (Rice, 1979), a distinction is made between couples who married with the idea that the wife would have a career and couples in which the wife embarked on a career after the couple had been married for some time. In this study, success seemed to depend, in part, on presence of very little or no ambivalence toward the wife's career. David Rice also notes that when the wife is invested in a full-scale career (as opposed to a job), both people in the relationship may well be classified as high achievers. Highly achievement-oriented people usually expect to be successful and often blame themselves when they are not, compounding whatever stress and difficulty they encounter.

Achievement-oriented people are usually quite persistent, even in the face of much stress, but they do require high levels of approval and support. Without support, high achievers often suffer from self-esteem problems, withdrawing from the relationship and thereby also withdrawing support from the spouse. A vicious cycle results, and both partners can turn to work for gratification and give up on the marriage.

Rice also points out that dual-career couples cannot often rely on society's conventional wisdom for marital success. These couples must create their own special structures over the years, particularly with regard to three areas: the management of time, the treatment of outside social relationships, and the raising of children. Without detailed scheduling and conscious planning, working partners often find it hard to spend meaningful time together. If their time is unorganized, one or the other partner will experience inequity. High achievers are especially sensitive to the issue of equity, or the fairness, of the marital situation. A careful assessment of how the couple uses time, Rice suggests, can help a therapist or social worker identify many of the problems the couple is facing.

Feelings of inequity are also likely to arise when the partners are rearing children. If the major responsibility for childrearing falls to the woman, she begins to feel tired, depleted, and guilty. Yet working wives often deny any conflict they feel over their performance as mothers. They have a special need to feel that both their marriage and their children are doing well since they are frequently confronted by strong, negative reactions from the rest of traditional, married society.

Another common form of denial is seen among dual-career couples, according to Rice. Achievement-oriented partners tend to ignore the subtle competition they feel in the struggle to "come through" as a spouse, a parent, and a worker. Moreover, the competition is often complicated when the wife feels she is at an unfair disadvantage, having started late or carrying the major responsibility for running the home and rearing the children. Many dual-career couples simply cannot function without outside domestic help. Otherwise, the women have little or no time left for the relationship. Furthermore, a "back-up system" should be available when the usual arrangements go awry, and there is a need to share in the arranging of the system. Feelings of inequity are often produced by the failure of domestic arrangements, particularly if the arranger is blamed for the problems that arise.

Finally, outside social relationships can be a source of difficulty in the dual-career marriage. Since these couples have so little social or leisure time together, many of their social needs are met at work, and strong social relationships outside the home can permit one to avoid dealing with the problems of the marital relationship.

In basic agreement with Rice, the Rapoports believe that large cultural changes are necessary to promote dual-career life-styles. They do believe, however, that these changes are on the way, including better child care and domestic services, convenient shopping, and efficient transportation. And, certainly, conventional one-career marriages are not immune to the strains of changing demands and roles in a complex world.

CONVENTIONAL ONE-CAREER MARRIAGES. The data suggest that men and women living in more conventional marital arrangements experience stress too. Although married men live longer, experience greater occupational success, and show lower suicide rates than never-married men, they also die younger than women, commit suicide more often, and suffer more frequently from stress-related health problems such as heart attacks and peptic ulcers (Bernard, 1973; Melville, 1977). These statistics might well reflect the emphasis placed on a man's performance as a breadwinner in the conventional marital situation. After all, a man's socioeconomic success was the most important determinant of marital satisfaction in several studies of the conventional, one-career marriage (Brenton, 1976; Hicks and Platt, 1970).

Women in conventional marriages become more submissive and conservative than they were before marriage, and they experience more neurosis and depressive symptoms than married men or single women (Murstein, 1973; Bernard, 1981). They are often quite dependent on their husbands for emotional and financial support as well as for their social and even personal identity. These conditions take their toll, and the women most committed to conventional marriage and family seem to suffer from the highest rates of menopausal depression. They are also admitted to mental hospitals more often than other women (Bart, 1970; Gove and Tudor, 1973).

Still, a great number of people seem not only to be satisfied, but to thrive in the conventional one-career marriage. Moreover, these couples generally report that, despite the stresses, they find their marriages quite rewarding. Obviously, a review of the problems reveals only half of the story.

Satisfaction over Time

The study of marital satisfaction as a general concept is really not a very satisfactory way to tackle the issues. Not only do the most satisfying aspects of marriage probably change over time, but the intensity of satisfaction clearly varies over the span of the marriage. Not only does it vary with the years and the stage of the family, but also with the goals of the partners and the kind of marriage they have established.

In the conventional, one-career marriage, women who lead less stereotypical, more egalitarian life-styles do very well for themselves and for their families. One study of 571 women in the Chicago area concludes that women who become involved in community and educational enterprises, who form close ties with other women, and who possess a fair degree of education, initiative, and administrative ability are likely to experience great satisfaction with themselves and their marriages (Lopata, 1971). More recent evidence from the Berkeley Institute of Human Development describes traditional, middle-class housewives at middle age as gregarious, nurturant, charming, and cordial (Livson, 1981). These conventional subjects moved through the years of midlife without experiencing crisis and appeared close, trusting, and poised.

In the same study, less conventional women, who were more likely to hold full-time jobs, seemed to have more difficulty negotiating the midlife transition, but by the age of fifty, they were closer and more trusting again. A recent study of some 15,000 readers of *McCall's* magazine (Jacoby, 1982) agrees. With age, working women seem to become more and more satisfied with their lives. Women over thirty-four were more satisfied with their two-paycheck marriages than those twenty-one through thirty-four, and women over fifty were the most satisfied of all.

Only 6 percent of *McCall's* working women felt their jobs had an adverse effect on their marriage, and more than two-thirds reported that their husbands were supportive and proud of their work. It is also important to note, however, that the compromise of the wife's career was often a central feature of the successful two-paycheck family. Most of the women in this survey said flatly that their husband's job took precedence and that they would simply quit their job and move if their husband was offered a better job in another city. Furthermore, such compromise was almost as common among managerial and professional women as it was among women in sales, clerical, or low-paying, unskilled jobs. Only a minority of the husbands (25 percent) were willing to help their wives with domestic chores, and younger men seemed no more willing than the oldest husbands in the survey.

Child care is the most important continuing problem that plagues the dual-career marriage during the years when the children are young. These complaints are not framed in terms of abstract problems. They are not obscure or difficult to understand. They are the everyday, practical problems created by a system that was not designed for working mothers. As one woman put it,

> I pay $16 a day for my four year old and $77 a month for an all-day kindergarten program (8:30 to 2:15), and $50 every two weeks to my mother-in-law (who lives two blocks away) to pick up my five year old at 7 A.M. and dress her, feed her, and put her on the school bus by 7:50, then pick her up at the bus stop at 2:30. If my in-laws are not well, I either miss work or have to pay $32 a day for my daughters.
>
> I also need a sitter on Saturdays since my husband and I get days off during the week. I have just hired two teenagers to job-share on Saturdays and during school vacations. I feel fortunate that I have been able to find loving, caring people to fill in the gaps—but I am also in a constant state of stress. If something goes wrong with just one person in my support system, everything blows up. I—not my husband—am responsible for working all this out (Jacoby, 1982, p. 127).

The central issue of child care affects conventional marrieds as well. A variety of researchers have examined the course of marital satisfaction over time in a marriage, and there is general agreement that people are most content with their marriages once they have helped their children successfully leave the family home.

In the late 1960s, Evelyn Duvall (1971) devised an eight-stage model of the family life cycle. This model is now widely accepted, and the stages will appear in later chapters of this book. In Duvall's model, four periods of marriage and family structure—the newlywed marriage, the parental marriage, the middle-aged marriage, and the retirement marriage—are subdivided as follows:

- Stage 1: Beginning families: 0–5 years of marriage, no children

- Stage 2: Childbearing families: oldest child less than 3 years of age

- Stage 3: Families with preschoolers: oldest child from 3 years to 5 years 11 months

- Stage 4: Families with school-age children: oldest child from 6 years to 12 years 11 months

- Stage 5: Families with teenagers: oldest child from 13 years to 20 years 11 months

- Stage 6: Families as launching centers: from departure of the first child to departure of the last child

- Stage 7: Families in the middle years: from departure of last child to retirement of first spouse

- Stage 8: Aging families: from retirement of first spouse to death of one spouse

According to Duvall, each stage of the family life cycle is characterized by specific tasks and goals. For instance, the newlywed or beginning family must establish its own, independent home while the parental family must accommodate the new roles and relationships associated with children. Studies by other authors also suggest that each stage is accompanied by change in feelings about the marriage, although there is some conflict about exactly what direction the changes take (Blood and Wolfe, 1960; Rollins and Feldman, 1970; Miller, 1976).

One version emphasizes a corrosion of affection and increasing disenchantment through at least the first twenty years of marriage. Most of the data clearly indicate that newlywed marriages are characterized by high levels of satisfaction and companionship, but the evidence also suggests that the honeymoon is soon over (Blood and Wolfe, 1960; Pineo, 1961; Campbell, 1975).

The controversy arises over whether love's labor and intimacy are forever lost or whether satisfaction is eventually recovered. Studies that suggest marriage is characterized by increasing disenchantment over the years (Blood and Wolfe, 1969) are sometimes cross-sectional and may, therefore, reflect important cohort differences, including educational and financial considerations and age at time of marriage. Others, like that of Pineo (1961), are longitudinal but consider only couples in the first twenty years of marriage, from Stage 1 (beginning families) to the end of Stage 5 (families with teenagers). Stage 5 couples have the most parental responsibility. Usually, the largest number of children are living in the parental home and other demands on the parents of the Stage 5 family are great. They are fully engaged in many adult roles, as parents, workers, homemakers, citizens, friends, and members of civic and other groups. Stage 5 parents may be under great role strain as they try to fulfill the varied expectations of the culture.

Researchers who have looked beyond Stage 5, to the attitudes and feelings of couples in the launching and retirement phases, often find evidence that marital satisfaction recovers as children leave the home. In fact, the married couples with empty nests may be among the happiest (Rollins and Feldman, 1970; Campbell, 1975; Miller, 1976).

The presence of children probably represents a barrier to the kinds of communication and interaction associated with high levels of marital satisfaction. Evidence has been found of a positive correlation between marital satisfaction and frequency of companionship, and other data indicate that the number of children and the socioeconomic class of the family are important predictors of marital satisfaction. Children demand much time and energy as well as money. Family size and the ability to pay for child care are probably factors that facilitate or interfere with positive interaction between husband and wife (Miller, 1976).

One final point about sex differences over the family life cycle: the bearing and launching of children seem to be the most important predictors of marital satisfaction for women. Events before and after the childrearing years have the more profound influence on many responses by male subjects. For example, husbands tend to report dissatisfaction during the years immediately prior to retirement; wives seem more dissatisfied with marriage during the parental years, from the time when children are toddlers to the departure of the first child (Rollins and Feldman, 1970).

So far, we have discussed love, companionship, work and childrearing in their relationship to intimacy and marriage. At least one other major aspect—sex—deserves attention. Marriage is, after all, the

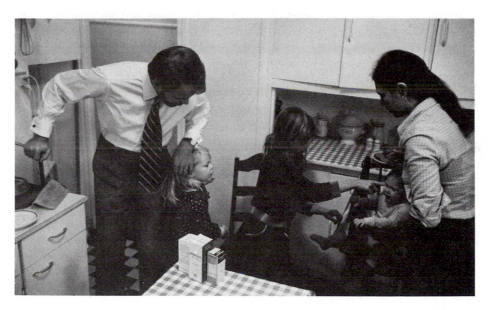

In a household with small children, if you are not too busy to carry on a meaningful conversation, then you are probably too tired.

only completely sanctioned outlet for human sexual desire in North American culture, despite the currents created by the changing tides of sexual customs and mores.

SEXUALITY AND RESPONSIVENESS

Sex in Marriage

In her novel *Fear of Flying*, Erica Jong complained that sex in marriage, like processed cheese, grows bland and boring. Was she right? Does sexual enjoyment decline over the course of married life? Certainly, the frequency of physical affection, from kissing to sexual intercourse, declines over years of marriage, but quantity doesn't indicate quality. In fact, recent evidence suggests marriage today may fulfill its sexual promise far better than it ever did (Reiss, 1980).

In the late 1940s and early 1950s, a pioneering series of studies of human sexuality was published, based on personal interviews. These became known as the Kinsey reports. In 1974, Morton Hunt again asked many of the same questions Kinsey and his associates had posed. Hunt (1974) wrote that "Western civilization has long had the rare distinction of contaminating and restricting the sexual pleasure of married couples more severely than almost any other." He was able to conclude, however, that sex in marriage has become steadily more acceptable, more pleasurable, freer, and more egalitarian since Kinsey published his first findings (1948). According to Hunt, part of the reason for the elaboration of sex in marriage lies in the general closeness of married partners compared with those in Kinsey's sample. Quicker access and great social acceptance of divorce may mean that those who remain married are more satisfied in a number of ways than used to be the case.

The average American married couple reports having sexual intercourse two or three times a week through young adulthood, tapering off to about once a week after the age of fifty (Masters, Johnson, and Kolodny, 1982). Large individual differences occur in every age range, however, and some couples seem to become more active with age rather than less so.

Moreover, Hunt (1974) reported substantial gains among married couples since Kinsey's studies, on every measure of sexual activity and pleasure he used, including frequency of orgasm during sexual activity, median duration of intercourse, and number of married persons who describe marital sex as "pleasurable" or "very pleasurable," as well as frequency of sexual intercourse. Hunt also found that the sexual techniques used by married couples today are much more varied than those Kinsey reported and include increased amounts of sexual play and a wider variety of coital positions. Not surprisingly, from this evidence he has concluded that marital sex is more pleasurable for contemporary couples than for those responding to Kinsey's survey.

People today, especially the youngest cohorts, come to marriage with greater sexual experience than in Kinsey's day. Women show more assertive and experimental attitudes. More external sources of information and stimulation are available today. So, too, are practical, accessible contraception and sexual therapy. All these conditions might be expected to facilitate the experience of sexual satisfaction in marriage.

Sexual Revolution

Hunt's findings about sex between married people are only one indication that impressive changes have taken place in both the attitudes people hold toward sexuality and their sexual behavior in and out of marriage and in every age group. Even among those who behaved most conservatively, among female American college students reports of sexual intercourse before marriage tripled in the ten years from 1958 to 1968. It is now generally accepted that by the age of 19 or 20, about one-half of all college women have engaged in sexual intercourse, although in some geographical regions, the proportion will be higher or lower (Dreyer, 1975; Zelnick and Kantner, 1977; 1979; 1980).

On the other hand, a number of writers point out that traditional attitudes have not disappeared completely. Although most young adults tend to condone a wide variety of sexual behaviors between consenting partners, Robert Sorenson found that they identify themselves as "serial monogamists," preferring one relationship at a time (while permitting occasional infidelity). In the same study, few adolescents agreed with the statement, "There is no kind of sex act that I would think of as being abnormal, so long as the people involved want to do it" (Sorenson, 1973). Young people also remain far more permissive toward male sexual behavior than female, especially with regard to casual encounters. As Hunt (1974) puts it, the "sex ethic of contemporary youth is essentially liberal-romantic rather than radical-recreational."

Not only are people more sexually active before and during marriage, but they are also more likely to remain active after marriage, whether they are divorced or widowed. In Hunt's (1974) sample, for example, not one male under age 55 described himself as sexually inactive after marriage, and only 10 percent of the females reported that they were inactive. In comparison, Kinsey found that 4 percent of his male subjects and 18 percent of the females were sexually inactive after marriage. Furthermore, it is reported often that postmarital sex is more pleasurable and fulfilling than prior marital experience (Masters, Johnson, and Kolodny, 1982).

Finally, as one might predict from the current data on sexual behavior, there is evidence of a trend toward increased extramarital sexual activity (that is, more married people report having sex with someone other than their spouse). For instance, Hunt (1974) found that among younger subjects, although nearly all extramarital sexual experience was suffused with guilt and conflict, three times as many women reported such experience as did in Kinsey's sample.

Extramarital Sexual Activity

One year after Hunt's report, a survey of *Redbook* readers reported that one-half of married respondents eighteen to thirty-four years old and nearly 70 percent of those over thirty-five claimed to have had extramarital sexual experience (Levin, 1975). A few years before, in 1970, a survey of *Psychology Today* readers indicated that 80 percent of respondents approved of extramarital sexual activity under some conditions. Admittedly, the readerships of these magazines are not representative samples of the American population, and more carefully designed research is clearly needed in this area. The figures reported are sufficiently dramatic, however, that we should not overlook their significance.

More thorough research seems particularly important if Hunt as well as Masters and Johnson are right in assuming that extramarital sex produces significant changes in both the marital and sexual behavior of the individuals involved (Hunt, 1974; Masters, Johnson, and Kolodny, 1982). Hunt argues that such activity, if discovered, always has negative consequences for the marriage. On the other hand, Masters and Johnson have commented that certain people become fully responsive for the first time in their lives as a result of extramarital sexual experiences (1966; 1970). Masters, Johnson, and Kolodny note that "some people find exactly what they're looking for: a release of pent-up tension, a means of getting even with their spouse for something, a way of satisfying their curiosity, a change of pace from their ordinary sexual diet, or a temporary form of escape." These authors also observe, however, that other people "find the experience to be empty, guilt-provoking, awkward, or frightening" and may develop significant sexual difficulties as a result of extramarital sexual involvement (Masters, Johnson, and Kolodny, 1982, p. 308).

Box 4.2 presents two examples of the types of reactions Masters and Johnson find common. What is the difference between an experience that benefits the individual and one that is harmful? How does extramarital sex affect marriage?

Historically, Americans have viewed marriage as both exclusive and permanent. Sociologist Jessie Bernard has suggested that male jealousy is the major support for sexual exclusivity and that female insecurity is the prop for permanence. As female insecurity and male jealousy wane in a modern world, Bernard believes, attitudinal changes toward extramarital sex will become widespread. Such changes are already apparent in the cautious suggestion by some researchers that extramarital sex may have a potentially positive function in meeting the variety of needs people develop in complex cultural settings (Bernard, 1975). Other writers have even suggested that extramarital sexual activity should be considered an extension of normal sexual behavior (Whitehurst, 1966; Libby, 1977; Roy and Roy, 1968).

A 1974 survey conducted by *Redbook* magazine indicated that at least half of the women reporting extramarital sexual activity also claimed to be happily married. A 1975 survey by Bell, Turner, and Rosen pointed to the same conclusion: of 2,262 married women respondents, 20 percent of those who rated their marriages as good or very good also reported extramarital sexual involvements.

BOX 4.2
From the files of Masters and Johnson

Masters, Johnson, and Kolodny use the following comments to illustrate the variety of ways people respond to extramarital sexual experiences. These married people were involved in sexual one-night stands, which Masters and Johnson believe are much more common than extramarital affairs. A one-night stand is, of course, easier to accomplish without the knowledge of one's spouse. People also seem to agree that a one-night stand poses less of a threat to the marriage since they do not generally see it as a love relationship.

A thirty-one-year-old woman: "I'd been married for almost ten years and had always been faithful, but I kept wondering what it would be like to have sex with someone else. One night I was out with some friends, and we met a few guys who bought us drinks and talked with us awhile. One of them was real good-looking and flirting with me, and I sort of flirted back. We went off to a motel for three or four hours, and it was beautiful sex, fantastic sex, just like in a novel. But that was the end of it, and it just felt good to know that I'd had the experience. I never told my husband and I don't plan to" (Author's files).

A thirty-six-year-old man: "My wife and I have very old-fashioned values and we both took our marital vows seriously, meaning no screwing around with anyone else. I never worried about it too much, since I wasn't the type to be running around anyway. But one night when I was working late a secretary asked me for a ride home, and then invited me in for coffee. Well, she was just divorced a few months, and she wanted more than coffee, and I was perfectly happy to oblige. But it was a stupid thing to do—not much fun, and lots of guilt about it afterwards—and I don't think I'd do it again" (Author's files).

SOURCE: W. H. Masters, V. E. Johnson, and R. C. Kolodny, *Human Sexuality* (Boston: Little, Brown, 1982), p. 308.

Although there is very little information about how people who consider themselves happily married handle extramarital sex, researchers in this area agree that deceitful adultery is not the most satisfactory of adjustments, and that a distinction should be made between *infidelity* (clandestine adultery) and *comarital sex* (consensual adultery) (Libby, 1977).

Consensual adultery, or comarital sex, seems most likely to occur in the context of what Cuber and Harroff (1965) have described as a vital marriage. In this context, extramarital sexual activity may serve to ease the strain created by the societal ideal of a lifelong union that admits of little social and no sexual variety. From this viewpoint, such behavior need not be viewed as a problem indicative of disorganization or a neurosis but may simply represent an emerging marital style (Libby, 1977).

Despite their apparently small number, couples engaged in consensual adultery have been described in some detail. Clanton (1977) has delineated three kinds of consensual adultery: *group marriage, open-ended marriage,* and *recreational adultery.* Little is known about the progress and development of open-ended marriages, and little work has been done on group marriage. Only recreational adultery has received much attention.

Recreational adultery between sexual partners who are married, but not to each other, is characterized by a relatively low level of emotional involvement and by the expectation of impermanence. Most participants believe strongly in traditional marriage and wish to maintain it. They are trying to provide a safe outlet for extramarital sexual expression. These people are often well-educated, middle-class, white married couples. They are surprisingly conservative in the nonsexual aspects of their lives and so value the discretion and respectability of potential sexual partners. The rules of recreational adultery, or "swinging" as it was once tagged, emphasize low commitment in the extramarital relationship, honesty with the spouse, and loyalty to the marriage (Denfeld and Gordon, 1973; Ziskin and Ziskin, 1973).

However, despite elaborate attempts to preserve the integrity of their marriages, couples who engage in this kind of sexual activity take substantial risks. One study of 124 couples practicing comarital sex (Ziskin and Ziskin, 1973) indicates that recreational adultery resulted in significantly more marital difficulties than agreements that permitted extramarital sex but did not call for the couple to participate together. Couples who had explicit agreements often believed extramarital sexual experience enhanced a marriage.

One thing the research clearly suggests is a need for better definitions of extramarital sexual activities. For instance, John Edwards and Alan Booth (1976) state that "the more negative the perception of the marriage, the greater the sexual deprivation in the marriage, and as the latter increases, the more likely one is to seek sex outside the relationship."

Couples practicing recreational adultery may have a negative perception of marriage (although they profess the opposite), but more independent comarital sexual arrangements may not necessarily be accompanied by sexual deprivation within marriage or by negative perceptions of marriage. Extramarital sexual behavior takes many forms. The impact of one set of rules may be very different from another. Any social scientist studying extramarital sex must consider the particular rules adopted by a couple for both marriage and sex, the historical and cultural context of the study, and the personality characteristics of the individuals in each couple. Only then will the data collected enable us to begin to appreciate the role of extramarital sex in a relationship.

One intriguing possibility remains totally unexplored in the literature on extramarital sexual activity. Extramarital sex may have significant historical and developmental aspects. As the attitude of the culture changes, the impact of extramarital sexual activity on márriage will probably change. Moreover, extramarital involvements may mean very different things to couples at different stages of the family life cycle. Consider this passage from *A Month of Sundays* by John Updike (1975, pp. 137–138):

> Adultery is not one but several species. The adultery of the freshly married is a gaudy-winged disaster, a phoenix with hot ashes, the revelation that one has mischosen, a life-swallowing mistake has been made. Help, help, it is not too late, the babies scarcely know their father, the wedding presents are still unscarred, the mistake can be unmade, another mate can be chosen and the universe as dragon can be slain. . . . The adultery of the hopelessly married with slowly growing children and slowly dwindling mortgages, is a more stolid and more domestic creature, a beast of burden truly, for this adultery serves the purpose of rendering tolerable the unalterable . . . not often understood as such by the participants, who flog themselves with blame while they haul each other's bodies into place as sandbags against the swamping of their homes. The adultery of those in their forties recovers a certain lightness, a greyhound skittishness and peacock sheen. Children leave; parents die; money descends; nothing is as difficult as it once seemed. . . . And then, in a religious sense, there is no more adultery, as there is none among schoolchildren, or slaves, or the beyond-all-reckoning rich.

DIVORCE AND REMARRIAGE

Few people solve their marital problems extramaritally, however. Most Americans choose exclusivity at the expense of permanence. Americans move gingerly from one monogamous relationship to the next, from the time they go steady in high school to their second or third marriage. Apparently, people learn the pattern of serial monogamy as adolescents and continue it in adulthood.

Reaching a low point in the early 1950s, the divorce rates for first marriages have risen consistently over the past thirty years. At mid-century, a larger percentage of the population married than ever before or since, and people married younger than at any other time in recent history. The divorce rate, which had peaked just after World War II, declined significantly, and the birth rate was extraordinarily high. Much of the American middle class moved to the spreading suburbs. Women left the work force and the rigors of collegiate and professional education. For middle America, these were the Eisenhower years—felt skirts, ducktails, and Sid Caesar.

Since the 1950s, every one of these statistics has changed dramatically. Singlehood has regained some of its earlier popularity; the trip to the altar typically occurs later in the 1980s than it did in the late 1950s; motherhood seems to have lost some of its luster; and the suburbs are strewn with the wreckage of lifelong monogamy gone awry.

Of females born between 1900 and 1904, about 12 percent have experienced divorce. The projection for females born in the middle to late 1940s indicates that 25 to 29 percent of them will divorce at least once by the age of sixty. In 1975, an estimated 25 percent of all marriages ended in divorce (U.S. Department of Commerce, 1975). People who complete college tend to show the lowest rates. But females who go on to graduate school experience divorce rates around 33 percent as opposed to the 22 percent typical of women with college degrees at the bachelor's level only. On the other hand, about 80 percent of men who go on to graduate school have intact first marriages (U.S. Dept. of Commerce, 1977). Figure 4.2 presents data on the first marriages, divorces, and remarriages for American women over the past half century.

The fact that about one-third of all first marriages now end in divorce does not necessarily mean Americans have given up on marriage. Census figures indicate that Americans remarry almost as quickly as they become divorced. In fact, 50 percent of all divorced males remarry within twelve months, and after fourteen months, half of the women are also remarried. Within three years, 75 percent of both males and females have found a second mate (U.S. Department of Health, Education, and Welfare (1973b).

Some psychologists and sociologists believe that the institution of marriage is now on shaky ground. Others have argued that rising divorce rates do not necessarily reflect a loss of faith in marriage as an institution, but rather a change in the functions of marriage. When marriage is seen as a context in which personal growth and self-fulfillment occur, (rather than a context for economic production), people want more satisfying emotional relationships within marriage. They are less likely to remain in a devitalized or combative-habituated marriage. Religious, legal, economic, and social sanctions designed to restrain divorce have weakened over the past twenty years. Women are more employable and more emotionally independent and have fewer reasons to stay in a unsatisfactory relationship (Melville, 1977; Reiss, 1980).

Some social critics have suggested that unsatisfactory marriages are best seen as functional disabilities, because they are associated with mental depression, feelings of isolation, and low morale. If marriage is a source of emotional problems, then divorce may be a reasonable solution (Renne, 1970). Clearly, many people ultimately perceive divorce as the right choice. Yet almost everyone who embarks on such a course experiences pain and

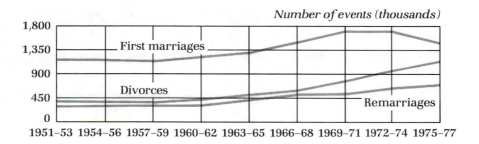

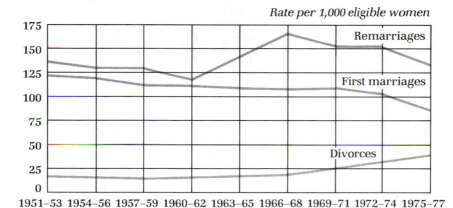

FIGURE 4.2
Number and rate of first marriages, divorces, and remarriages of women, 1951–1977

SOURCE: *U.S. Bureau of the Census, 1980.*

conflict. At least one major role is lost, an object of attachment (if not love) is gone, and with it goes an important source of security and identification. Children suffer, and relatives and friends are often deeply affected.

Divorce is not just an emotional trauma, however. It is also a hassle. The newly divorced or separated person often must make new financial and living arrangements, deal with child care or custody problems, set up housekeeping, and find a job. Evidently, the practical problems of day-to-day living are especially difficult for fathers. They "fumble along in what one father called a 'chaotic lifestyle,' " trying to manage the basic chores of running a household—shopping, cooking, laundry, and cleaning (Hetherington, Cox, and Cox, 1977).

Integrating children into a single life-style is a special challenge for men who have never before kept house or spent much time alone with their offspring.

Divorced people report significant emotional difficulties as well as practical problems. They show lower self-esteem than marrieds and suffer from feelings of anomie and loneliness. Marital separation may induce profound feelings of loss, guilt, anxiety, depression, and incompetence. In addition, divorced people with children feel they have failed as parents as well as mates and doubt their ability to adjust well in another marriage. Evidence suggests that separated couples experience great anxiety over social situations and an increase in sexual problems. Many men report that their work suffers as a result of separation (Melville, 1977; Hetherington, Cox, and Cox, 1977).

The degree of trauma an individual experiences during a marital separation or divorce depends to some extent on the length of the marriage, the age of the person, the number and ages of the children involved (if any), who suggested the divorce and how decisive that partner was. Some interesting sex differences seem evident as well. Women are more likely to experience distress prior to separation, whereas men report greater difficulties after separation. Several studies suggest that men do not seem to anticipate the extent of the impact of separation on their lives. Women seem significantly less unhappy than men immediately following separation; in fact, in some studies recently separated women did not appear to be significantly different from the total population in terms of the percentage reporting themselves to be unhappy (Chiriboga, 1978; Bloom and Caldwell, 1981).

The post-divorce problems some women report seem more sustained than those of men, however. Feelings of low self-esteem, confusion, anxiety, depression, and anger seem to plague some divorced women a long time. They feel unattractive, helpless, and incompetent. Furthermore, the presence of male children is a predictor of female distress even when there are no particular problems of discipline (Berman and Turk, 1981). It may be that since women so often retain custody of children, protracted problems of adjustment are more likely for women.

Perhaps because women seem to be more aware of the problems in a marriage before separation, they are more likely to ask for a divorce than are men. They also offer more specific reasons for the dissolution of their marriage. For instance, men are likely to talk about the impact of external events like work, a change in jobs, or a death in the family. Third ranked among the reasons men report is the simple confession that they are not sure what happened. (In contrast, "I don't know what happened" ranked twenty-ninth out of thirty-seven reasons given for divorce by women in one recent study [Kitson, and Sussman, 1982]). Women are much more likely to talk about specific dissatisfactions with the behavior of the spouse from untrustworthiness and immaturity to extramarital sexual activity, drinking, and "being out with the boys."

A comparison of recent studies of reasons for divorce with earlier data offers some clues about rising divorce rates. Comparing their findings with data collected in 1948, Kitson and Sussman (1982) concluded that the issues most likely to precipitate divorce today are affective or emotional. People expect their mates to offer personal support, encourage psychological growth, show maturity, and the like. In contrast, the divorcees of 1948 indicated that issues like drinking, authority problems, and nonsupport were critical in the decision to divorce.

Because emotional and affective problems head the list of reasons for divorce, it seems likely that more people will be dissatisfied with marriage than was the case in the past. Yet, the reasons themselves do not explain why some people leave unrewarding marriages and others do not. We need to know why some dissatisfied people never choose to leave. Fascinated by this question, one writer (Levinger, 1979) has proposed a three-factor model of marital cohesion. According to this hypothesis, whether or not a marriage will endure is determined by (1) the satisfactions or attractions of the marriage itself; (2) the perceived barriers to leaving the marriage; and (3) the attractiveness of alternatives to the marriage.

Taking the idea one step further, John Udry (1982) proposes that people are continually assessing the value of their current spouse against the value of potentially available alternatives. In the process, of course, they must also assess their ability to achieve those alternatives, including their own personal attractiveness and socioeconomic resources. To test his hypothesis, Udry carried out a longitudinal study of a hundred couples, as well as a cross-sectional analysis of another four hundred individuals, and reported that couples who saw themselves as having many alternatives to the marital relationship experienced disruption rates (divorce and separation) several times higher than those who assessed their alternatives as poor. In fact, Udry found that the assessment of alternatives predicted disruption better than marital satisfaction alone and that the combined use of satisfaction with marriage and assessment of alternatives predicted about 64 percent of the marital disruptions in his sample.

Even where one's alternatives are relatively clear and reasonably attractive, however, marital separation does not necessarily sever the bonds of attachment between husband and wife. Love may have fled, but attachment continues, creating confused, conflicted contact between separated spouses. Conflict and confusion are often enhanced, moreover, by the disapproval and withdrawal of friends and family, who feel threatened by newly single people or pressured to take sides (Weiss, 1975).

Such conflict also takes its toll on other family members. In one longitudinal study of families and divorce, the researchers were unable to identify even one case of victimless divorce (Hetherington, Cox, and Cox, 1977). Yet there must be some rubber in most family trees, for another such study concluded that even though almost all children of divorced parents show some distress at separation, by one year later, three-quarters of them have recovered (Wallerstein and Kelly, 1974). In general, the duration and intensity of family conflict seem to be the important determinants of the self-concept of a child caught in a marital maelstrom; most recent studies suggest little reason to assume that divorce per se does children any lasting psychological damage (Raschke, and Raschke, 1979; Longfellow, 1979; Rice, 1979). Figure 4.3 presents information about the number of children involved in divorces.

Nor does divorce seem to have a strong impact on attitudes about marriage, even among its victims. Second marriages, which occur almost as often as divorces, are likely to be perceived as happy by the participants (although the divorce rate for second marriages is about the same as that for first marriages). Eventually, 75 percent of all females and 85 percent of

Thousands

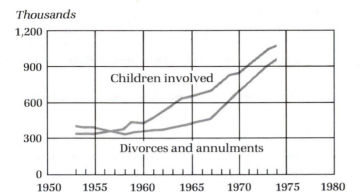

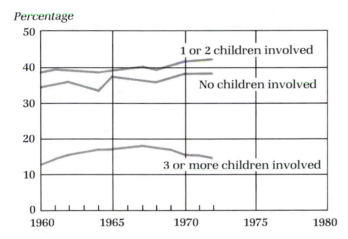

FIGURE 4.3
Divorces and annulments and estimated number of children involved, 1953–1974

Divorce decrees involving children, by number of children involved, 1960–1972

SOURCE: *U.S. Department of Commerce, Social Indicators, 1976 (Washington, D.C.: U.S. Government Printing Office, 1977), p. 54.*

all males who divorce will remarry, and they will typically report that their second marriage was less formal than the first, that their courtship was more likely to involve a sexual relationship, and that the sexual aspect of marriage is better in a second marriage than in the first (Reiss, 1980; Bernard, 1973).

On the other hand, the data on remarriage from the mid-seventies may suggest a trend toward singlehood. According to Arlene Skolnick (1978), "It is not clear as yet whether divorced people are simply waiting longer to remarry, or whether they are becoming disillusioned with marriage. As with a number of other statistical indicators, the slowdown in the rate of remarriage has demographers, social scientists, and policy makers anxiously waiting to find out whether people are simply postponing such commitments or opting out of them'' (p. 236). Not only are more people getting divorced, remaining single, living together, and having babies out of wedlock, Skolnick argues, but the plausibility of such options is increasing. Such significant changes in attitudes very likely mean that a basic transformation in family life is underway.

ALTERNATIVES TO TRADITIONAL MARRIAGE

The possible combinations and permutations of living arrangements are virtually endless in this highly diverse society. You can live alone, with another person of the same or the opposite sex, in a group, or in a crowd. Some people want to write down all the rules, and some prefer to work them out as a relationship develops. Social, financial, sexual, and emotional arrangements occur in contemporary America in great variety. Some are more socially acceptable than others, some more enduring; some provide great freedom; some offer financial security; and in some you may starve to death. In the rest of this chapter, we will look briefly both at the possibilities and at some of the important questions encountered in studying and evaluating the development of an alternative life-style.

The Single Life

During the 1970s, the number of men living alone increased by about 60 percent while the number of women living alone rose by about 40 percent (Reiss, 1980). Although many writers argue that young adults are not consciously choosing to remain single for life, there is some reason to believe that a slightly larger proportion of young people will remain single, if only because they cannot find appropriate partners. Because many babies were born in the 1950s and early 1960s, women who are now at a marriageable age encounter a shortage of men two to three years older, creating a "marriage squeeze" (Glick and Carter, 1976; Glick, 1977). Males born at the end of the baby boom face a shortage of women a few years younger.

Demographic realities aside, more people today are probably choosing the single life for positive rather than negative reasons. Singlehood has always been a more acceptable alternative to marriage than is suggested by United States statistics for the middle of this century. Historically, marriage has not always been available to everyone. In the Middle Ages, for example, marriage was a privilege generally reserved for the upper classes; two-thirds of the population never married. At the turn of the century, the single life was far more common than it had become by the 1950s. Recent trends toward postponement of marriage and the increasing popularity of the single life may simply represent a normalization of choice after the very-married fifties.

Although the vast majority of Americans still enter into marriage, most express some disillusionment with the institution. A number of forces are implicated in the increasingly critical attitude toward marriage and the increased attractiveness of singlehood. The emphasis placed by our culture on childbearing has clearly declined since the 1940s and 1950s. The emergent feminist influence is revising ideas about the place of women in the world. Men and women are encouraged to seek personal fulfillment as individuals instead of expecting to find someone capable of making them happy. Finally, there is a developing social territory and life-style specifically suited to the single person.

Mileski and Black (1972) have argued that alternative life-styles are most frequently chosen when the relevant social organization is available. Americans are currently offered housing, social groups, magazines, newspapers, and a host of material goods designed for the single life, from single-portion cans of soup to cruises of the Mediterranean. Moreover, changing cultural values allow single people opportunities to meet their sexual and social needs outside of marriage.

Singlehood is not only a tolerable way of life today, but a highly satisfactory way for many. Women, in particular, seem to find the single life to their advantage: single women of all ages report being happier than single males (Campbell, 1975), and they have lower rates of neurosis and depression than married women (Bernard, 1972).

Speaking of the advantages of being single in a married world, Margaret Adams (1971) cites the added opportunities for risk taking, social action, evaluation, and reform. She is, however, also forthright about the problems of singles and about the social sanctions that erode self-esteem and distort one's relationships. Singles, Adams points out, must learn to live with the tenacious cultural attitude that failure to marry is tantamount to failure as a person or that it represents a pathological state. (The image of the so-called spinster in this society is not an attractive picture; the bachelor over thirty is often suspected of being homosexual or neurotic.) Even more crucial is the difficulty of establishing an adequate social network as a single person, with the related problem of finding a congenial, trustworthy sounding board when one is often denied access to traditional lines of communication. Adams is particularly aware of the problems of single women, but most of her observations apply to singles of both sexes.

Happily, the expanding consciousness of our culture is beginning to override old images and make it possible for increasing numbers of men and women to go it alone if they choose. As more people choose the single life, the old, inaccurate stereotypes of the bachelor and the spinster (and, more recently, of the "swinging" single) will be replaced by more realistic attitudes about the single life.

Nontraditional Arrangements

Inadequate definitions complicate the study of the alternatives to marriage. When does a couple become a couple? At what point does a relationship become a courtship instead of a friendship? When does a sexual relationship become cohabitation?

HETEROSEXUAL COHABITATION.   The term *cohabitation* can be applied to a wide range of alternative life-styles, including weekend marriage between two people who live in different cities, term-contract marriage, common-law marriage, and homosexual marriage. Some of these relationships are little different from traditional marriage, save for the legalisms. Others are scarcely more committed than going steady, only one step removed from a casual date.

In part because the college-student population is easily accessible to academic psychologists, the most widely studied two-person alternative life-style is probably the arrangement in which a student couple shares living quarters, living expenses, and regular sexual activity. Although parents may not know or approve of such an arrangement (so that one partner may even continue to rent a separate apartment or maintain a different mailing address to avoid family censure), cohabitation at college, and afterward, represents an increasingly well-accepted, middle-class pattern. Similar arrangements may be even more frequent among young adults who are not attending college, but this noncollege population has not been studied.

On the basis of the limited research we have, one can scarcely draw firm conclusions, but Skolnick has suggested that the advantages and disadvantages of a cohabitation arrangement can be understood in terms of the tension between commitment and freedom. If the emotional bond between two people is the only basis for continued cohabitation, if they maintain the freedom to form other emotional and sexual relationships, how does either know where freedom ends and disengagement begins? If the commitments of the individuals involved in such a relationship are not clear, they may find themselves doing constant battle with insecurity and jealousy.

Recent figures suggest that well over a million couples live together today (compared with 50 million married couples), and that over 250,000 children are living with cohabiting couples. Most of these million or more couples do not want children, however, and they are by far the most efficient users of contraceptives among sexually active couples.

Ira Reiss (1980) interprets the data on contraception and attitudes toward marriage among cohabiting couples to mean that cohabitation is a form of courtship rather than a substitute for marriage. In another recent study, most cohabiting couples stated that they planned to marry someday, although the women in these relationships expected to marry more often than did the men (Risman, Hill, Rubin, and Peplau, 1981). On the other hand, the men saw fewer problems with the cohabiting relationship than did the women. The authors concluded that although cohabiting females do feel less powerful than noncohabiting females, they also expressed greater satisfaction with the relationship than noncohabiting females, including greater feelings of closeness, love, and self-disclosure. Generally, the study seemed also to demonstrate that couples living together in college do not differ from couples who are simply dating in terms of either the likelihood that they will marry or the likelihood that they will break up.

Cohabitation does not appear to pose a threat to marriage, but rather, to represent a step in the courtship process. In fact, many couples report that they are living together to learn how to relate to others in an intimate relationship. Therefore, it is not surprising to find that many of the problems people experience when living together are similar to the problems married people report. For instance, unstructured relationships produce the same conflicts over division of labor and role behavior that one might expect in a more traditional household (Stafford, Backman, and Dibona, 1977). Both married and cohabiting females do the lioness's share of the housework, even when holding full-time jobs. Although cohabiting men help with the laundry and dishes more often than do married men, cohabiting women do more gardening and home repair than married women and so lose some of the benefits they gain from assistance at laundry and other housework. A traditional ideology produces traditional behavior even in an unconventional relationship, creating traditional problems from decision-making to sexual functioning.

In addition to the problems everyone else experiences, of course, cohabiting couples have to cope with guilt and with pressure from others, especially parents, to enter a more traditional arrangement. In fact, one study suggests that cohabiting couples decide whether or not to marry sooner than dating couples do, in part as a response to parental pressure (Risman, Hill, Rubin, and Peplau, 1981). The effects of social pressure and guilt, which must be considered in the evaluation of any alternative life-

Public acknowledgment of homosexuality is a key force in the growing acceptance of homosexuals as part of the mainstream culture.

style, are even more evident in the cohabitation of people who express a sexual preference for someone of their own sex.

HOMOSEXUAL COHABITATION.   Perhaps the least accepted form of cohabitation is the homosexual marriage, although in many ways homosexual marriage is similar to heterosexual cohabitation. Homosexual relationships have been subject to the ravages of instability and guilt, just as are other socially ill-defined types of cohabitation. In ill-defined arrangements, the obligations and responsibilities of the partners are neither institutional-ized—as are sex-role distinctions—nor legally defined. The ambiguity of the relationship and the disapproval of society can combine to produce much guilt and instability.

Although Hunt's (1974) study of sexual behavior does not show any increase in homosexual behavior since Kinsey's day, it is clear that homo-sexuality is far more visible today than it was in the 1950s. As Keith Melville (1977) writes, probably not many homosexuals wish to change their sexual orientation, and homosexuality is no longer regarded as a mental illness by most psychologists and psychiatrists. Homosexuality is a part of modern life, probably a permanent part. But homosexuals still suffer the special difficulties associated with intense legal and social pressure to give up their life-style and conform to sexual and social norms.

Yet, one study of older homosexual men (Kimmel, 1982) points out that a number had been in relationships for as long as several decades. In this relatively small sample (fourteen men), two had experienced the death of a lover and gone on to establish a new, long-term relationship. Other research suggests that lesbian couples are even more likely than homosex-ual men to establish long-term close relationships (Bell and Weinberg, 1978). What is more, Masters and Johnson (1979) report that homosexual couples were able to communicate better and share more information about their sexuality than heterosexual couples. Homosexual couples also appeared more relaxed about sex, whereas heterosexual couples seemed to focus on achieving orgasm.

It is very likely that publicly acknowledged homosexuality and ho-mosexual cohabitation and marriage will become a more prominent part of the contemporary social scene. Many urban areas now provide environ-ments conducive to the development of a normalized homosexual subcul-ture, and homosexuals have increased opportunities to clarify the rules of approach and encounter—a prerequisite to the establishment of satisfac-tory long-term relationships (Mileski and Black, 1972). Rules of approach are the etiquette by which one knows whether a potential mate is avail-able or interested (or both). For example, wedding rings, engagement rings, the bestowal of fraternity pins, all signal different sets of rules for the heterosexual population. Such understandings allow relationships to pro-ceed more smoothly than is the case when the possibilities are unsignaled and the acceptable responses are vague.

As Gagnon and Greenblatt (1978) point out, it is only since the 1960s that a public, open homosexual culture has emerged. Openness means talking about one's sexual preference with others, disclosing those prefer-ences to parents and friends, shaping loving and caring relationships in an atmosphere of acceptance, and solving problems of identity and ideology.

Such developments will probably substantially change the course of homosexual relationships as well as the psychological development of homosexual individuals over the coming years.

ACCEPTABILITY AND ENDORSEMENT.   In *Family Systems in America* (1980), Ira Reiss makes the important point that every new social philosophy creates a new potential for dogma, a new tendency to state an opinion as if it were a fact. Those who experiment with new social forms, like cohabitation or premarital sex or extramarital sex, begin to think of those who are more traditional as narrow-minded and thoughtless.

In sorting out the dogma on both sides (that is, the traditional dogma versus the unconventional dogma), Reiss makes two distinctions: one between discrimination and inhibition, and the other between acceptance and endorsement. Although the experimenters, according to Reiss, are likely to see the traditional people as "inhibited," there is a difference between inhibition and discrimination. "The difference centers about being *unable* to allow oneself to do something because of the inability to even entertain certain thoughts and, on the other hand, the *desire* not to do something because one *has examined* a behavior and decided that it is not appropriate for oneself. Discriminating people and inhibited people can be found on *both sides* of this debate over new family forms" (Reiss, 1980, p. 464).

Moreover, Reiss argues, one can accept a possibility for other people without offering the endorsement that leads to dogma. "Rather than any increase in real freedom," endorsing a certain behavior as "*the* right way for everyone" restricts freedom. "Freedom involves choice, and choice is more in line with the concept of acceptance and . . . with the concept of discrimination rather than the concept of forced choice or endorsement of some lifestyle simply because it is old or new" (p. 465).

We live in an era in which expanding diversity of choice is viewed with great alarm by some and unbounded delight by others. The discriminating person seems unlikely to take either of these positions with regard to change. Discrimination implies the serious consideration of all possibilities, an understanding of the antecedents and consequences of new forms, and deliberate, conscious selection of the form best suited to the self. Discrimination also suggests no fear of change, but a welcoming of the opportunity to exercise choice, yet an awareness that not all possible choices are equally appropriate. Reiss has written:

> If I had to pick one characteristic that was a trademark of the family in twentieth-century America, I would pick the *legitimation of choice*. There is no question in my mind that as I write these words, the range of truly legitimated choices is far greater than it was in 1950, 1960, or even in 1970. . . . We

must learn to live with this, and we must learn to arrive at a judgment of our own preferences if we are to adjust to the type of society that has developed at this point in time. This does not necessarily call for a relativistic type of ethic in the sense of denying common values. What it does call for is the realization that although people feel that they can agree upon values such as integrity, honesty, concern for other human beings, happiness, and so forth, they may still disagree as to how best to achieve those values in their personal lives (p. 466).

SUMMARY

In this chapter, we have established some distinctions between various kinds of emotional relationships that are particularly important in young adulthood. We have defined an intimate relationship as one characterized by both self-disclosure and commitment, as well as mutuality, similarity, and dependency. Intimacy is said to depend, to some extent at least, on the development of a sense of identity and would, therefore, arise in late adolescence or early adulthood. However, it is clear that attachment may develop before adolescence or adulthood and appears to offer a greater potential for the life-span study of close relationships than the concept of intimacy.

Attachment is based on frequency of interaction and is thought to proceed from weak, diffuse bonds to closer, more complex ties. It has also been suggested that as attachment grows, attraction wanes. The concept of attachment is a relative one, meaning that not all attachments are experienced in the same way, allowing for the possibility of negative interaction within an attached relationship.

A variety of theories purport to explain the development of attached and intimate relationships; several are reviewed in this chapter. Social exchange theory offers the notion that love is the product of a reward-cost history in the exchange between two people where the outcome equals rewards minus punishments. In a variation on this theme, equity theory suggests that people become intimate in relationships where the outcome for both parties is equal. Both of these social-learning theories have been criticized for a seeming inability to explain the persistence of love in long-term, intimate relationships. Moreover, social exchange theory and equity theory focus on the matter of how intimate relationships are alike rather than explaining why some intimate relationships seem so different from others.

In particular, neither the concept of attachment nor the idea that love is a product of reward seems to explain why people make a distinction between loving and "being in love." Being in love adds to intimacy a dimension of desire or yearning for the physical presence of the lover as well as the feeling that the other person's welfare is central to one's own.

Some authors have suggested the propensity to be "in love" depends on the predominance of different values at different stages of the life cycle, whereas others believe that all romantic love proceeds through a life-cycle of its own, beginning with an intense phase that is transformed in the end to a less passionate form. According to another theory, different people define love differently; that is, there may be a list of basic styles or patterns of loving, a number of which might fulfill the basic criteria for intimacy.

Of these styles or types, those that are most likely to produce intimacy are those in which lovers experience feelings of commitment as well as desire and mutuality and an ability to engage in self-disclosure. Sacrifice and investment are characteristic of committed relationships, as is mortification, through the sharing of information that is potentially embarrassing. For most people, the matter of intimacy and commitment is resolved eventually in a more or less traditional way, with the decision to marry.

Marriage is a socially legitimate sexual union, begun with a public commitment and undertaken with some idea of permanence. Most societies specify reciprocal rights and obligations of the marriage partners in a legal sense, covering such issues as the ownership of property and the custody of children, but in the Western world today, people also expect that marriage will meet most, if not all, of their personal, social, and sexual needs. Although these expectations often produce disappointment, perhaps they rarely deter people from entering the institution.

The term *social homogamy* describes most American marriages: people marry someone of the same racial origin and of similar education and socioeconomic background. It is also fairly well documented that people choose to marry someone who is similar to themselves in terms of characteristics such as physical attractiveness, neuroticism, self-esteem, and degree of sexual desire. But it is not clear that similarity guides every level of mate selection. Some people have argued that complementarity, especially in such matters as dominance, nurturance, and orientation toward achievement may be important considerations in making a successful match.

What constitutes a successful match varies from one person to the next, however, and so a typology of marriage is probably necessary to make sense of the research on marital satisfaction. Marriages vary not only in the degree but also in the kind of satisfaction they offer. Categories such as instrumental versus companionship marriage have been suggested, and within each of these superordinate types a variety of subtypes may exist.

Another fast-growing category of marriage is represented by the two-paycheck family where partners typically report high levels of satisfaction, but also high levels of stress. Recent evidence shows that dual-career marriage is especially prone to difficulties concerning the responsibilities of childrearing, the scheduling and planning of time, and the development of a supportive social network.

In more traditional marriages, men are usually more satisfied than are women, and married women appear to be more vulnerable to depression and even institutionalization the more strongly they are committed to marriage. On the other hand, women who are able to develop less stereotypical, more egalitarian life-styles experience more satisfaction with themselves and their marriages.

Satisfaction varies not only with the kind of marriage one has, but also with the period of life in which one finds oneself. For instance, several studies suggest that marital satisfaction changes with the stage of the family life-cycle and that older married couples whose children are grown are among the most satisfied of all marrieds.

Marriage is, of course, the only completely socially sanctioned context for the expression of sexuality, and recent research also shows that marital satisfaction with the sexual aspects of marriage has increased dramatically over the past thirty or forty years. However, there is also an increased trend toward participation in premarital, extramarital, and postmarital sexual activity as well as the implication that people are finding all these forms of sexual expression more satisfactory and less difficult than ever before.

The conceptualization of marriage as the primary institution for the expression and development of intimacy has probably contributed to changes in the nature of marriage itself, and has undoubtedly been responsible for part of the increased probability that one will experience divorce. Divorce rates for the entire population hover around 25 percent, but certain groups, like highly educated women, find themselves at even greater risk; moreover, the probability of a second divorce is about the same as that for a first.

Divorce is experienced as a trauma by most of the individuals involved, although women are likely to experience more distress before separation while men seem to suffer most intensely during the first year after separation. On the other hand, women, who often feel unattractive, helpless, and incompetent as divorced people, seem more likely to suffer chronic post-divorce problems. As for the children of divorced parents, the literature shows that divorce per se is not nearly as important a predictor of childhood adjustment and self-concept as is the intensity and duration of family conflict.

Studies of the reasons cited for divorce show that people are more sensitive than ever to the emotional and affective aspects of marriage, although marital satisfaction alone is not the best predictor of marital cohesion. In fact, a person's perception of possible alternatives to marriage is probably the best single indicator of marital disruption, and one's assessment of one's own physical attractiveness and socioeconomic resources seems to be very important in establishing marital alternatives. Thus, as women become more financially independent, for example, they are more likely to perceive themselves as having alternatives to staying in an unsatisfactory marriage.

The skyrocketing divorce rate does not seem to indicate wholesale disillusionment with marriage as an institution, however, for as many as 80 percent of divorced persons will eventually marry again, and most will express satisfaction with this second marriage. On the other hand, the growing prominence of so-called alternative life-styles indicates that although the majority of young adults may still marry, a significant minority are willing to choose to remain single, to live with a partner without being married, or to experiment with other alternatives to marriage.

People are staying single longer, and at least a somewhat larger proportion may be choosing singlehood as a life-long course. The organization of a relevant social style and a deemphasis on childrearing as well as the greater career-orientation of women have probably contributed to the increased probability that one will spend a longer part of the life course alone.

One might also choose cohabitation, especially during the years of young adulthood, perhaps not so much as an alternative to marriage but as a new step in the decision-making process. However, many of the problems of marriage arise in the context of cohabitation too; in many ways a traditional ideology produces traditional problems even in an unconventional context.

Finally, people are freer to choose radically different solutions to the problems of intimacy, including the choice of a sexual partner from one's own sex. Homosexual cohabitation and even homosexual marriage are more acceptable today than has been the case in the American past, although it may be important to make a distinction between acceptability and endorsement. To endorse something is to imply that it is a good choice for everyone, establishing a new dogma of the unconventional in place of traditional doctrine. On the other hand, blind endorsement of the conventional is often narrow-minded and thoughtless. In all, one might best strive to become a discriminating person, someone who is able to consider almost any possibility with at least some degree of acceptance, in the attempt to assess what is most appropriate for oneself. The discriminating person welcomes choice as an exercise in freedom and judgment, but does not endorse all change as equally reasonable and good.

Chapter

5

The Expanded Context: Work, Family, and Friends

There is time for work. And time for love.
That leaves no other time.

COCO CHANEL

Adults are the caretakers, the ones who are responsible. We assume that adults have the skills to care for themselves, and to care for others when choice, chance, or circumstances require. To care for someone implies both emotional and physical support (Guttmann, 1975); and, in today's world, providing physical support means choosing, finding, and maintaining a job, whether one works at home or in a factory or an office, in a store or in the great outdoors.

Caring also implies a special closeness: the closeness of friends, and lovers, and children. In this chapter, we will explore the literature on work, family, and the development of friendship in young adulthood. Beginning with a survey of theory and research about vocational choice, job satisfaction, and the life cycle, we will examine how people choose jobs, why they become committed to them or why they change, and how they come to consider themselves successful or satisfied. In the course of our discussion, we will address the special problems of women and minorities in the job market, and, finally, we will broach the matter of integrating work and other aspects of one's life—especially family concerns.

The second half of the chapter deals with the other central developmental tasks of young adulthood: the establishment of family and a circle of friends. Here, we will look not only at the traditional choices but also at the growing trend toward alternative family careers, from single parenthood and stepparenting to the decision to forego childbearing. Of course, such issues and decisions are not limited to that part of the life cycle we call young adulthood. But, for most of us, these matters are central during the young adult years, whether or not they are permanently resolved.

WORK, OCCUPATION, AND CAREER

Almost all adults work. Unless you are lucky enough to be wealthy, you will have to labor to produce the goods and services that make possible personal, cultural, and species survival, as well as increments in the quality of life. The chances are, moreover, that even if you do not have to work, you will choose to do so; for *work*, whether or not it is remunerated directly, is a major social role of adult life. This social role, referred to as one's *occupation* or vocation, identifies a significant aspect of the self. An occupation provides an important social and personal anchor, a stronghold of identity. It is impossible to really understand adult life without a thorough understanding of the role of work during the life cycle.

Whereas the terms *occupation* and *vocation* are both generally applied to all forms of work, the word *career* is often reserved for prestigious occupations. Some writers believe that careerism is a minority, elite institution in Western society, in which the individual who has a career stays in one occupational field and progresses through a series of stages associated with upward mobility, achieving ever greater mastery, responsibility, and financial remuneration (Krause, 1971; Ritzer, 1977). Constructs such as being "on time" and "getting ahead" are central to the study of careers from this point of view. Insurance executives and university professors have careers; carpenters and domestic workers do not.

Adopting a different approach, other authors have defined a career as any organized path taken by an individual across space and time—as consistent involvement in any role over time (Van Maanen and Schein, 1977). In this sense, a doctor, a plumber, or a homemaker may have several concurrent careers: one as a worker, one as a spouse, one as a citizen, and so on. From this perspective, the study of careers is the study of change through the life cycle.

The concept of a career as involvement over time is especially useful for a life-span psychology. The study of an individual's occupational career can be expected to yield rich information about important life events that accompany progress in one's role as a worker. Events like being hired, promoted, fired, or retired are critical milestones in overall adult development. Plumbers, letter carriers, bookmakers, doctors, lawyers, and police officers all experience changes in occupational status—career changes.

Careers over Time

A number of writers have offered stage models of career development (Ginsberg, 1972; Super, 1957; Wanous, 1980). Table 5.1 presents one of the most comprehensive and detailed: an outline developed by John Van Maanen and Edgar Schein (1977) that divides the life span into four phases, and details the progress of both an external and internal career path. *External career paths* include the steps or milestones that are obvious to an outsider observing the career progress of another person. An *internal career path* includes all the personal, individual plans and expectations that make the work life of every individual unique.

Although all individuals will not progress through all stages of this model, since both cultural and personal differences influence the se-

TABLE 5.1
Stages of occupational career development

External career	Internal career
Exploration a. Occupational images b. Advice c. Success/failure in school test, sports d. Economic and historical constraints e. Educational choices f. Counseling, letters of recommendation g. Test results	**Exploration** a. Self-image of what's fun b. Self-assessment c. Development of goals, ambitions, tentative choices d. Enlarged self-image based on growing experience e. Need for real test of ability to work f. Anticipatory socialization based on models and images

Establishment
a. Mutual recruitment
b. Acceptance and entry
  1. Orientation
  2. Training
  3. Informal initiation
c. First job assignment
  1. Meeting boss and co-workers
  2. Learning period
  3. Period of full performance
  4. Leveling off and/or becoming obsolete
  5. Preparing for new assignment
d. Leveling off/transfer or promotion
  1. Feedback on meaning of move, performance review
  2. Repeat from (c) if transfer or promotion
e. Granting tenure
	Establishment
	a. Reality shock, insecurity, fear of rejection
	b. Develop image of organization
	c. First commitment to job versus taking on a task
	d. Maximum need for self-test
	e. Readjustment of self-image based on acceptance/rejection
	f. Developing a theme
	g. Expect first real test
	  1. Feelings of playing for keeps
	  2. Learning ropes
	  3. Testing commitment
	  4. Feelings of success/failure
	h. Reassessment of self-image and match to career
	  1. Sorting out family/work issues and achieving fit
	  2. Forming career strategy: how to make it?
	  3. Leave organization if necessary
	  4. Adjust to failure, revise theme
	  5. Turn to unions or other sources if threatened
	i. Period of maximum insecurity pursuant to tenure review
	  1. Crisis of full acceptance versus crisis of reassessment
	  2. Finding a new career versus new learning about self and organization

Maintenance (midcareer) a. Expect maximum productivity b. Occupational and organizational secrets shared c. Assume teacher/mentor role d. Deal with plateauing through remotivation	**Maintenance (midcareer)** a. New sense of growth, realistic assessment of ambition and potential b. Settling in, feeling security, danger of stagnation c. Threat of younger, ambitious recruits d. Thoughts of new pastures, second career, midlife crisis
Later career a. Assign jobs that draw on wisdom, perspective, judgment b. More community and society-oriented jobs c. More jobs teaching others versus being on the firing line	**Later career** a. Concern for teaching b. Psychological preparation for retirement c. Finding new sources of self-improvement d. Deceleration

SOURCE: Adapted from J. Van Maanen and E. H. Schein, "Career Development," in J. R. Hackman and J. L. Suttle, eds., *Improving Life at Work* (Santa Monica, Ca.: Goodyear, 1977), pp. 55–59.

quence, Van Maanen and Schein believe that every career may be described in developmental terms. According to their model, even jobs with little prestige, like domestic service or assembly-line work, and deviant occupations, like prostitution or burglary, can provide a context for the development of skills and the opportunity to be a mentor one day instead of a novice.

Furthermore, people develop in both the internal and the external sequences of their career paths. The external path includes the steps one encounters within a particular occupation. The career of restaurant manager, for example, usually includes such steps as helper or assistant cook, cook, assistant manager, and then manager. An internal career is a personal plan: it may include continued education, relocation, breaks in service, and the like, as well as external career changes. A young woman who envisions a career in education, culminating as a superintendent of schools, might begin an external career as an elementary teacher, then take a break during the early years of childbearing, later returning to work and running for the local school board. Here is a unique internal career involving several different external careers, some of them combined in what have until recently been rather unconventional ways for this culture.

In young adulthood, the first two stages of the Van Maanen and Schein scheme are a focus of concern for most of us. These two stages, exploration and establishment, are also the most thoroughly researched areas of vocational behavior. In particular, the process of exploration and choice of career has attracted much attention, both from researchers who are trying to help people make choices that produce both success and satisfaction and from those who are helping organizations to discover how to hire individuals who will be contributing, committed employees.

Exploration

In the voluminous literature on vocational guidance and selection, the occupational choices of adolescents and young adults are detailed, various occupations are minutely described, and enormous amounts of time, energy, and journal space are devoted to how successful matches between particular individuals and particular occupations occur. From this wealth of material, several major theoretical frameworks have emerged.

Perhaps the most elaborate point of view is that of the *differentialists*, who posit that in order to make a successful vocational choice, an individual must first thoroughly assess his or her abilities, interests, and personality characteristics (Holland, 1966, 1973; Strong, 1943; Roe, 1956, 1957; Smart, 1976). Adolescents are directed to take stock of themselves and seek a job

"The child was diseased at birth—stricken with an hereditary ill that only the most vital men are able to shake off. I mean poverty—the most deadly prevalent of all diseases." Eugene O'Neill

that is congruent with the resulting self-description. To this end, people often submit to endless questions, such as "Would you rather be a bricklayer or a short-order cook?" and "Would you rather sweep floors or answer telephones?" Generally, differentialist research shows a reasonable degree of predictive value for interest and personality inventories like the Strong Vocational Interest Inventory, and also demonstrates that several popular measures appear to yield very similar results, whether individual needs or personality characteristics are stressed (Lunneborg and Lunneborg, 1975; Meir and Ben-Yehuda, 1976, Cairo, 1982).

In a second, *developmental* approach, personality variables and early developmental factors are integrated using the notion of self-concept. According to this point of view, outlined first by Donald Super (1957), the vocational choice of adolescence is an implementation of the self-concept built during childhood. Each stage of childhood development is thought to affect one's self-concept and to lead one toward particular vocational decisions. Parental behavior, occupation, and socioeconomic status influence choice by influencing self-concept.

Super has postulated five stages of vocational development peculiar to young adulthood—*crystallization* of one's ideas about work (ages 14 to 18), *specification* of vocational preference (18 to 21), *implementation*, including training and first job (21 to 24), *stabilization* or settling down (25 to 35), and *consolidation and advancement* (35 plus). Unfortunately, although the idea of self-concept may be useful as a guide to vocational choice, it does not really explain the process behind vocational development. What, exactly, is a self-concept and how does it develop? Such empirical questions must be addressed before Super's ideas can be wholly understood.

Furthermore, recent evidence from a twenty-one-year longitudinal study of occupational development does not support the notion that career choice is a stage-like process or that closure is achieved in one's early twenties (Phillips, 1982ab). Super's stage theory implies that vocational choice culminates in a clear decision followed by a period of increasing commitment. From this perspective, job satisfaction and success should follow as one moves smoothly through the developmental stages. The longitudinal data from Super's own laboratory indicate, however, that it is not at all clear whether high levels of job satisfaction, job status, or job success are associated with decisiveness or increasing commitment. In fact, for many men in one group of subjects, job commitment remained provisional through the age of 36 (the last time these men were interviewed). Although increasing commitment throughout the stabilization phase was associated with early attainment, satisfaction and success seemed to be a product of flexibility. In the long run, change may be necessary, or at least beneficial, and very high levels of commitment may impede development (Phillips, 1982b).

Finally, the same longitudinal data have suggested that career exploration may not reasonably be limited to adolescence and young adulthood. Among the 95 subjects in the study, 37 percent were still involved, to some degree, in career exploration as late as age 36, and 19 percent experienced repeated career explorations over the course of the study. Furthermore, as the author of the latest articles on this sample, Susan Phillips, has pointed out, the last interviews were conducted before the men reached the restlessness of a mid-life crisis (Phillips, 1982a).

In light of the data from Super's lab, Phillips has proposed that a cyclical model of decision-making is necessary to describe vocational development over the life span (1982ab). Perhaps career stages should not be considered age linked at all, since the consideration of stages often leads researchers to overlook exploration or new beginnings after a certain age (Peacock, Rush, and Milkovich, 1980).

Of course, whenever we choose a career path, the act of choosing alone is not enough. We must also look for a job: choose an organization and be recruited by that organization or develop the resources to be an independent contractor or business owner. Unfortunately, little available research focuses on the career development of individuals who do not work for organizations of some kind. Obviously, it is easier to contact people in organizations than people who work alone. In addition, 90 percent of all Americans do work in organizations (Van Maanen and Schein, 1977), and most of these provide formal procedures for job search and recruitment, making it easy to study how people are selected for entry and how they adapt once they are chosen.

Job Search and Recruitment

People do not always use formal job search and recruitment channels provided by organizations, of course. It has been estimated, for instance, that 50 to 80 percent of all blue-collar workers use informal sources, like employee referral, to find jobs. Although white-collar workers do use formal sources more often, research also indicates that the use of informal sources is more often associated with job satisfaction. Turnover rates for new recruits who learned of a job opening through an ad in the newspaper or an employment agency are extremely high. For that matter, turnover rates for new employees in organizations are simply high in general. One study suggests that as many as 50 to 60 percent of all new recruits can be expected to leave within the first seven months (Wanous, 1980).

Why do so many people make choices they so soon regret? John Wanous (1980) contends that the fault lies with both the individual and the organization. During search and recruitment, the recruit hopes to maximize opportunities while the recruiter hopes to develop a large pool of job applicants. Therefore, both recruit and recruiter put their best foot forward. Rather than enabling job applicants and organizations to gain a realistic picture of each other, the situation promotes unrealistic expectations. Therefore, it is hardly surprising that the attitudes of new recruits become steadily more negative over the first few months and even years of employment. Decreasing satisfaction with one's employer occurs in the army, in the telephone company, in graduate students at prestige colleges, and in samples of people who have taken widely divergent jobs. Wanous believes that more realistic recruitment methods—methods that would reduce turnover—demand consideration of an individual's needs as well as abilities. Where the needs of the applicant are matched to the atmosphere of the organization, retention is most likely. Certainly, the question of job performance must be addressed. But other issues are equally important. Does the applicant expect a friendly, informal working situation? Is she or he only interested in earning top dollar? Do flexible working hours appear to be important? Does the organization offer child care? Potential for advancement? Independence on the job?

More informal hiring practices often seem to work because the applicant has a better idea of what the organization offers. Getting a job through a friend is at least informative. On the other hand, such methods tend to be discriminatory. In many places, affirmative action guidelines mandate the use of formal procedures; thus, realistic recruitment is more important than ever.

Acceptance, Reality Shock, and Commitment

Although unrealistic expectations inevitably produce disillusionment about one's new job and organization, not all of these expectations are created in the search-and-recruitment process. In many occupations, there is also great disparity between the image we gain of a job from education and anticipatory socialization (informal training) and the reality of the day-to-day demands of the job. Especially in those occupations for which the education or training is idealistic and principled but the job itself involves knowing and maintaining established procedures and routine bureaucratic functions, *reality shock* is a common entry phenomenon. For instance, the reality of teaching and social work is quite different from the image of the teacher or social worker as transmitted by a college or university curriculum.

The idealistic occupations are not the only shocking jobs. Reality shock is common to homemakers and secretaries and truck drivers. Entry information is almost always positively biased, and anticipatory socialization is most often unrealistic. Playing house and baby-sitting are not adequate preparations for the overwhelming and irrevocable responsibility of a career as homemaker and parent. Typing classes and television comedies don't offer a realistic picture of life as a medical receptionist or secretary, and law school provides at best only meager contact with the realities of the occupation of attorney.

Reality shock is associated with high turnover in the semi-professions like nursing or teaching, where there is little upward mobility (Ritzer, 1977) and the rewards for settling down after the shock wears off are minimal. If shock is deep, individuals may feel very disoriented and need to reevaluate their original career decision (Hughes, 1958). Shock may be increased if the first job assignment is too easy or too difficult for the recruit, or if the first group to which the new employee is assigned does not provide guidance and support. The formal use of such procedures as *stress inoculation* (in which recruits confront their own unrealistic expectations) and *psychodrama* (in which individuals expand on the potential risks and benefits of an occupational choice) have been specifically recommended for use in vocational counseling and education (Janis and Wheeler, 1978). More realistic entry information and training can also reduce shock and yield better performance over the long run (Macedonia, 1969).

In the final analysis, however, the most important career socialization experiences are provided by the organization, on the job. Various apprenticeship programs (such as the apprenticeship of a Ph.D. student to a major professor), as well as organizational rewards for satisfactory progress, are forms of socialization. In the more dramatic modes of on-the-job socialization, new recruits may even be thrown in over their heads deliberately, exposed to failing, or given menial tasks as part of the process. The point of such methods is not just to teach skills, but also to establish commitment—the development of which, as we noted in Chapter 4, is associated with the feelings and experiences of investment, mortification, and sacrifice.

Feelings of commitment are the product of one's investment in an organization or profession. Education constitutes an investment, and so does the learning of specific skills acquired on the job. Learning the ropes—the informal workings of the organization, the shortcuts, and the problematic situations—contributes to growing occupational commitment. Moreover, the organization's investment in the individual increases commitment. Pension plans, fringe benefits, stock options, promotions, and salary increases all serve to deepen such feelings (Ritzer, 1977). Similarly, the interests expressed by unions—medical and dental insurance, job security, and cost-of-living increases—foster commitment to the union and to unionized companies.

Investment is also increased by the personal bonds of sponsorship. Sponsorship does occur in most jobs within organizations and may even be an explicit part of the entry phase, as it is in occupations that involve apprenticeships. A sponsor, or mentor, takes a personal interest in the progress of the recruit, offering knowledge, help, support, providing recommendations or referrals, and assisting the novice in establishing contacts in the trade, business, or professional community. Success often depends on the acquisition of an appropriate sponsor. In academic life the power of one's sponsor, or major professor, can significantly affect one's professional attainments (Crane, 1965). In film, music, and the other arts, as well as in politics, the role of protégé is a common one in the lives of successful individuals—for example, the French director François Truffaut is considered a student of Alfred Hitchcock. Recall, too, that Jung studied under Freud.

In an article called "The Mentor Connection" (1977b), Gail Sheehy reviewed a study of twenty-five female executives done at Harvard by Margaret Hennig (1970). Hennig's research underlined the significance of women in the business world. Each of the most successful of these women had developed a close relationship with one powerful, successful man, and each was guided up the first rungs of the ladder by her sponsor. Because there were so few female executives in high places, all of the women discussed had male mentors. And all experienced the concomitant confusion of relationships laden with sexual and erotic implications as well as social and intellectual opportunities. A cohort effect may be present in these data: all of the women in the study were unmarried and under thirty-five at the beginning of the investigation. Attitudes may change enough to allow different kinds of work relationships to develop between men and women (Colwill, 1982).

Success, Job Satisfaction, and the Life Cycle

The new recruit, riding the white stallion of commitment and guided by a gentle but powerful mentor, gallops off into the sunset pursuing fame and fortune. At least that is the way this story is supposed to end. Yet it has become increasingly clear that Americans at all levels of the society are dissatisfied with their work in this bureaucratic, affluent society, and that many are not placated by the traditional economic incentives. Labor, management, and professional organizations are searching for ways to make work more meaningful and less autocratic within organizations of every kind. Gradually emphasis is being shifted to the noneconomic rewards of work, and efforts are being made to increase the challenge and value of work (Miernyk, 1975; Wanous, 1980).

The nature and organization of work is changing. Concepts like participatory management have evolved from our desire for less autocratic work environments. Workers are frequently organized into teams that make their own management decisions, sitting down with administrators to develop goals and objectives as a common project. Transitory groupings of individuals who are task oriented, rather than standing groups that perform the same function over and over again on every task, can provide a satisfactory solution to the problems of both worker and management (Toffler, 1970). Organizing employees in task-oriented groups allows workers to follow a project through each phase to completion. Instead of tracking the costs of several projects, for example, one accountant might be assigned to all phases of a specific project and be acquainted with all the workers assigned to a project. Sometimes this is called a team approach.

Other favored innovations are flexible scheduling, which allows workers to set their own hours (within limits) and even to pursue some occupational activities at home, and support for continuing education, through programs to provide both leave time and economic assistance. Indeed, support for continuing education is far more common today than ever before, and education seems to be a more important part of work at all levels. The revolution in work values and attitudes has contributed to an emphasis on learning and improving the quality of one's work (Abbot, 1977).

Most of those who are looking at the future believe we must move from a fixed to a flexible life-cycle design to meet the needs of workers. As Robert Butler has suggested in an article appropriately titled "The Burnt Out and the Bored" (1970), one approach to creating more productive and satisfying work environments is to reshuffle the life cycle. If people could schedule periods of work, leisure, retirement, or education throughout life, rather than being forced into long, boring blocks of the same activities for twenty, thirty, or even forty years, they might feel that all activities are more meaningful. People also need time to work through the conflicts among self, family, and work at different stages of the life cycle, returning to work refreshed and recharged. Butler makes five recommendations:

1. Employees should be allowed to accumulate leave for as long as they like and to use it in long, uninterrupted blocks.

2. Organizations should make greater provisions for employees to return to school, whether their course of study is job related or not.

3. Adolescents should be encouraged to work if they wish, rather than being forced to continue an education that seems meaningless.

4. Compulsory retirement should be abolished.

5. The rules of tenure, promotion, and seniority that encourage people to stay in the same job for forty years or more should be reassessed.

The American worker wants more than a paycheck. Workers are demanding job satisfaction, fair treatment, and involvement in decisions that affect their lives, as well as challenge, interest, and value in life both in and out of the occupational role.

Social consciousness is increasingly apparent in business, industry, and the professions. It has been said that this society is in transition, from a culture based on unconscious agreements to one based on conscious ones

(Babbie, 1977). As a result of that increasing consciousness, many workers are demanding promotion based on performance rather than on arbitrary decisions determined by race, sex, or the whim of a supervisor.

Sex, Race, and Work

Despite the growing concern over nonmonetary aspects of work, for many people in our culture a steady paycheck is still a major goal. Many simply want a good job rather than changes in the nature of work. Too often, people are still excluded from large areas of the labor force because the culture teaches that certain groups do not possess the abilities necessary for the successful pursuit of an occupation or that the primary duties and responsibilities assigned to a certain group are incompatible with the pursuit of particular occupations. Sexual discrimination and racial discrimination are two major reasons for the exclusion of large segments of the population from full participation in the occupational world.

WOMEN IN THE WORK FORCE.   Women are no longer excluded from taking some role in the marketplace, of course. Over the life span, nearly all of today's women will be members of the labor force. The number of working women has increased dramatically since 1950 (see Figure 5.1), and it is estimated that nearly 70 percent of females born betwen 1956 and 1960 will be members of the work force in the 1980s. (Compare this figure with the mere 45 percent of the cohort born in 1931 to 1935.) Nearly all women born in the last three decades will work at paying jobs during their lifetimes (Sawhill, 1979).

The effects of institutionalized sex discrimination are not apparent in these numbers. Women are working. The evidence is more subtle. Consider, for instance, the employment patterns of men and women. About one-half of all working women are employed in a handful of occupations—as secretaries, retail salesworkers, elementary-school teachers, bookkeepers, waitresses, nurses, typists, cashiers, sewers and stitchers, or private household workers. By comparison, the ten most populous occupational categories for males are filled by only about 20 percent of all working men (Cahn, 1979). Half of all women with high school educations, and one-sixth of all women with bachelor's degrees, take jobs classified as "clerical work" (Seidman, 1978).

Aside from the limited range of female occupations, these jobs tend to be less well paid, less prestigious, and offer less opportunity for advancement than the jobs typically held by men. On the average, women earn only about 60 percent of what the average male worker earns. Even when men and women with similar educational, work, and achievement experience hold similar jobs, the situation is little improved. Women earn only

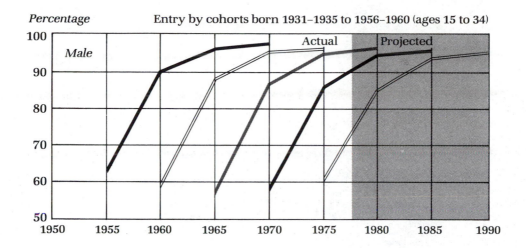

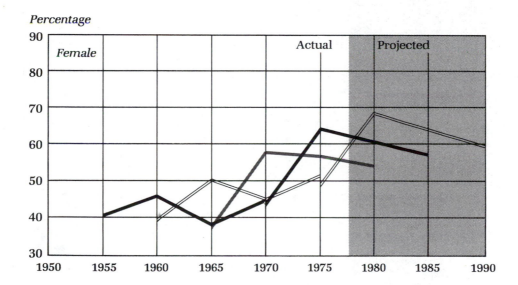

FIGURE 5.1
Labor force participation of selected cohorts, by sex, 1950–1990

SOURCE: *U.S. Department of Commerce*, Social Indicators, 1976 *(Washington, D.C.: U.S. Government Printing Office, 1977), p. 328.*

about two-thirds of what their male counterparts make at the same jobs (Seidman, 1978). Figure 5.2 presents some comparative information on the employment of women, minorities, and white males in each of several occupational categories. Figure 5.3 and Table 5.2 give comparative salary

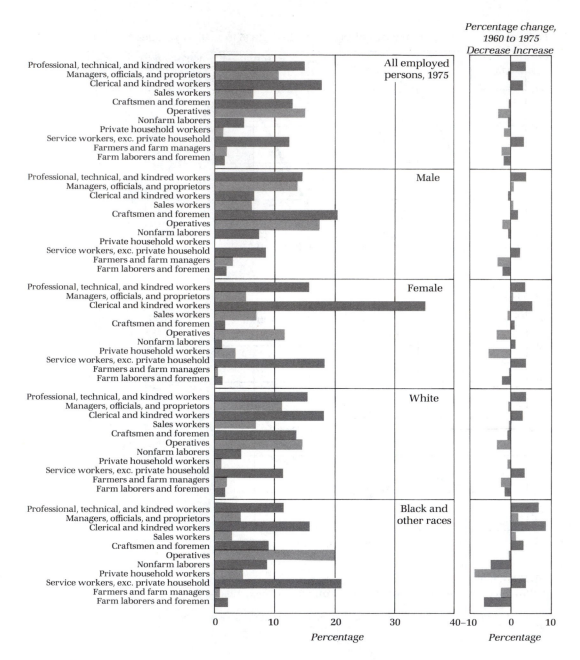

FIGURE 5.2
Occupation of employed persons, by sex and race, 1960 and 1975

SOURCE: *U.S. Department of Commerce*, Social Indicators, 1976 *(Washington, D.C.: U.S. Government Printing Office, 1977), p. 336.*

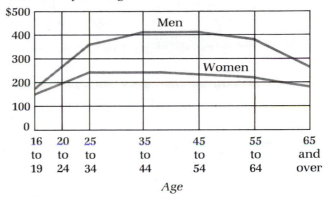

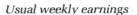

	White	Black		Hispanic	
			% of white		% of white
	Level	Level	earnings	Level	earnings
Total	$296	$238	80	$229	77
Men:					
16 to 24 years old	227	196	86	197	87
25 years and over	389	290	75	282	72
Women:					
16 to 24 years old	185	174	94	172	93
25 years and over	239	220	92	201	84

FIGURE 5.3
The male-female earnings gap: earnings profile of full-time wage and salary workers, by sex and age

SOURCE: *Monthly Labor Review* (*April 1982*), p. 17.

TABLE 5.2
The male-female earnings gap: Earnings by occupation, 1981 weekly medians for salaried workers

	Women's pay	Men's pay
Clerical workers	220	328
Computer specialists	355	488
Editors, reporters	324	382
Engineers	371	547
Lawyers	407	574
Nurses	326	344
Physicians	401	495
Sales workers	190	366
Teachers (elementary)	311	379
Waiters	144	200

SOURCE: *Time* (July 12, 1982), p. 23.

information for men and women and suggest that, if anything, the inequity has grown worse in recent years.

Women are less likely to be promoted than are men. "Women's jobs" tend to be dead-end jobs. Most of the occupations populated by women do not offer much hope of advancement. Seldom do waitresses become restaurant managers (although cooks sometimes do). Secretaries rarely become vice-presidents, and a nurse is a nurse is a nurse (she never becomes a doctor). Only one in a hundred women hairdressers becomes a shop manager. Policewomen tend to be assigned to clerical jobs, and almost all principals, even at the elementary-school level, are male (Ritzer, 1977; Cahn, 1979).

The same situation obtains in less traditionally feminine fields. Not only are women underrepresented in the ranks of the professions, but they are concentrated in relatively poorly paid positions at the lower ranks. Women are lawyers, but rarely judges. They seldom become chiefs of staff in hospitals. Less than one-tenth of all women college and university professors are full professors (Keyserling, 1979).

Moreover, at the highest levels of employment in organizations, there are few women indeed. Nearly 100 percent of all college presidents on coed campuses are men, for example. Over 90 percent of all graduate deans, deans of students, and registrars are male, and even in a government ostensibly committed to affirmative action, only 2 percent of the workers at the highest pay grade are female (Ritzer, 1977).

Finally, women are often faced with particularly trying pressures in their attempts to achieve congruence between family, self, and work. Women are expected to choose between children and work. Men are not. The woman who chooses to have a family and a career finds she is often pressured by both. The demands of an occupational career must be balanced with the responsibility for managing a household and for providing adequate child care in a world that is not designed for the dual-career family or for the female head of household.

The role of mother and homemaker is a full-time occupation. Whereas it has been estimated that executives and professionals spend about 55 hours per week in occupational activities, one study of homemaking reports that housewives spend 48 to 105 hours per week at work (Oakley, 1974). This work must be done by someone, and it is almost always the woman of the house who does it, whether or not she has another job outside the home (Rice, 1979).

A recent study by sociologist William Michelson confirms earlier surveys. Although husbands and wives in this study of 545 Canadian families reported that they shared child-care duties and housework, a more objective measure demonstrated that fully employed women spent 128 minutes a weekday on housework and 64 minutes on child care, while their husbands spent 57 minutes on housework and 22 minutes on child care—the same amount as husbands of nonworking mothers. In order to cope with the work, 94 percent of the working mothers said they did with less sleep. Half reported doing less cleaning, and about a third bought fast or frozen foods. What this means, according to Michelson, is that couples want to share the responsibilities, but "all things equal, she does it first" (*Los Angeles Times*, 1982).

For the full-time homemaker, dissatisfaction is often associated with the severity of demands at home versus the degree of aspiration a woman had for herself outside the home. For working women, conflicts between the demands of job, home, maternal duties, household duties, and marital obligations may create significant stress, even depression (Pearlin, 1975). Middle-class women seem especially affected by conflict between job and maternal duties when the job is valued for intrinsic rewards as well as economic benefits. Many professional women believe that such conflicts are more significant career obstacles than either professional and social stereotyping or explicit job discrimination (Jacoby, 1982; Hackman, 1977).

MINORITY WORKERS.   As one group of writers and researchers put it, "Racial prejudice against blacks by whites has been one of the most tenacious social problems in American history. It has resulted in an enormous catalogue of social ills, ranging from the deterioration and near bankruptcy of large cities to poverty, shorter life expectancy, high levels of crime and drug abuse, and human misery of all kinds among blacks themselves. Although whites today are much more accepting of formal equality than they were twenty years ago—supporting equal public accommodations, the right to run for public office, and fair housing, for example—there is still strong resistance to such notions as the forced integration of schools and affirmative action (Friedman, Sears, and Carlsmith, 1981, pp. 460–461 [quoted]). Moreover, unemployment figures for blacks and other minorities clearly reflect prejudice and discrimination. But simple unemployment statistics do not reveal the true extent of the problem. People leave the work force when they become discouraged about the prospects for finding a decent job. Once they drop out, they are no longer counted as unemployed. In addition, many minority workers are underemployed because their jobs do not adequately utilize or reward their abilities or because they are able to find only part-time jobs, even when they desire full-time work. Thus, unemployment figures, such as those for the late 1970s presented in Table 5.3, represent only those individuals still actively seeking work.

There are signs that the situation for black workers is improving slightly. Employment of blacks in the professions and white-collar jobs has risen since 1950, while the proportion of employed black people classified

TABLE 5.3
Unemployment[a] for males and females, 1960–1976

	1960	1970	1976
Males			
American Indian/Alaskan native	16.4	10.9	12.2
Blacks	8.6	7.1	15.9
Puerto Ricans	8.8	6.3	16.3
Majority	4.7	3.6	5.9
Females			
American Indian/Alaskan native	11.9	10.9	15.6
Blacks	9.0	8.4	18.9
Mexican Americans	9.6	9.1	14.6
Puerto Ricans	11.1	9.3	22.3
Majority	4.7	5.0	8.7

[a]Percentage of the labor force fifteen years of age or older who were out of work and actively seeking work.

SOURCE: Adapted from U.S. Commission on Civil Rights, *Social Indicators of Equality for Minorities and Women* (Washington, D.C.: U.S. Government Printing Office, 1978), p. 30.

as agricultural workers or unskilled laborers has declined. Moreover, during the 1970s the percentage of black males who were college bound increased, although the percentage of white males who considered themselves college bound declined. Still, the figures for the median weekly earnings of blacks, as presented in Figure 5.4, clearly show the continuing disparity between black and white males, as well as the extremely low wages earned by minority women.

For blacks, as for other minorities and women, the inequalities take two forms: institutional racism or sexism and overt discrimination. *Institutional racism* refers to all the ways in which a social structure prevents equality of opportunity. Unequal education as produced by housing patterns rather than by overt discrimination is an example. Other aspects of institutional racism depend on the acceptance of cultural stereotypes. Blacks are not encouraged to take the courses required for medical studies. Not only must blacks cope with the belief system (or ideology) of others, but they must often fight the tendency to internalize these negative attitudes. The ideology tells them that blacks are less valuable citizens, less important human beings than whites. Blacks may adopt all or part of that belief system without realizing it. When this happens, blacks perceive their environment as hostile and threatening and do not see themselves as respected, followed, or obeyed by others (Ziajka, 1972).

In a particularly interesting experiment designed to examine how belief systems can be internalized, subjects were given descriptions of the behavior of a "target" person with whom they were about to interact

Constant 1967 dollars

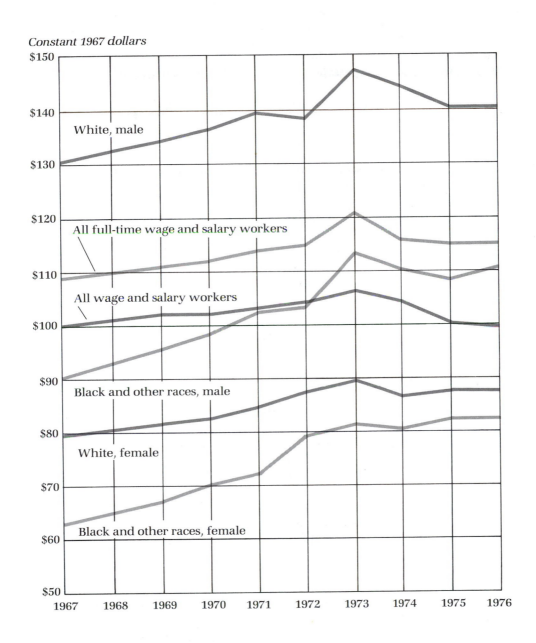

FIGURE 5.4
Median weekly earnings of wage and salary workers, by sex and race, 1967–1976

SOURCE: *U.S. Department of Commerce*, Social Indicators, 1976 *(Washington, D.C.: U.S. Government Printing Office, 1977)*, p. 345.

(Snyder and Swann, 1978ab). Sometimes, they were told that the "target" person would be hostile, cruel, and insensitive. After the interactions took place, the experimenters discovered that the informed subjects did perceive their target as hostile, even though the targets themselves were unaware that they had been described to the subjects. Moreover, more hostile behavior (the administration of loud, painful noise) actually occurred than in interactions in which the target had not been described as hostile. When, in the second step of the experiment, each target was introduced to a new person who had received no information from the experimenter, these same targets continued to act in a hostile way and were thus perceived by the new subjects as hostile. In contrast, targets who had been described (in the first step of the experiment) as cooperative and kind were not perceived as hostile; nor did they behave in a hostile way in the subsequent interaction. In sum, the experiment offered convincing evidence that the expectations people have affect not only how they perceive others, but probably how the other perceives the situation and, therefore, how that other person behaves.

Although very little has actually been done outside the laboratory about studying how such expectations affect minority groups, research on the impact of stereotypes is suggestive, and some such research has been done on Americans of Hispanic origin as well as on black Americans.

Americans of Hispanic origin constitute another minority group of great size and impact. Little information about this group is available, although it is the largest single minority in the United States, comprising up to 20 percent of the population of states in the southwest and west. The situation of Spanish-surname individuals in the labor market is perhaps even worse than that of blacks. Hispanic Americans are plagued by low income, high unemployment, migration, low occupational status, and discrimination. Among all youth of Spanish surname between the ages of sixteen and twenty-four, one in three is a school dropout. This figure is considerably higher for Hispanics than for whites or for blacks; the result is reflected in the figures in Figure 5.5. To compound the problem, many young, poorly educated Hispanics often become farm laborers instead of taking the clerical or craft jobs typically filled by white dropouts. In addition, people of Hispanic origin are not found in the service occupations as frequently as blacks, because of the language barriers they often encounter (Young, 1973).

Hispanic Americans face many of the same problems of self-image that afflict American blacks. A study of Mexican-American children born in the United States found, for example, that these children are more likely to describe themselves as "emotional, unscientific, authoritarian, proud, lazy, indifferent, and unambitious" than are Mexican-American children born in Mexico (Derbyshire, 1968). Again, it seems unlikely that people who have such self-perceptions will succeed in the occupational world.

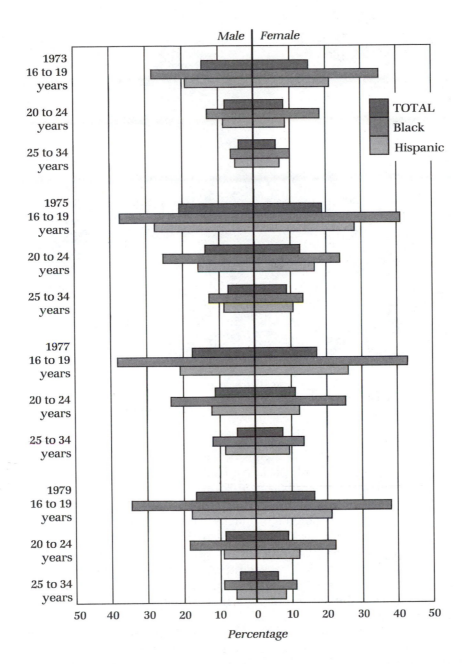

FIGURE 5.5
Unemployment rates of persons sixteen to thirty-four years old, by selected characteristics, for selected years, 1973–1979

SOURCE: *U.S. Department of Commerce,* Social Indicators, *1979 (Washington, D.C.: U.S. Government Printing Office, 1980), p. 334.*

It is all the more difficult to fight racial prejudice and struggle up the socioeconomic ladder if you cannot do so in English.

Most disturbing of all, perhaps, is the paucity of information about the vocational process, family structure, and self-concept formation of Hispanic Americans. Although texts and original source materials usually mention the special problems of blacks, most do not index or make any reference to research on the Spanish-surname population. Many such books simply refer to all minorities under the heading of "prejudice, effects of," or "discrimination," with little regard for the unique problems of bilingual or Spanish-speaking individuals. The preparation of a precise and useful analysis of the development of minority individuals as children and as adults awaits much needed research in this area.

Finally, if little can be said about Hispanic Americans, nothing at all can reasonably be reported about Native Americans. Although we know that their unemployment rates are astronomical and that their educational levels and income levels are for the most part very low, we find little psychological data. Perhaps because Native American subcultures are so diverse, the task of gathering information about them has seemed too complex. In any event, Native Americans are undoubtedly subject to many of the same problems faced by any group living in an unresponsive, uncaring, even hostile cultural milieu.

MAINSTREAM WHITE MALES.   An analysis of the problems of women, blacks, Hispanics, and Native Americans raises some questions about what it means to be a white male in this country. Whereas others may have problems finding employment, white males must have a job. There are no excuses. They must be competitive and task oriented. They must achieve, or at least try to do so. They must be aggressive, nonnurturant, brave, successful, and ambitious (Fasteau, 1974). If such a man does not have a job, he is not a person. Popular literature abounds with discussions of the working mother; but even after the significant social changes of the past two decades, there is little interest in the nonworking father.

The primary social and self-identification of the middle-class and working-class American male is derived from his occupation or from sports, friends, and machines. Men often find themselves ill-equipped for retirement and leisure. They die early of stress-related diseases. They are often isolated from the emotional rewards and support of family life.

Unemployment or underemployment in any form or for any reason is a major, if not the major, psychological and social crisis for the white male. Unemployment and underemployment probably affect most would-be workers, white and nonwhite, in this way; but the white, middle-class male who is unemployed is probably the most socially isolated of all Americans from individuals with similar experience and from people who can understand and sympathize with his dilemma.

Although the pressures and constraints imposed on white males by our society have been of concern to literary and artistic minds for some time, these issues have received wider attention only recently, with the publication of books such as *The Forty-Nine Percent Majority* (David and Brannon, 1976) and the emergence in the late 1970s and 1980s of a men's liberation movement. Still, interest in exploring the consequences of the masculine stereotype seems sporadic and tentative at best. Only in the study of fatherhood does there seem to be consistent progress.

Freud, upon being asked what it means to be an adult, is said to have answered "to work and to love." Vocational choices offer the opportunity for work; family and friends provide the context for love. In the last chapter we discussed the selection of marriage partners and the development of other intimate relationships; now we will turn to the choices that people make to establish a wider family and a social circle. First, we'll examine the decision to have children and the effects of children on parents as individuals as well as the effects of children on a marriage. Finally, we will look at the establishment of friendships in young adult life.

PARENTHOOD

Parenthood provides a special opportunity for loving, nurturing, and guiding the next generation. Children give people a unique stake in the shape and direction of their society. Thus, Erikson argues that we feel more investment in the betterment of the world of human beings when we are making a place for our own progeny. From this perspective, the evolution of the species is ensured not only by the birth of children but also by the caring evoked by children.

According to Erikson, children also fulfill important emotional needs, including the need to be needed, the need to be important to another person, and the need to be creative in an objective way—a way that makes a real difference in the world. Children can be a legitimate source of pride and of emotional growth not available to those who choose not to parent. Intense, fundamental experiences that can best be described as moments of great tenderness, awe, and wonder are often reported by parents who feel strong bonds with their young children. Finally, parenthood often enhances one's sense of a common human heritage, of universal kinship with other people and their children. As Ann Roiphe wrote,

> I remember the moment, now some twelve years ago, when I suddenly knew my child was being taken care of. I was bathing my daughter—who was trying to put soap in her mouth—and felt this sudden kinship with all other women who had done the same thing—this feeding, cleaning, disposing of urine and feces, smiling, hugging, and touching. And with this sense of a common bond, I entered a new phase in my life. I had grown to value my wonderful individuality a little less and my common humanity more.

For years, the literature on parent-child relationships described, explained, predicted, and otherwise concerned itself with the effects that parents have, or are presumed to have, on children. Then, in a seminal article, Robert Bell (1968) brought into clearer focus some important questions about the direction of these effects. Does parental use of punishment cause children to be more aggressive, or do the parents of an aggressive child finally turn to punitive measures? Do autonomous children have warm, permissive parents, or do the parents of an autonomous child feel more confident and positive about the child? Slowly but persistently, researchers and writers have turned their attention to the serious examination of how children affect parental personality development and self-perception. Now, there is a burgeoning literature in this area, as well as research on attitudes toward parenting and the impact of changing cultural expectations.

Clearly, the effect of childrearing on adult self-perception is profound. Adults consistently refer to the birth of children as a turning point in their lives (Lowenthal and Chiriboga, 1972). In one major study of 1,500 couples, for example, most people described the birth of children in terms of establishment of adulthood (Hoffman and Manis, 1978). Both men and women viewed parenthood as a major source of maturity and as a growth experience. Furthermore, the birth of children seems to affect changes in existing relationships with one's own parents. Often people express a more empathetic view of their parents during a woman's pregnancy, although they may also feel the need to "do better" (Lamb, 1978).

Bernice Neugarten (1968a) believes that parenthood affects self-concept, self-esteem, and most other aspects of adult identity. Neugarten's view suggests that the birth of children may constitute a crisis, in the Eriksonian sense: a turning point, an opportunity for growth.

Parenthood as Crisis

Most Americans feel that it is normal, necessary, and natural for individuals to replace themselves by bearing children. They expect to experience parenthood as joy-giving and fulfilling and tend to assume that good parents will be guided by instinctual love in the proper care of children. Anxious to demonstrate good, natural parenting, people often become secretly guilty when they don't know exactly what to do. Even child psychologists often have well-worn copies of Spock (1974) or Dodson (1974) tucked away for use at home.

According to Arlene Skolnick (1978), Americans seem to expect a "natural fit" between the needs of infants and the needs and behaviors of parents, reflecting a belief in *maternal* (and, perhaps, a paternal) *instinct*—a belief that denies the enormous role of culture and learning in all human behavior. In fact, there is little evidence that humans have any innate abilities as parents. Consider, for example, that for over two thousand years male psychologist-philosophers have been trying to convince mothers of the importance of breast-feeding their babies; and, for two thousand years, many mothers all over the world have rejected or resisted the idea (Kessen, 1965). Would this be the case for such a basic behavior pattern if so-called maternal instincts alone directed the mothers' choices?

The attitude that parenting is not only innate but also a basic source of joy, fulfillment, and adult maturity has been called the *pronatalist* position. Pronatalism is accepted by most members of this culture (Veevers, 1980). An individual who does not want to be a mother or father, or who does not think that parenting comes naturally, often feels abnormal or inadequate. People who discover they are not prepared for parenthood when the moment arrives feel guilty or immature. Since most people also believe that the course of a child's development depends heavily on the first few years, enormous anxiety, guilt, and even terror are sometimes in store for those who feel unprepared or unqualified for parenthood (Storr, 1972).

In the late 1950s and early 1960s, a number of researchers, thinking perhaps along the lines we've been discussing, began to present evidence that the birth of a first child was experienced as a crisis. In two of these studies (Le Masters, 1957; Dyer, 1963), 50 to 80 percent of the new parents interviewed expressed feelings of moderate to severe crisis when their first child was born. Later studies similarly suggested that the birth of the first child might best be conceptualized as a "moderately stressful" transition. These studies also yielded evidence, however, that parents experience their new role as adequately supplied with rewards as well as stresses (Hobbs, 1965; Russell, 1974; Hobbs and Cole, 1976).

It is possible that differences between the methods of these early and later investigations account for their differences in conclusions. The later studies relied heavily on mailed questionnaires rather than interviews, which generally yield higher crisis scores than do checklists. Moreover, return rates for the questionnaires were fairly low, often as low as 50 percent (Hobbs and Cole, 1976). Individuals who were experiencing great difficulty may have seen themselves as poor examples or felt their reports would not be socially acceptable and so may have been reluctant to reply.

The most recent research bridges these two sets of earlier studies by suggesting that parenthood has a rather paradoxical quality—it is experienced as both joyful and stressful. Preschoolers, for example, seem especially likely to make life both more difficult and more rewarding. On the one hand, couples with small children say the children brought them closer together as a couple. Children gave them a shared task, a common goal, and a common joy. On the other hand, these parents acknowledge that they have less time together as a couple and that the potential for disagreements over childrearing is always a problem, as is the loss of each spouse's attentiveness to the other as a husband or wife (Hoffman and Manis, 1978).

Both mothers and fathers repeatedly lament that children tie them down so completely. Parenting has the quality of "alwaysness": one loses the freedom to do things on the spur of the moment. Children are perceived as career limiting by women (Hoffman and Manis, 1978; Jacoby, 1982), and both parents experience a loss of individuality, a sense of fatigue, and the burdens of financial pressures and of worry over the children. Worries increase with the age of the children, culminating in the teen-aged years, when mothers and fathers outline long lists of troublesome areas from accidents to drugs, alcohol, sex, and self-doubts about how they have performed as parents. Despite these later pressures, however, the demands of preschoolers may well have the biggest impact on adults and are most likely to evoke paradoxical feelings (Hoffman and Manis, 1978).

The push-pull of parenthood brings married people closer together as they share a common joy, yet it is easy to drift apart when there is little time together as a couple.

Aside from changes in attitudes toward one's self and one's marriage, the most common response of young adults to the advent of the childrearing years appears to be a "traditionalizing" of sex-role behavior. In our culture, childrearing remains primarily a woman's responsibility, and the research indicates that women do, in fact, assume most of the burdens of child care. Fathers tend to react to the birth of their children in terms of greater concern about their role as provider. These conservative influences on sex-role behavior are obviously most difficult for women who are interested in pursuing careers, but the implications of such changes do not emerge clearly until after the first child is born (La Rossa and La Rossa, 1981; Hoffman and Manis, 1978; Lamb, 1978; Alpert and Richardson, 1980).

In one small but intensive study of the transition to parenthood by Ralph and Maureen La Rossa, the process by which these conservative role changes occur is suggested. The La Rossas see it in terms of a fight for free time between the parents, in which the woman is destined to be the loser. Noting that in the transition to parenthood, the human family becomes a kind of continuous-coverage institution, like a hosptial, La Rossa and La

Rossa underscore the "alwaysness" of parenthood. Someone must be immediately available at all times of the day and night. Someone must constantly be on hand to meet a baby's demands, and the demands of an infant are nonnegotiable: infants cannot be told to "wait a minute" or to "sit tight." Even when a child is asleep, parents don't have any real time off; the baby can wake up at any moment. The father's socially approved recommitment to the role of breadwinner buys him some time off, however. In the contest for free time, the father usually wins, simply because the social structure is on his side, and the traditional sex-roles of the money-earning father and the child-caring mother are perpetuated.

Still, the victory often costs the father dearly. Many men experience strong role conflicts between fatherhood and occupation. In the long run, research suggests that overall male life satisfaction is more strongly related to the quality of family life than to occupational achievement (Alpert and Richardson, 1980). For men, as for women, the establishment of a coherent role in the family is critical. A coherent role may take a number of forms. Some fathers play the teacher, some the pal, some prefer to be the authority figure, but the entire matter is severely complicated by social requirements that demand dedication to work outside the home (Lamb, 1978).

Research about the effects of childrearing is further complicated by the timing of parenthood. Children who arrive early in a parent's life are greeted differently than those who arrive later on. In one interesting study of timing, the early arrival of children (in one's early twenties) seemed to interfere with the parents' attempts to establish independence from their own parents (Daniels and Weingarten, 1980). Early parenthood also threatened the development of an intimate marital relationship. In contrast, although late-timing couples (late thirties to early forties) expressed greater dissatisfaction at the loss of intimacy as a couple, they seemed more aware of those moments when the marriage needed extra attention. The traditionalizing impact of childbearing also seemed less significant among late-timing couples, who have a better grasp of their identity as individuals and of their feelings for each other as a couple. Virtually every early-timing couple in this study said they would wait longer if they had the chance to do it over again. No late-timing couple expressed a desire to have had children sooner.

A variety of other factors undoubtedly influence adjustment to parenthood, but research exists on very few. Among these, social class seems to have the most well-documented impact. Perhaps because middle-class parents have adopted the pronatalist philosophy more completely than working-class parents, they continue to experience difficulty even after the preschool years (Hobbs and Cole, 1976). Middle-class couples tend to report fewer rewards from parenthood than working-class parents do, and they are more sensitive to the disruption of life-style that accompanies the birth of a child (Russell, 1974).

Alice Rossi (1968) has summarized some of the salient sources of stress that affect the experience of parenthood for most members of middle-class America:

1. Cultural pressure: The pronatalist position engenders blind commitment to parenthood in much the same way that other attitudinal systems promote the acceptance of monogamous marriage as the only normal adult life path.

2. Inception: Parenthood is not always voluntary or well planned.

3. Irrevocability: One cannot send a baby back. Almost all other life decisions can be revoked or at least modified. One cannot reject the parental role once a child is born, except through psychological withdrawal.

4. Preparation: There is no formal education for parenthood and very little realistic socialization. The transition from childlessness to parenthood is complete in one to three days, and little help is offered by social institutions, which operate on the assumption that parenthood is right and natural for all adults.

5. Guidance: No consensus exists, among lay people or experts, about which childrearing practices produce competent adults. Most advice seems to create pressure and anxiety.

Although these and other influences can contribute to making parenthood a crisis for both mothers and fathers, the experience of parenthood is, as we noted above, different for men and women. Women are supposed to accept most of the responsibility for meeting the day-to-day needs of children. Women are regarded by many psychologists, as well as by the society at large, as the primary influences on childhood development. And so it seems really to be the sins of the mother that are believed to be visited upon the child.

Mothering

In this country, the role of full-time mother is considered an essential step in the normal life path for women. Most Americans believe full-time mothering is critical for the successful development of children. It is assumed that substitute mothering, multiple mothering, and parttime mothering are inadequate. Research on maternal deprivation—especially the well-known work of John Bowlby (1958, 1969)—forms the basis for the scientific articulation of the dogma of full-time mothering. Bowlby was able to demonstrate that severance of the bond between mother and child is associated with deficient social, emotional, and intellectual growth among institutionalized infants. The uncritical generalization of these results to all care outside the home has reinforced the belief that a mother must give her undivided attention to a child for the first two or three years of life (Wortis, 1971).

For women, the dogma of full-time mothering and the conservative impact of childbearing have a variety of implications. Studies have shown that women suffer a loss of power in the marital relationship and that they receive less help with the housework from the father after the birth of the first born, even though they are assuming the primary responsibility for child care. With time, the balance of power seems to shift back, but the division of labor remains quite traditional, especially if the mother leaves work in order to bear children. Comparing women in the same age group, researchers have found that those without children are less likely to think that a man should make the decisions and provide the money for the family than are women with preschool children (Hoffman and Manis, 1978).

While her child is an infant, a mother must adjust considerably to meet the demands of a new role. If she has just quit her job, the change in her life-style is enormous. On the other hand, if she continues to work, the pressures and conflicts are very great indeed (Jacoby, 1982). In studying the timing of parenthood, Pamela Daniels and Kathy Weingarten (1980) discovered evidence that the new media image of the working mother has created unrealistic expectations. Women expect to ride "three mules at once," as Adela Rogers St. John once referred to being mother, wife, and career woman at the same time. When they cannot do it, they feel that their shortcomings are personal.

The data from the Daniels and Weingarten study suggest strongly that today's young women expect far more of themselves than older cohorts and are, therefore, less satisfied. Younger subjects who continued their careers after childbirth evidenced a sense of continuous compromise. For example, those who had been occupationally successful felt they were cutting corners for the first time in their lives. Furthermore, few younger women in this study experienced a sense of triumph at combining family and work. Only among the oldest cohorts did the combination of work and family seem to serve as a source of self-esteem as well as stress. Daniels and Weingarten conclude that young women will require much stronger institutional support if they are to ride those mules as successfully as everyone seems to expect.

Despite the problems, however, women also extoll the advantages of motherhood. Every couple in the Daniels and Weingarten study, whether early- or late-timing, said that children added an important dimension to their relationship, a quality of deepened love. In the Hoffman and Manis (1978) sample, subjects also repeatedly stated that children do bring married people closer together, giving them a shared task and a sense of interdependence. These parents talked about the satisfaction of feeling like a family, and how children add meaning to life.

For the fathers in these studies, the advantages of parenthood are perceived and explained in many of the same terms the mothers used. Fathers also believed children strengthen the marriage bond and add a new and meaningful dimension to life. Parenting behavior in the American family is very different among men than among women, however, and the differences have been the subject of a growing body of intensive research in recent years.

Fathering

"Fathers should be neither seen nor heard," Oscar Wilde once quipped. "That is the only proper basis for family life." And indeed, until a few years ago, the only research available on the subject of fathering concerned father *absence* rather than father *presence*. There have even been suggestions that the role of the American father is, in fact, rather unimportant because it is so diluted by a variety of cultural factors (Lynn, 1974). Fathers are often absent and emotionally detached from their families because of the demanding occupational lives they lead outside the home. Middle-class and upper-middle-class fathers, in particular, spend most of their waking hours in work-related activities. They may put in fifty-five hours a week at the office, plus additional hours spent in transit and recuperation. Family activities have almost disappeared as individual pursuits have become more popular. The knowledge explosion has undermined the role of the father as teacher and authority. Current trends in sex-role behavior have eroded his confidence, and divorce or separation often completes his disengagement from the family. Lynn has developed a theory of sex-role learning based on the assumption that male figures are not available as sex-role models for male children.

Rapid social changes and escalating occupational demands have left many men in a frustrating emotional limbo. No longer the authorities or bankers or protectors of the family, they have also not been expected to participate fully in the emotional and nurturant functions of parenthood. Some suggest that parenting is incompatible with the masculine image in

America today (Fasteau, 1974). Men are not taught to deal with emotions. Many men cannot express affection and cannot relate to the inner lives of their children. Men are not taught to value the personal kinds of rewards one can find in parenting.

Late in the 1970s, the work of Michael Lamb, Ross Parks, and their colleagues began to offer a different image of the role of father in the contemporary American family. First, and perhaps most important, they established that fathers can and do participate in vigorous interactions with their infants. Second, they established that fathers have a most important, if poorly understood, impact on the sex-role development of both male and female children.

In 1977, Parks and Swain presented a paper outlining the role of the father during childbirth. They reported that for both mothers and fathers in their subject group, childbirth was a profoundly moving experience in

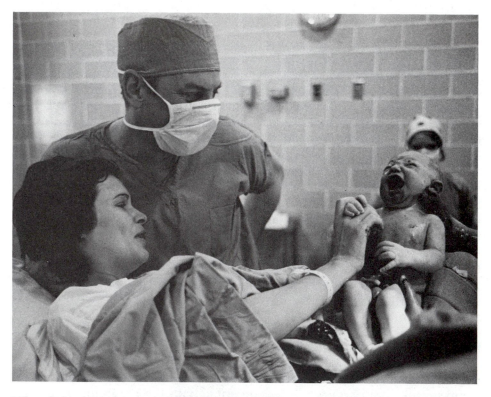

When fathers participate in the birth process, they are able to ease the pain and dis-
comfort of labor and share in the deeply moving emotional experience of childbirth.

which the men were able to reduce their partners' pain and discomfort through communication and emotional support: a basic tenet of the popular Lamaze method of natural childbirth. Lamaze, like other methods of preparation for childbirth, casts the father as an active participant in labor, monitoring the mother's progress, providing moral support, massaging and supporting her physically, and constantly reminding her to relax and concentrate.

In another landmark report, Parks and Swain (1976) concluded that both parents were sensitive to the cues offered by infants, but fathers were more likely to respond to an infant visually. Other studies confirm that most infants show attachment to both parents by seven to nine months of age. Infants greet their fathers as heartily as their mothers and show distress when separated from either parent (Lamb, 1981). It is also clear, however, that the kinds of interactions infants have with their fathers are quite different from the typical mother-infant exchange. Whereas mothers spend some time playing with their babies, almost all of the time fathers spend with infants can be characterized as play. Data from one study show, for instance, that mothers spend 10 percent of their time playing with their infant, while fathers play 50 percent of the time (La Rossa and La Rossa, 1981).

As his baby grows older, a father's behavior changes dramatically. He begins to pay much more attention to a male infant in the second year of life, and less to a female. A number of writers and researchers have suggested that the changes in a father's behavior during the second year of life are critical to the child's sex-role identification (Lamb and Goldberg, 1982).

Why do mothers and fathers display different kinds of behavior in parenting? Is their behavior to any extent biologically determined, or is it solely the product of social influences? As we might expect, such questions have provoked considerable controversy among researchers. For example, Michael Lamb contends that any biological predispositions directing sex differences in parenting are probably slight but exceedingly complex. He believes that social pressures exaggerate biological influences and that, given the right training, males and females can be equivalently good as parents (Lamb and Goldberg, 1982). Coming from an entirely different point of view, David Gutmann (1964, 1969, 1977) argues that a powerful biological phenomenon, which he has labeled the *parental imperative*, not only directs parenting behavior but also serves to organize much of adult personality development and provide an ultimate source of meaning as species needs intersect personal needs (Gutmann, 1975).

In extensive cross-cultural research using both longitudinal and cross-sectional data, Gutmann has made a case that, to a certain extent, men and women reverse roles as they age. In this process of role *involution*, as Gutmann calls it, men seem to become less aggressive with age, as well as more affiliative and more interested in love and community. They more often see energy emanating from outside the self, rather than from inside, and they seem to become more sensual and more sensitive to pain and pleasure. On the other hand, women become more aggressive, less sentimental, and more domineering as they grow older (Gutmann, 1964, 1969).

Extrapolating backward from his evidence on role involution in later life, Gutmann argues that sex-role distinctions are sharpened in young adulthood by the need offspring present for protection and nurturance. Gutmann believes one person cannot adequately meet both sets of needs. Therefore, biology dictates that men will protect and women will nurture. The biological needs of children are the imperative that organizes adult behavior more strongly along sex-related dimensions. According to this point of view, one parent cannot and should not try to meet both the physical and the emotional requirements of young children. The father is the expendable parent, the one who must leave the home to hunt or to sell refrigerators. The survival of the species depends on the ability of males to provide for and defend their families, while women provide the emotional security children need to become competent adults.

Gutmann is so adamant about the importance of the parental imperative that he believes new styles of family life may place the human race in grave jeopardy. In direct response to his position, Patricia Self (1975) has used the recent literature on fathering to take issue with Gutmann and to challenge the assumptions that young males are unable to exchange love and understanding and that they must continue to perform only traditional paternal functions. Infants do form active, close relationships with their fathers. Not only are men capable of providing emotional support for their children, they do in fact provide it. In agreement with Self, many social scientists are advocating the adoption of flexible life-styles that would allow both mother and father to parent part-time and work part-time. These writers believe that such flexibility would increase the desirability and interest people experience in both parenthood and work.

Work and Family

Traditional sex roles take fathers out of the home and into the marketplace, making the first years of a child's life perhaps the most difficult for mothers. For fathers, the early and middle stages of parenting seem hardest as mounting financial and occupational strains and declining job satisfaction create distress (Alpert and Richardson, 1980). Moreover, men are more likely to feel a conscious concern for family, and a strong desire to be with their children as the children grow up (Nydegger and Mittemas, 1979; Lowenthal and Chiriboga, 1973).

In the Daniels and Weingarten study, men who did not develop strong relationships with their infants often singled out a particular moment later on that symbolized their new appreciation of fathering. According to Daniels and Weingarten, this "click of fatherhood"—the moment when parental identity is translated into "hands-on parenting"— is all too often delayed for a man. The financial responsibilities of parenthood may galvanize his identity around the role of breadwinner, bringing occupational issues front and center and interfering with the development of a coherent family role. To create conditions that would allow fathers to experience that click as soon as possible, Daniels and Weingarten and other writers conclude that parents should share responsibilities more thoroughly, both at home and in the work place. This brings us to the matter of maternal employment.

A thorough review of the literature on working mothers reveals that almost anything can be said, depending on the population chosen, the time of the study, and the types of controls employed by researchers. Yet, considering the complexity of the problem, researchers have discovered surprisingly few significant relationships between maternal employment and any measure of child development thus far examined. (For data on the growth of maternal employment among ever-married women, see Figure 5.6.)

Several excellent reviews are available (Hoffman, 1961; Siegel, 1963; Propper, 1972; Hoffman and Nye, 1974). These articles present evidence of widespread societal disapproval of maternal employment, particularly when the children are of preschool age. In fact, one study (Komarovsky, 1973) reported that 64 percent of the male college population at one Ivy League college, and almost as many females, preferred a life path for married women that did not include employment outside the home during the childrearing years. Only 20 percent of the women and 7 percent of the men expressed attitudes compatible with uninterrupted maternal employment. In spite of these attitudes, shaped in part by the dogma of full-time mothering, the research simply does not support the notion that maternal employment will necessarily be accompanied by inadequate mothering or inferior development of the child.

When research includes adequate controls for socioeconomic class, divorce, education, and other relevant factors, few differences of any kind are found between the children of women who are full-time homemakers and the children of women who work.

Mothers who were happy with their jobs did not differ from satisfied full-time homemakers on measures of maternal behavior including control, emotional satisfaction, or adequacy of mothering. A comparison between women who were *not satisfied* with their lives as full-time homemakers and those who were *not satisfied* with lives that included

Percentage

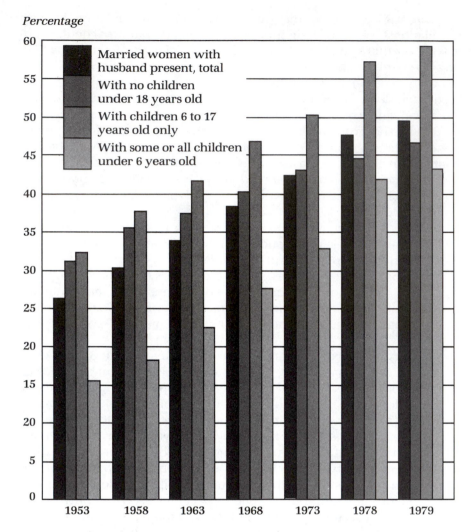

FIGURE 5.6
Married women, husband present, in labor force, by presence and age of
children, for selected years, 1953–1979

SOURCE: *U.S. Department of Commerce*, Social Indicators, 1979 *(Washington, D.C.: U.S. Government
Printing Office, 1980), p. 329.*

work and homemaking is also intriguing. The results indicated dissatisfied
working mothers demonstrated better control, more emotional satisfaction, greater confidence in their role, and superior adequacy of mothering.

Full-time mothering does not solve the riddles of child development for every mother and every child.

What a marvelous vision: every child with access to both its mother and its father, and every adult with access to both the satisfactions and the joys of parenthood and those of a career outside the home. Of course, for a growing number of single-parent families in this culture, there are no options. Then, mother or father must choose both parenthood and full-time employment, and the vision for them is often less than marvelous. Sharing the central tasks of adult life seems to be quite a different proposition from trying to do it all by yourself.

Single-Parent Families

Available information about single-parent families is badly in need of clarification. It is particularly difficult to sort out the effect of single-parenting from the economic, social, and often racial or ethnic differences that set these families apart from the usual nuclear family. Most single-parent families are headed by divorced or separated women, who often work at poorly paid jobs and have special day-care needs that the society does not meet. In fact, some social scientists have begun talking of the "feminization of poverty" (Time, 1982). Women may be discriminated against in both the job and the housing markets *because* of their children and their divorced or separated status. Employers often feel that a woman with young children is unreliable. Apartments and condominiums in better areas may refuse to rent or sell to families with children, especially to single-parent families.

In 1976, 20 percent of all children under eighteen did not live with both parents (U.S. Dept. of Commerce, 1978). And, most of the single-parent families are not doing well financially. Among white families, about 60 percent of those living on less than $4,000 per year were headed by one parent, although one-parent families make up only about 15 percent of all white families. Among blacks, nearly one-half of all families are one-parent families, but 80 percent of all one-parent families earn less than $4,000 per year. At the other end of the economic scale, fewer than 5 percent of families with incomes over $15,000 were headed by a single parent. For blacks, about 10 percent of families with incomes over $15,000 were one-parent families (Reiss, 1980).

Even single-parent families with sufficient economic resources have special problems with important psychological implications. The single parent must cope with the social isolation and loneliness of singlehood that we discussed in Chapter 4. These problems may be of even greater magnitude for the single parent, who is tied down by the care of young children and cannot take advantage of the opportunities that are available. Often single parents are completely cut off from most of the channels of communication in society.

In a study of single-parent families in Great Britain (Schlesinger, 1977), parents consistently reported feelings of loneliness and anomie. They also expressed frustration about the need to forgo sexual gratification because of the potential effects on the children or the adverse reactions of neighbors. Difficulty in meeting the physical demands of young children was a major problem for these parents, who also reported difficulty in finding ways to help the children cope with feelings of being different from "normal" families.

Few researchers have investigated the single-parent family created by the unmarried individual who adopts a child. The practice is not widespread and often involves the adoption of children with special physical or emotional problems. There is some evidence that these children adjust despite the odds against them.

Perhaps the biggest difficulty faced by all single-parent families is how to provide an adequate model for the behavior of the absent parent. Jane Burgess (1970) has pointed out that many single mothers manage to provide adequate models of male sex-role behavior through relatives and friends. Peers may also compensate to some extent for the absence of a father figure. For many of the children of single parents, the problem is eventually solved by marriage or remarriage, which raises the fairy-tale specter of the stepparent (Burgess, 1970).

Stepparenting

According to figures from the Bureau of the Census, the proportion of children living with one parent doubled from 9 percent to 19 percent between 1960 and 1978, while the proportion living with two parents declined from 88 percent to 78 percent. One of every eight children living with two parents lives with a natural parent and a stepparent. Two of every three children living with one parent is living with a divorced or separated parent (U.S. Department of Commerce, 1980).

Since 75 to 80 percent of all divorced people eventually remarry, and since many divorces involve families with children, many parents and children face the problems of integrating a new adult member into the family. In some families the situation is even more complicated when both adults have custody of children and the newly formed family includes the children of each of the parents.

A comprehensive (if now somewhat dated) review of the literature on stepparenthood (Walters and Stinnet, 1971) provides some insight into the process of constructing new family constellations. The data indicate that stepparents are more easily accommodated by very young children and by adult children. Stepparents are accepted more readily in families that have been split by divorce than in those in which the death of a parent precedes remarriage. The new parent will be most easily accepted by male children, especially if the new parent is also a male. This piece of information is particularly interesting when considered in the light of all the evidence on father absence. Apparently it is comparatively easy to provide an acceptable male role model through remarriage. On the other hand, children of both sexes tend to see a stepparent of the opposite sex as "playing favorites" more often than their biological parent, and stepmothers are believed guilty of favoritism more often than stepfathers. Of course, since women most often have primary responsibility for the day-to-day needs of children, there may be more opportunity for children to develop elaborate complaints about stepmothers.

Children continue to admire their absent biological parent, often more than their stepparent, which can produce feelings of inadequacy or rejection in a stepparent. A stepparent may be reluctant, even unable, to overrule the dictates or suggestions of the child's biological parent. If you cannot completely accept a role, it is hard for others to accept you in it.

Finally, stepparents and stepchildren often come to the newly constituted family with unrealistic expectations for their relationships (Stinnet and Walters, 1977). Instant love and togetherness are not the automatic result of the creation of a new family. Both parents and children must allow adequate time for trust and affection to develop. Family therapy can be useful in adjusting expectations that otherwise might, and often do, lead to disappointment and grief.

The process of learning to be a good stepparent is one about which little is known, despite a clear and pressing need. Surprisingly, the growing number of remarriages and so-called blended families has not provoked much interest in stepparenting, and few articles on parenting even mention the subject. It is not always easy to develop real affection for the children of another, especially when the absent parent of that child may be a source of difficulty or confusion in the child's current living situation. Experts have offered little assistance. What guidance and comfort are available come primarily from personal accounts by those who have lived through the situation.

One such account (Maddox, 1976) outlines the progress of a stepmother, a woman who married a man with two school-aged children. The author writes about her feelings and conflicts. She points out that stepchildren are a constant reminder of the former spouse. The bond with stepchildren has no legal permanence. The other biological parent, not the stepparent, will be given custody of one's stepchild should anything happen to one's spouse, the biological parent with whom the child resides. No incest taboo restrains stepparent-child sexual feelings. The children may try to maintain distance to protect themselves from another separation.

The role of stepparent is without essential social definition. It is a role we receive no preparation for, just as we are not prepared for biological parenting. There is little social consensus about how stepparenting should differ from or in what ways it is identical to parenting. New stepparents have no clues about how their duties, obligations, and rights might vary with the age, sex, or number of children in the family or how they might best interact with the biological parent not residing with the child. Guilt about one's performance under these circumstances may well inhibit the spontaneity needed to build loving relationships.

The number of stepparent adoptions in this country is increasing rapidly. Legal adoptions open the possibility for denying the biological parent visiting rights to the child. In fact, all official record of one of the biological parents may be expunged—a possibility that seems filled with important and unresearched implications. We are used to change, and we are ready to institutionalize it in many different forms. However, if this new wave of adoptive parents, or for that matter, the less formal stepparent arrangement, is to be successful, better information will be needed as well as more support from the legal, educational, and familial institutions of society. The rights and obligations of stepparents should be clarified, and the status and problems of stepparents must receive greater attention.

Childfreeness

Throughout human history some individuals have questioned the value of parenthood. But at the midpoint of this century in the United States, very few departed from the pronatalist philosophy so apparent in media representations of parenthood, from commercials for baby powder to family situation comedies. Nineteen out of every twenty couples today have at least one child. This does not mean, of course, simply that they have been misled by pronatalist philosophy or by folk beliefs that children are sweet and cute and childrearing is fun. As we have seen, most parents report that children add an important dimension to their experience of adulthood. Nonetheless, as we move into the twenty-first century, more and more individuals are choosing to have fewer children, or none. (Figure 5.7 shows the declining rate of population change for the past two hundred years.) We now have the word "childfree" rather than "childless." College-age women who report that they do not want children also report that the people they know endorse that decision (Houseknecht, 1977). Moreover,

Average annual rate of change
(percentage)

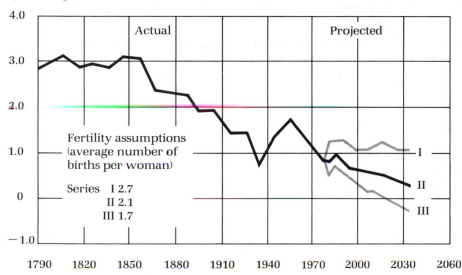

FIGURE 5.7
Average annual rate of population change, selected years, 1790–2040

SOURCE: *U.S. Department of Commerce,* Social Indicators, 1979 *(Washington, D.C.: U.S. Government Printing Office, 1980), p. 12.*

those who desire no children perceive support not only from others who question the value of childrearing, but also from those who desire to have children. Such general feelings of approval allow people to maintain positive self-images while making controversial life-style decisions.

Summarizing an extensive research program, Jean Veevers (1980) has outlined the decision-making process that underlies childlessness. She distinguishes between "early articulators" and those who simply postpone childbearing until it becomes obvious that a decision has actually been achieved. About one-third of the people she interviewed entered into marriage with the explicit understanding that there would be no children. Usually, the women in her sample precipitated the decision. Men generally chose to be childless because they married a particular woman; otherwise, they did not really consider childbearing in conscious ways.

Early articulators see not wanting children as a characteristic of the self: that is, they do not want children regardless of whom they marry or how the marriage is going. They are likely to seek sterilization. Postponers, in contrast, are much more likely to report that childlessness is related to their current marriage and to feel that, in another relationship, they might make a different decision.

Generally postponers progress through four stages in the establishment of a childless life-style. First, they postpone childbearing for a definite period of time—until he graduates or she is established vocationally, or until they buy a home. Later, the postponement becomes less definite—until they have enough money; until they have traveled a while. Finally, the couple consciously deliberate the pros and cons (the third stage), and adopt permanent childlessness as a life-style (the fourth stage).

Certain forces can speed up a couple's progress through these stages. A pregnancy scare may suddenly crystallize ambiguous feelings and elicit conscious deliberation. Sometimes a decision can be triggered by reaching a particular age, such as thirty or forty, or by achieving goals that were reasons for postponement, like buying a home. For some, the experience of owning a pet leads to a more serious discussion of the responsibilities of parenthood. For others, pet ownership may serve as a kind of substitute parenthood.

People choose a childless life for a wide variety of reasons, according to Veevers. Some have always felt children had a negative effect on marriage or adult development. Others are more concerned about pregnancy, viewing it as dangerous or unattractive. Some are unwilling to give up other pursuits for parenthood, especially occupational success, particularly for women. A few seem to think that only incompetent women choose motherhood. Others express the notion that motherhood leads to female incompetence, especially fulltime motherhood (which they see as their only option). Children may also be perceived as demanding and expensive. Moreover, some adults express not only disinterest but an active dislike of children and childish things, although they are uniformly reticent about expressing such an attitude. As Veevers points out, some of these individuals have had significant experiences with unattractive, even repellant children who were monsterously spoiled or, in some cases, deformed or retarded. Others express the opinion that parenthood is a kind of martyrdom. Believing that they offer little to their own parents, they see parenthood as generally unrewarding and unrewarded.

Couples who give reasons like these generally include at least one early articulator and express a high degree of consensus about the decision to remain childless. Veevers calls these couples "rejectors" and points out that they are usually quite committed to the establishment of a satisfactory childfree life-style. When asked how he would respond if his wife became pregnant, one of Veevers's male rejectors replied that his wife would have three choices: she could have an abortion, give the child up for adoption, or get a divorce.

Veevers also describes a group of couples she calls "aficionados." Unlike rejectors, these individuals tend to be postponers. Generally, they achieve a negotiated decision but show relatively low commitment. Most aficionados like children but also express favorable attitudes toward the positive aspects of a childless life-style. They report a deep appreciation for adult privileges—for the opportunity to be spontaneous and to pursue novel experiences. They also express an abhorrence of routine and great pleasure in adult leisure activities such as travel. Aficionados delight in the freedom to work hard and the freedom to quit work if they choose. They point to the tremendous expense involved in rearing a child (a cost estimated at $100,000, although it may be even higher if family income is substantially above the average).

Veevers notes that the number of childless couples has tripled since 1960. She also reports that many childless couples achieve high levels of personal and marital adjustment. Is it possible, she asks, that they are successful as individuals and as a couple precisely because they avoid parenthood? This would seem an especially pertinent question about those individuals Veevers describes as rejectors, since they seem to include childlessness as an element of self-definition.

Whether one chooses to parent or not, to marry or not, to follow a traditional career or not, these decisions are made more comfortable by the development of an appropriate reference group, by friends. The final section of our discussion of young adulthood deals with the task of building a social circle, with the need to develop meaningful, close relationships with those outside our kinship groups, to find *kith*, intimate friends.

FRIENDS

A review of the psychological literature on the subject of friendship reveals much that is similar to the literature on choosing a marital partner. One author has even suggested that, for a middle-aged man, friends are more influential than a spouse (Bischof, 1976). Men in this age group spend a great deal of time with their friends, often more time than they spend with their families. It makes sense, then, that many of the same thoughts we found in the literature on marriage are useful in understanding friendships. For example, similarity is believed to be a central factor in the growth of friendship, and there is some controversy over the role of complementarity in friendship (Schneider, 1976).

Physical Proximity

Perhaps the most important difference between choosing friends and choosing a marriage partner (aside from biological considerations, of course) is the central role of physical proximity in one's choice of friends. In our discussion of marriage, we discovered that people who wed, often lived close to each other before marriage. For friends, propinquity appears to be the best single predictor of bonding. One classic study of friendship (Whyte, 1956) provides a clear illustration. In this investigation, William Whyte plotted the growth of friendships among people who moved into a new residential community at approximately the same time. Whyte's data document the remarkable and overwhelming effect of proximity in the form of records of invitations and social sharing among these new neighbors. Figure 5.8 presents the social records Whyte collected. Subsequent studies of friendship patterns in apartment buildings and dormitories support the conclusions of Whyte's study (Friedman, Sears, and Carlsmith, 1981).

It has been noted that proximity implies a variety of things besides physical closeness. First, proximity guarantees availability. Second, people are generally motivated to view someone who lives nearby in positive terms because it is very difficult to avoid continued interaction with a neighbor and proximity affords the opportunity for people to learn how to avoid unpleasantness. Furthermore, familiarity, far from producing contempt, most often produces feelings of attachment if not affection where there are no strong conflicts (Friedman, Sears, and Carlsmith, 1981).

Proximity may also guarantee some attitudinal similarity. Most neighborhoods are fairly homogenous with regard to socioeconomic class, race, ethnicity, and age. Evidence indicates that similarity of attitudes (Byrne, 1961) and personality characteristics (Newcomb, 1961) encourages the development of friendship.

Beyond similarity, however, certain people are more likely to have friends than others because they are congenial. People who are socially rewarding—who are associated with pleasant experiences because they are attractive, warm, and friendly—tend to form friendships more easily and more often than those who are not. One finds, for example, that physically attractive people are assigned other positive traits that are considered valuable assets in the formation of friendships (Schneider, 1976). These traits include sincerity, honesty, understanding, kindness, sympathy, a happy mood, and friendliness (Freedman et al., 1981).

Self-disclosure is critical to the progress of intimate ties. Women are more self-disclosing than men (Jourard and Lasakow, 1958), and there is evidence that women develop more intimate friendships than men (Rubin, 1983). By the end of young adulthood, in the late thirties or early forties,

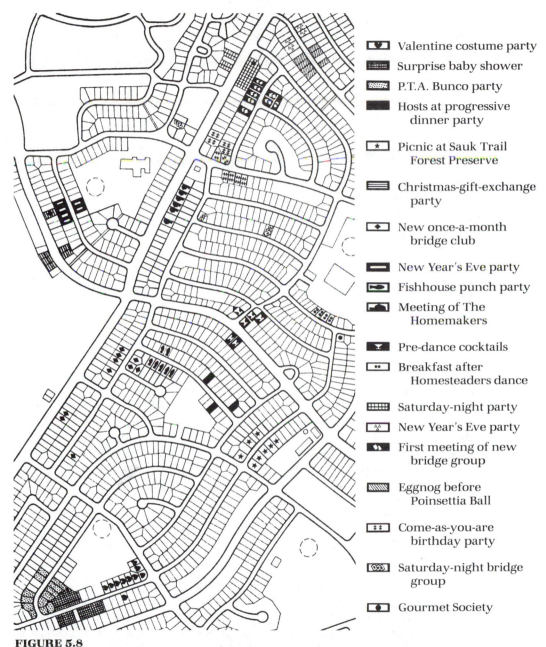

Valentine costume party

Surprise baby shower

P.T.A. Bunco party

Hosts at progressive
    dinner party

Picnic at Sauk Trail
    Forest Preserve

Christmas-gift-exchange
    party

New once-a-month
    bridge club

New Year's Eve party

Fishhouse punch party

Meeting of The
    Homemakers

Pre-dance cocktails

Breakfast after
    Homesteaders dance

Saturday-night party

New Year's Eve party

First meeting of new
    bridge group

Eggnog before
    Poinsettia Ball

Come-as-you-are
    birthday party

Saturday-night bridge
    group

Gourmet Society

FIGURE 5.8
Attendance at various social gatherings in Park Forest

SOURCE: *W. H. Whyte, Jr., The Organization Man (New York: Simon and Schuster, 1956), pp. 338–339. Copyright 1956 by William H. Whyte, Jr. Reprinted by permission of Simon and Schuster, a Division of Gulf and Western Corporation.*

most adults report that they have as many friends as they desire. People in this age bracket usually have three or four friends to whom they feel very close, although the number tends to decrease as one grows older (Haan and Day, 1974).

Friendship over Time

Levinger and Snock (1972) have suggested three stages of involvement in the development of intimate friendships. In the first stage, there is *unilateral awareness:* one person becomes aware of another and makes some tentative decisions about continuing contact. In the second, there is no self-disclosure; the interaction is called *surface contact* and is regulated by social norms and governed by social rewards. In these first two stages, proximity and similarity are important because they bring us into contact with some individuals and not others. In the final stage, *mutuality,* self-disclosure begins, a sense of commitment develops, and private norms for the regulation of the relationship emerge. Similarity and proximity create the necessary opportunity for the progress of a relationship, but absolute attributes such as honesty, sincerity, and sympathy are necessary for the interaction to proceed to the self-disclosure in stage three.

The friendships one makes as a young adult can become lifetime bonds. Relationships tend to persist over time and distance as one grows older (Hess, 1971; Lowenthal, Thurnher, and Chiriboga, 1975). In adulthood, one comes to appreciate the support and affection of old friends. In all probability, long-term friendships have an important effect on the development of identity of the adult, on feelings of continuity, and on the perception of time. How does it feel to be able to say, "Oh, we've been good friends for twenty, (thirty, forty, fifty) years. I knew them when . . ."?

SUMMARY

In this chapter, the focus of our concern has been work and family and friends in young adulthood. Each can be discussed in developmental terms, so that for our purposes it makes sense to consider the concept of a *career* not simply as a person's vocational identity but as a consistent involvement in any role over time, in both the work and the family life cycles. One may have a career as a plumber, a secretary, a corporate president, a mother, or a husband. In a sense, the study of careers is the study of change over the life span.

Researchers have outlined a number of stage models for occupational career development. In this chapter, we detailed the progress of an individual through both an external and an internal career path, placing the most emphasis on the stages of exploration and establishment. An external career path is simply a description of the objective steps in a particular career; an internal career path consists of the plans of a particular individual, plans that may involve one or more external careers.

The study of vocational choice, which has been of particular interest to psychologists, has been focused around two major schools of thought. First, we discussed the differentialist school, which suggests that career success depends on an optimal match between personality characteristics and the characteristics of individuals who have already demonstrated some degree of success in a particular field. Next, we reviewed a more developmental view, which presents the hypothesis that career choice develops in much the same way as self-concept or identity, through a series of stages from crystallization, specification, implementation, and stabilization to consolidation and advancement.

Generally, research has supported the notion that vocational success is more likely for people who choose careers that are congruent with their existing personality traits. The idea that people actually make such rational choices has been strongly challenged, however. Recent evidence also suggests that career choice is not an irreversible process, occurring in a series of stages that culminate in one's early twenties. Longitudinal studies of job satisfaction, job status, and success show that people are not likely to demonstrate inevitable increases in career commitment over time, and that as late as the age of thirty-six, nearly 40 percent of the subjects in one major study were still involved in some form of career exploration.

On the basis of such data, it has been proposed that a cyclical model of decision-making is necessary to describe career development over the life span, and that any stages that appear in such development are unlikely to show age-relatedness.

In addition to choosing a career, almost all Americans must seek out an organization in which to pursue that career. Therefore, in the first stage of career development, that of job search and recruitment, the decisions that govern organizational entry are salient issues for researchers. In particular, a good deal of work has focused on why the turnover rates for new recruits in organizations are so high. The conclusions suggest the importance of realistic recruitment procedures and of matching not only the abilities of the applicant to the job, but also the needs of a new recruit to the kinds of benefits offered by the organization.

The problems of realistic recruitment are related to another major area of thought and research: the evaluation of education, training, and anticipatory socialization. In many occupations, anticipatory socialization is so idealistic that new recruits are totally unprepared for the day-to-day reality of the job. This is an especially common problem in occupations where training is principled but the job itself involves many routine bureaucratic functions. Reality shock creates high turnover particularly in the semi-professions, like nursing and teaching, where upward mobility is limited and the rewards for settling down after the shock wears off are minimal.

The use of procedures such as stress inoculation and psychodrama, as well as more realistic recruitment practices, have been presented as solutions to the problem of reality shock. In the final analysis, however, socialization by the organization replaces the shock of reality with growing commitment to the job and the organization. Training and education, benefits and salary increases, even negative experiences like sink-or-swim situations, are all thought to contribute to occupational commitment. Research has shown that the development of commitment and, eventually, vocational success often depend on the acquisition of a powerful sponsor, or mentor. The relationship between sponsorship and upward mobility for women has been of special interest in recent years.

Issues of job commitment and success inevitably lead to an examination of job satisfaction. What do employees consider most important in return for their commitment and performance? In general, the data show that most people are actually fairly dissatisfied with their jobs, and not for the traditional reasons of economic remuneration. Today's workers want a less autocratic work environment; more flexible scheduling, not just on the job, but also over the years of employment; involvement in the decisions that affect workers' lives; and a job that offers some degree of challenge.

Recent social trends have also forced industry (and encouraged social scientists) to examine the extent of racial and sexual discrimination in the marketplace. Research has demonstrated, for instance, that despite the growing numbers of women in the work place, there has been very little change over the past few decades in the kind of jobs they hold or in the amount of money they make relative to men. It is also clear that women are less likely to be promoted than are men, whether in traditionally female jobs or not, and finally, that women are likely to be carrying the burden of housework and child care at the same time they are pursuing a fulltime career.

Racial prejudice and discrimination against blacks and other minorities are also evident in the statistics on employment and income as well as in information about life expectancy and susceptibility to the ills of urban life. Although whites today are certainly more accepting of formal equality than they were twenty years ago, there is also clear resistance to programs of school integration and affirmative action.

Unemployment for minority workers is direct evidence of some of these social problems. But the effects of prejudice and discrimination on self-concept, and even on behavior, are as yet poorly understood matters. Recent laboratory efforts have given us some insight into the process by which stereotypy affects not only the perceiver but also the target; however, the application of this research to the attitudes and behaviors of people in the social and occupational world awaits further investigation.

The data on stereotypy also suggest some interesting questions about the problems of white, middle-class males, as well as those of women and minorities. It seems likely that the acceptance and pursuit of occupational success as a way of life affects not only the length but also the quality of a white male's life.

Current research on parenting and the effect of children on adult development also suggests that stereotypy plays an important part in the lives of many men and women. Parenthood is considered by most people to be one of the most—if not the most—significant milestones in adult life. Both men and women view parenthood as a source of maturity and as an important source of life satisfaction.

Yet, most people also report that parenthood is a stressful and worrisome experience. The stereotype of the good parent, the parent well-endowed with natural love and wisdom, leaves most people unprepared for the realities of childrearing. In fact, the birth of a first child has been described as a crisis, and the evidence does suggest, at least, that most people have mixed feelings about parenthood, experiencing both joy and difficulty. This paradoxical quality of parenthood is especially clear among the parents of preschoolers.

Aside from the emotional impact of parenthood, a strong and fairly consistent impact on social behavior has been reported. The roles of husband and wife appear to be traditionalized by the birth of children. Children, especially infants, must be continuously monitored, and the greatest part of the burden falls to women, who generally do more child care and more housekeeping than men, even when both are working full-time. Yet strong role conflict between parenthood and occupation is also experienced by men, for whom the development of a coherent family role may be a critical predictor of overall life satisfaction.

The study of parenthood is further complicated by the role of timing. Couples who wait to have children until they are in their thirties or forties seem to express greater satisfaction with the progress of their experience as parents, and although they miss the intimacy of living without children, they are more sensitive to changes in their marriage that require attention than are younger couples.

In addition to differences caused by timing, there are definite sex differences in the experience of parenthood. For women, children often mean that occupational aspirations must be put aside, at least temporarily. Or they may find themselves under great stress trying to do everything at once, and do it all well. Changes in sex-role behavior have provided women with the opportunity to pursue a career outside the home at the same time they fulfill the roles of mother and wife; however, the social changes that are needed to support them in this attempt are not immediately forthcoming.

Of course, women also report immensely important emotional advantages to motherhood. They feel a sense of joy and interdependence in their marriages, and take pleasure in the feeling of family and a general enrichment in the meaning of marriage. Men report many of these same feelings, but until a few years ago, the infant-father and father-child relationships were relatively unexplored. Some have even argued that the father's role in the contemporary family is so diluted by cultural factors as to be unimportant.

Throughout the mid to late 1970s, however, research on infant-father interactions began to change the image of fathering, at least insofar as that image is projected by the psychological literature. Studies of couples starting families showed that fathers experienced childbirth as a profoundly moving experience and that infants demonstrate strong attachment to their fathers very early on. Evidence also suggests that fathers spend much more time in play with their infants than do mothers and that later, during their children's second year of life, they begin to pay more attention to male children and less to females. This focus of paternal attention and time may be an important factor in the sex-role development of both males and females.

The extent to which differences in the behaviors of mothers and fathers are biologically based is, not surprisingly, a matter of controversy among researchers. At least one major theorist has suggested, for example, that parenthood constitutes a biological imperative that traditionalizes the behavior of males and females. Although there is some evidence that men and women behave in less traditional ways later in life, it is difficult to say whether the conservative impact of parenting is a reflection of some biological imperative. Moreover, recent, dramatic social changes in the experience of work and family over the life cycle suggest at the least that if biological directives do exist, their effect is minimal.

Current research demonstrates, for instance, that many men feel a growing concern for the importance of parenting in their lives and are beginning to resent the emphasis society places on the role of breadwinner as a defining set of behaviors for them. As fathers contemplate stepping back some from the marketplace, mothers are working in ever growing numbers, apparently with no more negative effects on the development of children than occur in families in which mothers do not work.

Given the conflicting and complicated effects children and parenting have on the lives of adults, it is not surprising to learn that a growing number of people are choosing not to have children at all. Moreover, many adults find their situations even more complex because divorce and separation leave them in the position of rearing a family alone, or because remarriage requires that families be blended and that one partner take on the role of stepparent.

The number of single heads of household has doubled over the last decade, and many, if not most, of them must deal with difficult financial problems as well as the difficulties of meeting the demands of young children alone, or the social isolation of being single. Although little is known about stepparenting, this role too appears to pose some special problems and would seem especially worthy of more research since so many remarriages involve children under the age of eighteen.

There is at least some data on the decision to remain childless, however, thanks in large part to the efforts of one dedicated researcher. In her extensive study of couples without children, Jean Veevers has distinguished between early articulators and postponers. Early articulators tend to see the decision not to parent as a characteristic of the self rather than as a product of their marriage. Postponers, on the other hand, seem to progress through a series of stages, moving toward a more conscious choice of a childless life-style. Postponers are also more likely to see that choice as a product of their situation, and to choose a childless life-style because of the positive pleasures afforded by adult living rather than as a rejection of parenthood.

This chapter concludes with a consideration of one other important developmental arena for the young adult, the establishment of a circle of friends. Like marriage, friendship seems to depend, to large extent, on such factors as perceived similarity. Perhaps this is one of the reasons why so much of the research on friendship shows that proximity is an excellent predictor of who will become friends with whom, for people of the same socioeconomic class, educational background, race, ethnicity, and so forth are likely to live near one another. Proximity also guarantees availability and provides a motive for getting along well with someone as well as offering the time necessary to do so.

Over time, friendship progresses through surface contact to mutuality, characterized by increasing self-disclosure and a growing sense of commitment. Such attributes as honesty, sincerity, and sympathy are necessary for the interaction to proceed beyond the surface contact offered by physical proximity.

The friendships one makes in young adulthood can last a lifetime and persist not only over time but also over distance, affecting the development of identity and intimacy throughout the adult life span.

Perspectives

The Future and Young Adulthood

Alvin Toffler pointed out over a decade ago in Future Shock *(1970) that if we are to have a future at all, we had best think about how we want it to be and what we might do to channel the changes taking place in the world. For a social scientist, and especially for a student who wants to be a social scientist, it makes a special kind of sense to speculate about the future. If we are to formulate sophisticated research, it is very useful to try to anticipate the most likely course of human events beforehand. Longitudinal or sequential research designs require that one choose the kinds of methods and measures and ask the questions that will still be meaningful in five or ten or twenty years, often more.*

If predicting the future with any degree of accuracy remains beyond our reach, it is still prudent to consider the implications of some alternative scenarios. To begin with, the whole concept of young adulthood itself is a relatively new idea and likely to be redefined in a variety of ways over the next few decades, particularly since research on this part of the life span is currently so sparse. Few studies address this part of the life cycle specifically, in the way that childhood or adolescence or middle age and later life have

been examined. Consider, for example, the number of sociological and psychological journals that deal with the aged, including the Gerontologist, Journal of Gerontology, Experimental Aging Research, *and* Geriatrics. *Next, think about the number of books, as well as articles and conferences, that have focused on the problems of the middle aged;* Men at Midlife *by Farrell and Rosenberg (1981),* Past and Present in Middle Life *(Eichorn, et al., 1981),* Being and Becoming Old *(Hendricks, 1980), and* Women over Forty *(Block, Davidson, and Grambs, 1981) are only a few that we will be using in the next section of this book.*

In contrast, of the references used to prepare Chapters 3, 4, and 5, on young adulthood, none deals specifically with that period of the life span. All the literature referenced in Chapters 3, 4, and 5 is found in articles and books that deal either with the entire adult life span or with the topic at issue—marriage, divorce, friendship, and so on. This is despite the fact that we have been looking at the establishment phase of adult life, encompassing more than twenty years, during which one ordinarily experiences the fullest simultaneous participation in many of the major roles of adulthood, including spouse, parent, friend, worker, and citizen.

Given the length and complexity of this period, one of the important trends likely to affect the definition of young adulthood is the continuing differentiation of the life span into ever narrowing age strata. Age strata are those age groups a society recognizes in terms of changing demands, expectations, and privileges. Even now, there is evidence that at least one new stage, called youth, *may be emerging, at least for members of the middle class, at the end of adolescence and before the commitments of adulthood (marriage, parenting, career) are made. Kenneth Keniston (1970) has argued that the extension of higher education through the early and even mid-twenties has produced a period of "disengagement" from adult society and the opportunity to postpone adulthood. He believes that for many this period offers the opportunity for increased exposure to people who hold different beliefs and operate from different moral frameworks than those one grew up with. He contends that exposure to new ideas and the discovery of corruption in one's own social institutions are shaping the developmental tasks of this period.*

For those individuals who go on to college, especially for those who are able to live away from home, the period from seventeen or eighteen to twenty-two or twenty-three may offer the leisure to question the conventional moral and cultural wisdom of their social system, suggesting an important example of interaction or transaction between maturational forces and the environment. Only when certain cultural experiences are present at a particular time of life does the possibility of such a stage occur.

And what of those who do not go on to college during this period? We know that working-class people tend to say that middle age begins earlier than do middle-class people. Does this mean that working-class adults skip the period Keniston calls youth altogether? In particular, what happens to those who are unable to find rewarding jobs and are also denied access to higher education? The characteristics of young adult life for those who send their youth drifting from one place to another, for those who are chronically underemployed or who become involved in crime or drug addiction, should be defined. While the middle class enjoys the leisure to question social and moral values, do less affluent individuals reject those values out of hostility or despair?

What impact does either of these kinds of experience have on the tasks assigned to late adolescence and early adulthood: the consolidation of identity and the establishment of intimacy?

It is unrealistic to think that the task of formulating an identity is completed at the end of adolescence. Identity is never really fixed, but is continually reshaped by the changing roles and relationships that characterize the life span. Moreover, as historical time changes, there is probably also a change in the framework by which most people choose to define themselves. It may be that the task of identity formation has become so complex in modern societies that the period Keniston calls youth has emerged in response to the need for additional time. Veroff, Douvan, and Kulka (1981) have shown that young people are much less likely to use the traditional social roles as guides to identity formation. These authors believe that such weak ties to the social structure make the formation of identity more difficult and may also increase the social distance between any two people, since it is less likely that they will share the same social reality.

Of course, one of the major changes in those social roles is in the area of sex-role identity. Without a doubt, the question of sex differences will continue to be a major research issue in the study of adult life. As we look at current trends, there seems to be every reason to expect continuing change. As Issac Asimov (1981) wrote in Change!, "The aims of feminism will . . . no longer be the property of activists alone—it has already grown respectable and will have to become the settled and serious policy of society in general. The vast change in attitude will be brought about not by the angry or subtle persuasions of speeches, resolutions, or books, but as the inevitable consequence of the falling birthrate that the world will experience and want to continue to experience" (p. 11). Fewer and fewer women will have large families, and those that do choose to have children will probably devote less of their lives to mothering.

In this light, constant replication of the sex-role literature is in order. Time-lag studies (the design where the researcher tests the same age group over and over again at different times of measurement) would seem especially enlightening in the study of sex-role change. As society begins to acknowledge the importance of occupation in the lives of modern women, we might well expect that the development of identity and intimacy will be affected.

Current information on identity development in women shows that most experience a growing sense of self throughout most of the adult years (Marcia, 1980). One wonders if an emphasis on occupational choice might lead women to formulate a stronger, more stable identity earlier in adulthood, a pattern far more typical of males. How might that affect the growth of intimacy and mate selection?

Decreasing family size and increasing social pressure to stabilize the population are bound to have powerful effects on intimacy and mate selection. Some of these will be indirect, such as the effects we might expect from changes in sex-role behavior. Some will be more obvious. Smaller families mean less time must be devoted to the rearing of children. More and more years will be spent in the empty nest, especially if the average life span can be expected to increase. Already there is evidence that people are choosing to use some of that "empty nest" time before childbearing rather than afterward. The postponement of childbearing is a major demographic trend and has contributed to the emergence of the stage we called "youth." What other effects will be produced? If people postpone childbearing, they will probably also postpone marriage. We know that age at marriage is a good predictor of divorce. Is it possible that the divorce rate will stabilize or even decline if people wait longer to marry? Or will the extension of the life span and the decline of family size continue to push the divorce rate up?

Declining family size also allows people to choose childlessness and to opt for singlehood. As the social reality changes, it is no longer necessary for young people to marry in order to achieve success in adult life. The single man or woman is no longer a social outcast. Yet people continue to express a great need for social closeness and warmth in personal relationships. There is evidence, for example, that meaningful personal relationships are more important in the lives of young men than ever before (Douvan, 1975). What kinds of alternatives are likely to arise in these circumstances?

We will certainly have to redefine pair bonding in a way that makes more sense. Today, we do not even have the words to describe many of the relationships that exist in everyday life. What do you call the man or woman you live with and share a sex life with? What if you live with a person of the opposite sex, but do not share a sex life? What do you call someone with whom you have a sexual relationship but only occasionally share living quarters? The psychological and social realities of people's lives are often reflected in the words we have—or, in this case, do not have. American social relationships have become far more complex than the language permits, and the psychological impact of these relationships has never been examined. This seems a very important direction for researchers interested in the realities of young adulthood in the twentieth century.

In the arena of work, we can also expect some impressive changes. The one development most likely to affect the nature of work is the growth of the information-processing industry. It has been repeatedly suggested that the use of personal computers will allow a huge number of people who are currently isolated from the labor force to hook in via computer terminal or telephone. Might this include many young adults who might not otherwise be able to work? The college student or the young mother, the single parent or the handicapped person, may enter the work force in great numbers if work can be carried with them and done at any convenient time. It is even possible that relatively young adolescents could enter a work force where computer literacy was more important than work experience.

Computers will also revolutionize the traditional educational system that occupies such a large part of the life space of late adolescence and young adulthood. One could go to school at home, drop out from time to time, return at leisure. Information processing could, theoretically, make the finest education available to all who are capable, wherever they reside. Programmed learning could make literacy of all sorts—from reading and writing to computer technology—cheap, painless, and tailored to the individual. The impact of this technology on adolescents and young adults is likely to be the strongest, and now is the time to begin formulating the issues. The study of computers and their impact on society and on the lives of individuals is one of the most exciting frontiers of social and psychological research in adult development.

Finally, what physiological and biological forces might we expect to affect young adulthood? The use of drugs and alcohol, changes in diet and health habits, and improvements in the delivery of mental and medical health services are bound to change the way adult life is lived, from beginning to end. People are increasingly aware of the way stress affects both the quality and the length of their lives. Stress management, vitamin supplements, and regular exercise are more and more often routine, starting from the moment of

*birth. There are exercise classes for preg-
nant mothers, even ones for infants. Certainly, we can expect this growing
emphasis on preventative health care to
change the quality of middle age and later
life, but might not we also expect an impact on young adulthood (and especially
on work, a major source of stress)? People are demanding more flexible work
hours, more control over the design of
their work environment, and greater sensitivity to their needs as family members
outside the workplace.*

  *Might not these same concerns also
affect the nature of family life? If people
are to cope successfully with the stresses
of combining work and family, family is
also quite likely to change. Child-care facilities may become widespread; time off
for exercise class and relaxation become
a mandate; household help an essential;
children expected to behave more respon-
sibly. The challenge, as a June 1983* Time
*magazine pointed out in its cover article
on the subject, is "for each person to find
the level of manageable stress that invigo-
rates life instead of ravaging it" (p. 54).
Meeting that challenge will undoubtedly
have some spectacular effects on almost
all of our daily roles and activities, from
young adulthood through the last stages of
the life span.*

III

Middle Age

Chapter 6

The Inner Context: Biology and Cognition in Middle Age

The youth gets together materials for a bridge to the moon, and at length the middle-aged man decides to make a woodshed with them.

HENRY DAVID THOREAU

Until the early 1970s, anyone interested in the psychology of middle age would have been hard-pressed to find even the most rudimentary descriptive research. The years between forty and sixty generated little interest in experimental academic circles. Some clinical psychologists seemed dimly aware of the special circumstances of adults at midlife (Jacobs and Ritchie, 1961) but no one had approached the topic systematically. One might find an occasional reference to involutional melancholia in menopausal women or stumble on a few relevant remarks on cardiovascular disease in the medical literature. But, basically, development in the middle years was unexplored, and the now popular controversy over midlife crisis had not yet begun.

The next three chapters present some of the issues and questions that have now been raised about development during middle age. You will not find adequate solutions and explanations. We have less information about the middle-aged population than about any other age group in the life course. In fact, much of the data presented in Chapters 6, 7, and 8 has been gleaned from studies that focused primarily on other age groups. Adults between forty and sixty are often included in a study because a researcher needs a comparison group or control group, or simply because the format for presentation of results requires three age groups rather than the more common design requiring only two (young and old). The performance or behavior of the middle group is usually of no intrinsic interest to the reporter.

Undoubtedly, the general disinterest in the psychology of middle-aged people has reflected the prevailing cultural stereotype of midlife. Middle-aged people are considered pillars of society, conservative, dependable, and dull. Americans have traditionally regarded middle age as a stable, comfortable, predictable stage of life, a time of little excitement or change (Aronsen, 1966). Only in the last few years has midlife been considered unique and interesting by the lay audience or by academic researchers. Yet, as we shall see in this chapter, the years between forty and sixty may be second only to the teen-age years in the degree of biological, psychological, and social change experienced by most individuals.

Most of the existing information about midlife concerns the areas of biology and cognition. For example, of the three major works covering the subject of middle age that were published in 1977, one (Finch and Hayflick) is entirely devoted to the biology of aging, while another (Birren and Schaie) contains a great deal of information on physiology, perception, sensation, psychomotor performance, and the relationship between stress and disease. (The third volume, Binstock and Shanas, reviews research on the sociology of aging.)

In 1982, the *Handbook of Developmental Psychology* (Wolman, 1982) arrived. It offers only one chapter devoted exclusively to middle age (compared, for example, with eight chapters examining adolescence). Again, one must peruse the chapters on aging for information on the psychology of the middle aged. Progress is slow. But one chapter is better than no mention at all: at least research is underway that should gradually increase our understanding of this middle era in adult life.

We will begin our own review of what is known about the biology and cognition of middle age with a general description of body function and change, focusing most sharply on alterations in physical appearance and the relationship between stress and disease. Health problems and changes in appearance are the most obvious biological markers in the middle years of adulthood, and the ones that trouble middle-aged people the most. We will turn next to the unique biological events of middle age—the hormonal and reproductive changes so often considered the most influential at this stage of life, particularly for women—and, then, to the literature on sensation, perception, and psychomotor performance. In the final section of the chapter we will examine the cognitive and intellectual developments of midlife. A review of the developmental tasks of middle age is included to provide a context for the psychological and social issues discussed in Chapters 7 and 8.

THE BIOLOGY OF MIDDLE AGE

Appearance

For most of us, middle age makes its debut in the mirror. There is no need for sophisticated analysis of bone structure or the collagen content of the tissues; the burgeoning health and beauty industries in this country stand as testimonial to how most Americans react to the likenesses that stare back at them from over the bathroom sink.

The earliest physical sign that one is approaching midlife is increasing body weight and change in girth measurements. Most people are the heaviest they will be in their lives between the ages of thirty-five and fifty-nine, and the pounds add up very quickly after forty or forty-five. Weight gain is particularly rapid for middle-aged women (Kleemeer, 1959), who may feel that their extra pounds are less harmoniously distributed. The middle-aged man or woman is likely to carry excess baggage in the trunk of the body, rather than in the legs, as younger people do. A woman may

"Middle age is when your age begins to show around your middle."
Bob Hope

find that her waistline is much less defined than it used to be, and a man may need an extra inch or two (or four) at the end of his belt.

Everywhere in the body, fat is being redistributed. Middle age is a festival of lipid migration—fatty tissues disappear from the lips, breasts, and eyelids and orbits of the eye. The upper lip in particular begins to look much thinner, and the breasts lose their tone. The eyelids become more wrinkled and transparent, and the eyes may appear somewhat sunken. Although these changes are progressive, of course, and neither begin nor end in midlife, people seem most conscious of them during the middle years.

BONE AND CONNECTIVE TISSUE.   Changes in the bones and connective tissues contribute to the physical metamorphosis middle-aged people experience. The skin becomes thinner and flatter wherever it is constantly exposed to the environment (the face, hands, and forearms in particular). (In contrast, the unexposed skin of the back and buttocks changes very little in thickness over the years from twenty-five to seventy-six.) Most epidermal atrophy seems to be produced by exposure to the ultraviolet rays of the sun; so anyone who is really intent on preserving a youthful appearance would be wise to forgo the pleasures of sun worship. Darker complexions are less affected by sun, and the most dramatic change is usually seen in blue-eyed or green-eyed blonds and redheads. Black skin fares quite well and retains a youthful appearance longer than white skin (Selmanowitz, Rizer, and Orentreich, 1977).

You will remember from Chapter 3 that collagen progressively replaces other tissue proteins and produces increasing stiffness, while the remaining elastin becomes cross-linked and calcified. Skin loses so much elasticity by old age that it does not snap back when pulled up between the thumb and index finger but returns to its original position slowly. The skin also becomes coarser and more sallow as people grow older, and the hair not only grays but also stiffens as the hair follicles age. Hair is lost when the follicles begin to degenerate.

Some striking changes are apparent in the face. The nasal tip gets thicker; the straightness of the nasal profile decreases. The size of the eye opening seems diminished, and the effect is exaggerated by changes in the nose. The teeth wear down, and the vertical dimension of the face is reduced by changes in the structure of the bones (Brown, 1953; Selmanowitz et al., 1977). Moreover, as the eyes become increasingly opaque, a gray or yellowish ring may appear at the edge of the cornea. Figure 6.1 presents an example of changes in the face over the years of adult life.

Changes are noticeable in even the smallest ways. The rate of nail growth declines by 40 percent during the adult years, for example, and the nails become opaque and sometimes yellow or gray with age. Nails may also take on a ridged appearance (you may notice this already in your toenails), and they begin to show a tendency to split in layers. Age or "liver" spots proliferate and accumulate, especially on the hands.

PSYCHOLOGICAL REACTIONS. Middle-aged people—especially middle-aged women—register the physical transformations, both great and small, and worry about their appearance. Susan Sontag (1977), for one, believes women are especially sensitive to the changes of middle age because of our "double standard of aging": desirable women are young and beautiful, lithe and smooth. Aging decreases a woman's value. Middle-aged women often feel sexually ineligible at a depressingly early age. Sontag contends that such feelings are behind the tremendous demand for cosmetics and the growing popularity of plastic surgery among women at midlife: "A woman's face is the canvas upon which she paints a revised, corrected version of herself" (p. 290). That face is acceptable only as long as it remains unchanged, calm, unwrinkled. Older women are commonly viewed not only as ugly, Sontag argues, but as disgusting and sexually obscene. Despite

Age 25

Age 59

FIGURE 6.1
Changes in the face
during late middle
age

recent media hoopla about older women and younger men, there is still a fierce taboo about such sexual or romantic relationships, especially when the woman is middle aged or more and her male partner is fifteen or twenty years younger. Contrast that attitude with the casual acceptance (even the expectation) that older men will seek—and receive—the attentions of young women.

Midlife changes in physical appearance affect the judgments middle-aged women make about their own appearance more than such changes affect the judgment of other age groups of both men and women. Expressed concern about facial beauty peaks between forty-five and fifty-five. Women in these years seem particularly worried that the accumulating marks of time and experience will make them uninteresting to their spouses. They doubt the sincerity of their husbands' sexual advances. Many also exaggerate the unattractiveness and minimize the physical assets of other middle-aged women. Women of other age groups and men of all ages do not view women at midlife with as critical an eye (Nowak, 1977).

Lillian Troll (1977) has summarized the stereotype of the older woman in three words: "poor, dumb, and ugly." Troll maintains that until society values the experience written in a woman's face as much as it values worldliness on the face of a man, women will worry about appearance, spend enormous amounts of time and money on everything from turtle oil to diet pills, and feel they are condemned to sexless older years.

If you are a woman, especially a middle-aged woman, you have been taught to believe that physical attractiveness is a woman's most valuable asset. One day you discover your major asset is dwindling, and you begin to question the value of all your other assets. When you walk into a room and no one notices, you may begin to wonder about your social competence and your intelligence as well as your sexual allure. If the anxiety feeds on itself, you may feel uncomfortable in social situations and withdraw, experiencing even less approval and becoming even more withdrawn. Even if it never affects you that strongly, there is a sense of outrage that a forty-five-year-old woman should be "old" while the man she graduated with from high school is "in his prime." The gray in his temples is a mark of distinction, the lines in his face reflect his knowledge of the world, and he is respected and admired by old and young alike.

None of this means, however, that men sail through middle age without a care in the world. In fact, the literature suggests that middle-aged men often experience severe crises at midlife. They question their goals and values. They wonder if they have not missed the emotional, personal side of life in the process of building a career and acquiring worldly goods. They often see themselves as failures, even in the role of provider and worker. There is evidence, furthermore, that despite the fading of the bloom of youth, middle-aged women actually feel relatively positive about their general life situation, experiencing new freedoms and opportunities when their children leave home. Men often envy their wives these new pleasures and the chance to do something totally different with their lives. It is just that the problems of men and women at midlife differ, and for women aging is often summed up by what they see in their mirrors.

Health

One of the most important gauges of male aging is the height of the mercury during a blood pressure test. Many a middle-aged man spends increasing amounts of time in "body monitoring," fretting over the state of his health and the general condition of his physical machinery. Wives seem to pick up this concern, worrying about the health of their spouses far more often than middle-aged husbands worry over the health of their wives (Neugarten, 1968b).

Body monitoring probably reflects the very real vulnerability of the middle-aged man to life-threatening diseases. Death rates in middle age due to malignant neoplasms, vascular lesions, heart disease, ulcers, and infection are considerably above those of the general population. The mortality rates for males are higher than those for females in nearly every category and subtype of disorder.

Cardiovascular disease is the leading cause of death among the middle aged, accounting for nearly 40 percent of all deaths in this age group. Four out of five victims of heart attacks are men. Table 6.1 provides more information about the major causes of death among the middle aged and compares the figures for middle-aged people with figures for young adults and older adults.

In highly industrialized countries, where the average life span is more than seventy years, to die at forty-five is to die prematurely. The major causes for these premature deaths are cancer and cardiovascular disease, in part because people in technologically advanced nations generally survive the childhood infections common in less industrialized countries and therefore have time to develop some of the diseases typical of older people. Although medical advances lengthen lives, industrialization has also fostered environmental problems—pollution, radiation, and the proliferation of some chemical agents in food, water, and the atmosphere—that are important determinants of malignancy. Genetic background, viral infection, and hormonal imbalance influence cancer rates as well. So do related changes in the autoimmune system (Timiras, 1972). Theories about the etiology of cancer and cardiovascular diseases must account for the increased incidence of these ailments with age.

PERSONALITY TYPE.   It has been suggested that psychological as well as physiological factors play a role in the higher rates of cancer among people in industrialized countries. Because high levels of stress are a significant fact of life in technological societies, the relationship between stress and cancer warrants exploration. However, there is little data on the subject at this time. That is not true for the experimental study of heart disease, in which much has been made of the association between stress, life-style, personality, and susceptibility to coronary heart disease (CHD) and hypertension among middle-aged males.

The role of anxiety in CHD has become increasingly apparent, for example. Through most of middle age, the number of physical symptoms men report is related to anxiety, and hypertensive men of all ages report more physical and psychological symptoms. Longitudinal studies of the relationship between cardiovascular disease and personality show a clear relationship between the development of CHD and level of anxiety (Siegler, Nowlin, and Blumenthal, 1980).

Advancing age, elevated blood pressure, and high serum cholesterol, as well as obesity and smoking, are all associated with cardiovascular disease. Since factors like age or serum cholesterol level do not predict new

TABLE 6.1
Order of eleven leading causes of death, by death rate[a] for seven age groups, 1976

Total	25–34	35–44	45–54	55–64	65–74	75–84	85+
Diseases of the heart (337.2)	Accidents	Malignant neoplasm	Diseases of the heart	Diseases of the heart	Diseases of the heart	Diseases of the heart	Diseases of the heart
Malignant neoplasm (175.8)	Suicide	Diseases of the heart	Malignant neoplasm	Malignant neoplasm	Malignant neoplasm	Malignant neoplasm	Malignant neoplasm
Cerebrovascular disease (87.9)	Malignant neoplasm	Accidents	Accidents	Cerebrovascular disease	Cerebrovascular disease	Cerebrovascular disease	Cerebrovascular disease
Accidents (46.9)	Diseases of the heart	Cirrhosis	Cirrhosis	Accidents	Influenza and pneumonia	Influenza and pneumonia	Influenza and pneumonia
Influenza and pneumonia (28.8)	Cirrhosis	Suicide	Cerebrovascular disease	Cirrhosis	Diabetes	Diabetes	Arteriosclerosis
Diabetes (16.1)	Cerebrovascular disease	Cerebrovascular disease	Suicide	Diabetes	Accidents	Arteriosclerosis	Accidents
Cirrhosis (14.7)	Influenza and pneumonia	Influenza and pneumonia	Influenza and pneumonia	Influenza and pneumonia	Bronchitis, emphysema, and asthma	Accidents	Diabetes
Arteriosclerosis (13.7)	Diabetes	Diabetes	Diabetes	Bronchitis, emphysema, and asthma	Cirrhosis	Bronchitis, emphysema, and asthma	Bronchitis, emphysema, and asthma
Suicide (12.5)	Bronchitis, emphysema, and asthma	Bronchitis, emphysema, and asthma	Bronchitis, emphysema, and asthma	Suicide	Arteriosclerosis	Cirrhosis	Suicide
Bronchitis, emphysema, and asthma (11.4)	Arteriosclerosis	Arteriosclerosis	Arteriosclerosis	Arteriosclerosis	Suicide	Suicide	Cirrhosis

[a]Death rate per 100,000 estimated population per age group.

SOURCE: U.S. Department of Health, Education, and Welfare, *Monthly Vital Statistics Report, Final Mortality Statistics, 1976* (Washington, D.C.: U.S. Government Printing Office, March 30, 1978), pp. 20–21.

cases of CHD very well, however, many researchers expect to find that more specific personality traits combine with these factors to discriminate between those who develop CHD and those who do not. Although such attempts have been pursued since the early 1940s (Siegler, Nowlin, and Blumenthal, 1980), the most famous of these studies is the work of Rosenman and Friedman on the Type A behavior pattern.

Working with a large group of men between the ages of thirty-nine and fifty-nine, Rosenman and Friedman established a profile of the lives of people who seemed most likely eventually to suffer a heart attack. Dubbing their profile the Type A personality, they described Type A behavior as competitive and achievement oriented, aggressive, restless, and often hostile or impatient (see Figure 6.2). Rosenman and Friedman also outlined a contrasting profile, Type B, which is characterized by nonaggressive, patient, easygoing, and relaxed behavior. The Type A person seems to have a habitual tendency to increase the pace of life. He (or, less often, she) may be verbally explosive or argumentative and may always seem to have a grimace on his face (because of facial tension). In fact, interview data suggest that facial expression and speech style and volume are the most consistent clues to the Type A personality. In the group Rosenman and Friedman originally studied, about 10 percent of the men were classified as fully developed Type A, whereas another 10 percent were true to Type B (Friedman and Rosenman, 1974; Siegler, Nowlin, and Blumenthal, 1980).

Follow-up studies have demonstrated dramatic differences in the health of Type A and Type B men. Type A patterns were associated with

Cartoon by Jim M'Guinness

FIGURE 6.2
The type A personality

elevation in serum cholesterol levels, accelerated blood coagulation, and high daytime excretion of some of the stress hormones (Rosenman, Friedman, Straus, Jenkins, Zyzanski, Wurm, and Kositchek, 1970). Men who engaged in fully developed Type A behavior were twice as prone to CHD as those who exhibited Type B patterns.

Furthermore, it seems that CHD rarely if ever occurs before seventy *except* among those who live Type A lives. It doesn't even seem to matter how much fatty food a Type B man consumes, how many cigarettes he smokes, or how much exercise he gets: he probably will not die a premature cardiac death. Evidence is also accumulating that Type A behavior produces identical risks in women and men (Eisdorfer and Wilkie, 1977).

Of course, not everyone who is a victim of CHD leads a Type A life. Many of the men in the Rosenman and Friedman studies could not be classified as either fully developed Type A or Type B, and even an occasional Type B suffers a heart attack.

STRESS. General life stress may also play a role in increasing the potential for heart disease among those who are full Type As and among the few Type Bs who develop CHD. The likelihood of a heart attack has been associated with a significant increase in the number and type of life changes—alterations in relationships, activities, or environments—an individual experiences during any six-month to one-year period (Theorell and Rahe, 1974). The Holmes and Rahe Social Readjustment Rating Scale (SRRS) has been used to evaluate the degree of life change experienced by heart disease patients prior to the onset of the disease. The scale allows one to assign a particular number of points to each of a variety of major life events. The points are totaled over a limited time span for a given individual. Those who are assigned the greatest number of points for the time span are also those who most often suffer ill health in the following six months to one year (Holmes and Rahe, 1967). Table 6.2 presents the version of the SRRS we discussed in Chapter 2. You might want to check your score.

Refinements of the Holmes and Rahe Scale have been even more strongly associated with health, psychological symptoms, morale, self-concept, and life satisfaction than the original (Chiriboga, and Cutler, 1980; Horowitz, and Wilner, 1980). For instance, the version devised by David Chiriboga and Loraine Cutler (1980) not only expanded the 42 events on the original Holmes and Rahe scale to 138 items but also asked subjects to personally evaluate the impact of every item checked, by assigning points to each event themselves. Subjects were also required to evaluate whether a particular event was a negative or a positive stress.

Using their refined scale, Chiriboga and Cutler have found that although young adults seem to experience the highest levels of stress (be-

TABLE 6.2
The social readjustment rating scale

Life event	Mean value
1. Death of spouse	100
2. Divorce	73
3. Marital separation	65
4. Jail term	63
5. Death of close family member	63
6. Personal injury or illness	53
7. Marriage	50
8. Fired at work	47
9. Marital reconciliation	45
10. Retirement	45
11. Change in health of family member	44
12. Pregnancy	40
13. Sex difficulties	39
14. Gain of new family member	39
15. Business readjustment	39
16. Change in financial state	38
17. Death of close friend	37
18. Change to different line of work	36
19. Change in number of arguments with spouse	35
20. Mortgage over $10,000	31
21. Foreclosure of mortgage or loan	30
22. Change in responsibilities at work	29
23. Son or daughter leaving home	29
24. Trouble with in-laws	29
25. Outstanding personal achievement	28
26. Wife begin or stop work	26
27. Begin or end school	26
28. Change in living conditions	25
29. Revision of personal habits	24
30. Trouble with boss	23
31. Change in work hours or conditions	20
32. Change in residence	20
33. Change in schools	20
34. Change in recreation	19
35. Change in church activities	19
36. Change in social activities	18
37. Mortgage or loan less than $10,000	17
38. Change in sleeping habits	16
39. Change in number of family get-togethers	15
40. Change in eating habits	15
41. Vacation	13
42. Christmas	12
43. Minor violations of the law	11

SOURCE: T. H. Holmes and R. H. Rahe, "The Social Readjustment Scale," *Journal of Psychosomatic Research*, 11 (1967): 216.

Stress is ubiquitous in the everyday lives of those who live in complex societies. Even the most routine problems require concentration, speed, and patience.

cause they report a larger number of events), middle-aged people show the biggest increase in number of positive stresses as well as the highest number of negative family stresses. According to their findings, middle age represents both a crisis and a challenge for most people—a time of both negative and positive change.

Whether stress is positive *(eustress)* or negative *(distress)*, (Selye, 1976), the body undergoes a wide variety of physiological changes. The totality of these changes has been called the *General Adaptation Syndrome*, a term that describes the mobilization of the Sympathetic Nervous System (SNS). Whether you win the Academy Award (eustress), or find yourself in an automobile accident (distress), SNS mobilization produces changes in the cardiovascular, hormonal, respiratory, and temperature systems of the body. Such changes ensure more acute audition and vision (as you wait for Robert Redford to announce your name, or careen toward the open area on the right shoulder of the road). Glycogen is transformed into glucose for quick energy, and endorphins, the natural painkillers produced by the body, are released (just in case you lose the award or miss the shoulder). It has been argued that the continuous stimulation of urban life produces so much stress and so little opportunity for physical release (you probably will not screech with joy if you win or punch the driver of the other car), that people are constantly "overmobilized," eventuating in stress-related diseases of all sorts (Selye, 1976; Insel and Roth, 1982).

Heart attacks are not the only expression of cardiovascular disease, of course. The heart is only one part of the system. Changes in the blood vessels are also apparent by middle age. The large arteries become markedly less elastic with time. Stiffness of these blood vessels doubles between the ages of twenty and sixty and is related to the rising incidence of high blood pressure among subjects in longitudinal studies (Kohn, 1977).

Arteriosclerosis and *atherosclerosis* are diseases of the blood vessels that have in common the thickening of the arterial walls. Although both are related to high blood pressure and high serum cholesterol levels, the exact relation between blood pressure, cholesterol, and changes in the arteries remains something of a mystery (Robbins, 1967). The incidence of atherosclerosis increases in men after the age of forty, leveling off around age fifty-five; rates for women continue to rise until about age sixty-five.

In atherosclerosis, lesions or injuries to the arterial walls appear. The number of lesions increases with the passage of the years. Fat, cholesterol, collagen, mucopoly sacchrides, and small capillaries build up on the site of the lesions, forming *plaques*. The elastin fibers that make up the walls of blood vessels are split and fragmented at the site of the lesion. Plaques can be pictured as sandbars or reefs in the bloodstream, restricting flow through the arteries. Arteriosclerosis involves the same kinds of events as atherosclerosis, but occurs in smaller blood vessels and does not usually involve the formation of plaques. Often the words *arteriosclerosis* and *atherosclerosis* are used interchangeably (Robbins, 1967). It has been said that the changes in the large arteries and other blood vessels constitute a basic aging process, one that is intrinsic to the cells and tissues and is progressive, universal, and irreversible (Kohn, 1977).

The role of stress or environmental factors in the progress of arterial degeneration has not yet been clarified. We do know, however, that the General Adaptation Syndrome becomes less efficient with age. According to Hans Selye (1976), this nonspecific biological response has three stages. The first, called *alarm*, is accompanied by all the physiological mobilization changes we described above. The second stage, *resistance*, permits the body to repair whatever damage has been done during the first stage; but if stress continues unabated, adaptation is lost and the final stage, *exhaustion*, occurs. If Selye's stages are an accurate description, resistance may require more time in later life, and exhaustion may occur sooner.

It also takes longer for an older person to recover from stress because more hormones and other chemicals are required to produce alarm in the elderly. Therefore, researchers have been particularly interested in how aging of the endocrine system affects one's response to stress and disease (Timiras, 1972). As yet, however, no one has pinpointed the endocrine changes that are critical in the decreased efficiency of stress reactions. Relatively little is known about the action of individual hormones, and even less about the complex interactions between these chemicals as they circulate in the blood stream. Most of the available literature is descriptive and suggestive rather than experimental; and it is especially sparse on the subject of adrenocortical and pituitary hormones, although these appear to play a very important role in the General Adaptation Syndrome.

Most of the literature on hormone effects in adult life deals with the relationships between aging and the sex hormones. Although research in this area is still in its infancy, the questions raised by sex-specific aging have generated more interest than those raised by the relationships between stress and disease in middle age or later life. Perhaps the interest in sex hormones is related to the clarity of their effects. For women in particular, changes in the reproductive system are dramatic and universal.

The Reproductive System

More descriptive data on hormone levels and biological change is available about the climacteric than any other hormone-related event of adult life. The *climacteric* is the entire period during which significant changes in the reproductive system occur for both males and females.

Change in the female reproductive and genital tract is most dramatic between the ages of forty-five and fifty-four. These important midlife alterations begin with the progressive decline in the weight of the ovaries after the age of thirty. At about forty, a noticeable decline occurs in the number of oocytes (eggs) produced. From high school biology, you will remember that the first stage in the reproductive cycle is the growth of the Graafian follicle, the single layer of cells that encloses an ovum, or egg. After the ovum enters the Fallopian tube, the empty follicle in the ovary is referred to as the *corpus luteum* or "yellow body," and it begins to produce progesterone and estrogen. These hormones ensure that the lining of the uterus thickens and the uterine blood supply increases for the proper reception of a fertilized egg. If fertilization does not occur, the corpus atrophies, progesterone and estrogen levels decline, and menstruation ensues.

After the age of about forty, irregularities and disruptions occur with increased frequency at each step of the cycle. Fewer Graafian follicles appear with the passage of the months, and fewer corpora lutea form. Those that do form often fail prematurely, causing unusually short menstrual cycles. Menstrual cycles may be irregular for many months, even years, before complete cessation of the reproductive sequence. Menopause usually occurs between forty-five and fifty-four, preceded by one or two years of menstrual irregularity, including shorter cycles and skipped cycles. A woman may think she has stopped menstruating and then, after some months, start again (Neugarten, 1967).

Changes in the Fallopian tubes are probably involved in the premature failure of the corpora lutea that do form successfully. With advancing years there are fewer cilia (hair-like projections) to move the ovum down the tube, and there is less secretory material along the path from the ovum to the uterus. The alterations, seen with the aid of the electron microscope, are striking (see Figure 6.3). Uterine biochemical changes, increased fibrosis of the uterine wall, and mounting deposits of pigments in the uterus probably contribute to the decreasing likelihood of pregnancy in middle age.

Changes in the reproductive cycle are critical to the balance and production of hormones in the female body. The Graafian follicles are the source of much of the estrogen available in a woman's system. Naturally, if there are fewer follicles, estrogen levels will decline. Moreover, because progesterone is produced by the corpora lutea, the level of progesterone also drops dramatically between forty and sixty.

The entire female genital tract is believed to be directly affected by plummeting hormone production. The weight of the uterus declines by as much as 53 percent between the ages of thirty and fifty. During the middle years of adulthood, the vaginal walls shrink and become thinner, and vaginal secretion is much reduced (Masters and Johnson, 1966). Some atrophy of the external genitalia (in particular the labia) occurs in middle age, as well as some thinning of the pubic hair, but these changes are more apparent in very late life.

Many of the changes so apparent in the female genital tract can be delayed, or even reversed, with estrogen replacement therapy. For some years, such hormone replacement was popular, but controversy has developed over the long-term effects of estrogen therapy on health (Timiras and Meisami, 1972).

Physical alterations of the female reproductive system in middle age are often accompanied by a variety of physical and psychological symptoms. Such symptoms can be classified in at least three categories: (1) those related to disturbance in autonomic functions, including hot flashes, chills, sweating, tachycardia (excessively rapid heartbeat), and hypertension; (2) neurologic and psychosocial problems such as headaches, dizziness, nervousness, and bouts of depression; and (3) symptoms of somatic origin, such as the changes we have just discussed in the genital tract, as well as effects on hair, bones, and vascular system (Timiras and Meisami, 1972).

We do not know precisely how disturbances in autonomic function or neurologic and psychosocial problems are related to hormonal changes at midlife, although we do know that, for females between the ages of

FIGURE 6.3
Scanning electron microscopy of the uterine tubes of premenopausal and postmenopausal women

SOURCE: From E. Patek, L. Nilsson, and E. Johannisson, "Scanning Electron Microscopic Study of the Human Fallopian Tube. Report II: Fetal Life, Reproductive Life, and Postmenopause," Fertil Steril 23 (1978): 719. Reproduced with the permission of the authors and the publisher, The Fertility Society.

RIGHT: *Ampulla of a uterine tube of a premenopausal woman.*

BELOW LEFT: *Ampulla of a uterine tube of a woman fourteen years after menopause. Notice the absence of cilia.*

BELOW RIGHT: *Isthmus of a uterine tube of a woman twenty-seven years after menopause. Notice the flattened appearance of the cells.*

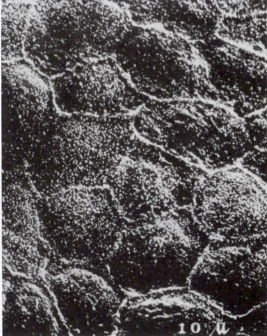

thirteen and fifty-four, menopausal women report the largest number of physical and psychological symptoms (Neugarten, Kraines, and Wood, 1965). The experience of distressing physical or psychological symptoms at menopause is not universal, however. Most women do report hot flashes or other mild autonomic disturbances, but only a few feel incapacitated. In one study (Paschkis, Rakoff, Cantarow, and Rupp, 1967), fully 16 percent of the women interviewed reported no symptoms whatever during menopause. To some degree, the experience of physical or psychological symptoms may depend on how a woman feels about infertility as her childbearing years draw to a close. Menopause is a significant symbol in the course of the female life span. To one woman, it may mean the freedom to redirect one's energies and develop new talents. To another, it may signify stagnation or unattractiveness and usher in feelings of emptiness (Newman, 1982). (We will explore the psychological impact of menopause in more detail as we discuss personality changes at midlife in Chapter 7.)

For men, the course of biological change in middle age proceeds quite differently. No single, abrupt physiological event occurs that can be considered analogous to the cessation of menstration in women. Changes in the male reproductive system occur quite gradually. Hormone levels and fertility decline over a relatively long period. The production of sperm declines by just 30 percent between the ages of twenty-five or thirty and age sixty, and by another 20 percent in the years between sixty and eighty, for an overall change of about 50 percent over forty or fifty years. Most of the changes that are being called male menopause involve psychological rather than hormonal or biological events (Newman, 1982).

Probably the most dramatic change in the male reproductive system during middle age is the involution, or degeneration, of the prostate gland. As the efficiency of this organ declines, less semen is produced, changing the experience of sexual intercourse to some degree. Eventually, the prostate becomes rigid and may obstruct the urinary tract. The incidence of prostate cancer is especially high in the middle years. It is the fourth common type of cancer among Americans; about 17 percent of the male population will develop the disease (Insel and Roth, 1982).

Throughout the male reproductive system and genital tract, aging does occur, if more gradually than for women. The degeneration of arteries and veins as well as increasing fibrosis (stiffness) of all the tissues of the body, including genital tissues, contributes to changing sexual function. For instance, erectal impotence occurs more frequently during middle age, although impotence is by no means an inevitable product of aging (Talbert, 1977). Erection and ejaculation occur less rapidly in middle adulthood than in late adolescence or early adult life. On the other hand, erection can be maintained for longer periods with age. Since premature ejaculation is the most common sexual dysfunction of early adulthood, age may also improve certain aspects of the male sexual experience (Masters and Johnson, 1966).

Some men do experience abnormally rapid decline in the functioning of the testes in their late sixties. When such hypofunction does occur, men report many of the same symptoms that trouble menopausal women, including hot flashes, chills, tachycardia, nervousness, and vertigo.

In sum, a variety of physical changes in the reproductive systems of both men and women during middle age have been documented. The entire genital tract is affected in both sexes, however, most of the alterations occur more slowly for men than for women. Although the available data have led many people to question the viability of sexual interest and activity in later life, the evidence on sexual behavior clearly indicates that many men and women go on leading healthy, vigorous sex lives well past the age of sixty.

Despite the physical changes, studies have reported that as many as 60 percent of men seventy-five or older still have involuntary morning erections and as many as three-quarters still feel sexual desire. Sexual activity for older men is closely related to the level of sexual activity they experienced as younger people. For women, however, sexual activity is more dependent on the opportunity to remain sexually active. This makes sense, since so many older women find themselves alone in later life. Among older married women, however, there is evidence that sexual desire may continue at about the same level as for men in the later years of the life span (Newman, 1982). Overall, the truth of the matter is aptly phrased by Masters and Johnson's (1966) injunction to "use it or lose it."

SENSATION, PERCEPTION, AND PSYCHOMOTOR PERFORMANCE

A second set of events begin in middle age, affecting people in fairly obvious and often annoying ways. By the age of forty or fifty, the first sharp declines in vision and hearing are usually noticeable. Although most of these changes are well within the range for which glasses and volume control knobs were designed, the deterioration is progressive and reflects again those basic processes of biological aging—increasing fibrosis of the tissues and the deterioration of the arteries and veins.

Vision

Important alterations take place in the function of the eye during middle age (see the drawing of the structure of the eye in Figure 6.4). First, the lens becomes less transmissive, and its ability to accommodate to shifts in focus

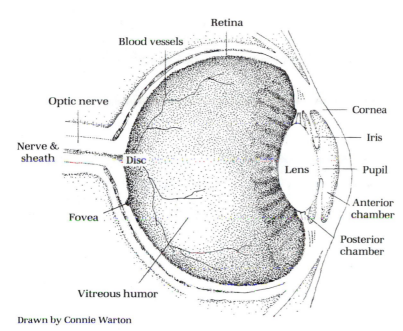

Retina

Blood vessels

Optic nerve

Nerve & sheath

Disc

Fovea

Vitreous humor

Cornea

Iris

Lens

Pupil

Anterior chamber

Posterior chamber

FIGURE 6.4
Major structures of the eye

Drawn by Connie Warton

declines. These changes produce noticeable differences in visual function as early as thirty-five or forty. Distant objects begin to appear blurred, and the closest object that can be seen without blurring is not as close as it used to be. The lens of the eye thickens with age, becomes stiff, and yellows. All these changes create increased opacity, and the eyes become more sensitive to glare. In addition, there is less sensitivity to the blue-green end of the spectrum as the lens yellows (Fozard, Wolf, Bell, McFarland, and Podolsky, 1977; Wolf, 1960).

The lens of the eye is rather like a piece of skin; and as with skin, new cells are constantly emerging. But cells cannot be sloughed off from inside the eye, as they can from our external layers. Thus, the cells of the lens become more and more compacted and the weight of the lens increases with age. During adulthood, the vitreous humor also begins to break down, and old cells and blood vessels collect, producing "floaters"—the dark spots that appear before the eye during rapid ocular movement (Corso, 1981).

As the lens is compacted and opacities appear, light from the external environment becomes increasingly scattered as it enters the pupil. Many of the problems of the aging eye, such as increasing sensitivity to glare, are produced by such scattering. Other difficulties—for example, depth perception—are related to the increased weight and stiffness of the lens.

Depth is judged in part by the accommodation of the lens to near versus far objects and by subtle distinctions based on brightness and contrast. The nearest distance at which an object can be seen clearly without a blur is called the *near point of vision*. "As a person grows older, the near point of vision recedes so that the range of accommodation becomes less and less" (Corso, 1981, p. 51). The ability to accommodate decreases markedly between the ages of ten and thirty, more slowly for the next ten years, and then at a rapid pace between forty and fifty, slowing again after fifty. Accommodation requires more and more effort to achieve, not because the muscles deteriorate, but because the lens is so much less flexible.

Muscular changes do account for a significant limitation of the upward gaze and for decreases in the extent of pupil dilation, however. Decreasing efficiency in the transportation and utilization of both sugar and oxygen combine with these muscular changes to affect dark adaptation and to cause shrinkage of the visual field. Interestingly, a smaller visual field can be produced in young subjects by reducing the amount of oxygen in the air they breathe. Continuing breadth of visual field is related to total vital capacity (Corso, 1981). As we shall see, there is reason to suspect that life-long physical fitness can make a difference in how sensory, perceptual, and cognitive changes proceed, perhaps because fitness is related to cardiovascular and respiratory function.

There is evidence that changes in the retina and nervous system are also at work in middle age. Rapid deterioration of depth perception between forty and fifty implicates the central nervous system. Furthermore, vascular changes in the retina are thought to be responsible for the deterioration of rods, the cells that govern vision at low levels of light. Night vision is impaired in very significant ways during middle age, with important implications for such skills as driving (Fozard et al., 1977; McFarland, Domey, Warren, and Ward, 1960).

All these changes are noticeable by the age of fifty. Most people begin to wear glasses when they want to see something clearly, but alterations in the sensory processes are probably not an important source of limitation in daily life until at least the age of seventy (Birren, 1964). Visual perception and the processing of visual information do not appear to change much during middle age. Unless subjects are tested under extremely adverse conditions, like reduced illumination or poor contrast, performance on tasks of visual perception is remarkably stable throughout the middle years (Comalli, 1970).

Audition

The most important and common problem associated with the aging ear is called *presbycusis*. It is most often associated with progressive loss of hearing for tones of high frequency and is caused by degenerative changes that

Glasses

I wear them. They help me. But I
Don't care for them. . . .
My gaze feels aimed. It is as if
Two manufactured beams had been
Lodged in my sockets—hollow, stiff,
And gray, like mailing tubes—and when
I pivot, vases topple down
From tabletops, and women frown.

JOHN UPDIKE

take place throughout the auditory system. Most of the loss occurs for the audiometric frequency spectrum over 1,000 cycles per second (c.p.s.). The implications of this loss become clear when you realize that the normal range of sounds that can be detected by the fully functional human ear includes frequencies between 20 and 20,000 cycles per second. The pure tone called middle C has a frequency of 262 c.p.s., and the pure tone one octave above middle C has a frequency of 524 c.p.s. The highest note on the piano has about 4,000 c.p.s., although the normal ear can detect overtones at least as high as 10,000 c.p.s. Figure 6.5 presents the fundamental and overtone frequencies of some common instruments and animal sounds (Cohen, 1969).

Older people do not lose the ability to hear high frequency sounds altogether. But if they are to detect tones above 1,000 c.p.s., the sound must be presented at greater volume than is necessary for younger subjects. Nearly all people over forty suffer some loss at high frequencies; males appear to be more severely affected than females (Corso, 1981).

Men may be subject to greater auditory loss because they are exposed to damaging levels of noise more often at work. Indeed, the ubiquitous noise of modern life is clearly responsible for some of the auditory problems all older people suffer. There is evidence, however, that even in iso-

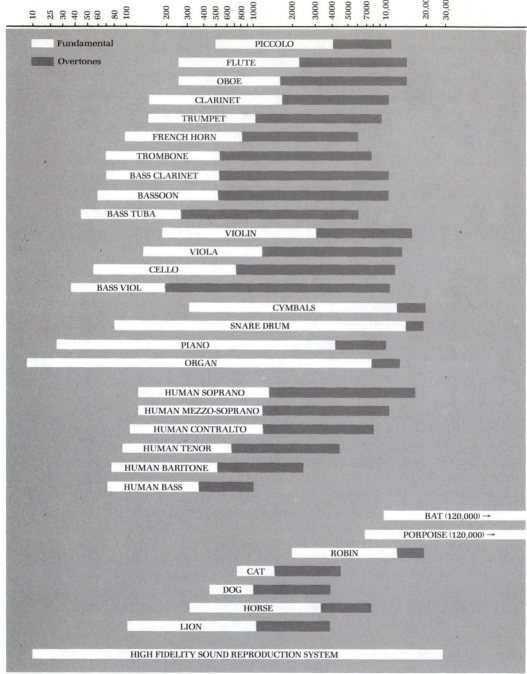

FIGURE 6.5
Frequency range of musical instruments and human and animal voices

SOURCE: *J. Cohen*, Sensation and Perception, II. Audition and the Minor Senses *(Chicago: Rand McNally, 1969), p. 10. Reprinted by permission of the author.*

lated, preindustrial groups, the ability to hear high-frequency noise declines throughout adulthood (Timiras and Vernadakis, 1972; Corso, 1981).

Four different forms of presbycusis have been identified, each of which is associated with a different kind of hearing problem among the elderly (Rupp, 1970; Schuknecht and Igarashi, 1964):

1. Sensory presbycusis: a loss of hearing for high-pitched tones that seems to result from atrophy of the hair cells in the inner ear

2. Neural presbycusis: problems of speech discrimination that suggest progressive loss of auditory neurons

3. Metabolic presbycusis: loss of pure tone hearing attributed to atrophy of the stria vascularis

4. Mechanical presbycusis: loss of high frequency hearing caused by decreasing flexibility of the basilar membrane

These four categories of auditory change occur in the spiral organ (organ of Corti) within the cochlea of the inner ear (see Figure 6.6). In addition, as the individual ages, impacted wax builds up in the ear canal and usually contributes to some of the hearing problems older people experience. Moreover, fluid often obstructs the eustachian tubes, and the bones in the middle ear become rather spongy, limiting their ability to conduct sound (Corso, 1977).

Degenerative changes in the auditory system are clearly present by the early years of middle age, but few people will be much affected by them. Many never even notice. One can simply turn up the stereo or buy better seats for a concert. At midlife, people can usually afford better seats anyway and probably buy them without noticing they need them. Auditory deficits, like those of the visual system, are troublesome only under stressful conditions. For example, when words are made to overlap or are frequently interrupted, subjects over forty have difficulty hearing sentences. Otherwise, speech discrimination is only minimally affected until very late in life (Corso, 1957, 1977, 1981).

For biologists and psychologists interested in sensory aging, the deficits of middle age are important not because they affect people's daily lives (they don't really), but because they raise significant research issues. Is damage to the sensory organ—for instance, the loss of hair cells in the inner ear or the stiffening of the lens—responsible for all the deficits associated with age? Or are changes in the central nervous system implicated? Questions about central versus peripheral mechanisms abound in the literature on sensation, perception, and cognition; but perhaps nowhere have they received more serious attention than in the study of psychomotor performance and response time.

FIGURE 6.6
The organ of Corti

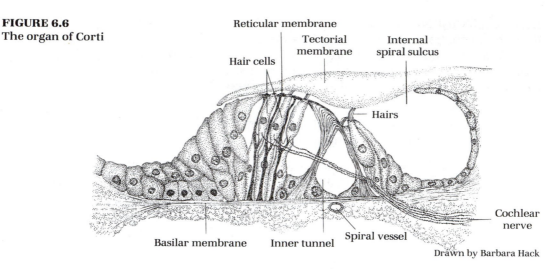

The organ of Corti of the inner ear contains the hearing receptors. It is here that many age-related hearing-loss changes take place.

Psychomotor Response and Reaction Time

You will recall from Chapter 4 that psychomotor skills are required for activities that demand dexterity and patterns of finely coordinated movements of the body or body parts, like dancing, driving, and dressing. Psychomotor responses require optimum preparation for and releasing of movements at the appropriate times (Birren, 1964).

There is overwhelming evidence that psychomotor responses slow with age (Welford, 1977) and that the effects of such slowing are ubiquitous (Birren, Woods, and Williams, 1980). Psychomotor slowing is thought to contribute to declining performance on general intelligence tests, information-processing tasks, and tests of memory function—both long and short term—as well as a variety of perceptual tasks that require complex or speedy decisions.

RESPONSE TIME.   Most of the basic research on psychomotor performance during adult life involves the measurement of response time in one form or another. Some studies present data on *simple response time*—the time it takes to respond to the onset or offset of a simple stimulus ("Push the button when the red light goes on"). Others involve *choice* (or disjunctive) *response* time—the time it takes to make decisions about whether to respond to a particular stimulus ("Push the button when the light is red but not when it is pink"), to decide which stimulus signals what response ("Push the button if the light is red, pull the handle if it is pink"), or to choose which of several possible responses to make ("When the light is red, choose one of the objects in front of you and put it on the other table").

The available evidence shows relatively little difference between the simple response time of healthy older people and that of young subjects. However, by middle age increments in choice or disjunctive response time are noticeable in situations that require a subject to withhold a response; to make one response and withhold another; to match one stimulus to another in order to make the correct response; or to perform a series of responses (Elias, Elias, and Elias, 1977). Differences between young and middle-aged people are most significant when both a complex decision and a rapid response are required.

A typical experiment on psychomotor performance might report that middle-aged people copy digits and words far more slowly than a younger group of people. In fact, between the ages of twenty and sixty there is a 97 percent increase in the time required for a task like copying (Birren and Botwinick, 1951). Such performance decrements are not universal, however. Occupation influences performance on this kind of test. For example, clerical workers tend to finish such tasks quickly throughout adult life.

The execution of unfamiliar tasks, such as writing numbers backward or carrying out an arbitrary series of movements, is also more difficult after forty. Whereas copying involves matching one stimulus to another, these more complex experimental situations require subjects to make long sequences of novel responses. A final category of response decrement has been illustrated in traditional word-association experiments and in those requiring subjects to substitute symbols for digits or decode a series of numbers. Choices are involved in the execution of these tests, and the ability to make complex and speedy reactions deteriorates substantially over adult life.

Although decline in psychomotor speed is easily demonstrated in the laboratory, research that might demonstrate how this change affects everyday life is sparse and inconsistent. For instance, studies of industrial output show that both speed and accuracy in daily work performance increase until middle age and then level off until retirement. Perhaps experience compensates for age-related slowness. It is also possible that, since these studies tend to be cross-sectional, the scores of older workers are inflated because poor performers leave their jobs earlier (Welford, 1977).

Other reports demonstrate that older workers do have more accidents related to speed requirements than younger workers. The accidents of young workers tend to be related to higher risk-taking. The same thing can be said of the differences in automobile accidents or traffic tickets that involve middle-aged or older people versus the young (Welford, 1977).

Beyond this limited data, there is very little objective information about daily life. Most of the discussion of psychomotor performance has focused not on the practical implications of slowness, but on the search for underlying physiological mechanisms. To this end, researchers have examined a variety of physiological evidence, including electroencephalograph records and measures of galvanic skin response (GSR) as well as patterns of evoked potential (a change in electrical activity in the nervous system as a response to stimulation).

PHYSIOLOGY OF PSYCHOMOTOR SLOWING.   Using the electroencephalograph (EEG) records of young and elderly subjects, researchers have demonstrated a very general change in the *alpha rhythm* of the brain over the adult years. The alpha rhythm—the regular pattern of brainwaves recorded during relaxation—usually has a frequency of nine to twelve cycles per second. A strong association has been demonstrated between both simple and complex response times and the frequency of the alpha rhythm. In fact, correlations between age and response time have been shown to be insignificant once the frequency of the alpha rhythm is taken into consideration. Figure 6.7 presents a hypothetical illustration of the alpha pattern of a young subject and an elderly one. In one experiment analogous to the hypothetical example, the median age of young subjects was 18.5 years and the median age of the older group was 63.0.

In young adulthood, the mean frequency of the alpha rhythm is about 10.5 cycles per second. By age seventy, the mean may fall by as much as two cycles per second. If it is true that information can be processed only during a specific part of the alpha cycle (see Figure 6.7), then older subjects, who exhibit fewer cycles per unit of time, may require longer to perceive the onset of a stimulus (Marsh and Thompson, 1977).

One intriguing study (Woodruff, 1972) reported that increasing the alpha rhythm of older subjects through biofeedback produced faster response times. The elderly were still not as quick as the young even after increases in the frequency of the alpha rhythm, however; other important forces must be at work as well. Moreover, even if we accept the importance of alpha wave slowing, there is still no reason to believe that alpha slowing *causes* response time to slow. Quite possibly, changes in the vascular system are responsible for both slowed response time and slowed alpha wave activity.

Certainly, there is evidence that cardiovascular diseases, especially atherosclerosis, reduce psychomotor speed. Reaction time can actually be manipulated in cardiac patients with pacemakers. Lowering the pulse rate by adjusting a pacemaker produces significant slowing of reaction time

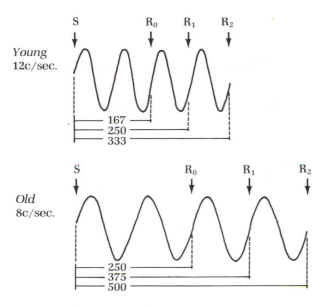

S   R₀   R₁   R₂

Young
12c/sec.

167
250
333

S   R₀   R₁   R₂

Old
8c/sec.

250
375
500

FIGURE 6.7
Comparisons of the EEGs and RTs of two hypothetical subjects, one a young adult and the other an elderly person

The interval between S and R₀ represents response time on a simple task, where the stimulus occurs at the same point in the alpha wave for both subjects and the response occurs at corresponding points in the alpha wave. Under these conditions, the older subject shows slower responses, because the alpha wave cycle occurs more slowly.

SOURCE: *Surwillo, W.W. Timing of behavior in senescence and the role of the central nervous system. In: F.A. Talland (Ed.)* Human Aging and Behavior. *New York: Academic Press, 1968. P. 14.*

and other indications of poor mental performance (Birren, Woods, and Williams, 1980).

The importance of cardiovascular health is also implicated by the data on physical fitness. Habitual exercisers have faster reaction times than do people who lead sedentary lives or exercise only sporadically. Some improvement has been produced in motor performance and related non-cognitive psychological tasks by programs of regular exercise. Maximum oxygen uptake has also been correlated with reaction time (Birren, Woods, and Williams, 1980).

Other research emphasizes the aging of neural cells. For example, *neural noise,* or random activity of the neurons, is thought to increase with age. If so, sensory signals may be more difficult to discriminate. Furthermore, stimulation may produce longer aftereffects, so that the activity produced by one decision or response begins to interfere with the progress of the next cognitive process. Studies of perceptual masking have given substance to the idea that duration of aftereffects increases with age.

Perceptual masking occurs when the presentation of one visual figure is followed after a short interval by another stimulus known to "erase" the perception of the first figure. Older subjects take longer to recover the perception of the first figure after perceptual masking. In fact, it takes 24 percent longer to overcome the masking of a visual stimulus at the age of

Physical fitness may improve the quality of life as we age, both prolonging the life span and delaying the onset of all the problems related to cardiovascular health— from reaction time and vision to hearing to the function of the central nervous system.

sixty-five than it does at twenty (Crossman and Szafran, 1956; Birren and Renner, 1977).

The neural noise hypothesis has been refined to include the possibility that older people spend more time monitoring incoming signals before they execute a response. Older people may be less willing or less able to cease monitoring previous responses and move on to the next part of a task. Increased monitoring may represent an attempt to compensate for increased neural noise and reduced signal strength (Welford, 1977).

Finally, there is a growing literature on *evoked* or *event-related-potentials* (ERPs) in the study of normal and abnormal aging. ERPs reflect specific brain activity synchronized with the onset of a stimulus. Although the measurement of such specific activity is plagued by technical and methodological problems, preliminary investigation suggests that ERPs reflect deficits in reaction time even among extremely healthy older people (Harkins, 1980; Ford and Pfefferbaum, 1980).

Like the research on ERPs, most of the available literature on the physiology of psychomotor response and other age changes is rudimentary as yet, although it does show promise. As one group of authors have pointed out, "The basic problem with these hypothetical notions about physiological bases of age changes . . . is that they are difficult to test. It is probably best to think of them as interesting, but oversimplistic" (Elias, Elias, and Elias, 1977).

Ultimately, research on speed and timing leads to a consideration of more general cognitive performance and intellectual behavior. For even when speed is not taken into consideration and the elderly are given untimed tests, scores on a variety of intelligence measures appear to decline in late middle age.

COGNITION

In the *Handbook of the Psychology of Aging* (1977), Jack Botwinick draws the general conclusion that, despite evidence of some decline in intellectual function with age, the decline starts later, is of lesser magnitude, and involves fewer functions than was believed as recently as the 1960s. On the other hand, Nancy Denney, in the *Handbook of Developmental Psychology* (1982), is struck by the number of researchers who report a discernible decline in performance by middle-aged subjects on many tests of problem solving and concept learning. The decline is especially noticeable when older subjects are required to search for a correct answer among a number of reasonable alternatives or to change strategies in the middle of a number of problems.

Denney and her colleagues have repeatedly demonstrated that the elderly cannot solve either traditional laboratory problems or practical, everyday problems as effectively as the young (Selzer and Denney, 1980; Denney and Palmer, 1982; Denney and Pearce, 1982). Although her research can be criticized as cross-sectional and, therefore, likely to reflect large cohort differences, Denney argues that cross-sectional studies may provide a realistic assessment of age changes despite all the recent criticisms. It is important to point out that, to date, sequential research has provided data on only a limited segment of the life span, whereas cross-sectional studies regularly report differences over forty to sixty years.

Typically, longitudinal studies report relative stability of intellectual performance throughout the years of middle age. (Longitudinal researchers do observe, however, decline in the performance of the elderly [Arenberg and Robertson-Tchabo, 1977].) It may be, of course, that longitudinal studies exaggerate the stability of performance in adulthood because the subjects who return to the study year after year become increasingly select. In the final stages, a longitudinal sample may consist primarily of individuals who demonstrate superior motivation and ability (Riegel and Riegel, 1972).

Longer-term sequential research may eventually clarify these issues. At present, however, the best strategy appears to lie in more detailed analyses of specific abilities. The distinction made in Chapter 4 between fluid and crystallized intelligence grew out of such an analysis. You will recall that fluid intelligence, based on the ability to organize and process new information speedily and effectively, is believed to decline after late adolescence, whereas crystallized intelligence, based on the accumulation of social and cultural experience, is thought to increase through a large segment of the adult life span (Horn, 1982).

Denney (1982) makes another important distinction, between what she calls exercised and unexercised abilities. Those abilities an individual

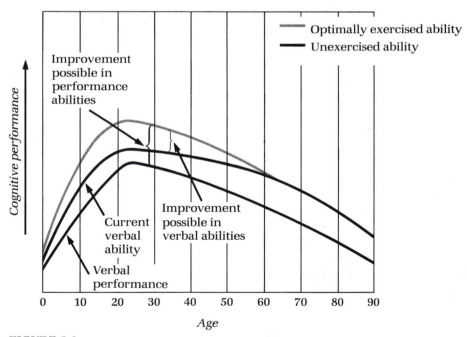

FIGURE 6.8
Amount of improvement possible in both verbal and performance abilities at ages thirty and fifty

SOURCE: *N. Denney, "Aging and Cognitive Changes," in B. B. Wolman, ed.,* Handbook of Developmental Psychology *(Englewood Cliffs, N.J.: Prentice-Hall, 1982), p. 820.*

exercises throughout the life span may age very differently from those that remain essentially unexercised. Although both kinds of abilities may improve throughout childhood and adolescence and decline in adulthood, for optimally exercised abilities one should find peak performances later in life, as well as longer periods of stability and slower decline. Figure 6.8 presents hypothetical curves representing the course of unexercised and optimally exercised abilities over the life span.

In two recent studies, Denney and her colleagues (Denney and Palmer, 1982; Denney and Pearce, 1982) presented data on traditional and practical problem solving that fit the hypothetical curves in Figure 6.8. Using the game of twenty questions to represent traditional problem-solving tasks, the researchers awarded higher scores to individuals who began with constraint-seeking questions (e.g., "Is it an animal?") when trying to guess which object in an array the questioner was "thinking of." Subjects who began with hypothesis-testing questions, simply suggesting one item after another (e.g., "It is the lamp?"), received lower scores. Although performance on this traditional task declined regularly with age after forty, twenty- and forty-year-olds performed in rather similar ways. The number of constraint-seekers was greatest in the group from thirty to thirty-nine. Subjects in various age groups were matched for educational level in this study (Denney and Palmer, 1982).

Examples of the kind of problems taken to represent practical problem solving are presented in Box 6.1. In one study (Denney and Palmer, 1982), performance on these practical problems increased to a peak in the forty-to-fifty group, declining thereafter. In a second study (from which the examples in Box 6.1 are actually drawn), the experimenters formulated practical problems for each age group, rather than presenting people of all ages with the same set of problems, because the kind of problems developed for the first study seemed most likely to occur in the lives of the middle aged rather than the young or the elderly.

Data for the second set of problems (Denney and Pearce, 1982) showed that young people solved all of the problems, even those designed specifically for the elderly, better than the elderly. Middle-aged adults, however, performed better than the young on problems designed for the elderly. High scores were assigned to those individuals who generated solutions involving actions one could take alone. Those who were unable to generate any acceptable solutions, and those who relied on the intervention of others (e.g., "I'd call the fire department") received lower scores.

On more traditional tests of intelligence, researchers most often report differences between the performance of young and middle-aged people for tests of digit symbol substitution, picture completion, picture arrangement, and other nonverbal tasks. Such differences are most commonly explained in terms of declines in psychomotor speed (Owens, 1966;

BOX 6.1
Real-life problems constructed for three different age groups

TWO PROBLEMS FOR YOUNG ADULTS

1. Let's say that a 25-year-old woman comes home to her apartment, where she lives alone, at 1:00 A.M. When she gets to the door she notices that the front door is unlocked and standing open. It is dark inside. The woman is surprised because she usually locks her door when she leaves her apartment. What should she do?

2. Let's say that a college student wants to go home to another state for Christmas but finds that he does not have enough money for the plane ticket. He also does not own a car. What should he do?

TWO PROBLEMS FOR MIDDLE-AGED ADULTS

1. If a middle-aged man is on vacation in a foreign country and he loses his wallet, which contains all his money and all his credit cards, what should he do?

2. The parents of a teenage daughter told her that she should be home from her date at 12:00 midnight on Saturday night. Although the daughter is usually very responsible, at 4:00 A.M. she is still not home. What should the parents do?

TWO PROBLEMS FOR THE OLDER ADULT

1. Let's say that a 60-year-old man who lives alone in a large city needs to get across town to a doctor's appointment. He cannot drive because he doesn't have a car, and he doesn't have relatives nearby. What should he do?

2. What should an elderly woman, who has no other source of income, do if her Social Security check doesn't arrive one month?

Cunningham and Birren, 1976; Birren, Woods, and Williams, 1980), although, as we noted above, the performance of older subjects ultimately falls short of performance among the young even when speed requirements are eliminated.

Further, when older subjects make a correct response to a test item, the response may be of lesser quality than the responses younger people make. If extra credit is given for superior answers (for example, on a test requiring people to produce synonyms), younger subjects achieve better scores. In general, however, deficits in response quality do not appear until after middle age. The issue in studying the performance of people at midlife is not ability per se, but whether the incipient processes of decline can be identified. If these processes can be identified in their early stages, it may be easier to intervene, reversing some of the less desirable effects of age before they become entrenched.

Another aspect of the complex literature on cognition involves the explanation of continuing optimal performance in some individuals. Denney (1982) touches on the matter when she suggests that optimally exercised abilities do not decline as early or as dramatically as those that are unexercised. Other researchers have also demonstrated that individuals who receive relatively high scores on intelligence tests given during childhood or young adulthood may actually show improvement on *both* verbal and nonverbal performance measures for the Wechsler Adult Intelligence Scale and the Stanford-Binet intelligence test, at least through the early years of middle age (Kangas and Bradway, 1971). Educational status and occupation also affect performance on tests of general intelligence. People who have attained high educational levels and high occupational status continue to achieve well on intelligence tests when compared with people of lesser educational and occupational status (Elias, Elias, and Elias, 1977).

Personality traits have also been linked to adult intellectual performance. For instance, intellectual decline has been correlated with *dogmatism* (resistance to change), which, however, is also inversely related to educational attainment, making it difficult to determine whether dogmatic thinking influences an individual's performance independent of educational level (Monge and Gardner, 1976).

In sum, it seems reasonable to conclude that the everyday performance of middle-aged people is relatively unaffected by the passage of time—whether we are speaking of sensory processes, perception, or cognition. If anything, middle age may be a period of optimal performance on practical, everyday problems. Under extreme conditions, of course, we would expect to find evidence for certain kinds of deficits by late middle age. It would seem wise to enlist the services of the young if one needed to receive and decode fast-paced messages transmitted at high frequencies by the light of the waning moon, especially if the messages were constantly interrupted by CB radio transmissions and masked by static noise. Still, it might be useful to have a middle-aged person on hand to decide how the information should be used. There are times when experience counts. And that brings us to the final topic for consideration in this chapter: the developmental tasks of middle age.

DEVELOPMENTAL TASKS

Erikson (1963, 1968a) discusses the central developments of middle age in terms of a conflict between *generativity* and *stagnation*. Generativity is an "expansion of ego interests and a sense of having contributed to the future" (1968a, p. 85). Erikson believes that the mature man or woman needs to be needed and to receive guidance and encouragement from what he or she produces. Generativity is reflected by a deep concern for the establishment and nurturance of the next generation. The central achievement of the generative stage is the direction of one's creativity and energy in a way that produces a lasting accomplishment worthy of sustained effort—a legacy. Impoverishment and self-indulgence are characteristic of individuals who fail to develop a generative personality and life-style in middle age.

Robert Havighurst (1972) expanded the concept of developmental tasks to include middle age. In middle life, he argued, achievement of adult civic and social responsibility and the establishment and maintenance of a standard of living are arenas of major growth and development. Teenagers must be assisted in becoming responsible, happy adults. The middle-aged adult must develop appropriate leisure-time activities and learn to relate to his or her spouse as a person. Middle-aged people must also meet and accept the demands of physiological change during these years and adjust to the aging of their own parents.

The outline of developmental tasks for middle age has also been explored in the work of Robert Peck, who elaborates four sets of important developmental challenges for the middle aged (Peck, 1968):

1. The individual must come to value wisdom over physical strength and attractiveness. One must accept inevitable losses of physical prowess with age and learn to use one's experience. Wisdom is defined as making "effective choices among the alternatives which intellectual perception and imagination present" (p. 89). (Notice that Peck is speaking not of speedy choices but of effective ones.) People who do not make the transition from physical prowess to wisdom in middle age often become bitter and depressed.

2. Socializing must replace sexualization as the major focus for male-female relationships. The middle-aged person redefines people as individuals and companions. Note the similarity of this suggestion to the belief that the middle-aged person comes to relate to the spouse as a person (Havighurst, 1972).

3. The individual must demonstrate *cathected flexibility*: the capacity to shift one's emotional investment to new people, activities, and

"All the strengths arising from earlier developments from infancy to young adulthood . . . now prove, on closer study, to be essential for the generational task of cultivating strength in the next generation." Erik Erikson

roles as old ones lose their potential for satisfaction. During middle age, children are launched from the home, and one experiences the death of one's parents, friends, and relatives. It becomes critical to participate in a wide range of relationships and events, in order to experience personal meaning and fulfillment.

4. Mental flexibility must become a central personal characteristic. In the middle years, the ability to use personal experience as a provisional guideline must emerge and replace the tendency to rely on experience as a rigid, automatic basis for rules of thought and behavior.

These four developmental patterns seem to imply a tendency toward increasing rigidity and withdrawal with age. As we will see in the next chapter, questions about rigidity and withdrawal have been central concerns in the study of personality throughout adult life.

SUMMARY

The biological clock in middle age marks off the days and months through a variety of physiological events that create significant signs of personal change in many individuals. The most obvious biological and physiological changes include the transformation of physical appearance, from increasing body weight and girth measurement to changes in bones, skin, and hair. The fat content of the body is redistributed; other tissues become increasingly stiff or fibrous; and coloration often changes.

Changes in physical appearance seem to have the greatest psychological impact on middle-aged American women. A double standard for male and female aging may be responsible for the concern middle-aged women express about facial beauty and their tendency to exaggerate the unattractiveness of other middle-aged women. Middle-aged women also seem to translate their worry over physical appearance into a fear that they are becoming boring and sexually undesirable or uninteresting at a time when most women still want regular, active sexual lives.

Middle-aged men are not nearly as concerned about physical appearance, either their own or that of most middle-aged women. But they do express anxiety about their health. They may spend increasing amounts of time in body monitoring, and their spouses may become involved in these observations. Just as middle-aged women's fears about their appearance are grounded in their vulnerability to the cultural double standard, men at midlife understandably react to their very real vulnerability to stress and disease.

In particular, middle-aged males are more susceptible to cardiovascular disease than are other groups of the population. Not surprisingly, incidence of this disease is predicted by behavioral attributes that are believed by many to be a part of the life-style of successful men in this country. The Type A personality—striving, competitive, aggressive, restless, and impatient—is twice as likely to be the victim of a heart attack as his easygoing, unambitious Type B agemate.

General life stress, as measured by the Holmes and Rahe Social Readjustment Rating Scale and related instruments, is also implicated in the development of coronary heart disease. Stress mobilizes the sympathetic nervous system, and with age, this mobilization becomes less efficient. Furthermore, arteriosclerosis and atherosclerosis are most often diagnosed for the first time in middle age. These diseases involve the thickening of the arterial wall and the breakage and disarray of elastin fibers. Plaques form in the arterial stream at the site of the elastin breaks and further restrict the flow of blood. It has been argued that the arterial changes observed in arteriosclerosis and atherosclerosis are basic age changes—universal, progressive, and irreversible.

Changes in the reproductive system represent another major set of critical physiological changes in midlife. For women, these events include progressive decline in the weight of the ovaries and increasing disruption of the reproductive cycle. Because fewer oocytes become mature and move down the Fallopian tube to the uterus, hormonal levels decrease dramatically between the ages of forty and sixty. Changes in hormonal production and balance produce further alterations in the genital tract. The vaginal walls shrink; there is loss of pubic hair; and the vagina may become weak and dry. Although most of these events can be reversed by estrogen replacement therapy, there is some controversy about the wisdom of routine administration of synthetic estrogen.

Aging of the male reproductive system affects the production of sperm and the size and weight of the prostate gland, alterations in the penis, and changes in sexual behaviors, including erection and ejaculation. Hormone levels decline over the adult years for men as well as women, but the decreases are rarely as abrupt for men as for women.

Sensation, perception, and psychomotor performance also change noticeably during midlife. Vision and hearing are usually significantly affected by the age of forty-five or fifty. Decreased transmissiveness of the lens of the eye and the lens's declining ability to accommodate make it more difficult to see things near and far and produce sensitivity to glare as well as changes in color vision. As a result of changes in the retina and in the nervous system of the eye, size of the visual field and sensitivity to low quantities of light and to flicker decline by the age of fifty-five.

Several different classes of auditory change also occur, all of which may be grouped under the rubric *presbycusis.* This term covers the loss of ability to hear high-pitched tones that follows from atrophy of the hair cells in the ear, loss of flexibility in the basilar membrane, loss of pure tone hearing consequent to atrophy of the stria vascularis, and problems of speech discrimination produced by loss of some auditory neurons.

Most changes in both hearing and vision during middle age can be adequately compensated for by optometry and volume control. The central issues in the research on biological changes brought about by aging do revolve not around decrements in daily function but around the question of whether central or peripheral factors are more important in the observed change.

The issue of central and peripheral factors has been most closely examined with regard to psychomotor developments at midlife. Available evidence clearly indicates that psychomotor activity slows with age. Reduced reaction times are observed in both simple and complex tasks. The decrements are most significant when experimental conditions demand that the individual withhold a response, perform a series of tasks, or match one stimulus to another in order to make the correct response. The greater decrement in speed when responding to a complex task than to a simple one and the careful observation of actual movement time have led investigators to emphasize the role of central mechanisms in the slowing of psychomotor performance.

Another focus of psychomotor research has been the search for a physiological basis for the relationship between aging and slowed response time. The alpha phase measure taken from electroencephalograph records of older persons has generated interesting research on improving psychomotor performance, but a causal relationship has not been established. One interesting theory of psychomotor aging involves the notion that neural noise increases with age. Studies of perceptual masking reinforce this hypothesis. The neural noise created by increasing stimulus aftereffects may be partly responsible for psychomotor slowing.

We do not yet have a clear and complete understanding of how these changes affect daily function, and the questions seem particularly complex when we try to assess the literature on cognitive change and age. Aging does seem to be associated with decline in the performance of people of average intelligence on tests of intellectual behavior. However, there is still much controversy about the role of psychomotor slowness in this decline, and about the inevitability of performance decrements. Individuals of high initial intelligence, and those of high educational attainment or occupational level, tend to maintain better performance on measures of general intelligence across the life span than do those with less intelligence, education, or lower occupational attainment.

On the other hand, a number of researchers have argued that some abilities, like those represented by nonverbal intelligence measures and laboratory tests of problem solving, decline substantially during middle age. In this regard, it may be very important to make a distinction between unexercised and optimally exercised abilities. In all probability, however, the critical practical performances of everyday life are relatively unaffected for most middle-aged people. These tasks have been described by Erikson as the development of generativity versus stagnation. Erikson defines generativity as the expansion of ego interests and a sense of having contributed to the future. Havighurst's and Peck's descriptions of the developmental tasks of middle age emphasize the need to value wisdom over physical power, to learn to socialize rather than sexualize in human relationships, to develop the flexibility to invest oneself in new roles, events and people, and to find ways to use one's personal experience as a provisional guideline rather than to formulate a set of hard-and-fast rules.

Chapter 7

The Personal Context: Stability, Challenge, and Change at Midlife

When more time stretches behind than stretches before one, some assessments, however reluctantly and incompletely, begin to be made.

JAMES BALDWIN

Until the past ten years or so, most Americans thought of middle age as a time of stability, a time characterized by conservative attitudes and behaviors at best, increasing rigidity at worst. More recently, however, we have increasingly come to think of middle age as a period of intense discomfort and stress. The great popularity of Gail Sheehy's book *Passages* (1976) in the late 1970s is only one of many signs that we are now quite likely to view crisis as a central feature of middle age. In some ways, the culture has exchanged one set of stereotyped ideas about middle adulthood for another equally unrealistic, if more romantic, set. In the classic variation of the new myth, the middle-aged, middle-class man abruptly abandons his wife, his family, and his friends for a new Porsche and a twenty-year-old blonde coed on a Honda. Although the wife, is of course, devastated, she soon finds that the single life has its advantages and so is unwilling to take him back when his fling is flung.

In another variation on the same theme, the gray-suited, gray-haired executive in his forties or fifties, chronically depressed and sexually bored, wastes away on alcohol and pills. And, of course, there is the stereotype of menopausal women, tearfully watching soap operas or sitting in an empty kitchen longing for the days when the floor was constantly marred by little heel marks. In the more modern version of the middle-aged fairy tale, she valiantly heads out for law school, battling opposition from her family, her friends, and her teachers.

Still, in the back of our minds is the legacy of the years before midlife crisis became an issue. There is the successful, middle-aged doctor, graying at the temples, president of the AMA, powerful, controlled, self-satisfied, with his smiling, competent wife at his side. They were always pictured on the society page, dancing at a benefit for the mentally retarded. The caption under the photo praised her skills as an organizer and administrator. To us they embodied the notion that middle-aged people are successful, confident—in charge.

Our conflicting stereotypes contribute to confusion about the experience of middle age. In this chapter we will explore that confusion. We will examine the evidence for both midlife crisis and for life satisfaction in middle age, as well as research that depicts fairly high levels of adjustment and productivity among people in their middle years. The attempt to make some sense of the contradictions will lead us to a discussion of stability, change, and personality in middle age. Finally, we will consider the available evidence on sex-role changes and sex differences, as we search for clues about how midlife crisis is engendered, experienced, or evaded.

MIDLIFE: CRISIS, CHALLENGE, OR CONSOLIDATION?

Mainstream America is not without professional company in its confusion over middle age. Certainly, the psychological literature on midlife crisis does not provide immediate enlightenment. In fact, much of the available information suggests two distinct points of view—two piles of paper. In the first stack, the "crisis" pile, one would find the work of the many psychiatrists and clinical psychologists who have described, often eloquently, the experience of midlife strife in both clinical and nonclinical samples. In the second stack, the "no crisis" pile, one might place the work of sociologists and research psychologists who have been able to demonstrate, over and over again, that most middle-aged people report feeling calm, satisfied, and stable, and are characterized by good judgment and feelings of control and achievement.

The clinicians describe case after case of personal disorganization, ranging from neurosis and psychosis to alcoholism. They talk about low marital satisfaction among the middle-aged people they see, and about stress and psychosomatic illness (Rosenberg and Farrell, 1976). The defenders of the "no crisis" position insist that the "normal life events of middle age do not in themselves constitute emergencies for most people" (Neugarten and Datan, 1974). As evidence, they refer to the many survey studies that report high levels of life satisfaction among the middle aged.

As we proceed to examine both of these arguments more closely, along with some of the most recent attempts to reconcile the contradictions, you will find that the solution may be a very complex one indeed. However, as Walter Mischel writes, the difficulty does not "prevent one from studying human affairs scientifically; it only dictates a respect for the complexity of the enterprise and alerts one to the dangers of oversimplifying the nature and causes of human behavior" (1969, p. 352).

The Potential for Crisis

At the top of the stack produced by the clinicians are the statistics: midlife marriage may represent a nadir in marital satisfaction (Pineo, 1961; Rollins and Feldman, 1970); the rate of first hospital admissions for psychotic disorders increases; the incidence of psychoneurosis may be highest during these years (Weintraub and Aronson, 1968), as are the totals for first admissions for alcoholism; and, of course, peptic ulcers, hypertension, and heart disease are most often diagnosed in middle-aged patients (Rosenberg and Farrell, 1976). Moreover, the rate of suicide rises alarmingly between the ages of forty and sixty, especially for men. One hundred and five men in one hundred thousand commit suicide in middle age, approximately three times the rate for males aged fifteen to twenty-four. Infidelity and desertion are major problems in the marriages of the middle aged. In the mid-1970s, about one hundred thousand middle-aged men left home every year, and in some of those years even more women left home (Bradbury, 1975).

Another important source of evidence in the crisis pile appears in case study and interview data from a number of influential psychiatrists and clinical psychologists, including Roger Gould at the University of California at Los Angeles (UCLA), Daniel Levinson at Yale, and George Vaillant and Charles McArthur at Harvard. Gail Sheehy's successful book *Pathfinders* (1981) was largely based on the work of Gould and Levinson, as was *Passages* (1976).

Gould's study (1972, 1980) contained interview and questionnaire data gathered from both individuals who were being seen at the UCLA clinics as well as a large number of nonclinical subjects. Levinson and his associates (1974, 1978) have presented very detailed descriptions of the life course for 40 middle-aged men over a four-year period; and Vaillant and McArthur (1972; Vaillant, 1977) have outlined the data from a forty-year longitudinal follow-up study of 268 men from the Harvard University classes of 1939–1941 and 1942–1944.

Taken together, these three studies have suggested the existence of a nearly universal transitional period of adult life occurring about age forty. This transition is said to be characterized by feelings of turmoil, a heightened awareness of aging, and a sense of the finiteness of time.

The following generalization from Vaillant and McArthur (1972, p. 423) is typical of the observations contained in all three of these studies as well as in the books by Sheehy:

> In any case, around forty a change occurred in the men. They appeared to leave the compulsive calm of their occupational apprenticeship, so reminiscent of grammar school days, and experience once more the *sturm und drang* (storm and stress) of adolescence. In fact, most subjects consciously perceived their forties as more tumultuous than they had their adolescence. . . . Just as adolescence is a time for acknowledging parental flaws and discovering truths about childhood, the forties are a time for reassessing and reordering the past.

The Harvard graduates described by Vaillant and McArthur experienced much more overt depression in their forties than they had in young adulthood. They often felt disenchanted with life and experienced agonizing bouts of self-appraisal and instinctual awakening. Yet these men had been selected as young adults because they were considered healthy and well adjusted. The Harvard Grant Study had been designed to illustrate how the male adult life cycle proceeds under the most favorable circumstances. On the average, men in the Harvard study had the income and social standing of a successful businessman or physician and the political viewpoint, intellectual tastes, and life-style of a college professor. By all ordinary standards, these men were successful, well-adapted adults.

Roger Gould's data from UCLA confirmed the notion that in the period "between forty and forty-three there is a series of temporary excursions from well-established lifelong baselines on statements dealing with personal comfort, indicating an acutely unstable period with a great deal of personal discomfort" (Gould, 1972, p. 530). (The results of a questionnaire developed at UCLA and administered to a large group of white, middle-class subjects between the ages of sixteen and sixty are summarized in Figure 7.1.) From interviews with patients in early middle age, Gould has crystallized their concerns as a definite tendency toward the existential questioning of "self, values, and life itself . . . quiet desperation and an increasing awareness of time squeeze" (p. 526).

Finally, Levinson and his associates (1974, 1978) have identified a period called *midlife transition* in their subjects too. They define some of the major issues as (1) bodily decline and a vivid recognition of one's mortality; (2) the sense of aging; and (3) the emergence of the more feminine aspects of the self. Middle-aged men in this study seemed to be confronting their own mortality and struggling with youthful illusions of omnipotence. They focused on healing old psychic wounds and learning to love formerly devalued aspects of the self. According to Levinson, "It is the changing relation to the self that is the crucial issue at midlife" (1974, p. 255).

Three studies, three different groups of subjects, three different sets of researchers—all reached strikingly similar conclusions. All three point to the importance of a relatively brief time span from thirty-nine to forty-three. All three make mention of an acute awareness of mortality and aging, of people encountering the finiteness of personal time. All three emphasize the conscious questioning and conflict of values during this period. All three repeat the themes of reassessment and reevaluation.

Why are all these middle-aged people so dissatisfied? Isn't it true that if we make the right choices in young adulthood (about marriage, home, job, family) we will be less restless and more stable? At least, we would imagine, the successful Harvard men ought to feel emotionally secure, sexually satisfied, and optimistic about the future. These questions hint that

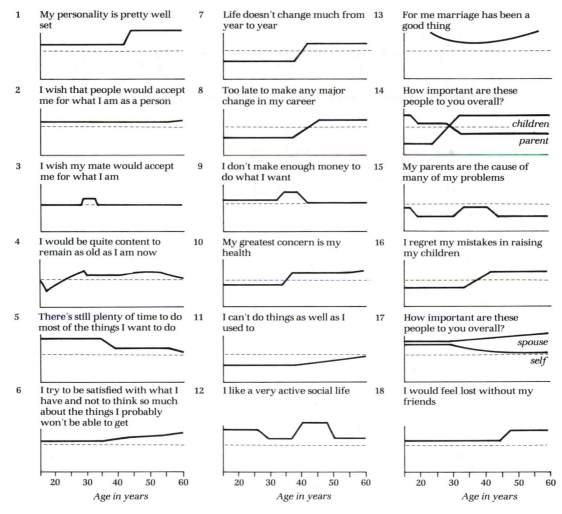

FIGURE 7.1
Sample curves associated with the time boundaries of the adult life span

SOURCE: *R. Gould, "The Phases of Adult Life: A Study in Developmental Psychology," American Journal of Psychiatry, 129 (1972): 528. Copyright © 1972 by the American Psychiatric Association. Reprinted by permission.*

many of us have bought the "Maturity Myth" of the middle class (O'Neill and O'Neill, 1977). Middle age is supposed to be a comfortable, satisfied time of life. Doesn't life begin at forty? In fact, success and maturity do not seem to come with lifetime, money-back-guaranteed peace of mind. And the disappointment may even produce despair, suicide, peptic ulcers, and coronary disease (Bromley, 1974).

The crisis pile is pretty persuasive taken alone. The confusion arises when the social scientists arrive with their scales and tests and passion for replication, numbers, and causal inferences. They want to know exactly how miserable "miserable" is, and how much more miserable it is at forty than it was at thirty or will be at fifty. Then they want to know why it's miserable. Surely turning forty itself does not cause midlife crisis! Is there a specifiable set or sequence of events that precipitates a problematic midlife transition?

The No Crisis Position

There are statistics on the top of this stack too. For example, the social scientists argue that suicide rates and the incidence of psychosis increase throughout the life span. Rates for the middle aged look high only if you compare them to rates for the young. Taken in context, the statistics simply suggest that aging may be accompanied by difficulty. Yet, most middle-aged people report that early adulthood was the period of greater emotional strain (Gurin, Veroff, and Feld, 1960).

Certainly, there is little reason to believe that the normal events of middle age precipitate inevitable crisis. Even as dramatic an event as menopause does not appear to be universally experienced as traumatic. This is especially interesting in light of our deeply ingrained image of the sorrowing "change of life" woman. In actuality, young women appear to be the ones who see menopause in unrelentingly negative terms—as a depressing, unpleasant, disturbing eventuality. Older women, especially postmenopausal women, usually report feeling calmer, more confident, and happy to be released from the hormonal shifts of the reproductive cycle. Although older women do often find the symptoms of menopause disagreeable, they also report some degree of control over the extent and severity of their symptoms. In general, they see the climacteric as a temporary inconvenience, but do not regret losing their reproductive capacity. To the contrary, they emphatically welcome freedom from pregnancy (Neugarten, Wood, Kraines, and Loomis, 1963; Neugarten and Datan, 1974; Datan, 1971; Newman, 1982).

Climacteric changes in men seem far too gradual to account for any abrupt or critical changes in adjustment or emotional state during middle age. Of course, the probability of sexual dysfunction in males increases with age, but nearly all forty-year-old males are functioning within normal ranges. Thus, it is unlikely that changes in sexual potency or hormonal balance, or physical alterations of the reproductive system, are of great significance in the years between thirty-nine and forty-three (Newman, 1982).

Continuing the search for critical events, the social scientists have looked into the problems of transition from parenthood. After all, as Kurt Vonnegut captures the mood in *Slaughterhouse Five*, it appears potentially devastating:

> Billy Pilgrim could not sleep on his daughter's wedding night. He was forty-four. . . . The moonlight came into the hallway through doorways of the empty rooms of Billy's two children, children no more. They were gone forever. Billy was guided by dread and by the lack of dread. Dread told him when to stop. Lack of it told him when to move.

Billy's experience is certainly dreadful, but the launching of children is thought to be even more difficult for women. Women in this stage are sometimes described as victims of the *empty-nest syndrome.* Clearly, women define their lives more closely in terms of the family cycle than do men. Even single women without children often perceive the life cycle in terms of the family they might have had or the families of their friends (Neugarten, 1968b). Nonetheless, the research shows that most women do not view the departure of their children as an unhappy prospect. Instead, they look forward to the launching of their offspring with some eagerness, and experience a new sense of freedom and delight in having time to use latent abilities and talents in ways that were impossible with a houseful of children (Neugarten, 1968b).

Increasing levels of life satisfaction for females of all life-styles are associated with the so-called empty-nest period. Confirmation comes from articles in psychological journals, popular magazines, and the results of a variety of national surveys (Jacoby, 1982; Newman, 1982; Glenn, 1975; Neugarten, Kraines, and Wood, 1965). Intensive longitudinal studies offer similar observations. The empty nest is not usually a source of unhappiness. The years when children are going through adolescence are experienced as more uncomfortable, and most women seem to look forward to the years when the children will be on their own with positive feelings of anticipation. Furthermore, many field studies have shown improved functioning and psychological health for a large number of women in late middle age (Livson, 1981a, and 1981b; Lowenthal and Chiriboga, 1972).

For middle-aged men, however, the launching of children does not produce increasing satisfaction or improved functioning. The family life cycle is simply not as influential in structuring the lives of men. Awareness of middle age for males seems to be more strongly related to cues provided by their occupational roles than to changes in the family. These cues include the deference of younger employees and a heightened sense of mastery and expertise (Neugarten, 1968b).

For men, the life cycle may well be defined at work by terms such as "new recruit," "assistant representative," "supervisor," and "retiree."

Yet, the social scientists point out that midlife crisis is not directly associated with occupational satisfaction or career progress either. For example, most men report relatively high occupational satisfaction during middle age (Clausen, 1976). Furthermore, neither the anticipation of retirement nor retirement itself seems to be accompanied by crisis. Only those who retire unexpectedly experience much dissatisfaction with leaving the work force, and most middle-aged men look forward to retirement (Barfield, 1970; Atchley, 1976).

Generally, middle-aged men describe themselves as satisfied and tend to see middle age as the prime of life. They want to feel young, but they do not want to be young again. They experience a heightened capacity to manage their environment, an increased sense of authority and autonomy, and feelings of expertise. Upper-middle-class men, such as those in the Harvard sample, are particularly positive. They feel powerful, and they view themselves as decision-makers and the standard-bearers of society. They take great pride in their own objectivity, polish, ease of operation, and incisiveness (Neugarten and Datan, 1974). Overall, like middle-aged women, they describe these years as an improvement over the "life-cycle crunch" of young adulthood, when one must meet extensive familial and occupational demands (Harry, 1976).

Studies of fun and happiness fall in line with the rest of the data presented by the creators of the no crisis pile. For example, in one series of interviews with nearly seven thousand males and females from 4 to 103, researchers found few relationships between age and mood or degree of current happiness and opportunities for fun (Cameron, 1972a, 1975). Longitudinal data from Duke University (Palmore and Luikart, 1974) confirm that reported life satisfaction neither rises nor declines as subjects pass through the middle years of life. In this study, perceived health—not age—was by far the strongest factor predicting life satisfaction. Perceived health was more important than either objective health, as rated by a physician, or income and education.

And so, we have come full circle, from the argument that middle age is a critical stage of life, perhaps the most stressful period in the life cycle, to the contention that there is no relationship at all between age and emotional state. What happened between the time we started out at UCLA and ended up at Duke University?

Denial and Crisis

A number of writers and researchers have addressed themselves to the conflict in the literature we have been reviewing. For instance, some of the more clinically oriented believe that middle-aged people tend to rationalize and to deny the experience of crisis. In a psychiatric interview, the experimenter is able to see through the apparent calm, to the real inner turmoil. But the questionnaires of the survey researchers simply pick up what the subject believes to be the socially desirable response—not how life is really going, but how it should be going (Rosenberg and Farrell, 1976).

Recently, the major proponents of the denial hypothesis, Michael Farrell and Stanley Rosenberg, published a study of personality development based on a sample of five hundred men in young adulthood and middle age. In their book, *Men at Midlife* (1981), Farrell and Rosenberg point out that the literature on midlife crisis is plagued by the use of differing methods and quite different samples of men. They also reiterate the notion that questionnaires are likely to reflect denial and a reluctance to report negative experience. They do not, however, claim that all middle-aged people will experience a crisis.

Farrell and Rosenberg discovered that a variety of resolutions were achieved when the men in their own sample encountered the central tasks of midlife development—tasks such as assuming the role of "patron" of the family, becoming a source of financial and emotional stability for both the older and the younger generations, learning to live with increasing physical vulnerability, and accepting one's inability to achieve the unfulfilled dreams of youth. In assessing different responses to these tasks, Farrell and Rosenberg developed a four-part typology of their subjects. They pointed out that the men differed along two major dimensions: the ability to confront stress and the degree of life satisfaction reported. Table 7.1 outlines the four types and shows how they are defined along these two dimensions of stress confrontation and life satisfaction.

About 12 percent of the Farrell and Rosenberg sample fell into category I: the *anti-hero* type. These individuals appeared to be alienated from the community and the mass culture. They expressed little satisfaction with their occupational careers, and they seemed to possess little or no sense of the future. Often, they talked about wanting to "start all over

TABLE 7.1
A typology of responses to middle-age stresses

Denial of stress	Open confrontation with stress
Dissatisfied	
IV Punitive-Disenchanted	**I Anti-Hero**
1. Highest in authoritarianism	1. High alienation
2. Dissatisfaction associated with environmental factors	2. Active identity struggle
3. Conflict with children	3. Ego-oriented
	4. Uninvolved interpersonally
	5. Low authoritarianism
Satisfied	
III Pseudo-Developed	**II Transcendent-Generative**
1. Overtly satisfied	1. Assesses past and present with conscious sense of satisfaction
2. Attitudinally rigid	2. Few symptoms of distress
3. Denies feelings	3. Open to feelings
4. High authoritarianism	4. Accepts out-groups
5. High on covert depression and anxiety	5. Feels in control of fate
6. High in symptom formation	

SOURCE: M. P. Farrell and S. P. Rosenberg, *Men at Midlife* (Boston: Auburn, 1981), p. 32.

again." More of the "anti-hero" subjects were married to working women than in any other group. But the men were not dissatisfied with their marriages, although they often expressed disappointment about the way their children were turning out. More often than any other type, the anti-hero was likely to experience a strong, personal sense of midlife crisis, and unlikely to deny or project these feelings. Men in this group also tended to suffer from physical as well as psychological symptoms.

The largest group in the sample, 32 percent of the men, classified as *transcendent-generative*, appeared to negotiate the midlife transition with no experience of crisis or turmoil, but rather with a deep sense of personal satisfaction in marriage, family, and work, along with good health, continuing faith in the future, openness, and feelings of confidence and self-assurance.

About 26 percent of the sample fell into the *pseudo-developed* group, who also reported satisfaction and showed few psychological or physical symptoms. Farrell and Rosenberg believe, however, that these men simply deny the stress they experience. They do not report any real hopefulness about the future and seem to have problems thinking and deciding. They just can't get going. They admit to dissatisfaction with their sex lives, and experience their children as a source of trouble. They are ethnocentric and authoritarian and likely to accept the social prescription that middle age is a comfortable, successful time in the life cycle. The pseudo-developed man copes with the problems of the period by sticking his head in the sand.

Finally, nearly 30 percent of the sample was classified as *punitive-disenchanted*. The vast majority of these men were in crisis, despite their ability to deny any problems. They were likely to be dependent and unhappy, to feel restless and irritable, and to use alcohol to alleviate their symptoms. They were unhappy with their wives and their children and showed very low tolerance for ambiguity, often appearing bigoted as well as authoritarian. Farrell and Rosenberg classify Archie Bunker as a member of the punitive-disenchanted group.

Obviously, since over one-half of the Farrell and Rosenberg sample used denial as a major coping mechanism, and since another 32 percent reported that they did not really experience what has been described in the literature as "crisis," survey and questionnaire research is unlikely to show high levels of psychological discomfort among middle-aged men as a group. Nevertheless, as Farrell and Rosenberg put it, "though we do not find 'crisis' in the sense of conscious disruption of identity to be a common pattern as men confront middle-age, we do find a range of responses, some of which may be just as problematic as a crisis" (1981, p. 208).

Of special interest is Farrell and Rosenberg's finding that the overwhelming majority of the transcendent-generative men in their sample came from affluent, middle-class areas. They often began life with a wealth of economic and emotional resources and by young adulthood had been able to develop multiple coping strategies. Farrell and Rosenberg believe disappointment and insurmountable crisis in middle age may be, in good measure, an injury of class. In this culture, male vocational failure is most likely to be accompanied by a devastated self-concept and feelings of estrangement from the society and even the self. Consider the fact that a great many of the punitive-disenchanted men were the sons of semi-skilled or unskilled laborers, or had suffered a childhood of abuse and neglect. Farrell and Rosenberg argue that our society establishes criteria for success that most men will never be able to attain. As a result, the majority end up as psychological casualties, experiencing their failure as a personal deficiency, and seeing themselves as inadequate.

Farrell and Rosenberg's emphasis on the importance of socioeconomic class and the opportunities of childhood suggests a related hypothesis. It is possible that the experience of midlife crisis is mediated by cultural, historical, and generational differences. Perhaps some groups or even whole generations of people are more likely to encounter crisis than others; changing social and historical conditions in postwar Germany provide a dramatic example (Bradbury, 1975). For those whose adult lives were shattered by World War II, middle age was a very different experience than it was for those who entered middle age in the economic boom years of the 1960s. Certainly, the experience of middle age in this country may be different for those who entered the prime of life in the boom of the 1960s when compared to those who entered it in the economic slump of the late 1970s and early 1980s.

It is also possible that midlife crisis emerges only in those cultures and historical times that offer the basic affluence required for extensive introspection or concern for the psychological quality of life. As a society becomes wealthier and more leisure time is available, people have the opportunity to pursue more narcissistic concerns, especially introspection and self-expression (Cytrynbaum, Blum, Patrick, Stein, Wadner, and Wilk, 1980). This cultural-historical hypothesis may explain why midlife crisis does not seem to occur in some parts of the world. It is more frequent in highly industrialized, affluent nations (but it is also more apparent in the United States and England than in Germany and France [Bradbury, 1975]).

Undoubtedly, important cohort influences affect the experience of middle age. Yet, such forces cannot explain why some individuals in a given cohort report crisis and some do not. Even when people from very similar economic and social circumstances enter middle age in approximately the same time frame, there are those who make the transition with little or no difficulty, and those who experience midlife as a difficult time indeed. Furthermore, careful evaluation of personal reports even suggests that within the same individual, midlife is often experienced in a paradoxical way—as a period of both difficulty and opportunity.

Defining Crisis

At this point, it may be helpful to focus on the word "crisis." Our ordinary understanding of the term may not be a satisfactory definition for the uncertainties of middle age. A midlife crisis is not necessarily a catastrophe. Take into consideration, for instance, the Harvard Grant Study subjects who described their forties as more tumultuous than their adolescent years. "Despite this turmoil, the best adapted men tended to perceive the period from thirty-five to forty-nine as the happiest in their entire lives" (Vaillant and McArthur, 1972, p. 423).

These men saw their forties as a time for reordering their lives and for reassessing the past. They experienced more overt depression during middle age than during other periods of adult life, but at the same time they seemed able to acknowledge and accept depression and turmoil as a part of the life-style of a successful man. Among the men Levinson followed, midlife transition was also characterized by feelings of vitality, and by the freedom to express compassion and reevaluate formerly suppressed aspects of the self.

Crisis need not be defined in an unrelentingly negative way. Although social scientists tend to emphasize the pathological and fatalistic implications of the term, stability and crisis do not have to be seen as positive and negative poles. Positive development can emerge from crisis—from upheaval, uncertainty, and change. As one writer has noted, the notion that crisis is always negative would lead us to "emphasize sexual satisfaction but not excitement" (Riegel, 1975b, p. 366). Or, as Washington Irving observed, "There is a certain relief in change, even though it be from bad to worse; as I have often found travelling in a stage-coach, that it is often a comfort to shift one's position and be bruised in a new place."

New behavior, attitudes, and solutions often arise out of conflict. Even in the view of learning theorists, conflict creates variability in behavior, offering the possibility for discovering new solutions. Solomon Cytrynbaum and his associates (1980) offer a systems approach to the study of midlife as a way to integrate and understand the existing research. They assume that personality differences affect one's capacity to adapt at midlife, when the coping and defensive strategies one has learned are pitted against a variety of challenges. The biological changes of middle age combine with cultural and social transitions such as launching children, career changes, and the death or illness of family and friends, as well as with a growing sense of time running out and of personal confrontation with one's own mortality, to demand a new integration of personality and life-style. Table 7.2 outlines the phases of destructuring and reintegration that Cytrynbaum and his co-authors have described.

Cytrynbaum et al., along with a growing number of researchers engaged in work along similar lines, do not believe everyone is able to seize

TABLE 7.2
Developmental phases in midlife

	Precipitators of the destructuring process →	Reassessment →	Reintegration and restructuring →	Behavioral and role change →
Conscious	Biological change and decline. Life-threatening illness. Cultural and social structural transitions such as "empty nesting," parental imperative, early retirement, status loss. "Time left to live."	Reassessment of primary relationships and current identity and life structure. Denial and externalization leads to defensively premature role change (in family or work). Emergence of real or fantasized transitional partners.	Testing in reality, and/or rehearsing in fantasy different visions of primary relations to men, women and children. Integration of the more creative forces in personality in the form of a revised dream or legacy and of existing and emergent masculine and feminine components of personality.	Recommit, modify or dramatically change behavior and/or relationships to primary family and/or work systems. Act on creating legacy, sense of community, mentoring, or other expressions of generativity.
Unconscious	Confrontation with death, mortality, death anxiety.	Mourning and grieving losses: dream, mentors, idealism, legacy. Oscillate between depression and elation. Internal distress, reemergent contrasexual and other suppressed components of personality. Reactivation of mother-son, mother-daughter separation/individuation struggle.	Realignment of defenses and consolidation of primary polarities, such as male-female and destructiveness-creativeness.	

SOURCE: S. Cytrynbaum et al., "Midlife Development: A Personality and Social Systems Approach," in L. Poon, *Aging in the 1980s* (Washington, D.C.: American Psychological Association, 1980), p. 469.

the creative opportunity of a life-span transition. Some individuals do not experience middle age as a period of positive growth. Some become disenchanted with life. Some are unhappy and dissatisfied. For some, middle-age *is* a catastrophe, and they do not adapt. When the time comes to reassess the life course, some count themselves failures and are unable to accept the accounting. Failure or perceived failure may precipitate dissatisfaction and despair. Individual differences are clearly of central importance.

Personality, Timing, and Midlife Transition

Beyond the social and economic circumstances that might insulate one from the experience of disillusionment in middle age, there is evidence that, as with most developmental phenomena, timing is important in negotiating the midlife transition. Those who progress through the adult life course in a normal, expectable way are able to anticipate and predict the life course more accurately. They experience fewer difficulties than those who do not follow the normal sequence and rhythm—the social clock—of adult life (Neugarten and Datan, 1974).

Data from the Oakland Guidance sample illustrate the importance of timing. Those who proceeded through a normative life course without detours like divorce, unemployment, and widowhood were the most satisfied. Among the Harvard men, those who achieved stable marriages before age thirty and continued to lead normal, predictable marital lives were also among the best-adjusted men. You might recall from Chapter 3 that Orville Brim and Carol Ryff (1980) contend that anticipatory socialization is a key element in successful stress adaptation.

People who are *off-time*, that is, who are going through events like marriage or parenthood or widowhood either early or late, may be isolated from the common knowledge or wisdom of the culture, making it difficult for them to use the normal lines of support and communication available to those in transition. We know how a young parent is supposed to respond to a baby, but how is a middle-aged woman supposed to deal with childbirth? How should a fifty-year-old student treat a teacher who is twenty-five?

Being off-time is not, however, an inevitable disaster. In fact, at least 7 percent of the best-adjusted men in the Harvard studies had marched along to a different drummer; whereas 23 percent of those who were the least well adjusted were considered on-time.

Why are some people able to cope with the untimely, while others are dissatisfied and poorly adjusted even when things proceed in normal,

People are not often socially prepared to cope with events that occur in their lives at times very different from when their cohorts had the same experience.

predictable ways? If upheaval, turmoil, and conflict provide the opportunity for new solutions, they also offer the prospect of failure. If one is unwilling to risk failure, the necessary adjustments may not emerge. If fear of failure produces withdrawal and constriction, growth cannot take place. As Sir James Barrie summed it up, "We are all of us failures—at least the best of us are."

The best-adjusted men in the Harvard studies were able to "accept their own tragedy" (Vaillant and McArthur, 1972, p. 424). Paradoxically, these men appeared both depressed and vibrant with energy. How can that be? Can a person be both depressed and satisfied?

Here the psychiatric literature and the social sciences converge. "As a result of the life history with its accumulating record of adaptations to both biological and social events, there is a continually changing basis within the individual for perceiving and responding to new events in the outer world" (Neugarten, 1964, p. 194). Not the events of midlife themselves, or age alone, or timing, can explain individual responses to the challenges of middle age. Rather, it is the perceptions of those events, the personal context in which they are experienced, that is central.

PERSONALITY: CHANGE AND SAMENESS

Even though the study of personality is central to the understanding of human development, personality research is rarely done from a developmental point of view. Personality is usually defined in terms of the stable, basic attributes of individuals, as an enduring set of dispositions. If there were no stable traits or capacities or skills, if human beings changed radically over the life span, then the study of personality would be pointless. In a sense, people would not have personalities (Livson, 1973).

If we make the assumption, as many developmental psychologists do, that change is constant, then most current personality research and theory are incompatible with the study of psychology over the life span. Consider, for example, the fact that good personality tests are supposed to exhibit reliability. That is, people are not supposed to change their answers from one time of measurement to another. If too many people do change their response to a particular item, that item is most often removed from the test and the opportunity to study change is lost. Klaus Riegel contended that "since human beings are changing all the time, they cannot be appropriately described by instruments that are supposed to reflect universal and stable properties" (1975b, p. 357).

Given the interests and assumptions of traditional personality researchers, it is not surprising that most studies of personality over the life course emphasize sameness, continuity, and stability. Of course, stability is not an illusion created by personality tests. People do develop enduring characteristics. Much of the available research may focus on continuity in personality at the expense of developmental change, however.

Change need not imply complete unpredictability or discontinuity. Change may be predictable, even when it is relatively dramatic. Thus, there may be *genotypic continuity* of personality without *phenotypic persistence*, which means that individuals who share certain kinds of personality characteristics may all change in the same kinds of ways, even though some of those ways are quite unexpected. For example, people who were happy, dependent, anxious youngsters may become independent, dissatisfied, assertive adults. In this instance, no single trait or characteristic has remained stable, but the course of change was the same for everyone who fit the original description. If one expects genotypic continuity, it might be necessary to develop a typology: a description of groups of individuals with the same personality traits.

Phenotypic persistence, on the other hand, is the extent to which particular traits or dispositions are stable over different times of measurement (Livson, 1973). If a researcher expects to find phenotypic persistence, then a simple study of characteristic personality traits over the life span should provide an adequate basis for prediction.

Phenotypic Persistence

Dozens of studies, both cross-sectional and longitudinal, have demonstrated the stability of a wide variety of personality traits over time. (Just a few of the characteristics mentioned in the literature on phenotypic persistence appear in Table 7.3.) Almost all of the cross-sectional research suggests that personality dispositions are stable over the life span. However, if subjects in different age groups are well matched according to socioeconomic status, education, and marital circumstance, evidence for change sometimes emerges (Neugarten, 1977).

Of course, the cohort influences that operate in a cross-section make such research extremely difficult to interpret (Schaie and Parham, 1976). Longitudinal studies report stability most often when very general characteristics (like adjustment) are employed and only one set of responses is used as a measure (Neugarten, 1977). Despite these difficulties, such research has unearthed some interesting and unexpected information.

TABLE 7.3
Selected cross-sectional studies of phenotypic persistence

Dimension	Investigator	Date
Egocentrism	Looft	1972
Dependency	Kalish	1969
Introversion	Chown	1968
Dogmatism	Botwinick	1973
Rigidity	Angleitner	1974
	Botwinick	1973
	Chown	1961
Cautiousness	Botwinick	1973
Conformity	Klein	1972
Ego strength	Sealy and Cattell	1965
Risk-taking and decision-making	Robins	1969
	Welford and Birren	1969
Need-achievement	Veroff, Atkinson, Feld, and Gurin	1960
Perceived locus of control	Brim	1974
Creativity	Kogan	1973
Hope	Haberland	1972

SOURCE: Based on B. L. Neugarten, "Personality and Aging," in J. Birren and K. W. Schaie, eds., *Handbook of the Psychology of Aging* (New York: Van Nostrand Reinhold, 1977), pp. 635–640. Copyright © 1977 by Litton Educational Publishing, Inc. Reprinted by permission of Van Nostrand Reinhold Company.

"An old codger, rampant, and still learning." Aldous Huxley

For instance, although the stereotype of middle age includes the belief that consciousness becomes increasingly narrow and restricted, there is little evidence that rigidity or dogmatism increases with age. Although older subjects are likely to persist in the use of inappropriate solutions in new problem-solving situations, most of these difficulties are caused by the slowing of psychomotor skills, or by the requirement that subjects demonstrate new learning or memory. In other words, older people do not seem to suffer from an inability to unlearn old habits or solutions, as the stereotype implies. It is just that it may take them longer to learn new ones (Botwinick, 1973).

Tests of simple rigidity most often involve situations that tap psychomotor skills. Dogmatism is a much more complex form of resistance to change. Tests of dogmatism usually measure the ability to tolerate the ideas or beliefs of others and other aspects of authoritarianism. In most of these studies, age alone accounts for less than 20 percent of the differences between people, and at least half of the age-related changes occur after the age of fifty-five. Intelligence is a much more important predictor of rigidity, no matter how it is measured, than is age (Chown, 1961; Botwinick, 1973; Riegel and Riegel, 1960; Hollander and Hunt, 1967).

Older subjects do appear to be more cautious than the young. They are less likely, for example, to make a change or to venture a response that might produce a gain but that might also risk what is already in hand. Older subjects are disinclined to take any action. They tend to choose alternatives that require no action and afford no risk, even when the probability of success for an action alternative is extremely high (Botwinick, 1966).

Even when subjects over the age of sixty-five are excluded, a trend toward cautiousness is evident with advancing age. For example, in political polls, middle-aged subjects with only a high school education choose "no response" far more frequently than the young. Once again, however, higher levels of education seem to override age effects. Furthermore, there is no evidence that the middle aged become more politically conservative as a group. Cohort differences, time-of-measurement factors, and education are much more important predictors of political attitudes than is age (Douglass, Cleveland, and Maddox, 1974; Glamser, 1974).

While studies measuring one or two specific personality dimensions at a time suggest stability over the years, multidimensional personality studies often point to areas of change, particularly when they focus on the developmental progression of different personality types.

Genotypic Continuity

One of the earliest and most influential multidimensional, longitudinal studies of personality and aging was carried out over twenty years ago at the University of Chicago (Neugarten, 1964). Information from interviews, projective tests, and questionnaires were collected from a large and representative sample of people aged forty to eighty over a period of ten years.

Although the Chicago researchers found evidence of stability for the socioadaptational processes—styles of coping, life satisfaction, and strength of goal-related behavior—important areas of change were discovered as well. In particular, they were impressed by a shift from *active* to *passive mastery* among male members of the sample. At forty, the men in the sample felt in charge of their environment: they viewed risk-taking in a positive light and perceived themselves as wellsprings of energy and change. By sixty, all this had been transformed. These same men began to see the external environment as dangerous and threatening, and the self as passive and accommodating (Neugarten, 1964, 1973).

Movement from active to passive mastery has been observed in cultural groups as diverse as the Navajo Indians, Lowland and Highland Mayans of Mexico, and culturally isolated groups in Israel. Over time, people show an increasing tendency to accommodate the self to outside influences (Gutmann, 1964, 1977, 1979). Throughout middle age, both men and women become more preoccupied with their inner lives. They pay greater attention to their feelings, experiences, and cognitive processes. Increasing interiority is among the best-documented phenomena discovered in the developmental study of personality. *Interiority* is defined by some of the traditional aspects of introversion, but it also refers to decreasing attachment to persons and objects in the external world (Neugarten, 1973).

The Chicago group was also intrigued by changes in the way people think about time. Sometime during middle age, people stop perceiving their life cycle in terms of time since birth and begin to view life in terms of time left to live. In a second major multidimensional study of personality at the Institute of Human Development in Berkeley, Florine Livson (1981a, and 1981b) has found that changing time perspective and an increased awareness of death is one of the main forces behind the kind of personality change she and her colleagues have observed over the middle years of adult life.

Over the forty years or so of the Berkeley study, evidence has accumulated that psychological health and well-being does not draw on the same resources at different phases of the life cycle. For this reason, psychological health is not particularly stable over the years of adult life, and different individuals have difficulty at different points. For instance, in the Berkeley study, responsibility and intellectual competence in adolescence predicted psychological health in men subjects at age forty. At age 30, however, such adolescent traits had not predicted psychological health well at all. This evidence confirms that the concept of genotypic continuity may be very useful in understanding development over the life span (Livson and Peskin, 1981; Peskin and Livson, 1981).

The Berkeley studies have also reported some rather interesting sex differences. For women, the process of predicting psychological health from adolescence was almost the inverse of the process for men. Women seemed to draw heavily on adolescent traits during early adulthood. By age forty, however, women who had been described as independent, bright, and interesting in adolescence were depressed, irritable, and conflicted (Livson, 1981a, and 1981b). By age fifty, these women had rebounded.

In a more detailed analysis of women who were among the best adjusted by age fifty, Livson (1981a) found that it made sense to divide all the subjects into two distinct groups: traditionals and independents. Traditional women were described as gregarious, nurturant, conventional, charming, and cordial. They exhibited a tendency to handle anxiety by repressing it, and to show rather frequent signs of *somatization*—the expression of anxiety in terms of physical symptoms like headaches or indigestion. Independents were ambitious, skeptical, and unconventional. They seemed to be able to cope with anxiety through insight and other, more direct forms of expression. One-third of the independents were divorced or widowed; many held full-time jobs. Traditionals tended to be primarily committed to the role of housewife.

Traditionals moved through the years from forty to fifty without difficulty. They did not experience midlife crisis and, at forty, appeared close and trusting, giving and poised. By fifty, they had a strong protective attitude toward others and were very nurturant. At forty, in contrast, the independents were quite dissatisfied and in the midst of what looked like a crisis. Out of touch with their own creativity and intelligence, they were bothered by demands of work and family and exhibited low levels of psychological health. By fifty, they had survived the transition and seemed much more able to trust and to be close. Livson feels that the change in these women occurred as they were able to respond to unfulfilled needs for achievement when the children began to leave home (Livson, 1981b).

In a parallel analysis of psychologically healthy men, Livson found a similar pattern. Men who improved in psychological health between forty and fifty were described as expansive, sensuous, outgoing, and gregarious, but less controlled and more unrealistic than their stably adapted counterparts. At forty, these men had chosen to suppress their emotionality and impulsiveness, adopting a sort of macho exaggeration of the masculine stereotype—angry, hostile, defensive, and ruminative. At fifty, the improvers were able to give up this dubious adaptation and move toward greater closeness and intimacy in their interactions with others. In sum, Livson suggests that for both men and women, inability to conform to the conventional gender stereotype is often associated with unhappiness and dissatisfaction as one enters middle age; but, over the years from forty to fifty, it is possible to learn to cope with stereotyped, external demands in a more personally gratifying way.

A final example of genotypic continuity from the Berkeley researchers is found in their work on intelligence and personality (Eichorn, Hunt, and Honzik, 1981). Using the Stanford-Binet, the Terman-McNemar, and

Perhaps the most significant change that has been reported in the lives of men at midlife is a growing appreciation of and desire for increased intimacy and caring in their relationships with others.

the Weschler Adult Intelligence Scale as measures of intelligence, the Berkeley researchers have found no evidence of decline in I.Q. over the years of adolescence and adulthood to age fifty. Neither did they find any reason to make a distinction between verbal and nonverbal skills; and they believe that their results cannot reasonably be explained by either practice effects or the tendency of low scorers to regress toward the mean or average of the sample.

The Berkeley group did, however, find evidence of an average gain of about 6.2 I.Q. points, and one report focused on the personality characteristics associated with changes in I.Q. This report described I.Q. gainers as balanced people—well socialized but not timid or conforming, and highly but not extremely independent, adaptable, and self-confident. Of special interest is their observation that people who as adolescents were "highly controlled (perhaps especially in sexual expression), dependable, calm, and somewhat aloof from their peers," had higher I.Q.s in middle adulthood as well as at adolescence, but that by adulthood (even young adulthood) they had changed in many other significant ways. In fact, by middle age, the men who increased in I.Q. showed a whole new list of personality correlates including insightfulness, rebelliousness, and the tendency to have interesting, unusual thoughts. Another victory for genotypic continuity!

Again and again, it appears that the intellectual aspects of personality tend to be more stable and a better predictor of the direction of personality change than other aspects of personality. For instance, data from the Oakland Guidance Study show that intellectual capacity is a much better predictor of late-life adaptation than is either psychological health in early adult life or a variety of other personality measures (Kuypers, 1981). In this study, the people who seemed to cope best with the challenges of aging were objective, logical, flexible, tolerant, and able to concentrate. Those who showed greater personality disorganization with age appeared unable to appraise life realistically and demonstrated a definite tendency toward tangentiality and confabulation in thinking. They also showed withdrawal, delusion, and preoccupation. Joseph Kuypers concludes that self-actualization is rooted both in intellectual capacity and in the limitations or advantages one's environment offers in using that capacity.

Probably the most extensive use of the concept of genotypic continuity can be found in a study, published in 1974 by part of the Berkeley group, focusing on the parents of the subjects in the other Berkeley studies and thus covering the life span from forty to seventy (Maas and Kuypers, 1974). Tables 7.4, 7.5, and 7.6 present some of the typologies and the resultant developmental patterns that emerged in this study. As Table 7.4 indicates (pp. 322–323), a wide variety of personality types and characteristics were assessed, using three different kinds of response measures (interviews, tests, and questionnaires). Table 7.5 (p. 324) offers a typology of life-styles for the female subjects, and Table 7.6 (pp. 324–325) defines each of the components of life-style that appear in Table 7.5.

Genotypic continuity was found for both personality type and life-style, although some clusters were characterized by greater change over the adult life course than were others. For example, life-style indicators changed more for women than for men, with the most dramatic changes occurring for work-centered mothers. This finding supports the conclusions reached by Livson (1981a) when she interviewed the offspring of the people in the Maas and Kuypers study.

THE BERKELEY MOTHERS.   Both work- and group-centered mothers experienced positive changes of life-style over the years from thirty to seventy. At thirty, the work-centered mothers were dissatisfied with their marriages, and reported more financial problems than the other mothers. By middle age, however, these women had ventured "into a totally new and apparently highly gratifying style of life" (Maas and Kuypers, 1974, p. 118). They had developed independence from marital ties, adequate economic rewards, and a new circle of friends. These women may well be the mothers of Livson's independents.

The group-centered mothers also seemed to be able to lead more fulfilling lives with the advent of middle age and launching. On the other hand, uncentered mothers (those who focused almost exclusively on the role of mother), who had been happy and healthy at thirty, had the lowest economic status at the age of seventy and were in poor health. Many of these women were widowed in their seventies, too late to change the course of their lives. Most had lost their homes, and few of them even had much interest in their children or grandchildren later in life.

THE BERKELEY FATHERS.   The most dramatic shifts for male subjects occurred for personality type rather than for life-style clusters, especially among the "conservative-ordering" fathers. As young adults, these fathers were described as withdrawn, shy, distant, and conflicted, and they seemed to have many marital problems. At seventy, although their marital problems had declined in importance, the men had become conventional, controlling, and even more distant.

Active-competent fathers also showed some noteworthy development over the years. As older men they were conforming, direct, capable, and charming, if somewhat critical of others and rather distant in their personal relationships. They saw themselves as active in the role of friend, despite the fact that they spent much of their leisure time alone. As young adults, these same men had been demonstrative and outgoing and had felt a strong sense of personal adequacy. But they were also described as explosive and irritable, tense, and nervous. Over the years, most of them had been occupationally successful, and the personal and economic rewards of success seemed to allow them to develop the charming, attractive personalities that characterized their later years.

What is remarkable about this study is the degree to which people who were alike as young adults were also alike in later life, despite the general instability of particular personality traits and life-style characteristics. Different types developed along the same track, lending predictability to the course of change. If the authors of this study had averaged scores over all the people in different groups, few patterns might have emerged. The value of typologies for the study of personality seems quite clear from this kind of data.

Multidimensional studies of personality, like those we have been reviewing in this section, indicate that development is characterized by both stability and change over the life course. In general, the most important

TABLE 7.4
Personality groups and personality characteristics[a]

Data source	Area	Measure
Interview ratings	Intellectual functioning	Estimated intelligence capacity
		Mental alertness
		Mental speed
		Accuracy of thinking
		Use of language
	Presentation of self	Personal appearance
		Energy output
		Freshness
		Restlessness
		Talkativeness
		Excitability
		Self-assurance
		Criticalness
		Openmindedness
		Frankness
	Relation to child-S	Critical
		Interest
	Mood	Cheerfulness
		Worry
		Satisfaction with lot
		Self-esteem
		LSR
Questionnaire	Perception	Locus of control
		Locus of evaluation
Test	Intelligence	Full-scale IQ
		Verbal IQ
		Performance IQ
		Total number of parents

[a]All entries in columns indicate significant difference of .05 or below between identified group and all remaining parents of the same sex, with the exception of the WAIS I.Q. scores, where no significant differences were observed.

SOURCE: H. S. Mass and J. A. Kuypers, *From Thirty to Seventy* (San Francisco: Jossey-Bass, 1974), pp. 150–151.

TABLE 7.4
(*continued*)

	Mothers' groups				Fathers' groups		
Person-oriented	Fearful-ordering	Autonomous	Anxious-asserting		Person-oriented	Active-competent	Conservative-ordering
Higher	Lower						
Alert	Remote						
Active	Sluggish						
Accurate	Inaccurate		Inaccurate				
	Halting						
Positive							
	Sluggish						
Fresh	Worn						
			Restless				Placid
	Mute		Talkative				Mute
	Apathetic		Excitable				
Self-assured	Not assured		Not assured				
			Critical				
Open		Closed					Closed
	Covers thought						Covers thought
			Critical		Not critical		
High	High	Indifferent	Indifferent				
Cheerful	Depressed						Depressed
Little worry	Worrisome		Worrisome				
High	Dissatisfied		Dissatisfied				
High	Low	High					
High	Low		Low				
Internal	External						
(117; 11.9)[b]	(112; 8)	(116; 11.3)	(118; 12.8)		(129; 10.6)	(127; 23.2)	(130; 10.2)
43	11	7	8		13	9	12

[b]First number is mean full-scale score; second number is standard deviation.

TABLE 7.5

Life-style clusters and life-style characteristics for three female life-style types

Arenas	Uncentered	Disabled-disengaged	Work-centered
Home and visiting	High involvement as guests	Low involvement as hostess	More visiting than in forties
	Visits others more than once a month		
Work and leisure	A few interests pursued with others	A few interests pursued alone	High involvement and satisfaction with work
	Not satisfied economically	A moderate number pursued with others	Many leisure interests
Marriage	Not presently married	Open, communicating, close marriage	Not presently married
		High involvement as spouse	
		Sees marriage as having changed for better	
Parenting	Sees children often	Mixed satisfaction and dissatisfaction	Very satisfied with children's visits
		Little expression of affect	
Grandparenting	Sees grandchildren often	Low involvement	
		Mixed satisfaction and dissatisfaction	
Friendship		Has less meaning than in forties	
Clubs	Low involvement and low satisfaction	Low involvement	
Health	Not satisfied	Has seen a doctor and been hospitalized in the last year	
		Not satisfied	

SOURCE: Based on H. S. Mass and J. A. Kuypers, *From Thirty to Seventy* (San Francisco: Jossey-Bass, 1974), pp. 47–80.

TABLE 7.6

Examples of life-style components from the Berkeley Parents' study

Arenas	Interaction	Involvement	Satisfaction	Perception of change
Home and visiting	As host(ess): Frequency For whom? Informality As guest (visitor): Frequency With whom? Informality	As home dweller, homemaker As neighbor As host(ess) As guest	With home With neighborhood	Change in frequency of being host, guest (since forties)

TABLE 7.6
(*continued*)

Arenas	Interaction	Involvement	Satisfaction	Perception of change
Work and leisure	Extent of present work for pay (full time, part time, none) Total recreational activities Number pursued alone Number pursued with others Ratio with others/alone	As worker As retiree	With present work With present financial situation With retirement	Change with retirement (for worse or better) Nature of change with retirement Changes in recreational activities (number; ratio of, with others/alone)
Marriage	Closeness of relationship Mutual instrumentality of partners Activity interdependence of partners Modes of decision making Openness of communication	As marital partner	With current marriage With decision making	Generally (changes in people's marriages these days) Changes in own marital relationship (for better or worse)
Parenting	Frequency of seeing most frequently seen child/least frequently seen child Closeness of relationship with child-S Pattern of exchange of advice between parent and children With child-S (degree of): expressiveness instrumentality control	As parent	With child-S With visiting patterns of children	Change in relationship with child-S with increasing age (closer/more remote)
Grandparenting	Frequency of seeing Informality and mutuality	As grandparent	With grandchildren With child-S's raising of grandchildren	Generally (changes in ways children are raised nowadays) Specifically (differences in rearing of grandchildren and rearing of child-S)
Family of origin	Frequency of seeing closest sibling Closeness of relationship with closest sibling	As member of family of origin (e.g., sibling)	—	Change in relationship with closest sibling
Friendship and informal relations	Closeness of relationship with "person most important to me" Instrumentality in relationship with important person Openness of communication with important person	As friend	—	Change in meaning of friendship

SOURCE: H. S. Mass and J. A. Kuypers, *From Thirty to Seventy* (San Francisco: Jossey-Bass, 1974), pp. 14–16.

changes seem to take place in how people perceive their lives and how intensely involved they are in the external world, its demands and roles. These dimensions of personality, which have been called the *executive processes*, refer to changes in one's sense of self, in the way time and the life cycle are conceptualized, and in the way emotions are experienced.

EXECUTIVE PROCESSES.   Researchers who are interested in the study of cognition tend to emphasize the internal nature of personality change with age. For example, Hans Thomae (1970, pp. 4–8) offers three basic postulates about age-related personality change:

1. It is the *perception* of change in the self, rather than the more objective cues, that is related to behavioral change. If you think you are or will be different, then you begin to behave differently.

2. How an individual perceives change is influenced by that individual's central concerns and expectations. Expectations and beliefs determine perception, and perception is basic to developmental change.

3. Adjustment to aging depends on the balance one is able to achieve between cognition and motivation. Adaptation requires either cognitive restructuring or change in the motivational structure of the individual. In other words, with age, either what you want or how you plan to acquire it must change as your life circumstances change.

Fortunately, age-related changes in perception are a positive experience for most people. According to Nancy Haan, "The life span seems typified by movement toward greater comfort, candor, and an objective sense of self" (Haan, 1976, p. 64). Moreover, Haan was able to strengthen her contention that these changes are age related after the results of a more recent analysis (1981) of two different cohorts of the Berkeley Studies showed that no consistent differences could reasonably be attributed to the different historical contexts of the cohorts. In other words, Haan found no important differences in personality trends for the two cohorts. (Curves representing development for males and females in each cohort appear in Figure 7.2, pp. 328–329).

Haan's work supports the general conclusion that the intellectual aspects of personality are most stable. That is, the people who were interested in intellectual matters as adolescents were also more interested in intellectual matters as adults. For example, *cognitive investment*—the value subjects placed on intellectual matters, ambitiousness, breadth of interests, fluency, dependability, and propensity for introspection remained quite stable between the ages of fourteen and forty-seven. Although cognitive investment did become more important over time, and although everyone in the sample seemed to become more cognitively invested, everyone maintained approximately the same rank order.

Another strong trend in Haan's study emerged along a dimension called "open/closed to self." People who were rated as very open appeared insightful, introspective, interesting, and able to think unconventionally. People who were described as closed were also conventional, uncomfortable with uncertainty, defensive, fastidious, and power-oriented. The strongest overall finding in the study was the development of greater openness, especially among those of the highest socioeconomic class. Interestingly, adolescent males had appeared more open than females, but by adulthood they had become more closed, suggesting that adult life, at least through age forty-seven or so, is more difficult for males than females.

Haan's subjects also moved toward greater nurturance, and most developed greater self-confidence over the years of adult life. In general, everyone progressed toward more effective use of cognitive abilities and became more confident, more nurturant, and more likely to view themselves as self-guided, psychological beings. Another interesting trend was discovered for interest in the opposite sex, and eroticism. Haan found that sexuality peaked in late adolescence, assuming less importance in young adulthood, but showing a definite resurgence in middle age.

In sum, Haan concludes that adaptation at midlife "appears to reflect the accrued wisdom of people who have grown tolerant and become instructed, socially and psychologically. . . . Our middle-aged had also become considerably more giving and self-extending . . . , as well as interpersonally predictable and accountable to others—or generative, to use Erikson's term" (pp. 150–151). Haan does not believe that stage-specific theories like those of Gould and Levinson can account for this data; moreover, she does not find evidence for a midlife crisis. Adults do undergo impressive changes in personality, but, this study suggests, there is no compelling reason for the definition of tightly organized stages. The most interesting observations concern the relationships between how people view themselves and how they cope with the changing demands of the environment and the changing nature of their own expectations.

Cross-sectional research on adult personality development between the ages of twenty-five and eighty-two also indicates strong developmental trends along the openness dimension (Costa and McCrae, 1981). However, the sex differences discovered in this study were quite different from

FIGURE 7.2

Average scores on PARAFAC factors

SOURCE: N. Haan, "Common Dimensions of
Personality Development: Early Adolescence
to Midlife," in Dorothy Eichorn et al., eds.,
Present and Past at Midlife (New York: Academic Press, 1981), pp. 132–133.

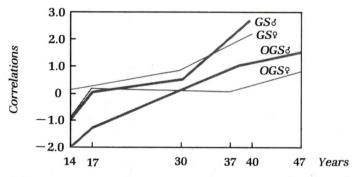

a) Average scores on PARAFAC Factor 1: Cognitively invested

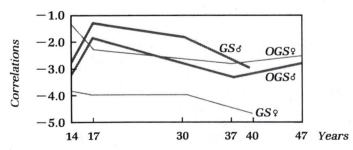

b) Average scores on PARAFAC Factor 2: Emotionally under/over controlled

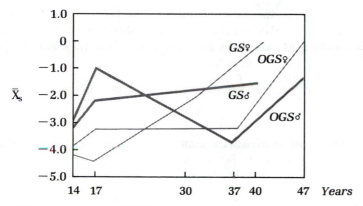

c) Average scores on PARAFAC Factor 3: Open/closed to self

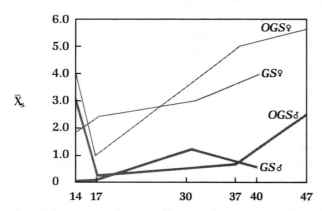

d) Average scores on PARAFAC Factor 4: Nurturant/hostile

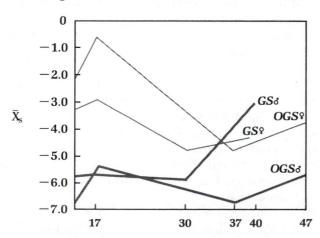

e) Average scores on PARAFAC Factor 5: Under/over controlled, heterosexual

those outlined by Haan. Costa and McCrae included people who were much older than those in the Haan study; and, probably because of the age difference, they found that openness increases with age in men. In the oldest men, thinking no longer precluded feeling, and the entire group appeared more "tender-minded." Costa and McCrae provide evidence for Albert Camus's notion that "to grow old is to pass from passion to compassion." Their findings also support the conclusion that sex-role stereotypes are more likely to dominate personality organization in young adulthood than in middle or later life, bringing us back to a question of great interest in the study of aging personality: Does sex-role behavior change in any significant way as people move through middle age?

Personality and Sex-Role Behavior

In order to understand current theory and research in this area, we must return to the original work of the Chicago group (Neugarten, 1968a, and 1968b). The finding that middle-aged people tend to move from active to passive mastery has formed a context for much subsequent work in personality and sex-role behavior, because such movement is more characteristic of male than of female development. Men appear to become less aggressive and domineering with age and also more in touch with the sensual and familial aspects of life. At the same time, evidence indicates, women move toward greater independence, less sentimentality, and greater dominance in middle age (Gutmann, 1975).

As was discussed in Chapter 5, Gutmann attributes the "normal unisex of later life" to the resolution of the parental emergency, and tends to see the sex-role changes of middle age as part of an inevitable, genetically based process. Other authors (Self, 1975) adamantly disagree. However, whether or not there is a biological imperative that directs sex-role behavior, there is little doubt that the course of personality development differs in important ways for men and women over the adult years.

For example, we have seen in several studies that men appear to progress toward greater sensuality and openness in middle age, although, in the Haan study, men remained less open than women through age forty-seven. All the males in the Haan study showed greater sexuality over time, more markedly so than did the females, but only the older cohort of males showed much progress toward increased nurturance with age. Even in the older cohort, however, the women continued to be much more nurturant than the men at all ages.

Florine Livson (1981b) indicates that many of the men in her sample who displayed a macho, exaggerated, angry, defensive style at age forty, moved toward more nurturant, intimate styles later on. However, both the independent and the traditional women in her sample also showed greater nurturance with age; the independents, in particular, were able to demonstrate greater intimacy and closeness at age fifty than at forty. In this study, it appears that those who did not conform to conventional gender roles, whether male or female, were more likely to develop real intimacy and tenderness as they moved toward old age.

Another researcher studying the Berkeley sample (Brooks, 1981) discovered some interesting relationships between sex-role behavior and *social maturity,* which she defined as the ability to live comfortably with others, to respond appropriately to both ordinary and extraordinary stress, and, when necessary, to depart from the conventional mores and institutions of a society. As men and women pass through middle age, they become more and more similar in social maturity. Brooks goes on to speculate that as women in their late fifties and sixties take responsibility for heading the household, they will begin to function like men in their thirties, while the men, withdrawing from the work force, function more and more like young women.

Brook's speculation fits the notion of "sex-role involution" as outlined by Gutmann. *Sex-role involution* is a term for sex-role reversal. In other words, Gutmann expects women to begin to function in more and more masculine ways, while men adopt more feminine modes of responding. The process eventually results in complementary roles but reverses the dominance-submission patterns of the parental years.

The evidence for sex-role reversal in the later years is scant. Even Gutmann's work has been roundly criticized on procedural grounds and because his samples have been very small (McGee and Wells, 1982). Generally, research in this area suggests that men and women move toward *androgyny*—the acceptance of both male and female personality characteristics—rather than sex-role inversion. The Haan study clearly demonstrates increasing openness and nurturance for both sexes. Furthermore, women may not actually become more aggressive or achievement-oriented with time, but simply may have greater opportunities to express themselves in instrumental ways. Over the adult years, women with the highest need for achievement tend to go back to work. The experience of employment may have more to do with the direct expression of achievement needs and aggression than the decay of parental roles (Baruch, 1967).

Finally, although personality traits may change with age, there are more overt aspects of gender typing to be considered in addition to the subjective experience we have been discussing. People develop a *gender identity*—that is, a self-concept that is masculine or feminine. They also hold certain beliefs about what is appropriate behavior, and they behave in more or less traditional ways. Research has focused on how well a person's verbal report of his or her self-concept matches the cultural sex-role stereotype, or how closely scores on tests and in interviews match this stereotype; but little work has been done on other kinds of overt behaviors or on beliefs.

The research that does exist suggests that sex-role involution, or even androgyny, does not occur in the everyday behavior of men and women. When men retire, for example, they do not begin to help out with the housework; women continue to do it and often complain of less leisure and independence with the husband's retirement. The wives of retired men report a loss of privacy and less time for their own social network because they must begin to cater to the needs and desires of their retired husbands. Furthermore, inequalities of language, both verbal and nonverbal, continue in old age. Women speak when spoken to in old age as in youth. They lower their gaze and generally behave in more submissive ways. Men retain control of the conversation at senior citizen's centers, just as they did at the Rotary Club in their youth (Keating and Cole, 1980; McGee and Wells, 1982). Clearly, more research along these lines seems warranted before we can speak of the "normal unisex of later life."

SUMMARY

The literature on middle age has been characterized by controversy over the past few years. Whereas the efforts of the psychiatric and clinical research communities clearly suggest that the middle years are characterized by great turmoil, at least for men, the objective research of social psychologists and sociologists does not support the notion of a midlife transitional crisis. Middle-aged people themselves do not describe their lives in terms of crisis. They tend to report feeling happy, satisfied, confident, and in control.

Middle-aged people do not view the normal events of the adult life cycle as emergencies. Some events generally regarded as negative, such as the climacteric for women and retirement for men, are regarded with rather positive feelings by older people. Certainly, some aspects of middle age produce discomfort, but the negative aspects are described, by the people who have experienced them, as inconveniences rather than as disasters.

It may be that questionnaire and survey data really reflect denial and the social desirability of responses. Middle-aged people may be unwilling or unable to admit that they are experiencing crisis. Based on this hypothesis, several attempts have been made to develop a typology of middle age that might reflect the propensity for crisis. One major study, for example, has classified males along two dimensions: openness to conflict and degree of life satisfaction. Using this simple system, the researchers were able to identify groups likely to experience crisis, and those likely to negotiate the midlife transition smoothly, developing a deeper sense of satisfaction, confidence, and faith in the future.

It is also possible that certain historical periods are more likely than others to be associated with the experience of crisis. Social or economic upheaval may produce greater difficulties among the middle aged, or the shift toward greater introspection and self-expression in affluent, industrialized nations may be central to the experience of crisis.

Neither the hypothesis of denial nor the concept of cohort differences can explain, however, the kind of individual differences that seem to characterize the research on midlife crisis. Part of the solution may lie in adopting a different definition of crisis. If we look at middle age as a time of opportunities for growth and development as well as a difficult transitional period, we can begin to see the variety of experience and resolution that may proceed from the events of middle age.

Some people do not grow and develop. For some, middle age is a catastrophe. Perhaps the experience of being off-time produces a disruption of the normal sequence and rhythm of the life cycle. Certainly, the evidence suggests that it is more difficult for people who experience a disruption of sequence or timing to make optimal adaptations to middle age. It is also possible that some individuals are unable to make the necessary adjustments because their behavior is restricted by a view of adulthood that does not permit failure, mistakes, and therefore learning.

Although the issue of midlife crisis is unresolved, both the psychiatric literature and the research of social scientists point to areas of developmental change in personality over the course of adult life. It has been suggested that the researchers who investigate personality typically underestimate such change because of their focus on the stable, universal aspects of personality. For this reason, the concept of genotypic continuity has received special consideration in the developmental study of personality.

The study of stability in traits and characteristics over the life span documents phenotypic persistence in personality. These studies have challenged long-standing stereotypes about increasing dogmatism and rigidity in older people. There is little evidence that middle-aged people, or even older people, become increasingly rigid.

Multidimensional studies of personality have been more fruitful in identifying areas of personality change than the typical study of one or two traits that appears in the literature on phenotypic persistence. These studies usually include a wide variety of personality variables and life-style characteristics, often presenting the results in terms of developmental progression for a number of personality or life-style types rather than for the sample as a whole.

In general, development over the adult years seems to occur most dramatically in the intrapsychic processes, or the ways in which the individual perceives the self and the outside world. Cognitive theorists have extrapolated from this finding that perceived change is the key to behavioral development. Perceived change is mediated by the beliefs and expectations of the individual. Adjustment results from the balance the individual is able to achieve between cognitive processes and motivational structures.

In terms of empirical research, the evidence suggests that when a number of personality dimensions are defined, those that are most closely associated with the intellectual aspects of personality tend to show increasing importance with age, but relative stability. Personality characteristics that seem to reflect openness to the self, nurturance, and sexuality show change over time. Openness and nurturance increase in both males and females, whereas sexuality seems to go through a period of relative inhibition in young adulthood, followed by a resurgence in later life.

Life-style indicators, such as work- or group-centeredness, appear to influence life satisfaction differentially over the adult years, especially for women. Although both work- and group-centered women show increasing levels of satisfaction through middle age and later life, women who are unfocused appear to become increasingly dissatisfied and poorly adjusted as the years go by.

Finally, the sex differences that are so prominent throughout all this research have generated an important set of issues regarding the potential for sex-role involution or androgyny in later life. Most of the evidence suggests a shift from active to passive mastery for men and a movement toward increasing dominance and independence for women, throughout middle age and later adulthood.

Nevertheless, many of the personality trends identified in the research we have reviewed in this chapter are valid for both males and females. Both sexes become more open, more nurturant, and more self-confident. It may be too that the apparent sex-role inversion described by some authors is the result of a wider variety of expression available to older women, especially the opportunity to express achievement needs more directly; or, perhaps sex-role involution merely reflects the increasing opportunity for people who have never been comfortable with the traditional stereotypes to express themselves in more personally gratifying ways.

It is also important to point out that although we do not yet have adequate research on many kinds of sex-role behaviors or on beliefs about gender typing, the work that does exist is at odds with the evidence suggesting involution or even androgyny. Men and women continue to be-have in fairly traditional ways when it comes to the everyday behaviors of life. Until a wider variety of research has been undertaken on the matter, it is unlikely that an accurate picture of gender-role development in later life will emerge.

Chapter 8

The Expanded Context: Family, Home, and Leisure

The man coming toward you is falling forward on all fronts. . . .
His hair is loosening, his teeth are at bay, he breathes fear,
His nails send tendrils into the belly of the atmosphere;
Every drop of his blood is hanging loose in the universe;
His children's faces everywhere bring down the college doors;
He is growing old on all fronts; his foes and his friends
Are bleeding behind invisible walls bedecked with dividends;
His wife is aging, and his skin puts on its anonymous gloves;
The man is helpless, surrounded by two billion hates and loves; . . .
The man coming toward you is marching on all fronts.

OSCAR WILLIAMS

Oscar Williams's lines illuminate the militant, inexorable sense of time passing and the strong currents of circumstance that carry people along as they reach the midpoint of adulthood. Middle-aged people are driven by obligations, responsibilities, hopes, dreams, and ambitions, at a high tide of interdependence and expectation. Long past the beginnings of adult life—of marriage, family, and work—yet not near the end, they are in midstream, and few change horses there. Most simply spend their energies trying to stay in the saddle.

The struggle to maintain balance is a major theme in this chapter. The tasks of middle age focus on the maintenance of one's position while the whole world shifts. Marriages alter, children leave home, one's own parents retire and begin to show the signs of advanced age, and the relationship of work and leisure to life-style is transformed.

In this chapter we will examine the major social forces that threaten equilibrium in the middle years. We will explore the impact of adolescent children on family structure and parental psychology, continuing through the launching and marriage of those once troublesome teens; and we will look also at the changing relationship between middle-aged people and their own parents, for as the society ages as a whole, more and more people are both parents and children for a longer portion of the life span.

Finally, we will discuss the changing roles of both work and leisure in the lives of middle-aged people. The intricate balance between work and play is altered as one moves into the empty-nest stage of marriage and on to the retirement years, and many middle-aged people are essentially unequipped to deal with lives that do not revolve around the traditional roles of parent, worker, and homemaker. We will define the concept of leisure and look into the possibility of developing a leisure career in later life.

LOVE AND MARRIAGE

When Charles Dickens wrote, "They were the best of times; they were the worst of times," he could have been describing marriage at midlife: full of promise and disappointment, satisfactions and turmoil. For some, the transition from parent-of-an-adolescent through launching to the empty nest comes as a relief. Now there is time and energy for a real husband-wife relationship again. For others, the exit of children means looking across the empty nest at a stranger. Our discussion begins with a look at marriage and family in the fourth stage of the family life cycle, when parents are confronted by the adolescence of their children. (As outlined in Chapter 4, a family enters Stage 4 with the adolescence of the oldest child.)

Adolescent Children and Middle-Aged Parents

Most of the available evidence points to deterioration of relationships within the nuclear family after the very earliest years of childrearing. Some researchers have reported a plateau and some have even noticed slight recovery as the children move outside the home during the school hours, but by the time the children reach twelve or fourteen, friction begins increasing again among all members of the family group.

What is going on in the fourth stage cannot fairly be characterized as war, maybe not even as full-scale rebellion. It is more a series of nagging, bickering, quarreling skirmishes. Psychologists armed with questionnaires still find much continuity between generations in such long-term dimensions as basic value structure, respect, and need for approval. But the day-to-day interaction between parent and child involves much that is disagreeable (Hurlock, 1975; Lurie, 1974).

In one of the more interesting and detailed longitudinal analyses of marriage and family at midlife, Michael Farrell and Stanley Rosenberg have documented the trend toward lower satisfaction, finding a nadir as the children leave home. However, they did not find the same pattern for all of the four personality types described in *Men at Midlife* (1981) (see Chapter 7 for descriptions). The worst declines in marital satisfaction occurred for the punitive-disenchanted men, fully 45 percent of which expressed the notion that marriage is simply no longer rewarding after twenty years. On the other hand, 80 percent of the transcendent-generative men found their marriages rewarding, and more than half of them described themselves as still feeling quite close to their wives. Although the forces affecting these families were similar in many ways, different families adopted very different strategies in dealing with the pressures of launching and the empty nest.

In most of the families, the women became more autonomous in middle age, often returning to work or pursuing an education and changing the power structure of the marriage. Furthermore, women were generally closer to the children throughout adolescence, often forming alliances that further upset the balance of power. Frequently, these alliances were based on secretive and deceptive attempts to protect the husband from

"Oh, to be only half as wonderful as my child thought I was when he was small, and only half as stupid as my teenager now thinks I am." Rebecca Richards

dealing with his loss of control. For instance, a wife might support the oldest daughter's bid for independence, even secretly helping her pay for an apartment despite her husband's disapproval. She avoided open confrontation, overtly nodding in agreement, but she let the child know she considered the husband's disapproval irrational and ill-guided. Husbands, especially among the pseudo-developed men, collaborated in these subterfuges by pretending that nothing was happening and describing their marriages as close and happy, when, in fact, husband and wife had ceased sharing much in the way of important feelings and experiences.

Eventually, both husband and wife began to resent the pretense and the inauthenticity. Sometimes spouses even came to view the partner as alien and dangerous because there was so little honesty in the relationship. The transcendent-generative men seemed able to cope better because they were able to confront the conflict, risking marital dissolution at times, but unable to settle for a devitalized relationship.

In his novel *Bread Upon the Waters*, Irwin Shaw writes about a family enmeshed in this kind of situation. For years the father has been protected from the realities of both the children's lives and his wife's life. Finally, his college-aged daughter lets him in on the plot:

"... Oh, Daddy, boys and girls aren't like what they were when you and Mummy were young. You know that."

"I know it. And I hate it."

"Mummy knows it. She doesn't keep her nose in a book day in and out," Caroline said harshly. "Who do you think gave me the pill on my sixteenth birthday?"

"I suppose you're going to say your mother," Strand said.

"And you're shocked." Strand saw, with pain, that there was malice and pleasure on his daughter's face as she said this.

"I'm not shocked. Your mother is a sensible woman," Strand said, "and knows what she's doing. I'm merely surprised that she neglected to tell me."

"You know why she didn't tell you? Because she's in the conspiracy."

"What conspiracy?" Strand asked, puzzled.

"We all love you and we want you to be happy." There was a hint of childish whimper as she spoke. "You have an impossible picture in your head of what we're all like—including Mummy. Because we're yours you think we're some sort of perfect angels. Well, we're not, but for your sake, we've been pretending, since we were all babies, that we are. We're a family of actors—including Mummy, if you want to know the truth. With an audience of one—you. As for Eleanor and Jimmy—I won't even go into it. Nobody could be as good as you thought we could be and I've told Mummy we shouldn't try, that you'd find out and you'd be hurt more than ever. But you know Mummy—she's made of iron—if she decides to do something, there's no bending her. Well, now you know. I'm not saying we're *bad*. We're just human. *Today* human" (Shaw, 1981, pp. 482–483).

Farrell and Rosenberg believe that men at midlife use their families as a primary source for the experience of both love and control. The maturation of the children threatens them, and in the ensuing struggles, a child may be viewed as a traitor, or even an enemy, especially during launching. When the children are still in early adolescence (the "pre-launch cocoon"), mothers tend to set the limits, and the father's role includes backing her up. As the offenses become more adult and therefore more serious, the father becomes more involved. Both mother and father see threats to the cocoon from "outside forces," rather than from the maturation of the children, and they tend to exaggerate the differences between family beliefs and ideals and those of the outside world.

As launching approaches, open battles with the children become more intense. At this point, family rules, routines, and beliefs, laid in cement by the parents, are often threatened by the identity excursions of the adolescent. As Farrell and Rosenberg point out, new ideas can produce growth in both parents and child. Limited deviance can serve a positive function, and apparently many transcendent-generative men are able to

For some middle-aged parents, the lives of their children represent the only opportunity for the fulfillment of their own youthful dreams.

take advantage of their child's search. Too often, however, less positive dynamics develop.

The problems are complicated by the fact that parents seem consistently unwilling to let their children go; yet children do need assistance in their battle for independence. Adolescents may need the most help just when they are being the most difficult, lashing out in severe opposition to parental values and attitudes and evoking strong fear of abandonment in their parents. Both parties frequently wish for greater love, understanding, and consideration. Often adolescents reawaken the ambitions and dreams of parents or express suppressed parental conflicts, especially about issues like sexual freedom and achievement.

Some parents overidentify with the child, pushing for the fulfillment of their own youthful plans, hoping to vindicate themselves through their children. For others, one or more children become scapegoats representing the parent's own unconscious impulses and eliciting from the parent confusing double-bind communications that give permission with the left hand and take it away with the right. (The standard joke "If you can't be good, be careful" is such a double-bind statement, as are the injunctions "Don't do anything I wouldn't do" or "I know you'll do the right thing.")

Farrell and Rosenberg contend that men actually have a harder time letting go of their children than women, who, perhaps because they have been closer, seem more prepared. The men seemed to experience a stunned sense of loss, clinging to the past, while the women pushed to move on to the next stage of life. (Although the father's role is usually considered peripheral, Farrell and Rosenberg point out, the father's emotional involvement is often intense, even when he is unable to see what is going on or to evaluate his own contribution.) When the experience of launching is very different for husband and wife, that difference can itself become an additional source of consternation.

Marriage and the Middle-Aged Woman

The men and women in the Berkeley and Oakland studies we reviewed in Chapter 6 have shown an unusual degree of marital stability. Only about 20 percent of both groups were divorced after an average fifteen years of marriage. Yet, research reports underline the difference between "his" marriage and "her" marriage by the time a couple reaches middle age. The correlation between recent ratings of marital satisfaction given by wives and those given by husbands averaged only about .31; that is, husbands and wives show surprisingly low levels of agreement with regard to how satisfying their marriage is (Skolnick, 1981).

Those individuals who continue to put up with unsatisactory marriages are especially interesting. In Arlene Skolnick's sample, the men in stable but unsatisfying marriages tended to exhibit low levels of self-confidence, while the women were more aggressive and less nurturant than either divorced women or those in satisfactory marriages. People in unsatisfactory marriages often are critical of each other, have discordant personalities, and engage in serious conflicts. Not that people in happy marriages have no conflicts. They do. But they are able to deal with problems more constructively. Skolnick (1981) believes that the differences between happy and unhappy marriages are differences not of *content*, but of *process:* that is, not what is at stake, but how it is handled.

Looking a little closer at the feminine perspective, Janice Stroud (1981) has considered longitudinal data on the Oakland Guidance sample of women in their early forties. In this group, women who were full-time homemakers were likely to report the most stable, happy marriages. Homemakers had the highest morale and self-esteem and were described as giving, warm, and conventional. College-educated homemakers seemed perfectly suited to be the wives of high-status men. These findings make sense in terms of Skolnick's (1981) analysis too, for she reported that personality assessments for men and women in satisfying marriages show a striking degree of similarity in cognitive investment and intellectual capacity, social character, coping style, social maturity, and need for achievement.

Continuing her analysis, Stroud looked at the lives of working women who were equally committed to home and family (dual-track), those who had worked off and on but were presently unemployed (unstable workers), and those who were working and very committed to their careers (work-committed). She found the work-committed women to be equally as warm and giving as the homemakers and to be the least negative of the group. Although many of these women were parents too, 80 percent of them were currently single, leading Stroud to conclude that during this stage of the family life cycle at least, work and family commitment are virtually incompatible.

The dual-track and unstable workers in Stroud's sample seemed to find middle age least satisfying. Dual-track women were assertive and independent but exhibited low self-esteem and poor morale. They also appeared rather cold. Stroud believes these women were probably very uncomfortable in the traditional feminine role during the adolescence of their children: "With marriages less happy than the homemakers and jobs less rewarding than the work-committed, double-track workers seem to have the worst of both worlds" (p. 376). These women may be Florine Livson's (1981a) independents, who reached a low point in life satisfaction in early middle age.

Stroud's unstable workers seemed to live in a kind of despair. In adolescence, they had been indistinguishable from their peers, but by early middle age these women had become hostile, angry, depressed, socially unaware, and negative. They did not enjoy their marriages or their children and had been unable to find jobs that might provide some sense of satisfaction.

We might also recall, however, that a number of studies have demonstrated the growing independence and aggression of middle-aged women and the growing passivity and sensuality of midlife men, suggesting that these changes are developmental phenomena. The effect such changes may have on the balance of power in the marital relationship can create considerable strain: "Put together the mounting strong-mindedness of the midlife wife and the strange stirrings of emotional vulnerability in the midlife husband, and what have we got? A mystery story at the peak of its suspense" (Sheehy, 1976, pp. 196–197).

It is little wonder that Stage 4 marriages are often characterized by low marital satisfaction when compared to other stages of the marital or family career (Pineo, 1961; Rollins and Feldman, 1970). Divorce rates for middle-aged people reflect the intensity of some of these pressures. In the period between 1970 and 1974, the incidence of divorce and separation rose spectacularly for all women, but particularly for those approaching forty (Bernard, 1975). The increase for women over forty has also been staggering. Between 1960 and 1969, for example, divorce rates for females aged forty to forty-nine increased by well over 40 percent (Krishman and Kayani, 1974).

Given the strains of raising adolescent children and the readjustments required by changing sex-role behaviors, it seems remarkable that most middle-aged couples stay together, but they do. Even though divorce rates are rising for this group, as they are for all age groups, it is still true that the frequency of divorce and separation declines over the family life cycle. It is also true that relationships with adolescent children begin to improve as they establish themselves as adults.

In the discussion of midlife crisis in Chapter 7, we considered the potential for growth in the midlife transition. Certainly adolescent children can be a stimulus for new development on the part of their parents as well as a source of strain. Today's adolescents appear to be flexible, tolerant people. Many are concerned with issues of public responsibility and are better able to cope with the magnitude and pace of change in their society than were former generations. Their freedom and freshness can reactivate old conflicts, but these same qualities can also provide a challenge and stimulate growth in their parents. As John Conger (1972) phrased it, "This requires both patience and the courage of self-analysis, but it is vital."

Changing sex-role behavior can also provide a context for growth, for self-analysis, and for renegotiation of significant interpersonal relationships. A midlife marriage may wither, but it can also flourish. For those who do transcend midlife readjustments, there appear to be ample rewards hidden in the empty-nest marriage.

The Empty Nest

Although marital satisfaction never again reaches the romantic heights of the years before the first child is born, marriage after the nest is empty may well be more satisfactory than marriage during most of young adulthood or early middle age (Glenn, 1975). Since women are particularly dissatisfied with both the marital relationship and the spouse during the Stage 4 marriage, the improvements in satisfaction may be a function of launching. The positive effects of launching do appear to outweigh whatever anxiety and loss is experienced by middle-aged women, and thus the women's reactions may serve to enhance the marital relationship. Moreover, middle-aged men seem to be changing in a way that is compatible with improved marital relationships. If they become less work-oriented and more concerned with family life and with the marital relationship, it may contribute to increased satisfaction (Lowenthal and Chiriboga, 1972; Deutscher, 1967).

The successful empty-nest marriage is built around common interests and increased companionship. Joint and shared leisure activities now become an important predictor of marital satisfaction. Joint leisure activities require a high degree of communication and interchange; parallel or shared activities are performed together, although they may require little interchange. Figure 8.1 shows the relationship between marital satisfaction and joint leisure activities for different periods of the marital career. Period IV in the figure corresponds to the period of the empty nest; period II represents that part of the family life cycle devoted to the rearing of preschool and school-aged children.

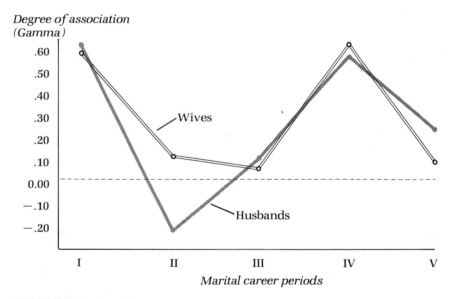

FIGURE 8.1
The association between leisure time spent jointly and satisfaction over marital career periods

source: D. K. Orthner, "Leisure Activity Patterns and Marital Satisfaction over the Marital Career," Journal of Marriage and the Family, 37 (1975): 91–102. Copyright © 1975 by the National Council on Family Relations. Reprinted by permission.

Although it has been noted that the u-shaped curve describing marital satisfaction between periods I and IV is rather flat (there is neither a deep trough nor an extremely pronounced recovery), such a curve is found with a fair degree of consistency when couples are followed over the family life cycle into the empty nest (Rollins and Galigan, 1978). The curve could be related to other phenomena, like changes in occupational careers, but it has more often been explained in terms of the pressures created by childrearing. During the rearing of children, the number of family roles (mother, father, husband, wife, homemaker, provider) is great, and not all of them can be fulfilled equally well. When the level of conflicting demand creates *role strain*, couples find that they have less and less time for companionship and joint leisure activities. The launching of children not only gives married people time to have more fun together, but also gives them time to spend on separate activites. Livson's (1981a) observation of increasing satisfaction for independent women, as well as Stroud's work suggesting that work and marriage are incompatible for women in the pre-launch cocoon, fits the notion of role strain.

Even in studies where a u-shaped function has not been found, (Skolnick, 1981), there is little evidence that marital satisfaction simply corrodes with the passage of time. In Arlene Skolnick's study, for instance, marriages did change, some for the better and some for the worse, and most of the change was attributable to situational factors: more or less money, the intensification or alleviation of problems with children, changes in health, and the like. There is great potential for better or for worse over time in marriage, and the renegotiation of a marital relationship during middle age is critical to adjustment in later life. Married older people tend to be much happier than singles (Peterson, 1968). Skolnick wonders if the same problems couples in her study have managed might not lead younger cohorts to the divorce courts. She feels that today's young adults are unaware that a marriage can improve, even after a period of real discomfort and dissatisfaction.

On the other hand, if the divorce rate among younger adults goes up, the remarriage rate in middle age may show a similar increase. Perhaps those who remarry in middle age will find companionship and harmony in their later years. The culture is changing rapidly, and data collected over the next ten or twenty years will contribute substantially to our understanding of middle age, middle-aged people, and the culture of middle age. We can expect to find some influential cohort differences as the postwar generation moves in this phase of life.

Yet, cohort differences can be overestimated, even exaggerated, by both social scientists and families. Although research suggests a substantial number of similarities in the events, attitudes, values, and beliefs that shape the lives of family members from one generation to the next, current emphasis on instability and change can create its own mythologies.

Perhaps one of the most important of these is the unsupported notion that the extended family is dead. Not only are the middle-aged parents operating in a nuclear family, but they are also members of a *lineage family*, consisting of an older, a middle, and one or more younger generations (whether married or unmarried).

THE LINEAGE FAMILY

The term *lineage family* refers to three generations: the middle generation and their parents and children. (The *lifetime family*, often called the *nuclear family*, refers to only two generations: parents and children.) Over the years, the middle generation has been roundly criticized for its behavior toward both its progeny and its parents. The media often paint a picture of a generation who have spoiled their children and then lost touch with them, and who have neglected their own parents, carting them off to understaffed, unsanitary institutions and abandoning them. Studies of exchange and visitation in the lineage family simply do not support this kind of exaggerated image, however. Evidence about the transmission of beliefs and values across the generations also shows surprising generational continuity suggesting both contact and communication (Troll and Bengtson, 1982).

Core Values in the Lineage Family

The media are not solely responsible for overestimating the generation gap. Family dynamics seem to be involved as well. Both parents and children tend to exaggerate generational differences, reflecting the *generational stake*. For parents, the generational stake is defined by the need to see their children carry on family traditions and beliefs; for children, it is a matter of finding how to express their own uniqueness. Generally, however, investigators have found that political and religious affiliations are very strongly transmitted from one generation to the next. Liberalism, egalitarianism, and dedication to causes is transmitted moderately well; and attitudes toward work and achievement are readily handed down from one generation to the next.

Changes in the social climate over different cohorts tend to affect the expression of values most strongly. For example, children may continue to go to the same church but be less conventionally moralistic than their parents. Both father and son may view themselves as very "dedicated to causes," but the son may spend his time trying to prevent the building of new atomic energy plants while the father fights a local planning commission over zoning restrictions.

Of course, there are important generational differences too. Research suggests that sex-role orientation and attitudes toward sexual behavior have not been strongly transmitted across generations of the last few years. Furthermore, whereas achievement orientation and motivation apparently are handed down, belief in specific statements of the so-called Protestant work ethic, like "hard work always pays off," is not transmitted as consistently (Troll and Bengtson, 1982).

Surprisingly, the quality of family life or the warmth of family interactions does not seem to influence the degree of transmission very strongly (Troll and Bengtson, 1982). Parents and children may relate out of love and caring, from guilt, or from a sense of duty. Warmth and involvement between generations is, however, associated with greater similarity of self-assessed personality traits (Clausen, Mussen, and Kuypers, 1981).

In terms of personality, there are more similarities between generations in intellectual traits than in other characteristics. "Placing high value on intellectual matters and being insightful and fluent are also clear and compelling characteristics that many . . . share with their parents" (Clausen, Mussen, and Kuypers, 1981). These and other personality effects are observed both in families that are close and in those that are not close. For instance, the degree of negativism a father shows is likely to be strongly related to rebelliousness and the lack of insight in the son. If mother and daughter are not close, the mother's negativism is likely to be associated with undercontrol, defensiveness, and negativism in the daughter. In close relationships, negative attitudes do not have as strong an effect (Clausen, Mussen, and Kuypers, 1981).

It appears that our parents are likely to influence our thinking and behavior whether we like it or not, or even whether we like them or not. When adults are asked to "describe a person," they make more spontaneous references to their parents than to anyone else in their lives, and this is the case even for adults who are seventy or eighty years old.

Studies of exchange and visiting are compatible with the data on beliefs and attitudes. The middle generation does not stand on a solitary peak, surrounded by chasms of generational differences on either side. In fact, one classic study of transactions over three generations suggests that the image of a bridge is much better suited to the middle-aged (Hill, Foote, Aldous, Carlson, and McDonald, 1970).

Exchange in the Lineage Family

Help and comfort are extended across the lineage family, traveling in all directions, but most often from the middle generation to both the old and the young. Such help includes the provision of services and goods, outright gifts of cash and necessities, and emotional and physical assistance. While it is true that the elderly do not often live with their middle-aged children, the middle-aged pay the lion's share of the taxes that support Social Security, Medicare, and all of the public services provided to the elderly. These services along with the education of the young are a part of the legacy of the middle generation in a modern social system (Sussman, 1972).

Most young adults want to live near their parents, especially once the fourth generation is born. Furthermore, although elderly parents prefer to live in physically separate quarters, they like to be near their middle-aged children, and there is a good deal of visiting. In fact, one study estimates that about 70 percent of all young adults see their parents weekly, and about 40 percent of all middle-aged children also visit their parents weekly (Troll and Bengtson, 1982). Young or middle-aged children who have moved to other parts of the country are also likely to stay in touch by letter or phone. Often members of the extended family who strike out for new places serve as "family scouts," exploring new territory. If the scouts are successful, the rest of the extended family follows (Troll and Bengtson, 1982; Sussman, 1977).

As young adults grow older and establish their own homes and families, they perceive greater closeness and family solidarity than they did during the explosive years of launching. Newlyweds often report, for example, that family relationships improved after they moved from their parent's home. Interaction with the older generation is also best during the years when all three generations are able to live independently. Elderly people who are forced to move in with their children (and about one-third eventually will) do so because they are in deteriorating health. Relationships suffer from such close quarters, but it is not clear whether the problems stem from physical proximity itself or from the waning strength and growing dependence of the old (Troll, 1971; Johnson and Bursk, 1977).

As elderly parents become progressively less able to care for themselves, *role reversal* may occur: the middle-aged child takes on some of the obligations and responsibilities of a parent. Role reversal undoubtedly creates anxiety, even resentment, on both sides. New learning is required. And the middle generation may find that providing a home for the aged is especially burdensome while they are putting one or more children through college or boarding a divorced son or daughter and a grandchild or two (Sussman, 1977).

Some authors have questioned whether caring for the physical health of a very elderly person is not more stress than middle-aged children can handle (Hess and Waring, 1978) at a time when life can be extended far beyond the physical capacity of the individual for self-help. Perhaps as middle-aged women return to the work force, the number of elderly living with their own children will decline, especially as the empty nest of their middle-aged children is refilled more and more frequently by the instabilities of their grandchildren's lives. Hess and Waring suggest that in the future kin ties may more often be experienced as voluntary, as the nature of middle and old age changes.

Certainly, the changing nature of life in the middle years has altered how some family roles are fulfilled. Notably, the role of grandparent has changed in recent times. Most adults become grandparents for the first time in middle age (the average age is forty-seven), and few fit the old image of the white-haired, bespectacled, checker-playing or cookie-baking grandparent. In fact, most grandmothers and grandfathers are still very active outside the home. Many, if not most, are working at full-time jobs, and some have difficulty accepting the idea that they are really old enough to be grandparents. Nevertheless, most middle-aged people are happy with their position in the family matrix. Many prefer grandparenting to parenting, and almost all agree that grandparenting is easier (Robertson, 1977).

The Middle Aged as Grandparents

The current descriptive literature on grandparenting is notable in that it illustrates the wide variety of role behavior among middle-aged and elderly people. Until much more work is done, it is difficult to generalize about either the role of grandparents in general or the meaning of grandparenting, for there is so much difference from one family to the next (Troll, 1980). What we do know is that about 75 percent of all middle-aged and elderly people have grandchildren, and most visit them about once a week.

Age does make a difference in how people respond to the role of grandparent. People in their forties and their seventies feel less positive about becoming grandparents than people in their fifties and sixties. The age of the grandchildren is also important: grandparents tend to be closer to young children, becoming less involved as the children become adolescents (Troll, 1980). It is clear, however, that grandparents can play an important role in the lives of children. They are involved in the transmission of political and religious attitudes, and they often play a part—sometimes positively, sometimes negatively—in family problems. In one Chicago sample of grandparents and grandchildren, 80 percent of the subjects reported trying to influence one another, especially with regard to values and life-style (Troll, 1980).

The data on grandparenting underline the potential importance of grandmothers, in particular, for family functioning. Grandmothers often provide baby-sitting and may even serve as a surrogate parent for the

The American family is linked through its women; the emotional heritage flows from mother to daughter rather than from father to son.

children of widowed or divorced parents. They also serve the lineage family as interveners in crisis situations and as the bearers of tradition. Parent-child tensions are often relieved through the good offices of a grand-mother, who may provide rest and recuperation for exhausted parents (Robertson, 1977). Moreover, lineage families tend to be linked through middle-aged women, their daughters, and their mothers. In a sense, the extended family in America is an emotional matriarchy.

Of the two major studies that have been devoted to the description of types of grandparents, one included both grandfathers and grandmothers, and the other focused exclusively on grandmothers. The first study, by Neugarten and Weinstein (1964), offers an analysis of the meaning of the grandparent role and a five-part typology of grandparenting (see Table 8.1). According to Neugarten and Weinstein, grandparenting seemed to take on several major kinds of meaning in the lives of their subjects. Most frequently, their subjects reported a sense of both biological renewal, expressed in statements about carrying on the family line, and emotional self-fulfillment, reflected in reports of companionship and good times

TABLE 8.1
A typology of grandparenting

Style	Characteristics
Formal	Always interested in child, provides special treats, indulges child, may even babysit, but leaves parenting to the parent, does not interfere or give advice
Fun-seeker	Informal, playful relationship like a playmate; authority is irrelevant, expects mutually satisfying emotional relationship; sees grandparenting as leisure
Surrogate parent	Grandmother assumes actual care-taking responsibilities, as when the mother is working
Reservoir of family wisdom	Distinctly authoritarian grandfather dispenses special skills or resources; parents are subordinate to him as well as the child
Distant figure	Visits on holidays and special occasions; contact infrequent and fleeting; benevolent but remote

SOURCE: Based on B. L. Neugarten and K. K. Weinstein, "The Changing American Grandparent," *Journal of Marriage and the Family,* 26 (1964): 199–204.

with the grandchildren. Acting as a resource person also provided a source of meaning for some members of the sample, who emphasized the potential of the role for providing experience, financial aid, or time that the parents cannot offer. A few of the grandparents suggested a fourth theme: the vicarious satisfactions derived from the accomplishments of grandchildren, who may be able to achieve goals that preceding generations were not able to fulfill.

Some of Neugarten and Weinstein's grandparents found little or no meaning in the role: slightly less than one-third of the sample were characterized as *remote* from their grandchildren. Many of these grandparents felt uneasy about their remoteness and offered rationalizations based on the ages of the grandchildren, on their own busy life-styles, or on strained relationships with children.

The second major study (Robertson, 1977) also presents a typology but is limited to the description of grandmothering. About 26 percent of the women in the Robertson study were labeled *symbolic* grandmothers. Their primary focus is on what is morally right for the child: on setting a good example. The symbolic grandmother seems similar to the formal type as described by Neugarten and Weinstein (see Table 8.1). Another group, *individualized* grandmothers, were more concerned with deriving emotional satisfaction from their relationships with grandchildren than in seeing that the grandchildren were reared properly. A third group, about 29 percent of the sample, were described as the *apportioned* type. The apportioned group were concerned both about doing what is right for the child and deriving emotional satisfaction from the relationship. Robertson, like Neugarten and Weinstein, found that about one-third of her sample was remote, uninvolved, or unconcerned with the grandmother role.

Robertson also found that socioeconomic level was a good predictor of the type of grandmother a woman would become, and that life satisfaction and marital status also seemed important. Yet, despite their differences, 80 percent of the grandmothers agreed that a good grandmother is a person who loves and enjoys her role, sets a good example, provides help, and is a good listener, but does not interfere.

We have talked a good deal about the middle-aged, middle-generation woman. She is the center of the lineage family, the mother, the grandmother. Much less is known about the role of the middle-aged, middle-generation man in the lineage family. Occasionally one can glean some clues about his attitudes and behaviors in a study of parenthood or grandparenthood, but he is usually underrepresented in any study sample.

In their study, Neugarten and Weinstein (1964) do state specifically that the theme of biological renewal might have proved more important if the sample had contained more paternal grandfathers. The study produced one particularly helpful observation, however. The theme of emotional self-fulfillment was most salient among grandfathers, who in their middle years had the leisure time to relate to their grandchildren in ways they had found impossible with their own children.

As the studies of grandparenting indicate, middle-aged males infrequently appear in the literature on home and family, just as middle-aged women do not receive much attention from social scientists who study occupational life. This does not mean that the middle-aged male has no significant role in the family; nor does it mean that the role of worker is unimportant for the middle-aged woman. We simply do not have enough data on women workers or on middle-aged fathers and grandfathers to support lengthy discussion. For the middle-aged male, we can begin to get a sense of role development only in the literature on occupational psychology; that is, in the literature on work.

Without a doubt, the entry of unprecedented numbers of women into the labor force is changing the structure and meaning of work. It may be that the financial independence of women will offer more occupational independence to men. Or, perhaps the needs of women will change the structure of work in ways that will be important to men. It is also possible that data on working men and women at midlife will show very different dissatisfactions and rewards. We simply don't know. What we do know is that as the twentieth century draws to a close, some important changes are taking place in how middle-aged men perceive their role as workers.

WORK

Robert Benchley once quipped that "the thing to do is to make so much money that you don't have to work after the age of twenty-seven. If this is impractical, stop work at the earliest possible moment, even if it is a quarter past eleven in the morning of the day when you find you have enough money." American workers at midcareer now seem more attuned to Benchley's message than they once were. Moreover, as the United States, and most of the highly industralized countries of the world, move into the postindustrial era, we are experiencing a tremendous change in the nature and meaning of work. Today, about 65 to 70 percent of all workers hold jobs that provide services, and, by the year 2000, it is estimated that only about 10 percent of the labor force will still engage directly in the manufacture of goods. Vigorous growth of the white-collar, middle-class occupations is expected through the turn of the century (Havighurst, 1982). Figure 8.2 presents the shifting job scene since 1900.

Because both the nature of work and attitudes toward it are changing, American business and industry face unprecedented challenges of the assumptions on which they have operated for the past hundred years or so. People no longer want to work just to have a job; nor are they content simply to make more and more money. There is a general cultural emphasis on the importance of personal growth and interpersonal relationships. These new values have led to demands for interesting, meaningful work and increasing disaffection with the conforming world of the gray flannel suit.

These problems are particularly clear to those who study management and organizational behavior and especially those interested in changing attitudes toward work (Van Maanen, 1977; Beckhard, 1977). Many middle-aged men are turning down top job offers because they do not want to make the kinds of personal sacrifices that prestigious positions often demand. Remember that 95 percent of all Americans are employed by organizations of one kind or another. Organizations demand that people work long hours, travel, and even transfer to other parts of the country. They often offer more money, challenge, and responsibility, harder work, and greater prestige as rewards. Apparently, middle-aged men are no longer so readily willing to jeopardize their health, families, friendships, and free time just for a promotion.

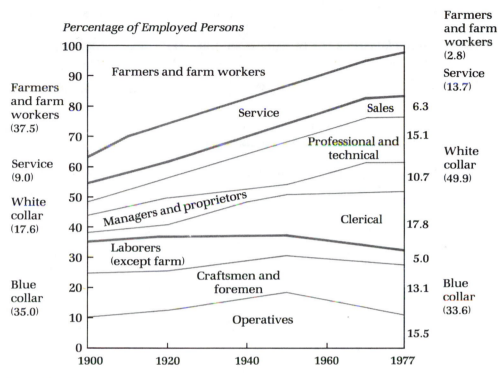

FIGURE 8.2
Occupational trends in the United States

SOURCE: *U.S. Bureau of the Census,* Occupational Trends in the United States, 1900–1959; Manpower Report of the President, 1968; Employment and Training Report of the President, 1979.

Researchers and writers in organizational behavior have often suggested that if business and industry are going to retain and promote their best and brightest, they will have to accept substantial changes in the characteristics of the successful career. The personal and familial needs of middle-aged workers, from foremen to executives, must be met, or the most competent people will simply leave (Beckhard, 1977).

The motivations of middle-aged, middle-class men are no doubt varied, but perhaps the most widely discussed factor in recent years has been the increasing value middle-aged men are placing on marriage and family. As children are launched, the marital relationship gains renewed significance, and husbands often want to spend more time with their wives. Don't forget the research on changing sex-role behaviors: husbands at midlife may become less aggressive, less assertive, more sensual, and more passive than they were as young men.

The economics of modern life are probably influential as well. To-day's middle-aged man feels little obligation to leave his heirs a large estate. As the financial pressures of caring for the children ease, monetary in-ducements become less effective. Moreover, many middle-aged wives re-turn to full-time work, adding to the family coffers and reducing or eliminating their husbands' freedom to transfer. Finally, Social Security, pension plans, and retirement planning allow some middle-aged men the option of early retirement, more leisure, greater freedom, and even the opportunity for a second career (Beckhard, 1977).

It is not clear whether such trends among middle-aged men are rela-tively new phenomena or whether the culture is simply allowing the ex-pression of an underlying developmental tendency. One classic study from the early 1950s did clearly foreshadow today's organizational dilem-mas, however. In 1952, Raymond Kuhlen and George Johnson conducted a study of schoolteachers that documented a shift in focus from "expansion-seeking motives" (such as getting a different job or being promoted) to "contracting motives" (such as retirement). According to Kuhlen (1968), these shifts could be predicted by the kind of need hierarchy described by Maslow (1970): whereas young adulthood is consumed by the need for economic security and success, middle age is devoted to the fulfillment of needs for affiliation and service.

Whatever the causes may be, there is less intense competition now than in the past for upper rungs of the organizational ladder. Lotte Bailyn (1970, 1977) has called those who do not choose to compete the "nonaccommodators." Nonaccommodators derive satisfaction from their families, are more people-oriented than accommodators, show signs of better marital adjustment, and are not as success-oriented. If more men are becoming nonaccommodators, how will organizations change at the top? Nonaccommodators are loyal to their organizations and are concerned with the problems of the people around them and with the larger society as well. Surely, organizations will suffer if all of these loyal, people-oriented individuals refuse top management positions.

Job Enrichment

The disaffection, alienation, and resignation of middle-aged workers, from the assembly line to the executive suite, has sparked much new research on job enrichment. How can you make work more satisfying for those who are not inspired by the achievement ethic? In an attempt to explore this question, Katz and Van Maanen (1974) defined three areas of job en-richment:

1. Job characteristics: Enrichment can be achieved by redesigning daily tasks so that they are less boring, more efficient, and more rewarding.

2. Interactional factors: Enrichment can be accomplished by improving the work environment, particularly the human processes and relationships.

3. Organizational policy: Enrichment can be facilitated by offering flexible hours, increasing the opportunities for advancement, providing greater job security, and improving fringe benefits.

It has been suggested (Katz, 1977) that workers need different kinds of enrichment at different times in their tenure on a job. In the beginning, organizational policies will be more important, then interactional factors, and finally job characteristics will become most salient. For the first few weeks or months (or even years if the job is very complex), job safety and security are dominant. One needs to be accepted and to feel important. Such job characteristics as autonomy and challenge may interfere with optimal performance by a new employee.

Later in one's tenure on the job, autonomy, challenge, and the completeness or wholeness of the result one produces become important. In assessing the careers of the men in the Berkeley and Oakland Guidance studies, John Clausen (1981) concluded that, in addition to income, three intrinsic features of career at midlife predict high levels of satisfaction for most middle-class males in white-collar jobs: (1) a good match between personal interests and job characteristics; (2) the opportunity to utilize their abilities; and (3) the freedom to develop their own ideas. Among blue-collar workers, security was more important than these intrinsic factors, and blue-collar men were especially happy when their jobs offered good hours and entailed little stress. Whether in a blue- or white-collar job, convenience and security were more important predictors of satisfaction among older men.

A surprisingly large proportion of the men Clausen studied were satisfied with their jobs, regardless of job status. About 75 percent felt that their current job represented what they wanted to do, or approximately what they wanted, and 67 percent were judged "well satisfied" on the basis of interview data. Older workers generally seemed to be more satisfied and to believe their jobs were more important than did the young. In fact, in another study of work satisfaction, about 45 percent of the older men stated that they would not change jobs even if they were offered more money (Havighurst, 1982).

Yet, there are those who not only want to change jobs, but do in fact change jobs during midlife. In recent years, about 10 percent of men between the ages of forty and sixty voluntarily changed their career paths; it has been suggested, however, that the poor economic conditions of the late 1970s and 1980s have produced a climate in which the number of people who claim to be interested in changing careers is artificially low. After all, if unemployment is rampant, why rock your own personal boat by grousing or wishing for a different job? Better to accentuate the positive. You can't always have what you want, but, on the other hand, you can't always want what you have either. And so there are those who risk the economic undertow and set sail for a new course. The middle-aged woman reentering the job market is prototypal, but the trend can also be seen among men, even those who have been highly successful in their first careers (Havighurst, 1982; Sheppard, 1971).

Second Career

Not much hard data has been developed about the decision to change careers at midlife. Researchers have even had some difficulty deciding what to study. A variety of factors and considerations may motivate a midlife career change. Different motives for change may yield different results and lead to different conclusions. Technological advances eliminate some jobs, sending individuals scurrying for second careers. Early retirement sometimes allows people to look for a completely different kind of work while they are relatively young. Early retirement simply means coming to a natural end of an external career at a young age—perhaps by becoming too old for it, as in the case of professional athletes or dancers, or through personal choice. Retirement is not necessarily voluntary, even when it occurs at an early age. This is true, for example, not only among athletes, but among military career people, police personnel, and photographers' models.

In addition, some people deliberately choose to leave one career for another. This group is not easy to describe. Ewan Clague (1971) has suggested that people make such choices when unexpected opportunities arise, because of changes in their family lives, because they are bored, because they have not been able to achieve, or because they feel the need for more leisure time. And this list is by no means exhaustive.

It does seem clear that many more people would voluntarily embark on a second career if the way were eased. A 1971 report on blue-collar workers shows that as many as 35 percent of the subjects interviewed wanted to change to different occupations. There are also definite signs of interest among management and professional people. At some eastern colleges that encourage the enrollment of older students, as many as 20 percent of the graduate students are over the age of thirty-five (Kay, 1974).

General economic problems are not the only inhibiting force, of course. Even in the best of times, it is more difficult for older men and

Early retirement presents some with an unprecedented opportunity to begin again, to widen their horizons no matter how successful they were in a first career.

women to find satisfying jobs. Unemployment rates for males begin to skyrocket after the age of forty, and those who are unemployed remain so longer during the later years. Government statistics show that nearly 25 percent of men over sixty are unemployed, but this figure is probably lower than the actual number. Many men in this age bracket have dropped out of the labor force because they cannot find jobs. Older people believe that age discrimination is widespread, and they are probably right. If they are, there may be a large group of workers who would like but have not found second careers (Kay, 1974).

Unemployment among older workers is often the product of stereotypic ideas about whether older workers can learn new jobs and be as productive as young workers. The available data challenges negative attitudes. Workers in late middle age complete retraining programs as often as younger ones, and there is scant evidence that production in the context of one's occupation (as contrasted with the laboratory context) declines over the career (Siegler and Edelman, 1977). Nevertheless, the specter of unemployment undoubtedly discourages many from attempting a midlife career shift. Morever, the immobility that characterizes occupational life for many older workers has many unfortunate effects for the organization as well as for the individual, and these effects may act to reinforce the negative stereotype. Dissatisfaction and boredom can lead to withdrawal from or hostility toward the organization and to an increasing emphasis on life roles outside the organization.

Organizations could provide long-term employees with greater opportunities for lateral transfer, emphasizing increased satisfaction rather than demanding high levels of achievement. Companies could make provision for second careerists—for those who want to leave and those who want to enter the organization. They could also provide more flexible career designs, permitting an older worker to return to school or even to take a sabbatical leave. Such practices might well produce substantial dividends in morale, productivity, and interpersonal relations for both the individual and the organization. People who cannot move from an anxiety-provoking or dissatisfying situation can be difficult and unpleasant co-workers.

A number of authors concerned with the occupational arena have suggested that the postwar generation may add momentum to the developments we have been discussing. As those in the "class of '67" (the birth cohort of approximately 1945) approach middle age, they may dramatically increase the pressure on organizations. This group is the largest affluent generation this country has produced, and they will expect to maintain the standard of living to which they are accustomed. They already have great accessibility to early retirement programs. They are raising smaller families and increasing their economic and geographic mobility. They have more education than earlier generations and seem less likely to believe that they cannot be reeducated (Kay, 1974).

As Robert Havighurst concludes, "It has become clear that there is likely to be a growing amount of movement from one job to another in the age period forty-five to seventy. The most desirable situation is one that maximizes freedom of choice for the individual so that he (she) can change jobs if he (she) wants to, retire early or late, take a part-time job, and combine a changing work role with developing leisure and community member roles" (1973b, p. 616). Many experts agree with Havighurst about the need for and the advantages of the flexible career. Research has led to promotion of the four-day work week and extended educational or experimental sabbaticals, and to the notion that industry should adopt the nine-month academic year, which would allow workers to transfer or change from one job to another.

Much of the fervor for flexible careers stems from attempts to solve the occupational and organizational problems we have been discussing. Many have also argued that a flexible career pattern will make it easier for Americans to handle their leisure time in increasingly creative and fulfilling ways.

LEISURE

Even though the research on work suggests that Americans these days are less willing to sacrifice for the sake of a promotion or an increase in pay, the middle-aged American in the last quarter of the twentieth century is still very work-oriented. In fact, current interest into the effects of providing for flexible career paths abolishing mandatory retirement ages is, at least in part, a reflection of the general concern about the way Americans use (or fail to use) leisure time.

Generally, leisure time is not given a high priority in the value hierarchies of most middle-aged people, and it seems that few researchers have given it much thought either. Yet, this state of affairs seems bound to change. Retirement is no longer a period of preparation for death, but is an important and substantial part of the normal life span. Many retirement communities now are open to people over fifty, not sixty-five, and retirement in late middle age is not uncommon. Furthermore, the withdrawal of the middle-aged male from the work role and his increased dissatisfaction with the work environment suggest that middle age is the optimal time to develop leisure interests.

Some view the prospect of so many individuals with unstructured time on their hands as a rather frightening possibility. Lord Arran asks, for example, "What are they going to do with their spare time? Judging by present social habits one envisages a great sea of blank gaping faces stretching out before innumerable television screens from midday to midnight with short pauses for the absorption of tinned foods recommended by the advertising programmes" (1976, p. 113). This Englishman's comments indicate that Americans are not alone in their conviction that idle hands are the devil's workshop. There is a general distrust of leisure in industrialized Western cultures: industrialization requires that people value hard work. Moreover, industrialization depends to some extent on the worker's ability to delay gratification, to forgo the consumption of immediate rewards in favor of larger rewards that are gradually accumulated. Leisure can be defined as enjoyment of immediate gratification, and as such it may be a difficult concept to promote in a highly industrialized nation.

Types of Leisure

To be clear about what we are discussing, it is useful to distinguish between *instrumental activity*, which has as its objective some form of future gratification, and *expressive activity*, which offers immediate gratification—satisfaction in the process of doing. There are some important problems inherent in making this distinction. One person's work may be another's play. If you paint for the money, it is instrumental activity, even if you enjoy painting. If you paint for pleasure, it is expressive activity, even if you sell your paintings (Gordon, Gaitz, and Scott, 1977).

To minimize the problems of defining leisure, some researchers have simply studied how people spend the time they do not spend at work. Although this kind of study does yield some interesting information, it seems a rather inadequate way to approach the subject of leisure and does little to advance our understanding of how to help people deal with large amounts of free time. As Figure 8.3 indicates, almost all this leisure time is spent watching television. In one study only one-half of the sample spent any time at a sport or hobby. Few even participated as spectators in any outdoor activities. Volunteer work as leisure is nearly nonexistent.

It is little wonder that so many men over sixty-five complain of having too much free time and say they derive more satisfaction from work than from leisure activities. Between 82 and 90 percent of the subjects in various surveys have said they would work even if they did not need the money. For most of these people, leisure is a marginal activity to be enjoyed only if one has worked long and hard and deserves a vacation (Pfeiffer and Davis, 1974; Parker, 1975).

A very different approach to understanding leisure begins with an operational definition along a continuum of leisure activities from mild relaxation to intense involvement. For example, Gordon, Gaitz, and Scott (1977, p. 316) have defined leisure as "personally expressive discretionary activity, varying in intensity of involvement from relaxation and diversion at the low end of the continuum, through personal development and creativity at higher levels, up to sensual transcendence at the highest levels of cognitive, emotional, and physical involvement." In Table 8.2, various leisure activities are classified by intensity.

Gordon and his colleagues offer the developmental hypothesis that leisure activity can balance or bridge role conflicts at different stages of the life cycle. For example, the leisure activities of parents probably become less home-centered as children grow and there is less conflict between the need for stability in family life and the drive toward accomplishment at work. Whatever its developmental role, however, leisure is rarely seen as a legitimate activity in and of itself. Most people feel leisure activities are justified by their relationship to work. Leisure is seen as legitimate because it allows people to get some "well-deserved rest" and return to do yet a

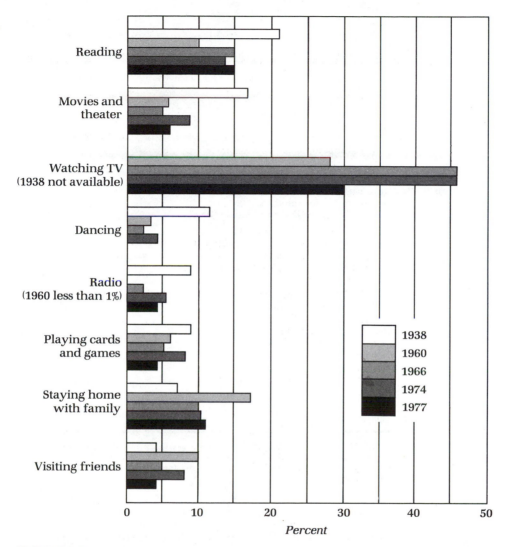

FIGURE 8.3
Favorite leisure activities: selected years, 1938–1977

SOURCE: *U.S. Department of Commerce, Social Indicators, 1979 (Washington, D.C.: U.S. Government Printing Office, 1980), p. 539.*

better job. The retired person, especially, faces a crisis of "legitimacy" (Decker, 1980). For most Americans, the only leisure careers that are acceptable are those that retain some meaning as work.

For example, the activities at the lower levels of the Gordon, Gaitz, and Scott typology in Table 8.2, such as relaxation and sleeping, would

TABLE 8.2
Qualitatively varying forms of leisure activity according to intensity of expressive involvement

	Forms of leisure activity
Very high	Sexual activity Psycho-active chemical use Ecstatic religious experience Aggression, "action" (physical fighting, defense or attack, verbal fighting) Highly competitive games and sports Intense and rhythmic dancing
Medium high	Creative activities (artistic, literary, musical, etc.) Nurturance, altruism Serious discussion, analysis Embellishment of instrumental (art or play in work)
Medium	Physical exercise and individual sports Cognitive acquisition (serious reading, disciplined learning) Beauty appreciation, attendance at cultural events (galleries, museums, etc.) Organizational participation (clubs, interest groups) Sight-seeing, travel Special learning games and toys
Medium Low	Socializing, entertaining Spectator sports Games, toys of most kinds, play Light conversation Hobbies Reading Passive entertainment (as in mass media usage)
Very low	Solitude Quiet resting Sleeping

SOURCE: C. Gordon, C. M. Gaitz, and J. Scott, "Leisure and Lives: Personal Expressivity Across the Life Span," in R. Binstock and E. Shanas, eds., *Handbook of Aging and the Social Sciences* (New York: Van Nostrand Reinhold, 1971), p. 314. Copyright © 1977 by Litton Educational Publishing, Inc. Reprinted by permission of Van Nostrand Reinhold Company.

hardly serve as a way of life. The diversions listed at the second level—socializing, attending sporting events, playing games, pursuing hobbies, reading, and watching television—are also unlikely to gain much acceptance as leisure careers. On the other hand, activities like exercising, learning, participating in clubs and interest groups, traveling, and attending cultural events might qualify because they require cognitive, emotional, and physical energy. The creative activities, like painting, writing, playing music, and so on are clearly legitimate. In fact, they are work roles for many people and thereby obvious career material. At the highest level, sensual transcendence, few activities might be viewed as legitimate career interests. Sexual activity and the use of psycho-active drugs or ecstatic religious experience have little relationship to work. On the other hand, competitive games and sports might gain some acceptance, if the participants were accomplished.

Unfortunately, the elderly retiree is unlikely to perform well at the most culturally acceptable leisure pursuits, like the creative activities or sports. Decker (1980) notes that the *portent of embarrassment*, that is, fear of making a fool of oneself through poor performance, predicts that older people will be forced to accept low levels of expressive involvement in leisure activities. Clearly, we need to develop a concept of leisure independent of, or at least in addition to, its work-related meanings: a *leisure ethic*.

A Leisure Ethic

The activities of life can be classified not only in terms of the amount of energy they require, but in many others ways. For instance, we might classify both work and leisure activities with regard to the degree of freedom they permit, or the ability to proceed at one's own pace. The opposite of freedom in this sense is constraint: the ways in which the activity or the environment demands an activity be done in a particular way. For instance, constraints include demands for speed, either from the activity itself, as in the case of playing a video game like Pac-Man, or from the environment, as when a music teacher demands that one pick up the pace of a particular piece. We might also classify activities with regard to the kind of satisfaction they provide. Some activities are satisfying just because we enjoy them. In contrast, some are so distasteful you couldn't pay someone to do them: they lack any intrinsic reward whatever, or may even be so aversive that no amount of extrinsic reward will suffice to make people do them voluntarily.

Using these two dimensions, three "pure" types of activities that occur in everyday life can be identified. *Pure leisure* is activity that provides both high levels of freedom and intrinsic motivation. *Pure job* is defined by high levels of constraint and high extrinsic motivation. And *pure work* lies in between leisure and job, offering both high levels of constraint and high levels of intrinsic motivation. In this view, leisure and work are not mutually exclusive, but leisure is simply the freedom to "work" with something one likes to do at one's own pace. The challenge, then, is to find the things one really likes to do (Neulinger, 1980).

Ideas like these are part of the evolution of a leisure ethic. Currently, however, most of us do not have much experience of freedom when we are at leisure. Instead, we feel we have nothing to do. And so the concept of "leisure education" has also evolved—not a particularly clear idea at best. As Lord Arran asked in 1976, "What is meant by this aim leisure education, and how is it to be achieved? How as a subject is leisure to be evaluated and how does it relate to the rest of the curriculum?" (p. 108). Many educators see leisure in terms of sports, games, and practical activities such as woodworking, metalworking, and technical drawing. The assumption is that leisure activities can be taught in an educational environment. But how do you teach someone to have fun? You can teach people to play football or to crochet, but can you teach them to enjoy these activities? After a lifetime of training in the delay of gratification, can people really be expected to find immediate rewards sufficiently valuable and important? Can they be expected to be able, or to allow themselves, to enjoy the immediate rewards that are characteristic of leisure activities?

Decadence, decline, and social instability are all thought to be natural consequences of too much leisure time, and the notion of leisure education is not free of this underlying set of assumptions. Educators are exhorted to teach people to use their free time wisely. Using one's leisure time wisely sounds a lot like work. Until we are able to observe and define our attitudes toward leisure more precisely—until we are able to see how these attitudes may affect the results of our research—it seems unlikely that much progress will be made toward a comprehensive, workable program of leisure education.

Was Lord Arran justified in his concern for the masses as a great sea of gaping blank faces, or was Disraeli the better prophet when he observed that "increased means and increased leisure are the two great civilizers of man"?

SUMMARY

In this chapter we have explored some of the changing events and circumstances that are part of American life for many middle-aged people, and we have traced the development of some of the major concerns and themes that flow from those events. The issues of importance in middle age are not static. There is a shading of one theme into another even over this fairly circumscribed period of adult life.

During middle age, the adult moves from a lifetime family that usually includes adolescent children to the family of the empty nest. The individual's perception of self as a person, a parent, and a spouse is influenced by the course of these events. Midlife marriage is a source of both great satisfaction and great turmoil. Relationships within the nuclear family deteriorate from the earliest years of child-rearing, reaching a nadir in the years of the pre-launch cocoon and launching.

Some couples are able to transcend these difficult years, confronting the conflicts and experiencing personal development. Others are unable to make the necessary adjustments. One particularly common pattern involves the growing independence of both the wife and the children in the midlife family. Wife and children secretly collude to sustain the husband's image of himself as central to the family decision-making process, when, in fact, they may consider his notions irrational and ill-guided.

Parents often seem unwilling to let their children go, and both parties yearn for more love, understanding, and consideration. Children may reawaken parental conflicts and dreams, becoming scapegoats or idealized extensions of the parent's youthful self.

Open warfare with the children is but one of the great changes of the midlife marriage. In many homes, the mother returns to a full-time job, demanding many new adjustments in the family. Apparently, marriage and work are not compatible for most women in early middle age. Data show that dual-track women are not as satisfied or well adjusted as are homemakers in their early forties. By age fifty, however, these dual-track mothers will usually have found how to express themselves in more gratifying ways. The most dissatisfied midlife women seem to be those who have led unstable occupational lives, finding satisfaction neither in work nor in marriage.

For those who deal successfully with the midlife transition, marriage can provide ample rewards. Marital satisfaction improves during the empty-nest period, and general life satisfaction increases for many women who were not well suited to the domestic life of a young wife and mother.

Middle-aged women occupy a central place in the lineage family throughout the launching years and into the empty-nest phase of the lifetime family. They are at the intersection of the American three-generation, lineage family, extending aid and comfort to both the younger and the older generations. Although interactions proceed more smoothly when the three generations maintain some degree of physical independence, there is much intercourse between the elderly and their adult, middle-aged children.

Problems can arise when an elderly parent requires full-time care. The decision to institutionalize a failing parent can be very difficult, and role reversal can create anxiety and resentment in both parent and child. However, the general tenor of relationships between middle-aged people and their parents seems to reflect a growing understanding and acceptance of the older generation by the middle aged.

Research on the transmission of core values in the lineage family suggests that basic political, social, and religious orientations are handed down from one generation to the next, but that the way in which these values is expressed may differ with the historical times. Parents tend to exaggerate the similarities between themselves and their children, whereas children tend to overestimate the differences. This phenomenon has been attributed to the generational stake, the need of the parent to see family traditions carried on and the desire of the children to establish their own uniqueness.

Family warmth and the quality of interaction do not seem to affect the transmission of either values or personality characteristics. Personality effects, especially the transmission of intellectual traits, have been observed in both families that are close and those that are not. Negative attitudes in the same-sex parent seem especially likely to evoke undercontrol and defensiveness in children.

Studies of exchange and visiting are compatible with data on values and attitudes. Most middle-aged children visit their parents when it is geographically possible, whether out of desire or a sense of duty, obligation, and guilt. Not only by visiting, but by extending financial assistance and help up and down the lineage family, the middle-aged generation serves as a bridge between the young and the old.

During middle age, many couples see a fourth generation added to the lineage, as they become grandparents for the first time. Usually they still lead vigorous, active lives outside the family. Many grandmothers work full-time, but most still manage to derive satisfaction and meaning from the grandparent role.

All grandparents do not function in the same way. Some value grandparenting as biological renewal; some see it as an opportunity to serve as a resource person; and others value it as a form of emotional self-fulfillment and for the experience of vicarious accomplishment. Styles of grandparenting also vary widely, from formal and remote to fun-seeking.

Less is known about the feelings, behaviors, and attitudes of grandfathers than of grandmothers. Although the role of the middle-aged man in his family has come in for greater scrutiny in recent years, we probably still have more data on the relationship of the midlife man to his work than to any other aspect of his life-style. Women return to the labor force in great numbers at midlife (and many never leave), but the research still tends to focus on the meaning of work for men in middle age.

Generally, today's middle-aged males are not as committed to their jobs as they were twenty or thirty years ago, and they seem to be expressing a greater interest in marriage and family. Early research on motivational changes at midlife suggested these developments, but many organizations were still taken by surprise and are now concerned about losing the best and most qualified of the "nonaccommodating" middle-aged men, many of whom are refusing promotions that would require diminished family involvement and loss of whatever roots they have in the community.

The trend toward less intense competition within organizations has led to detailed study of such policies as job enrichment and second careers.

The men who express the greatest satisfaction at midlife not only are making a good living, but also are experiencing their jobs as a good match between personal interests and job characteristics and as an opportunity to utilize their abilities and develop their own ideas.

Whereas a surprisingly large number of middle-aged men express satisfaction with their current careers, there are also those who wish they could be doing something else. Moreover, there are those who actually do change careers—perhaps 10 to 20 percent, although the proportion might well be higher if the general economy and the attitudes of employers toward the older worker were to change in a positive way.

It has been suggested that the postwar generation may add momentum to the movement toward second careers in middle age. Not only are many of these people educated and affluent enough to consider second careers, but, since they are not having nearly as many children as their parents, they may be greeted by a much greater demand for older workers as their generation ages.

Besides the option of career change, some have suggested that more flexible career designs might also be a great advantage in middle age. By mixing leisure activities and work, people would find it easier to enjoy their work over the years of midlife and also to develop creative and fulfilling ways to use their leisure time.

Research has clearly demonstrated, however, that although Americans may not be as driven to work as they once were, neither are they prepared for a life of leisure. Americans do not value leisure-time pursuits, and most retired men complain of too much free time. Americans spend most of their leisure time watching television. Flexible career planning would make it possible for individuals to explore other leisure activities and also to begin to value them. Thus, nonwork pursuits would become part of a more complete and continuous life-style that would facilitate transition to and enjoyment of retirement.

Another solution to the problem of increasing leisure is leisure education, a concept that is not yet clearly defined. (Nor do researchers even agree about what *leisure* is: some have defined it as free time; others describe it as expressive activity.) But it seems unlikely that leisure education will help Americans to develop fuller leisure lives until we better understand, and perhaps have changed, the basic attitudes and values of this work-oriented society. Until then, the end of mandatory retirement and the extension of such ideas as the flexible career may offer the most practical alternatives for the growing number of Americans who arrive at an extended period of retirement with few nonwork interests and an abhorrence of idleness.

Perspectives

The Future and the Middle Aged

Over the next two decades or so, it is very likely that some spectacular cohort changes will emerge in the way middle age is lived in this country. As you will remember from the Introduction, the post–World War II baby boom is now on the brink of middle age, and the sheer size of this group of people is bound to have a substantial impact on every social institution through which it passes. This is an exciting time to begin a study of the midlife transition. In particular, a series of time-lag studies might prove of great value. Time-lag designs involve the study of one age group, for instance people between the ages of thirty-nine and forty-three, at several different times of measurement, for instance in 1985, 1990, 1995, and the year 2000.

If we were to embark on such a series of time-lag studies, what kinds of effects might we expect? Looking back at the history of this cohort and how it has affected the way we view childhood, adolescence, youth, marriage, family, and work, there seems little doubt that the effects will be both impressive and unpredictable. Certain common themes appear likely, however. The size of this group has always been of great importance. There were not enough classrooms when these people were in elementary and secondary schools. There were not enough spaces in colleges and universities. There were not enough jobs when they became young adults, and there was not enough housing when they began to establish families. In all probability, the unemployment rate will begin to decline as this group finally establishes itself in the economy, and per capita income is likely to rise (Bower, 1980). But there is also reason to believe that many in this cohort will continue to experience failures of the system.

At midlife, so the stereotype suggests, we are finally able to rest on our laurels. Success and life satisfaction are the rewards of hard work and dedication during young adult life. Nevertheless, the energy crunch, the entry of women into the labor force, and the large number of people entering middle age do not set the stage for the majority to see this part of the American Dream fulfilled. Perhaps the baby boom cohort will learn to lower its expectations, thus averting some general cultural midlife crisis. Perhaps they will accept the postponement of economic or social success until later in middle age—at fifty or sixty—combined with a change in the retirement age from sixty or sixty-five to seventy or seventy-five. Or, this generation may change the meaning of middle age in a more significant way. Perhaps they will seize the opportunity offered by smaller families and longer lives to change direction at middle age. Mor people may choose reeducation and a second career. Women, especially, will no doubt continue to reenter schools and the market place at a tremendous rate during the middle years.

The effects we will see will not only be a product of size, however. They will also depend on some of the other important historical changes reflected in the lives of the postwar baby boom. This cohort will live longer, on the average, than any before it, and its members will probably be healthier throughout their life span. In general, people in this cohort can be expected to engage in more political and social activism, to be more critical of governmental policy, and to have a positive attitude toward change. As this generation takes the reins of government and industry, they will be in a position to make some important long-term contributions to the social scene. We would certainly want to include a survey of political attitudes and opinions in the time-lag studies we planned. Since the culture has often responded poorly to the needs of these indi-

viduals, it will be interesting to see what kinds of changes they propose. Or will they become more content with the system as they become more established? The next ten or twenty years should provide an unparalleled opportunity to test the time-honored cliché that the younger generation grows up to be just like the older one.

The meanings of sex, marriage, and divorce have been revolutionized during the adolescent and adult years of this cohort. If the trends continue, we can expect that second and even third divorces may become fairly commonplace. Questions about how people relate to adult stepchildren, and to the children and grandchildren produced by former marriages, have never been asked. How do people respond to stepgrandchildren? Do the adult stepchildren feel any responsibility toward an aging stepparent? Do adults continue to engage in relationships with half- or step-siblings?

It will also be interesting to see whether this cohort accepts aging more or less gracefully than older people do now. Will they be less affected by the changes in appearance and sexual function that accompany age because they are better informed? Or will they be more strongly affected because sexual function and attractiveness have become so culturally important? Will the double standard of aging begin to disappear as double standards for sexual behavior have? As older women enter the labor market and become wealthier, more successful, and more powerful, they may also be considered more attractive. Furthermore, today's middle-aged man may date a younger woman more easily than tomorrow's. Because there are so many women in the postwar baby boom, there are a relatively large number of available younger women today. When the boom is middle-aged, however, the number of available younger women will shrink considerably. Older women may seem increasingly attractive as the number of young people in the culture diminishes.

Aside from the impact of divorce, sexual liberation, and the employment of women on family life, there are other reasons to suspect some significant differences in the way the baby boom

generation carries out the adult role of parent. It has been suggested by John Conger (1968) that one of the most important sources of the infamous "generation gap" of the 1960s and 1970s was a cohort difference between adolescents of that era and their parents. People who were the parents of teenagers in the 1960s and 1970s were generally people who had gone through their own adolescence in the years before World War II. Prewar America was a very different place indeed from the America of the late twentieth century. Nearly 50 percent of the population still lived in rural areas, and most adolescents did not complete high school. In a sense, very few people born in the 1920s or 1930s experienced an adolescence at all. Adolescence as a general cultural phenomenon is really a product of postwar America.

How will those who have experienced an adolescence of their own react to their own adolescent children? Most of the members of the baby boom cohort who have chosen to parent now have children of elementary school age. As they become the parents of adolescents, one might well expect less anxiety and bewilderment over the behavior of their teenagers. The baby boom cohort grew up with loud rock and roll. They had to sort through more alternatives regarding sexual decisions than their own parents, and they have encountered drug abuse as young people. As adolescents, the baby boom generation were mostly urban dwellers. The majority completed high school and at least attempted college. One would think they might be in a position to offer more guidance and less resistance to their own adolescents, partly because they should be less fearful and more often able to see the opportunities of a modern adolescence as well as the pitfalls.

Will the "generation gap" close? That seems a question worth exploring in our time-lag studies. It is also possible, of course, that the gap will not only continue to exist, but become more extensive. The children of the postwar baby boom may consider it important to rebel, and their parents may consider it not only acceptable, but necessary. As parents of adolescents, the baby boom generation has set an example their children will find hard to ignore. There is little doubt that the 1960s and early 1970s is seen today in a romantic haze. My own son (who is just thirteen) has said, "Mom, how exciting to grow up in the sixties. I wish I had grown up in the sixties." Will he be driven to recreate that experience? Will he (and his cohorts, of course) consider it necessary to find some way to drive a wedge between himself and me? He already has discovered a truly obnoxious noise (arcade games on a home computer). Perhaps he will find an equally obnoxious political and social position as he passes through late adolescence. We shall see, and it will be fascinating.

There are also likely to be some very significant changes in the way aged parents are treated. For one thing, members of the postwar baby boom have become accustomed to condominiums and apartments and often do not have the facilities to care for a parent. For another, there is some evidence that this generation feels less personally responsible for its progenitors than did previous generations. Finally, if they have any sense, the postwar babies will begin to look at the future for themselves and plan for their own later years. For all these reasons, we will probably see an increase in the number of acceptable alternatives available in the care of aging parents. Improvements in retirement communities, convalescent homes, and other such facilities are likely, and a reconstruction of the Social Security system and other pension plans is critical if the society is to provide for an aging baby boom.

All of these trends suggest an impact on the design of work and the importance of leisure. If people live longer, healthier lives and if they are able to lower their expectations for financial success in middle age, there is some possibility that they will be free to try new things at midlife. Career changes may be routine, but we might also expect a change in how people view leisure. Certainly, this cohort has added several dimensions—such as sexual activity and the use of psychoactive drugs—to our definition of leisure, not to mention a host of new sports and activities that have emerged in the last twenty years, from surfing and dirt-biking to skiing, hang-gliding, and disco roller skating. This generation is leisure-oriented, and our theoretical time-lag studies should include a variety of items designed to measure changes in attitudes toward leisure as well as the kind and frequency of leisure activities people pursue.

This is a very exciting time to be thinking about a time-lag study of middle age. An endless number of areas might be included, for middle age is indeed the prime of life in the sense that one is active and involved in all the major roles of adulthood. A longitudinal study of this particular cohort would also answer important questions, of course. What are the long-term effects of the changes we see? Are people generally happy with the kinds of changes they make at midlife? Does an increased interest in leisure contribute to overall life satisfaction? How will more liberal attitudes toward sex and divorce affect people as they move through middle age and into the empty nest? And, of course, the questions we can formulate at this point will only constitute the tip of the iceberg. With luck, someone will be there to ask more questions before it is too late to get the answers.

IV

Later Life

Chapter 9

The Inner Context: Biology and Cognition in Later Life

If I did not keep telling myself my age over and over again, I am sure I should scarcely be aware of it. Although every hour of the day I tell myself, "My poor fellow, you are seventy-three and more," I cannot really persuade myself of it.

ANDRE GIDE

In *A Good Age* (1976), Alex Comfort distinguishes between biological aging and "sociogenic" aging—the product of the role that society imposes on people as they reach a particular chronological age. Although no one escapes all the psychological and biological changes that accompany age, some of the least pleasant changes may appear simply because they are expected. Our perception and assessment of the physical or cognitive changes that accompany old age (or any age, for that matter) may yet be proved to be of the greatest significance to psychological life (Lowenthal and Chiriboga, 1972). Certainly, elderly people display a wide variety of adaptations. Because immense forces are at play—and have been for a long while—it is not surprising to find that individual differences among the elderly are so great that it is nearly impossible to use normative data to describe any elderly individual.

Nevertheless, our cultural stereotypes of the aged suggest they can all be described with a few words. Comfort points out, for example, that old people are generally considered "unintelligent, unemployable, crazy, and asexual" (1976, p. 10). And the older one becomes, the dimmer the outlook. Near the end, the aged are seen as "aimless, apathetic, debilitated, disruptive, hypochondriacal, insecure, . . . out of control, sluggish, and temperamental" (Smith, 1979, p. 333).

Such attitudes are bewildering, not only because they are unjustified by the facts but because all of us can expect to be old. Old people cannot properly be described in a few words or even a few volumes. Children, adolescents, even young adults are more likely to behave like one another than are the elderly, and it does not take very much thought to see why; a few examples should suffice. Consider, for instance, that most adults in their twenties are married, have children, are employed (especially if they are males), and are in reasonably good health. In contrast, some older people are married, but many are divorced, separated, or widowed. Most older people have not only children but also grandchildren, and some have great grandchildren. A few have outlived their own children. Many older men are still working full-time in their first-chosen career, while others are employed part-time, are fully retired, or have entered second or even third careers. A good many older people are in excellent health (although most have at least some chronic diseases); some are in fair health; and some are in very poor health. As life experiences accumulate, the chances that any two people will have similar histories diminish. It is quite predictable, therefore, that personality, cognition, perception—all of the psychological processes we have been studying—will vary more dramatically from one elderly person to another than from the young adult or child to another.

Keeping in mind the extent of individual variation among the aged, let us look at some of the available normative data. As we age, all of us can expect to find ourselves changing in some predictable ways, and it seems prudent to be advised of the nature and direction of these developments. If we are prepared for and have a clear understanding of the extent and variability of the changes that occur in later life, we may be less easily persuaded or frightened by the ageism of our culture and better able to relate to the old people around us as well as the old person in ourselves.

This chapter covers biological and cognitive change in later life. It begins with a discussion of those observable, outward changes in appearance that are so evident to us all and proceeds to a review of the literature on the less tangible, more abstract developments in sensation, perception, cognition, problem solving, and creativity. For the most part, we must be

"We grow neither better nor worse as we get old, but more like overselves."
May Lamberton Becker

content with a review of research on *age differences* rather than a discussion of *age change* (see Chapter 1). As is generally true in discussions of adult development, most of the research reported in this area is cross-sectional in design. It is especially important to keep this in mind when considering the data on biological and physiological development, because one can easily fall into the trap of accepting physical changes as universal, inevitable, and irreversible, even when there is little objective evidence for such a point of view. This chapter, therefore, emphasizes the kinds of cohort or personality issues that are important in the interpretation of the data.

BIOLOGICAL AND PHYSIOLOGICAL CHANGE

Appearance

The trends that are already evident in the appearance of middle-aged people progress throughout later life, and some accelerate. The skin becomes more wrinkled and dry, less elastic and thinner. Unlike the wrinkles of middle age, however, wrinkling in later life is no longer closely related to the structure and function of muscles. Middle-aged crow's feet and laugh lines persist, but wrinkling increases as the fat tissues atrophy. In very old age the skin may take on the criss-cross look of soft, crumpled paper (Rossman, 1977).

Among the skin changes that are particularly apparent late in life are senile warts on the trunk, face, and scalp and an accelerated proliferation of pigmented plaques, or age spots. The small blood vessels become increasingly frail, break more easily, and frequently produce black and blue spots (Rockstein, 1975; Agate, 1970).

Perhaps the most pronounced development in physical appearance during later life is the postural slump or stoop that characterizes many older people. The head is held slightly forward of the rest of the body and upper limbs are often bent (see Figure 9.1). The shrinkage of muscles, the decrease in elasticity and increase in calcification of the ligaments, the shrinkage and hardening of tendons, and the flattening of vertebral discs now add their effects (for many of us) to the cumulative effect of years of poor posture. Although the slumping posture of many old people may well account for all or most of the decline in average height that seems to occur with age, alterations in the bones and vertebrae may also play a role in the data on height.

FIGURE 9.1
Stooped posture in an elderly person

CPH Biomedical/Scientific Photography, Robert
Walker, photographer

Skeletal Change

It is probable that apparent declines in height with age involve actual loss
of bony materials. There is a decrease in bone mass over the adult years, a
fact unknown as recently as thirty years ago. At one time it was thought
that only delicate older women who drank too little milk became weak
and frail of bone. Today it is clear that the skeletal weight of both sexes
declines with age (Garn, 1975).

In older people, the bones become hollow and therefore weak rather
than brittle. Figure 9.2 shows how changes proceed at the inner and outer
surfaces of the long bones. Concurrent with such change in the long bones,
the vertebral discs become thinner, and height changes may occur as the
vertebrae collapse. Vertebral collapse or fracture is more common among
females than among males.

Other important alterations occur in bony tissues and affect the aging
individual. Bones become porous and in some places may appear moth-
eaten. Some porousness is considered a normal part of aging, but in extreme cases *senile osteoporosis* may be diagnosed. The exact point where
normal bone loss becomes osteoporosis is unclear, and the causes of severe
bone loss seen in victims of this disease are unknown (Tonna, 1977).

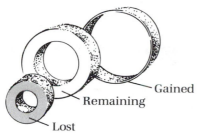

Remaining

Gained

Lost

Female bone remodeling from ages 30 to 80

FIGURE 9.2
Age changes at the inner and outer surface of a tubular bone

SOURCE: *Adapted from S. M. Garn, "Bone Loss and Aging," in R. Goldman and M. Rockstein, eds.,* The Physiology and Pathology of Aging *(New York: Academic Press, 1975), p. 45.*

The probability of bone fracture over the course of adult life parallels the progressive loss of bony material seen with age (see Figure 9.3). There are great individual differences in the rate of bone loss and susceptibility to fracture, and there are also evident sex and race differences. Unfortunately our knowledge about developmental changes in bony matter is limited to available statistical descriptions of sex and race differences. A variety of causal hypotheses have been offered and some forms of prevention, including the ingestion of large doses of vitamins and minerals, have been unsuccessfully tried. The most we can say is that bone loss is least likely for those with the largest skeletal mass, for males rather than females, and for those with genes of West African origin (Garn, 1975).

It has been argued that the changes in the skeletal system are universal, progressive, presently irreversible, and functionally harmful. Still, some of the changes reported in the literature, especially changes in height, may be at least in part a function of cohort differences, especially since so many of them are usually assessed only during autopsies—a circumstance that will always yield cross-sectional data (since one cannot, obviously, perform autopsies on the same subjects at different points in their lives). When such methodology is used, there will be no longitudinal research designs.

Differences in stature can be assessed without autopsy, but even for such an objective attribute, how much is a cohort difference and how much a developmental change is unclear. For example, although evidence indicates that younger generations are taller than older ones (a *secular trend*), with cross-sectional studies reporting age differences of as much as three inches between males aged twenty-five and sixty-five, the few longitudinal studies that exist suggest changes more on the order of one centimeter, or about a half an inch (Daman, Seltzer, Stoudt, and Bell, 1972).

There is similar confusion in much of the data on biology and physiology. Researchers are uncertain about the optimal measurement procedures in many areas we will cover, such as gastrointestinal development

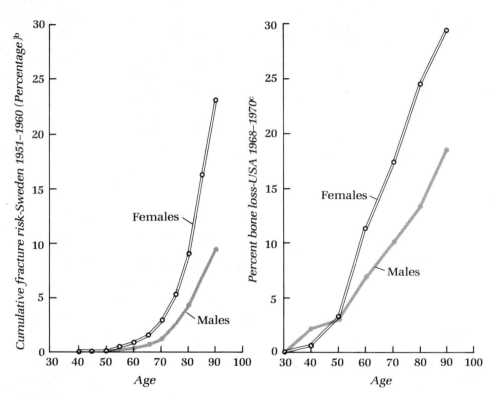

FIGURE 9.3
Cumulative fracture-risk curves and cumulative percentage bone-loss curves[a]

[a]Cumulative bone loss minus 10 roughly equals the cumulative fracture percentage.
[b]Swedish data.
[c]United States data.

SOURCE: *S. M. Garn, "Bone Loss and Aging," in R. Goldman and M. Rockstein, eds.,* The Physiology and Pathology of Aging *(New York: Academic Press, 1975), p. 43.*

or kidney function. Moreover, longitudinal study is often impossible with present technology, and much controversy has arisen over the interpretation of data.

Furthermore, decline and deterioration are not the only continuing processes of note over the adult years. Bone growth actually continues throughout life (although the hollowing process pictured in Figure 9.2 proceeds more rapidly). The most obvious instances of continued growth are apparent in the face and head. The nose becomes a bit broader (two to three millimeters in males) and longer (two millimeters). Cranial growth continues off and on throughout adulthood, even into the ninth decade.

Ribs and leg bones increase in diameter even as they become weaker and increasingly ossified (Israel, 1968; Garn, 1975).

The structure and function of almost every organ and system in the human body is affected by the passage of the years. We have little real knowledge of the relative influences of age, environmental and experiential forces, and cohort differences. But much descriptive material is available on the procession of changes in the heart, the nervous system, the respiratory and digestive systems, the kidneys, and the pancreas.

Muscles and Heart

Muscle weight decreases relative to general body weight late in life. Significant changes occur in the structure and composition of the muscle cells, including shifts in chemical balance and the accumulation of collagen and fat. Both the number and the diameter of muscle fibers decrease in later life, and sometimes the remaining fibers *hypertrophy* (become enlarged) (Guttman, 1977).

As it is usually defined, the basic *motor unit* consists of a single motor neuron and all the fibers it innervates. Age brings occasional fragmentation of the myelin sheath that surrounds the neuron, and other structural irregularities occur. The transportation of protein through the axons may be disturbed, the membrane may become thicker, and the synaptic cleft may become larger.

The time it takes for a muscle to relax or contract and the time it requires before it can be restimulated increases in later life. The maximum rate of tension development—the rate at which tension develops in a muscle that is contracting—decreases. These changes probably account for some of the decline in motor function that is observed in older people. However, most researchers agree that one must postulate changes in other parts of the nervous system in order to account for the magnitude and variety of age differences in motor performance.

The heart is primarily a muscular structure, and as is true for other muscles, age differences in cardiac function become quite apparent in later life. Although the cardiovascular problems of middle age are often arterial, in later adulthood the heart muscle begins to show alterations. The valves become thicker and less flexible and the aged heart has more fat tissue. The left ventricle may atrophy while the left atrium and the aorta enlarge. Each stroke of the heart is less effective, and by the age of sixty, maximum blood flow through the coronary arteries has declined by 35 percent. Despite these changes, the evidence does not support the view that heart failure in old age is a direct result of deterioration in the heart muscle. Instead, heart failure is more likely to be caused by the advance of the arterial changes outlined in Chapter 6 or by chronic pulmonary problems (Harris, 1975).

Vascular degeneration can interfere with the heart's blood supply. In very old age, declining heart function and deteriorating vascular condition may produce blueness of the extremities, even gangrene of the lower limbs (Sinclar, 1969). Vascular degeneration is also reflected in climbing blood pressure. At age twenty-five, the average blood pressure in males is 120/75, whereas at age sixty-five, it has increased to 160/90 (Rockstein, 1975).

The primary function of the heart is the distribution of oxygen and nutrients to the body and to itself. It is the motor behind the circulatory system. But if the heart is to provide an adequate supply of oxygen, the lungs must transfer oxygen in adequate amounts into the bloodstream. Alterations in the structure of the lungs can interfere with this vital and delicately balanced system.

Lungs

With advancing age, total and vital capacity (see Chapter 3) continue to decrease. The muscles that lift the ribs weaken, and changes in the structure of the rib cage interfere with the expansion of the lungs. There is a reduction in the number of alveoli (air pockets through which gases are exchanged in the lung), and the bronchioles (the small tubular extensions of bronchial tubes) become less elastic. Shortness of breath is a common complaint among older people, and some degree of *emphysema* is almost always present in the elderly. Emphysema is much more severe and occurs much earlier in those who smoke (Agate, 1970; Rockstein, 1975).

Kidneys

Another critical adjunct of the circulatory system, the kidneys, are responsible for the elimination of most of the nonvolatile waste products from the body. They cleanse the bloodstream and maintain a constant fluid volume in the body and an exceedingly precise balance of electrolyte and hydrogen ion concentrations. With age, renal failure becomes one of the most common causes of death.

Nevertheless, even in very old age, the kidneys maintain the delicate liquid balance of the body quite well as long as the body is functioning within normal limits. Under stress, however, major declines in kidney function may be apparent. Moreover, the rate at which the kidneys filter the blood decreases with age, even in very healthy people. Because the system loses the ability to replace injured renal cells, a reduction in the number of basic *nephron* units occurs, and the remaining units must compensate for the loss of these tiny filters (Lindeman, 1975).

Filtration declines by as much as 50 percent over the years from the age of twenty-five to eighty. Some have argued that most of this decline may be due to decreased blood flow through the kidneys, but other research suggests that a decrease in the number of functional nephrons is directly responsible (Rockstein, 1975; Lindeman, 1975).

Kidneys, heart, and lungs are intricately interrelated in the proper function of the circulatory system and therefore in the oxygenation and nutrition of every cell in the human body. Another important part of the process occurs in the digestive tract, where nutrients are prepared for and transferred to the blood stream.

Intestinal Tract

The general nutritional problems of older people—problems caused by poor diet and the deteriorating teeth—are compounded by the fact that stomach motility declines with age, as does peristalsis in the intestine and colon. The mucosa that protect the gastrointestinal lining atrophy, and the volume of gastric juices secreted is reduced. These changes contribute to general intestinal distress as well as to poor nutrition and are responsible for one of the most frequent complaints of age, constipation (Agate, 1970; Rockstein, 1975).

Other Organs

The trends we have noted for the heart, lungs, kidneys, and intestines occur in the other organs in the body. Increasing amounts of fatty and fibroid tissues, declining muscle function, and impeded blood supply affect many other functions, including those of the endocrine system, the pancreas, and the lymphoid tissues. Increasing rates of diabetes, greater susceptibility to bacterial infection, and declining basal-metabolism rates reflect the deterioration of major organ systems with age.

One other major biological system requires extensive coverage and leads us into the gray area between biology and psychology—between physiology and cognition. We have arrived at the interface between who you are and what you are: the nervous system.

Nervous System

It is time to bring up some methodological considerations once again. The study of change in the nervous system is difficult for several important reasons. Most of the research must be done at autopsy, and the tissues of the nervous system are extremely sensitive to environmental conditions. The determination of whether an individual was neurologically diseased, never easy, is particularly difficult post-mortem. A large part of the data, then, is hard to interpret because one cannot say which changes are the result of secular trends or cohort differences, which are the product of possible environmental damage or neural diseases, and which represent developmental change (Brody and Vijayashankar, 1977).

Perhaps the most consistently replicated data suggest an overall loss in brain weight observed between the ages of twenty-five and seventy. On the one hand, because brain weight is correlated with body weight, it is likely that much of the hundred-gram weight difference between old and young brains is actually a cohort difference. On the other hand, there is some evidence that the number of brain cells declines dramatically with age. By the age of eighty or ninety, some researchers believe, losses may run as high as 44 percent for most cortical areas (Brody and Vijayashankar, 1977). Others argue that such claims are exaggerated (La Rue and Jarvik, 1982).

Chemical differences between old and young brains have also been documented. Water content declines substantially with age; lipids or fats increase. The amount of protein per brain dry weight declines from about 140 grams at about age twenty to 100 grams by age ninety. Amounts of some inorganic salts, including calcium, chloride, and sodium, decrease; potassium and phosphorus levels rise. Important alterations have also been noted in cerebral blood flow (calculated as flow per minute per 100 grams weight), which declines from 62 milliliters at age twenty-one to about 58 milliliters at age seventy-one (Ordy, 1975).

Chemical and metabolic changes as well as declining blood flow may produce cell loss and, therefore, cognitive and motor impairment. Although the exact significance of cell death for human behavior is not understood, all behavior may be considered a product of the nervous system, and researchers repeatedly refer to the deteriorating function of central mechanisms, from simple sensory-motor functions to the most complex aspects of perception and cognition, when discussing psychological aging (Ordy, 1975).

The study of brain-wave functions and the study of medical problems in the elderly have given us more direct information about the correlation between biological change and psychological events. One example is found in the literature on the electroencephalograph (EEG) patterns of the elderly. EEG and neurological evaluations indicate that degree of brain impairment is inversely related to longevity in people over seventy, and age-related changes in sleep seem directly associated with changing EEG patterns (Wang and Busse, 1974; Kales, 1975).

Sleep

EEG patterns during normal sleep indicate a succession of four stages from lightest to deepest sleep, plus one regularly occurring pattern known as REM (rapid eye movement) sleep. REM sleep is characterized by low amplitude, fast-frequency brain waves, and a marked decrease in muscle tone. Subjects are more likely to recall dreaming when awakened during or immediately after REM sleep than they are if awakened during any of the four non-REM stages. Of these, the fourth stage is thought to represent the deepest kind of sleep. Stage four sleep is observed once every seventy to hundred minutes during the young-adult sleep cycle, but in older people, this fourth stage is nearly absent. The amount of REM sleep is about equal in young and old subjects, but REM sleep is more frequently interrupted by second-stage sleep in older people than in young adults or in the middle aged (Kales, 1975).

Insomnia is a frequent complaint of older people, especially women over sixty. Reports suggest that insomnia is often related to depressive syndromes involving apprehension about physical health. It is, however, one of the classic symptoms of depression at all ages, and the frequency of depression increases with age. Older people do have more health problems than do the young, of course, and the relationship between physical and mental health is of special interest in dealing with the elderly.

MENTAL AND PHYSICAL HEALTH

What does it mean to be healthy? If it means, as the World Health Organization has suggested, that one experiences complete mental, physical, and social well-being, then few older people can be considered healthy. Of all people over sixty-five, 85 percent report at least one chronic illness, and about one-half of the older population report some limitation in their daily activity due to a chronic disorder (Hendricks and Hendricks, 1977). But the application of absolute standards is not often useful in talking about the aged. One's perception and cognitive assessment of both stress and illness are as important as objective stress and illness, if not more so. At times it seems most accurate to say that a healthy person is one who feels healthy. At the very least, we must consider the resources people have for coping as well as the severity of any impairments they experience (Lowenthal and Chiriboga, 1973).

The most common nonfatal chronic diseases among the elderly are arthritis and rheumatism, which affect as many as 80 percent of all people over the age of seventy and are second only to heart disease as causes of impairment in the normal activity of older people.

Osteoarthritis is a condition caused by the changes in bone and cartilage that normally accompany aging. *Rheumatoid arthritis* is believed to be an immunological disease that develops early in life and becomes more debilitating with age (McKeown, 1965).

Heart disease, cancer, and cerebrovascular lesion account for about 70 percent of all deaths after middle age. Influenza and pneumonia become prominent in the mortality rates after sixty-five, but the frequency of cirrhosis of the liver declines. Arteriosclerosis becomes much more deadly as one ages: the fifth most frequent cause of death in elderly populations, it is not listed among the ten most frequent causes of death in the middle aged (National Center for Health Statistics, 1971).

Of all the ills of humankind, those most closely identified with aging are probably the cerebrovascular and arteriosclerotic diseases that affect the brain. Each year two hundred thousand people in the United States die of strokes. A stroke is a *cerebrovascular accident* caused by an *embolism* that has traveled from elsewhere in the body to one of the cerebral arteries, or by a *thrombosis* or obstruction that develops in the brain (Hendricks and Hendricks, 1977; Insel and Roth, 1979).

Cerebrovascular disease is often associated with cognitive and personality changes that may frighten patients and those around them. People often use the word *senile* to sum up the effects of cerebrovascular disease; they are unaware, however, of the complexity of diagnosing the exact problem involved or of the variety of possible outcomes. It is possible to recover completely from a cerebrovascular accident, or to suffer irreversible change. Moreover, some brain syndromes are caused by chemical and metabolic disorders rather than by cerebrovascular accidents, and some are the result of degenerative changes in the brain cells.

Aging, Senility, Psychopathology, and Social Pathology

Senescence refers to the changes that accompany the process of aging. As we noted above, although the term *senility* is commonly used to refer to cognitive and personality changes that accompany some brain disorders, the word is so widely misused that it has come to have little if any real meaning. People even use it to refer to purely psychiatric problems, implying that psychiatric symptoms are a routine part of being old. The diagnosis of physiological, psychological, and sociological problems in the elderly is much more difficult than the cultural stereotype suggests. Many elderly people are isolated from normal social intercourse. They may be suffering from malnutrition, or from debilitating drug interactions, especially if they have several chronic health problems.

Diagnosis is further complicated by the fact that periods of depression are a common experience in old age. Age is associated with a variety of losses, from loss of role (as when an individual retires), to loss of financial, social, or political power, and the loss of close relationships. Eventually, the oldest members of a cohort have lost most of the essential people, places, and things that define their personal history.

Although depression is more common among the elderly than among other age groups, there is little evidence that psychiatric disorders in general increase with age (Srole, Langner, Michael, Opler, and Rennie, 1962). In other words, older people are not more likely to suffer from mental illness than the rest of the population—but if they do develop an emotional disorder it is more likely to be diagnosed as depression. Hypochondriasis, paranoid reactions, and chronic anxiety are also more common in elderly populations than in other age groups (Pfeiffer, 1977). Furthermore, the suicide rate for those over sixty-five is about three times that of the general population, especially among males aged seventy-five to eighty-five (U.S. Public Health Service, 1974).

There is reason, however, to suspect strong environmental influences whenever an elderly person develops psychiatric symptoms. The mental illness of old age is all too often accepted as a natural outcome of the aging process itself, and, therefore, considered untreatable. Factors such as health, economic resources, and the responsiveness of the older person's social network (or lack of it) are ignored. Let us say, for example, that an elderly person begins to exhibit paranoid behavior and hypochondriasis. Both of these problems may easily alienate those who live with or near the person. As friends and relatives become more irritated, the paranoia increases, often aggravated by hearing and vision losses. The hypochondriasis, too, is an understandable response to the sensory changes and other normal physical complaints of age. The victim is dismissed as hopeless because of his or her age, despite clear evidence that the elderly respond favorably to a warm, supportive environment and to the treatment of cognitive and sensory deficits (Gallagher, Thompson, and Levy, 1980).

Norms for most of the traditional psychological tests are inadequate for the diagnosis of elderly patients, and attempts are rarely made to assess such factors as environmental stress, functional capacity, or prognosis in psychotherapy. For instance, an elderly person complaining of memory impairment is much more likely to be seen as a victim of brain dysfunction than of depression, although it is widely recognized that depression can produce memory impairments. Even when brain damage is present, it does not mean that the symptoms are untreatable. In fact, one group of authors (Gallagher, Thompson, and Levy, 1980) warns that a diagnosis of chronic or organic brain syndrome should be suspended until all treatment alternatives have been exhausted.

Organic Brain Syndromes

Organic brain syndromes are those behavioral and cognitive patterns caused by physical pathologies of the brain tissue, or by chemical and metabolic conditions that affect the functioning of the brain. At first, organic brain syndromes may be mistaken for psychological disturbances. Early prominent signs often include mood changes, irritability, fatigue, and agitation. Eventually, memory deficits, problems of visual-motor coordination, and difficulties in learning, abstraction, and the assimilation of new information appear. Severe brain disorders may produce gross disorientation, confusion, and bewilderment. Finally, even the memory of one's own history may be affected. A few patients become unable to communicate at all and are unable to respond to their own names (Pfeiffer, 1977).

Even when the symptoms of such disorders are extremely severe, however, they may be reversible. Of all organic brain syndromes, 20 to 30 percent are completely reversible, and in the irreversible cases some degree of function can usually be restored through therapy and retraining.

Although they are often referred to as *acute syndromes*, reversible brain syndromes are not necessarily characterized by sudden onset. The quality of the symptoms, rather than their severity or the nature of their onset is most important. A fluctuating level of awareness is a positive sign, even when hallucinations, space and time disorientation, and memory loss for both recent and remote events are present. If the individual has some lucid moments, no matter how severe the symptoms are at other times, there is reason to be optimistic. Reversible syndromes may be caused by metabolic malfunctions like those that accompany a heart attack, diabetes, hypoglycemia, and renal toxicity. Vitamin deficiencies, alcoholism, or the use of cardiac and diuretic drugs, steroids, or antihypertensives can also produce reversible brain syndromes.

In fact, one recent review article (Levy, Derogatis, Gallagher, and Gatz, 1980) suggests that the major causes of brain disorder among elderly patients are the overprescription of drugs and the use of alcohol simultaneously with over-the-counter preparations and prescriptive drugs. Elderly people are extremely sensitive to drugs, yet most are using some form of chemical intervention. Only 5 percent of the elderly do not use any drugs, and one-half of them use alcohol and over-the-counter preparations as well as drugs. Often *synergy* is responsible for confusion and disorientation. Synergism, which occurs when the effect of one drug intensifies the effect of another, is a particular problem in institutions. Patients are frequently given several different drugs daily, as often as needed, with minimal consideration of synergistic effects, the interaction of health and psychological problems, or the problems elderly people have metabolizing drugs (Levy et al., 1980).

Diagnosis of brain syndromes often requires extensive knowledge of neurophysiology and gerontology. As Sandra Levy and her associates (1980) have pointed out, nearly a hundred acute brain syndromes mimic a

Diagnosis of the psychiatric problems of the elderly is confounded by negative stereotypes, by the expectation of disability, and by the social and economic disenfranchisement of the old.

few chronic conditions. Although Levy et al. admit that massive efforts, including intensive psychotherapy, do not seem to pay off for many elderly patients, the use of many simple behavioral interventions—from music therapy, art, or physical therapy to simply an occasional party with beer and wine and dancing—have all proved successful. Often patients seem to benefit from *any* intervention, especially in an institutional setting. If the intervention is discontinued, however, patients may deteriorate faster than would have been predicted if no intervention had been attempted.

Indeed, sometimes brain syndromes caused by cerebrovascular accidents and accompanied by paralysis and aphasia are still reversible; such famous cases as that of the actress Patricia Neal are illustrative. On the other hand, full recovery is not possible for the victims of *chronic brain syndromes*, although substantial improvement may be effected by proper treatment and therapy. There are two known types of chronic brain syndromes: *senile psychosis* (or senile dementia) and the psychosis associated with cerebral arteriosclerosis.

The psychosis associated with cerebral arteriosclerosis is somewhat better understood than senile dementia. Arteriosclerosis in the brain is much like the process described for other arteries in Chapter 6. Onset may occur as early as fifty, and it is much more likely to attack males than females. In general, the progress of the disease is erratic, and resultant impairment is often temporary; the patient may be disoriented or even delirious at times and later regain full or nearly full capacity. In some respects, this disease is difficult to differentiate from a reversible brain disorder, and the victim may behave more like a cardiac patient than a person with chronic brain syndrome. People who develop cerebral arteriosclerosis most often die of heart disease or pneumonia (Butler and Lewis, 1973).

Senile dementia is something of a mystery to medical and psychiatric researchers. It appears to be caused by the dissolution of brain cells and is independent of arterial changes. Dementia is more common in females than in males, and the average age of onset is about seventy-five. The weight of the brain actually declines as cells atrophy; but the progress of the disease is slow, gradually becoming more severe over a period of years. Errors in judgment increase; personal care habits deteriorate; the ability to abstract is progressively impaired; and anxiety, depression, or irritability become more and more frequent. Sleeplessness, wandering, fabrication, and the loosening of inhibitions are common (Butler and Lewis, 1973).

The degeneration and death of nerve cells probably occur to some extent in all older people; however, some researchers believe that damage must reach a critical level before the symptoms associated with dementia occur. Microscopic study of brain cells suggests dementia may be associated with an increase in cells containing an abnormal number of chromosomes. There is also some evidence that the production of antibodies designed to work in the brain may be severely impaired. Nevertheless, a precise understanding of the disease has thus far eluded researchers (La Rue and Jarvik, 1982). It is eventually fatal: the average survival rate is only about five years, although some individuals live ten years or more.

Obviously, to enhance the accuracy of research about brain syndromes such as senile dementia, it is extremely important for researchers to assess the health status of elderly subjects. Some of the processes involved in the appearance of senile dementia are present in most older people, and the prevalence of arteriosclerosis approaches 100 percent in the very old. Mortality due to heart disease doubles each decade past middle age for males, and triples for females. Most studies of general health suggest that health is more important than age in predicting cognitive performance. For example, formal operational thought is seen among elderly people who are in excellent health much more often than those who are not. In fact, in one study, the authors report that once health, education, and sex are considered, age alone is not useful in predicting the presence of formal operations (La Rue and Waldbaum, 1980).

It is both surprising and discouraging, given these facts, that so few researchers inquire about the health of their subjects. For example, only 9 percent of the studies in the *Journal of Gerontology* during 1978 adequately specified the health of elderly subjects (La Rue and Jarvik, 1982). As we discuss changes in perceptual and intellectual function with age, it is essential to remember that one can rarely be sure whether or not disease processes are implicated in declining performance among elderly subjects. The presence of disease is a theoretical problem even when attempts at assessment are made. The number of people with undiagnosed health problems probably increases greatly later in life; without an attempt to assess subjects' health status, data may be uninterpretable.

Finally, it should be noted that the relationship between brain damage and the severity of psychiatric symptoms is not really clear. Constitution, personality, heredity, and environmental conditions play important roles in determining how impaired a person becomes. Our ignorance of the borderland between biology and psychology is dramatically illustrated by the facts of organic brain syndrome, and as we move through the literature on normal aging, the relationships between the physical and the psychological become more and more obscure. Investigations of such subjects as problem solving and creativity involve very little, if any, discussion of biology. At the level of sensation and simple perception, the relationships would seem more readily understood. But even in this area so much variability occurs in performance that one cannot assume any simple interrelationships between biological and behavioral changes.

SENSATION AND PERCEPTION

Vision

Throughout later life, the alterations of the lens of the eye that began in middle age proceed, and a second set of changes occurs, affecting the retina and producing further decrements in acuity and color vision. Older people must look about ten times as long as young adults before they can describe a gap in a picture of a ring presented for just a fraction of a second using a tachistoscope. If a moving stimulus is presented for such a brief period, age differences in acuity are exceedingly large (Fozard, Wolf, Bell, McFarland, and Podolsky, 1977).

Color discrimination is affected too, declining dramatically after the age of seventy. Before seventy, older subjects are able to perceive colors as accurately as younger subjects about 76 percent of the time. After eighty or ninety, many older people label colors incorrectly as much as half of the time, especially when the stimulus colors are in the blue-green range. Interestingly, although the elderly are less accurate in labeling various shades of blue and green, they usually prefer the color blue, and like yellow least despite the fact that accuracy for reds and yellows remains fairly high throughout the life span (Gilbert, 1957; Dalerup and Fredericks, 1969; Corso, 1981).

This increasing difficulty of color discrimination may be caused by the yellowing of the lens of the eye or by the effects of arteriosclerosis. Both eyes do not seem to degenerate at the same rate, however; one eye usually leads a person to make more mistakes on a color discrimination task than the other (Corso, 1981).

Arteriosclerosis produces a decline in the availability and utilization of oxygen in the central nervous system, which may damage the retina or the brain centers that process visual information. In combination with continued yellowing and inelasticity of the lens, vision eventually becomes blurred and fuzzy. Figure 9.4 presents a black-and-white version of how the world might look to an individual who has reached the age of eighty or ninety. Notice especially the lowered contrast and increased glare that are characteristic.

Visual Perception

It is easy to see how the aging of the lens, vitreous humor, and retina might produce decrements in depth perception, acuity, and color vision. It is not as simple to understand why pronounced changes in visual perception— the interpretation of visual information—develop during later life. The

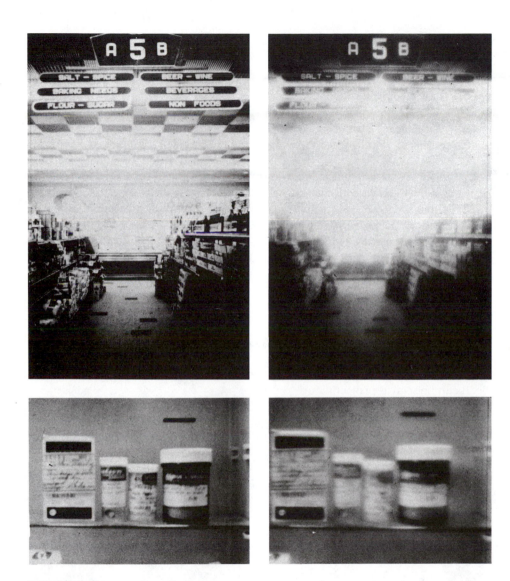

FIGURE 9.4
Photographic simulation of scenes as seen by people in their late seventies or
early eighties

*The elderly's increased susceptibility to glare is illustrated by the two upper photos.
Visual problems associated with poor contrast are illustrated in the two lower
photos.*

SOURCE: *J. L. Fozard, E. Wolf, B. Bell, R. A. McFarland, S. Podolsky, "Visual Perception and Communication,"
in J. Birren and K. W. Schaie, eds.,* Handbook of the Psychology of Aging *(New York: Van Nostrand
Reinhold, 1977), p. 516. Copyright © 1977 by Litton Educational Publishing, Inc. Reprinted by permission of
Van Nostrand Reinhold Company. The prints were made from color slides prepared by Dr. Leon Pastalan.*

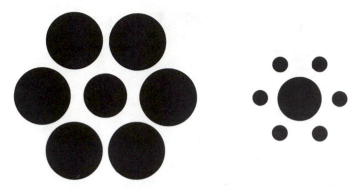

Are the center dots in both figures the same?
Tichner's Circles

FIGURE 9.5
Commonly used visual illusions

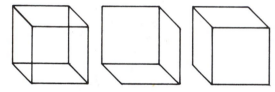

The Necker Cube. It can be seen as projecting up
or down in three dimensions in the first cube. In the
other two cubes the perspective is stabilized.

The Müller-Lyer illusion

Do you see an old lady or a young girl?

Do you see two profile faces?
Or a wine glass?

fact that older people sometimes perform more like adolescents than like young adults or the middle aged has been of special interest to researchers interested in visual illusions. Figure 9.5 presents some of the traditional visual illusions frequently used in perceptual research.

Older people, like teenagers, are more susceptible to illusions such as the Müller-Lyer than are young and middle-aged adults. This phenomenon has led some researchers to propose that there is *perceptual regression* in old age and to speculate that similar processes might be found in other perceptual and intellectual functioning. It does appear that the old perform more like adolescents than like younger adults on a variety of tasks besides the visual illusions. Some of these include the "tilted room" and "tilted chair" situations, in which the subject is asked to judge vertically when his or her body is supported at some unusual angle. (You have probably been in a similar situation in a "fun house" when the floor tilts at a crazy angle.) Older adults also perform poorly when they are required to place luminous shapes straight ahead or at eye level in a dark room. Moreover, the oldest groups perform more like adolescents on tasks involving the discovery of embedded figures or recognition of incomplete forms (Wapner, Werner and Comalli, 1960; Comalli, 1970). Figure 9.6 presents typical results of perceptual-regression research.

Other research suggests that older people show less perceptual flexibility than do the young. In viewing the Necker Cube or the old/young woman figures shown in Figure 9.6, older subjects do not report seeing the figure reverse as often as the young. Whereas 80 percent of a young sample eventually report seeing both versions of the old/young woman, only 24 percent of the old do so. Older people also have difficulty reading the name of a color if it is printed in an incongruous hue—for example, if the word "red" is printed in green ink.

The perceptual-regression hypothesis has been popular as an interpretation of these data. Not all the data on perception support the regression hypothesis, however. In particular, it has been difficult to demonstrate regression in the perception of Tichner's Circles (see Figure 9.5). Older people seem *less* susceptible to this illusion than do young adults (Elias, Elias, and Elias, 1977).

No doubt cohort differences are responsible for some of the apparent regression of elderly subjects. Younger subjects have more education about and exposure to such phenomena as the Necker Cube and Müller-Lyer illusions. This is particularly true of subjects in studies in which the younger subjects were drawn from college populations (Eisner and Schaie, 1971).

The idea that older people are more susceptible to unusual variations in stimulus configurations provides the basis for one major hypothesis currently competing with the regression hypothesis. It may be that older people are more vulnerable to the stress involved in novel situations or that

FIGURE 9.6
**Data typical of that
used to support the
perceptual regres-
sion hypothesis**

*SOURCE: P. E. Comalli, Jr.,
"Life-Span Changes in Vi-
sual Perception," in L. R.
Goulet and P. B. Baltes, eds.,
Life-Span Developmental
Psychology (New York: Ac-
ademic Press, 1970), pp. 212,
222.*

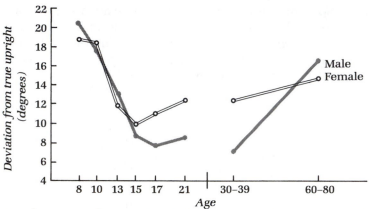

Age changes in adjustment of the body to an upright position in a tilted room

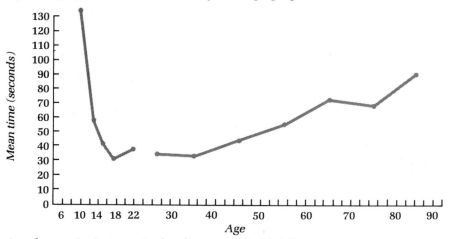

Age changes in time required to discover embedded figures

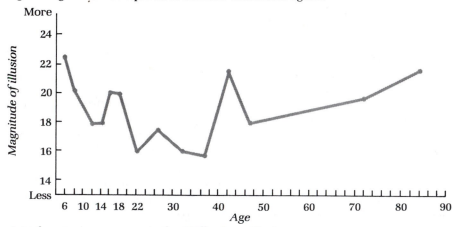

Age changes in responses to the Müller-Lyer Illusion

they are simply not accustomed to as much novelty as are the young (Fozard and Thomas, 1975). More sequential or longitudinal research on this point would be useful. The experimental manipulation of novelty might also help researchers sort out the various possibilities.

It may also be that the elderly are simply unmotivated when faced with a task like the reversal of the Necker Cube. These sorts of problems may seem trivial or meaningless. Or perhaps reversals fail to occur because the elderly eye shows less spontaneous random movement than the eye of a younger person. In any event, there is evidence that with practice, elderly people can be taught to perform more like young adults, suggesting that at least some motivational or cohort effects are present.

Whether or not we are able to discover the exact locus of change in vision and visual perception, the research does have important practical implications. For instance, it makes good sense to color-code tools or medications for the elderly in red or yellow. Environmental designers would be well advised to provide more illumination and to take special care in avoiding visual stimuli that might produce glare. Larger numbers and letters are in order when designing for the older person, and the use of novel or unusual stimulus features should be carefully controlled.

Audition

As is true for vision, the auditory changes of middle age progress through later life, and more advanced symptoms may be observed. Of all those over sixty-five, 13 percent suffer severe presbycusis and require professional help for their hearing difficulties. As presbycusis advances, there are new implications for emotional and social behavior change that can affect the quality of life for the older person.

In its more advanced stages, presbycusis affects one's ability to perceive and understand speech. At age eighty, adults make about 25 percent more errors than twenty-five year olds in the discrimination of single-syllable words. Predictably, these deficits are aggravated under stressful conditions, such as accelerated or filtered speech and the overlapping or interruption of words (Bergman, 1971; Corso, 1977, 1981).

The ability to use auditory stimuli and information from the environment is a critical factor in personal effectiveness, comfort, security, and enjoyment. The loss of one's ability to hear is stressful. It interferes with personal relationships and cuts one off from much that is interesting and exciting in life. Depressive states are quite common in people with moderate to severe hearing loss (Knapp, 1948; Corso, 1977, 1981).

Audiological services are often of great benefit in some forms of presbycusis. Hearing aids are expensive, however, especially the most helpful ones, which intensify only the high tones most elderly people hear least well. Moreover, the degree of loss, especially in speech perception, cannot be accounted for solely in terms of sensory deficits. Researchers often note that aging of central mechanisms as well as changes in the ear must be involved in age-related hearing loss (Bergman, 1971; Corso, 1977, 1981).

Summarizing research on audition, Jack Botwinick (1981) offers a list of sensible prescriptions for speaking with an elderly person:

(1) speak slowly and pronounce words carefully;
(2) avoid unfamiliar words, for example, slang . . . ;
(3) avoid distracting background sounds when possible;
(4) speak louder than usual but not too loudly [very loud speech is annoy-ing and makes it difficult to give and take in a conversation]; and
(5) have the listener look at you. This focuses attention and minimizes distraction (p. 94).

Audition and vision are the major channels through which informa-tion flows from the environment. However, the other senses also make important contributions, and some attempts have been made to describe age-related development in gustation, olfaction, and pain.

Gustation, Olfaction, and Pain

Although the evidence is sparse, it appears that older people are less likely to correctly identify any of the four primary tastes (sweet, salty, bitter, and sour) when these tastes are presented in low concentrations. Sensitivity for the taste of sugar declines most rapidly. Reduction in the number of taste buds after fifty or sixty, as well as decreasing elasticity in the mouth and lips and decreased saliva flow, probably all contribute to the aging of gusta-tion. However, smoking and certain kinds of food preferences (very spicy foods for instance) may add to declining sensitivity. The effects of spicy foods and smoking probably account for more rapid loss of taste discrimi-nation in men (Corso, 1981).

In one of the most straightforward studies of taste and smell, blind-folded subjects tasted a variety of foods, from different kinds of fruits and vegetables to combinations of all sorts. Elderly people were able to label food correctly less often than the young and used fewer adjectives to de-scribe taste and smell. In this study, the elderly identified salty tastes best, and recognized the taste of tomatoes more often than the young. They also identified apples, fish, coffee, and sugar fairly well. Older subjects had the most difficulty with lemon, pineapple, strawberries, corn, celery, carrots, and beans. Not one single elderly person was able to identify the taste of broccoli, whereas 30 percent of the college-aged subjects were able to do so (Corso, 1981). It is quite possible, of course, that differences in cohort familiarity with certain foods, such as pineapple and broccoli, magnified some of the most pronounced age differences.

The loss of discrimination for food tastes is probably due more to olfactory changes than to changes in gustation, but the two are obviously interdependent. Consider how difficult it is to enjoy food when you have a bad head cold. Older people are less sensitive to odors than the young, although no one is sure whether health problems or peripheral or central mechanisms are responsible. By the age of sixty, the population of sensory cells in the nose has declined substantially, and those cells that remain are misshapen and receive a reduced blood supply (Corso, 1981).

In addition to changes in taste and odor discrimination, age differences in preferences have been documented as well. Older people apparently dislike bitter tastes more than young adults, although they do not appear to be more sensitive to bitter substances. Few comparative statistics are available, but the fact that elderly people say they don't like hamburgers and they do like fish sets them apart from the very young. On the other hand, elderly people like milk, toast, vegetable soup, and pie for dessert—not an objectionable meal to a child or a young adult, especially the pie for dessert. As for olfaction, children prefer the odor of flowers. Adults like fruits and more sophisticated floral scents like lavender oil and hyacinth (Moncrieff, 1966; Engen, 1977).

The general trend toward declining sensitivity is also found in the literature on pain. The number of pain sensors (*Meissner's corpuscles*) and the number of peripheral nerve fibers that carry pain impulses decline with age. These changes may be directly responsible for decreasing sensitivity to pain; or older people may simply be adapted to greater levels of pain or may be more reluctant than the young to report it (Corso, 1977, 1981).

John Corso (1977, 1981) has been one of the most productive writers on the effects of aging on the sensory and perceptual processes. He believes the changes that have been observed are multiply caused by degeneration in receptors, nerve fibers, and brain projection areas. He also argues that declining sensitivity may not be apparent when the environment is planned to compensate for age-related change or when the individual learns to use information from several senses to compensate for loss in one. Although the gathering and processing of sensory information may become less efficient with age, education, experience, and intelligence can help maintain normal functioning. Finally, Corso assumes that age-related changes in sensation and perception are associated not just with peripheral changes but with alterations in central mechanisms, which makes it possible to account for the performance of older people when interference is present and on complex tasks like decoding or abstracting information from complex visual arrays.

Meanwhile, let us not forget that there have been very important historical changes that might well affect sensation and perception. Changes in eating habits, smoking and drug use, health habits and problems—even such a general change as environmental pollution—may affect one's ability to receive sensory data. Generational differences in motivation and in experience with novel situations or with laboratory tests may also be at play in this data. With these facts in mind, we turn to the literature on the more complex cognitive processes and, in particular, to the study of learning and memory: two areas that have served as a wellspring for research and theory in geropsychology.

LEARNING AND MEMORY

People usually talk about learning and memory as though the differences between them were clear, but this is not always so. *Learning* has been defined as the acquisition of information or behavior. *Memory* is said to involve the retention and recall of learned material. But how can learning be tested unless an individual recalls something? And how can a person recall something unless it was acquired in some way? Obviously, one cannot test learning without testing memory, or memory without learning; and the problems don't end there.

It is also necessary to make a distinction between learning and performance or between memory and performance. If subjects are anxious about making mistakes, or if they don't like the experimenter, or if they think the experiment is silly, the data may be more reflective of these attitudes and feelings than of learning and memory. In considering this literature, one must be keenly aware of the factors that influence performance in order to evaluate whether a researcher is likely to have assessed the competency in question.

Learning

Most studies of learning among elderly people address the problem of *verbal learning*, usually assessed by testing for the acquisition of lists of words, sentences, or even groupings of letters known as nonsense syllables. The words or syllables may be presented in *serial* fashion, one after the other, or as *paired associates*. In a paired-associates study, the learner responds to one word or syllable with another word or syllable specified by the experimenter. For instance, the experimenter may present two nonsense syllables, like "yug" and "dak," together. After the first presentation, the learner is shown the syllable "yug" alone and is supposed to say "dak." If the response is incorrect, both syllables are presented together again. The interval during which both words are presented together is called the *inspection interval.* The period during which only the first member of the pair appears and the subject must remember the second syllable is called the *anticipation interval.*

In both longitudinal and cross-sectional studies, older people have consistently showed slower learning on both serial and paired-associate learning than the young. The data seem quite convincing on this point, but they do not imply that the old do not or cannot learn, only that the old may take a little longer (Gilbert, 1973; Arenberg and Robertson-Tchabo, 1977).

The question of how large a decrement occurs at what age has been of less interest recently than the study of what constitutes an optimal learning environment for adults. Such inquiry has practical ramifications, of course, but is also a useful way to ferret out the mechanisms behind age-related changes in learning and to supply the answers to some important theoretical questions.

Pacing

Creating an optimal learning environment for the older adult requires careful consideration of the timing or pacing of a task. When the anticipation interval is very brief, the performance of older people is especially poor. But brief inspection intervals do not have an adverse effect on performance. Such data have led some researchers to conclude that age-related learning decrements are never as important as changes in memory functions since the anticipation interval is thought to be the period during which the subject is retrieving learned material from memory (Eisdorfer, Axelrod, Wilkie, 1963; Arenberg, 1973).

In addition to memory deficits, changes in motivation as well as declining tolerance for stress may masquerade as learning decrements. For example, in analyzing the errors people make during learning, researchers have found that older subjects tend to omit responses rather than to make incorrect responses. Younger people make both kinds of errors (omission and commission) less frequently than do the old, but both types of errors occur equally often. In some instances, older people may really know the right responses but may be unable to give them quickly enough.

Studies like these have led to a search for ways to improve the performance of the elderly, and a number of methods have proved successful.

Yet, even under optimal conditions older people do not generally do as well as young adults. It is possible that older people require more time to perform all the processes of learning and memory, but several more specific hypotheses have been formulated too.

One such hypothesis about the origin of performance decrements is based on the notion that older people handle stress less well than the young. Carl Eisdorfer and his associates at Duke University suggested older people experience much higher arousal than the young, under conditions that require fast responding. Responses recorded from the *autonomic nervous system* (ANS) during learning experiments provided support for the *overarousal hypothesis*, and Eisdorfer also demonstrated that when ANS arousal was reduced using drugs, the performance of elderly subjects improved substantially (Eisdorfer, 1968; Eisdorfer, Nowlin, and Wilkie, 1970).

Overarousal does adversely affect the performance of the old under some laboratory conditions. However, if subjects are accustomed to experimental conditions, ANS-inhibiting drugs no longer improve performance, and young people continue to perform better than the elderly. Furthermore, some researchers have also shown that even when subjects are permitted total control over the pacing of a learning task, young people still learn faster than the old. Self-pacing and a supportive, familiar environment make important contributions to improving the performance of older subjects, but other forces are also at work.

THE MEANINGFULNESS DEBATE.   In the late 1960s, classic studies by Irene Hulicka (1967) raised some important questions about the interpretation of research on both learning and memory. In the first study, subjects were required to learn a list of paired-associate nonsense syllables. Hulicka found that when given the opportunity, 80 percent of the oldest subjects refused to participate in an experiment that seemed so "silly."

Clearly, older people perform far better when they are asked to learn materials that make sense to them. Moreover, taking advantage of well-established learning as an aid to new learning can lead to better performance among older subjects. For instance, word pairs that have high *associative strength* are acquired with relative ease by older people. Associative strength reflects the likelihood that one member of the pair will elicit the other. The pair "chair-table" has high associative strength; the pair "chair-bed" does not. It is possible that the learning decrements older people exhibit are partially due to the interference of well-established material with new responses. Over the years, various forms of the *interference hypothesis* have been offered, but it is likely that interference simply reflects the fact that older people didn't learn the material well in the first place. If initial learning is carefully controlled, and if the anticipation interval is long enough, interference rarely affects older people more than it

"It's a man's own fault, it is from want of use, if his mind grows torpid in old age." Samuel Johnson

affects the young (Arenberg, 1967; Botwinick and Storandt, 1974; Hulicka, 1967; Hartley, Harker, and Walsh, 1980).

Although meaningful material is easier for old people to learn than nonsense, it is also true that they do not show the level or speed of acquisition the young exhibit even when the material is meaningful. If the researcher requires subjects to make abstractions about the meaning of the material, age differences are increased (Botwinick, 1981). Again, however, Irene Hulicka and her associates have made the debate more interesting, this time by demonstrating that young people use more *mediators* than the elderly. A mediator is an internal, unobservable response (a thought or idea) that changes the type or quality of a subsequent response. For instance, images serve as mediators. If you were introduced to Mr. Sweet and you imagined him eating a pound of bon bons, you would be using a *mnemonic* device, a mediator, to encode Mr. Sweet's name. *Encoding* is the "symbolic representation of one thing by another; that is, it is the unknown internal code of the nervous system for physical objects or events" (Arenberg and Robertson-Tchabo, 1977, p. 426). Hulicka's study of mediation indicated that older people may encode information in different ways than young people do (Hulicka and Grossman, 1967; Treat and Reese, 1976; Hartley, Harker, and Walsh, 1980).

On traditional learning tasks, some researchers have produced dramatic improvement in the performance of the elderly through instruction in mnemonics; but not all the data are positive. Results vary depending on precisely what stimulus materials are involved, how the subjects are chosen and instructed, what kinds of measures are employed, and so forth (Hartley, Harker, and Walsh, 1980). Furthermore, research on mediation requires a consideration of memory. If older people do not use mnemonic systems or mediators, they may not seem to learn as well as the young, and they also will not remember as much. Where does learning end and remembering begin?

Memory

Although learning and memory probably depend on the same underlying mechanisms, it is useful to make some distinctions between them. To quote Fergus Craik (1977), one of the premier researchers and theorists in the study of memory:

> Learning may be thought of as referring to the acquisition of general rules and knowledge about the world, while "memory" refers to the retention of specific events which occurred at a given time in a given place. We have learned that Paris is the capitol of France, that $8 \times 9 = 72$, that our telephone number is 864–2967—the time and place of learning is not important for our utilization of these pieces of knowledge. On the other hand, time and place is of the essence when we recall a specific incident—who was at the party last Saturday or what we were doing on July 7, 1973 (p. 385).

Learning is the retention of general rules. *Memory* is the retention of events. Both learning and memory require the encoding, storage, and retrieval of information. The study of learning and memory, as well as decision making, problem solving, and related behaviors is often combined in the study of *information processing*. When compared with more traditional forms of research in learning and memory, information-processing approaches focus more closely on how we go about storing and retrieving ideas, events, and facts, rather than how well we do so.

Most models of information processing are based on analogies with the functioning of a computer. In the study of memory particularly, a computer-based three-process stage model has been useful. When working at a computer, one generally has three functions with which to contend. First, information must be entered through the keyboard. Next, this information must be manipulated in some way while it is in the immediate or working memory of the system. Finally, if the information is to be re-

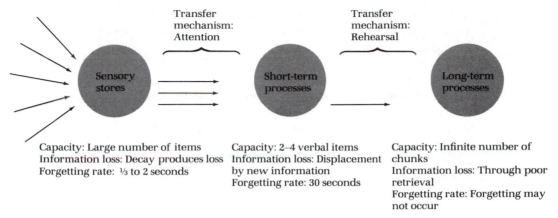

FIGURE 9.7
Three-process model of memory

tained for later use, it must be transferred from working memory to long-term storage in a special part of the computer or on a disc or tape.

Similarly, human memory is assumed to involve at least three basic stages, the input or entry stage, called *sensory memory;* an intermediate or short-term memory, called *primary memory;* and a long-term memory, often referred to as *secondary memory.* Figure 9.7 is a schematic representation of such a model.

The computer analogy can lead us astray if we begin to think of memory as a series of stores into which information flows automatically. It is better to think of each stage in terms of the processes that control the encoding and retrieval of information rather than the nature of the memory store. In the first stage, *sensory memory,* information is registered in a literal or eidetic manner, as an exact copy. Attention, rehearsal, or organization of the information is not required, but information decays very rapidly here. A sensory trace persists for only .25 to 2 seconds, and, unless one attends to the information during that interval, it will be replaced by new incoming information (Murdock, 1967; Craik and Lockhart, 1972; Walsh, 1975; Craik, 1977).

Everything that happens in the environment may well be available in sensory memory, but only information to which one *attends* is transferred to *primary memory.* Using the computer analogy again, we might say that information in primary memory exists as single items, or *bits.* The capacity of primary memory is limited. Only about 2.6 to 3.4 words or 5 to 7 digits can be retained here at a time. If information is to be retained longer, it must be transferred again, this time to *secondary memory*, which is assumed to be of unlimited capacity and indefinite duration.

One of the most important aspects of this computer-based model is its description of the way in which people transfer information from primary to secondary memory, by *processing* (manipulating) the information. The processing may be as simple as *rehearsal*—for instance, repeating a telephone number over and over again. The more elaborate the process, however, the more likely it is that one will have rapid, accurate access to the stored information. More elaborate, deeper processes include using mnemonics and imagery, organizing the new information, drawing inferences, or making generalizations—almost any kind of manipulation qualifies, although processes do vary in their effectiveness. The more effort required, the more likely one is to retain the information being processed.

In the study of aging and memory, there has been little argument over whether performance declines with age. Both longitudinal and cross-sectional data amply demonstrate that people find it more difficult to remember certain kinds of information as they grow older. Instead, the research has focused on discovering the point at which the bottleneck occurs. Which stage of memory is the most affected by age?

SENSORY MEMORY.   There is some reason to believe that fewer pieces or bits of information are available in sensory memory per unit of time in later life. Sensory and perceptual changes with age probably mean that older people need more time to discriminate among environmental stimuli (Walsh, 1975; Elias, Elias, and Elias, 1977).

Experiments that focus on sensory memory have demonstrated that older adults require longer to identify a single letter when it is presented for a few milliseconds, and that it takes them longer to improve at such tasks than the young (Smith, 1980). It has also been demonstrated that the elderly have more difficulty remembering things that are presented orally than those presented in written form. This may well be a problem of attention. When information is presented verbally, one must perceive what is being said and simultaneously process the meaning of it (Hartley, Harker, and Walsh, 1980; Craik and Simon, 1980).

On the other hand, despite some changes in sensory memory with age, most researchers appear convinced that the major bottleneck is not at the input stage, but is more likely in the processes defining primary and secondary memory.

PRIMARY MEMORY.   The study of attention is an important aspect of research on primary memory. Evidence suggests that primary memory is affected by age, at least under stressful conditions such as those present in a *dichotic listening* experiment. In dichotic listening tests, one short series of digits (series 1) is presented to the right ear, while at the same time a different short series (series 2) is presented to the left ear. The subject is then asked to repeat series 1. Typically, older people recall the first string the experimenter asks for as easily as younger subjects do. If, however, they must recall series 2 as well, older people perform poorly when compared with younger subjects (Inglis and Caird, 1963; Clark and Knowles, 1973).

Dichotic listening requires subjects to divide their attention between two incoming channels. Older people seem especially vulnerable to error in situations that require divided attention, perhaps because they must shift back and forth between perception and processing for recall (Craik, 1977). Of course, under normal conditions, people are rarely required to divide their attention so consistently, and when subjects are presented with simple tasks involving primary memory, like the recall of a short list of numbers, there is little evidence that age affects primary memory in very important ways (Craik, 1977).

From a review of the current literature it seems far more likely that the most significant changes occur in the processes by which information is transferred from primary to secondary memory. Instructions that require the reorganization or elaboration of information produce consistent decrements in the performance of elderly subjects. For instance, if older people are asked to repeat a short string of numbers backward, they must reorganize the input and are likely to experience difficulty.

SECONDARY MEMORY. There are three possible ways in which information may be lost from long-term or secondary memory. First, it may be that, rather than forgetting information more easily, older people never store it effectively in the first place. A second possibility is that information is lost from memory because of biological defects; in other words, it decays more readily with age (we might think of this idea as the "leaky storage bin" hypothesis). Finally, it may be that information is encoded and stored reasonably well, but elderly people have trouble retrieving it.

There is a good deal of evidence that older people encode information differently from the young, as exemplified by their failure to spontaneously use mediators when trying to encode paired associates, or even when trying to remember meaningful materials. Still, some researchers believe that all retrieval deficits are not caused by deficits in encoding (Hartley, Harker, and Walsh, 1980; Fozard, 1980). Data on the ability of elderly people to recall information versus their performance on tests of recognition are cited as evidence of a separate retrieval problem. Typical experimental results found in studies of recall and recognition have shown that elderly people do far better on tests that require recognition than on

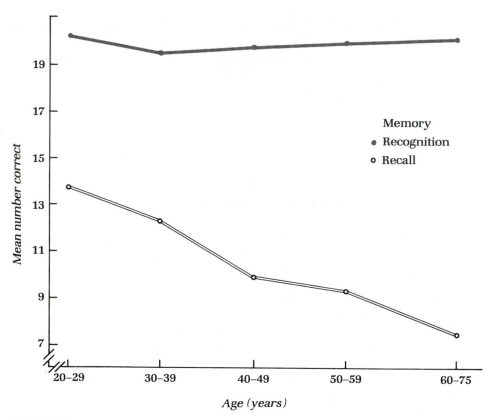

FIGURE 9.8
Mean recall and recognition scores as a function of age

SOURCE: *Based on data in Schonfield (1965) in Jack Botwinick,* Aging and Behavior, *2nd ed. (New York: Springer, 1978), figure 18.1, p. 338. Copyright © 1978 by Springer Publishing Company, Inc., New York. Used by permission.*

those that require recall (see Figure 9.8). Even when older people are encouraged to process more elaborately, these differences appear. Such results suggest that retrieval is the problem, if we assume that processing is the same for recall or recognition (Walsh, 1975).

Other writers insist that the difference between recall and recognition is, in fact, best explained in terms of encoding. Poor processing or encoding, they point out, will inevitably lead to difficulties in retrieving information. Returning to the computer analogy for a moment, let us imagine that you want to store your homework on a disc or tape for retrieval later. In order to do this, you will have to enter your homework in the computer, tell the computer to keep all the information in the same place, and give that place, or "file," a unique name so when you ask the computer to retrieve your homework later, it knows where to look. If, however, when entering the file name, you accidentally type in the label "homewok," the computer will not be able to retrieve a file when you request "homework" later on. Poor processing produces poor retrieval: the information is there, but you can't get access to it. Luckily, if you ask your computer for all the files you have currently stored, it will list "homework," and you will be saved. In the same way, when elderly people are given a few hints, they often remember information they could not retrieve on an earlier test. Perhaps they organized or labeled the information badly.

In addition to the problem of faulty encoding, it may be that recognition and recall depend on different types of processing. At least one writer has suggested that recall follows from very elaborate forms of encoding, such as reorganization and drawing generalizations, whereas recognition depends on simpler processes, such as sorting items into categories. Although young people tend to use processes that are appropriate for recall—reorganizing, summarizing, and so on—this form of organization may not give them an edge in recognition (Smith, 1980). (There is some evidence, however, that although recognition is easier than recall for the elderly, even recognition tests are easier for young subjects.)

James Fozard (1980) argues that the most effective way to eliminate competing explanations lies in the study of intervention. As one begins to study how to treat the problems of the elderly, the explanations for those problems may be clarified. Some of the evidence shows, for instance, that personality variables like activity level, energy, productiveness, responsibility, self-restraint, and impulsivity are related to memory performance. Other researchers have shown that cautiousness may produce decrements in performance on memory tasks. When older people are given large rewards for correct responses, but some reward for any response at all, performance seems to improve. Ordinarily, the elderly tend to make errors of omission; that is, they simply fail to respond rather than make a mistake. Mistakes may be essential to learning information well (Erber, Freely, and Botwinick, 1980).

A complete understanding of memory also requires an examination of how people learn more about things they already understand fairly well. Most of the studies we have been discussing focus on the encoding of new information, from nonsense syllables to written passages. The process of elaborating what one already knows—of becoming an expert—may be different. Consider the computer again, only this time think about the operator. Imagine you are learning to play a video game like Pac-Man. At first, you learn one move at a time; then you might memorize a sequence of moves—right, up, left, right, down, and so on—while at the same time learning how the monsters move and how to escape them. Eventually, however, you start to think of the pattern for the first game board as a whole. Now you can learn the patterns for new game boards in terms of variations on what you already know rather than beginning from scratch. This process of assimilating new material into old information has not yet been included in the traditional experimental study of memory (Hartley, Harker, and Walsh, 1980).

TOP-DOWN VS. BOTTOM-UP PROCESSING.   This last point brings us to one of the central theoretical arguments in the study of aging and memory. Usually, researchers assume that information is processed from the "bottom-up": the individual perceives incoming information, finds a way to organize it, and then processes it for storage. The implication is that age changes in the brain make it more difficult to use elaborate forms of processing.

An alternative view describes "top-down" processing. Over time, certain types of processing may become very strongly automated; it may become difficult to handle information in any other way or to deal with new or unusual information. Perhaps flexibility of processing decreases with age because certain modes of thought are essentially unused. If so, one must expect important cohort effects in memory performance. Memory may be a transaction between incoming information and what an individual already knows (Meacham, 1977; Hultsch and Pentz, 1980; Labouvie-Vief and Schell, 1982).

Two kinds of evidence tend to support the top-down, or transactional, view. First, memory often changes an unfamiliar idea or story to fit existing information. For instance, remember the cartoon called "Cinderfella" (or was it a movie?). I recall that the main character was a man, and the story was supposed to be humorous, but everything else I recall may be little more than an analogy from Cinderella. It is quite probable that things I remember from Cinderfella are only transformations of my knowledge of the Cinderella tale that seem to fit the silly title. I might have more accurate recall of *Cinderfella* if I didn't know *Cinderella* at all.

Another line of evidence for top-down processing shows that older people recall dated information better than the young, and that they recall everyday facts nearly as well. Dated information might include questions like "Who was Tom Mix?" or "What is tatting?" (Hultsch, and Pentz, 1980). Elderly people also perform far better on memory tests when dated materials (for instance, items from the 1908 Sears and Roebuck Catalog) are used than when modern test materials are employed (Labouvie-Vief and Schell, 1982).

Finally, there is reason to suspect that the ways in which people learn to process information change over generations. We know, for instance, that formal operations do not occur nearly as frequently in pre-industrial cultures as they do in modern, industrialized nations. It seems reasonable to assume that complex societies demand changes in the ways people deal with information. In the face of the "information explosion" fostered by electronic media, younger people are probably better prepared to deal both with more information and with greater novelty of information. Although this premise is difficult to research, it is clear from anecdotal data that the formal teaching of memory has changed radically in the last fifty years. People in their seventies still believe children ought to memorize the Declaration of Independence or the Preamble to the Constitution. On the other hand, today's children are appalled by the suggestion that they learn dates and names or be able to quote passages. They expect to be taught the basic principles and central ideas that will allow them to reconstruct details if necessary. There is too much information to store it bit by bit; one must file the basic ideas immediately, and go on.

Cohort differences in information processing might also be expected to affect a wide variety of cognitive operations in addition to memory, including problem solving and creativity.

PROBLEM SOLVING AND CREATIVITY

The literature on aging contains relatively few studies of problem solving. It is a complicated matter to pursue. Measurement is difficult at best, and interpretation is often impossible. What are the relationships among learning, memory, and problem solving? How does problem solving differ from creativity? How do motivation and education or intelligence affect either? In spite of the difficulties of answering such questions, some provocative attempts to define the areas of concern have been offered and some tentative hypotheses developed.

Early studies showed age differences in performance on problem-solving tasks of all sorts, from those requiring the subject to sort and classify items to brainteaser problems involving discovery of the sequence in which a number of electric switches must be pressed to activate a light (Welford, 1959; Jerome, 1962).

Later, researchers analyzed the performance of older subjects in greater detail. For example, it has been demonstrated that older subjects tend to make inquiries that yield little information and to treat redundant information as though it were new and different. Older subjects also tend to handle both positive and negative examples of a concept as though they were positive. In other words, if an older subject is told that *A*, *B*, and *C* are examples of a concept but that *D* and *E* are not, an elderly subject may still attempt to include *D* or *E*, or both, in the concept, ignoring the fact that the information about *D* and *E* was negative. If an individual cannot profit from negative information, inappropriate (or old) solutions may persist in spite of disconfirming evidence. The individual may seem to be rigid (Wetherick, 1966; Wetherick, 1969; Arenberg, 1968).

More recently, investigators have addressed the area of *concept learning*—the ability to identify exemplars of some well-defined universe of objects and to describe the rules for distinguishing between objects that belong to that universe and those that do not. In one study, middle-aged people performed better at such tasks than either older or younger age groups. As is the case in other problem-solving situations, the tendency of the elderly to retain a hypothesis that has been disproved seems to interfere with general concept learning (Giambra and Arenberg, 1980).

Piagetian-type tasks have also been employed in the study of problem solving, but the results are somewhat confusing. For instance, when Diane Papalia-Finlay and her associates (Papalia-Finlay, Blackburn, Davis, Dellman, and Roberts, 1982) set out to replicate earlier findings that elderly women could be trained on Piagetian tasks of conversation, they were unable to complete the study because none of the thirty-four subjects they tested (mean age 73.7) was unable to perform the task in the first place. Of course, these women were an unusually well-educated group, and all were living independently and in good health. Papalia-Finlay concluded that educational level is probably a better predictor of conservation than age.

In a similar vein, however, Nancy Denney and her colleagues (Selzer and Denney, 1980; Denney, 1982; Denney and Palmer, 1982; Denney and Pearce, 1982) report that performance on Piagetian tasks involving classification as well as performance at the traditional problem-solving task of "Twenty Questions" declined regularly with age, from the ages of twenty through seventy-nine. "Twenty Questions" is a game in which the players have twenty guesses in which to name the person, place, or thing the experimenter has in mind. The best way to approach the game consists in asking questions that eliminate as many possibilities as one can with any one question. For example, "Is it a person?" is usually followed by "Is it a male?" thus eliminating one-half of all the possibilities with one question. A poor strategy uses up guesses by asking specific questions (e.g., "Is it Roy Rogers?") before enough general information is known to formulate a good specific guess.

Denney's research also showed that middle-aged people performed best on the kind of practical problems discussed in Chapter 6, and that the elderly can be trained so that their performance at "Twenty Questions" is substantially improved. Denney believes that many traditional laboratory problem-solving tasks like "Twenty Questions" draw on abilities that are essentially unexercised in the everyday lives of older people. She argues that practice and training will produce improvement, at least to the level of performance indicated by the responses of older people to practical problems. Despite the benefits of practice, however, Denney argues that problem-solving ability does decline with age. The more complex the strategy or organization required to complete the task, the less likely that older people will perform very well. But, as is true for learning and memory, simple notions such as the idea that old information interferes with the acquisition of new ideas do not adequately account for the apparent deterioration of problem solving (Rabbitt, 1977).

Problem-solving research has also focused on intervention strategies. The performance of elderly people has been improved by modeling, by strategy hints and memory aids, and by using operant conditioning to override the disruptive effects of irrelevant stimulation (Denney, 1982; Sanders, Clausen, Mayes, and Sielski, 1976; Layton, 1975; Sanders, Sterns, Smith, and Sanders, 1975). Significantly, however, in many cases practice alone seems to have as great an effect as training does. Perhaps, given time, the elderly can improve their own performance without intervention.

In light of the conflicting and often confusing results of research about intervention, Leonard Giambra and David Arenberg make the somewhat radical suggestion that studies designed to identify age differences in problem solving be abandoned. "This Prohibition-Against-Aging-Studies would help move us out of the 'gee-whiz, look at the age difference' mentality (which represents the least taxing, thoughtful, and useful of all mentalities) to an insistence that age differences or changes be explained by specifying the nature of the modifications that must be made to theories that account for the standard (young adult) age group's performance" (1980, p. 257).

If the study of problem solving seems frustrating at times, the study of creativity is downright maddening. We lack even a reliable definition of the phenomenon. As Jack Botwinick (1981) has pointed out, research on creativity is too often confounded by the presence of other characteristics. For example, because historical studies of creativity rely on written records, they are heavily influenced by the subjects' prominence (we have written records only about people who achieved a certain level of prominence in their lifetimes). Laboratory studies, on the other hand, often measure the number of different or unique responses an individual makes rather than the quality of those responses. Botwinick argues that this kind of research also inadequately gauges creativity—a multifaceted phenomenon that involves an originality, flexibility, and independence of thought along with a tolerance for ambiguity and a preference for complexity.

A book that is now more than thirty years old, *Age and Achievement* (Lehman, 1953), is sometimes cited as the definitive work on the subject of publicly recognized creative achievement over the adult years. After analyzing the life work of dozens of famous artists, scientists, scholars, and technicians of the past four hundred years to determine the age at which they produced their most outstanding contributions, Harvey Lehman concluded that most major creative achievements occur relatively early in a career, some time between the ages of twenty and forty. *Age and Achievement* does not, however, stand without challenge. Foremost among those challenges is the work of Wayne Dennis (1966).

First eliminating from Lehman's sample all those who died at an early age, Dennis examined the creative productivity of those who lived to produce during their later years. Creativity, he showed, continues well past middle age, especially in areas where much of the legwork can be done by younger people. Unlike Lehman, Dennis did not attempt to evaluate the importance of any particular work, but simply counted the number of contributions people made during each age range. Lehman has argued that quality is the important measure and can be shown to be maximal during early adulthood, even for those who do not die early (Lehman, 1960).

The creative work of the elderly he studied, wrote Lehman, was most likely to consist in formal preparation and presentation of earlier ideas and the recording and interpretation of a lifetime's work, as well as the assumption of leadership roles. As Jack Botwinick (1981) points out, however, the assumption of leadership may actually be one of the reasons why creative people appear to be less productive with age. Working time declines as people accept the roles of teacher, advisor, administrator, and leader—roles that often accompany success and recognition.

Whether or not Lehman is correct, one is struck by the number of important exceptions, especially the great painters, sculptors, and architects, who made lasting, often critical, contributions to the history of art late in life. These people are all the more noteworthy since they engaged in the kinds of creative activities most often associated with young adulthood. Leonardo produced the *Mona Lisa* after the age of fifty; Titian finished *Christ Crowned with Thorns*, considered by many his most important statement on light and color, when he was eighty-two. Although Rembrandt lived to be only sixty-three, he rendered two of his most remarkable works, *The Polish Rider* and *Christ Preaching*, in his fifties. At the age of forty-seven, August Rodin created his most daring sculpture, the bust of *Balzac*. Vincent van Gogh did not even become a painter until he was twenty-seven. And finally, in the field of architecture, Le Corbusier designed Notre Dame du Haut at the age of sixty-four. This building has been called the "most revolutionary building of the mid-twentieth century" and

*Ah, nothing is too late
'Til the tired heart shall
   cease to palpitate.
Cato learned Greek at
   eighty; Sophocles
Wrote his grand Oedipus,
   and Simonides
Bore off the prize of verse
   from his compeers
When each had numbered
   more than fourscore years.*
HENRY WADSWORTH LONGFELLOW

a mirror of the "spiritual condition of Modern Man—which is a measure of its greatness as a work of art" (Janson, 1962, p. 545).

Of course, these are just a few examples, drawn only from a limited area of human endeavor. Table 9.1 lists a few more late-life masterpieces

TABLE 9.1
Some late great events

George Bernard Shaw writes his first play	Age: 48
Sophocles writes *Oedipus Rex*	Age: 75
Freud writes his last book	Age: 83
Pope John XXIII is elected	Age: 77
Konrad Adenauer wins the election that allows him to lead West Germany to reconstruction	Age: 72
Benjamin Franklin invents the bifocal lens	Age: 78
The Durants write the *Age of Napoleon*	Age: 89
Coco Chanel comes back into the world of fashion	Age: 72
Von Benden discovers the reduction of chromosomes	Age: 74
Bertrand Russell forms the Committee of 100, a radical organization devoted to nuclear disarmament	Age: 88
Karen, Baroness Blixen writes her first book	Age: 49
John Wayne wins an Oscar	Age: 62
Michelangelo creates St. Peter's and frescoes the Pauline Chapel	Age: 71–89
Mahatma Gandhi launches the Quit India movement, leading to India's independence	Age: 72
Frank Lloyd Wright completes the Guggenheim Museum	Age: 91
George Burns launches a new movie career, winning an Oscar for *Sunshine Boys*	Age: 80
Cecil B. De Mille produces *The Ten Commandments*	Age: 75
Claude Monet begins his Water Lily series	Age: 73
Charles de Gaulle returns to power in France	Age: 68

from a number of other fields. It is worth noting that if one of the late achievers listed there, Sigmund Freud, had died before he reached forty, no one would have ever heard of him. One wonders where psychology might be without the contributions of Freud, or how twentieth-century architecture would have evolved without Notre Dame du Haut. Could younger men have produced such work? It seems unlikely that someone in their twenties, for example, might develop the depth of understanding reflected in the later work of a Freud or a Le Corbusier.

What are the factors that facilitate and maximize the creative potential of older people? Most of the laboratory evidence on creativity deals with the study of *divergent thinking,* or the number of alternative correct or possible answers to a problem, asking for instance, for all the different ways one could use a junked automobile. The available evidence on divergent thinking does not show much decline with age, but divergent thinking may be more closely related to intelligence in adulthood than it is in childhood.

Research such as that on divergent thinking suggests that it may be inappropriate to use the same measure of creativity for different age groups, because creativity may involve different sets of abilities at different stages of the life cycle. Irving Taylor (1974) has even developed a scheme representing different stages of creativity over the life cycle. A brief summary of his hypothesis is presented in Table 9.2.

If we cannot decide how to measure creativity, then it will be difficult to determine how to optimize it. There are compelling arguments in support of the notion that the present experiential and environmental conditions of older people stultify creativity in old age. Poverty, illness, malnutrition, lack of education, racism, sexism, and the negative view our society has of the aging personality all contribute to declining creativity. If this is so, the situation is not new. Humankind has always shown conflict and fear over the process of aging, and we can find anecdotal evidence for the effect of such attitudes everywhere (Butler, 1974b; Bromley, 1974).

Particularly instructive is the apparent influence that such stereotyping has had on even the very great creative figures of history. Thomas Jefferson, for example, seemed to be convinced that he was becoming an imbecile at the age of sixty-eight, though to all appearances he continued to

TABLE 9.2
Creativity over the life course

Type of creativity	Age range
Expressive spontaneity: Creativity that may have a biological base and may be suppressed by formal education; shows up in children's games, dance, drawings	Childhood, appearing again in the late thirties
Technical proficiency: Creativity that is a function of the refinement of skills, as in concert instrumental work, dance	Typical of the twenties and forties
Inventive ingenuity: Creativity as it is expressed in idealized drawing, gadgetry, tinkering	Typical of the thirties and fifties
Innovative flexibility: Creativity that allows one to modify and adapt basic ideas, systems, and organizations for new purposes	Ages twenty-five to fifty
Emergentive originality: Creation of totally new or original ideas	After fifty

SOURCE: Based on I. Taylor, "Creativity and Aging," in E. Pfeiffer, ed., *Successful Aging: A Conference Report* (Durham, N.C.: Center for the Study of Aging and Development, 1974).

function as well as ever. In a letter to Benjamin Rush, Jefferson wrote, "Had not a conviction of the danger to which an unlimited occupation of the executive chair would expose the republican constitution of government made it conscientiously a duty to retire when I did, the fear of becoming a dotard and of being insensible to it would of itself have resisted all solicitations to remain" (Comfort, 1976).

To be creative, the individual must be free to change, to invent, and to reinvent the world and the self. Creative people continue to question, to search, and to actively participate in life. We should not be surprised, in a society where the full participation of older people in life is seldom required, if older people are less creative. In fact, it is remarkable that the people listed in Table 9.1 were able to overcome the pressures to limit themselves and their horizons with age.

Why some individuals remain creative and productive throughout the life span remains an intriguing but essentially unanswered question. Why did Monet begin his series of water lily paintings at the age of seventy-three, yet Jefferson worried about becoming an insensible dotard at sixty-eight? What can be done to make all of life, including old age, more creative? The creative researcher, young or old, could contribute much to human knowledge of creativity.

SUMMARY

In this chapter we have covered the physical and biological changes of later life as well as sensory, perceptual, and cognitive development. Moving from the outside in, we have seen evidence of many varied age-related changes and age differences in almost every aspect of human structure and function. Important alterations occur in outward appearance, in the structure and function of organs and organ systems, in sensation, perception, learning, memory, problem solving, and creative thought.

Changes in outward appearance include continued wrinkling and atrophy of skin tissues, hair loss, and the exaggeration of slumped or stooped posture. Outward appearance is also affected to some extent by skeletal changes, including the collapse of spinal vertebrae and subsequent height loss.

The most profound skeletal changes are not outwardly apparent, however. These involve increased porosity and hollowness of bony structures. Extreme age changes in the bones may be diagnosed as senile osteoporosis, although it is not clear where normal age-related changes end and this pathological condition begins.

The chemical composition and the number and diameter of muscle fibers of voluntary muscles and heart are also affected by age. Some alterations occur in the nerves that innervate individual motor units; and contraction time, latency, and relaxation periods increase. Changes in the structure of the heart result in decreased maximum blood flow through the coronary arteries. Arterial changes and increasing blood pressure combine with changes in the heart to predict rising rates of heart failure in later life.

Nor are the lungs as efficient in later life as they once were. The number of alveoli decreases, and the lung tissues become increasingly stiff. Pulmonary changes contribute to the incidence of heart disease and lead to some degree of emphysema in most older people.

The kidneys and intestinal tract, like the heart and lungs, show the effects of age in decreasing functional capacity. Loss of nephrons produces reduced filtration in the kidney. Lowered motility of the stomach, along with declining peristalsis in the colon, probably play a role in the inadequate nutrition commonly observed among older populations.

Although methodological difficulties plague the study of nervous-system development, some age-related change has been demonstrated. The number of brain cells has decreased dramatically by the age of eighty or ninety, and there are important alterations in the chemical composition of the remaining brain tissues. Although the relationship between these biological changes and psychological change is not clear, we do have direct evidence for the association of changing physiological measures and changing psychological phenomena in some areas, such as sleep.

Despite the assumed relationship between brain and behavior, however, we have yet to delineate the basic nature of the interface between biology and psychology. This is true even for extensive physical changes such as those observed in organic brain syndromes. Psychological function may change without evidence of physical alteration, as is seen in the functional disorders of later life. Moreover, the extent of biological damage is not a good predictor of the severity of psychiatric symptoms associated with organic brain disorders.

A distinction is made between acute and chronic brain syndromes. The symptoms of acute brain syndrome may be entirely reversed with appropriate care and treatment. The progress of chronic brain syndromes cannot be entirely halted, but substantial restoration of function may be achieved through therapy and retraining.

The precise effects of physiological age changes are equally unclear in the study of sensation, perception, and cognition. Color vision and acuity are particularly affected among the visual abilities, and declining speech perception reflects the auditory decrements of later life. Changes take place in the receptor organs and peripheral nerves of vision and audition, but psychologists must look to deterioration of central mechanisms for fuller explanation of the nature and severity of sensory change.

Documentation of age-related alterations in perception has given rise to several major, competing hypotheses about the nature and direction of development in later life. The regression hypothesis suggests that the performance of older people can be compared with that of children and adolescents. Some data on visual illusions and the judgment of verticality and horizontality support the regression hypothesis. Other evidence suggests that the perceptual changes of later life may be related to the greater susceptibility of older people to unusual variations in stimulus configurations.

The major area of research on cognitive change in older people involves the study of learning and memory. It is difficult, at times, to distinguish between these two processes. The study of learning focuses on how well information is stored; the study of memory centers on questions of process. Both cross-sectional and longitudinal research suggest that there are age-related decrements in performance on tasks designed to test both learning and memory. The major concern in recent years has been to identify the conditions under which the performance of older people can be optimized.

Researchers have found that pacing and task meaningfulness influence the learning performance of older people. Older people perform at higher levels when they can pace themselves and when the material to be learned is meaningful to them. Another reason that older people do not seem to learn as well as younger subjects is that they do not use the same mediating and mnemonic devices. It has been demonstrated that significant improvements in the performance of the elderly can be achieved if they are encouraged to use more elaborate encoding processes.

The emphasis on encoding processes is echoed in the literature on memory. One popular theory of memory offers a three-stage model and suggests that the major difference between one stage and the next is in the degree of elaboration required to transfer information to or from that stage. The research supports the position that older people do not encode as elaborately as the young. This data would predict that, in the context of a three-process model of memory, the most important decrements would be found in long-term memory. At present long-term memory does seem to be the site of most age-related memory change.

An alternative view stresses the importance of what is already in memory for the processing of new information. This theory of "bottom-up" processing predicts important cohort differences in the way people deal with new information.

This chapter closes with a discussion of the most complex and abstract arenas of cognitive research: problem solving and creativity. Much of what has been said about learning and memory can be applied to the literature on problem solving, because problem solving can be viewed as a complex learning or memory task. It has been demonstrated that many of the same methods that might be expected to improve learning and memory also improve problem-solving behavior in the old. These methods include strategy hints, memory aids, and the use of operant conditioning to help older people overcome the disrupting effect of irrelevant stimulation.

The study of creativity, on the other hand, has not centered on the discovery of optimal conditions. It has, instead, tended to focus on the development of some appropriate measure for creative potential. Until this basic problem is solved, it will be difficult indeed to outline the nature and direction of age-related change in creativity.

Chapter 10

The Personal Context: Personality and the Social Network

Age only matters when one is aging. Now that I have arrived at a great age, I might just as well be twenty.

PABLO PICASSO

In this chapter, we will be looking at the interaction between social attitudes, social demands, social opportunities, and the aging of personality. What people believe and what they expect influence how they behave and how they perceive themselves. At every age, there are certain behaviors that are acceptable, or *age appropriate*, and certain behaviors that are labeled "immature." Of course, it is also possible to be considered "old before your time." Some age-appropriate behaviors are clearly positive developments. For example, two year olds are expected to be able to play nicely with other children, at least for short periods of time, and to be capable of rudimentary verbal interactions. Age-appropriate behavior in adolescence includes a fair degree of independence and poise. Other behaviors are less commendable but are age appropriate nonetheless. Two year olds are expected to be difficult, demanding, and unruly. Adolescents are expected to be argumentative and to resist adult authority.

Although some writers believe that the last few years of the life cycle are characterized by fewer and fewer social strictures, elderly people are supposed to be kind and gentle and wise. On the other hand, they are thought to become resistant to change, slow to learn, less ambitious, and more opinionated than the young (Schonfield, 1982). One wonders how elderly people might behave if social attitudes were different. The same question might be raised about any stage of the life cycle.

In this chapter the tasks or trends that characterize development in later life are discussed in terms of the prevailing social attitudes toward older people in this country. Keeping the literature on social attitudes in mind, we will also review the research on successful aging and will examine different life-styles and adaptations in old age, from rocking-chair solitude to Gray Panther activism, in terms not only of external behavior and social role performance but also of inner, psychological developments, emotional changes, and alterations in time perspective and reference.

The second section of the chapter focuses on the details of the social network in later life, including dyadic relationships, family ties, and community involvement. Particular attention is paid to the inevitable losses of the later years, and especially to the death of a spouse. The emotional aspects of grief, bereavement, and dying are examined in greater depth in Chapter 12. In this chapter, we will concentrate on the social changes encountered by those who lose people close to them late in life.

We will also consider the role of friendship in later life, especially in comparison with the function of family ties, and in light of the growing trend among older people toward retirement in age-segregated communities. Finally, we will look at some recent suggestions for supporting and reinforcing family efforts to care for and relate to the most disabled elderly individuals.

ATTITUDES AND TASKS

This life a theatre we well may call,
Where every actor must perform with art,
Or laugh it through and make a farce of all,
Or learn to bear with grace his tragic part.
                                                     Palladas

Thousands of years before Erik Erikson began to study Freud, the Greek dramatist Palladas captured the notion of integrity, defining it as an attempt to carry off one's performance in life as a significant character. In Erikson's twentieth-century version, the individual confronts the proposition "I am what survives of me"—the faith, will, purposefulness, competence, love, care, and wisdom that flow from an individual into the lives of others and the institutions of society. The task is to find a narrative line that sums up one's own life, to make sense of the passage of years and events, to finish the puzzle, to complete the picture. It has been described as the drawing up of a balance sheet, and the literature repeatedly refers to the retrospection of the elderly as evidence of the significance of this final reevaluation, this tying together of loose ends (Butler, 1963; Erikson, 1968a; Frenkel-Brunswik, 1970).

Retrospection and reminiscence were assigned a central role in the development of integrity by one of the most influential students of aging in America, Robert Butler. Butler (1963) argues that reminiscence, or the process of *life review*, produces candor, serenity, and wisdom in old age. He believes that constructive retrospection facilitates a creative, positive reorganization of the personality. Recently, a similar concept, oral history, has been popularized by Alex Haley's *Roots*. Haley has championed the importance of retrospection, not just as a tool for working with the elderly, but as a legacy, an invaluable contribution to younger generations (Haley, 1982).

As Butler notes, however, integrity is not the only possible outcome of life review. The other side of the coin is despair: the inability to accept one's own fate. Those who despair cannot accept death and are victimized

"When I was younger, I could remember anything, whether it happened or not; but I am getting old, and soon I shall remember only the latter." Mark Twain

by the feeling that time is too short. Despair is accompanied by regret, frustration, discouragement, and the feeling that one's life has been meaningless. One speculates about how things might have been, if this or that or the other had only been different. Certainly, most of us wonder how our lives would have turned out if we had taken the road less traveled (or perhaps the one more often chosen). The despairing person feels that the achievement of meaningful goals was rendered impossible by the choices or surprises of life. Death becomes the ultimate usurper, ending any hope of fulfilling one's lifetime hopes and ambitions.

    The achievement of integrity may be difficult in a society that devalues the aged. Optimistic or comforting visions of old age are rare in the literature of the social sciences, in fiction, in verse, or in humor. They exist, of course, but more often one finds echoes of the despair expressed by Macbeth:

I have lived long enough: my way of life
Is fall'n into the sere, the yellow leaf,
And that which should accompany old age,
As honour, love, obedience, troops of friends,
I must not look to have . . .

Attitudes

A few years ago, it was routine to argue that the elderly are devalued, stereotyped, and excluded by the rest of society; and that they lose most of their significant major social roles, suffering a reduction of meaningful responsibility and a limitation of function. Older people were most often described as lonely, bitter, poor, and emotionally or physically ill, subject to a reality limited by the few meaningful roles left to them by the cultural dictates of later life.

Research strongly supported this negative view. Consistently, investigators reported that the elderly were held in low esteem by all age groups in our society, including themselves. All sorts of evidence was marshalled in favor of this position, from reports that people of all ages believed the death of a seventy-five year old was less tragic than the death of a younger person, to studies that listed the negative terms people chose to describe the elderly—tired, ill, sexless, mentally slow, forgetful, unable to learn, grouchy, withdrawn, self-pitying, isolated, unhappy, unproductive, and defensive (Hickey and Kalish, 1968; Butler, 1974a; Kalish, 1975; Kalish and Reynolds, 1976; Collete-Pratt, 1976).

The elderly were accused of making the situation worse by refusing to acknowledge their age—by clinging to youthful self-images, creating strain between their view of themselves and the way the rest of society viewed them (Rosow, 1977a). Finally, it was often argued, the problems of the elderly were not taken seriously enough: doctors and nurses did not perceive the difficulties of the old as urgent, and those who offered psychological services did not view the elderly as attractive, valuable patients. Eventually, the elderly themselves participated in the devaluation, not caring for their health or feeling resigned to poor physical conditions, depression, and isolation (McTavish, 1971; Kalish, 1975).

In the past few years, this entire line of evidence has been questioned. In the late 1960s and through the 1970s, most researchers seemed to set aside their own bias—the idea that people undervalue the elderly—when trying to define societal attitudes. Recent research has shown that subjects who are given a chance to cite exceptions to statements about the elderly (statements like "older people require longer to learn anything new") usually say that there are many exceptions. In fact, subjects have often suggested that as many as 50 percent of the elderly cannot really be described by a general statement about aging (Schonfield, 1982).

Perhaps we have been prejudiced about stereotypes. Stereotyping in and of itself need not be unfair. A stereotype is a distillation of beliefs and attitudes toward a class of people or objects. In a complex, fast-paced social system, stereotypes can serve an important function. For instance, if you go to the supermarket and actually read the labels on every brand of each item you purchase, it might take you a year and a half to finish shopping. You could be paralyzed by indecision in the canned-goods aisle. Instead, it may make sense to adopt some stereotypic attitudes like "All aspirin are alike." You can then buy the cheapest aspirin, or the one in the bottle that matches your bathroom wallpaper, without pondering the real merits of each brand.

In the same way, stereotypes help one decide how to behave toward people. If a nine-year-old boy is invited to a birthday party for a male classmate, his mother will probably not send along a Barbie doll as a present. Certainly her response is stereotypic; but, unless she wants to make a political statement, a doll is not a choice that will charm most nine-year-old boys. The mother may know that there are exceptions, or believe that this state of affairs is not necessary or even good. Her stereotype worked for her, however: it made buying a present more efficient, particularly if she doesn't know the boy in question well enough to be aware of his individual likes and dislikes.

Similarly, in speaking to an elderly person one does not know, it might be best to avoid the latest slang, to speak up a little, and to expect some resistance to suggestions that require great change. That doesn't mean that all elderly people are rigid, old-fashioned, or deaf: it is important at the same time to remain open to the possibility that this particular person is familiar with the latest slang, has very acute hearing, and is looking for an exciting change. Stereotypes become dangerous when people begin to feel that the stereotype defines *normal* behavior (when ambitious old people are considered crazy), or when the stereotype is accepted as a reflection of biology (if waning ambition is thought inevitable).

David Schonfield (1982) believes that the social sciences have been extremely critical about the treatment of the elderly and that such harsh criticism is simply not justified. Most Americans, he maintains, do not in fact have overly negative attitudes toward the aged; but they believe they do. For instance, 71 percent of the general public believes that the elderly are not given enough respect. Only 40 percent of the elderly agree, and only 1 percent of the public believes the elderly receive too much respect. These statistics do not suggest the aged are devalued. Even in areas that have been treated by social scientists as controversial, the general public does not seem to be nearly as biased as one might guess. In one national survey, for example, 90 percent of the respondents stated that they did not believe sex to be inappropriate for married people over seventy.

There is evidence, however, that people fear aging and believe that life loses its promise in the last part of the life cycle. Moreover, although it may be true that Americans feel less negatively about the elderly than social scientists have assumed, it is also true that both aging and the aged remain the objects of fear and ignorance. *Ageism*, defined as "discrimination based on age," especially "against middle-aged and elderly people" (Morris, 1979, p. 24), cuts across all races, religions, and socioeconomic groups and applies to both sexes. It is no coincidence that positive terms related to age are rare (mature, mellow, sage, venerable, veteran), whereas native terms abound (old bag, bat, biddy, battle axe, dirty old man, codger, coot, fogy, fossil, fuddy-duddy, geezer, goat). How about "over the hill," the "Geritol generation," the "declining years," "second childhood," and even "little old lady"—harmless, sexless, helpless? Then there are the terms that deride the disabilities of age—decrepit, crotchety, doddering, senile. Not a pretty picture (Nuessel, 1982).

What is surprising is that the opportunities of age are so often overlooked. Once the children are gone, and retirement (or at least semi-retirement) becomes a real possibility, real freedom is also possible, for the first time since late adolescence (if one had the chance then). No more fighting rush-hour traffic or hauling carloads of kids to school and lessons and extracurricular activities. No need to be up every morning at 7 A.M. At seventy, you can sleep all day if you want to; nobody cares. You might think, "How sad, nobody cares." But the other possible reaction is, "Great! Finally, everyone's minding their own business."

Successful Aging

Because so few longitudinal studies have followed people throughout the life span into old age, it is safe to assume that much of what we believe about aging reflects the poorer health and lower socioeconomic and educational status of older cohorts—all of which are important in the interpretation of data on self-image, attitudes toward aging, and morale. Cohort differences do not explain all the data, however. Even among the lowest socioeconomic groups and those in the poorest health, there are individuals who maintain high levels of self-esteem and life satisfaction. In fact, some studies show no age-related changes in self-concept, and some even suggest increases in self-esteem with age (Kaplan and Pokorny, 1970; Bennet and Eckman, 1973; Edwards and Klemmack, 1973; Haan, 1981).

Bernice Neugarten has argued that some of these data reflect impor-tant historical trends (Neugarten and Hagestad, 1977). She believes that age-ism is waning and that increased consciousness has already wrought improvements in the status of older people. Neugarten has even suggested that the culture may be conferring economic preference on the elderly. Some older Americans are a visible and contented leisure class. Further-more, recent studies have demonstrated that younger people are not unre-mittingly negative toward the elderly (Green, 1981). Investigators have found that positive adjectives like happy, friendly, stable, and responsible are more often used to describe the elderly now. Many times a study will report more positive than negative results (Kahana, 1982). Researchers have also discovered that life satisfaction does not necessarily decline with age.

Information about how satisfied the elderly perceive themselves to be, what kind of behavioral patterns they adopt, and how others respond to them varies with the instruments researchers have chosen, the way elderly people are presented, and the characteristics of the people who participate in the study. Too often, researchers simply survey and report what older people do rather than how they feel about it or how involved they are. It may be the quality of participation in life that determines satisfaction, however, rather than what one chooses to do. Activity per se is not necessarily a good predictor of satisfaction. For some people, many activities and roles maintain meaning in later life. For others, few seem worthwhile. What may be most important is the degree of freedom one has to discard activities that have lost their meaning and pursue those that remain (Lowenthal, Thurnher, and Chiriboga, 1975; Neugarten and Hagestad, 1977).

ACTIVITY AND ADJUSTMENT.   One of the most influential early theories of adjustment in later life was formulated by Cumming and Henry in 1961. On the basis of data collected in the 1950s, these authors posited that *disen-gagement* from the roles and activities of adult life produced successful aging. It was assumed that such withdrawal was a mutual process, occur-ring both within the individual and from the social setting, and that it constituted a universal phenomenon.

Over the years since disengagement theory was first presented, how-ever, it has become apparent that optimal aging cannot be predicted by social activities and role involvement alone. Research has shown that some satisfied elderly people disengage; but it has also demonstrated that contin-ued *engagement*—high levels of activity and involvement—is optimal for others (Palmore, 1979). Like younger adults, older people derive satisfac-tion from a variety of life-styles. For example, in the typology developed by Robert Havighurst (1969) for one classic study of successful aging, eight

TABLE 10.1
Eight patterns of aging

Personality type	Life-style	Description	Degree of life satisfaction
Integrated	Reorganizers	Competent, engaged, and involved; substitutes new activities for old	High
	Focused	Integrated personality, moderately active, centered in one or two role areas	High
	Disengaged	Low levels of activity and role involvement, reduced role commitment, high self-esteem	High
Armored-defended	Holding on	Holds on to midlife roles and activities; when successful, maintains adequate levels of life satisfaction	High[a]
	Constricted	Low to medium involvement in a few role areas	Medium to high
Passive-dependent	Succor-seeking	Medium to high activity levels; if successful at gaining attention from others, maintains adequate levels of life satisfaction	Medium to high[a]
	Apathetic	Low role activity; does not expect much from or give much to life	Low to medium
Unintegrated	Disorganized	Deteriorated cognitive processes, poor emotional control	Low to medium

[a]These individuals maintain adequate levels of life satisfaction only where they are able to successfully maintain the corresponding life-style pattern.

SOURCE: Based on R. J. Havighurst, "Research and Development in Social Gerontology: A Report of a Special Committee of the Gerontological Society," *The Gerontologist*, 9 (1969): 1–90.

major personality types or life-styles are described, a number of which can be considered satisfactory (see Table 10.1).

Although no single pattern of aging is best for everybody, it may be possible to predict adjustment from one's earlier personality (Neugarten and Hagestad, 1977). If an individual has always been active, involved, and satisfied, and if the environment provides opportunities for continued involvement of similar quality, a satisfactory life-style can emerge in old age. In contrast, for a person who has never been deeply involved in many of the activities and roles of adulthood, later life may present a welcome opportunity to shed responsibilities and activities one never really wanted.

Although disengagement theory has been strongly challenged as the sole explanation of successfully adaptive aging, the basic idea has been reworked and redefined to produce several more recent hypotheses. Some believe disengagement must be measured in terms of emotional involvement: concern for internal rather than for external events. Evidence for this view shows that older people are less likely to become emotionally invested in environmental circumstances than are the young (Havighurst, Neugarten, and Tobin, 1968) and that they tend to exhibit some decline or restriction in the flow and expression of physical energy, along with a rejection of the more "vulnerable, volatile, or emotional components of personal existence" (Lowenthal, Thurnher, and Chiriboga, 1975, p. 64). Older subjects also report fewer emotionally charged experiences, either negative or positive, than do younger groups. This type of data has been construed as a reflection of inner, or psychological, disengagement.

On the other hand, some argue that intrinsic disengagement is natural and adaptive only for "self-protective or emotionally bland individuals" (Lowenthal, Thurnher, and Chiriboga, 1975, p. 237). Even then, these authors maintain, the process of withdrawal is limited to "a deliberate sorting out and sloughing off of unwanted responsibilities." Others contend that observed disengagement may be directly attributable to stress-inducing environmental and circumstantial disturbances, such as widowhood or failing health (Palmore, 1968; Tallmer and Kutner, 1969).

A number of hypotheses about disengagement—the conditions under which it occurs and is adaptive—remain unexplored. Does disengagement happen in societies which value productivity and activity less than twentieth-century America? Does disengagement occur in some areas of life more often than in others? Is disengagement usually a consequence of trauma or failing health? The case is not easily closed. As much as some would like to eliminate disengagement theory from the possible explanations of successful aging, it cannot easily be dismissed.

Marjorie Lowenthal (1978), for example, has formulated an important variation on the engagement-disengagement theme by suggesting that adaptive adjustments in the relationship between goals and behavior are the key to successful aging. People who respond to the losses of later life by limiting their goals and behaviors fit the picture painted by disengagement theory, but other possibilities abound. Some people expand their goals and behaviors when they encounter loss, substituting new roles and relationships for old ones. Lowenthal calls this pattern *transcendence*. An older woman who, after the death of her husband, seeks a career outside the home may transcend the crisis of widowhood. A man who looks forward to sailing around the world when he retires has a transcendent approach.

Other possibilities exist for those who expand or constrict their goals during a life transition but fail to change their behavior. Lowenthal labels this pattern *escapism*. People who talk in a booming voice of travel and adventure but never pack a suitcase, or who plan a party once a month but never get out the invitations, are escaping. Lowenthal also describes the pattern of *denial* followed by those who manage to ignore a life transition, changing neither goals nor behaviors. A man who continues to come home every night and act as though nothing has happened after his wife asks for a divorce denies the change. A woman who continues working toward a big promotion although she has just been passed over for the second time is exhibiting denial.

Lowenthal believes that disengagement is often adaptive because engaged life-styles are difficult to maintain in later life. In fact, a disconcerting finding of her report, *Four Stages of Life* (1975), concerns the fate of individuals given to complex, involved life-styles. Outlining four major life-styles, from the *simplistic*, characterized by limited role involvement and limited social activities, to the *complex*, involving a wide range of roles and role behaviors, Lowenthal and her associates found that the happiest young adults were those judged most complex. Among the oldest subjects, however, complex people seemed to be the least happy. According to Lowenthal, the low levels of satisfaction found among older, complex personalities reflect reduced opportunities for participation and self-expression in old age. Although younger complex people experienced deficits and difficulties, they also possessed the greatest resources for coping with the ups and downs of their lives. By late middle age, however, the simplest types—those reporting the fewest emotional experiences, the lowest levels of stress, and the fewest turning points in their lives—were the happiest.

If a society closes many avenues of self-expression and involvement to its oldest citizens, they will have difficulty maintaining a complex life-style, and they may be forced to disengage rather than transcend the problems of aging. In the absence of opportunities for engagement, disengagement is too often involuntary: complex people may grow old happily only if they belong to those relatively small and privileged groups whose life-style options remain varied.

As our society becomes less age conscious, however, and as more people live to be very old, the social structure of old age is likely to change. Already compulsory retirement has been abolished in many organizations. One can now continue to work until seventy, even beyond. Income from full or part-time work provides greater flexibility. If Lowenthal and her associates replicate their study in the year 1990 or 2000, they may well find that adults with complex personalities have been more successful at maintaining their life-styles over the years. It will be fascinating to see how changing demographics affect the lot of the elderly.

Surely, other historical forces will affect the adjustment of elderly people too. The women's movement, the sexual revolution, and the general diversification that accompanies the postindustrial society will all probably influence adjustment. Such changes could spell trouble, if they mean greater stress and more rapidly shifting demands. On the other

As the population ages, particularly if the life span is much increased, people will undoubtedly be forced to spend a greater proportion of that increased span as active members of the labor force.

hand, they might provide growing options and produce greater flexibility in people of all ages. One of the more intriguing lines of evidence and speculation in this regard concerns the impact of changing sex roles and the interaction of sex differences in aging.

PERSONALITY, SEX DIFFERENCES, AND AGING.   In *Four Stages of Life* (1975), Lowenthal, Thurnher, and Chiriboga reported an intriguing trend that might be characterized as a kind of disengagement. Many of the men they studied progressed, with age, from insecurity and discontent through buoyancy and nearly uncontrolled energy to order, control, and industry, and, finally, to a mellow, less dissatisfied attitude about themselves, characterized by a tendency to make fewer demands on both the self and the environment (Lowenthal, Thurnher, and Chiriboga, 1975; Gutmann, 1977). For women, however, the progression was quite different: they seemed to proceed from dependency and helplessness to a more assertive, aggressive, or energetic stance. That older women resembled middle-aged men in many respects presented a clear challenge to the idea of disengagement.

Four Stages of Life reported that sex differences were larger than age differences in almost every area of investigation. Only on measures of self-concept did differences between age groups appear as important as sex differences.

There is much evidence that healthy, older women become more assertive while remaining nurturant and warm, whereas healthy older males remain assertive but become more expressive, nurturant, and caring. Over time in a marriage, women are seen more and more often as the dominant partner—a shift that has been associated with positive attitudes toward the changes of later life (Turner, 1982).

Yet, these are tempered changes. The evidence also shows that pugnaciousness, assertion, and rejection of passivity are adaptive in later life for both men and women. Moreover, among well-adjusted men, the trend toward nurturance, warmth, and shared decision making is not accompanied by passivity and submissiveness, even though increased passivity may be common in male development after middle age (Lieberman, 1981; Turner, 1982).

Thus, as we might expect, changes through the last part of the life cycle represent continuing adaptation and adjustment rather than discontinuity. Preliminary evidence suggests that successful aging can be predicted from early adult adjustment, especially for women (Kuypers, 1981). In a continuing analysis of the data from the Berkeley studies, Joseph Kuypers has defined adaptation in later life in terms of a fluid responsiveness to both the external and the internal world. The well-adapted subjects in his sample appeared self-directed, empathic, and firm but flexible, and they were able to suppress their own anxieties when necessary or redirect anxiety into productive activities (sublimation).

Kuypers also describes subjects who tended to rationalize and were haunted by doubt as *defensive* adapters, whereas *disorganized* personalities exhibited tangential thinking and often appeared immobilized. Repression rather than sublimation characterized defensive individuals, while withdrawal, preoccupation, and even delusional thinking were characteristic of the disorganized personality.

Adaptation in women, according to Kuypers, showed greater stability than adaptation in men from early to later adulthood, and it seemed more strongly related to family life events. Overall, for both men and women, socioeconomic class and intellectual ability were the best predictors of adjustment in later life. These findings may ultimately mean that success in one's major life roles is in fact the best predictor of late-life satisfaction. Socioeconomic class is usually a reflection of occupational achievement for males, and marital disharmony is related to the success a woman experiences in the traditional female role. Is it possible, Kuypers wonders, that certain individuals, especially certain women, are "locked" into ego failure from the earliest years of adulthood because they are unsuccessful at the major life roles? If it is accurate to hypothesize that adult role fulfillment is important in determining adaptation, then we might also expect historical changes in the determinants of adaptation. If roles change substantially from one generation to the next, there may be concomitant changes in the factors that best predict adjustment.

Thus, the exploration of successful aging may be an endless project. As the society evolves and needs and expectations change, the possibilities for adjustment and satisfaction later in life may be continuously altered. Futurists like Alvin Toffler (1970, 1980) predict enormous increases in cultural diversity in the next generation, and these trends can be expected to influence adults of all ages. It may be that such concepts as "successful aging" are too general to yield valuable information, particularly in the context of rapid social change. The conditions and circumstances that favor one pattern of aging over another may not be static long enough for anyone to make even temporarily definitive statements about optimal patterns. Studies like those of Lowenthal and her associates are most provocative when they address circumscribed phenomena. For example, substantial age differences have been found in some aspects of time perception.

Time Perspective

The study of time perspective has offered some productive research about the ways in which our perception of time may be related to other attitudes and behaviors. Children in Western cultures learn to associate time with distance, for example, and have a strong tendency to view time in a linear way. Time is perceived by most of us to pass, moment by moment, each second disappearing as it is ticked off by the clock. Americans, in particular, grow up with the notion that time passes in a definite, measurable way, just as the miles fly past in a speeding car. In America, time marches on. It may come as some surprise, then, to learn that time evidently passes quite differently for people of different age groups. Although we know that "time flies when you are having fun" or that the days before your birthday party drag when you are six and race when you are thirty-nine, the subjective experience of time holds a mystery for most of us. Why does time seem to go faster as one grows older?

It has been suggested that time passes faster for adults because each moment represents a smaller proportion of one's total life. If this were so, old men and women should perceive time as passing more swiftly than the middle aged. In actuality, however, more middle-aged men describe time as passing quickly than do members of any other age group. Could it be, then, that one's orientation toward the present or the past, rather than the future, best predicts the experience of time pressure? Middle-aged men spend a good deal of time rehashing the past, reworking and reorganizing their lives. Perhaps people experience a sense of time pressure at transition points throughout the life span rather than at one point or the other (Lowenthal et al., 1975).

Older people too may spend a lot of time thinking about the past. There is evidence, however, that older people evaluate the past in a positive and satisfied way more often than do young adults or middle-aged people (Cameron, 1972a; Lieberman, 1970). Older people also report less experience of eventfulness, or density of time than those at the threshold of middle age. Subjects in their fifties and sixties report fewer turning points and fewer frustrations in their lives than do people in their forties. They also express less involvement in the events they do experience. Perhaps changes in the experienced density of time may eventually explain age differences in the sense of time pressure people feel.

In contrast with the differences in the subjective perception of how time passes, researchers have found little age difference in the ability to estimate the objective passage of time. While older people may engage in more vigorous life review, there are no data that indicate older people

"Nothing is inherently and invincibly young except spirit." George Santayana

dwell on the past while younger subjects live in the future. It does seem true, however, that the future is seen as better than the present or the past throughout the first half of the life cycle. Sometime around the age of fifty, the past, present, and future are all perceived as about equally negative or positive. After the age of seventy, the past is evaluated as better than the present, and the present is seen as better than the future (Bortner and Hultsch, 1972).

Most older Americans do not believe the future is likely to be the best period in their lives. Many young people do. Younger subjects project much farther into the future than do the old. About three-quarters of the high school students and newlyweds in the Lowenthal study projected into their eighties, but only 66 percent of the middle-aged subjects and only 46 percent of the preretirement group did so. Interestingly, the happiest of the preretirees were found in that 46 percent. In the oldest group, two-thirds of those individuals who were rated as "impaired" in adjustment showed limited ability to project themselves into the future. Thus, although the happiest group might not have a rosy vision of the future, they appear willing to plan for and accept it anyway. As Arthur C. Clarke quipped on quoting Robert Browning's lines "Grow old along with me/ The best is yet to be": "I think he's whistling in the dark, but I'm going anyway."

One last finding about time perception from Lowenthal and her associates has some interesting implications. Time perspective may have more predictive value for the old than for the young. We have seen that in older groups the ability to project into the future is associated with adjustment. There are also data to support the notion that the most competent older people are those who are *not* heavily invested in the future. They may plan for the future, but they do not live in it. Neither do they dwell in the past, although they have learned to consider the past as well as the present and future. Older people may actually be in a position to achieve balance in time. An older person has a past long enough to be a history, to contain triumphs and defeats, to be as exciting as the future; and so the future becomes less demanding and less impressive.

The alteration of one's perspective on time may be part of the process by which *integrity* develops. In describing integrity Erikson (1963, p. 268) says that it is in part "the acceptance of one's one and only life cycle." This acceptance is accompanied by a diminished need to rush toward the future to achieve unfinished goals and tie up loose ends. Again, we are standing at a juncture of developmental trends and social structure. The social structure dictates acceptable goals and achievements, which are also defined and interpreted in the context of a particular personality. These social and personal events combine with a changing sense of time to determine the developmental course of later adulthood. Ruth Benedict expressed the interaction eloquently when she wrote that "Society in its full sense . . . is never an entity separable from the individuals who compose it. No individual can arrive even at the threshhold of his potentialities without a culture in which he participates. Conversely, no civilization has in it any element which in the last analysis is not the contribution of an individual."

THE SOCIAL NETWORK

It has been argued that all present theoretical frameworks for the study of adult development underestimate the importance of the interaction between biological and environmental forces. Even more specifically, some contend that, unlike the first seven stages of Erikson's scheme, the eighth stage is too often described almost exclusively in terms of internal, developmental factors. Too little consideration is given to the influence of external, environmental experience and the problems of coping constructively with the physical, psychological, and social losses of the later years (Glenwick and Whitbourne, 1978).

What are the important social facts and events of later life, and to what extent do they interact with other age-related changes? It is often tempting to ignore the enormous variety of life experiences encountered in later adulthood. Some older people are married, some are not, and some are remarried. Some are close to distant kin; some distant with their closest relatives. Some retire and some do not; some are semi-retired. Some develop or extend ties with the community and are politically involved in later life. Others withdraw. A few live in institutions; some live alone; some live with relatives and others with friends. As the numerical imbalance between the sexes increases, a few talk of radical polygamous relationships or homosexuality as an alternative to life without sex at all. Others think it is inappropriate for older people to even think about such things. The social forces that affect and are affected by older people are of nearly endless variety, and in this chapter we will be able only to address the most basic issues.

Nonetheless, we can begin to consider some important environmental events in relationship to the general developmental trends we have discussed so far. What effect does the life-style of an elderly person have on adjustment, satisfaction, health, morale, and survival? In this chapter, information about marriage, family, and friendship is surveyed. Economic, ecological, and work-related issues will be covered in Chapter 11.

Marriage

That time of year thou may'st in me behold
When yellow leaves, or none, or few, do hang
Upon those boughs which shake against the cold,
Bare ruined choirs, where late the sweet birds sang.
In me thou see'st the twilight of such day
As after sunset fadeth in the west;
Which by and by black night doth take away,
Death's second self, that seals up all the rest.
In me thou see'st the glowing of such fire,
That on the ashes of his youth doth lie,
As the death bed whereon it must expire,
Consumed with that which it was nourished by.
This thou perceiv'st which makes love more strong,
To love that well which thou must leave ere long.

                          William Shakespeare

Shakespeare's sonnet leaves little doubt that intimacy can be as sweet in the last years of life as the early ones. Perhaps, as instrumental roles become less urgent, the expressive ones assume greater importance; and for many older people, especially men, intimacy is synonymous with marriage. Nearly eight out of ten males over 65 are married (only four of ten females are), and the remarriage rate for men over 65 is seven times the rate for women. Whereas one in three older women live alone, only one man in seven does (Reiss, 1980). Figure 10.1 represents statistics on marital status in later life.

Much of the available evidence, such as that we reviewed in Chapter 7, suggests that the last years of married life are characterized by great satisfaction. However, since most of these studies are cross-sectional, nagging questions remain. Is it possible, for example, that marital satisfaction is high among older married couples because unhappily married people have gotten divorced or been separated? Once the children are gone, even the more traditional couples may be willing to face the fact that they are not getting along very well. Staying together for the sake of the children is commonly cited as a reason for the survival of an unhappy marriage through the first twenty years or so (Atchley, 1980).

Satisfaction does not imply, of course, that older marriages are trouble-free. We discussed some of the complaints of older women in Chapter 7: the loss of freedom and the added demands they experience once their husbands retire. Moreover, as Barbara Turner (1982) points out, the data on personality change imply that women in older marriages act increasingly like mothers to their husbands, and many of them seem to resent this turn

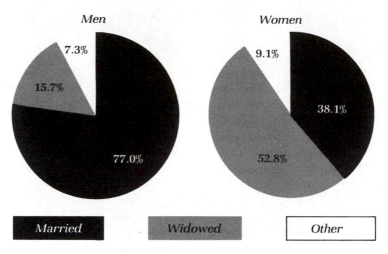

Percentage Distribution of Older Persons by Marital Status, 1900 and 1972

Status	1972 Men	1972 Women	1900 Men	1900 Women
Married	77.0	38.1	67.1	34.2
Widowed	15.7	52.8	26.4	59.3
Other				
Divorced	1.8	2.5	0.5	0.3
Never married	5.5	6.6	5.7	6.0
Total	100.0	100.0	100.0	100.0

FIGURE 10.1
Marital status of older persons, 1900 and 1972

SOURCE: *U.S. Department of Health, Education, and Welfare,* Facts About Older Americans, 1976 *(Washington, D.C.: U.S. Government Printing Office, 1976).*

of events (Keating and Cole, 1980). Throughout the middle years of marriage, women express a great desire for greater communication with their husbands. In old age, men also seem to feel a heightened desire for closeness, but Turner (1982) notes that often they have not developed any real capacity for it.

Although older men report that they are more interested in family and friends than they have ever been, researchers have found that they actually spend most of their time alone. Women continue to have more friends than men do in later life, and they do not see their husbands as closest confidant nearly as often as husbands name wives in that capacity. Men apparently depend heavily on their spouses for the expression of

Marriage may be more important in the emotional lives of men than women, especially in old age, since men derive feelings of intimacy almost exclusively from their wives while women are connected to a broader network of significant others.

TABLE 10.2
Perceptions of older husbands and wives
concerning the most troublesome and most
rewarding aspects of marriage relationships
during the later years

	Percent
Rewarding aspects	
Companionship	18.4
Mutual expression of true feelings	17.8
Economic security	16.2
Being needed by mate	12.0
Affectionate relationship with mate	11.2
Sharing of common interests	9.3
Having physical needs cared for	7.6
Standing in the community	7.0
Troublesome aspects	
Different values and life philosophies	13.8
Lack of mutual interests	12.5
Mutual inability to express true feelings	8.6
Unsatisfactory affectional relationships	8.5
Frequent disagreements	8.5
Lack of companionship	7.7
Other	8.5
Nothing troublesome	36.2

SOURCE: N. Stinnett, L. M. Carter, and J. E. Montgomery, "Older Persons' Perceptions of Their Marriages," *Journal of Marriage and the Family* (November 1972), p. 667. Copyright © 1972 by the National Council on Family Relations. Reprinted by permission.

intimacy while women turn to friends and family outside the marriage. In this light, it seems likely that women continue to be unhappy with the level of communication in the marriage, although they may not experience the marriage as unsatisfactory. After all, they have chosen to remain married through the family life cycle. A finer analysis of the rewards and problems of older marriages seems required if we are to make sensible statements about the nature of the marital relationship in the aging family.

A study by Nick Stinnett and his colleagues (Stinnett, Carter, and Montgomery, 1972) is relevant here (see Table 10.2). In their sample of older married couples, more than 90 percent described their relationship as "very happy" or "happy," and well over half stated that their marriages had improved with time. The majority felt that the later years were the happiest years of marriage. Still, most experienced some troublesome problems. They were especially likely to note differences in values and life philosophies as well as lack of mutual interests. Although nearly 18 percent thought that the expression of one's true feelings was a rewarding aspect of long-standing marriage, this was the third most common problem area as well. Similarly, the affectional side of marriage stood out as a source of satisfaction in marriages where affection was available, and dissatisfaction where it was difficult to come by. Stinnett et al.'s list of rewards and problems differs substantially from that offered by younger couples. For example, sexual problems, disagreement over finances and in-laws, as well as disagreements over the rearing of children are most frequently mentioned by younger married couples (Landis and Landis, 1973).

One final note about older marriages: as social expectations decline, the resurfacing of personal needs may have an important impact on sexuality (Lowenthal, Thurnher, and Chiriboga, 1975). As we noted in Chapter 7, longitudinal data from the Berkeley and Oakland studies showed a resurgence of heterosexual interest during middle age (Haan, 1981). Men in the empty-nest stage of the family life cycle have even been described as hedonistic. Furthermore, as society becomes less negative about the romantic and sexual interests of the elderly, there appears to be a trend toward increasing romanticism in the later years. For instance, a study from the late 1960s showed that older couples remarry because they desire a companion and a confidant and want to feel necessary and useful to someone. Romantic love was not often cited as a primary force in December marriages, and few couples mentioned sex directly as a major reason for remarriage (McKain, 1969). Newer evidence (Decker, 1980), however, shows just the opposite—an increasingly romantic view of love in people who have been married twenty years or more and frequent mention of romance as an important force in December marriages.

It is possible, of course, that the meaning of sexuality changes over the life course. McKain (1969) has noted that sex in later life becomes less specifically genital, less demanding—that "the sex of an older marriage is not confined to the bedroom" (p. 36). A gentle touch, a word of endearment, can go a long way toward satisfying the need to be close to someone of the opposite sex. Little experimental work exists on the subjective experience of sexuality in later life. However, biological changes in the experience of sexuality for most older people have been documented, and these changes probably have important psychological implications.

Sexuality

We have already noted that there is a general slowing of the sexual response after middle age and probably some lessening of intensity. Age changes are more pronounced for men, including less complete and less rapid erection and longer refractory periods. Moreover, males report that, during orgasm, feelings of inevitability and readiness are less distinguishable from ejaculation. Men may even experience less demand or need for ejaculation in later years (Masters, Johnson, and Kolodny, 1981).

In women, the orgasmic phase may be shorter and the refractory period longer in later life, but women do not lose the capacity for orgasm or for sexual enjoyment. Those men and women who manage to remain sexually active into their later seventies will probably continue to engage in sexual activity for the rest of their lives. We already know that continued sexual activity throughout adulthood is the best predictor of a healthy, active sex life in old age. Masters, Johnson, and Kolodny (1981) note that it can be crucial to recognize the basic facts of sexual aging and establish realistic new standards for sexual performance.

Those who never really enjoyed sex will probably not be sexually active older people. A negative body image or the feeling that one is unattractive are common obstacles to continued sexual activity. With age, people even become ashamed of their sexual desires and begin to feel like "dirty old men (or women)." Considering the social barriers, it is rather surprising that there are so many examples of individuals who led lives obviously characterized by eroticism in later years: L. N. Tolstoy, Victor Hugo, H. G. Wells, Pablo Picasso, Charlie Chaplin, Henry Miller, Pablo Casals, and Bernard Berensen (de Beauvoir, 1977) to name a few. All the names are masculine because we know much more about the sex lives of men than women and because men have always had more sexual freedom. Yet women have, do, and will live sexually active lives throughout the life course.

In addition to continued activity, one's marital state has considerable effect on an older person's sex life. Marriage lends sexuality a comfortable, respectable context for older people. By the same token, however, widowhood leaves many people sexually stranded. They do not condone nonmarital sexuality, and remarriage can be difficult to achieve. Not only are there a good many more women than men among the elderly, but older people who remarry often encounter opposition from children, family, and friends. And such pressure is effective: the approval of children and friends is strongly associated with marital success in later life.

Rejection by family and friends may produce failure, resentment, and alienation in a December marriage, and rejection is certainly not uncommon. Younger people often feel that the elderly do not need to marry, or that love and marriage in later life are ridiculous or even vaguely disgusting. Children and other family members may worry about the disposition of the estate after remarriage, and such matters are important. In the most successful December marriages, partners give first priority in financial matters to each other (Stinnett and Walters, 1977; Atchley, 1980).

As attitudes toward aging change, the romantic love and sexual expression more typical of younger groups may well become more socially acceptable for older people. If love and sexual desire are considered inappropriate for older adults, it is not likely that many research subjects will report such feelings. It is even likely that older people do not experience intense feelings of love and sexual desire because love and sex are thought to be inappropriate for them. On the other hand, there is no reason to believe that sex is an imperative for healthy aging.

Defining what is sexually normal or appropriate for others is risky business at best, and despite the best of intentions it is often oppressive. In a whimsical but earnest article entitled "Sexuality and Aging: Essential Vitamin or Popcorn?" Larry Thomas (1982) warns that recent changes in attitude have actually overemphasized the importance of genital sex in the lives of elderly people. The media are now beginning to focus on sexuality in later life, and even researchers like Masters and Johnson have promoted sex like a kind of essential vitamin, implying that an active sex life is basic to mental, or even physical, health. Thomas reminds us that sexual activity is not essential to life, or a key to healing all mental or emotional problems. Sex is rarely a person's primary interpersonal activity.

Sex, Thomas quips, is like popcorn. Why popcorn? Because there are so few prescriptions about it. Nobody says, "Eat your popcorn, it's good for you," nor does one hear, "Don't eat that popcorn; it will ruin your teeth." Furthermore, popcorn is fun and not too serious. No one is likely to suggest a steady diet of popcorn, and it probably isn't carcinogenic. Like sexual activity, researchers are likely to find that healthy, happy elderly people eat more popcorn than those in poor health. Moreover, once you give up eating popcorn, you may never take it up again. But use it or lose it? That implies causality, and we cannot infer causality from the data we have. Thomas also cautions that too much attention to popcorn might produce all kinds of interesting effects—like popcorn anorexia or popcornoholism. Sex, like popcorn, might best be left out of the limelight.

A variety of generational changes are likely to affect the intimate lives of elderly people over the next few decades. For instance, today many more women survive to old age than men. There are presently only about seventy-five men for every one hundred women over the age of sixty-five, and the situation is even more lopsided after seventy. If the current trend toward increasing longevity for males continues, the numerical imbalance may be corrected to some extent, and the options for older women will expand.

Today's young and middle-aged adults will undoubtedly change the social structure of old age as they enter the ranks of the elderly. Attitudes about sex, marriage, and divorce are more liberal among younger cohorts.

Even if developmental changes produce more conservative intimate behavior, cohort differences may be substantial. Still, some of the harshest facts of later life are not likely to change much for the foreseeable future. Although the life span may soon be increased by a few years, or even a few decades, older people will continue to be affected by the losses of later life. And, of all the changes and predictable events of the life span, the death of a spouse is the one generally considered most traumatic.

Widowhood

Death and loss are certainly not the exclusive province of the old. In fact, since the average age of recent widows in this country is fifty-six, it might have been as appropriate to discuss this issue in the section on middle age. Widowhood and loss appear in this chapter only because there is more information on the subject as it applies to later life, not because the subject is irrelevant to other age groups.

Fifty-two percent of the female population and 19 percent of the male population in the United States are widowed before age sixty. By age eighty, one-third of the male population and over 70 percent of all females are widowed. Widowhood transforms one's social position as well as one's personal life. Beyond the loss of a significant person, perhaps the most significant person in one's life, one loses a primary source of financial support or personal services, as well as access to socially accepted forms of sexual expression.

Furthermore, widowhood brings a special kind of social stigma. Widows and widowers are tainted by death. Widowhood may evoke fear or embarrassment in friends and family. No one knows quite how to help a bereaved person, and people often decide it is best to leave the grieving individual alone. There is even an exonerating mythology that grieving people want to be left alone.

As a consequence, someone who loses a spouse also loses those friends and family members who are unable to deal with bereavement or with the bereaved's new status as a single person. After the pain of loss begins to recede, a new kind of discomfort arrives. A single person is a fifth wheel or even a threat to married friends.

Bereaved men and women must learn to deal with all the ways in which widowhood embarrasses or threatens others. Some societies go to great lengths to exclude the widowed. Many practice the seclusion of widows; some have even encouraged ritual suicide by the surviving spouse. We are certainly more tolerant, but there are many obvious signs of strain. It is common, for example, to separate the widow or widower and the immediate family from the rest of the mourners at a funeral. At times, the mortuary secludes the family behind a curtain. The bereaved are driven in a separate car, often a limousine with tinted windows. The family enters and leaves the funeral home and the gravesite before or after the other mourners.

Embarrassment and fear are only two of the emotional responses the bereaved encounter. Grief is often viewed as a kind of self-indulgence, rather than as a psychological necessity. Samuel Johnson wrote, "Grief is a species of idleness." Johnson died in 1794, but his attitude is still part of our chin-up, stiff-upper-lip, pull-yourself-together heritage. The show must go on. Grief is seen as self-pity rather than as a response to loss, to loneliness, and to deprivation. Feelings of grief are the natural consequence, the price, of committing oneself to another human being. Grief derives from the need for interaction and intimacy, feelings of danger and insecurity, and the loss of comfort, information, and financial security that follow the death of a spouse.

Mourning—the feeling of a sense of duty to the dead—may last a lifetime. But acute grief occurs within a few days of bereavement and is severe for several months. Recovery usually takes place in twelve to eighteen months, although several turning points are ordinarily experienced within the first year, times when a major change for the better in feelings, attitudes, and behavior occur. Positive changes can be seen in such mundane activities as moving the furniture around, as well as more obvious steps such as getting a job or going on a holiday (Parkes, 1972).

Acute grief is accompanied by physical symptoms as well as emotional distress. About one-half of all widowed people complain of headaches, digestive upsets, rheumatism, asthma, and other stress-related disorders. Health is generally poorer than before bereavement. The number of widows and widowers who die during the first year of bereavement is substantially higher than the death rate for individuals of the same age who are not bereaved. The most frequent cause of death during this period is heart disease. To date, no adequate explanation for increased mortality has been found. It may be that widowed individuals alter their personal habits too dramatically, from smoking and eating to sleeping and exercise. Ultimately a physiological explanation may be provided by those who study stress and health. For the moment, however, the old notion that the surviving spouse dies of a broken heart is at least as good as any that science can offer (Parkes, 1972).

Surprisingly, young adults who are widowed are most likely to be categorized as health risks and to suffer from prolonged or delayed grief. It is among the young that grief is most likely to interfere with work or social life for several years rather than months. The younger a widowed person is, the more likely he or she is to express ideas of guilt or self-reproach about the circumstances surrounding the spouse's death (Glick, Weiss, and Parkes, 1974).

Younger people most probably suffer extreme disorganization in bereavement. They are likely to be left to raise children alone, and they are less likely to have friends who have been widowed. The spouse is likely to have died unexpectedly and to have left financial and personal accounts disorganized or to have made no provision for surviving family members. Young adults are unrehearsed. Older people, especially women, seem to spend a substantial amount of time rehearsing for widowhood, thinking about how they will act, what they will do, how they will get along. Preparation, anticipatory socialization, and planning ease the way through any transition (Lowenthal, Thurnher, and Chiriboga, 1975).

Almost all the evidence supports the idea that widowhood is more difficult for the young. But there is some controversy about whether it is harder for men or for women. Widowhood may have different meanings for males and females.

WIDOW.   Some contend that since the male role is more prestigious than that of the female, the loss of a husband is more devastating than loss of a wife. Furthermore, it is harder for a widow to find a new husband than it is for a widower to find a new wife. A widow loses a friend, a companion, and a sexual partner. She also loses an escort and a provider. Usually, her socioeconomic status plummets. Many widows are unable to support themselves. Some 26 percent have never worked, and 40 percent have not worked during the time they were married. Through the late 1970s, the majority of the widows in this country got by on less than $3,000 a year (Zarit, 1977b): that means $250 a month for housing, food, transportation, utilities, clothing, and medical expenses. Considering that the average elderly person spent about $1,200 per year on medical expenses alone, it is not surprising that few older women can hope to maintain independent lives.

Especially among older cohorts, a woman is likely to depend on her spouse not only for financial support but also for a large share of her identity and for her links with the social fabric of the community. The social costs of widowhood are especially high for the educated, socially active, middle-class woman who has built a rich, complex life based on the presence of her husband and family (Lopata, 1975). Most of the activities and friendships of the educated middle class are based on pairs. Social gatherings of every kind are built around couples. If a woman's income is dramatically affected by the death of her spouse, she may have to give up her social life because she can't afford the price of admission. She may have to move to a less expensive neighborhood, sacrificing all the stable, day-to-day relationships and informal activities based in the old neighborhood. Many married females lose their major roles in life with the death of the spouse, and there are no comparable roles to assume as a widow.

More traditional societies, and some preindustrial cultures, have well-defined roles for the widow. Later life can even be characterized as a matriarchy in some settings. The role of shaman or sometimes witch is ascribed to widowed women in older cultures; more modern traditional societies emphasize the roles of grandmother and mother-in-law (Gutmann, 1977; Lopata, 1975). In most of American society, however, the role of the widow is not a major feature of the social landscape. It is assumed that the younger widow will marry again and the older one will become inactive. Widows are forced to choose between these limited options, because they seldom are affluent enough to be independent with style.

Still, there are examples of successful styles of widowhood at all socioeconomic levels and among all social and ethnic groups. In a classic study of more than three hundred widows living in the Chicago area, Helena Lopata (1973) described three particularly adaptive but widely divergent styles. First, *self-initiating widows* maintained those aspects of old roles that were appropriate to their new status; related freely and independently with their children; and moved away from couple activities and friends, often entering into or strengthening involvement in community roles. Gradually, these women took over, reassigned, or gave up the role functions of their husbands, and engaged in a conscious reexamination of life and society in an attempt to adjust to their new position in the social network.

Lopata's second category consisted of women who were members of an ethnic group and had lived in a sex-segregated world all their adult lives. Often relatively unaffected by their loss, these widows became immersed in family, peers, and neighbors, and continued their daily habits and routines with little disruption. The third style of widowhood was embodied by women who became downwardly mobile social isolates, unable to maintain the social interactions and activities typical of marrieds. These widows suffered substantial loss of status, believed that old friends could not be replaced, tended to see people as hostile and unhelpful, and withdrew from family, peers, and friends. Probably always marginal members of society at best, they appeared fearful and possessed of few skills and little confidence. Paradoxically, adjustment to the role of widow was relatively easy for them, because isolation and loss of status fulfilled the expectations they had of widowhood and society.

Lopata points out that active, engaged, self-initiating widows were found most frequently among the highly educated, upper socioeconomic groups. The isolated, downwardly mobile widow was actually closer to the norm. Many American women spend their lives committed to home and family and cannot develop an active, socially engaged life-style after a spouse dies. Lopata reported upper middle-class women experienced the most acute grief, but were also the most likely to make excellent recoveries because they had greater resources, including money, education, contacts outside the home, and so on. Recovery was related to resources. Depth of grief was related to the centrality of the spouse in the individual's married life-style.

Studies of widowhood repeatedly refer to economic and role losses in the lives of bereaved women (Kastenbaum, 1981). The meaning of widowhood for men has been approached in a different way. The literature shifts from the detailing of social and economic consequences to more personal and interpersonal dimensions.

WIDOWER.   Those who argue that widowers have more difficulty adjusting to the loss of the spouse believe that a man may experience his wife as a part of the *self*, "my flesh and blood." A wife may well be a man's only close friend and confidante, the only one who really knows him (Glick, Weiss, and Parkes, 1974).

Moreover, men are relatively unprepared to live out their lives alone. Fewer men than women are widowed, and men are usually widowed at a later age than women. The death of a spouse may ruin a man's plan for life in retirement. He never imagined what life might be like as a widower (Atchley, 1980).

Widowed men often find themselves emotionally estranged from other family members but dependent on them for the necessary tasks of daily life—cooking, shopping, and keeping house since they lack these mundane skills. Nor do they have the social skills that permit the development of meaningful new relationships with family and friends, a new confidante or sex partner (Bernardo, 1968; 1970).

Men are usually widowed at a later age than women. Therefore, if men do have more difficulties in developing a single life-style than women, some of these problems are probably attributable to their greater age. If age is controlled, widows report greater anxiety than do widowers, but widowers seem to suffer from greater feelings of anomie (Atchley, 1980).

Although men have more options available to them for new heterosexual relationships, women seem to have the advantage in developing significant same-sex confidantes and friends. Men are less likely to form new, significant relationships after bereavement than are women, but they also tend to have had fewer close relationships prior to bereavement.

The loss of a spouse is traumatic regardless of one's sex, and our culture is not organized in a way that facilitates recovery and reintegration for the recently widowed. It has been said that Western society has deinstitutionalized the rituals of mourning and bereavement to such a degree that they are not adequate for the individual faced with the shock, confusion, and grief that follow a great loss (Lopata, 1975).

SERVICES. In recent years, however, some new resources have become available for bereaved people. Perhaps the best known of these is an organization called Widow-to-Widow, a group of widowed people who provide comfort and services to those in bereavement. Widow-to-Widow tries to create a safe environment in which grief can run its course. Helpers offer companionship and acceptance (Silverman, 1977). They wait out the ambivalence, the demanding or irritating behavior, even the paranoia, that accompany grief, and they let the bereaved person decide what is best for herself or himself.

Widow-to-Widow usually initiates contact without being asked, and each helper is matched, for socioeconomic level, education, and other characteristics, with the bereaved person. The helper is there to assist in the transition from being married to being a widowed person, to help the individual learn the new role. No effort is made to minimize mourning or to cheer up a grief-stricken person.

The organization stresses that most people are unprepared for widowhood, because most of us are reluctant to face dying or death. Bereaved people are often surprised and frightened by the overwhelming intensity of their feelings. They sometimes believe they are going crazy, having a nervous breakdown. They are unprepared for the degree of emotional distress and disorganization that accompanies widowhood.

Sometimes a person from outside the family can be more helpful than kin in situations that threaten self-esteem, especially if the family has no traditions for the expression of grief. An outside helper who has lost a spouse is not alarmed, frightened, or surprised by the intensity or duration of the grief process, and that alone can provide great reassurance (Silverman, 1977; Parkes, 1972).

Widow-to-Widow was designed to create a social network where none existed before or to strengthen an existing network where it is inadequate. Friends and family are often too unfamiliar with death and bereavement to fill the need. Yet older people often do have strong, complex social networks available in their lives. In many ways—as we have seen in the chapters on middle age—the social ties of older people are much healthier and stronger than the cultural stereotype suggests.

FRIENDS AND FAMILY

Friends

Partly because of scholarly interest in engagement and disengagement, we have a good deal of information on the course of social interaction over the last part of the life span. As is true for so many areas we have reviewed, one can safely say that a variety of friendship patterns appear to be satisfactory for older people. For some individuals, continued—even increased—social intercourse is very rewarding. For others, a few close relationships suffice. For a few, fairly complete social isolation is experienced as satisfactory, if isolation is an extension of earlier personality characteristics and life-style choices.

An association between friendship and high morale has been established, but we do not have much evidence that this relationship is a critical one (Lowenthal and Robinson, 1977). The existence of at least one confidant may be a key factor in adjustment, but that confidant need not be a peer. An adult child or other family member can fill this role adequately. Even the need for one confidant has been challenged, for there is evidence that individuals who have been lifelong isolates may find old age a relatively satisfactory time of life, even when they are completely alone (Lowenthal and Robinson, 1977; Gubrium, 1975). Again, the importance of earlier personality type and life-style is underscored (Riley and Foner, 1968; Maas and Kuypers, 1974). If one were to make a generalization, however, it would seem that for most of the elderly citizens of this country, relationships with family are paramount. For most, they are the major source of intimacy, mutuality, and emotional support.

Family

Despite all of the rhetoric about the disintegration of family ties and the specter of institutionalization in old age, research on the American family shows that older people turn to their families first when they are in need, and they attend to their families when there is conflict between kith (friends) and kin. In later life, older people are most likely to name a family member as the person closest to them (Lopata, 1975; Lowenthal and Robinson, 1977; Black, 1977; Troll and Bengtson, 1982).

Of course, norms for family interaction between children and elderly parents are quite different from those for the young family. Elderly parents are expected to stay out of the affairs of their adult children and not to strain the resources of the middle-aged generation. Optimal relationships develop when there is little physical dependence between parent and child and neither attempts to place limits on the behavior of the other. Obviously, such good will and independence is most likely among individuals of relatively high socioeconomic status (Atchley, 1980; Hess and Waring, 1978). Most families prefer "intimacy at a distance," and the elderly are very careful not to place their emotional relationships with middle-aged children in jeopardy by asking for financial help (Decker, 1980).

Parent-child interaction is a two-way street, of course, and norms for the behavior of children also change with age. An adult child is expected to develop *filial maturity*, to learn to view the parent as a person, acknowledging that the parent-as-person was formed by a social history much of which took place before the child was born. Adult children must give up adolescent rebellion and grow in a way that eventually permits their parents to depend on them and eases the shock of role reversal (Blenkner, 1965).

Most older people find their relationships with adult children satisfactory, but these ties are also clearly influenced by personality type and life-style. Community-oriented, socially active, engaged men and women of high socioeconomic status and high educational level do not report family relationships are as significant as do those individuals who have always been very family centered and who have less education and less financial security. Disengaged older people in poor health may be dissatisfied with their family relationships and distant from their children and grandchildren. Studies done so far on family life and the elderly rarely include large numbers of extremely involved or disengaged individuals. We must, therefore, be cautious in making generalizations about the importance of family ties (Riley and Foner, 1968; Lowenthal, Thurnher, and Chiriboga, 1975; Maas and Kuypers, 1974).

Furthermore, one is well advised to consider the evidence on family life and aging in the light of current cultural norms and stereotypes. The responses of older people to their adult children have been characterized by some as a mixture of "sterility, formality, and ritualism" (Lowenthal and Robinson, 1977, p. 438). There is strong sentiment in this culture that older people ought not to be a burden to their children and ought to let their children live their own lives. Current norms do not permit older people to demand intimacy or attention from the young. Lowenthal and

Robinson argue that when older people say that they see their children as often as they like, or that they are as close to their children as they hoped to be, they may really be expressing "superficially assimilated norms," not personal experiences, needs, or wishes. Elderly people might actually benefit from more intimacy and less independence from their adult children. These suggestions pose a substantial research challenge. Distinguishing between superficially assimilated norms and real personal experience seems a demanding task indeed.

Taking the suggestion even further, one might contend that kin ties become more voluntary as the society becomes more affluent. Two-thirds of the people interviewed in one national survey believed that children have no obligation to their parents and that parents should have their own lives even if it means spending less time with their children. If these attitudes become entrenched, future generations may see less exchange between all living generations of the lineage family (Hess and Waring, 1978).

Although relationships between elderly parents and their children certainly bear more examination, there is also a surprising lack of research on the role of siblings and other close relatives throughout the life span. Of all human relationships, those between siblings have the longest duration, and the majority of people over seventy have one or more living siblings. Yet, little information is available on the quality and the nature of sibling relationships in youth or later life (Circirelli, 1980). There is some evidence that actual contact decreases between elderly siblings, but most still report that they feel close to a brother or sister. Relationships tend to be especially durable between same sexed siblings, and sisters in particular. In fact, a sister will often take on the role of mother with the death of the female parent. Many elderly people end their lives living with a sibling, but no information is available on how such arrangements develop or progress. Certainly, this area has rich research potential for those interested in close attachment over the life cycle.

Some final observations on the future of the family network are in order. It is easy to underestimate the strength of family networks. After all is said and done, they persist in the face of institutions and norms that "result in treating people as commodities rather than human beings" (Sussman, 1977, p. 238). If the society is to accommodate increasing numbers of elderly individuals in a humane, healthy way, we must investigate the potential of the family for care of the aged. Perhaps the family network should be supported by services and economic incentives under contractual arrangements between the government, institutions, and families. Money now channeled through institutions might go directly to families instead, and the growth of mobile services for patients living at home might be encouraged or directly subsidized. In the long run, this approach could cut hospital costs substantially. Paraprofessionals could be used more widely. Families might, with appropriate community support, provide special facilities in their homes. Contracts with individual families could provide for the nurturance, intimacy, and privacy older people require, as well as health care, physical rehabilitation, and economic relief. Benefits could be transferred through tax write-offs, property tax waivers, and low-cost loans for renovating or building independent quarters for the older person. Further, specific care and therapeutic services from established agencies might be made available to the family.

Sussman (1977) urges that removing sacrifice and deficit living from the linkage between elderly people and their families will engender a modern version of filial responsibility. Dependence need not create the mutual sense of guilt and neglect that can develop when "filial piety" is taxed to the breaking point. The alternatives currently available so often result in unsatisfactory or even disastrous situations that suggestions such as institutional support for the family deserve serious consideration.

SUMMARY

From an Eriksonian viewpoint, the central crisis of later adulthood involves the resolution of conflict between integrity and despair. Integrity is characterized by "the acceptance of one's one and only life cycle" as meaningful and significant, whereas despair is described in terms of frustration, discouragement, and fear. Development in the last stages of adult life seems to focus on the search for a narrative line, on the task of making a sensible whole of one's life and finding courage and wisdom in the process.

Recent research suggests that current attitudes toward aging and the elderly are not nearly as negative as they once appeared to be. People often make negative generalizations, but they are also willing to admit that a great many people don't fit the stereotype. The positive aspects of later life, including the potential for freedom and change, can begin to emerge in this more encouraging atmosphere.

Clearly, many elderly people do evolve satisfactory life-styles, but research has not revealed one best way to age. Both active and inactive individuals at all economic levels and with varying degrees of health and education manage to maintain or develop high levels of self-esteem and life satisfaction in old age. Moreover, a strong argument can be made that with ageism on the wane (and given reasonable economic growth), we may see even greater diversity in the future. Successful aging seems most likely to occur when an individual has the opportunity to choose a lifestyle congruent with earlier personality development and the option to sort out and slough off unwanted responsibilities.

Researchers have not yet been able to find universal, culture-free patterns of personality development. And they have had little success in postulating trends based on observation of overt social and behavioral data. Some interesting hypotheses about late-life development have evolved out of disengagement theory, however. One trend, described as inner disengagement, seems to involve a decline or restriction in the flow of physical energy and a rejection of the more emotional components of existence. The evidence for intrinsic disengagement is stronger for men than for women; but it is possible that the cultural context presents so many barriers to those who would lead complex, engaged lives that we cannot currently assess the extent to which inner disengagement is a natural consequence of the aging process.

Other researchers are convinced, however, that successful aging is an extension of earlier personality trends. There is evidence that adjustment can be predicted from early adulthood patterns, especially for women. These data suggest the importance of lifelong success in the major adult roles.

It is simpler to look for clear developmental trends in specific aspects of the aging process. One area of special interest has been the investigation of how time is experienced by older people. Although the notion that time passes more quickly in later life appears to be a myth, older people do appear to experience time as less eventful or less dense. Older people do not project as far into the future as do the young, and they seem to evaluate the past in more positive terms. This positive evaluation is not tantamount to living in the past; the best adjusted older people seem to achieve a balance in time that is not characteristic of younger adults.

Developmental trends are not easily understood in isolation from the social context in which they occur. The influence of environment may be underestimated in many current theoretical explanations of later life. We need more data on the variety of social and environmental events that influence development in old age before we can look at the interaction of developmental and environmental forces. These issues can only be addressed in the most primitive way as yet, but they cannot be ignored.

Available information on the social network in later life includes data on marriage, family, friends, and organizations. Later-life marriage is characterized by relatively high levels of satisfaction and by a greater emphasis on the affective aspects of the marital relationship than is found among younger adults. Companionship, love, and the expression of true feelings are some of the most frequently mentioned sources of satisfaction among older married. More than 90 percent of all older married people report their marriages are "happy" or "very happy."

A variety of explanations have been offered for the high level of satisfaction among older marrieds, including the possibility that unhappily married people eventually divorce and leave the sample. Another possibility involves the hypothesis that sex-role distinctions are leveled in later life, producing more egalitarian relationships. It has also been suggested that the launching of children and the arrival of retirement finally afford older couples the luxury of each other's company.

Love in later life may not have the romantic or sexual implications of love in youth, but many older people do remain sexually active to the end of their lives. A healthy, active sex life through the rest of adulthood predicts a healthy, active sex life in old age. Social mores make it difficult for older people to find acceptable avenues for sexual expression outside of traditional marriage, however, and so widowhood leaves most older individuals sexually stranded. Remarriage among the old is not readily condoned by family and friends, and the numerical imbalance of the sexes in later life makes remarriage unlikely for many older women. On the other hand, it may be unjustified to focus on sexuality as a critical aspect of life satisfaction in later life. Sex, like popcorn, should probably be taken with a grain of salt.

Because there are so many more widowed women than men, widowhood has been most thoroughly studied for females, but both men and women are bereaved by the loss of spouses and must face the emotional distress and societal fear or embarrassment that surround dying and death in this culture. Grief is too often viewed as a form of self-indulgence rather than as a psychological necessity, and mourning is often prematurely curtailed.

A widow loses not only a friend, a companion, and a sexual partner, but also an escort and a provider. Her social and financial standings plummet, and she may become withdrawn and isolated. Although our social structure offers few options for the widow, women do make adjustments, ranging from an active, self-initiating life-style to a life of relative social isolation.

The maintenance, reassignment, or resignation of both male and female role functions is a major focus of the literature on widowhood. Researchers studying widowers have been most concerned with the loss of the affective and emotional support of a spouse. A wife may well be a man's only friend, and men are often relatively unprepared to live out their lives alone. They do not rehearse or plan for widowhood as women often do, and they find themselves estranged from their families and unable to care for themselves and the daily, routine household tasks.

There are fewer widowers than widows, however. Because marriage between an older man and a younger woman is more socially acceptable and more common than marriage between an older woman and a younger man, some avenues for recovery are more available to men than to women. Women, on the other hand, have skills and life-styles that more readily permit the cementing of significant same-sex friendships after bereavement.

The loss of a spouse is, for both women and men, a difficult, even traumatic, experience in a culture that does not provide strong rituals of mourning and bereavement. New services and directions are required, such as those being provided by Widow-to-Widow, an organization that offers help in the transition from married person to widowhood. The support offered by Widow-to-Widow allows the bereaved person to grieve, to be frightened, angry, hostile, and even to feel crazy, in an accepting, supportive relationship. There are times when the social fabric fails, and new networks must be created where old ones no longer exist or are inadequate to the task.

For most older people, the social network may fail in some respects but remain surprisingly strong in others. Most Americans currently maintain stronger ties with their adult children and other kin than they do with peers. Families come first, in times of need and when the demands of friends conflict with those of kin. Most important of all is the relationship between parent and child, the nature of which changes dramatically over the years. In later life parents are expected to be relatively undemanding and to let their children live their own lives. In return, adult children are expected to show filial maturity, to view the parent as an individual, and not to show signs of "adolescent" rebellion.

Most older people seem to be able to develop satisfactory relationships with their adult children, but some question has been raised about the extent to which we should generalize on the basis of the information we have on the family in later life. Both the active, engaged and the disengaged older adult may be underrepresented in the research samples currently available, and there seem to be some unresolved problems of interview and survey interpretation. Does older peoples' apparent satisfaction with their relationships to adult children reflect real experiences and needs? Or is there an element of lip service to the social norms that dictate that elderly parents be undemanding and stay out of the lives of their adult children? ·

As the population ages and the number of elderly people increases, some of the questions we have asked may be answered and some new questions undoubtedly will be raised. Currently, many social scientists are seeking ways in which our society can evolve nurturant, intimate, yet independent arrangements for the care of its older citizens. It has been suggested that the family network is consistently overlooked as a resource by our bureaucratic society, and that governmental support of the family could be the optimal solution to the challenge of providing a healthy, human environment for the older person. This arrangement could strengthen the family and support its potential for intimacy and love.

Chapter 11

The Expanded Context: The Ecology of Aging

I could be handy, mending a fuse
When your lights are gone.
You can knit a sweater by the fireside,
Sunday morning go for a ride.
Doing the garden, digging the weeds,
Who could ask for more?
Will you still need me, will you still feed me,
When I'm sixty-four?

PAUL McCARTNEY

E *cology* is the science of plants and animals as they are related to their environment. Humans are included among the animals studied by ecologists, reminding us that we are part of an ecosystem, that we adapt to our niche, and that our niche changes as a result of that adaptation. A high-rise apartment building is as much a niche as a fox's den. And, as is the case for other animals, the impact of the physical environment changes with age. People see and hear less well as they grow old. They become less sensitive to some aspects of the environment and more sensitive to others. The relationship between people and their physical and social world is always evolving, changing both the people and the environment (Lawton and Nahemow, 1973; Lawton, 1980).

Some of the objective changes that occur with age are explored in this chapter—changes in income, work, housing, and mobility. Some of the processes and possible outcomes associated with various patterns of adaptation are described. In a sense, however, we have been studying the ecology of aging from the first page of this book. M. P. Lawton (1970) contends that the *individual environment* (the biological, psychological, and social conditions of a particular life), the *interpersonal environment* (the world of interactions with others), the *social environment* (the world of norms and institutions), as well as the *physical environment* (housing, neighborhoods, and transportation), must be considered in defining a human ecology.

In Chapters 9 and 10 we examined the individual and interpersonal environments of the elderly and considered some information on the social environment. This chapter focuses in greater detail on those aspects of the social environment associated with retirement and leisure, and on the physical environment. There will be facts, of course, such as how many people retire at what age, how much money they make, how they structure their time, and where they live. But we will also consider a variety of questions researchers have only begun to explore. How do people adapt to age-related changes in their social and physical world? Do most people enjoy retirement? Why do some resist it? What happens when an older person is forced to move? What physical conditions are associated with feelings of well-being and optimal physical or psychological functioning?

THE DEMOGRAPHY OF AGING

During the past hundred years, the number of people over the age of sixty-five living in the United States has increased approximately sixfold. By most of the standards traditionally used to characterize national populations, the United States is an aged population. Aged populations are those in which more than 7 percent of the residents are currently over the age of sixty-five. Worldwide, the elderly constitute the fastest growing segment of the population. In 1980, there were fifty-seven million more people in the world over sixty-five than there were in 1970.

The growing proportion of elderly in this country and others reflects two important trends: larger numbers of people are living to very advanced ages, and the birthrate in the population is declining.

Countries with aged populations still account for only a small proportion of the world's total population. But most highly industrialized, affluent nations are aged, including the nations of Western Europe, Scandinavia, North America, and Japan. Most of those people who are now sixty-five will live an average of fifteen years more and will be in good health for ten of those years (Hendricks and Hendricks, 1977; Bradbury, 1975).

Most of America's elderly are concentrated in smaller cities, in rural areas, and in the central cities of our great urban areas. Few live among the more affluent in the suburbs. As the population moves from the plains of the midwest to the cities, and finally to the suburbs, the oldest citizens tend to stay behind. Thus both rural and inner city populations become relatively aged (U.S. Department of Health, Education, and Welfare, 1976a).

Contrary to popular misconceptions, nearly all Americans over sixty-five live in community settings in their own homes or with family. Current statistics indicate that 75 percent of all elderly heads of household own their homes and live quite independently. About 8 percent are housebound—that is, they live in the community but cannot get out alone. This includes those who still live with their spouses and those who live with a sibling or a child. Only about 5 percent of the aged live in institutional settings, and of this 5 percent, it is estimated that at least one-quarter could live in the community if enough financial aid were available (Carp, 1977; Struyk, 1981; Bradbury, 1975). Table 11.1 summarizes this information.

Throughout the 1970s, the financial situation of the elderly improved steadily. Increases in Social Security benefits, growth in the availability and value of private pension funds, and increased tax benefits have all contributed to the affluence of the elderly in the 1980s. Some of the latest figures show that only one in five elderly families live on less than $4,500 per year. "Poverty level" income is currently defined by the U.S. Bureau of Labor as

TABLE 11.1
Living arrangements of the elderly

Arrangement	Percent
Own their own homes	75
Live with spouse or family member	70
Live alone or with nonrelative	25
Live in institutional setting	5

$3,000 to $4,000 for a couple and $2,500 to $3,200 for a single person over sixty-five.

Of course, the figures obscure some important exceptions. As is generally the case in discussions of economic issues, there are large and important differences associated with race, sex, and geographic location. For example, one-half of all retired, single females receive only the minimum benefit of $1,125 per year, and about one in four black males draws the minimum. On the average, blacks receive about $20 per month less than elderly whites.

In addition, although older couples tend to maintain a standard of living comparable to that of younger people, elderly singles are very often living at or below the poverty level (Atchley, 1980). Still, there is little doubt that the circumstances of older people have improved dramatically since the early 1970s, when six in every ten elderly Americans were classified as poor (Atchley, 1980).

Most of the improvement can be attributed to a 210 percent increase in Social Security benefits since 1965 (although this increment represents only about a 57 percent increase in purchasing power). At present, Social Security is the sole source of income for 80 percent of the elderly. It is quite possible that the elderly will continue to become more affluent over the years, because younger people are likely to contribute to private pension funds, or to set up their own retirement accounts with the blessing of the Internal Revenue Service. Even in the last few years, there is evidence of substantial change. Among those who retired most recently, about 60 percent of the males and 40 percent of the females have some source of income aside from Social Security. With a private pension, income is often twice that of other elderly retired people (Atchley, 1980; Decker, 1980).

Finally, there are those who do not retire. In 1975, about 21 percent of all males over sixty-five and 8 percent of all females reported direct earnings. Those who work average twice the annual income of those who do not—a fact that has created much controversy over the so-called Social Security "earnings test." As it currently stands, one dollar in Social Security benefits is lost for every two dollars an elderly person earns over $3,480 each year. The minimum unpenalized wage is scheduled to increase over the next few years, but many believe it will still be a major obstacle in the road toward an increased standard of living for retired persons. Others believe that the earnings test is unfair primarily because income from investments and interest is excluded, allowing relatively wealthy people to collect Social Security benefits, but penalizing those who must continue to work.

In any event, for most Americans, retirement is the central economic event of later life. Therefore, it is not surprising that the study of retirement usually begins with exploring an individual's relationship to work but ends up focusing on the individual's relationship to money. Our discussion also will trace this path, and will include an examination of attitudes toward retirement, adjustment to retirement, and the role of leisure in retirement.

RETIREMENT

Retirement is a relatively unexamined area within the field of psychology, although sociologists have been somewhat interested in it over the years. Of course, retirement is a fairly new phenomenon, first gaining recognized status in the United States only after the Social Security system was introduced in 1935. People who were twenty in 1935 and have paid for Social Security all their working lives are part of the new American retired. Only in America and other highly industrialized nations, where mortality is low and the life span is great, could such a phenomenon emerge. With advanced technology, fewer hours are required from workers, so fewer people have to work at any one time to support economic growth (Sheppard, 1977).

At some point, in fact, not only are fewer people required to work but fewer people may have the opportunity to work, because technological advances reduce the number of jobs necessary to sustain economic growth. "Given that there are more people than jobs," Robert Atchley (1980) has pointed out, "a good case might be made that an individual is entitled to hold a job only so long" (p. 168). In this sense, retirement in a highly technological society may be seen as a necessity rather than a privilege. Certainly, rules making retirement mandatory follow from such reasoning.

As economic growth becomes possible with fewer workers and as technology eliminates many kinds of jobs, profound changes in attitudes toward work and retirement result. People begin to view retirement as a right—a novel idea in a country where work has long been considered a moral duty. Americans no longer seem to believe that it is sinful to be unemployed, especially after contributing a number of years to the labor force. And, since Social Security is conceptualized as a savings plan rather than welfare, it reinforces the notion that retirement is a reward for a lifetime of work rather than an embarrassment.

Other very general changes in the meaning of work have accompanied automation and advanced technology and have popularized retirement. As workers become separated from the products of their labor, few feel that their jobs are intrinsically rewarding. Today, few people practice a craft or a vocation; nor do they produce anything for their own consumption. Most people simply hold jobs. Work is a less critical aspect of one's identity if that work is boring, repetitious, or unrelated to one's life in any meaningful way aside from the income it produces.

For all these reasons, more and more people are likely to be attracted to retirement at an early age. Currently, the people most likely to retire early are those who have the early retirement plans offered by organized labor or those with health concerns. In the foreseeable future, however, it is likely that people will retire early from all walks of life. Retirement has become a predictable and even expected part of the normal life cycle— which may mean in part, that the retirees of the future will have a better chance of enjoying themselves, for, as we shall see, planning can make all the difference when the time comes to leave the work force.

Retirement Defined

Who is retired? Certainly, an older woman who has been a homemaker all her life, cannot collect Social Security, and finds herself living with a daughter is not "retired" in the usual sense. Neither is the director of admissions for a local state college who collects both a salary from the state and a pension earned during twenty years of military service. Generally, retirement refers to a time of life when someone does not hold a regular job and collects at least part of his or her income from Social Security or another pension fund. Not all researchers use the same definition, however; and conflicts in the research literature are often generated by differences in how retirement is defined.

"Retirement" sometimes refers to a decision, sometimes to an event. It may also denote a role or a process. Although most researchers agree that it is important to view retirement as a process, they also regard it as a decision and a role. As a process, it may begin very early, when young people first begin to develop attitudes toward retirement (Atchley, 1980). This process of retirement includes the formation of attitudes about, preparation for, and transition or adjustment to a life-style and a set of expectations: a new role.

The Role of Retiree

Although it has been argued that the role of a retired person is ambiguous, there are certain definite social expectations, including both rights and duties. A retired person in this society has the right to be supported without having either to work or to bear the stigma of unemployment. Retired people can expect to have autonomous management of their time and other resources and often to be given certain privileges associated with valuable service to a particular profession or occupation. For instance, retired college professors are usually accorded emeritus status, allowing them to use the library and research facilities of the college, the faculty club, the recreational facilities, and often conferring a parking space (at a premium on some city campuses).

In return, retirees are expected to refrain from full-time work (regulations like the earnings test of the Social Security Act enforce this demand). They are also required to manage their own lives, live within their incomes, and remain independent. More and more often they are also expected to maintain their skills and to provide free consulting services to the community when necessary. Organizations like the Association of Retired Businessmen channel the skills of the elderly. The relative vagueness of the retiree role, beyond these basic rights and duties, is probably necessary if people are to have the flexibility to adjust to the physical changes of age and still maintain independent lives (Atchley, 1980). However, some social scientists believe that role ambiguity is usually associated with poor adjustment (Sussman, 1972). Unfortunately, it is nearly impossible to compare the role of retiree with the other roles of life, because it is so strongly associated with age.

It is possible that people consider the role ambiguity of retirement more legitimate than role ambiguity at other points in the life cycle. Ambiguity is a two-sided coin. It can be confusing or bewildering, but it can also offer freedom. Years ago, a seventy-year-old student convinced me that retirement was one of the great opportunities in life. At sixty-five, he had traveled to Canada, learning to repair boats along the way. He returned to California and joined a communal household with a group of young adults, and realized his dream of owning a boat repair shop at the beach. He was taking a course in developmental psychology because he had recently met a new woman. She was thirty-five and had a fourteen-year-old son. Tom

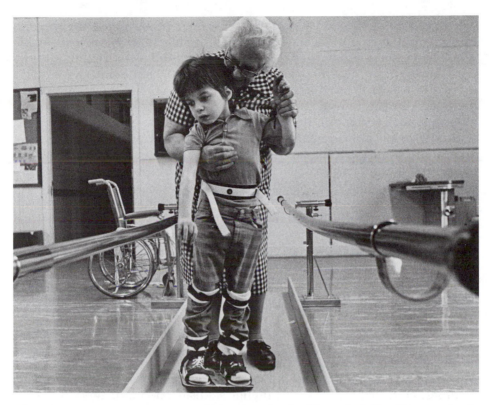

There is a growing expectation in this society that healthy, relatively affluent retired people will give freely of their skills and their time to the community.

wanted to understand the boy better and loved listening to the lectures, but he had trouble reading the book and wasn't earning a passing grade in the course. Concerned about his progress, I called him over one night to suggest he turn in some extra credit. But he demurred, pointing out that he was enjoying himself immensely and did not plan to go to graduate school anyway! He confided that he loved being old because people thought he was cute and he could get away with things he never would have been able to do in middle age.

Retirement as a Process: Attitudes

Obviously attitudes about retirement are strongly influenced by how an individual feels about work. Since work is no longer cherished as an end in itself by a majority of people, it is not surprising to find that most workers see retirement as an active, busy, involved, expanding, full, fair, hopeful, relaxed, and independent state of affairs (Atchley, 1974). However, people who have rewarding jobs are usually less interested in retiring than those with boring or unfulfilling jobs. Blue-collar workers generally express more enthusiasm toward retirement than people with professional jobs. A high degree of autonomy on the job is associated with less favorable attitudes toward retirement, whereas little variety or responsibility, coupled with low levels of task quality, predict a desire to retire early. The most favorable attitudes toward retirement are produced by the desire to escape from repetitious, unrewarding work (Barfield and Morgan, 1978; Streib and Schneider, 1971).

For white-collar workers, such as sales clerks and service people, income is the most useful predictor of attitudes toward retirement. If these workers have enough money, they look forward to retiring. In fact, income predicts attitude toward retirement so well among white-collar workers that some researchers believe the relationship of workers to money is the key to understanding attitudes toward retirement (Shanas, 1972).

Educational level also seems to be related to attitudes toward retirement, but evidently it does not play the same role for men as for women. Harold Sheppard (1977) reported that highly educated men are less willing to retire, whereas the best educated women leave the work force earlier. There are conflicting findings, however. In one study, women with higher incomes, better educations, and higher status occupations tended to continue working longer. It is possible that the inconsistency occurs when female professionals are overrepresented among the women in the sample (Streib and Schneider, 1971).

Finally, age or cohort has been associated with some specific perceptions of retirement. Younger workers tend to be more favorably disposed toward retirement, perhaps because work is a less central value for the young. Older workers, who are closer to actual retirement, worry more about finances and are more likely to have negative feelings about retirement. Perhaps older workers are less positive about retirement because they hold positions of greater authority and prestige than do the young. Or it may be that the oldest workers are the most negative because those with the most favorable attitudes tend to take early retirement and drop out of the work force (Sheppard, 1971; Atchley, 1976; Rose and Mogey, 1972).

Because attitudes shape decisions about when to retire, the forces that influence attitudes—including income, educational and occupational status, and age—prove to be the most important predictors of which workers will choose early retirement and which will stay in the work force. Mandatory retirement policies affect a vast number of workers, from the assembly line to the college campus; and early retirement programs are rapidly decreasing the number of men and women over fifty-five or sixty in the labor force.

Some individuals choose to leave the work force as early as possible, generating great interest in the factors that motivate such decisions. According to one study, perceived inability to work is the primary reason people retire early. Age or failing health, or both, were cited most often by those who retire before the age of sixty-five. Mandatory retirement policies are based on the notion that older people are unable to produce as well as the young, despite all the evidence that age alone is an inadequate criterion for biological, psychological, or social functioning (Palmore, 1971).

Federal regulations enacted by Congress in 1978 have abolished mandatory retirement policies involving federal employees and have raised the retirement age to seventy in many organizations and industries that depend on federal funds. Social scientists will be watching to see how such changes affect the decision to retire. It may be when older workers are given a choice, some will view retirement less enthusiastically than they do now.

Finally, the attitudes and opinions of friends and family influence the decision to retire. The emotional support and acceptance of those close to a worker may be important factors in setting a date. Early retirement is seen most favorably by those who find it acceptable not only to themselves but also to significant others (Chown, 1977).

Retirement as a Process: Phases

The retirement process can become a central feature of life as an individual becomes a "short-timer" in the labor force. Atchley (1980) defines six stages in the progress of an individual nearing retirement age, beginning with a *preretirement* phase. In preretirement, people who are short-timers entertain a number of fantasies about retirement, including images of how they will feel, what they will do, and how life will develop once they retire. In the second phase, the *honeymoon*, newly retired people play out these fantasies, if they are able to. Of course, the fantasies must be realistic if there is to be a honeymoon at all. If the fantasies are not really in the realm of the possible, or if they turn out to be unsatisfactory, *disenchantment* sets in, and the individual must begin restructuring his or her time in a constructive, meaningful way. Disenchantment is followed by a phase called *reorientation*, in which disenchanted retirees pull themselves together and discover how to become realistically involved in the world around them. With luck and effort, reorientation will produce choices that lead to a comfortable, satisfying life-style, ushering in a period of *stability*. *Termination* is the final phase. Retirement may end because an individual goes back to work, but more often it is terminated by illness or disability. Retirement requires that one be independent, and it comes to an end when grave disabilities begin. The transition from stability to termination is usually gradual, however, and is never complete unless the individual is institutionalized.

Not all people will go through all of these stages, of course. Some individuals may have developed plans so realistic and satisfying that they proceed from preretirement to stability without a hitch. Others are more or less disenchanted throughout the retirement period. Perhaps as many as 30 percent or so are never really satisfied (Streib and Schneider, 1971; Atchley, 1980). Nevertheless, less than 10 percent truely miss their jobs. What most people dislike about retirement is the feeling of economic dependence or being forced to retire because of mandatory retirement policies or health problems.

Given the opportunity, most people choose to be partially rather than fully retired in the later years. In one longitudinal study of some eleven thousand self-employed workers, most elected to continue working part-time after retirement age. Among wage and salary workers, in contrast, more elected to retire completely than to look for a different job or take a job that paid less in order to remain employed part-time. Significantly, many more completely retired wage and salary workers than completely retired self-employed described themselves as "not very happy" (15 percent versus 40 percent). Having a choice seems to make the difference (Quinn, 1981). As in other areas of the literature on adjustment and aging, we find a recurring theme: the greater the number of options available to individuals, the more likely it is that they will develop satisfying life-styles.

Retirement as a Process: Adjustment

Early or late, the last day of work eventually arrives. As an event, a day in the life, retirement has not been a particularly comforting rite of passage. Traditionally, retirement ceremonies have emphasized the problems of separation and loss rather than new opportunities or freedoms. The usual retirement gift is supposed to symbolize gratitude for years of service, but is often so standardized as to be a cold, impersonal signal that an important part of one's life is ending. Of late, however, things are changing, and it is not unusual to see signs of envy at the retirement banquet. Gifts more often suggest new horizons—airplane or cruise tickets for travel to some distant place, a typewriter or set of paints for developing one's artistic side. As

Atchley (1980) points out, retirement ceremonies are an emerging ritual and an excellent arena for interesting new research.

New attitudes toward retirement have also created major revisions in the theories of social scientists. A look at one of the more popular early theories of adjustment to retirement tells the tale. *Substitution theory* was based on the assumption that giving up work necessarily entails loss. Adequate adjustment, therefore, was assumed to depend on whether the individual developed new activities that offered the same kinds of gratification provided by the role of worker (Shanas, 1972; Friedman and Havighurst, 1954).

Substitution theory quickly led to much research on the kind of gratification Americans find in work. As we noted earlier, one of the clearest findings to emerge was that, especially for blue-collar workers, the primary meaning of work is money. Even among white-collar workers, what Americans miss most about their work is the money they earned (Shanas, 1972).

In light of the overwhelming importance of money for the American worker, it has been difficult to give much credence to a theory of retirement based on the importance of activity substitution. The growing significance of leisure as a legitimate pursuit in retirement also challenges the notions offered by substitution theory. People do not always derive the same kind of gratification from leisure as they derive from work. Some people show genuine interest in leisure, not as escape or as rest and relaxation from work, but as a valued and preferred activity. If a large proportion of the population develops a leisure ethic in retirement, substitution theory would seem to be of limited value—unless one is prepared to argue that leisure and work provide the same kinds of gratification.

Substitution theory is a variation on the theme that retirement creates crisis, a less formal version of which is the hypothesis that people who retire are likely to experience physical illness or disability. The incidence of physical illness and disability does increase with age, of course, but there is little evidence that retirement is a critical factor in this increase. On the contrary, researchers have found that health improves slightly after retirement (Streib and Schneider, 1971).

The conceptualization of retirement as a crisis has also led to the notion that psychological problems, social disturbances, and cognitive changes accompany departure from the work force. What is probably the most comprehensive investigation of the crisis position (Streib and Schneider, 1971) begins with the broad hypothesis that "retirement is a major disruption in an adult's role and would tend to have deleterious consequences for the individual" (p. 5). These researchers carried out a longitudinal examination of more than four thousand men and women in forty-eight states during the late 1960s. The subjects were employed in jobs ranging from production-line work and unskilled labor to professional services, teaching, administration, and sales. Objective and subjective measures of health were used, as well as objective and subjective appraisals of economic well-being. A variety of social and psychological dimensions were assessed, including self-image, feelings of usefulness, satisfaction with life, and adjustment to retirement.

On every measure, the majority of the retired subjects in this study seemed satisfied and well adjusted. These individuals described their health and their incomes as adequate, and three-fourths reported that retirement had made no difference in their general life satisfaction. Few felt that retirement was very difficult; fully one-third reported that it had turned out better than they expected. Only 4 to 5 percent said retirement was worse than they had anticipated. Furthermore, the authors argued that a sizable number of their subjects had overestimated the adverse effects retirement would have on feelings of satisfaction, and earlier researchers may have done the same thing.

It should also be noted, however, that even in this generally positive sample there were individuals who were not able to accept the role of retiree. In fact, 10 percent of the subjects eventually returned to work. Although the loss of work may not be experienced as crisis by most retirees, any comprehensive theory of the retirement process must allow for those individuals who do not adjust easily, if at all.

The formulation of disengagement theory by Cumming and Henry (1961) offered an alternative to substitution theory and to the notion that retirement is experienced as crisis. As you may recall, disengagement theory suggests that mutual withdrawal between the individual and the society is a normal developmental event. In a variation on this theme, called "differential disengagement," it has been argued that disengagement does ultimately underlie adjustment in retirement, but that it occurs at different rates and in different amounts for the various roles in an individual's role set (Streib and Schneider, 1971). Differential disengagement allows for the development of new roles and activities within a framework of withdrawal.

Similarly, the notion that men progress from active to passive mastery late in middle age suggests that disengagement may be an important feature of adjustment to retirement. From this point of view, retirement constitutes a crisis only for those individuals who have not achieved, or at least begun, the transition from active to passive mastery in middle age, those who are "holdouts against strong internal and perhaps external pressures toward passive receptivity" (Guttmann, 1972, p. 297).

Marjorie Lowenthal (1972) contends that a shift in balance between instrumental and expressive goals—such as the transition from active to passive mastery—insures adjustment to retired life. This shift, too, is thought to take place during middle age rather than at retirement age. Thus, only those who remain heavily invested in instrumental goals are expected to experience a crisis of retirement (Lowenthal, 1972).

WORK LIFE AND ADJUSTMENT.   Outlining a typology of success in retirement, Lowenthal argues that individuals who have always been obsessively driven to work, who view work as an end in itself, will find retirement most traumatic. Unless the obsessive/instrumental personality is able to achieve substitution, she or he will be vulnerable to depression in retirement and will be especially threatened by the growing probability of dependence.

A second major approach to work, described by Lowenthal as instrumental/other-directed, is based on the perception of work primarily as a means to an end, the end being social acceptance and approval. Because the instrumental/other-directed person is empathic and appreciative of others, a reorientation usually occurs in midlife, although it is sometimes postponed until retirement. If so, retirement may represent some degree of crisis and include a period during which some form of substitution is required to ease the transition. But Lowenthal predicts that the instrumental/other-directed type will eventually accommodate to the loss of the work role.

There is some evidence to support the predictions Lowenthal and Atchley have made about the person who is very work oriented. Of those subjects in the Streib and Schneider (1971) study who returned to work after retiring, 73 percent reported that work was the major source of life satisfaction for them. Only 55 percent of the other subjects in the sample made such statements. Those who return to work may be obsessively instrumental people or have job-oriented goals that are important even after retirement. On the other hand, retirees who returned to work were also objectively healthier than those who did not. Many of those who went back to work were well-educated white-collar workers who had a wide range of options available to them. We may find, when mandatory retirement policies end, that many people will choose to stay on the job longer or will return to work.

The schemes presented by Lowenthal and Atchley allow a wider range of individual differences than either substitution theory or disengagement theory imply. They also suggest that a variety of patterns might be associated with reasonable levels of life satisfaction and adjustment. Such flexible frameworks are likely to yield productive hypotheses for future research and a deeper appreciation for the complexities of human adjustment.

Interestingly, one fairly obvious adjustment strategy, the substitution of leisure as a major goal during later life, has not been closely examined. The available data suggest, however, that leisure is rarely an important element in the upper-level value structure of today's elderly American.

Retirement and Leisure

In a culture that has traditionally placed great value on hard work, most men, and increasing numbers of women, may be unable to see leisure as an intrinsically valuable activity. Yet, as we have already heard from several studies, most Americans do not derive intrinsic satisfaction from their work. When they retire they miss the money, not the work. Unfortunately, most people don't seem to consider leisure activities an acceptably gratifying or meaningful alternative.

Consistently, researchers report that most middle-aged and elderly people do not spend much time engaged in leisure activities of any sort. Elderly people derive greater satisfaction from their work than from their leisure activities, and only a small number feel that they do not have enough free time (Pfeiffer and Davis, 1974). Futhermore, education does not seem to make much of a difference in these data. College-educated people are no more likely to have a wide range of leisure activities than are the semi-skilled (Atchley, 1980).

A variety of explanations have been offered for the apparent reluctance people feel about involvement in leisure activities. At least two, and probably three, minimal conditions must exist before leisure activities can be viewed as appropriate, valuable role behaviors. The primary condition is economic: people must have adequate funds that they are free to spend on leisure. Older adults who have enough disposable income for leisure activities find that many such activities are available to them. Those who are well-off financially are most likely to achieve congruence among leisure activities, individual competence, personal preferences, and needs.

The second requirement involves the development of a true leisure ethic in a work-oriented culture. The issue here is whether leisure activities can be seen as a legitimate source of identity—as an important contribution to the individual and to the rest of the society. Some contemporary observers see the emergence of a leisure ethic among the young. Consider Michael Harrington's suggestion that "more and more university students are convinced that work in American society is morally empty, esthetically ugly, and, under conditions of autonomation, economically unnecessary." John Kenneth Galbraith has observed that "the students react to my praise of toil with great applause and loud demands for a holiday from work." Of course, a leisure ethic is more than a denial of the central role of work. It is also a positive affirmation of the role of leisure. "If the soul has food for study and learning, nothing is more delightful than an old age of leisure," Marcus Tullius Cicero wrote over two thousand years ago. "Leisure consists in all those virtuous activities by which a man grows morally, intellectually, and spiritually. It is that which makes life worth living."

The third condition, education for leisure, both follows from and contributes to the development of an ethic. People have to learn positive attitudes toward leisure, just as they are taught positive attitudes toward work, and they must learn the leisure skills necessary to use their time in creative and fulfilling ways. Furthermore, a leisure education should begin early. The data we have strongly suggest that leisure education cannot begin in adulthood if much is to be accomplished. Leisure behavior is remarkably stable over the life course. Even people who predict that they will spend more time in leisure after they retire, rarely do so (Teague, 1980; Basse and Ekerdt, 1981). The ability to participate successfully in leisure activities probably begins in childhood and may simply not be possible after middle age (Basse and Ekerdt, 1981; Atchley, 1980).

Only a very small number of individuals take up new activities in old age. Old habits often interfere with the learning of new ones, and everyday activities like shopping, housekeeping, tinkering, and puttering begin to take up more and more of one's time. At the moment, there is little or no direct data on elderly competence to assume the leisure role, but a number of writers have bemoaned the tremendous emphasis of American education on job skills, leaving people unprepared to restructure their time around other activities.

Perhaps a fourth condition might be added, with the caveat that it is necessary for most people and most activities, but not every person in every moment. A companion, an audience, a fellow participant may be required and is usually preferable. An individual who is cut off from the social world has fewer leisure options available and may not enjoy those that remain.

Undoubtedly, the study of leisure will continue to increase in importance as larger and larger numbers of people are freed from the necessity of work, especially if there is any substantial increase in the normal, healthy life-span (Neulinger, 1980). One of the more interesting aspects of this study involves speculation about the future of retirement as new cohorts move from the labor force into the leisure years.

Retirement as an Institution

If Robert Atchley is correct, the future of retirement is assured by a number of trends. The decline in commitment to vocation as an end will continue, according to Atchley, and the attitude of the public toward retirement will become progressively more positive. One kind of development, almost certain to have an important impact on the level of adjustment retired people experience, is the end of compulsory retirement. As the number of working-age people in the population declines, Social Security becomes more and more expensive for each remaining worker. For this reason, it is likely that more flexible retirement programs will emerge, allowing workers to continue full- or part-time for as long as they are able. Under such a program, retirement benefits are introduced as the number of hours worked declines, and adjustment may be more easily achieved.

Retirement education programs may also have a beneficial effect on adjustment among the elderly of the future. These programs are increasingly available through industry and adult education facilities. Among their major objectives are the exploration of options and the selection of activities and reference groups.

Not only does one choose an area of activity (such as political, social, or creative), one also often chooses groups with which to participate. There are many possibilities within each activity area, and these vary with the nature of the individual's participation. For example, one could choose to work for a political party or for the League of Women Voters (a nonpartisan group), or for any of a number of special-interest groups such as NAACP, NOW, or Green Peace. Each group engages in political activity, and many of the same skills are needed in all of the groups; but the experience of one is quite different from the experience of another.

It is important for older adults to learn how to be competent in selecting and handling interactions with groups and organizations. Older people need to deal with a variety of institutions, including both those they choose (such as senior citizen centers) and those they need (such as welfare bureaucracies, housing developments, and rehabilitation or convalescent hospitals). When older adults are familiar with the options and resources available to them, they experience increased life satisfaction. And the efficiency and benefits of the providing organizations may be improved as well (Sussman, 1972).

Preretirement programs also provide a forum for financial planning and should be made available to workers of all ages. Atchley (1977) points out that most people do not even know how much Social Security they will be entitled to and how it will compare with their salaries before retirement. Moreover, workers are not often aware of the uncertainties or shortcomings of their companies' pension programs. Left to their own devices, they tend to make little or no preparation for coping with the financial limitations of retirement and seldom consider how inflation is likely to affect them when they are living on fixed incomes.

Finally, preretirement education should include information about basic health care, the importance of good nutrition and how to achieve it, the benefits of regular exercise, and the significance of physiological, psychological, and social events of later life. Preretirement education and realistic planning for retirement are associated with higher levels of adjustment among retired people and more favorable attitudes toward retirement during the work years (Atchley, 1980; Chown, 1977; Green and Tyron, 1969).

The need to increase the options available at retirement is repeated throughout the literature on the physical environment and financial well-being of the elderly. It is, in fact, probably the major concern of those who study such matters as housing, transportation, and the variety of available services and support systems in the community.

THE PHYSICAL ENVIRONMENT

As we noted above, most older Americans do own their own homes, but these houses tend to be of less value, to be older, and to have fewer rooms and fewer amenities (such as central heating or air conditioning) than the homes of younger people. It is estimated that as many as one-fifth of the homes owned by the elderly living in rural areas do not have adequate plumbing. Moreover, although people who own their own homes often have low monthly payments or own their homes free and clear, they still spend a large proportion of their income on housing. On the average, older people spend 23 percent of their income on housing, although only one in six has a mortgage. Younger homeowners spend only 20 percent, despite the fact that three in four have a mortgage. Of the elderly who rent, 38 percent spend over one-third of their income on housing, as do over 80 percent of the elderly who still have a mortgage (Atchley, 1980). Maintenance costs are higher for an older home. Thus, even an old house with a small mortgage can be quite expensive.

Elderly people also tend to live in older neighborhoods, and complaints about noise and traffic head the list of headaches among the urban elderly. Those who live in the inner city are also worried about crime and litter. A home is more than a few rooms, a bath, and a yard. It also encompasses a territory—a neighborhood, a social group, and access to the larger world. The entire community is an important ecological unit for older people, because so many depend upon their immediate surroundings to supply all their needs. Public transportation is very poor in most cities in this country. Even in New York City, where public transportation is more readily available than in most American cities, it does not meet the needs of older citizens. A 1971 study of older New Yorkers concluded that they might best be described as "block bound" (Nahemow and Kogan, 1971).

If you are block bound, the size of your psychological neighborhood or community is dramatically limited. You spend almost all of your time within walking distance of your home. Walking distance for most elderly New Yorkers is about one-half mile, or nine blocks in any direction. Most of the subjects in the New York study walked wherever they went—to doctors, shopping, social gatherings, and so on. Few neighborhoods, even sophisticated urban communities, provide all needed services within walking distance of one's home, and so older people do without the services they cannot reach by walking.

The elderly are also limited by the nature of the communities where they live. Older Americans are concentrated in central cities and rural areas. Those in rural districts may not be subject to the smog, social tension, and decay of urban life, but they are the most isolated members of the older population. The cities provide more options and opportunities than rural areas. But most elderly residents have below-average incomes, live in the oldest, poorest neighborhoods, and are unable to take advantage of the possibilities inherent in city life (Birren, 1970).

Curiously, the data show that older people report they are satisfied with these seemingly unfortunate circumstances, and we also know that they do not often move. Some interpret these data as evidence that the elderly really are satisfied with their living arrangements. Others argue that, since six out of ten elderly people express the desire to move and never do so, it is likely that they are dissatisfied with their arrangements but unable to change them. Moving is, after all, expensive and difficult. Often elderly people value the familiar aspects of the old neighborhood enough that they feel moving isn't worth the trouble, even though they don't really like the condition of their houses or the deterioration of their communities. Older residents tend to rate their own housing as satisfactory even when experimental observers assess the same structures as poor. Perhaps the ratings and reports of older people function as defense mechanisms. As evidence for this position, it has been noted that older people express less satisfaction with their present arrangements once the possibility of moving into new living quarters in public housing occurs (Keller, 1968; Britton, 1966, Carp, 1977).

For these reasons, one of the major concerns of researchers in this area has to do with the problem of "timely relocation." How can elderly people be convinced to move to suitable housing, in a better neighborhood, near better transportation, with easier upkeep, before they become too frail to function in the inner city or an inaccessible rural area?

New trends in housing for the elderly seem likely to encourage more timely relocation in the future. For instance, the growing availability of condominium and cooperative housing offers the elderly low maintenance along with a social setting conducive to interaction. At the same time, these housing arrangements provide the attraction of fixed monthly payments. Another promising trend can be seen in the increasing popularity of module and mobile homes, especially since the federal government has ruled that mobile homes are eligible for assistance programs. Although mobile homes depreciate, the upkeep on a new one is very modest compared with the expense of maintaining more conventional housing. Moreover, in some areas it is possible to purchase the land on which a mobile or module home sits, thus insuring that part of the investment will appreciate over the years (Struyk, 1981).

At the moment, however, no research exists on the comparative satisfaction of elderly living in conventional, condominium, cooperative, or mobile housing. Most of the research on housing for the elderly focuses on the impact of planned housing, specially designed for the elderly and usually constructed under the supervision of the government. Generally, studies of government housing projects and planned communities suggest that expressed life satisfaction and social behavior are affected in a positive way by such environments. Typically, statements about the effects of housing on physical health have been more difficult to interpret, with some investigators reporting positive effects and some finding no evidence for improvement (Sherwood, Greer, Morris, and Sherwood, 1972; Carp, 1966; Lawton and Cohen, 1974; Parr, 1980).

Growing numbers of module and mobile homes give the elderly a housing alternative that is inexpensive, efficient, and modern and provide the opportunity to live in a community planned with their needs in mind.

Planned Housing

Because we have so few systems for describing the environment, and because we know so little about its potential impact, it is difficult to design measures that will communicate the "quality of life" or the "contribution of housing." Investigators have used a variety of instruments and scales in the measurement of dimensions such as morale, adjustment, even health, leaving us many unanswered questions. For instance, how do self-ratings of health relate to a doctor's appraisal? How does the objective design of an environment affect the ways in which people generally describe it? (Parr, 1980). Despite these obvious problems, some interesting results have been presented. Some of the most detailed and intriguing are from a study conducted by Frances M. Carp (1966, 1977) following the progress of a government-planned apartment building called Victoria Plaza in Texas.

In the original study and in a recently published eight-year follow-up (1966, 1975), Carp concluded that the Victoria Plaza project seemed to have had favorable effects on the social and psychological well-being of its tenants. Follow-up data also suggested favorable effects on physical health. Residents of Victoria Plaza exhibited unusually low rates of death and institutionalization (Carp, 1975; Carp, 1977). In addition to reports on psychological, physical, and social well-being, Carp offered some insights into the practical day-to-day lives of Victoria Plaza residents. These observations provide a unique framework for viewing the life-styles of older people—their needs, desires, and habits.

Residents were questioned about their likes and dislikes after they had moved into their new lodgings. Among the things these older adults liked best were the clean, modern rooms and conveniences, including stoves, refrigerators, private baths, elevators, and access to transportation and community facilities. They also appreciated the physical security in the building and the closeness of other people their own age. They praised the idea of a complete maintenance staff and seemed happy to be living in age-segregated quarters where there were no children as full-time residents.

Although the residents of Victoria Plaza liked the closeness of other old people and the absence of children, a number of residents felt that middle-aged residents would provide more interesting company and stimulation. Most studies of age-segregation compare communities that are completely age-segregated with those that are not controlled for age. A few investigators have considered the effects of high *age density* (a large proportion of residents of a particular age group) versus low age density, but all of these studies present problems. Often subjects in age-segregated, specially designed environments have just moved into bright, new housing, clearly superior to what they left behind. Residents in older age-dense neighborhoods may show high levels of morale because they have lived in the same area for a long time and appreciate the familiar surroundings. In Europe, new housing that provides a mix of all age groups seems to be quite successful. Because no American units with residents of various age groups have been studied, we have nothing with which to compare the data we have (Carp, 1977; Rosow, 1967; Sherman, 1974).

The residents of Victoria Plaza seemed to prefer age-restricted housing, but they also noted some important drawbacks. Competent residents were especially concerned about living with people who could not take care of themselves or were unable or unwilling to engage in the flow of social life in the project. Residents of the Plaza often expressed high standards of cleanliness and behavioral propriety. They seemed especially dissatisfied with one older man who insisted on bringing his women friends in through the fire escape. Some residents felt the presence of competent, proper, middle-aged people might inhibit such behavior.

A number of residents lodged design complaints that provide insight into the details of everyday life at the Plaza. The building had been constructed around one major entrance lobby, where much social activity took place. The only elevators in the building opened into this lobby. Many residents felt the building should have had at least one private, quiet back entrance where people could come and go unnoticed. Special problems were created by the single entrance when a resident fell ill or died. Because everyone and everything had to enter and leave through the same set of elevators, residents never knew if they might be confronted by death or illness when the elevator doors opened.

Tenants also complained about the weight of the lobby doors, which had to be pushed open by hand. And they objected to the heavy window draperies, which did not provide privacy and sunlight simultaneously. There were also some curious blindspots in special areas. For instance, refrigerators had been installed high off the ground in an attempt to prevent stooping, but short residents were unable to reach the upper shelves. Bathroom doors had been widened to allow the passage of a wheelchair, but the bathroom was too small for a wheelchair to turn around in.

These problems underline the importance of consulting older people throughout the design process. Such consultation is not yet common, but it always produces interesting results. At one conference, sponsored by a builder in cooperation with a local community college and a council on aging, the elderly participants mentioned a variety of facilities that might be beneficial. Many said they would like Jacuzzi-type therapy pools in housing facilities. And, although questionnaire responses indicated that the cost of housing was the single most important concern of these older people, other possibilities also generated enthusiasm. Most insisted on being allowed to keep a pet—one woman commented that her cat was "the only warm thing that has touched me in years" (Ryon, 1978), and the majority wanted a small piece of land nearby where they could grow flowers and vegetables, not just for recreation but for the table. Some small, inexpensive details were also revealed as important, including sliding rather than swinging doors, extra wide tubs, seats built into showers, electric wall plugs installed eighteen inches to three feet above the baseboard, and windows placed low enough that someone sitting in a wheelchair or lying in bed could see outdoors. Some comments emphasized the need for security and convenient transportation.

Not everyone asked for special amenities, however. One man is quoted as follows: "I believe a major problem with senior housing is the increasing tendency to provide these kinds of extras. This is the kind of coddling most of us resent, and friends of mine who live in such places object to their cost" (Ryon, 1978). The issue of whether special planning and services is tantamount to coddling brings us to one of the central points of many current theoretical formulations—the role of supportive environments.

Theory and Environment

Environmental planners commonly assume that because older people are less independent, they need supportive environments. It is possible, however, for the environment to be oversupportive, robbing the individual of the opportunity to experience a sense of mastery and the self-esteem that proceeds from successful functioning (Carp, 1977).

Here we should distinguish between *prosthetic* and *therapeutic environments*. Prosthetic devices are permanent supports, such as glasses or artificial limbs, that allow the individual to function fully only as long as they are present, and can, therefore, encourage dependence. Therapeutic environments offer rich and varied opportunities, even challenges, and the security and permissiveness that lead to new growth and adaptation (Carp, 1977; Birren, Butler, Greenhouse, Sokoloff, and Yarrow, 1963).

The balance between prosthesis and therapy is critical in the maintenance and encouragement of adaptive behavior. One especially sophisticated treatment of this issue has been offered by M. Powell Lawton and his associates. Lawton assumes that the most adaptive outcome will occur where the *demand quality* of the environment is within the range of the individual's competence, particularly when the demand quality approaches the maximum capacity of that individual. *Competence* is defined here as combined biological, sensory motor, and cognitive capacity. The demand quality of the environment refers to the potential of the physical setting for evoking the desired behavior. From this point of view, either very high or very low levels of challenge or stress will be associated with poor outcomes (Lawton and Nahemow, 1973; Lawton, 1977; Lawton, 1975; Lawton, 1980). Figure 11.1 presents a graphic representation of the relationship between demand quality, competence, and adaptation.

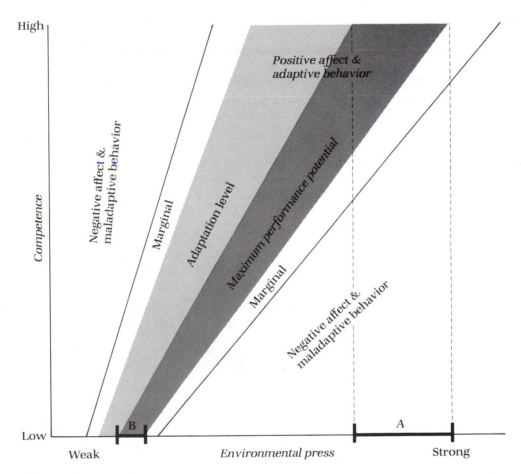

FIGURE 11.1
Behavioral and affective outcomes of person-environment transactions

This figure indicates that an individual of high competence will show maximum performance over a larger range of environmental situations than will a less competent individual. The entire range of optimal environments will occur at higher levels of environmental press (A) for the most competent person than for the least competent person (B).

SOURCE: *M. P. Lawton and L. Nahemow, "Ecology and the Aging Process," in C. Eisdorfer and M. P. Lawton, eds., The Psychology of Adult Development and Aging (Washington, D.C.: American Psychological Association, 1973), p. 661. Copyright © 1973 by the American Psychological Association.*

Lawton's presentation focused on the hypothesis that *person-environment congruence* is an important principle of housing design. Optimal person-environment congruence is found in environments that are person-specific. People must be individually matched to their environments to assure the proper balance between therapy and prosthesis. Prosthesis cannot be denied when it is necessary; that would be as ridiculous as denying someone glasses if he or she needed them. The proper level of prosthesis can prolong independence rather than create dependence. At the same time, it isn't desirable to remove all challenge from the environment. The important consideration is the fit between the needs and abilities of the individual and the degree of support and challenge offered by the environment (Lawton, 1975; Kahana, 1973; Kahana, 1975).

Lately, Lawton's theory has been criticized as too broad to encourage much research. Concepts like "adaptive behavior," "environmental press," "competence," and "maximum performance potential" are rather vague. Recent attacks on the problem of definition may help. For example, Paul Windley and Rick Scheidt (1980) have defined the following eleven important dimensions of the environment in studying environmental press.

1. Sensory stimulation: To what extent will redundant cues (such as both color-coding and labeling directional information) compensate for sensory decline?

2. Legibility: Is press affected by the degree to which designers use spatial organization to facilitate orientation and direction finding?

3. Comfort: How do dimensions such as the level of illumination and temperature affect either perceived press or behavior?

4. Privacy: In what ways can the control of unwanted stimulation be enhanced?

5. Adaptability: Is it possible to increase the ways in which a particular space can be adapted by its inhabitants as their needs change?

6. Control: In what ways does individual ownership and jurisdiction over space affect functioning, and how can such control be facilitated?

7. Sociality: What kinds of spaces encourage interaction between inhabitants or interaction with the community at large?

8. Accessibility: How can mobility be enhanced within a particular space as well as making entrance and exit as easy as possible?

9. Density: How does the perception of crowding affect social interaction and well-being?

10. Meaning: Do people behave differently in spaces that have symbolic meaning (such as the design of a church) or personal meaning (memories and social history) connected to them?

11. Quality: In what ways does the aesthetic appeal, design utility, and the size of a space affect behavior?

All of these are interesting questions, and the few partial answers offered by Windley and Scheidt are fascinating. Designers have found, for example, that reducing the size of areas set aside for social interaction but increasing their number results in greater frequency of social interaction. Even more interesting, some studies suggest that one effective way to involve people in their social setting is to design space so that one moves from private, enclosed, personal space through semi-private space (like a front porch), to public space (like a sidewalk). The house/porch/street configuration substantially increases social interaction over more conventional designs.

In a similar article, Joyce Parr (1980) proposed that researchers might profitably choose a behavior and study how it is influenced by a variety of environmental characteristics. One might focus on the number of social interactions initiated by a particular set of people, or in a particular space. Changes in the design of a space could then be assessed in a very specific way. For example, it has been demonstrated that the location and length of the path from a front entrance to an elevator affects social interaction (Howell, 1978).

Parr also believes that researchers ought to study the meaning of environmental characteristics for individuals as well as their impact on behavior. How do people interpret the installation of rails in a bathroom? Do they see it as helpful and supportive, or do they feel it implies incompetence? Parr underscores how important it is for social scientists interested in this arena to spend more time in interdisciplinary research. In particular, the architectural literature must be considered if recommendations about the creation of space are to be developed.

A final note drawn from an interesting set of studies (Howell, 1980) cautions us about the concept of "adaptation." The responses people make to environmental change are not always adaptive; they can also be historical. Sandra Howell has argued that the major motive people bring along with them to their environments is the desire for continuity of identity. This need is reflected, for example, in the way people everywhere display their personal effects in the spaces they inhabit. Often, people break institutional rules and suffer punishment in order to keep their own things around them. Such behavior is hard to explain in terms of adaptation. What difference does it make whether you hang up the picture of your son or keep it in your drawer? When they move to smaller housing, people most often miss their bedroom set and formal dining room table, even though they have no need of the double bed or a huge walnut table and six chairs. Why? It hardly seems adaptive to maintain these outmoded, space-eating items. Sometimes, the person-place history of an event is a better explanation for behavior than adaptation.

Ideas about support, structure, adaptation, and person-place history are especially helpful in coming to grips with the literature on institutionalization. More than any other topic in the study of aging, the prospect of institutionalization suggests marginal behavior, the loss of well-being, and the disruption of person-place history.

Institutionalization

Assessing the impact of institutionalization on the well-being of elderly people is a tricky business. In the first place, an older person is usually admitted to an institution because he or she is no longer fully competent. In most cases, that individual is not expected to improve dramatically, and is not often expected to return home again. What kind of control or comparison group should a researcher use? Older people who are still in the community do not generally have such severe physical problems. Even those on the waiting list for an institution differ from those who have been on the list long enough to gain admission. Certainly, it is difficult to make comparisons between individuals living in different institutions. What is required are longitudinal studies of large groups of elderly, comparing those who are eventually institutionalized with those who are not (Lieberman, Prock, and Tobin, 1968).

Without good information about the effect of institutionalization, the family who must deal with a failing elderly person often finds itself in grave crisis. Institutionalization is considered a last resort by families, which means that when the family reaches the point at which it can no longer care for an ailing member, two upsetting things are going on. First, the individual who needs the care is usually very ill indeed, and, second, the family must evaluate a situation about which there is little cultural wisdom and no well-accepted expert guidance. Most of the existing research is descriptive, and much of it is biased by the negative attitudes that Americans in general have toward the day when independent living is no longer possible.

Through the considerable confusion and complexity, however, a few consistent results have begun to emerge. The environmental characteristics of institutions undoubtedly have an impact on patient behavior and well-being. In particular, those that offer environmental warmth, that foster independence, and that provide adequate health care seem to produce positive outcomes, especially for the most responsive elderly (Lieberman,

Tobin, and Slover, 1971). One recent study of three different nursing homes (Montgomery, 1982) showed that family interaction improved after a family member was admitted to an institution, regardless of the care policies of the particular home involved. This data support the notion that nursing homes are not used as a dumping ground for the old, but as a last resort. They provide the family with the support necessary to resume more nearly normal relationships.

Nonetheless, there are important differences between institutions, and some guidelines both for choosing an institution and for interacting with that institution on behalf of an elderly patient have emerged. One important set of dimensions involves the degree of *segregation* (isolation from the outside world), *congregation* (how often members are required to perform the same activities in the same place at the same time), and *control* (the degree of autonomy permitted to patients). Generally, the more segregated, controlled, and congregate the setting, the more dehumanizing the atmosphere (Kahana, 1973; Lawton, 1977).

At the same time, greater segregation, congregation, and control may be required to care for the patients who are the least able to care for themselves. As Barbara Kahana (1982) has pointed out, the needs of the elderly individual must be matched with the degree of congregation, segregation, and control. In her research, Kahana has demonstrated that the fit between a patient's need for structure and support and the degree of congregation and segregation offered by the environment predict patient morale better than environmental characteristics alone. She argues for a distinction between congregation/segregation and crowding or surveillance. Many elderly people are socially isolated by the time they reach an institution, and the chance to interact with a number of the peers may offer new opportunities for relationships and activity. Institutional control does not seem to fit the picture in the same way, however.

In fact, it seems likely that the most important negative features of institutions are related to power and control. In one interesting sociological analysis (Schmidt, 1981–82) two different residential settings for the elderly were evaluated in terms of social exchanges and power. Both of these homes were well regarded, and both drew from white, middle-class populations with unusually high levels of education for their cohorts. Both homes had boarding facilities characterized by high levels of privacy and autonomy, and both also had nursing units where control, segregation, and surveillance were the order of the day. Eventually, all boarders entered the nursing care facilities, becoming a "patient" instead of a "boarder." Part of the analysis describes how boarders were able to delay demotion to patient.

Schmidt writes that "patienthood was at once a threat and a demotion." Furthermore, since these homes did not take Medicare payments, patients were also threatened with being sent away to a home that accepted Medicare. Boarders who were competent enough to walk to town and to do favors for the staff were typically given prestige-enhancing jobs and were able to delay transfer to the nursing unit. The possession of a color television set, or the attention of an interested relative was also instrumental in delaying transfer. Boarders' resources were many, including mobility, independence, and the freedom to renounce the care offered by the institution. Since boarders were allowed to control their own money and since they often had their own transportation, they could simply leave the institution as a protest.

Patients, on the other hand, possessed very few resources. Since both homes asked relatives to handle all monies, it was impossible for elderly patients to deploy even the most basic financial resources. Without mobility or independence, patient resources were so scarce that competition between patients made solidarity improbable. In other words, patients were not likely to cooperate in confronting the staff with a grievance. For patients, the only remaining resources were emotional, and so they used guilt, anxiety, or abrasiveness to coerce the staff. Patients also showed less conformity to peer or staff norms, for they were less likely to be rewarded. Schmidt argues that payments to institutions should be made contingent upon the progress of the patient, thus allowing an elderly person to exchange progress or improvement for control.

If control and responsibility are given to patients, activity, social interaction and well-being are affected in a positive way. Even such simple changes as the establishment of a patient forum for airing complaints and the permission to structure one's own time have had a beneficial effect. In one intervention, patients were given a plant to care for, and in another they were rewarded for simply remembering the answers to questions about the daily routine in the institution. Both interventions had positive effects upon the patients (Beck, 1982), perhaps because they involve treating the patient more like a functioning human being and less like a ward. Programs of visiting, occupational therapy, and music and art activities have all been effective in institutional settings (Arthur, Donnan, and Lair, 1973; Kosberg, 1973; Gottlieb, 1978).

The tendency to treat patients like wards is, to some extent, a product of the instrumental focus found in many institutional environments. Staff members spend most of their time and energy attending to the physical and medical needs of their patients and tend to ignore the personal, social, and affective aspects of the setting. Staff tend to define care with regard to physical well-being, whereas patients define it in terms of personal dignity. For example, in one study of a midwest nursing home given the fictitious name Murray Manor (Gubrium, 1974), patients repeatedly ex-

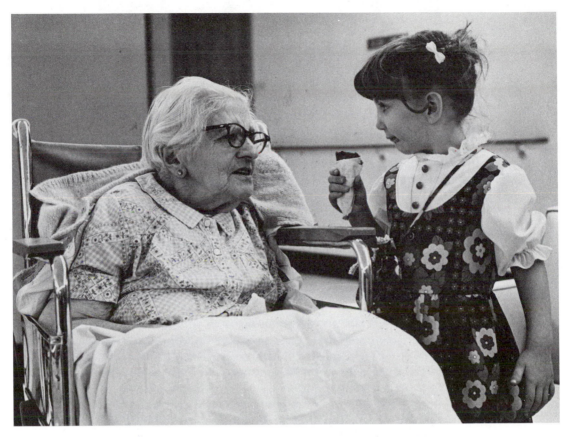

Institutions need be neither inhumane nor dehumanizing if the concept of caring is extended from the physical to the social and psychological needs of the patient.

pressed the sentiment that patients are people who deserve respect, and they defined their "own good" with regard to social relationships rather than physical concerns. Staff, in contrast, were relatively inattentive to any but medical concerns.

Here, perhaps, lies a legitimate role for the family. Research has shown that in cases in which families visit, the elderly receive more attention, feel less alone and are more integrated with the community at large (Shuttlesworth, Rubin, and Duffy, 1982). Contact with family seems to be more important than relationships within the institution in predicting patient well-being (Tesch and Whitbourne, 1981). And the more an institution treats the family as a client, rather than a tool, the greater the family integration. It has been suggested that families be included in treatment plans and staff conferences, that separate activities be planned to include families, and that visitation, transportation, and provision for families to take meals with residents be made (Montgomery, 1982). Families might well take responsibility for the personal, social, and affective needs of patients when they are included in the regular treatment regimen offered by an institution. Perhaps such a program might change Marjorie Lowenthal's observation that the central problem in most institutions is "overworked, undertrained, and highly harassed staff who are unable to cope with physical needs of their patients, to say nothing of the psychosocial needs" (1977, p. 449).

Finally, it is important for families to recognize that an institution that tries to meet the social and psychological needs of the elderly is probably more valuable than one with modern, costly facilities. In particular, an institution must provide the patient with continuity, offering a bridge between the present and the past, the old and the new, the personal and the institutional. "The social psychological milieu which would respond to these needs would be one where residents can be alone without being lonely, where people are available to each other without crowding one another, where personal attention is available without surveillance, where one can be cared for without giving up the feeling of caring for one's self and for relevant others, where one can depend on others without giving up one's independence" (Kahana, 1982, p. 880).

Obviously, we have a long way to go if the huge number of aging people in this population are to have the range and quality of facilities that will permit them to live lives that are as satisfying and independent as possible to the very end of the life cycle. Professionals in the field of institutional care must work toward more voluntary, nonauthoritarian community structures, greater choice, and the creation of responsibility and meaningful social relationships in the context of adequate medical and physical care.

Relocation

Each of the subjects in this chapter—retirement, new housing, institutionalization—implies the possibility of *relocation*. Relocation is believed to have an important impact on older people and is critical to understanding research on other environmental aspects of aging. It should be considered in the interpretation of information about institutionalization, for example. If the elderly deteriorate after admission to an institution, some of that decline may be a product of the move itself rather than the quality of the institution or even the nature of the illness. At the same time, relocation is also associated with positive effects for those elderly who are able to meet and master the challenge of moving.

The Kahanas (Kahana, Kahana, and McLenigan, 1980) have studied one group for whom relocation is an exciting, overwhelmingly positive choice. These are the adventurous elderly, who decide to move away when they retire. In this study, 80 percent of the participants felt their status had improved since they retired, and saw themselves as "young-old." Adventurers tend to measure life satisfaction in terms of the challenge and interest they experience, rather than dissatisfaction. The Kahanas believe that the number of adventurous elderly will increase in the near future.

"I pray . . . /That I may seem, though I die old, /A foolish, passionate man."
William Butler Yeats

Of course, voluntary relocation and forced relocation are different experiences, and among the very elderly and those who are already institutionalized, there is evidence that declining health and morale often accompany a move. Those who are forced to relocate by urban renewal projects or who are admitted to institutions show the highest mortality rates and the highest probability of illness in the first few months after transfer (Markus, Blenkner, Bloom, and Downs, 1972; Chown, 1977). Even among those who are relocated involuntarily, however, the most competent individuals may well show improvement if the new environment is warm and permits a good deal of autonomy. Moved into an unfavorable environment, competent patients tend to deteriorate (Marlowe, 1973; Lawton, 1977). The least competent, by contrast, do not seem to improve even when moved to the best settings.

One recent review summarized fourteen studies of relocation (Coffman, 1981), eight of which reported no increase in mortality rates, and six of which showed increased mortality in relocated samples. Generally, it seems that increased mortality occurs no more often than increased survival rates, and relocation can be a positive experience when the proper support and attention is available and the new environment constitutes an improvement. "The message seems to be that relocation itself is virtually irrelevant to survival so long as the support system is made adequate, whether for the purposes of 'therapy' or prevention of 'transfer trauma' " (Eustis, 1981, p. 494). High staff morale and careful handling of the personal possessions of patients are also important in the planning and execution of successful relocation.

Relocation is but one of many issues that could be independently studied in the context of understanding the interaction between the individual and the physical environment. In one sense, if we are trying to understand how retirement or institutionalization affects older people, relocation effects seem only a nagging problem. As is often true, however, confounding variables can be valuable and interesting as a focus of study themselves.

SUMMARY

This chapter is devoted to a discussion of the ecology of aging and to a review of the literature on retirement. The environment may be viewed as including the individual's biological, psychological, and social condition—

the interpersonal environment or social world, and the physical environment in all its many manifestations, from housing and community to transportation.

A study of the environment of older adults might begin with a simple statistical survey of the dimensions of the elderly population. The population of the United States is considered aged because it is characterized by a large number of people who live to advanced ages and by a declining birthrate. Most of America's elderly are concentrated in rural areas and central cities, and most live in homes they own.

Most people over the age of sixty-five do not work; thus, it is necessary to understand the implications of retirement for the older person— the financial, psychological, and social impact—in order to gain a sense of the environmental forces that are important to the aging person. Retirement is a relatively new phenomenon. Because a sizable community of retired people in this country has come into being only since the end of World War II, we have not had much time to learn about retirement as an institution in the United States.

The growing numbers of retired people and an evolving trend away from the rigid work ethic are creating a view that retirement is the right of any individual who has worked for long enough. A retired individual does not engage in year-round, full-time work and receives at least some pension or Social Security benefits. Retirement is a role with few mandatory responsibilities or activities beyond some behavioral and attitudinal patterns, including independence, self-respect, and financial and social responsibility. The retirement role is canceled by severe illness or disability, although most individuals maintain at least part of the dignity of retirement for some time before they become severely ill or disabled.

Retirement has been viewed as a process that starts when people begin to develop attitudes toward leaving their jobs and that terminates when one can no longer maintain the independence and responsibility demanded by the role.

The kind of job a person has can influence his or her view of retirement long before the event occurs. Blue-collar workers show relatively favorable attitudes toward retirement, whereas professionals register much less enthusiasm. Autonomy on the job appears to be a predictor of attitudes toward retirement, as is task quality. Blue-collar workers may be showing an escape effect in their enthusiasm for retirement.

For the huge number of people in the middle, income seems to be the best predictor of attitudes. The effect of education on attitudes toward retirement varies. Education seems to be more likely to produce favorable attitudes in women than in men, although there is conflicting evidence on this point. Finally, age is an important variable in retirement attitudes.

Younger workers seem to look forward to retirement more enthusiastically than do older workers.

Attitudes toward retirement shape the decision about when to retire; illness and beliefs about one's continuing ability to produce are also important. Other determining forces include regulations and policies about compulsory retirement age, early retirement pension programs, and the attitudes of family and friends.

Most retirement ceremonies have emphasized the negative aspects of the new role and reflect the generally bleak cultural perception of life in retirement. A more positive ritual is emerging, however, and research is beginning to show that retirement doesn't necessarily represent a significant loss and, therefore, an important crisis.

Early theory proceeded from the assumption that retirement created significant loss by depriving the individual of satisfactions obtained through work. Nevertheless, research on the meaning of work has not led to the conclusion that Americans generally find their work intrinsically satisfying. What they miss about work, after retirement, is the money they earned. Thus, loss of work does not constitute a significant crisis for most workers, although the reduction of income causes problems.

Neither has research yielded support for the notion that retirement creates many important behavioral or physical disturbances. After conducting a comprehensive examination of the crisis position and inspecting a number of measures ranging from objective and subjective physical health and financial status to self-esteem, age identification, and life satisfaction, Streib and Schneider rejected the hypothesis that retirement has deleterious consequences for the individual. They have concluded instead that some form of the disengagement hypothesis seems best to fit their data, and certainly the disengagement theory has afforded an important theoretical framework for those who study retirement. Data on passage from active to passive mastery and from instrumental to affective goals seem to support the notion of disengagement. Some individuals who have not disengaged from instrumental goals, or even from their jobs, also make successful adjustments, however.

Typologies based on the relationship of the individual to his or her work have been offered as explanatory frameworks for adjustment to retirement. It is hypothesized that individuals who are unable to reorganize their value systems in preparation for retirement will fit the substitution model and may experience crisis; those who successfully reorganize their value hierarchies or who have always had value hierarchies congruent with retirement are not expected to experience difficulty.

One example of a value hierarchy consistent with retirement is presented in Lowenthal's hypothesis that middle age is usually accompanied by a shift from instrumental to affective goals. Another kind of structure that would be congruent with retirement would include acceptance of leisure as a valuable and significant activity. The literature suggests, however, that few Americans are able to view leisure as a legitimate use of time. The culture has long been characterized by a strong sense of the moral validity of work, and few adults develop a leisure ethic or many leisure activities. It is not impossible to find Americans who think of leisure as honest and important—just difficult. It has been suggested that at least two, and probably three, requirements must be met before leisure will be accepted as a legitimate alternative for the older population: older adults must be able to finance leisure activities from funds they consider rightfully theirs; both the elderly and other age groups must come to view leisure as worthwhile; and leisure education must be expanded to offer people an opportunity to explore the range of leisure-time activities available and to match abilities, needs, interests, and opportunities.

The future of retirement is difficult to predict, because it is still a relatively young institution in a rapidly changing culture. It does seem important and possible, however, to expand the level and accessibility of opportunities available to the retired older person. This goal can be fostered by more flexible retirement programs and the abolition of compulsory retirement policies. Preretirement education—including information on financial planning, recreation, health care, nutrition, and strategies for dealing with institutions—would also be helpful. In reviewing the options available to the elderly, the restrictions of the physical environment seem to be as important as those of the interpersonal and individual environments. Those who would develop opportunities for the elderly must examine carefully their needs for housing, community, transportation, and support services.

Most elderly people live in inner cities or rural areas. Those who live in cities are limited to the services and facilities available within walking distance of their homes. Those in rural areas are often isolated, from other people and from needed services. Schemes aimed at solving these problems are most often designed by younger people and developed to serve the community at large. Thus, elderly citizens too often find themselves in the midst of large urban renewal projects that have clean, modern shopping centers, medical plazas, and entertainment facilities—and impersonal, uncaring atmospheres.

Housing that is planned specifically for the elderly can relieve some of the hardships of older people. Planned environments have been shown to have a decisive impact on life-style and well-being, although the impact on health and morale is not as clear. One long-term, comprehensive study was made of a government housing project, Victoria Plaza. The reports of this study support the hypothesis that housing can have a significant positive effect on the lives of older people. This study also provides enough detail on design and resident behavior to offer some important insights for students of the psychology of aging. In particular, the residents of Victoria Plaza made it clear that they were most concerned about the kinds of people they live with, and they had very high standards for the conduct of their neighbors. They were concerned about the ability of other residents to function independently. In discussing the competence of the elderly, one must examine the value of prosthetic versus therapeutic environments. Several popular theories of environmental planning require an understanding of this distinction.

A prosthetic environment provides a permanent support system. A therapeutic environment offers a number and variety of opportunities that can lead to new growth and development. One important theoretical hypothesis, offered by M. Powell Lawton, is based on the notion that the balance between prosthesis and therapy is critical. Lawton believes the most adaptive outcomes occur when the demand quality of the environment is within the range of the individual's competence, and particularly when the demand quality approaches the maximum capacity of that individual.

The practical implications of matching the person and the demands of the environment are nowhere more apparent than among the disabled elderly who enter institutions. Because most institutional administrators and staff members emphasize the physical and medical care of the aged, the degree of support versus challenge provided by the environment is seldom given much attention. Descriptive evidence suggests that few if any of the social and psychological aspects of the environment are ever formally considered in institutional settings.

This distressing state of affairs is caused, in part, by the notion that individuals who are mentally disabled or very old will not benefit from environmental enrichment. The data do not support this view. A wide variety of therapies and rehabilitation programs have been shown to be effective with elderly patients in many settings. Yet rehabilitation and therapy are not funded by the governmental agencies responsible for monitoring the quality of care in nursing homes. Much remains to be done, in studying and in optimizing institutional environments. New data strongly demonstrate that institutions can provide the support necessary to normalize family interactions and that when patients retain power and responsibility, improved social interaction and well-being can be associated with institutionalization.

The final issue considered in this chapter is relocation, as a methodological problem and as a variable of some import and interest. Relocation is believed to have a negative impact on the lives of elderly people. Nevertheless, it is possible to describe relocation conditions under which improvement occurs: if a move is voluntary, if the new environment is perceived as favorable, if the individual is adequately prepared for relocation, then moving has been associated with improvement in the condition of the most competent older people. At the same time, unfavorable moves appear to produce deterioration in the most competent. For the least competent, the quality of the new environment seems to make little difference, and relocation of any kind is a high-risk situation. Relocation is an example of the kind of issue that at first may seem interesting only as a confounding variable, but one that on closer examination generates a new area of research.

Chapter 12

Dying and Death:
A Final Context
for Human
Development

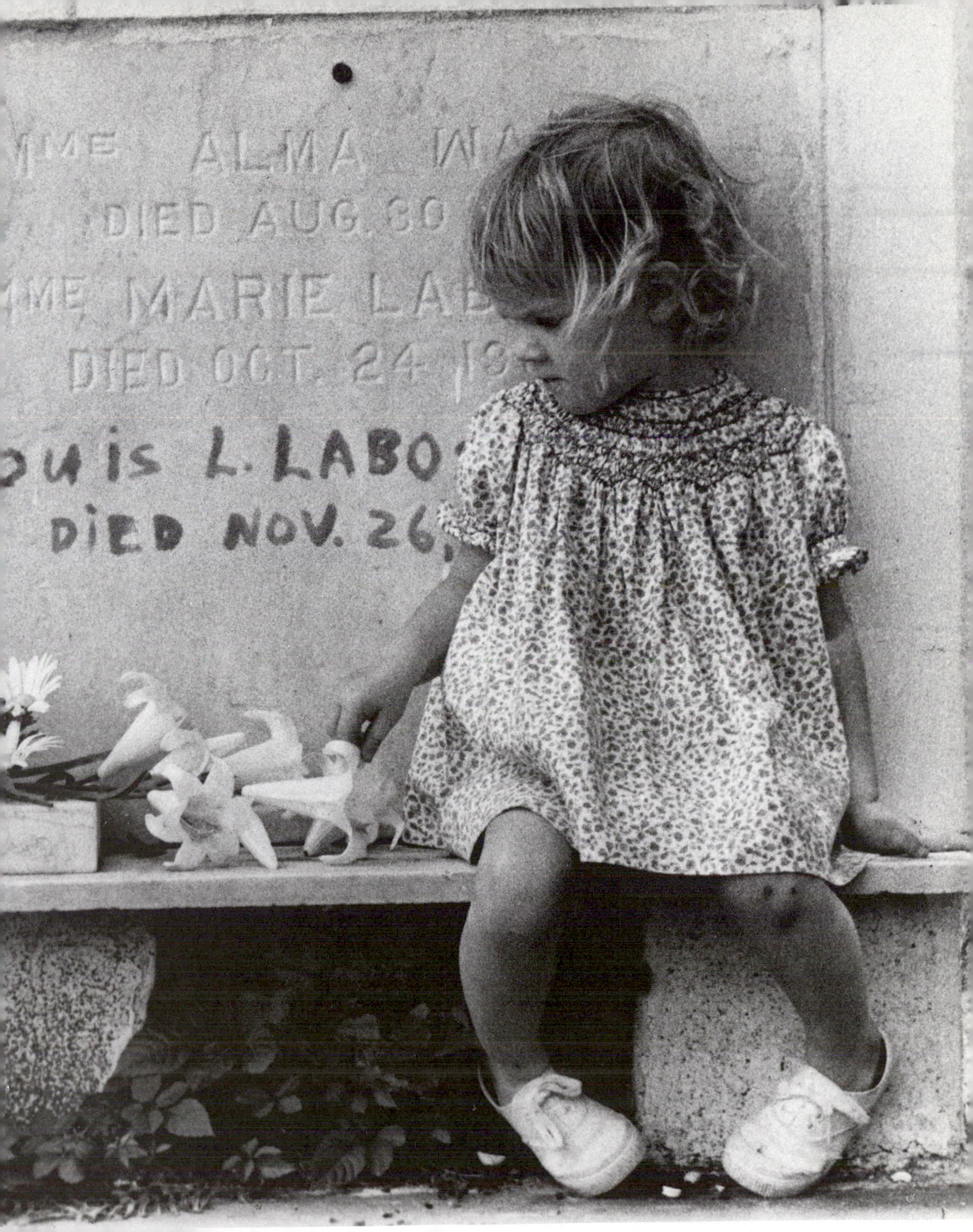
ALMA
DIED AUG. 30
MARIE LAB
DIED OCT. 24
ouis L. LABO
DIED NOV. 26

*It is impossible to experience one's own death
objectively and still carry a tune.*

WOODY ALLEN

It has been said that recognition of our own mortality is what separates human beings from the other creatures that inhabit the earth. This chapter explores that uniquely human understanding and the effect it has on development, especially in the last stages of the life cycle. Of course, a truly life-span treatment of this subject would examine the impact of death and dying during every period of life. But here we can only graze the subject, beginning with a general discussion of attitudes toward death and then focusing on the meaning of death in later life, particularly the meaning of death for those who are aware of its imminence.

The death of an older person has different meanings than the death of a child, a young adult, or an adult at midlife. Cultural attitudes and values vary with the age of a dying or deceased person, and, as we shall see, one's own attitude toward dying and death changes with age. The medical and biological meanings as well as the psychological and social meanings of death are different for the old and the young.

This chapter begins with a broad discussion of such meanings, from the personal ones conveyed by attitudes and emotional responses, to the legal and medical definitions that are often a subject of heated controversy. We will look at the traditional signs of death, examine the concept of brain death, and review the literature on the intellectual and emotional changes associated with the *terminal stage* of life.

The terminal stage is that period during which the individual has a "persistent awareness of the prospect of death from natural causes in late life" (Bromley, 1974). Most of the research and theory in this chapter are products of the investigation of the terminal stage. Thus, a good deal of space is devoted to the possibility that there are predictable stages or optimal patterns of emotional development among people who are terminally ill.

The second part of the chapter is devoted to the interpersonal and social context of dying, including how professional care-givers interact with those who are dying and how survivors deal with the experience of grief and bereavement. In the final section of the chapter, dying and death are explored as a social institution. We will consider not only how concrete experience with dying and death affects the survivors, but also how the concept of death and the dying of a particular individual has significance for development over generations.

DEATH AS A SOCIAL AND PSYCHOLOGICAL CONSTRUCT

"Death is a biological event, a rite of passage, an inevitability, a natural occurrence, a punishment, an extinction, the enforcement of God's will, separation, reunion, and a time for judgment" (Kalish, 1977, p. 483). Dying, in contrast, is a part of life. One's dying can be influenced by the social environment and by one's past experience, beliefs, attitudes, and the like. Dying can be understood; death cannot. Yet, death need not be considered senseless, and in order to make sense of dying one must make some sense of death. So we begin with a discussion of the definitions and, more important, the significance of death.

Death is the ultimate paradox of human existence. In childhood, recognition slowly dawns that death may not be just another kind of life. Very small children believe, for instance, that death is a sort of low-level living during which one is not very happy a lot of the time. With time, children understand that death is different, perhaps the opposite of life. Later they accept the notion that it is also permanent, inevitable, and universal. It occurs to everyone, and it happens every day. Despite that knowledge, however, one's own death remains a unique event. It will happen only once. We know that, like all creatures, we will die; yet with every breath we take, that knowledge is challenged. We wake up alive every day of our lives. We have no personal experience of waking up dead (Kastenbaum, 1981a; Guthrie, 1971).

For the social scientist, death produces another important paradox. Although it only occurs once, at the end of life, it seems to affect the whole course of individual development. It is a primary source of motivation for the living. Can you imagine life without death? Immortality transforms the meaning of life completely. Time, love, work—all our significant roles and values would be radically altered in a deathless universe. It might well be that a deathless universe is a lifeless one. Life draws its vitality, its intensity, its value, in some measure from its very perishability.

Still, one of the most persistent themes in human history is the search for immortality, either physical or spiritual. Existential philosophers and psychologists contend that anxiety about death is a primal experience and that human beings require a strong belief system as a defense against the fear of death. A belief in life after death lends a significance to life that is impossible when death is viewed as a void, an end to existence. In modern societies, where belief in spiritual immortality is waning, the existential thinker would predict that life is experienced as less meaningful. In consequence, individuals are unable to encounter death with equanimity. They deny its reality (Becker, 1973; Kastenbaum, 1981a; Lifton, 1981).

The Existential Position

In place of spiritual immortality, modern societies have emphasized social immortality—the importance of generativity, living through one's progeny, one's contribution to society. Speaking from an existential perspective, however, Robert Lifton contends that the nuclear age even robs us of a belief in social immortality (Lifton and Olson, 1974; Lifton, 1981). He argues that the specter of the holocaust and the possibility of Armageddon offer the indelible image of death as senseless tragedy and an absurdity rather than a fitting end to life. If nothing can endure the atomic age, then nothing matters. Life is meaningless and so, therefore, is death.

Lifton draws his conclusions from years of working with those who survived some of the great tragedies of modern times: German concentration camps, the bombing of Hiroshima, and the war in Viet Nam. He believes that all of us are, in a sense, survivors of these horrors. Those who were there personally are most extreme in their attitudes, but all of us are affected. Lifton's studies reveal the following common themes among survivors, themes he contends are found in all modern cultures.

1. The death imprint: All survivors report vivid, indelible images of death as grotesque and absurd, images produced in moments of tremendous anxiety.

2. Death guilt: To a greater or lesser extent, all survivors experience guilt because they did not die. This is not moral or legal guilt; it is paradoxical. It is a product of the vulnerability and helplessness created by situations in which it is impossible to act, or even feel appropriately.

3. Psychological numbing: Survivors also experience a paralysis of mind in moments of horror. Lifton believes that psychological numbing is an adaptive response because the intensity of feelings appropriate to such horror would cause insanity.

4. Suspicion of counterfeit nurturance: Survivors often resent any offer of help. They may see the need for assistance as a sign of weakness, or they may reject help because they are in conflict between accepting the horror as reality and rejecting it.

5. Struggle for meaning: Finally, survivors often spend much of the rest of their lives and their energies in a struggle to make sense, to produce meaning from their experience. The creation of Israel and the crusade of Viet Nam veterans for recognition represent this kind of struggle. Lifton believes that the mission is an expression of unrelieved mourning for those who died.

Lifton has consistently argued that these five themes all reflect an emotional denial of the reality of death. Dying and death become taboo subjects when they rob life of its meaning. Unfortunately, this is a terribly hard proposition to research. Denial is an unconscious process: people are unaware that they are denying their anxiety. Therefore, it is difficult, if not impossible, to document such denial. Survey research showing that only 10 to 25 percent of the population feel death is an important source of fear in their daily life does not satisfy the existential psychologist who believes this is simply evidence of how widespread denial is (Kalish and Reynolds, 1976; Greer, 1965; Schmitt, 1982–83).

Another approach to the existential hypothesis is offered by naturalistic observation (Schmitt, 1982–83). For example, one study brings several lines of evidence to bear, including the remarks of important public figures, interviews with ordinary working adults, and the responses of parochial school children. The author found that most Americans, from important public figures like Hubert Humphrey and Richard Nixon, to the waitresses and truck drivers described by Studs Terkel in *Working* (1974) seem to believe in some form of social immortality. Either they believe they will be immortalized through their achievements, or they believe their descendants will allow them to "live on." Even the media promote the idea of immortality, consistently using phrases like "He will always be remembered for . . . ," or "her immortal portrayal of . . . " Furthermore, the interviews with parochial school children suggest that many people continue to believe in God and in traditional spiritual immortality.

This author concluded that a wide variety of forces shield Americans from experiencing existential crisis in the nuclear age. Nuclear weapons have no relationship to the roles people play in everyday life. Most of us do not know the facts of atomic warfare well enough to discern whether nuclear weapons might ever be relevant. The government shrouds such information in secrecy and complexity, if not fabrication. Furthermore, Americans see nuclear weapons in terms of protection rather than destruction and find it difficult to imagine their own death, much less the collective death of the species. The belief that one can overcome any obstacle also shields Americans from the reality of nuclear disaster. Even the antinuclear power alliances have not focused on nuclear weapons until recently. Finally, traditional beliefs, such as those of the parochial school children interviewed in this study, are certainly not dead.

Even if such traditional religious modes were gone, however, there is little evidence that they form the strongest bulwark against death anxiety. Some researchers have reported that intense religious beliefs are associated with less anxiety about death, but that the absence of religious beliefs has also been linked to low death anxiety. It is intermediate levels of religiosity that seem to be most strongly related to fear of death (Kalish and Reynolds, 1976; Feifel and Branscomb, 1973; Kalish, 1963).

What is more, some secular practices not associated with strong belief systems seem to be related to low death anxiety. For instance, college students who used psychedelic drugs and those who practiced Zen meditation showed less intense galvanic skin responses (a measure of palmar sweating) and fewer changes in heart rate in response to death-related stimuli in one study (Garfield, 1974). This research is particularly important because of the measure of fear that was employed. Verbal reports are more likely to be influenced by denial or suppression than are physiological measures.

If fear of dying and death has not been generated by the great historical changes of our times, why has it become an uncomfortable, unpleasant, even taboo subject for some? Perhaps this American fear of death is simply learned and not a universal feature of experience. It may be, for example, that fear of death is related to the dominant value system of Western thought. Westerners see death as defeat. Nature is the enemy, and death brings about the ultimate victory of nature.

The Learning of Death Anxiety

If we learn to fear death, then we must do so by analogy, for we cannot fear death from our personal experience—we have no personal experience of it. One important source of the fear, however, is the death of someone else, the experience of separation. As some have noted, people cannot make distinctions between how survivors feel and how someone who is dead feels. We have no idea how it feels to be dead, but we associate death with loss and attendant feelings of grief and anxiety. Furthermore, from the survivor's point of view, dead people are also inactive, and most Westerners value productivity and fear loss of mobility (Howard and Scott, 1965; Kastenbaum, 1981b).

The notion that death is not threatening to all people is partially supported by cross-cultural data. To illustrate, a study of one Polynesian kin group shows a very different set of attitudes toward death than are familiar to most North Americans. Although essentially without any strong beliefs in immortality, these people believe that death must be pleasant if one is freed from work and responsibility. This Polynesian culture does not foster a strong work ethic. Kinship is broadly recognized, and most members of the group develop numerous, diffuse emotional relationships and so rarely experience separation anxiety. They do not, in fact, seem to experience such simple forms of separation anxiety as homesickness (Howard and Scott, 1965).

Death as a social and psychological construct is very complex, and we have only begun to explore its developmental implications. It is little wonder that there is much competing thought and research. It seems far too soon to define a mature attitude toward death. We can't even say with any certainty whether there is such a thing as a mature attitude. The general tenor of the literature, however, is that Americans ought to be coping with dying and death better than they do. The most persistent theme is that Americans deny the reality of death, and this is generally considered a pathogenic attitude. This position needs to be examined carefully. Students of dying and death have begun to ask valuable questions, and though we are still far from the answers, the situation seems much improved by the attempt.

THE INNER CONTEXT: BIOLOGICAL, COGNITIVE, AND PERSONALITY PROCESSES

There are at least three important ways in which death must be defined: biomedically, psychologically, and socially. *Biological death* occurs when all physical signs of life cease. *Psychological death* refers to the cessation of thoughts, feelings, and needs as well as to the disappearance of the personality characteristics associated with a particular individual. *Social death* is the end of the institutional and cultural processes, such as the funeral service and mourning, surrounding the death of an individual. These three aspects of death seldom, if ever, occur simultaneously; increasingly, they are separated by long periods.

A common (if much feared) occurrence of modern life occurs, for example, when psychological death precedes medical-biological death. The use of artificial life support systems has made the gulf between psychological and biological death one of the most controversial areas in medicine. It is also possible for social death to precede the demise of biological processes. This happens when a dying person is treated as an object rather than a person. Elizabeth Kübler-Ross (1974) has been adamant that artificial life support systems, used for extended periods of time, create withdrawal of family, friends, and even hospital staff, who may treat the patient as an object to be turned, cleaned, or moved. The living begin to speak of the patient in the third person.

There is even startling evidence that biological death, at least as it is currently defined, can precede psychological death. This is one way to describe the experiences reported in such books and articles as *Life After Life* (Moody, 1975). Box 12.1 presents a summary of the characteristic aspects of such experiences. Furthermore, it appears that in some cultures social death often precedes (and even causes) both psychological and biological death. Cases of so-called voo doo death are essentially accounts of the potential effects of social death.

BOX 12.1
Life after death (life?)

On the basis of extensive interview data, Dr. Raymond Moody—in his book *Life After Life*—suggests a number of common features of the psychological experiences of individuals during a period in which they may have been biologically or clinically dead. Although there are many individual differences, several aspects of the experience often reported include:

1. awareness of a loud noise that is "sensed" rather than heard and is often described as a buzzing or drumming sound;

2. the sensation of moving rapidly through a dark tunnel, funnel, or cave toward an intense light;

3. seeing or feeling the presence of dead ancestors and relatives who are present to help the individual through the transition from this life;

4. the interpretation of the light as a power or presence that did not judge, but required the individual to review his or her own life—the presence is sometimes experienced as love;

5. the experience of "seeing" their lives pass in front of their eyes, a panoramic view of their own actions and thoughts;

6. awareness that their time had not yet come and they must return to complete their normal life span.

SOURCE: R. A. Moody, *Life After Life* (New York: Bantam, 1975).

Clearly, it has become very difficult to define death or, for that matter, life. We do not even have a really satisfactory medical-biological definition, and the problem is as old as medicine itself. For example, numerous certified cases of premature burial occurred in the eighteenth and nineteenth centuries. Individuals believed to be dead were apparently in the grips of a trance-like hysteria that mimicked physical death, even to the cessation of observable heartbeat and respiration (Mant, 1968).

Today, rapid advances in medical technology require the constant redefinition of death and dying. People diagnosed as terminally ill ten years ago are still alive today. People who died ten years ago, according to traditional criteria, live on with the aid of artificial life support systems. Karen Quinlan is such a person.

The traditional definition of death in terms of heartbeat and respiration has been replaced by a very complex set of criteria for electroencephalographic brain death (see Box 12.2). These Harvard criteria, as they are

BOX 12.2
A summary of the Harvard criteria for brain death

1. *Unreceptivity and unresponsivity:* The individual is totally unaware of externally applied stimuli and inner need and completely unresponsive.

2. *No movements or breathing:* Observation of at least one hour reveals no spontaneous muscular movements, spontaneous respiration, or response to stimuli such as pain, touch, sound, or light. Total absence of respiration after the patient is on a mechanical respirator may be determined by turning off the respirator for three minutes and observing whether there is any effort on the part of the patient to breathe spontaneously.

3. *No reflexes:* The pupils of the eyes are fixed and dilated and do not respond to intense light. Ocular movements, in response to head turning or irrigating the ears with ice water, and all blinking movements are absent. There is no swallowing, yawning, or vocalization and no postural activity. There are no tendon reflexes or plantar response, and the application of noxious stimuli has no effect.

4. *Flat electroencephalogram:* Given that the EEG electrodes are properly applied, the apparatus is functioning properly, and the personnel in charge are competent, a flat EEG is of "great confirmatory value," if hypothermia (temperature below 90 degrees Fahrenheit) or the use of central nervous system depressants, such as barbiturates, are excluded.

5. All of the above tests shall be repeated at least twenty-four hours later with no change.

SOURCE: Based on "A Definition of Irreversible Coma: Report of the Ad Hoc Committee of the Harvard School to Examine the Definition of Brain Death," *Journal of the American Medical Association*, 205 (1968), 337–340.

called, are widely accepted and rely on the concept of *total brain death*—cessation of function in both the neocortex and the brain stem.

To some writers in this area, however, the Harvard criteria seem unreasonable, too conservative, and too rigid. The electroencephalogram (EEG), for instance, does not always reliably indicate brain function. Overdoses of hypnotic drugs can result in an EEG that mimics brain death. On the other hand, EEG recorders sometimes produce meaningless marks that can be interpreted as signs of life (Devins and Diamond, 1977; Veatch, 1976; Jeffko, 1980).

It has been suggested that the use of EEG records be abandoned, that the presence of brain-stem reflexes be deemphasized, and that attention be focused more strongly on neocortical function. One alternative demands that being human be defined in terms of personhood as well as biological function. This approach leads to a definition of death as the total and permanent cessation of spontaneous activity in the organism as a whole, but uses the Harvard EEG test as a criterion for spontaneous activity in the neocortex (Jeffko, 1980). It also implies that spontaneous neocortical activity, respiration, or circulation ought to be present when heroic life-saving measures are deployed.

Determining when heroic measures will be used is a critical issue, of course. Controversy exists over the role of the physician because of the possibility that emergency considerations (such as the need for organs for transplant operations) may color the decisions of medical personnel. It is also argued that the family cannot be solely responsible for such decisions. The use of a document known as a living will (see Box 12.3) is one attempt to consider the patient's wishes in the process—to make it possible for the patient to guide physicians and family in this most difficult decision.

Defining Dying: The Terminal Stage of Life

If it is difficult to say when someone is dead, it is often impossible to say when he or she is dying. In some sense, the processes that will terminate in death may begin many, many years before we become aware of them. Sometimes the beginning of the terminal phase is clear: a physician informs a patient that he or she has a deadly disease. But often, death approaches, even late in life, without any obvious warning. Still, subtle changes do occur, even when the individual is unaware that death is imminent. Research shows that dying is accompanied by progressive cognitive and personality changes, sometimes noticeable only in retrospect.

In a classic study of these changes, Klaus Riegel reported intellectual decrement in the last years of life on standard intelligence tests like the Wechsler Adult Intelligence Scale. He found that those elderly subjects who scored very low died sooner than those who performed well. Riegel attributed this *terminal drop* to the physiological deterioration or damage ultimately leading to death. Terminal drop could be seen in people's performance several years before biological death, and it was of such magnitude that Riegel believed most or all of the age differences between young and old subjects in cross-sectional studies of intellectual performance might be due to the phenomenon (Riegel and Riegel, 1972; Riegel, 1971).

Other research has demonstrated that performance on learning and retention tests as well as time and spatial orientation deteriorate as a subject nears death. In the terminal phase, people also appear to be less emotionally complex, less introspective, and more docile and dependent.

BOX 12.3
A living will

TO MY FAMILY, MY PHYSICIAN, MY LAWYER, MY CLERGYMAN TO ANY
MEDICAL FACILITY IN WHOSE CARE I HAPPEN TO BE TO ANY INDIVIDUAL
WHO MAY BECOME RESPONSIBLE FOR MY HEALTH, WELFARE OR
AFFAIRS

Death is as much a reality as birth, growth, maturity and old age—it is the
one certainty of life. If the time comes when I,_____
can no longer take part in decisions for my own future, let this statement
stand as an expression of my wishes, while I am still of sound mind.

If the situation should arise in which there is no reasonable expectation of
my recovery from physical or mental disability, I request that I be allowed
to die and not be kept alive by artificial means or "heroic measures." I do
not fear death itself as much as the indignities of deterioration, dependence
and hopeless pain. I, therefore, ask that medication be mercifully
administered to me to alleviate suffering even though this may hasten the
moment of death.

This request is made after careful consideration. I hope you who care for
me will feel morally bound to follow its mandate. I recognize that this
appears to place a heavy responsibility upon you, but it is with the intention
of relieving you of such responsibility and of placing it upon myself in
accordance with my strong convictions, that this statement is made.

Signed _____

Date _____

Witness _____

Witness _____

Copies of this request have been
given to
                                    _____

                                    _____

                                    _____

                                    _____

SOURCE: Euthanasia Educational Council, New York.

Especially interesting is the observation made in one study that those subjects who were extremely ill but eventually recovered did not show the same deterioration as those who eventually died (Lieberman and Coplan, 1969).

Increased withdrawal in those near death as well as reduced attachment to people, groups, possessions, and ideas has also been noted. A number of studies emphasize the frequency of contemplation and reminiscence among older people in the terminal phase (Kalish, 1977; Kübler-Ross, 1969).

Without a doubt, however, the most popular description of psychological and social events during the terminal phase is the series of stages developed by Elizabeth Kübler-Ross in her famous book, *On Death and Dying* (1969).

Stages of Dying and the Acceptance of Death

In the course of her work at the University of Chicago teaching and research hospital, Elizabeth Kübler-Ross conducted clinical interviews with dying patients. Using these interviews, she outlined the characteristic course of emotional development that she saw among patients who made the best personal adjustments to their confrontations of death. The scheme includes five stages, now fairly well known—well enough known, in fact, to cause some problems for those who do not quite fit the pattern, especially if the people around the patient are committed to promoting acceptance of death. The five stages are (1) denial, (2) anger, (3) bargaining, (4) depression, and (5) acceptance.

DENIAL AND ISOLATION. Among most of the patients Kübler-Ross interviewed, initial reactions to news of their terminal conditions were dominated by shock and disbelief. Many felt a mistake had been made. Some sought a second opinion or shopped around for a more positive diagnosis. A few seemed to find assurance in the occult. Some tried "miracle cures." Eventually, however, most developed enough acceptance or belief to feel distressed and angry.

ANGER. In this stage, patients often experienced feelings of resentment, hostility, and envy. These feelings were frequently directed at members of the medical team, hospital staff, friends, and family. For some, death represented the ultimate frustration. Unable to finish any unfinished plans, to reach unreached goals, the patients experienced anger and aggression.

Once anger subsides, according to Kübler-Ross, bargaining becomes the dominant response.

BARGAINING.   Often dying people seem to be looking for a way out. Because no rational ways are available, irrational responses may emerge. They may try to make a deal with God, or the staff, or even with the disease. Kübler-Ross points out that such bargains are never kept, and if the patient outlives the bargain, a new one is struck.

DEPRESSION.   The next stage is characterized by grief. A dying person feels great loss and sorrow and may experience some sense of guilt and shame, just as one may when someone else dies. Kübler-Ross believes that if patients are allowed to express their grief, and communicate it to others, they will eventually come to accept the imminence of death and develop a sense of calm about it.

ACCEPTANCE.   In this final stage, people may become quite detached from the outside world, from the objects and people that were part of their lives. They achieve a peace of mind that is different from resignation; it is not characterized by despair or remorse, but by a sense of "rest before the long journey," by quiet expectation.

Kübler-Ross has done a great deal to humanize death and dying in the United States, but her work has sometimes been badly misrepresented. As she herself writes, if these five stages are interpreted as a series of invariant, universal steps to a mature death, that can do a good deal more harm than good to the dying patient (Kübler-Ross, 1974). Her recent work emphasizes individual differences and stresses the importance of discovering the patient's response pattern and accepting it. She points out that it is not the role of the medical staff or of the families to break down the defenses of dying patients and push them through the stages. Some patients, for example, continue to deny that they are going to die. It may be cruel and counterproductive to undermine hope that sustains them, however unrealistic that hope may seem to others.

Nonetheless, Kübler-Ross still thinks that passage through all five stages represents a classical, optimal pattern. A number of writers have taken issue with this position. Kübler-Ross does not offer the kind of systematic observation that most experimentally oriented researchers require, and there are several important alternative theories. One particularly thoughtful hypothesis emphasizes the recurrence of denial throughout the whole process of dying. From this perspective, dying involves a clustering of emotional responses that are constantly waxing and waning. Hope, disbelief, anger, bewilderment, and acceptance are all part of the emotional life of a terminally ill patient at any moment (Shneidman, 1973).

Systematic observation suggests a variety of other common emotional patterns. In one early study, only about one-quarter of the terminally ill showed acceptance and positive composure, whereas another quarter welcomed death only as an end to pain. This report emphasized the finding that many patients go on denying the possibility of death part of the time up to the very end, and that they derived some benefit from the denial. Life utterly without hope for the future is very difficult to acknowledge on a moment-to-moment basis (Hinton, 1967).

Furthermore, denial may have certain social functions as well. Denial may be necessary to forestall the withdrawal of friends and family and to promote the role enactments required for continuing medical treatment. Most research has demonstrated that as the patient approaches death, there is mutual withdrawal between the patient and his or her social circle. When terminally ill people become completely resigned to death, they abandon the "sick role." Sick people are exempted from the ordinary responsibilities of life, but they are expected to seek help and cooperation in curing their illness. When people are sick, it is assumed they will get well. It may be important to normal social relations for a dying patient to continue the sick role even when hope is gone in the mind of the medical care-giver (Beilin, 1982–83).

Another important point of view stresses individual differences during the final phase of life. Each person dies a different death. This hypothesis suggests that those who deal with dying patients should focus on individual needs and desires in order that patients may achieve an *appropriate death*. An appropriate death is one that fulfills the ideals and expectations of the patient, not the hospital staff. Patients must be supported in making their own decisions and finding the style best suited to the self (Weisman, 1972).

No universal or optimal series of stages is assumed by the concept of an appropriate death, but three general phases have been described: an acute phase, a chronic living-dying interval, and a terminal phase. The onset of the acute phase coincides with the patient's initial awareness that his or her condition may be terminal. The acute phase represents a crisis, accompanied by very high levels of anxiety. Denial, anger, and bargaining, as well as anxiety, are thought to be prominent during this first phase (Weisman, 1972; Pattison, 1977a).

As the patient adjusts to the idea of being gravely ill, anxiety gradually diminishes and the chronic living-dying phase begins, as illustrated in Figure 12.1. In this phase, the patient experiences fear of the unknown and

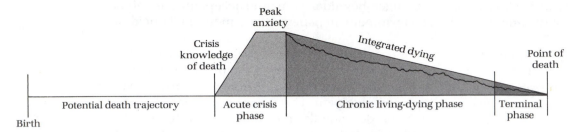

FIGURE 12.1
Terminal-stage anxiety

SOURCE: *Adapted from E. M. Pattison,* The Experience of Dying *(Englewood Cliffs, N.J.: Prentice-Hall, 1977), p. 44.*

fear of loneliness, anticipatory grief over the loss of friends, of body, of self-control, and of identity (Pattison, 1977a). It is also possible that anxiety and sorrow can be expected to alternate, even coexist, with hope, determination, and acceptance (Shneidman, 1973).

The terminal phase begins when the patient starts to withdraw from the people, objects, and events in the outside world. Although the patient may still experience a kaleidoscope of emotional states, as is true for all three phases, one kind of response may dominate a particular phase. Anxiety is most typical of the acute phase, grief is most characteristic of the chronic living-dying interval, and withdrawal dominates the terminal phase.

A final facet of this three-phase formulation requires an understanding of *dying trajectories*. A dying trajectory is a way of representing the most probable duration and shape of the dying process for an individual. Duration refers to the length of the dying process. Shape refers to whether the process can be expected to go steadily downhill, to include stable periods, periods of improvement, and so on. The following four basic trajectories have been described (Glaser and Strauss, 1967, 1968; Strauss and Glaser, 1970):

1. *Certain* death is expected at a known time (for example, the patient is given six months to live).

2. *Certain* death is expected, but the time is *unknown* (for example, the patient is told it could be six months or six years).

3. It is *uncertain* whether the patient will die and there is *a known* time when the question will be resolved (for example, if surgery is effective, the patient will recover).

4. It is *uncertain* whether the patient will die and there is *no known* time when the question will be resolved (for example, the patient has a chronic heart problem).

The ambiguity and uncertainty of the last two trajectories are thought to produce great anxiety. The acute phase is prolonged when there is uncertainty, and the final trajectory is believed to be the most difficult for any patient. Great ambiguity, as represented by the last trajectory, may produce dysfunctional behavior and hypochondriacal fixation on one's physical state. Adjustment is possible, however, when doctors are able to arrest or manage the disease. For example, individuals who wear pacemakers, especially the young, are able to cope successfully with the fourth trajectory (Pattison, 1977a).

In all, it appears that the terminal phase of life is no more easily characterized than any other stage of the life cycle. There seem to be levels and types of denial or acceptance, and these two processes can occur simultaneously. Furthermore, the patient can display *hope* even when it is clear that no cure can be found. Hope can be seen in someone who looks forward to seeing a new grandchild, or another birthday, or another spring. A patient may, for instance, plan for a vacation in Hawaii while rewriting a will, "just in case" (Saunders, 1981; Pattison, 1977b).

Furthermore, denial or acceptance may be very different experiences for different people. Robert Kastenbaum (1981b) points out that some people make energetic attempts to control the process, whereas others spend their energies trying to establish continuity between themselves and their survivors. In either case, there may be acceptance, or denial, or both. At other times, resistance may be mistaken for denial. Denial is fairly primitive, but resistance can be sophisticated and resourceful. The patient who resists death may deliberately attend to certain positive events because it seems inappropriate to dwell on dying or because there is still much to accomplish in the time remaining. Many dying people simply choose to leave their thoughts about dying unspoken, focusing on living instead.

We must learn to respect the desire to maintain a personal identity and independence through the final stage. These thoughts seemed well summarized by Claire Ryder and Diane Ross (1981) when they wrote that "the crux of dying with dignity is in retaining one's individuality, be that in acceptance or denial, anger or serenity" (p. 169).

The burden of helping a patient maintain independence and individuality most often falls on those least well-equipped to deal with the problems. Because most people die in institutions under the care of medical personnel, the task is all the more difficult. Like living, dying is strongly influenced by the environment, and the standardized, congregate, controlling atmosphere of the traditional hospital is not designed to facilitate dignity in the terminal phase.

Dying in a Hospital

A dying patient entering a hospital becomes a ward of the culture's *death system*—a "socio-physical network by which the relationship to mortality is mediated and expressed" (Kastenbaum, 1981a, p. 67). People are part of the system: doctors, nurses, clergy, funeral directors, florists, lawyers, even life insurance agents. Places are included too, from battlefields and cemeteries to mortuaries and churches, and, of course, hospitals. Nearly every elderly person dies in a hospital. Hospitals provide care for the terminally ill, and they are an important part of the system for disposal of a body. Knowledge of how to care for a corpse in the home has nearly vanished in the twentieth-century world.

The dying patient is not the only one who has difficulty adjusting to the institutional aspects of the death system, however. Doctors and nurses are trained to save lives, to fight death every inch of the way. For many of them, death represents defeat and personal failure. They find themselves frustrated, upset, even angry when a patient dies despite all of their best efforts. One study even reported that doctors are more fearful of death than most people (Feifel, 1965), and another demonstrated that nurses consider anxiety about death and dying more socially acceptable than other groups of subjects (Martin, 1982–83).

Anxiety and fear probably produce avoidant behaviors in medical care-givers. They may focus on paperwork or the maintenance of equipment and the administration of medication rather than the social and emotional needs of someone who is dying. Until recently, many patients were not even informed that they were dying. In the late 1960s and early 1970s, it was common practice to withhold information about a terminal condition altogether, or to tell a family member rather than the patient.

Such practices came under attack for a number of reasons, but especially because it became clear that most patients were at least partially aware that something was horribly wrong, and that no one wanted to discuss it. Dying people found themselves engaged in mutual pretense with the hospital staff, friends, and family. Although patient, staff, and family know that death is imminent, everyone continues to act as though nothing out of the ordinary is going on. Dangerous topics are avoided, and all the actors focus on minor complaints. If some difficult subject must be handled, no one is allowed to break down, and any slips or outbursts are scrupulously ignored (Glaser and Strauss, 1965).

Things have changed radically in recent years, however. By the mid-1970s most doctors reported feeling that their patients have an absolute right to know about their condition (Rea, Greenspoon and Spilka, 1975). A 1978 study provided information about the attitudes of physicians, nurses, chaplains, and a group of college students. Table 12.1 presents a summary.

Most recently, the debate over patients' rights has led to a related question: does the patient have the right to refuse to listen? Some patients will want to know and some will not. Some will want more details than others. Some can accept the truth, but won't want to discuss it. Others will ask the critical questions, or intimate that they already know the answers early on. Sometimes a patient may not be ready to hear the answer although the question slips out, forcing the care-giver to hedge or temporize. Some want to know more than can reliably be said about their diseases. Once the patient has a clear, simple explanation of the disease and its seriousness, and understands the treatment or kinds of management available, he or she is in a position to lead the way. The responsibility of the

TABLE 12.1
Summary of interview data on the disclosure of information to the terminally ill patient, 1978 (selected questions)

Questions	Percent responding "yes"			
	Physicians	Nurses	Chaplains	Students
1. If terminally ill patients request information, do they have an unqualified right to know the truth about their conditions?	87	86	79	81
2. As a general rule, the physician should:				
give complete information without waiting for the patient to ask	29	45	25	47
take the initiative in revealing the terminal condition, but then only answer specific questions	42	43	50	26
answer specific questions, but not take the initiative	27	11	21	18
answer patients' questions only to the extent the physician feels is appropriate	2	2	4	9
3. Should a doctor allow a patient to take pain medication even if it hastens death?	93	98	93	88
4. Do you support "passive euthanasia," that is using ordinary means of maintaining life but otherwise allowing nature to run its course?	91	100	96	87

SOURCE: R. G. Carey and E. J. Posavac, "Attitudes of Physicians on Disclosing Information to and Maintaining Life for Terminally Ill Patients," *Omega*, 9 (1978–79): 67–77.

caretaker or informant now lies in keeping in touch and making information available to the patient as needed (Hinton, 1976; Saunders, 1981).

Kübler-Ross (1974) describes the role of the medical staff and other helpers in terms of listening rather than talking. Once the basic facts are outlined, the patient needs a chance to share, to talk, to ventilate, even to scream. Helpers have only to be available and to remember that grief lasts a long time.

Still, it is very hard for personnel trained to fight death to be responsible for easing the way. Often, care-givers in hospitals grieve like members of the family. In fact, the level of stress among nurses in Intensive Care Units may be as high as the patient's. Furthermore, once a patient nears the end, the family may accept it and begin to withdraw. In this case, the care-givers become surrogate grievers. The family may be better prepared than the staff, who now see the family as unfeeling. The institutionalization of the dying seems to increase stress all round—for the dying person, for the care-giver, and for the family, who feel confused by the emotional responses of medical personnel (Fulton, 1981). These are just a few of the reasons why there has been such a rapid and positive acceptance of alternative care for the dying, either at home or in specially designed hospital facilities. Such facilities are often called *hospices.*

Hospices

The focus of concern in a hospice is shifted from the medical to the psychological, from the possibility of death to the quality of life. The efforts of hospice workers are directed at making the patient comfortable and peaceful, rather than delaying the moment of death. A hospice is something between a hospital and a home. Sometimes it is simply an organization within a hospital, the primary medical concerns of which are aimed not at treatment but at the restoration of normal daily functioning to the dying patient.

In an ordinary hospital, for example, pain medication is given only when a patient asks to be medicated. Moreover, patients are usually restricted in their activities and functions. Both of these procedures are designed to prolong biological life, but neither contributes much to the quality of psychological life. In a hospice, pain medication is given every two to four hours, before any pain occurs, and there is no maximum dose. Patients are given enough medication to free them from the fear of pain as well as the experience of it. Dimorphine, cocaine, and gin are recommended because the combination, known as a Brompton's Cocktail, leaves the patient alert as well as pain free. Patients are allowed complete freedom to come and go and to choose their activities and tasks. It is assumed that the *patient* knows what is best (Saunders, 1969).

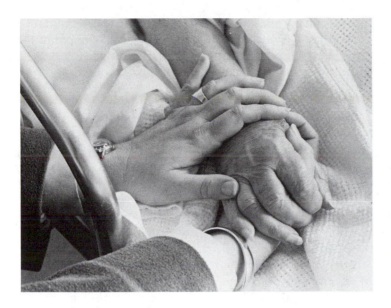

The role of the hospice staff is not defined in terms of doing for the patient, for much of the time there is nothing objective that can be done, but simply being with the patient.

The role of a hospice staff member is not seen in terms of doing for a patient (because often nothing objective can be done), but simply being with the patient. Patients are never treated as objects, even when they are unconscious. More attention is paid to appearance and to personal needs than to tests and medical procedures. Hospices usually provide enormous support for the family that wants to keep the patient at home all or most of the time.

Cicely Saunders (1976), a major figure in the hospice movement, contends that once patients are freed of pain and have regained their independence and dignity, few desire to end their lives before nature runs its full course, and there is little worry or depression. In fact, the environment Saunders envisions seems to come very close to providing the conditions for "appropriate death" (Weisman, 1972):

1. Patients must be maintained free of pain.

2. Emotional and social impoverishment must be kept to a minimum.

3. Patients must be supported in maintaining competent behavior.

4. Patients must be given opportunities to resolve conflicts and fulfill realistic wishes.

5. The patient must be able to seek or relinquish relationships and control.

A hospice is a place where an appropriate death is seen as an attainable goal and where everyone is devoted to the protection of the patient's autonomy and dignity. Often, however, a hospice is not a place at all. It is an organization within a hospital that provides support for the family that wishes to keep a dying person at home.

Dying at Home

For many decades now, the major trends in medical treatment have led away from home care. Procedures have become more and more sophisticated, specialized, and often bewildering. Once sophisticated medical treatment ceases to confer reasonable benefits, however, institutionally supported home care becomes an intriguing possibility. Hospice organizations are especially well equipped to provide both the medical information and the emotional support that is critical to family care. As we shall see, the family must cope with grief and bereavement at the same time they attempt to meet the medical and psychological needs of a terminally ill patient.

Some writers believe that many people fear death in modern societies because they fear institutionalization and the unreasonable prolongation of life. This kind of anxiety can be alleviated by home-based, hospice-supported care. Furthermore, home care may also ease the family's guilt and anxiety, especially when the anxiety is related to feelings of helplessness. On the other hand, the twenty-four-hour, seven-day-a-week care of a dying person is a tremendous physical and emotional burden. Hospice support enables the family to integrate home care in an existing life-style with minimal disruption. Hospice support also means that the family will be able to take a vacation from care once in a while, or have a regular day off (Buckingham, 1982–83).

A significant objective of the hospice movement is the reorganization of health insurance and Medicare so that families can maintain a terminally ill patient. It is extremely important to remember that pain is physical and emotional, but it can also be financial. Few insurance programs completely cover the costs of a catastrophic illness, and often the costs run to two and three times the median family income. Patients experience guilt over the expenses their families must bear. Older children may have to give up college or go to work in order to foot the bill. A homemaker may find herself job hunting. Dying at home is, obviously, much less expensive and can relieve some of the financial distress experienced by both patient and family (Ryder and Ross, 1981).

At the same time, as Kastenbaum (1981b) warns, "financial issues may warp our expectations and affect our ability to concentrate on the caring process itself and its adequate evaluation" (p. 205). Costs should not be the primary focus of the hospice movement or the central issue in family decisions. If they are, the emotional benefits derived from home care, such as the alleviation of guilt and anxiety, may not be forthcoming, and the family may be quite unable to deal with grief and bereavement either before or after death. One of the most positive effects of home care may be the opportunity to deal openly and honestly with the emotional loss of someone close.

Grief and Bereavement

Grief is an emotional response to a real loss, and we expect to grieve when someone close to us dies. Less universally recognized is the fact that grief can and does begin before the biological death of a terminally ill person. Kübler-Ross contends that the family and friends of a dying person often go on a classical journey through all the stages of dying—including shock, anger, bargaining, depression, and acceptance—when they learn of the patient's condition. She notes, also, that family, friends, and medical staff members generally lag behind the patient through each phase (Kübler-Ross, 1969, 1974).

Because family and friends progress more slowly, Kübler-Ross believes counseling the family of the terminally ill patient is quite important. Family members need help following the patient's emotional development. If the family is unable to face or discuss the patient's death, the patient may be unable to encounter death in an appropriate way.

If family members can catch up with the patient and share their feelings openly, Kübler-Ross believes the process of mourning will be eased. When people have a chance to complete their relationship with a dying person, to finish unfinished business, there is less remorse and guilt. Kübler-Ross refers to the anger, guilt, and self-recrimination bereaved family and friends often experience as *grief work*. She believes grief work is the most debilitating aspect of mourning and can be accomplished before the patient dies.

Even so, the family will grieve. Open awareness and counseling will help, but feelings of sadness and mourning are a natural part of bereavement, even when death comes as a relief from a long and difficult illness. Reactions vary in intensity, of course, depending on the age of the individual who dies, the importance or centrality of the relationship between a survivor and the deceased, the cause of death, the kind of care a survivor was able to provide, and so on.

In general, the death of an elderly person is less disruptive to the lives of survivors than the death of someone young, although there is some controversy over why this might be so. On one hand, since the culture places less value on the elderly, their deaths may seem less tragic. On the other hand, older people are said to have "lived full lives," and death at the end of the life cycle may simply seem part of the changing of the seasons rather than a cause for alarm. The death of an older person does have grave implications for the surviving spouse, however. Still, even in widowhood, older people seem to make better adjustments than do the young (Parkes, 1972).

Sudden or unexpected death is associated with more intense bereavement than death following an extended chronic living-dying phase. Sudden death deprives the survivors of an opportunity to complete their relationship with a dying person. Furthermore, friends and family are often relieved when someone dies after a prolonged, debilitating illness. Of all the possible kinds of death, suicide is probably the most disruptive for friends and family. Intense feelings of distress, failure, and guilt haunt the survivors of someone who commits a suicide (Kalish, 1977).

The intensity of grief is also related to the nature of the relationship between the survivor and the deceased. Obviously, the death of a great aunt one scarcely knew will be experienced as less difficult than the loss of a father or mother. The death of a spouse is usually more disruptive than the death of an aged parent. The loss of a child triggers extremely intense grief, especially if the parents have been deeply invested in the parental roles. Most difficult of all, perhaps, is the loss of a parent in a child's early years, an event with serious implications for long-term psychological development (Kastenbaum and Aisenberg, 1972).

Edwin Shneidman (1976) contends that the death of a very significant person can be viewed as a natural disaster, like an earthquake or a devastating flood. Emotional dullness, depression, a sense of worthlessness, sleeplessness, amnesia, and a general psychic numbing are common responses. Shneidman even suggests that the shock that accompanies the sudden death of a close person resembles a kind of partial death.

Emotions are difficult to define or describe, but common reactions to bereavement include misery, despair, apathy, and waves of yearning that sometimes produce physical sensations like tightness and choking. Physical distress may be experienced every twenty minutes at first, even when the death was long expected. Bereaved people often show agitation and restlessness or self-doubt, anger, shame, and guilt. The anger may be directed at others, including medical staff, no matter how helpful and competent they have been. Anger may even be directed at the self, regardless of how much the survivor was able to do for the dying person (Hinton, 1967; Kalish, 1977).

Intense grief can be both emotionally and physically incapacitating, and bereavement is associated with mortality rates that are higher than average. It has been suggested that bereaved people should be treated as though they were physically ill. In Chapter 10, we discussed the association between bereavement and heart disease. Other data (Fredrick, 1976–77) show a relationship between infectious disease or cancer and bereavement. The latter report shows that grief may be characterized by the "oversecretion" of very powerful hormones, known as the corticosteroids, for extended periods. Figure 12.2 presents the mortality rates for one group of bereaved people. Figure 12.3 contains data on the secretion of corticosteroids. The researchers who did this work feel that grief may be considered a disease process if it can be shown that the secretion of corticosteroids suppress the body's immune mechanisms (Fredrick, 1976–77).

Obviously, survivors need emotional support from others, especially following a sudden death. Typically, however, there is little organized help available to the bereaved, and medical treatment is usually limited to

"A man's dying is more the survivors' affair than his own." Thomas Mann

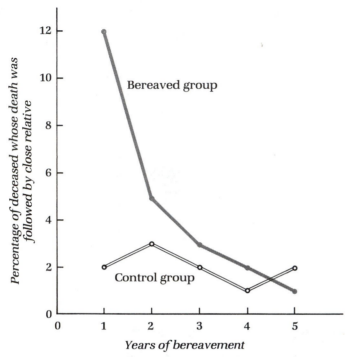

FIGURE 12.2
Mortality of the bereaved

SOURCE: *W. D. Rees and S. G. Lutkins, "The Mortality of the Bereaved,"* British Medical Journal, 4 (1976): 13–16.

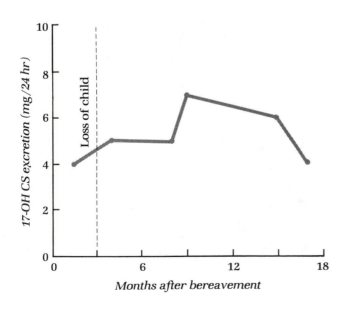

FIGURE 12.3
Corticosteroid levels following bereavement

SOURCE: *M. A. Hofer, C. T. Wolff, S. B. Friedman, and J. W. Mason, "A Psychoendocrine Study of Bereavement,"* Psychosomatic Medicine, 34 (1972): 492–504.

the use of sedation. Kübler-Ross argues that the bereaved should never be sedated. Bereaved people need to express their feelings and should not bottle them up or try to sleep them off, especially when their reactions are intense. They need counseling and follow-up care. It might even help if hospitals had "screaming rooms" where people could say or do whatever they require to express their grief. Sometimes this expression may include or even depend upon the opportunity to see the body, to touch or talk to the deceased. Such responses are not morbid or unusual and probably help the survivor overcome the initial denial and disbelief (Kübler-Ross, 1974).

The opportunity to express negative feelings and sympathy is usually enough for those who are bereaved. But some people may require the help of professionals. Edwin Shneidman has proposed the development of specialized *postvention* programs for those who experience very intense or prolonged grief. Postvention includes a variety of therapeutic techniques, from simple talk and reassurance to interpretation, gentle confrontation, and attempts to have the patient experience intense feelings. Shneidman believes it is essential for survivors to eventually face their negative feelings, including anger, shame, and guilt. He doesn't recommend immediate postvention, but thinks it should begin within the first three days. Simple forms of postvention ought to be viewed as a part of the total care of the dying patient (Shneidman, 1976).

Professional treatment is available to a small number of those who are bereaved, but most manage with very little organized help and often with little continuing support from friends and family. We are seldom comfortable with someone who is grieving. We don't know what to do or say. We feel awkward and we may be tempted to avoid doing or saying anything for fear of doing or saying the wrong thing. We leave people to bury their own. The participation of outsiders is usually limited to attending the funeral, sending a card to the family, and making a contribution to the cancer society or the heart fund. The most dependable form of social support for the bereaved seems to come from the American funeral industry, and there is much controversy about the role and the practices of this particular segment of the country's business and service community.

Mourning customs serve many social and psychological functions. They allow bereaved people some ritual emotional expressions and give the friends and acquaintances of the deceased some acceptable, prescribed form of participation in the family's sorrow. Some believe such customs and rituals as the viewing of the body, the funeral service, and even the obituary in the local paper are exceedingly important. They help make the death real and acceptable for the bereaved. They give people a sense of structure, and they serve as a way to muster social support for those most affected by the death.

Yet the American way of death has been roundly criticized for nearly every conceivable reason. Some argue that American customs and funerals are too simple; others say they are too elaborate. In the center of this controversy is the bereaved family, trying to make what seem like overwhelming decisions and to do what is decent and right in the eyes of the culture.

THE EXPANDED CONTEXT: RITUAL, CUSTOM, AND THE CYCLE OF GENERATIONS

Funerals

There are two very vocal, competing schools of thought about American funerals and mourning rituals. On the one hand, it has been said that American customs are too simple, too informal. Mourning dress is not required; survivors need not cancel their social engagements; there is no prescribed period of bereavement. Such complete absence of formal ritual is thought by some to produce maladaptive responses in the bereaved (Gorer, 1965).

On the other hand, there are those who argue that American funerals are too expensive and too elaborate, even gruesomely so. Critics contend that the whole notion of the open-casket funeral is unnecessarily costly and upsetting. Embalming and the use of cosmetics are criticized as ridiculous, even morbid. The purchase of an expensive casket is similarly described, and it is suggested that funeral arrangements be as simple and frugal as possible (Baird, 1976; Mitford, 1963).

Criticism of the American funeral industry has been derived from historical analysis, from cross-cultural comparison, and from estimates of the average cost of mortuary services. Very little in the way of systematic research has been done on the psychological aspects or functions of a funeral. Journalistic exposés generally focus on ills and abuses in the delivery of mortuary services rather than on the needs and reactions of the bereaved.

What are the functions of a funeral or a mortuary service? The most vocal critics believe the funeral industry is almost entirely self-serving, reflecting the economic system and exploiting generally negative attitudes toward death and dying. In her now famous book *The American Way of Death*, Jessica Mitford (1963) suggested that American funeral practices emphasize the physical rather than the spiritual aspects of death in order to sell such expensive items as elaborately sealed metal caskets and the ser-

There are those who argue that death is the ultimate commercial transaction, the last rite of the American consumer.

vices of embalmers and cosmeticians. She saw the funeral industry primarily as a profit-oriented business that trades on the inability of Americans to face death or see it as a natural part of the life cycle.

Mitford also pointed out that embalming and the use of cosmetics have been practiced only in ancient Egypt and twentieth-century America and that the use of metal caskets is almost unknown in other parts of the world. To Mitford, these practices seemed senseless. She believed that people buy such items because they fulfill an irrational desire to preserve the body. In fact, caskets and embalming don't help preserve the body and even if they were effective, they would seem only to prolong or to reinforce the fantasy that the deceased hasn't really died, but has only "gone away," as at least one commercial sympathy card put it.

Funeral directors justify the use of embalming and cosmetics as part of creating a beautiful picture for the survivors to remember. But survivors find these memory pictures unreal and unacceptable and often, critics note, the only real function they serve is to increase the cost of mortuary service. The practice of selling funeral and mortuary services or cemetery lots to people before they need them has also been taken to task on financial grounds, since dwindling supplies increase the price of remaining burial plots. Even memorial societies that guarantee simple, cheap, decent burials have not escaped scrutiny. Many young people join such organizations, paying substantial entry fees that are then used for years by these organizations at no interest charge (Baird, 1976).

An analysis by Consumer's Union (1981), however, outlines how some memorial association members benefit through substantially lower prices on conventional funeral arrangements if they choose an association carefully. There are several different types of societies and associations. Societies, like those discussed above, provide burial arrangements per se. Associations never actually provide services; they simply refer their members to mortuaries with which they have arranged, formally or informally, for a discount on conventional funeral needs. Membership usually costs around $25 per family member. In the best arrangement, the association enters into a formal contract with a local undertaker who offers low prices to members in return for a volume of reliable business. Total costs (even for burial instead of cremation) usually average about $500 for members of contract associations.

Other arrangements are less reliable, but probably worth investigating. In a *cooperating assocation*, the members have a verbal agreement with a local undertaker. Sometimes the relationship with that individual deteriorates, however, and the association can no longer guarantee its members a discount. The *advisory association* does not refer its members to any particular undertaker, usually because undertakers in the area are uninterested in cooperating. It does offer advice and information, however, that can be useful to a family in making funeral arrangements before the need arises. This is the main goal of all such associations: education and the discussion of funeral and burial plans before the family is under the stress of a recent death.

The average costs of cremation and funeral services at a conventional mortuary and cemetery are about $1,800, although it is not atypical for a family to spend $3,000 or $4,000 dollars on these last rites, especially when the body is interred in the ground. This means that, for many families, a funeral may well be the third or fourth most expensive purchase they ever make. Although many argue that such expense is unnecessary, it is important to note that average figures do not really give one enough information, because less expensive services are available. Moreover, middle-class families today can expect to buy many items that fall in the same price range, from a used car for a teenaged child to orthodontia. Weddings (for the two average children of an average family) can be a lot more expensive.

Nonetheless, alternative funeral arrangements not only are available, they are becoming more popular. These services tend to stress the gathering of friends and family and focus on feelings and personal histories rather than on the trappings of the standard funeral service with its elegant casket and expensive floral arrangements. In one exploratory study, the researchers examined the effect of such an alternative funeral on the family and on the congregation that participated. Keeping in mind that the people interviewed were all members of a church attended by the deceased, the authors pointed out some of the positive and negative aspects of one alternative plan. In this particular case, the deceased was buried on his own land in a casket the family made. A memorial service was held in the church the next day. Seventy percent of the people in the congregation favored the alternative, and most noted that they felt it increased the significance of the funeral. Of interest, however, is the finding that many of those who favored the alternative plan also thought that the burial of the body prior to the service was not a particularly helpful idea. Many people apparently feel the need for the presence of a deceased person. Everyone agreed that the alternative plan offered an important sense of personal involvement in the planning of the service and insured the availability of the congregation as a source of emotional support for the family (Bergen and Williams, 1981–82).

One of the more interesting questions raised by this line of inquiry involves what might be pared from the average funeral and burial without sacrificing its function for the family. For instance, Elizabeth Kübler-Ross has argued that survivors ought to view the deceased. Seeing is believing, or so the saying goes; and for some bereaved people, seeing the body helps prevent long-term denial and promotes acceptance. One recent investigation concludes that the more "difficult" the death is for the family and close survivors to accept, the more importance they are likely to attribute to the funeral (Swanson and Bennett, 1982–83).

This study also offers a preliminary analysis of how different aspects of the conventional funeral and burial serve the survivors. The researchers divided survivors into two groups, those who considered themselves "close" to the deceased, and those who considered themselves "very close." They surveyed both groups about the following seven common funeral practices: (1) the presence of friends at the service; (2) the presence of family; (3) personal references to the deceased at the funeral; (4) an open casket; (5) the giving and receiving of gifts; (6) the purchase of flowers; and (7) being at the burial site.

Of the "very close" group, 75 to 87 percent perceived all of these seven practices as helpful. What is especially interesting is the difference in the perception of some practices by the group who described themselves as "close" versus "very close." Less than one-half of the close group saw any of the practices as helpful. This group was also much more likely to be concerned about the long-term effects of funeral costs on the quality of family life, and the open-casket funeral and presence at the grave site were not perceived as helpful by people in the close group. In all probability, the function of a funeral is not the same for everyone. For those who were most closely related to the deceased, the funeral may be part of the process of realization and acceptance. For those who are less close, seeing and comforting the most bereaved survivors may be the point of the funeral. Therefore, the presence of the deceased may have little positive value.

When the presence of the deceased is important, it may mean embalming, especially if the family is scattered throughout the country and time is required for everyone to gather. For many reared in the tradition of the open casket, the body is convincing evidence of death and the desire to view it is not gruesome or morbid. One bereaved woman, affected by the current literature on funeral practices, ordered the casket closed during the funeral service of an aunt with whom she had lived. She later felt the closed casket had been more secretive and morbid than an opened one. She worried that she had snubbed her aunt by refusing to look at her (Stevens-Long, 1978).

The important point here is that general pronouncements about what is or is not morbid or unnecessary appear unwise. It is the survivors who must decide what will or will not meet their needs. Sometimes what you are used to is what you need, no matter what current customs or criticisms dictate. People often find great comfort in conventional, traditional procedures and practices, especially in times of stress; whether the procedures make much sense (either rational or economic) makes little difference. This is certainly an area in which much more objective evidence, based on much larger and more varied samples, is required before general changes can be recommended with much confidence.

For the moment, the dissemination of realistic and complete information about the decisions and costs of funeral and mortuary services may be the most sensible step toward the modification or tailoring of current customs. Whether or not one decides to purchase burial property or to plan a funeral service, whether one is young or old, a visit to a mortuary and cemetery can be an enlightening experience. A pre-need visit to Forest Lawn at Glendale, California, serves as an example (Stevens-Long, 1978).

Forest Lawn is a popular, successful business. Over two hundred thousand people are interred at Forest Lawn in Glendale, which is the smallest of the three Forest Lawn mortuary and cemetery establishments in southern California. It has been written that Forest Lawn "stands squarely in the main line of American funeral ritual," emphasizing the traditional Christian symbols—including religious statuary and stained glass—while deemphasizing individual monuments, such as costly and elaborate tombstones (Pattison, undated).

Especially relevant is a series of radio advertisements by Forest Lawn. The campaign is built on personal testimonials and encourages people to comparison shop before deciding on a cemetery and mortuary. Robert Wheeler, director of community affairs for Forest Lawn, suggests that the major reason people overspend is that they do not make plans, arrangements, and decisions before a death occurs, but wait until the last moment when emotional distress may overwhelm common sense (Stevens-Long, 1978).

Box 12.4 presents a list of the basic decisions that must be made in planning a funeral service. A common response to such a list is, "It doesn't matter anyway; let's figure it out when the time comes." This is precisely the pattern that leads to distress and emotional overspending after a death, when survivors try to second guess the deceased. A second likely response is, "What do I really want?" In this phase, people often ignore the needs and desires of the survivors, leaving them torn later on between their needs and the instructions of the deceased. A final stage involves the question, "What would be most appropriate for my family and friends?" as well as "What makes sense for me?" Funeral and burial decisions ought to be made by families together, if possible. If not, certainly the survivors should be considered. Let's suppose, for example, that you decide you want to be cremated and have your ashes scattered. You might want to consider the idea that interment in the ground, mausoleum, or cremation vessel is concrete evidence of finality, sometimes an important point for survivors (Pattison, undated).

In any event, the goal is to provide a level of ritual appropriate to family and friends while preventing the purchase of costly and unnecessary items and services simply because no one knows what to do. Box 12.5 presents a list of minimum prices provided by Forest Lawn, Glendale, and might be useful in understanding the financial implications of various decisions. Notice that a simple cremation without funeral services can be obtained for $695, whereas a basic funeral service and burial total about $1,100, including the burial plot but excluding flowers.

Even when planning exists, however, it may be difficult to protect survivors from the impulse to overspend. Funeral expenditures have become a kind of secular ritual, serving as evidence of the concern and decency of the survivors (Pine and Phillips, 1970). The responses of survivors in industrial societies organized around the nuclear family may be especially intense. Individual deaths are *less* important to the culture as a whole in the complex society, and so the customs and rituals surrounding death and dying are deemphasized at the psychological expense of the bereaved.

In any event, as the people at Forest Lawn are quick to point out, things do change in the funeral industry, but only very slowly, which seems as it should be at this point. We have little systematic knowledge

BOX 12.4
Some important decisions about funerals, burials, and cremations

1. Which mortuary and cemetery are most appropriate?

   Considerations: Cost, distance, family mobility patterns, philosophy and training of the service personnel, range of services available.

2. What kind of funeral is most appropriate for the survivors?

   Considerations: Open or closed casket versus memorial services before or after interment, degree of formality, use of eulogy or personal statement.

3. Who should officiate?

   Considerations: Denomination of officiant, officiant's knowledge of deceased and family, designation of individual if officiant to be nonreligious.

4. Where should the funeral take place?

   Considerations: Choice of a specific church, within the mortuary-cemetery complex or in a traditional place of worship, any special nontraditional preferences such as services in the home or outdoors.

5. What kind of creative or artistic works might be used at the funeral or memorial service?

   Considerations: Choice of instruments and/or singers, type of musical composition, use of special poetry or prose selections, use of visual art.

6. What kind of interment seems appropriate and where shall it take place?

   Considerations: Cremation versus burial, scattering of ashes versus interment in the ground or in cremation urn, location of cemetery property, costs.

7. What arrangements should be made with regard to the body?

   Considerations: Type and cost of casket for burial or cremation, type and cost of sectional concrete box for grave, clothing and disposition of jewelry that is ordinarily worn, use of religious symbols (rosary, Bible), use of a slumber or viewing room prior to funeral.

8. What exchanges between family and friends seem most appropriate?

   Considerations: Use of flowers, suggestions for contributions to charity, special wishes with regard to cards or memorial notices.

BOX 12.5
Minimum prices for various funeral purchases and mortuary services at
Forest Lawn Cemetery, August 1983

BURIAL
Property:
   Glendale: $295
   Hollywood Hills: $245
   Covina Hills: $245

Endowment care (includes
maintenance of streets, art work,
grounds and burial property):
   Glendale: $45
   Hollywood Hills: $34

Sectional concrete box: $125

Interment and recording (includes
opening and closing grave, use of
greens, setting up chairs,
replacements of grass, record-
keeping): $255

Casket: $165 and up, plus sales tax

CREMATION
Niche:
   Glendale: $120
   Hollywood Hills: $90

Endowment care:
   Glendale $20

Cremation casket (cardboard): $29

Scattering of ashes: $40

Funeral casket: $165 and up (replaces
cremation casket for casket-present
funeral)

MORTUARY AND FUNERAL COSTS
Mortuary services only (includes the call to pick up the body, the disposition
of the body, and record-keeping): $535

Mortuary services and funeral services (includes the first call, disposition of
the body, record-keeping, embalming, the use of a slumber room, church
attendants, and use of any Forest Lawn church, hearse rental, funeral
direction and counselor services, an organist, valet services, transportation
of the flowers, direction of the procession): $775

Total with funeral (minimum): $1,700 (burial) $1,100 (cremation)
Total without funeral (minimum): $1,460 (burial) $695 (cremation)

about the importance or effect of any particular practice. And so it seems most sensible to counsel that people begin to think about what they want and about the needs of their families and friends, uninfluenced (if possible) by the bountiful rhetoric on the subject.

Renewal and Recovery

In describing the history of grief and mourning, Philippe Ariès (1981) argues that the prohibition of mourning in the twentieth century may well be an overreaction to the elaborate demonstration of grief that characterized the nineteenth century. He also believes that grief and mourning are not necessarily innate responses to the loss of someone close, but may be socialized to some extent. He has pointed out, for example, that in at least one preindustrial culture, women mourn for their fathers and brothers, but seem to experience little sense of loss at the death of a spouse.

In Western cultures, however, and especially in the United States, the death of a spouse is experienced as an extremely stressful event. In fact, most people consider it the most stressful event of the average life history (see the Holmes and Rahe stress survey in Chapter 7). Because the nuclear family is often very close and may be isolated from an extended emotional and social network of close relationships, the death of a member is that much more traumatic. It is not at all unusual for a bereaved person to experience intense grief reactions in the first year of mourning. Although most survivors report a tapering off of the reaction after six months or so, strong anniversary reactions are not uncommon. Sometimes survivors must live through the kaleidoscope of the year's events—the changing of the seasons, the Fourth of July, Christmas, or Passover—before grief really abates. Each new instance of a familiar event brings fresh memories and a renewed sense of loss (Lifton and Olson, 1974; Kalish, 1977; Kastenbaum, 1981a).

Even after one year, there may be continuing grief among the elderly survivors of a marriage. Although follow-up visits from family, clergy, physicians, and friends can make a difference, those who experience extreme grief in the first few weeks often remain poorly adjusted at one year (Carey, 1979). Kastenbaum (1981a) believes that long-lived people are especially vulnerable to extreme grief reactions, not because they are more seriously affected by a particular loss, but because they so often experience multiple losses in short periods. The death of a dear friend may be closely followed by the death of a sibling and then loss of the spouse. Before the individual can work through one loss, another arrives bringing with it what Kastenbaum calls *bereavement overload*.

In a society which is reluctant to stop for death, family and friends often become impatient with someone who appears to be in perpetual mourning. It is not surprising, then, that the best predictor of recovery, like so many other of life's adjustments, is not the relationship between survivor and deceased, but the personality of the survivor (Saunders, 1976). The theme of continuity in personal development recurs consistently in the literature on old age. People die as they lived, and they survive bereavement in much the same way that they have survived life's other difficult transitions.

In one sense, the recovery of the survivor signals the last stage of death and dying. Social death occurs only when all the institutional, cultural, and personal processes associated with death have run their course. Throughout the twentieth century in the United States, the death system has encouraged a swift, and sometimes premature, social death. In the process, the significance of death and dying for the living has been obscured, and it may be that the search for new concepts and images of death should begin with a look at the processes of social death.

If Americans are to face death and dying with equanimity, it can not be viewed as an abomination or a defeat, but must be seen as a meaningful and valuable addition to life and to living. Erikson believed that the mark of integrity was the acceptance of one's own death as a natural and fit culmination of a completed existence. He also argued that basic trust depended upon the development of meaning and the communication of integrity to the next generation (Erikson, 1963).

It is in the process of dying and in the rituals of death that one is given the last opportunity for the expression of integrity. Our common belief is that death is deplorable, evil, and unnecessary. Many psychologists and sociologists fear that full knowledge of one's terminal condition may trigger a suicidal state or, at the very least, a severe depression accelerating an impending death (Weisman, 1972).

Our review suggests that none of these beliefs stands close scrutiny. People do often die with equanimity and grace. The terminal stage of life has its own merits, styles, and forms of experience, experience sometimes not readily available at other points in our lives.

Although the certainty of death creates fear of one kind, it undoubtedly reduces another kind. We need no longer fear life once it is clear that we are dying. Dying offers one an opportunity for courage, audacity, determination, humor, and, perhaps above all, for the communication of personal meaning. The special merits of the terminal phase of life are most readily available, of course, to the elderly, to those who have lived out their full life spans and have the opportunity to look back, to review, and to achieve a sense of completion. The literature seems to bear out this prediction. Older people are judged more accepting of death than are the young, at times even welcoming it and often considering it more appropriate than continued living. Some even express a sense of adventure and fascination about dying and death (Bromley, 1974; Nettler, 1971; Marshall, 1975).

There are many styles and patterns of dying. Some people are completely aware of their own dying; others are aware but totally unable to accept their fates, expressing only distress and anxiety. Some are unable to speak of death at all. Not all people die with acceptance and peace, nor should they. Strength and beauty can be communicated even in denial, as Dylan Thomas beautifully illustrated in this poem to his dying father:

> Do not go gentle into that good night,
> Old age should burn and rave at close of day;
> Rage, rage against the dying of the light.
>
> Though wise men at their end know dark is right,
> Because their words had forked no lightning they
> Do not go gentle into that good night.
>
> Good men, the last wave by, crying how bright
> Their frail deeds might have danced in a green bay,
> Rage, rage against the dying of the light.
>
> Wild men who caught and sang the sun in flight,
> And learn, too late, they grieved it on its way,
> Do not go gentle into that good night.
>
> Grave men, near death, who see with blinding sight
> Blind eyes could blaze like meteors and be gay,
> Rage, rage against the dying of the light.
>
> And you, my father, there on the sad height,
> Curse, bless, me now with your fierce tears, I pray.
> Do not go gentle into that good night,
> Rage, rage against the dying of the light.

All dying people probably experience stress and anxiety, and denial most often alternates or even occurs simultaneously with acceptance throughout the chronic living-dying and terminal phases. Although denial is sometimes considered a primitive coping mechanism, it does not exclude the use of more mature behaviors like humor and the redirection of one's energy or anxiety to productive, creative work—sublimation (Pattison, 1977b).

Finally, the existentialists point out that our encounters with dying and death lead us to reassess our lives, to reassess our values, and that they create a sense of urgency in fulfilling our own plans and dreams. Contact with the dying can actually serve as a source of personal courage for the survivor, as a wellspring for action, decisiveness, and motivation, propelling one toward a more meaningful, integrated existence (Kastenbaum, 1965).

Dying can free one to be oneself, to grow and develop, to be creative in a way not possible when one's perspectives are bounded by the ordinary sense of risk that accompanies daily life. Encounter with the dying can help us integrate the experience of death and lend meaning to life rather than rob life of its meaning. The dying have much to offer the living.

SUMMARY

This chapter begins with a general discussion of the meanings of death and dying in the course of human development. Death has been defined as a biological event, a rite of passage, an extinction that can never be really understood, although we have concepts and beliefs about it that influence our behavior. Dying, in contrast, can be understood as the terminal stage of life. The terminal stage is that period during which the individual has a persistent awareness of the prospect of death in later life.

Two basic views about the role of death in development were presented in this chapter. The first might be labeled the existential view. Existential philosophers and psychologists have argued that the fear of death is a universal human experience. Strong belief systems are fostered and maintained by this universal fear, and these systems allow people to find a sense of personal meaning in life and to encounter death with equanimity. Without a strong belief in some form of immortality, the existentialists argue, people will deny the reality of death. From the existential view, this is an unfortunate state of affairs, because encounter with our own mortality lends an intensity and decisive quality to our lives.

The other point of view suggests that the fear of death is not a primal experience, but a learned anxiety. Experimental data indicate that many people do not experience any conscious fear of death most of the time. In fact, many people seem to believe in a kind of generational or social immortality. Moreover, a fear of death is not strongly related to the strength of one's belief system. Cross-cultural data have been mustered to demonstrate that in some societies people generally demonstrate little or no fear of death, despite the lack of a strong belief in any form of immortality.

In almost every research area of interest to those who study dying and death, there is little agreement in the evidence or even in the basic definitions researchers use. An important illustration is provided by the work on the biological definition of death. The medical-legal problems of defining death have become hopelessly intertwined with the difficulties of defining psychological death. And controversy continues over such issues as the importance of total brain death versus death of the neocortex.

If death is difficult to define, dying is even more elusive. For most people, the medical predictions made by physicians mark the onset of the terminal stage. Research shows, however, that cognitive changes and personality changes are apparent in those subjects near death, whereas these changes cannot be seen in gravely ill subjects who survive or even in those who are thought to be terminally ill but eventually recover. These cognitive and personality precitors are part of the phenomenon known as terminal drop.

The best known personality changes associated with dying are those outlined by Elizabeth Kübler-Ross in her five-stage hypothesis about emotional development in the terminal part of the life span. Her stages include denial and isolation followed by anger, bargaining, depression, and finally by a peaceful acceptance of death characterized by a sense of calm and quiet expectation. In recent years, Kübler-Ross has emphasized individual differences in progress through these stages. She still believes her original scheme represents an optimal pattern of emotional adjustment, however.

A number of other writers have contended that it is premature to talk about an optimal death. Many have observed that in even the best adjusted terminally ill patients, denial may alternate with acceptance or even seem to be present with acceptance throughout the terminal stage.

One popular alternative construction of the terminal phase offers the notion of an appropriate death, one that fulfills the needs and expectations of the patient rather than the attendant medical staff. This construction also involves the conceptualization of the terminal stage in three phases: acute, chronic living-dying, and terminal. Although one kind of emotional response may appear most dominant in each of these phases, the patient may also exhibit a wide range of feelings throughout the whole dying process. The intensity of each phase and the probability of adjustment is thought to be related to the patient's individual dying trajectory. Trajectories include estimates of the duration of the dying process and the extent to which the patient may be expected to experience periods of stability or even recovery. Ambiguous or uncertain trajectories are thought to be associated with greater levels of anxiety.

Kübler-Ross's construction of the terminal phase and the concept of appropriate death both strongly suggest that the medical worker or helper should not attempt to orchestrate a patient's pattern of adjustment, but simply to be available as a source of information and support. The issues surrounding information and support from medical personnel have been of great interest for some years. This concern has generated changes in the attitudes and perhaps the behaviors of some of those to whom the care of the dying is assigned. Survey research suggests dramatic changes in the attitudes of physicians, nurses, and clergy about the disclosure of information to a patient about his or her terminal condition. The inability or unwillingness of medical personnel to disclose such information in the past is thought to have generated elaborate and perhaps destructive behaviors.

It is now generally agreed that the patient must be given a simple and honest description of the seriousness of a terminal condition and the medical treatments and management available. It is also thought that counseling should be provided for both the terminally ill patient and the affected family. It seems unlikely, however, that traditional hospital settings and medical personnel can ever offer an optimal milieu for the care of dying patients. In recent years there has been much interest in alternative settings, and hospices in particular have received much attention.

A hospice is something between a hospital and a home, an environment specifically designed to care for those who are dying. The focus at a hospice is on making the patient as comfortable and peaceful as possible, and on the restoration of freedom and function rather than on the prolongation of life. It may well be that a hospice is best able to provide the conditions thought necessary for an appropriate death. Hospice staff members also provide support for families who wish to keep dying patients at home, an important alternative. These kinds of alternative solutions to the problems of terminally ill patients deserve much closer and more systematic investigation.

The need for closer and more systematic investigation is also clear in the present literature on grief and bereavement. There seems to be agreement that grief is experienced very intensely in a modern, bureaucratic society—indeed, that it may even be considered a disease process because it is associated with higher than average mortality rates. But there is little agreement about the kinds of practices and societal support systems that ought to be available to the bereaved.

Programs of professional counseling have been proposed, but these are not likely to be available to all of those who are bereaved. Social customs and rituals are the forms of postvention most readily available and acceptable to most grieving people. Yet the rituals and customs made available by the culture have been under heavy attack in recent years.

Funerals are criticized as expensive, gruesome, and morbid. In particular, the practices of embalming the body and the purchase of expensive caskets have been attacked. At the same time, some writers have suggested that the mourning customs we have are not elaborate or formal enough to serve the needs of the bereaved. The viewing of the body and the gathering of the family at a funeral service, as well as interment in the ground or vessel, are defended by those who believe that funerals and mourning rituals are an important source of structure and support for those experiencing the loss of a close relationship.

As a society we are beginning to accept dying and death and to deal with these significant, if also mysterious and frightening, aspects of life.

"The more complete one's life is, the more . . . one's creative ca-
pacities are fulfilled, the less one fears death. . . . People are not
afraid of death per se, but of the incompleteness of their lives."
Lisl Marburg Goodman

One critical step in this process must be the dissemination of objective and complete information about the costs of funerals and the decisions that must be made when someone dies. Moreover, people must be encouraged to make such decisions well in advance of their own deaths, in consultation with those who will be most affected. This kind of reflection by those who are not near death can help in the search for new concepts and images of death.

We must learn not to view dying and death, funerals and mourning, as unnecessary or valueless abominations. Each dying person has his or her own style, and the terminal stage merits and offers opportunity for the experience and expression of some of the most important aspects of humanity. Courage, audacity, determination, and humor are all possible when we are closer to the experience of our own mortality. Finally, it is in the terminal stage of life that one is given the last opportunity for the creation of personal meaning, for the experience of one's life as complete, for the communication of integrity to those we leave behind.

Perspectives

The Future and the Later Stages of Life

It may be that over the next few decades, we will see some significant increases in the length of the average human life span. Certainly, there are those who believe that even with the incomplete knowledge available at this point in history, some strides can be made to increase longevity. Popular books, for example, recommend a variety of strategies, from extensive diet changes that include fasting to the ingestion of vitamins, minerals, and amino acids. We should note, however, that we do not yet have any convincing evidence from human studies for any of these recommendations. At the moment, the most credible, if rather conservative, prediction does not call for life spans of 100 or 120 years, but rather for more and more individuals to live past the age of 75 and for them to be healthier and function more fully throughout all of those final years.

In the most likely case, the number of infant deaths will decline and the number of acute and chronic diseases in the later years will decline as well, creating a "rectangularization of the survival curve" (Fries and Crapo, 1981). Rectangularization means that nearly all individuals will live to a ripe old age, generally estimated to be about 85 years, after which the mortality rate will rise very rapidly. In other words, people will live long, healthy lives and die rather suddenly of "old age." This position requires that we accept three premises: (1) that the human life span is fixed; (2) that the age of first infirmity will increase; and (3) that, therefore, the duration of infirmity will decrease (Fries and Crapo, 1981).

It may, of course, be that the first premise is wrong and that people will begin living longer than the 85 years Fries and Crapo foresee. What would happen, for example, if people routinely lived 120 to 150 years? Without a doubt, such a change would alter the meaning of every major social institution, the meaning of most interpersonal relationships, probably the meaning of life itself, and certainly the meaning of death. Can you imagine being married to the same person for 100 years? What about 150? What impact would it have on the parent-child relationship for the parent to be 120 and the child 100 years old? How many career changes could you go through in an 80-year work life? Or, could you retire at 60 and live another 60 years? If there is a significant increase in the life span, there will also be some radical changes in store for those who are heir to the extra years.

In any case, even if we only accept the more conservative prediction that most people will live to be 85 or more, there will be some critical issues to consider. Society cannot support a huge, vulnerable, nonworking elderly population. Therefore, the health and well-being of older adults will have to become a top social priority. Moreover, there is little doubt that this goal depends on people making good personal health decisions from early on, in childhood and adolescence, before any decline occurs. People must learn the value of physical activity, of dietary and weight control, and of managing problematic habits such as cigarette smoking or alcohol and drug consumption. They must also learn to exercise their mental abilities and their social skills throughout life.

Looking around us, we can be reasonably certain that efforts toward this end are underway. Data on health and well-being in middle age and later life already suggest the impact of information and education. Declining rates of heart disease and the improvement of survival rates for cancer patients are examples. Exercise programs are extremely popular, and schools are now instituting them at the elementary level. The natural food movement, although waning some from its initial peak in the late 1960s and 1970s, has made us all more aware of the dangers of consuming fat and sugar and food additives. And no one is more dogged in their warnings about the dangers of smoking than one's own children, fresh from health science class.

Along with physical preparations for longer life spans, we must also change the negative age stereotypes of the past if society is to be spared the burden of a dependent senior class. Older people must continue contributing to the social system through many more years of their lives; this is especially so in the next forty to seventy years when the giant population bulge of the second postwar baby boom enters the last stages of the life span. It will be impossible for a dwindling number of younger workers to provide complete retirement security for this cohort. Undoubtedly, the retirement age will rise, or the concept of complete retirement will be replaced by a more gradual withdrawal from the labor force. In order to maintain productivity in the later years, people will have to reject the notion that older workers are less competent or less able. You cannot put the horse to pasture if there is no one left to draw the cart.

As stereotypes about competence and ability change, many other negative attitudes are likely to disappear. If elderly people are considered socially competent, *then why not socially attractive? If they are active in the labor force and the community, why not sexually? Certainly the attitudes of today's middle-aged adults are compatible with such changes. The postwar baby boom will soon be middle aged, and this cohort has generally been a force for change in American attitudes, ideas, and institutions. They have altered our conceptions of marriage and divorce, sexual behavior and leisure, even politics and religion. From adolescence, they have been social activists, and we can probably expect them to react to each stage of life in a questioning, challenging way. It is true that most of the trends we are discussing began many years before the postwar baby boom—perhaps around the turn of the century. But it is through this cohort that these changes have become part of the mainstream of American life, as acceptable as apple pie.*

How, then, will they serve up the last slices of the life span? Perhaps they will seize some of the long-neglected opportunities of age. Once their obligations to family and community are fulfilled and their years as full-time members of the labor force are over, they may be able to

make the most of the freedom available to the elderly. Certainly, this cohort has always been more sensitive to the freedom inherent in any situation. They have even been criticized as narcissistic and irresponsible, the "me generation." If they are able to apply that attitude toward life to its last stages, the world of the elderly could be revitalized, even become a time of experimentation.

If communes didn't work out when the kids came along, maybe they will work out after the kids are gone. If hippies sold out to the establishment when it came time to settle down and get a job, maybe they will have the cash to buy out when it comes time to retire. Old people hitchhiking through Europe staying at senior hostels (as opposed to youth hostels)? If they are healthy and vigorous, why not? And what special contributions to art and science and philosophy and religion can we expect from a mentally and physically vigorous elderly population? Many great artists and thinkers from Picasso and Casals to Mao and Tito, George Bernard Shaw, Charles de Gaulle and Albert Schweitzer suggest the potential of older people in a rectangular society. Zorba the Greek said men of his sort should "live a thousand years" (Fries and Crapo, p. 141). What contribution might some of the great geniuses of young adult life have made had they lived to be a healthy 85? There are bound to be some very special footprints in the sands of time when the elderly walk as steadily and in as great a number as the young.

Finally, how will the meaning of death and dying change if nearly everyone lives a full and vigorous life right to the very end? There is some evidence that those who have been most satisfied in life also accept death with the greatest sense of equanimity. This is the basic premise Erikson adopts in his description of integrity. Given enough time and energy, will greater numbers develop integrity? Or will death be all the more difficult when there is no great suffering or long period of debilitation in the terminal stage of life? More rigorous empirical evidence about the role of life satisfaction and integrity in the acceptance of death and dying seems justified.

Quite probably an awareness and acceptance of death while one is still living a full and vigorous life will have some extremely interesting effects. Consider, for example, some elderly friends of mine, Joe and Sue. They are in their mid-seventies and have known each other for decades. Two years ago, Joe's wife left him (the rumor is he wanted too much sex) and moved to Florida. Sue's husband died some time ago. Suddenly, they saw each other in a new light. They started dating and fell in love and the experience has some important meanings because it occurred so late in life. They have the freedom to go everywhere and do everything together. There is no clock to watch, no children to tend; no job troubles them. On the one hand, they have more time and energy to devote to one another than at any other point in the life span. On the other hand, their love is infused with a very special quality. They are always aware that their time together may be limited. They hope for five good years together, and every hour of it seems doubly precious for its vulnerability.

It is reported that the romantic involvements of the elderly are less passionate, less sexual than those of younger people. Certainly, there is some evidence that older people see sexuality in a less specifically genital way than do the young. Sexual feelings are more general and perhaps less urgent. But does that mean one feels less romantic or less passionate? You would not think so if you saw Joe and Sue looking at one another across a room full of chattering friends and relatives. They can hardly wait to be alone. They walk with their arms around one another and smile and talk in that exclusive way all lovers have. In fact, if the elderly are healthy and energetic, we may see the last stage of life is more romantic and more poignant in many ways than the earlier years when one feels immortal and most of life was ruled by obligation and routine.

Of course, even rectangularization may never come to pass. People may go on living and dying in much the same ways they have for the past few decades. Perhaps the economic pressure generated by the specter of a huge, aging class of citizens will be too great and the social system will cease to encourage the personal decisions necessary to achieve a rectangular society. Perhaps people will decide the cost of regular exercise and good health habits is too great when weighed against the few extra healthy years to be gained. Or, the young may be unwilling to offer any coherent role to the elderly—although I suspect the new breed of elderly will not wait for their children to offer them a role any more than they waited for their parents to do so. In fact, one of the more interesting questions about the future concerns the transfer of power from the baby boom generation to its children.

Some have predicted the establishment of a gerontocracy, a society run by a numerous and powerful elderly unwilling to pass the reins of the government and industry—an interesting dilemma.

As usual, there are so many intriguing questions and so few answers: a frustrating situation at times, but also an exciting one. If you ever find yourself thinking that it has all been done or said, just remember some of the issues that have been raised in these Perspectives sections. This is a wonderful time to be studying and researching human development because there is a rapidly growing awareness of the questions and a newly sophisticated technology for exploring the answers. The development of sequential and time-lag research design is one of the more exciting sets of events in any area of psychology. The emergence of a transactional or dialectic perspective is both challenging and seductive. The study of adult life offers an endless variety of subjects, a burgeoning portfolio of method and theory compiled to pursue an intensely interesting and personal question: What will become of us as we grow old?

Glossary

Active mastery   A mode of dealing with the environment; thought to be characteristic of young and middle-aged men; the environment is viewed as malleable and the self is seen as a source of energy and change; independence and energy are valued.

Activity theory   The hypothesis that successful aging is associated with the maintenance of social, physical, and intellectual activity.

Acute brain syndrome   A reversible, organic brain disorder characterized by fluctuating levels of awareness, emotional and intellectual dysfunction.

Adjustment model of marriage   The clinical representation of a good marriage as one in which there is agreement between the partners and with the conventional standards for a successful marriage.

Agape   One of the six basic styles of loving; unselfish love.

Age density   The proportion of a particular neighborhood or population belonging to a specified age group.

Age equivalence   An attribute of a measure, experimental task, or observation that implies that (1) the same set of abilities or traits is measured for all ages in the sample and (2) the abilities or traits are equally important, in the experimental hypothesis, for all age groups.

Ageism   The notion that chronological age is a primary determinant of human traits and capacities and, thus, that one age is superior to another.

Age-related change   Change occurring over the life course and correlated with chronological age.

Age simulation   A form of experimental research in which developmental researchers try to create in the laboratory the conditions thought to produce age-related change.

Allocentrism   One of Heath's five dimensions of maturity; the ability to take on multiple perspectives, to put oneself in someone else's shoes.

Alpha rhythm   Brain-wave patterns with a frequency of from 9 to 12 cycles per second.

Androgyny   The acceptance of both male and female characteristics in oneself.

Anticipatory socialization   The process by which people are rehearsed and prepared for an event by the social delivery of information and training.

Anti-hero   Male midlife personality type described by Farrell and Rosenberg as experiencing a strong sense of crisis and feeling alienated and dissatisfied.

Apportioned grandmother   A type of grandmother defined by her concern about doing what is right for the grandchild and by her ability to derive significant emotional satisfaction from the role of grandmother.

Appropriate death   A death that fulfills the ideals and expectations of the dying individual.

Arrangement   An agreement between an unmarried male and female to share living quarters, expenses, and regular sexual intercourse.

Arteriosclerosis   A disease of the blood vessels in which the walls of the smaller arteries thicken and harden.

Associative strength   The power of one word to call up or be associated with another.

Assumption   A fact or statement taken for granted or believed to be correct.

Atherosclerosis   A disease of the blood vessels involving hardening of the arteries, as in arteriosclerosis, but affecting the larger arteries and usually including the formation of plaques.

Attachment   A relationship characterized by feelings of intimacy and commitment but not necessarily by current positive feelings or by self-disclosure.

Autoimmune theory   The hypothesis that biological aging is primarily attributable to detrimental changes in the autoimmune system that diminish its ability to identify foreign material.

Autonomic nervous system   The part of the nervous system that supplies smooth muscles in the internal organs, the cardiac muscle, and glandular tissues with nerves and governs involuntary action.

Autonomy   One of Heath's five dimensions of maturity; with stability, allows an individual to think independently of the particulars of a situation and frees cognitive processes from emotional bias.

Axiom   A statement regarded as a self-evident truth.

Basal metabolic rate   The rate at which energy is used by an organism at rest.

Baseline data   Information about the frequency or intensity of behavior prior to experimental intervention in a behavioral analysis design.

Bereavement   The state of having lost a significant relationship, usually through death.

Biocultural context   The biological, social, and historical forces associated with an individual's psychological development.

Biological death   The cessation of all physical signs of life, including heartbeat, respiration, and reflexes.

Biological renewal   A type of meaning attributed to the role of grandparent; refers to perpetuation of the family.

Brain death   One of several definitions of biological death; involves the measurement of activity in the neocortex and brainstem.

Cardiac output   The quantity of blood ejected each minute by one of the ventricles of the heart.

Career   Any organized path taken by an individual across space and time; consistent involvement in any role over time.

Cataract   Opacity in the lens of the eye.

Cathected flexibility   The ability to invest a new role or activity with emotional meaning.

Central nervous system   Neural and supportive tissue comprising the brain and spinal cord; controlling voluntary behavior, cognition, and intelligence.

Cerebral blood flow   The quantity of blood flowing through each 100 grams of brain weight per minute.

Cerebrovascular accident   The rupturing of a cerebral blood vessel; a stroke.

Chronic brain syndrome   An irreversible organic brain syndrome from which full recovery is not possible, as in senile psychosis and the deterioration associated with cerebral arteriosclerosis; affects emotion and social and cognitive behavior.

Classical conditioning   The pairing of a neutral stimulus and a stimulus known to evoke a reflexive response until the neutral stimulus evokes the response when presented alone; association through temporal contiguity.

Closed system   A theoretical framework for the study of development; characterized by an ultimate stage of growth.

Cognition   Internal mental activity, including knowledge, consciousness, thinking, imagining, and dreaming.

Cognitive investment   The value an individual places on intellectual matters; breadth of interests, fluency, and introspection.

Cohabitation   Living together as husband and wife without being legally married; common-law marriage.

Cohort   A group of people all born during the same period of time.

Cohort difference   A difference between people of different age groups and attributable to the different social and cultural experiences or other environmental conditions associated with those particular age groups.

Collagen   A protein that makes up about one-third of the protein in the human body.

Collagen theory   The hypothesis that biological aging is primarily attributable to the progressive cross-linking of large protein molecules, particularly collagen, that make up the tissues of the body.

Comarital sex   Extramarital sexual activity under a consensual arrangement.

Companionship marriage   A marriage in which the relationship between husband and wife is of paramount concern to the partners and serves as a primary source of marital satisfaction.

Compensation   Extra effort or attention to a sensory or motor task to maintain or improve performance on that task.

Competence   An individual's sensorimotor, emotional, and cognitive capacities; used to predict adaptation to the environment.

Complementarity hypothesis   The notion that individuals who choose each other as mates are similar in most physical, intellectual, and psychological traits.

Conditionability   An individual's capacity for acquiring classically or operantly conditioned responses.

Conditioning   A process by which response frequency is altered by association with external environmental events, as in classical or operant conditioning.

Conflict-habituated marriage   A subtype of institutional marriage; characterized by constant arguments, bickering, and nagging; discord is seen not as a basis for ending the relationship, but as normal communication.

Congregation   The requirement that people in institutions do things at the same time and place.

Consolidation   The strengthening or securing of useful knowledge gained in childhood; takes place during the development of formal operations in adolescence or young adulthood.

Content-free ability   An intellectual capacity or cognitive operation that can be applied to various subjects.

Control   The degree of autonomy permitted in institutional settings.

Corpus luteum   An empty follicle in the ovary, left by the egg when it enters the Fallopian tube; produces progesterone and estrogen.

Correlation   A statistic that reflects the degree to which two events or phenomena are associated—the frequency with which two phenomena are found together; degree of correspondence.

Cosmic perspective   Kohlberg's concept of the most mature stage of moral reasoning; a feeling of unity with the whole of nature.

Cross-linking theory   The hypothesis that biological aging is primarily a product of the loss of elasticity and flexibility in tissues; this loss results from the linking of large molecules, such as collagen, or from mutations that occur when DNA or RNA become cross-linked.

Cross-sectional design   A research format that includes the observation of subjects from two or more cohorts as representatives of as many different age groups; observations are made at one and only one time of measurement.

Crowning   The moment during birth when the infant's head emerges from the birth canal and is surrounded by the labia, which form a crown.

Crystallization   One of five proposed stages of vocational development postulated by Super; characterized by the firm establishment of one's ideas about the type of work one desires to do.

Crystallized intelligence   Mechanical and social knowledge, spatial reasoning and visualization, accuracy of perceptual and motor performance, vocabulary, and information skills; thought to increase with age.

Cultural bias   The tendency to reflect the values or beliefs of one's own society or class when making generalizations about a larger population and to hold one's own beliefs or values as good, true, or natural.

Cybernetic capacity   The ability of the organism to adapt to and control the environment; the capacity to organize and to utilize energy efficiently.

Dark adaptation   The gradual increase in visual sensitivity that occurs under conditions of low illumination.

Death clock   A hypothetical genetic mechanism or program that controls the number of divisions of the labile cells and thus ensures that tissues will eventually die.

Decay   Loss or erosion of information from the sensory stores of the memory.

Decrement model   The notion that the aging process is characterized by continual decline or degeneration of abilities.

Demand quality   The degree to which the environment requires the individual to exercise competence in order to achieve a maximum level of adaptation.

Denial   The defense mechanism in which external reality is not recognized; thought to be common in the very young and the very old.

Deoxyribonucleic acid (DNA)   An acid that is the part of genetic material that determines heredity; a complex molecule composed of strands of sugars and phosphates and chemical bases arranged in a double helix.

Development   Orderly changes presumed to be evidenced by individuals as they progress in time toward maturity and through adult phases toward old age.

Developmental school   A group of theorists who suggest that vocational choices are determined by one's early experiences.

Developmental task   A prescription, obligation, or responsibility thought to contribute to healthy, satisfactory growth in a particular society.

Devitalized marriage   A subtype of institutional marriage in which the partners are congenial but are bored or disenchanted with their relationship.

Dialectical model   A general set of assumptions about human nature and developmental change; represents the organism and the world around it as existing in a state of continuous change.

Dichotic listening   A memory task involving the recall of a short series of digits presented to one ear when a different series of digits is presented simultaneously to the other ear.

Differential approach   A mode of developmental study devoted to discovery of predictable relationships through research that proceeds from a framework consisting of assumptions common to several theories.

Differentiation   In biological development, the process by which cells become different one from the other in terms of both structure and function.

Disengagement theory   A theory positing a process of mutual withdrawal between older people and society. Thought to begin in middle age, disengagement has been described as successful adjustment to growing old.

Displacement   Loss of information from short-term memory through the substitution of new information from the sensory stores.

Distribution   An objective property of an event, referring to whether the event is experienced by many people, whether it is age-related, and whether it is likely to occur in the life of a particular person.

Divergent thinking   The intellectual process that allows an individual to generate alternative correct or possible solutions to a problem.

Dogmatism   Resistance to change, particularly in one's ideas or opinions.

Double helix   The intertwining spiral structure of the DNA molecule.

Dying trajectory   The patterning of the terminal stage of life of an individual, including the duration of this stage and the amount of decline and recovery expected.

Ecology   The science of plants and animals in relation to their environments.

Efficiency quotient   A measure of an older person's performance on tests of intellectual capacity relative to the performance of an average adult at the age of twenty.

Elastin   Large protein molecules that make up the elastic fibers of the body; similar to collagen but more flexible.

Elementarism   The philosophical position that human behavior can be productively analyzed and understood in terms of its basic elements.

Embolism   An abnormal particle, such as an air bubble, circulating in the bloodstream.

Emergence   The philosophical position that human behavior cannot be meaningfully reduced to a series of simple events but is governed at every level of organization by principles that transcend those governing simpler forms.

Emotional self-fulfillment   A kind of meaning found in the role of grandparent by those who value the companionship and good times they have with their grandchildren.

Empirical definition   A statement of the meaning of a term or concept, based on observation and experience rather than on theoretical principles or deductions from some set of assumptions or axioms.

Empiricist   A scientist who takes the position that the study of a particular phenomenon is best carried out by objective observation and data-gathering without reference to theory.

Empirico-inductive thought   Reasoning based on generalizations from direct experience rather than on abstraction and deduction.

Empty-nest syndrome   A group of symptoms thought to be associated with launching children from the home; most often described in terms of depression or anxiety.

Encoding   Conversion of information from the environment to the memory systems or to the kind of symbolization useful in the memory process.

Engagement   Maintenance or increase of activity level and involvement in social roles during later adulthood.

Entropy   The relationship between the amount of organization in a system and the amount of energy available for useful work; a measure of the disorganization of a system.

Epigenetic principle   Erikson's statement that anything that grows has an internal ground plan that determines the special times or critical periods during which specific developments can occur.

Equity theory   A theory which proposes that successful intimate relationships are based on equality of the outcome for both partners, where outcome is equal to the sum of a person's assets minus the sum of his or her liabilities.

Eros (erotic love)   One of the six basic styles of loving; romantic love.

Error catastrophe   A critical accumulation of cellular errors; the result of mutation that is thought to curtail functioning enough to cause the death of the organism.

Ethnic endogamy   Marriage within one's own racial and ethnic group.

Ethnocentrism   The tendency to see the behaviors that are valued in one's own culture as universally optimal or mature.

Evoked potential   Specific brain activity correlated with the onset of a stimulus.

Executive processes   Subjective aspects of experience, such as self-awareness, perception of environmental quality, perception of time, and mode of dealing with the environment.

Experiential change   Personality change characterized by an increase or decrease in the strength of a particular trait from one time of measurement to another, and by changes in the rank ordering of individuals tested on that trait.

Experimental mortality   The phenomenon of dropout, or refusal of subjects to continue to participate in a longitudinal developmental research study.

Expressive activity   Behavior that offers immediate gratification or satisfaction; leisure.

External career path   The stages encountered in the pursuit of a particular occupation, such as apprentice, journeyman, master.

External validity   The degree to which conclusions drawn from data about one sample can be generalized to other samples with similar characteristics.

Family life cycle   A proposed division of married life into eight stages; includes beginning families, childbearing families, families with preschool children, families with school-age children, families with teenagers, families as launching centers, families in the middle years, and aging families.

Filial maturity   The ability to view one's parent as a real and separate person—acknowledging that the parent was formed by a social history that took place before as well as after one's own birth, relinquishing adolescent rebellion, and allowing the parent to develop some dependence on oneself.

Fluid intelligence   Innate general cognitive capacity reflected in performance on tests that require relational thinking (such as memory span and block design); believed to peak in late adolescence or early adulthood.

Forbidden clone   A mutant cell thought to trigger an autoimmune reaction in which body tissues are destroyed; central to the process of aging and death.

Formal operations   The final stage of cognitive development, as described by Piaget, in which the individual is able to think abstractly and systematically about complex propositions and problems.

Free-radical theory   The hypothesis that biological aging is primarily due to the cross-linking and mutations that occur when the body produces molecules with fewer or more than the ordinary complement of electrons; these molecules are thought to be involved in cross-linking or to be responsible for detrimental autoimmune reactions or mutations.

Functional syndrome   A psychiatric disorder or set of symptoms that have no apparent physiological basis.

Gender identity   Psychological identification of the self-concept as either masculine or feminine.

Generativity   The positive pole of the crisis of middle age as proposed by Erikson; a deep concern for the establishment and nurturance of the next generation; direction of one's creativity and energy in a way that will produce a lasting accomplishment.

Genetic error   A mutation produced during the replication or repair of cellular material of DNA.

Genetic imperative   A theoretical construct suggesting that parenthood constitutes a social emergency and sharpens the sex-role distinctions of the parents.

Genotypic continuity   Changes in the personality that are predictable but are not necessarily characterized by the persistence of particular traits.

Gerontology   The study of aging and the problems of the aged.

Grief   Emotional suffering caused by bereavement or deprivation; characterized by sadness, anger, depression, and often by physical symptoms such as nausea.

Grief work   The anger and self-recrimination that accompany bereavement.

Hierarchical stage   A stage, as in Piaget's theory, that is built on and includes the elements of previous stages.

History-graded influences   The general social and historical background of a particular group of people born into a culture at the same time.

Holism   The philosophical position that the organism can be understood only as an entity that is greater than the sum of its parts and cannot be analyzed as a series of simple events.

Homogamous marriage   Marriage between individuals of similar social and educational backgrounds, intellectual and personality characteristics, physical attributes, and value structures.

Hospice   A facility for the dying patient; offers medical services necessary to allay pain or restore function, but focuses on emotional care of the patient and his or her family.

Hypothesis   A set of assumptions stated as a tentative explanation and used as the basis for experimentation.

Hypothetico-deductive thought   The process of forming a hypothesis about the explanation for a phenomenon, deducing a prediction, and suggesting a test of the prediction.

Implementation   One proposed stage of vocational development; usually occurs between the ages of eighteen and twenty-one; includes training for and entry into one's first job.

Incipient process   A process that is beginning to be or is becoming apparent.

Individualized grandmother   A grandmother who is concerned primarily about deriving emotional satisfaction from her grandchildren, rather than about seeing that they are properly reared.

Infidelity   Clandestine adultery; deceitful adultery occurring in the absence of an explicit agreement with one's spouse.

Institutional marriage   A marriage in which the partners derive their major satisfactions from relationships and activities outside of the husband-wife relationship (for example, from parenting or from community activities).

Institutional racism   Indirect discrimination on the basis of race, such as inadequate education and training rather than denial of employment.

Instrumental activity   Behavior that is rewarded by future gratification, such as work for pay, rather than by immediate gratification intrinsic to the activity.

Instrumentation   The use of instruments and tests for observation, measurement, and control.

Integration   One of Heath's five dimensions of maturity; an integrated person has a coherent system of values, motives, personality traits, and beliefs that permit the organization of life events in a meaningful way.

Integrity   The central achievement of Erikson's final stage; the accrued sense of order and meaning that allows one to see one's own life as meaningful and as a contribution to the human world.

Intelligence   The ability to learn or to reason and solve problems; the potential or innate ability of the individual to adapt.

Intelligence quotient   The score one receives on a traditional test of intelligence (such as the Stanford-Binet or the Wechsler Adult Intelligence Scale); used as a measure of general ability to learn.

Interference hypothesis   A tentative explanation of the learning decrements associated with age; asserts that well-learned material may become an obstruction to the learning of new material.

Interiority   Increased awareness of and emphasis on one's own experience and inner thought processes; believed to accompany old age and to be associated with a decline in sensitivity to events in the immediate environment.

Internal career path   A set of individual expectations and perceptions about one's career; may include transitions through several external career paths.

Internal validity   The degree to which a particular piece of research or a general research format allows one to draw unambiguous conclusions about the relationships observed in the data obtained.

Intersexual convergence   Increasing similarity in the attitudes and behaviors of males and females, particularly sexual attitudes and behaviors.

Intervention   Intrusion of the experimenter into the research design in order to manipulate or control some aspect of the environment and so produce an observable change in a developmental process.

Intervention research   Any research format based on the observation of phenomena resulting from manipulation of the experimental environment by the researcher.

Intimacy   The quality of closeness and rapport found in relationships characterized by self-disclosure, mutuality, similarity, and compatibility.

Intrapropositional thought   The process by which one develops a set of hypotheses about reality and tests them against one another and against reality.

Intrapsychic phenomena   The inner processes of the personality, such as self-awareness, perception of time, and perception of the environment.

Intuition   An aspect of cognitive function which permits one to discover the existence of conflict or paradox and to grasp or sense a relationship without really understanding it. Permits the questioning of accepted principles and solutions.

Invariant sequence   A sequence of stages that are believed to occur in the same order for each individual, regardless of social or cultural circumstances.

Inversion   A reversal of the usual relationship between two phenomena, such as sex-role inversion in later life when some men become increasingly feminine and some women develop masculine traits.

Involution   The reversal of some aspects of biological development as when the uterus and other sex organs return to normal size and condition after pregnancy or when changes occur in the genital tract and reproductive organs during climacteric.

Irreversible decrement   A general decline or degeneration of biological, emotional, and social capacities; characteristic of development in later life as pictured by the cultural stereotype.

Labile cell   A cell that reproduces itself repeatedly over the course of the normal life span.

Learning   The acquisition of new information, skills, or rules.

Leisure ethic   A set of attitudes and beliefs about the value of leisure as a role in adult life.

Life review   The tendency to review one's life course in old age; reminiscence in later life.

Life span   The entire course of human life from conception to death.

Lifestyle   The environmental characteristics, social choice of personal and group relationships, degree of involvement in leisure and work, and investment in various roles that typify an individual's life.

Lifetime family   The nuclear family, including two generations only.

Lightening   An event in the final month of pregnancy, when the fetus drops, or settles, down into the pelvic area.

Lineage family   The extended family, including the older, middle, and younger generations (married or unmarried); may be more than three generations.

Lipid migration   Movement of fat from one part of the body to another.

Longitudinal design   A research format that involves the observation of one cohort over two or more times of measurement (the same individuals are observed repeatedly).

Long-term memory   The process by which, or the stores into which, information is transferred as it exceeds one's immediate capacity for retention; believed to be of infinite capacity and of infinite duration.

Ludis   One of the six basic styles of loving; game-playing love.

Macroscopic theories   In research on biological aging, theories that focus on forces that affect the organism as a whole.

Mania   One of the six basic styles of loving; possessive love.

Maternal instinct   The degree to which a natural fit exists between the needs of an infant and the needs and behavioral repertoire of a female parent of any species.

Measurement   Appraisal of a phenomenon through the application of tests, observation of performance, description of natural behavior, or any other objective means.

Mechanical mirror model   A set of assumptions about human nature and developmental change; represents the organism as if it were a machine; suggests that behavior can be analyzed and understood as a series of simple events or elements.

Mediator   An unobservable, internal process or response that influences external behavior by evoking related prior experience or stimulation.

Memory The several processes by which, or the stores in which, information from current experience is filed and retrieved later; each process has different characteristics, capacities, and functions.

Metamorphosis Change in vocational status, from novice to probationary member; sometimes acknowledged by the ritual of a new title or position.

Methodology The principles and strategies involved in the pursuit of knowledge about any scientific question or problem.

Microscopic theories In research on biological aging, theories that focus on changes in individual cells or the relationships among cells.

Midlife transition A period of turmoil and reassessment identified by the clinical literature and thought to occur between ages 39 and 43.

Mnemonics A technique for improving the memory through the use of codes to help one store and recall information.

Model A general set of assumptions about, and definitions of, the nature of a phenomenon—specifically, human nature and human development—from which theories and hypotheses proceed.

Molecular level A level of theory formulation based on analysis of a complex phenomenon (such as intimacy, commitment, or parenthood) into simple stimulus-response chains.

Mortification Sharing information and feelings about oneself that are potentially embarrassing or humiliating; a practice often observed in successful communal living arrangements.

Motor unit The motor neuron and all of the muscle fibers it affects.

Multiple orgasm Two or more orgasms during a single episode of sexual activity, as defined by contractions of the vaginal musculature.

Multiple regression A statistical technique that yields a set of correlations—statistics that indicate how often two phenomena are found together.

Mutation A genetic error produced during the reproduction or repair of cellular material, or occurring spontaneously at some time in the history of the organism, and thought to be generally harmful to cellular function.

Mutuality A proposed final stage in the development of friendships; includes shared knowledge of each other, a sense of commitment, and behavior regulated by private rather than general social norms.

Nature/nurture controversy Debate among developmentalists over how much of human behavior is determined by external, environmental forces and how much by internal, maturational forces.

Near point of vision The nearest point at which an object can be seen clearly without a blur.

Nephron unit One of many tiny filters in the kidney that constitute the central mechanisms by which waste is removed from the blood stream.

Neural noise Random activity of neurons in the cortex; assumed to increase in frequency with age and believed to make it more difficult to detect sensory signals from the external environment.

Nonnormative influences Environmental and biological events that do not occur to everyone or cannot be specified as most likely to occur at a particular phase of life.

Normative age-graded influences   The biological and environmental events that are strongly associated with chronological age.

Occupation   The principal business of one's life; vocation.

Off-time individual   One who enters some role or activity at a point in the life course generally considered too early or too late to be optimal or appropriate.

Ontogenetic change   Age-related change, which can be expected to occur regardless of the social or historical context of the subject.

Open system   Any theoretical conception of human development that represents the organism in continuous and cumulative change and so suggests the possibility of unlimited growth.

Operant conditioning   Use of punishment and reward to produce changes in the frequency of behavior.

Optic disc   Blind spot in each eye; occurs at the point where the optic nerve is attached to the retina.

Optimization   The process of making something as perfect or as functional as possible.

Ordered transposition   Changes in personality traits; subjects retain relative positions despite changes in the intensity or strength of a particular trait.

Organismic model   A set of assumptions about human nature; presents the organism as active, organic, and holistic, and presents human development as structural and emergent.

Orgasmic platform   The extension of the vaginal barrel during sexual arousal; produced by the vasocongestion of the major and minor labia.

Orthogenetic principle   The proposal that development is characterized by change from a state of relative globality and lack of differentiation to a state of increasing differentiation, articulation, and hierarchical integration.

Osteoarthritis   Inflammation of the joints, due to changes in bone and cartilage.

Overarousal hypothesis   The proposal that older people perform poorly on tests of learning because they experience greater excitement of the autonomic nervous system under conditions of fast pacing than do the young.

Overt behavioral measure   A test designed to quantify an observable response or some characteristic of an observable response.

Paired associates   Two nonsense syllables used in a verbal learning experiment. Subjects must learn to call out one in response to hearing or seeing the other.

Parental imperative   The genetic emergency believed to occur at the birth of the first child and to sharpen sex-role distinctions between father and mother.

Passive-congenial marriage   A type of institutional marriage; described as amicable but characterized by a lack of emotional involvement between the partners.

Passive mastery   The tendency to cope with environmental change, or with dissatisfaction with the environment, by accommodating to circumstances rather than by attempting to alter external events.

Path analysis   A statistical technique that allows researchers to determine which factors analyzed in a multiple regression act through other factors included in that regression.

Perception   Interpretation of sensory stimulation in terms of prior experience, environmental demands, or other personal and situational factors.

Perceptual masking   The presentation of a visual figure followed, after a short interval, by another stimulus known to erase the perception of the first figure.

Permanent cell   A cell that does not reproduce itself in the course of the life span.

Phenotypic persistence   Stability of personality traits or dispositions over the life course.

Plaque   Abnormal formation on the wall of a blood vessel where fat, cholesterol, and other wastes build up, eventually forming an obstruction to normal circulation of blood.

Pluralistic ignorance   A situation in which individuals are unaware of each other's opinions and feelings on a subject because they are unable or unwilling to discuss the subject.

Portent of embarrassment   The fear of appearing foolish due to poor performance at a new activity.

Postvention   A program of therapeutic intervention for the bereaved, begun as soon as an individual experiences a loss or offered to those who experience very intense or prolonged grief.

Practice effect   Changes in subject behavior produced by repeated exposure to a test or an experimental task.

Pragma   One of the six basic styles of loving; logical love.

Presbycusis   Progressive loss of hearing for high frequency tones; associated with degenerative changes in the auditory system.

Problem-finding   A proposed final stage of cognitive development; believed to occur in adulthood; characterized by the ability to formulate questions about transformations and implications.

Problem solving   A stage of cognitive development postulated by Arlin; characterized by the formulation of questions that request specific information or classification about relations or systems.

Process research   Developmental study that focuses on description of events believed to be responsible for normal development, rather than on discovery of ways to induce, reverse, or optimize in a controlled setting.

Programmed theory   The hypothesis that biological aging is based on a definite order of events built into the human genetic structure as a result of natural selection.

Projection   A defense mechanism by which the individual attributes his or her unacceptable impulses to other people.

Pronatalist attitude   The beliefs and emotional responses underlying the position that childbearing and childrearing are natural, basic, and necessary activities for all human adults.

Prosthetic environment   An environment that provides some form of permanent support for functioning; allows the individual to function more fully as long as the supports are present, but produces no permanent therapeutic effect.

Pseudo-developed   Male midlife personality type identified by Farrell and Rosenberg as denying the stress of the midlife transition and experiencing dissatisfaction and hopelessness.

Psychological death   The cessation of thought, feelings, and needs and the disappearance of the personality characteristics and abilities associated with a particular individual.

Psychomotor skill   An ability that requires dexterity and agility and is believed to improve with practice.

Punitive-disenchanted   Male midlife personality type identified by Farrell and Rosenberg as denying crisis and functioning in a bigoted, authoritarian way.

Quickening   The sensing of fetal movements during pregnancy; usually begins in the fourth or fifth month.

Random sampling   A technique—such as flipping a coin or drawing names from a hat—by which subjects are chosen entirely by chance for a study.

Rationalization   Shift of a function from the family or individual to an institution or group in the society.

Reaction time   The amount of time an individual requires to respond to a stimulus that signals a response.

Reality shock   The experience of disparity between the conception of an occupation created by education or by anticipatory socialization and the reality of that occupation.

Recreational adultery   A subtype of consensual adultery in which sexual activity is considered as recreation, not as an aspect of interpersonal involvement (swinging).

Reductionism   The philosophical position that human behavior can ultimately be reduced to a series of simple events or elementary forms.

Refractory period   The period after a response when an individual cannot be rearoused (for example, the period following ejaculation in the male sexual response).

Rehearsal   A form of processing that transfers information from short-term memory to long-term memory; involves repetition of information in short-term stores.

Reliability   The extent to which a subject's response to an item on a test, or performance on an experimental task, is stable from one time of measurement to another.

Reminiscence   Review of one's past life during old age; a part of the life review process.

Residential propinquity   Physical closeness of one's dwelling to that of another individual.

Resource person   A conceptualization of the grandparent role that emphasizes the potential of the role for providing experience, financial aid, or time that the parent cannot offer.

Respondent conditioning   The pairing of a neutral stimulus and a stimulus known to evoke a reflexive response (as food evokes salivation) until the neutral stimulus comes to evoke the response when presented alone; *see* Classical conditioning.

Retirement   A period late in life when an individual does not hold a full-time, year-round job and receives at least part of his or her income from social security or a pension program.

Rheumatoid arthritis   Inflammation of the joints caused by immunological dysfunction; develops early in life and becomes progressively worse.

Ribonucleic acid (RNA)   An acid present in all cells; a complex molecule carrying information about protein synthesis.

Rigidity   Inability to unlearn old habits in order to develop new ones; often included in stereotypic descriptions of the thinking and behavior of the elderly.

Role cycling   The relationship between peak periods of demand in each of the careers of a dual-career couple and peak periods of demand in their roles in the home.

Role involution   The leveling of sex-role distinctions that is believed to occur during middle and later life, as men exhibit a tendency toward passive mastery and women display more aggressive, active forms of mastery.

Role overload   Conflict between the demands and expectations of two or more roles; characteristic of particular life styles (for example, the conflict between the mother/wife role and the career expectations of a woman in a dual-career marriage).

Role reversal   The taking on of some of the obligations and responsibilities of a parent by adult children as their parents become very elderly.

Sample   A group of individuals included in an experimental study and thought to be representative of a particular segment of the population.

Scientific method   A set of rules for obtaining observations and for generalizing from and integrating those observations to develop a theory or explanation of a phenomenon; one way of knowing or understanding the world.

Segregation   The degree to which people in institutions are isolated from the outside world.

Self-disclosure   Revelation of personal information; considered essential to the development of an intimate relationship.

Self-produced feedback   Any sensory, cognitive, or emotional stimulation following self-initiated behavior.

Semantic differential   A measure of connotative or emotional meaning in which subjects rate words or concepts on a series of bipolar adjectives.

Senescence   Changes that accompany the aging process.

Senile osteoporosis   Pathological or extreme porousness of the bones of an elderly individual.

Senile psychosis   A chronic, irreversible brain syndrome associated with the dissolution of the brain cells; senile dementia.

Senility   The characteristics associated with old age, especially mental and physical infirmities.

Sensation   Awareness of simple stimuli in the environment.

Sensory register   The first stage in a three-process model of memory, in which information is registered automatically as an exact copy of the environment.

Sensual transcendence   Cognitive, emotional, or physical activity of great intensity; provides high levels of involvement and gratification of the senses; peak experience.

Sequential design   A format for developmental research; uses two or more simple cross-sections or longitudinal studies in one research project.

Short-term memory   The second stage in a three-process model of memory; in this stage information exists as bits or single items and memory is characterized by limited capacity and the rapid displacement of old information by new data from the sensory register.

Similarity hypothesis   The proposal that mate selection proceeds on the basis of similarity of values and attributes, including physical attractiveness, intelligence, and beliefs about role behaviors and lifestyle.

Simple response time   The time it takes to respond to the onset or offset of a simple stimulus used to signal the beginning of a response.

Social clock   The culturally accepted ordering and scheduling of social and environmental events; provides information about whether an individual's life is meeting the expectations of society.

Social death   Cessation of institutional and cultural processes surrounding the life and death of an individual (for example, mourning and bereavement).

Social-exchange theory   Interpretation of close relationships by social-learning theorists positing that intimacy is the product of a reward-cost history in the interaction between two people.

Social gerontology   The study of the influence of social and environmental events and processes on the life course in adulthood.

Social intelligence   The abilities and skills that are predictive of success and adaptation.

Socialization   The process of learning skills, attitudes, and values, as well as the cognitive and emotional patterns that relate people to their sociocultural settings.

Socialized control   A label for the description of middle-aged people often found in studies of attitudes toward aging emphasizing the belief that middle-aged people are dependable, conservative, and rigid.

Social-learning theory   The notion that human development proceeds through the asssociation of environmental events or learning.

Social maturity   The ability to live comfortably with others, respond appropriately to stress, and depart from conventional norms when necessary or desirable.

Socioadaptive process   Overt, objective, social behavior related to adaptation and to one's ability to cope with environmental events.

Somatic theory   The hypothesis that biological aging is primarily a function of an increasing number of genetic errors or mutations in cellular structure that lead to a decline in cellular function.

Somatization   The tendency to express one's psychological tensions or anxieties through physical symptoms rather than through behavioral channels.

Specification   A proposed stage of vocational choice; believed to occur between the ages of 18 and 21; characterized by development of an explicit vocational choice.

Speech discrimination   The ability to differentiate between different sounds in the language one hears.

Sponsor   An experienced member of an occupation who takes a personal interest in the progress of a recruit, providing information and support and assisting the novice in establishing contacts.

Stability   One of Heath's five dimensions of maturity; with autonomy, enables a person to think independently of the particulars of a situation and frees cognitive processes from emotional bias.

Stable cell   A cell that reproduces itself only when appropriately stimulated.

Stagnation   The negative pole of the developmental crisis of middle age as proposed by Erikson; characterized by impoverishment and self-indulgence.

Stepparent adoption   Legal adoption of a child by a stepparent.

Storge   One of the six basic styles of loving; the love of best friends.

Striped muscle   A muscle that produces discrete, voluntary movements (such as lifting the leg or flexing the arm).

Structural analytic stage   A proposed final stage of cognitive development; believed to occur in adulthood and to follow from and build upon formal operations, enabling the individual to analyze relationships between whole systems and paradigms of thought.

Swinging   A form of recreational adultery; characterized by low levels of emotional involvement between sexual partners who are not married to one another and by the expectation that extramarital sexual relationships will be impermanent.

Substitution theory   The proposal that successful adaptation to retirement is based on the replacement of the work role with activities that provide similar kinds of gratification.

Surface contact   A proposed second stage in the development of friendships; characterized by lack of self-disclosure and regulated by social norms and social rewards.

Symbolic grandmother   A grandmother who reports that the most important aspects of grandparenting involve doing what is morally right for the child and setting a good example.

Symbolization   One of Heath's five dimensions of maturity; the degree to which a person can represent feelings and ideals in words.

Syndrome   A group of signs and symptoms that occur together and characterize a particular abnormality or disorder.

Synergy   An intensification of effect produced when one force is combined with another, as when the effect of one drug is heightened by simultaneous use of another.

Taxonomy   An orderly system for classifying plants and animals according to their relationships to each other.

Terminal stage   The period of life during which an individual has a persistent awareness of the prospect of death from natural causes.

Test-retest effect   Any change in subject behavior or performance produced by repeated exposure to an experimental test or measure; practice effect.

Theme   The basic motivation for pursuit of an occupation at a particular point in one's career.

Theorem   An idea that is proposed as a demonstrable truth; often occurs as part of a general theory.

Theory   A principle or set of principles offered as an explanation for some phenomenon.

Threshold   The point at which sensory stimulation is intense enough to produce an effect that is psychologically noticeable.

Time compression   The speeding of natural processes that often is produced in the laboratory to facilitate experimental observation of some long-term developmental change.

Time-lag design   Observation of one age group over at least two different times of measurement.

Time of measurement   The moment in history when a set of observations is made in the course of a developmental research project.

Time perspective   The way an individual experiences the passage of time; the way an individual regards the past, present, and future.

Time-related change   Developmental change that occurs over the life course as a result of an individual's personal history and social, economic, and historical circumstances.

Timetable   A subjective deadline for evaluation of progress in one's occupational career, especially progress related to the theme one has developed for a particular stage of that career.

Total brain death   Cessation of function in the brain and the brainstem as defined by such criteria as the cessation of spontaneous breathing and movement and the presence of a flat electroencephalogram record.

Total marriage   A subtype of companionship marriage, in which the marital couple share every area of their lives, including feelings, responsibilities, hobbies, thoughts, and dreams.

Toxemia of pregnancy   A metabolic disturbance characterized by a rise in blood pressure and fluid retention in the early stages; can be life threatening if untreated.

Transactional change   Change in which the elements themselves are altered. There is an exchange of influence in a transaction, and each element is affected by the presence of the other.

Transcendent generative   Male personality type identified by Farrell and Rosenberg as experiencing no crisis of midlife yet exhibiting growth, self-confidence, and satisfaction.

Transformation   A major change in the form, nature, or function of a thing so that it can be put to a use not originally intended.

Trimester   A three-month period (as the first three months of pregnancy).

Typology   An orderly system of classification based on groups of objects, people, or events with similar characteristics (for example, a system based on clusters of personality traits).

Vacuole   A small space or cavity in a cell; may contain air or fluid.

Validity   In experimentation, a term referring to how accurately research procedures measure what they are supposed to measure.

Vasocongestion   The flooding or congestion of an area with blood from the capillaries; occurs in many areas of the body during sexual arousal.

Verbal mediation   An internal use of language that affects one's response to a particular stimulus (for example, the use of a rhyme or a system of key words to aid memory).

Vicarious achievement   A perception of the grandparent role as one who values the possibility that grandchildren may be able to achieve goals preceding generations have not achieved.

Visual acuity   The ability to see accurately small details in the visual field.

Visual mediation   Use of imagery in a way that affects one's response to an external stimulus (for example, the generation or adoption of an image as a device to aid memory).

Vital capacity   The sum of the excess capacity of the lungs, both for inspiration and for expiration, after a normal breath has been taken and expelled.

Vital marriage   A subtype of companionship marriage; the marital couple participate in and share many common activities and areas of concern, such as social and family activities and financial management.

Wear-and-tear model   A model of aging that stresses the importance of accumulated physical insults over the life span.

References

Abbott, W. Work in the year 2001. *The Futurist*, February 1977, pp. 25–29.

Achenbach, T. *Research in developmental psychology: Concepts, strategies, methods.* New York: Free Press, 1978.

Adams, M. The single woman in today's society: A reappraisal. *American Journal of Orthopsychiatry*, 1971, *41*, 776–786.

Adelman, R. C. In pursuit of molecular mechanisms of aging. In A. Cherkin & C. Finch et al. (Eds.), *Physiology and cell biology of aging.* (Aging Series, Vol. 8.) New York: Raven Press, 1979.

Adler, W. An autoimmune theory of aging. In M. Rockstein (Ed.), *Proceedings of a symposium on the theoretical aspects of aging.* New York: Academic Press, 1974.

Agate, J. *The practice of geriatrics.* Springfield, Ill.: Charles C Thomas, 1970.

Albrecht, G. L., & Gift, H. C. Adult socialization: Ambiguity and adult life crises. In N. Datan & L. H. Ginsberg (Eds.), *Life-span developmental psychology: Normative life crises.* New York: Academic Press, 1975.

Alpert, J. L., & Richardson, M. S. Parenting. In L. W. Poon (Ed.), *Aging in the 1980s.* Washington, D.C.: American Psychological Association, 1980.

Anderson, B., Jr., & Palmore, E. Longitudinal evaluation of ocular functions. In E. Palmore (Ed.), *Normal aging II.* Durham, N.C.: Duke University Press, 1974.

Arenberg, D. Age differences in retroaction. *Journal of Gerontology*, 1967, *22*, 88–91.

Arenberg, D. Concept problem-solving in young and old adults. *Journal of Gerontology*, 1968, *23*, 279–282.

Arenberg, D. Cognition and aging: Verbal learning, memory, and problem-solving. In C. Eisdorfer & M. P. Lawton (Eds.), *The psychology of adult development and aging.* Washington, D.C.: American Psychological Association, 1973.

Arenberg, D., & Robertson-Tchabo, E. A. Learning and aging. In J. E. Birren & K. W. Schaie (Eds.), *Handbook of the psychology of aging.* New York: Van Nostrand Reinhold, 1977.

Ariès, P. The denial of mourning. In R. Fulton, E. Markusen, G. Owen, & J. L. Scheiber (Eds.), *Death and dying: Challenge and change.* San Francisco: Boyd & Fraser, 1981.

Arlin, P. K. Cognitive development in adulthood: A fifth stage? *Developmental Psychology*, 1975, *11*, 602–606.

Arlin, P. K. Piagetian operators in problem-finding. *Developmental Psychology*, 1977, *13*, 297–298.

Aronsen, D. S. Personality stereotypes of aging. *Journal of Gerontology*, 1966, *21*, 458–462.

Arthur, G. L., Donnan, H. H., & Lair, C. V. Companionship therapy with nursing home aged. *The Gerontologist*, 1973, *13* (2), 167–170.

Asimov, I. *Change!* Boston: Houghton Mifflin, 1981.

Atchley, R. C. Respondents and refusers in an interview study of retired women. *Journal of Gerontology*, 1969, *24*, 42–47.

Atchley, R. C. The meaning of retirement. *Journal of Communications*, 1974, *24*, 97–101.

Atchley, R. C. *The sociology of retirement*. Cambridge, Mass.: Schenkman, 1976.

Atchley, R. C. *The social forces in later life*. (2nd ed.) Belmont, Calif.: Wadsworth, 1977.

Atchley, R. C. *The social forces in later life*. (3rd ed.) Belmont, Calif.: Wadsworth, 1980.

Babbie, E. *Society by agreement: An introduction to sociology*. Belmont, Calif.: Wadsworth, 1977.

Baldwin, A. L. *Theories of child development*. New York: Wiley, 1980.

Baer, D. M. The control of the developmental process: Why wait? In J. R. Nesselroade & H. W. Reese (Eds.), *Life-span developmental psychology: Methodological issues*. New York: Academic Press, 1973.

Bailyn, L. Career and family orientations of husbands and wives in relation to marital satisfaction. *Human Relations*, 1970, *23*, 97–113.

Bailyn, L. Involvement and accommodation in technical careers: An inquiry into the relation to work at midcareer. In J. Van Maanen (Ed.), *Organizational careers: Some new perspectives*. New York: Wiley, 1977.

Baird, J. The funeral industry in Boston. In E. Shneidman (Ed.), *Death: Current perspectives*. Palo Alto, Calif.: Mayfield, 1976.

Bakerman, S. (Ed.) *Aging life processes*. Springfield, Ill.: Charles C Thomas, 1969.

Baltes, P. B. Life-span developmental psychology: Some converging observations on history and theory. In P. B. Baltes & O. G. Brim, Jr. (Eds.), *Life-span development and behavior*. Vol. 2. New York: Academic Press, 1979.

Baltes, P. B., & Goulet, L. R. Status and issues of a life-span developmental psychology. In L. R. Goulet & P. B. Baltes (Eds.), *Life-span developmental psychology: Research and theory*. New York: Academic Press, 1970.

Baltes, P. B., Reese, H. W., & Nesselroade, J. R. *Life-span developmental psychology: Introduction to research methods*. Monterey, Calif.: Brooks/Cole, 1977.

Baltes, P. B., & Reinert, G. Cohort effects in cognitive development of children as revealed by cross-sectional sequences. *Developmental Psychology*, 1969, *1*, 169–177.

Baltes, P. B., & Willis, S. L. Toward psychological theories of aging and development. In J. E. Birren & K. W. Schaie (Eds.), *Handbook of the psychology of aging*. New York: Van Nostrand Reinhold, 1977.

Baltes, P. B., & Willis, S. L. Life-span developmental psychology, cognitive functioning and social policy. In M. W. Riley (Ed.), *Aging from birth to death*. Boulder, Colo.: Westview Press, 1979.

Barfield, R. *The automobile worker and retirement: A second look*. Ann Arbor,

Mich.: Institute for Social Research, 1970.

Barfield, R. E., & Morgan, J. N. Trends in satisfaction with retirement. *The Gerontologist*, 1978, *18*, 19–23.

Bart, P. Mother Portnoy's complaint. *Transaction*, 1970, *8*, 69–74.

Baruch, R. The achievement motive in women: Implications for career development. *Journal of Personality and Social Psychology*, 1967, *5*, 260–267.

Bassé, R., & Ekerdt, D. Change in self-perception of leisure activities with retirement. *The Gerontologist*, 1981, *21*, 650–654.

Beaubier, J. Biological factors in aging. In C. L. Fry (Ed.), *Aging in culture and society*. Brooklyn, N.Y.: J. F. Bergin, 1980.

Beck, P. Two successful interventions in nursing homes: The therapeutic effects of cognitive activity. *The Gerontologist*, 1982, *22*, 378–383.

Becker, E. *The denial of death*. New York: Free Press, 1973.

Beckhard, R. Managerial careers in transition: Dilemmas and directions. In J. Van Maanen (Ed.), *Organizational careers: Some new perspectives*. New York: Wiley, 1977.

Beilen, R. Social functions of the denial of death. *Omega*, 1981–82, *12*, 25–35.

Bell, A. P., & Weinberg, M. S. *Homosexualities: A study of diversity among men and women*. New York: Simon & Schuster, 1978.

Bell, R., Turner, S., & Rosen, L. Multivariate analysis of female extramarital coitus. *Journal of Marriage and the Family*, 1975, *37*, 375–385.

Bell, R. Q. A reinterpretation of direction of effects in studies of socialization. *Psychological Review*, 1968, *75*, 81–95.

Bennett, R., & Eckman, J. Attitudes toward aging: A critical examination of recent literature and implications for future research. In C. Eisdorfer & M. P. Lawton (Eds.), *The psychology of adult development and aging*. Washington, D.C.: American Psychological Association, 1973.

Bergen, M., & Williams, R. R. Alternative funerals: An exploratory study. *Omega*, 1981–82, *12*, 71–78.

Bergman, M. Hearing and aging. *Audiology*, 1971, *10*, 164–171.

Berman, W. H., & Turk, D. C. Adaptation to divorce: Problems and strategies. *Journal of Marriage and the Family*, 1981, *43*, 179–189.

Bernard, J. Sex-role learning in children and adolescents. Paper presented at the meeting of the American Association for the Advancement of Science Meetings, Washington, D.C., December 1972.

Bernard, J. *The future of marriage*. New York: Bantam, 1973.

Bernard, J. Notes on changing life styles: 1970–1974. *Journal of Marriage and the Family*, 1975, *37*, 582–593.

Bernard, J. *The female world*. New York: Free Press, 1981.

Bernardo, F. M. Widowhood status in the United States: Perspectives on a neglected aspect of the family cycle. *Family Coordinator*, 1968, *17*, 191–203.

Bernardo, F. M. Survivorship and social isolation: The case of the aged widower. *Family Coordinator*, 1970, *19*, 11–15.

Berscheid, E., & Walster, E. Physical attractiveness. In L. Berkowitz (Ed.), *Advances in experimental and social psychology*. Vol. 7. New York: Academic Press, 1974.

Berscheid, E., Walster, E., & Bohrstedt, G. The body image report. *Psychology To-*

day, 1973, *7*, 119–131.

Bierman, E., & Hazzard, W. Biology of aging. In D. Smith & E. Bierman (Eds.), *The biologic ages of man*. Philadelphia: W. B. Saunders, 1973.

Binstock, R. H., & Shanas, E. (Eds.) *Handbook of aging and the social sciences*. New York: Van Nostrand Reinhold, 1977.

Birren, J. E. (Ed.) *Handbook of aging and the individual*. Chicago: University of Chicago Press, 1959.

Birren, J. E. *The psychology of aging*. Englewood Cliffs, N.J.: Prentice-Hall, 1964.

Birren, J. E. The abuse of the urban aged. *Psychology Today*, March 1970, pp. 36–38, 76.

Birren, J. E. Progress in research on aging in the behavioral and social sciences. *Human Development*, 1980, *23*, 33–45.

Birren, J. E., & Botwinick, J. The relation of writing speed to age and to the senile psychoses. *Journal of Consulting Psychology*, 1951, *15*, 243–249.

Birren, J. E., Butler, R. N., Greenhouse, S. W., Sokoloff, L., & Yarrow, M. R. (Eds.) *Human aging*. Washington, D.C.: U.S. Government Printing Office, 1963.

Birren, J. E., Kinney, D. K., Schaie, K. W., & Woodruff, D. S. *Developmental psychology*. Boston: Houghton Mifflin, 1980.

Birren, J. E., & Morrison, D. F. Analysis of the WAIS subtests in relation to age and education. *Journal of Gerontology*, 1961, *16*, 363–369.

Birren, J. E., & Renner, J. V. Research on the psychology of aging: Principles and experimentation. In J. E. Birren & K. W. Schaie (Eds.), *Handbook of the psychology of aging*. New York: Van Nostrand Reinhold, 1977.

Birren, J. E., & Schaie, K. W. (Eds.) *Handbook of the psychology of aging*. New York: Van Nostrand Reinhold, 1977.

Birren, J. E., Woods, A. M., & Williams, M. V. Behavioral slowing with age: Causes, organization, and consequences. In L. W. Poon (Ed.), *Aging in the 1980s*. Washington, D.C.: American Psychological Association, 1980.

Bischoff, L. J. *Adult psychology*. (2nd ed.) New York: Harper & Row, 1976.

Black, D. The older person in the family. In S. H. Zarit (Ed.), *Readings in aging and death: Contemporary perspectives*. New York: Harper & Row, 1977.

Blackman, A. Over 65 set growing at 1,600 a day in U.S. In H. Cox (Ed.), *Focus: Aging*. Guilford, Conn.: Dushkin, 1978.

Blenkner, M. Social work and family relationships in later life with some thoughts on filial maturity. In E. Shanas & G. Streib (Eds.), *Social structure and the family*. Englewood Cliffs, N.J.: Prentice-Hall, 1965.

Block, M. R., Davidson, J. L., & Grambs, J. D. *Women over forty: Visions and realities*. New York: Springer, 1981.

Blood, R. O., Jr., & Wolfe, D. M. *Husbands and wives: The dynamics of married living*. New York: Free Press, 1960.

Bloom, B., & Caldwell, R. A. Sex differences in adjustment during the process of marital separation. *Journal of Marriage and the Family*, 1981, *43*, 693–701.

Boothby, W. M., Berkson, J., & Dunn, H. L. Studies of the energy metabolism of normal individuals. A standard for basal metabolism with a nomogram for clinical application. *American Journal of Physiology*, 1936, *116*, 468–484.

Bortner, R. W., & Hultsch, D. F. Personal time perspective in adulthood. *Developmental Psychology*, 1972, *7*, 98–103.

Botwinick, J. Drives, expectancies, and emotion. In J. E. Birren (Ed.), *Handbook of aging and the individual*. Chicago: University of Chicago Press, 1959.

Botwinick, J. Cautiousness in advanced age. *Journal of Gerontology*, 1966, *21*, 347–353.

Botwinick, J. *Aging and behavior: A comprehensive integration of research findings*. New York: Springer, 1973.

Botwinick, J. Intellectual abilities. In J. E. Birren & K. W. Schaie (Eds.), *Handbook of the psychology of aging*. New York: Van Nostrand Reinhold, 1977.

Botwinick, J. *We are aging*. New York: Springer, 1981.

Botwinick, J., West, R., & Storandt, M. Qualitative vocabulary test responses and age. *Journal of Gerontology*, 1961, *16*, 363–369.

Bower, L. America's baby boom generation: the fateful bulge. *Population Bulletin*, 1980, *35*, 29–33.

Bowlby, J. The nature of a child's tie to his mother. *International Journal of Psychoanalysis*, 1958, *39*, 350–373.

Bowlby, J. Attachment and love. Vol. 1. *Attachment*. New York: Basic Books, 1969.

Bradbury, W. (Ed.) *The adult years*. New York: Time-Life Books, 1975.

Brash, D. E., & Hart, R. W. Molecular biology of aging. In A. Behnke, C. Finch, & G. Moment (Eds.), *The biology of aging*. New York: Plenum, 1978.

Brenton, M. The breadwinner. In D. S. David & R. Brannon (Eds.), *The forty-nine percent majority: The male sex role*. Reading, Mass.: Addison-Wesley, 1976.

Brim, O., & Ryff, C. On the properties of life events. In P. B. Baltes & O. G. Brim, Jr. (Eds.), *Life-span development and behavior*. Vol. 3. New York: Academic Press, 1980.

Britton, J. H. Living in a rural Pennsylvania community in old age. In F. M. Carp (Ed.), *Patterns of living and housing of middle-aged and older people*. Washington, D.C.: U.S. Government Printing Office, 1966.

Brody, H., & Vijayashankar, N. Anatomical changes in the nervous system. In C. E. Finch & L. Hayflick (Eds.), *Handbook of the biology of aging*. New York: Van Nostrand Reinhold, 1977.

Bromley, D. B. *The psychology of human aging*. (2nd ed.) Baltimore: Penguin, 1974.

Brooks, J. B. Social maturity in middle-age and its developmental antecedents. In D. Eichorn, N. Haan, J. Clausen, M. Honzik, & P. Mussen (Eds.), *Present and past in middle life*. New York: Academic Press, 1981.

Brown, A. M. Surgical restorative art for the aging face. *Journal of Gerontology*, 1953, *8*, 173–190.

Buckingham, R. W. Hospice care in the United States: The process begins. *Omega*, 1982–83, *13*, 159–171.

Buck-Morss, S. Socioeconomic bias in Piaget's theory: Implications for cross-cultural studies. In A. Buss (Ed.), *Psychology in social context*. New York: Irvington, 1979.

Buhler, C. The course of human life as a psychological problem. In W. R. Looft (Ed.), *Developmental psychology: A book of readings*. New York: Holt, Rinehart &

Winston, 1972.

Burch, P. R. J. *An inquiry concerning growth, disease, and aging.* Edinburgh: Oliver & Boyd, 1968.

Burgess, J. K. The single-parent family: A social and sociological problem. *Family Coordinator*, 1970, *19*, 141.

Buss, A. R. Dialectics, history and development: The historical roots of the individual-society dialectic. In P. B. Baltes & O. G. Brim, Jr. (Eds.), *Life-span development and behavior.* Vol. 2. New York: Academic Press, 1979.

Buss, A. R. Methodological issues in life-span development psychology from a dialectical perspective. *International Journal of Aging and Human Development*, 1980, *10*, 121–164.

Butler, R. N. The life review: An interpretation of reminiscence in the aged. *Psychiatry*, 1963, *26*, 65–76.

Butler, R. N. The burnt out and the bored. *The Futurist*, June 1970, p. 82.

Butler, R. N. Successful aging and the role of the life review. *Journal of the American Geriatric Society*, 1974, *22*, 529–535.

Butler, R. N. The life review: An unrecognized bonanza. *International Journal of Aging and Human Development*, 1980, *12*, 35–38.

Butler, R. N., & Lewis, M. I. *Aging and mental health: Positive psychosocial approaches.* St. Louis: Mosby, 1973.

Butler, R. N., & Lewis, M. I. *Aging and mental health.* (2nd ed.) St. Louis: Mosby, 1977.

Byrne, D. Interpersonal attraction and attitude similarity. *Journal of Abnormal and Social Psychology*, 1961, *62*, 713–715.

Cahn, A. F. Summary. In A. F. Cahn (Ed.), *Women in the U.S. labor force.* New York: Praeger, 1979.

Cairo, P. C. Measured interests versus expressed interests as predictors of long-term occupational membership. *Journal of Vocational Behavior*, 1982, *20*, 343–353.

Cameron, P. Stereotypes about generational fun and happiness versus self-appraised fun and happiness. *The Gerontologist*, 1972, *12*, 120–123, 190.

Cameron, P. Mood as an indicant of happiness: Age, sex, social class, and situational differences. *Journal of Gerontology*, 1975, *30*, 216–224.

Campbell, A. The American way of mating: Marriage si, children, only maybe. *Psychology Today*, May 1975, pp. 39–42.

Campbell, D. T., & Stanley, J. C. Experimental and quasi-experimental designs for research. Chicago: Rand McNally, 1963.

Carey, R. G. Weathering widowhood: Problems and adjustment of the widowed during the first year. *Omega*, 1979, *10*, 163–174.

Carp, F. M. *A future for the aged.* Austin: University of Texas Press, 1966.

Carp, F. M. Long-range satisfaction with housing. *The Gerontologist*, 1975, *15*, 27–34.

Carp, F. M. Housing and living environments of older people. In R. H. Binstock & E. Shanas, *Handbook of aging and the social sciences.* New York: Van Nostrand Reinhold, 1977.

Cattell, R. B. Theory of fluid and crystallized intelligence: A critical experiment. *Journal of Educational Psychology*, 1963, *54*, 1–22.

Chester, N. L. Pregnancy and new parenthood: Twin experiences of change. Paper presented at the meeting of the Eastern Psychological Association, Philadelphia, April 1979.

Chiriboga, D. Personal communication, April 1978.

Chiriboga, D., & Cutler, L. Stress and adaptation: A life-span perspective. In L. W. Poon (Ed.), *Aging in the 1980s*. Washington, D.C.: American Psychological Association, 1980.

Chown, S. M. Age and the rigiditics. *Journal of Gerontology*, 1961, *16*, 353–362.

Chown, S. M. Morale, careers, and personal potentials. In J. E. Birren & K. W. Schaie (Eds.), *Handbook of the psychology of aging*. New York: Van Nostrand Reinhold, 1977.

Circirelli, V. Sibling relationships in adulthood: A life-span perspective. In L. W. Poon (Ed.), *Aging in the 1980s*. Washington, D.C.: American Psychological Association, 1980.

Clague, E. Work and leisure for older workers. *The Gerontologist*, 1971, *11*, 9–20.

Clanton, G. The contemporary experience of adultery: Bob and Carol and Updike and Rimmer. In R. W. Libby & R. N. Whitehurst (Eds.), *Marriage and alternatives: Exploring intimate relationships*. Glenview, Ill.: Scott, Foresman, 1977.

Clark, L., & Knowles, J. Age differences in dichotic listening performance. *Journal of Gerontology*, 1973, *28*, 173–178.

Clausen, J. A. Glimpses into the social world of middle age. *International Journal of Aging and Human Development*, 1976, *7*, 99–106.

Clausen, J. A. Men's occupational careers in the middle years. In D. H. Eichorn, N. Haan, J. Clausen, M. Honzik, & P. Mussen (Eds.), *Present and past in middle life*. New York: Academic Press, 1981.

Clausen, J. A., Mussen, P. H., & Kuypers, J. Involvement, warmth and parent-child resemblances in three generations. In D. Eichorn, N. Haan, J. Clausen, M. Honzik, & P. Mussen (Eds.), *Present and past in middle life*. New York: Academic Press, 1981.

Clayton, V. P., & Birren, J. The development of wisdom across the life span: A reexamination of an ancient topic. In P. B. Baltes & O. G. Brim, Jr. (Eds.), *Life-span development and behavior*. Vol. 3. New York: Academic Press, 1980.

Coffman, T. L. Relocation and survival of institutionalized aged: A reexamination of the evidence. *The Gerontologist*, 1981, *21*, 483–500.

Cohen, J. *Sensation and perception II: Audition and the minor senses*. Chicago: Rand McNally, 1969.

Colby, A. Developments in a theory. Unpublished paper, Harvard University, 1978.

Collette-Pratt, C. Attitudinal predictors of devaluation of old age in a multigenerational sample. *Journal of Gerontology*, 1976, *31*, 193–197.

Colwill, N. *The new partnership: Men and women in organization*. Palo Alto, Calif.: Mayfield, 1982.

Comalli, P. E., Jr. Differential effects of context on perception in young and aged groups. Paper presented at the meeting of the Gerontological Society, Miami Beach, Florida, October 1962.

Comalli, P. E., Jr. Cognitive functioning in a group of eighty to ninety year old men. *Journal of Gerontology*, 1965, *20*, 14–17.

Comalli, P. E., Jr. Life-span changes in visual perception. In L. R. Goulet & P. B. Baltes (Eds.), *Life-span developmental psychology: Research and theory*. New York: Academic Press, 1970.

Comalli, P. E., Jr., Wapner, S., & Werner, H. Perception of verticality in middle and old age. *Journal of Psychology*, 1959, *47*, 259–266.

Comfort, A. *A good age*. New York: Crown, 1976.

Commons, M. L. Personal communication, July 1982.

Commons, M. L., & Richards, F. A. The structural analytic state of development: A Piagetian post-formal operational stage. Paper presented at the meeting of the Western Psychological Association, San Francisco, April 1978.

Commons, M. L., and Richards, F. A. A general model of stage theory. In M. L. Commons, F. A. Richards, & S. Armon (Eds.), *Beyond formal operations: Late adolescent and adult cognitive development*. New York: Praeger, 1982.

Conger, J. J. *Adolescence and youth: Psychological development*. New York: Harper & Row, 1968.

Conger, J. J. A world they never knew: The family and social change. In J. Kagen & R. Coles (Eds.), *Twelve to sixteen: Early adolescence*. New York: Norton, 1972.

Consumers Union. Funerals: The memorial society alternative. In R. Fulton, E. Markusen, G. Owen, & J. L. Scheiber (Eds.), *Death and dying: Challenge and change*. San Francisco: Boyd & Fraser, 1981.

Corso, J. F. Confirmation of normal discrimination loss for speech on CID auditory test W-22. *Laryngoscope*, 1957, *67*, 365–370.

Corso, J. F. Auditory perception and communication. In J. E. Birren & K. W. Schaie (Eds.), *Handbook of the psychology of aging*. New York: Van Nostrand Reinhold, 1977.

Corso, J. F. *Aging sensory systems and perception*. New York: Praeger, 1981.

Costa, P. T., & McCrae, R. R. Age differences in personality structure revisited: Studies in validity, stability, and change. In J. Hendricks (Ed.), *Being and becoming old*. Farmingdale, N.Y.: Baywood, 1981.

Cox, H. *Focus: Aging*. Guilford, Conn.: Dushkin, 1978.

Craik, F. I. M. Age differences in human memory. In J. E. Birren & K. W. Schaie (Eds.), *Handbook of the psychology of aging*. New York: Van Nostrand Reinhold, 1977.

Craik, F. I. M., & Lockhart, R. S. Level of processing: A framework for memory research. *Journal of Verbal Learning and Verbal Behavior*, 1972, *11*, 671–684.

Craik, F. I. M., & Simon, E. Age differences in memory: The role of attention and depth of processing. In L. W. Poon, J. L. Fozard, L. S. Cremak, D. Arenberg, & L. W. Thompson (Eds.), *New directions in memory and aging: Proceedings of the George Talland Memorial Conference*. Hillsdale, N.J.: Lawrence Erlbaum, 1980.

Crain, W. C. *Theories of personality*. Englewood Cliffs, N.J.: Prentice-Hall, 1980.

Crane, D. Scientists at major and minor universities: A study of productivity and recognition. *American Sociological Review*, 1965, *30*, 699–713.

Crossman, E. R. F., & Szafran, J. Changes with age in speed of information intake and discrimination. *Experiential Supplement*, 1956, *4*, 128–135.

Cuber, J. F., & Harroff, P. B. *Sex and the significant Americans*. Baltimore: Penguin, 1965.

Cumming, E., Dean, L. R., Newell, D. S., & McCaffrey, I. Disengagement: A tentative theory of aging. *Sociometry*, 1960, *23*, 23–25.

Cumming, E., & Henry, W. *Growing old*. New York: Basic Books, 1961.

Cunningham, W. R., & Birren, J. E. Age changes in human abilities: A twenty-eight year longitudinal study. *Developmental Psychology*, 1976, *12*, 81–82.

Curtis, H. J. The somatic mutation theory. In R. Kastenbaum (Ed.), *Contributions to the psychobiology of aging*. New York: Springer, 1965.

Cytrynbaum, S., Blum, L., Patrick, R., Stein, J., Wadner, D., & Wilk, C. Midlife development: A personality and social systems perspective. In L. W. Poon (Ed.), *Aging in the 1980s*. Washington, D.C.: American Psychological Association, 1980.

Dalderup, L. M., & Fredericks, M. L. C. Color sensitivity in old age. *Journal of the American Geriatric Society*, 1969, *17*, 388–390.

Daman, A., Seltzer, C. C., Stroudt, H. W., & Bell, B. Age and physique in healthy white veterans at Boston. *International Journal of Aging and Human Development*, 1972, *3*, 202–208.

Daniels, P., & Weingarten, K. *Sooner or later: The timing of parenthood in adult lives*. New York: Norton, 1980.

Datan, N. Women's attitudes toward the climacteric in five Israeli subcultures. Doctoral dissertation, University of Chicago, 1971.

David, D. S., & Brannon, R. (Eds.) *The forty-nine percent majority: The male sex role*. Reading, Mass.: Addison-Wesley, 1976.

De Beauvoir, S. Joie de vivre. In S. H. Zarit (Ed.), *Readings in aging and death: Contemporary perspectives*. New York: Harper & Row, 1977.

Decker, D. L. *Social Gerontology*. Boston: Little, Brown, 1980.

Denfeld, D., & Gordon, M. Mate swapping: The family that swings together clings together. In M. E. Lasswell & T. E. Lasswell (Eds.), *Love, marriage, and family: A developmental approach*. Glenview, Ill.: Scott, Foresman, 1973.

Denney, N. W. Aging and cognitive changes. In B. B. Wolman (Ed.), *Handbook of developmental psychology*. Englewood Cliffs, N.J.: Prentice-Hall, 1982.

Denney, N. W., & Palmer, A. M. Adult age differences on traditional and practical problem-solving measures. Unpublished manuscript, University of Kansas, 1982.

Denney, N. W., & Pearce, K. A. A developmental study of adult performance on traditional and practical problem-solving tasks. Unpublished manuscript, University of Kansas, 1982.

Dennis, W. Creative productivity between the ages of twenty and eighty years. *Journal of Gerontology*, 1966, *21*, 1–8.

Derbyshire, R. L. Adolescent identity crisis in urban Mexican-Americans in East Los Angeles. In E. B. Brody (Ed.), *Minority-group adolescents in the United States*. Baltimore: Williams & Wilkins, 1968.

Deutscher, I. Socialization to postparental life. In A. Rose (Ed.), *Human behavior and social process*. Boston: Houghton Mifflin, 1967.

Devins, G. M., & Diamond, R. T. The determination of death. *Omega*, 1976–1977, *7*, 277–296.

Diamond, N. Cognitive theory. In B. B. Wolman (Ed.), *Handbook of developmental psychology*. Englewood Cliffs, N.J.: Prentice-Hall, 1982.

Dodson, F. D. *How to father*. New York: New American Library, 1974.

Douglass, E. B., Cleveland, W. P., & Maddox, G. L. Political attitudes, age, and aging: A cohort analysis of archival data. *Journal of Gerontology*, 1974, *29*, 666–675.

Douvan, E. Sex differences in the opportunities, demands, and developments of youth. In R. J. Havighurst & P. H. Dreyer (Eds.), *Youth: The seventy-fourth yearbook of the National Society for the Study of Education*. Chicago: University of Chicago Press, 1975.

Douvan, E. Interpersonal relationships: Some questions and observations. In G. Levinger & H. L. Raush (Eds.), *Close relationships and the meaning of intimacy*. Amherst: University of Massachusetts Press, 1977.

Douvan, E. Learning to listen to a different drummer. *Contemporary Psychology*, 1983, *28*, 261–262.

Dowd, J. J. The problems of generations and generational analysis. *International Journal of Aging and Human Development*, 1980, *12*, 197–181.

Dowling, C. *The Cinderella complex*. New York: Pocket Books, 1982.

Dreyer, P. H. Changes in the meaning of marriage among youth: The impact of the "revolution" in sex and sex role behavior. In R. E. Grinder (Ed.), *Studies in adolescence*. (3rd ed.) New York: Macmillan, 1975.

Dulit, E. Adolescent thinking à la Piaget: The formal stage. *Journal of Youth and Adolescence*, 1972, *1*, 281–301.

Duvall, E. M. *Family development*. Philadelphia: Lippincott, 1971.

Dyer, E. D. Parenthood as crisis: A restudy. *Marriage and Family Living*, 1963, *25*, 196–201.

Eckensburger, L. H. Methodological issues of cross-cultural research in developmental psychology. In J. R. Nesselroade & H. W. Reese (Eds.), *Life-span developmental psychology: Methodological issues*. New York: Academic Press, 1973.

Eckland, B. K. Theories of mate selection. In M. E. Lasswell & T. E. Lasswell (Eds.), *Love, marriage, and family: A developmental approach*. Glenview, Ill.: Scott, Foresman, 1973.

Edwards, C. P. The comparative study of the development of moral judgment and reasoning. In R. H. Munroe, R. L. Munroe, & B. B. Whiting (Eds.), *Handbook of cross-cultural human development*. New York: Garland STM Press, 1980.

Edwards, J. N., & Booth, A. Sexual behavior in and out of marriage: An assessment of correlates. *Journal of Marriage and the Family*, 1976, *38*, 73–81.

Edwards, J. N., & Klemmack, D. L. Correlates of life satisfaction: A reexamination. *Journal of Gerontology*, 1973, *28*, 497–502.

Eichorn, D. H., Hunt, J. V., & Honzik, M. P. Experience, personality and I.Q.: Adolescence to middle age. In D. H. Eichorn, N. Haan, J. Clausen, M. Honzik, & P. Mussen (Eds.), *Present and past in middle life*. New York: Academic Press, 1981.

Eisdorfer, C. Arousal and performance. In G. A. Talland (Ed.), *Human aging and behavior*. New York: Academic Press, 1968.

Eisdorfer, C., Axelrod, S., & Wilkie, F. L. Stimulus exposure time as a factor in serial learning in an aged sample. *Journal of Abnormal and Social Psychology*, 1963, *67*, 594–600.

Eisdorfer, C., & Lawton, M. P. (Eds.) *The psychology of adult development and aging.* Washington, D.C.: American Psychological Association, 1973.

Eisdorfer, C., Nowlin, J., & Wilkie, F. Improvement of learning in the aged by modification of autonomic nervous system activity. *Science*, 1970, *170*, 1327–1329.

Eisdorfer, C., & Wilkie, F. Stress, disease, aging, and behavior. In J. E. Birren & K. W. Schaie (Eds.), *Handbook of the psychology of aging.* New York: Van Nostrand Reinhold, 1977.

Eisner, D. A., & Schaie, K. W. Age change in response to visual illusions from middle to old age. *Journal of Gerontology*, 1971, *26*, 146–150.

Elder, G. H., Jr. Historical change in life patterns and personality. In P. B. Baltes & O. G. Brim, Jr. (Eds.), *Life-span development and behavior*. Vol. 2. New York: Academic Press, 1979.

Elias, M. F., Elias, P. K., & Elias, J. W. *Basic processes in adult developmental psychology*. St. Louis: Mosby, 1977.

Elsayed, M., Ismail, A. H., & Young, R. J. Intellectual differences of adult men related to age and physical fitness before and after an exercise program. *Journal of Gerontology*, 1980, *35*, 383–387.

Engen, T. Taste and smell. In J. E. Birren & K. W. Schaie (Eds.), *Handbook of the psychology of aging.* New York: Van Nostrand Reinhold, 1977.

Erber, J., Freely, C., & Botwinick, J. Reward conditions and socioeconomic status in the learning of older adults. *Journal of Gerontology*, 1980, *35*, 565–570.

Erikson, E. H. *Childhood and society*. (2nd ed.) New York: Norton, 1963.

Erikson, E. H. Generativity and ego integrity. In B. L. Neugarten (Ed.), *Middle age and aging.* Chicago: University of Chicago Press, 1968. (a)

Erikson, E. H. *Identity, youth, and crisis.* New York: Norton, 1968. (b)

Erikson, E. H. *The life cycle completed: Review.* New York: Norton, 1982.

Eustis, N. Symposium: Relocation-interpretation and application. *The Gerontologist*, 1981, *21*, 481, 483.

Farrell, M. P., & Rosenberg, S. D. *Men at midlife.* Boston: Auburn House, 1981.

Fasteau, M. *The male machine.* New York: McGraw-Hill, 1974.

Feifel, H. The function of attitudes toward death. In Group for the Advancement of Psychiatry (Eds.), *Death and dying: Attitudes of patient and doctor.* New York: Mental Health Materials Center, 1965.

Feifel, H., & Branscomb, A. B. Who's afraid of death? *Journal of Abnormal Psychology*, 1973, *81*, 282–288.

Feifel, H. Death in contemporary America. In H. Feifel (Ed.), *New meanings of death.* New York: McGraw-Hill, 1977.

Feiring, C., & Taylor, J. The influence of the infant and secondary parent on maternal behavior: Toward a social systems view of infant attachment. *Merrill Palmer Quarterly*, in press.

Finch, C. The brain and aging. In J. Behnke, C. Finch, & G. Moment (Eds.), *Biology of aging.* New York: Plenum, 1978.

Finch, C. E., & Hayflick, L. (Eds.) *Handbook of the biology of aging.* New York: Van

Nostrand Reinhold, 1977.

Flavell, J. H. *The developmental psychology of Jean Piaget*. New York: Van Nostrand Reinhold, 1963.

Flavell, J. H. *Cognitive development*. Englewood Cliffs, N.J.: Prentice-Hall, 1977.

Ford, J. M., & Pfefferbaum, A. The utility of brain potentials in determining age-related changes in central nervous system and cognitive functioning. In L. W. Poon (Ed.), *Aging in the 1980s*. Washington, D.C.: American Psychological Association, 1980.

Fozard, J. L. The time for remembering. In L. W. Poon (Ed.), *Aging in the 1980s*. Washington, D.C.: American Psychological Association, 1980.

Fozard, J. L., & Thomas, J. C. Psychology of aging: Basic findings and their psychiatric applications. In J. G. Howells (Ed.), *Modern perspectives in the psychiatry of old age*. New York: Brunner-Mazel, 1975.

Fozard, J. L., Wolf, E., Bell, B., McFarland, R., & Podolsky, S. Visual perception and communication. In J. E. Birren & K. W. Schaie (Eds.), *Handbook of the psychology of aging*. New York: Van Nostrand Reinhold, 1977.

Fredrick, J. F. Grief as a disease process. *Omega*, 1976–1977, 7, 297–305.

Freedle, R. Some ingredients for constructing developmental models. In K. Riegel & J. Meacham (Eds.), *The developing individual in a changing world*. Chicago: Aldine, 1976.

Frenkel-Brunswick, E. Adjustments and reorientation in the course of the life-span. In R. G. Kuhlen & G. G. Thompson (Eds.), *Psychological studies of human development*. (3rd ed.) New York: Appleton-Century-Crofts, 1970.

Freedman, J. L., Sears, D. O., & Carlsmith, J. M. *Social Psychology*. (2nd ed.) Englewood Cliffs, N.J.: Prentice-Hall, 1981.

Friedman, E. A., & Havighurst, R. J. *The meaning of work and retirement*. Chicago: University of Chicago Press, 1954.

Friedman, M., & Rosenman, R. H. *Type A behavior and your heart*. New York: Knopf, 1974.

Fries, J. E., & Crapo, L. M. *Vitality and aging*. San Francisco: Freeman, 1981.

Fulton, R. Anticipatory grief, stress, and the surrogate griever. In R. Fulton, E. Markusen, G. Owen, & J. L. Scheiber (Eds.), *Death and dying: Challenge and change*. San Francisco: Boyd & Fraser, 1981.

Gagnon, J. H., & Greenblatt, C. S. *Life designs: Individuals, marriages and families*. Glenville, Ill.: Scott, Foresman, 1978.

Gallagher, D., Thompson, L. W., & Levy, S. M. Clinical psychological assessment of older adults. In L. W. Poon (Ed.), *Aging in the 1980s*. Washington, D.C.: American Psychological Association, 1980.

Garfield, C. A. Psychothanatological concomitants of altered state experience: An investigation of the relationship between consciousness alteration and fear of death. Doctoral dissertation, University of California, Berkeley, 1974.

Garn, S. M. Bone loss and aging. In R. Goldman & M. Rockstein (Eds.), *The physiology and pathology of human aging*. New York: Academic Press, 1975.

Gergen, K. J. The challenge of phenomenal change for research methodology. In D. F. Hultsch (Ed.), *Implications of a dialectical perspective for research methodology*. *Human Development*, 1980, 23, 254–265. (a).

Gergen, K. J. The emerging crisis in life-span developmental theory. In P. B. Baltes & O. G. Brim, Jr. (Eds.), *Life-span development and behavior*. Vol. 3. New York: Academic Press, 1980. (b).

Giambra, L. M., & Arenberg, D. Problem-solving, concept learning and aging. In L. W. Poon (Ed.), *Aging in the 1980s*. Washington, D.C.: American Psychological Association, 1980.

Gilbert, J. G. Age changes in color matching. *Journal of Gerontology*, 1957, *12*, 210–215.

Gilbert, J. G. Thirty-five year follow-up study of intellectual functioning. *Journal of Gerontology*, 1973, *28*, 68–72.

Gilligan, C. *In a different voice: Psychological theory and women's development*. Cambridge, Mass.: Harvard University Press, 1982.

Ginsberg, E. Toward a theory of occupational choice: A restatement. *Vocational Guidance Quarterly*, 1972, *20*, 169–176.

Glamser, F. O. The importance of age to conservative opinions: A multivariate analysis. *Journal of Gerontology*, 1974, *29*, 549–554.

Glaser, B. G., & Strauss, A. *Awareness of dying*. Chicago: Aldine, 1965.

Glaser, B. G., & Strauss, A. *The discovery of grounded theory*. Chicago: Aldine, 1967.

Glenn, N. D. Psychological well-being in the postparental stage: Some evidence from national surveys. *Journal of Marriage and the Family*, 1975, *37*, 105–109.

Glenwick, D. S., & Whitbourne, S. K. Beyond despair and disengagement: A transactional model of personality development in later life. *International Journal of Aging and Human Development*, 1978, *8*, 261–267.

Glick, I. O., Weiss, R. S., & Parkes, C. M. *The first year of bereavement*. New York: Wiley, 1974.

Glick, P. C. Updating life cycle of the family. *Journal of Marriage and the Family*, 1977, *39*, 5–15.

Glick, P. C., & Carter, H. *Marriage and divorce: A social and economic study*. (2nd ed.) Cambridge, Mass.: Harvard University Press, 1976.

Goldstein, M. S. Physical status of men rejected through selective service in World War II. *Public Health Reports*, 1951, *66*, 587–609.

Gordon, C., Gaitz, C. M., & Scott, J. Leisure and lives: Personal expressivity across the life span. In R. H. Binstock & E. Shanas (Eds.), *Handbook of aging and the social sciences*. New York: Van Nostrand Reinhold, 1977.

Gordon, M., & Shankweiler, P. J. Different equals less: Female sexuality in recent marriage manuals. *Journal of Marriage and the Family*, 1971, *33*, 459–465.

Gordon, T. J. Aging in America. In M. W. Riley (Ed.), *Aging from birth to death*. Boulder, Colo.: Westview Press, 1979.

Gorer, G. *Death, grief, and mourning*. Garden City, N.Y.: Doubleday, 1965.

Gottlieb, H. Personal communication, January 1978.

Goudy, W. Changing work expectations: Finding from the retirement history study. *The Gerontologist*, 1961, *1*, 644–649.

Gould, R. L. The phases of adult life: A study in developmental psychology. *American Journal of Psychiatry*, 1972, *129*, 521–531.

Gould, R. L. Transformations during early and middle adult years. In N. J. Smelser & E. H. Erikson (Eds.), *Themes of work and love in adulthood*. Cambridge,

Mass.: Harvard University Press, 1980.

Gove, W. R., & Tudor, J. F. Adult sex roles and mental illness. *American Journal of Sociology*, 1973, *78*, 812–835.

Green, M., & Tyron, H. *Preretirement counseling: Retirement, adjustment, and the older employee*. Eugene: University of Oregon Graduate School of Management, 1969.

Greenfield, P. M. Cross-cultural research and Piagetian theory: Paradox and progress. In K. F. Riegel & J. A. Meacham (Eds.), *The developing individual in a changing world*. Chicago: Aldine, 1976.

Greenfield, P. M., & Childs, C. Weaving, color terms and pattern representation: Cultural influences and cognitive development among the Zinacantecos. *International Journal of Psychology*, in press.

Gubrium, J. F. On multiple realities in a nursing home. In J. F. Gubrium (Ed.), *Late life communities and environmental policies*. Springfield, Ill.: Charles C Thomas, 1974.

Gubrium, J. F. Being single in old age. *International Journal of Aging and Human Development*, 1975, *6*, 29–41.

Guilford, J. P. The structure of the intellect. *Psychological Bulletin*, 1956, *53*, 267–293.

Gurin, G., Veroff, J., & Feld, S. *Americans view their mental health*. (Joint Commission on Mental Illness & Health. Monograph Series No. 4.) New York: Basic Books, 1960.

Guthrie, E. R. The status of systematic psychology. *American Psychologist*, 1950, *5*, 97–101.

Gutmann, D. L. An exploration of ego configurations in middle and later life. In B. L. Neugarten & Associates (Eds.), *Personality in middle and later life*. New York: Atherton Press, 1964.

Gutmann, D. L. The country of old men: Cross-cultural studies in the psychology of later life. *Occasional Papers in Gerontology* (No. 5.) Ann Arbor: Institute of Gerontology, University of Michigan–Wayne State, 1969.

Gutmann, D. L. Ego psychological and developmental approaches to the "retirement crisis" in men. In F. M. Carp (Ed.), *Retirement*. New York: Behavioral Publications, 1972.

Gutmann, D. L. Parenthood, key to comparative study of the life cycle. In N. Datan & L. Ginsberg (Eds.), *Life span developmental psychology: Normative life crises*. New York: Academic Press, 1975.

Gutmann, D. L. The cross-cultural perspective: Notes toward a comparative psychology of aging. In J. E. Birren & K. W. Schaie (Eds.), *Handbook of the psychology of aging*. New York: Van Nostrand Reinhold, 1977.

Gutmann, D. L. *Personal transformation in the post-parental period: A cross-cultural view*. Washington, D.C.: American Association for the Advancement of Science, 1978.

Gutmann, D. L., Grunes, L., & Griffin, B. The clinical psychology of later life: Developmental paradigm. Paper presented at the meeting of the Gerontological Society, Washington, D.C., December 1979.

Gutmann, E. Muscles. In C. E. Finch & L. Hayflick (Eds.), *Handbook of the biology of aging*. New York: Van Nostrand Reinhold, 1977.

Haan, N. Personality organization of well-functioning younger people and older adults. *International Journal of Aging and Human Development*, 1976, 7, 117–127.

Haan, N. Common dimensions of personality: Early adolescence to middle life. In D. H. Eichorn, N. Haan, J. Clausen, M. Honzik, & P. Mussen (Eds.), *Present and past in middle life*. New York: Academic Press, 1981.

Haan, N., & Day, D. A longitudinal study of change and sameness in personality development: Adolescence to later adulthood. *International Journal of Aging and Human Development*, 1974, 5, 11–39.

Hackman, J. R. Work design. In J. R. Hackman & J. Lloyd Suttle (Eds.), *Improving life at work*. Santa Monica, Calif.: Goodyear, 1977.

Haley, A. Commencement address. California State University, Los Angeles, June 1982.

Hammar, S. L., & Owens, J. W. M. *Adolescence*. In D. Smith & E. Bierman (Eds.), *The biologic ages of man*. Philadelphia: Saunders, 1973.

Harkins, S. W. Psychophysiological issues: Brain evoked potentials. In L. W. Poon (Ed.), *Aging in the 1980s*. Washington, D.C.: American Psychological Association, 1980.

Harris, R. Cardiac changes with age. In R. Goldman & M. Rockstein (Eds.), *The physiology and pathology of human aging*. New York: Academic Press, 1975.

Harrison, D. E. Is limited cell proliferation the clock that times aging? In J. Behnke, C. Finch, & G. Moment (Eds.), *The biology of aging*. New York: Plenum, 1978.

Harry, J. Evolving sources of happiness for men over the life cycle: A structural analysis. *Journal of Marriage and Family*, 1976, 38, 289–296.

Hartley, J. T., Harker, J. O., & Walsh, D. A. Contemporary issues and new directions in adult development of learning and memory. In L. W. Poon (Ed.), *Aging in the 1980s*. Washington, D.C.: American Psychological Association, 1980.

Hatfield, E., Utne, M. K., & Traupmann, J. Equity theory and intimate relationships. In R. L. Burgess & T. L. Huston (Eds.), *Social exchange in developing relationships*. New York: Academic Press, 1979.

Havighurst, R. J. Personality patterns of aging. *The Gerontologist*, 1968, 8, 20–23.

Havighurst, R. J. Research and development in social gerontology: A report of a special committee of the Gerontological Society. *The Gerontologist*, 1969, 9, 1–90.

Havighurst, R. J. *Developmental tasks and education*. New York: McKay, 1972.

Havighurst, R. J. Social roles, work, leisure, and education. In C. Eisdorfer & M. P. Lawton (Eds.), *The psychology of adult development and aging*. Washington, D.C.: American Psychological Association, 1973.

Havighurst, R. J. The world of work. In B. B. Wolman (Ed.), *Handbook of developmental psychology*. Englewood Cliffs, N.J.: Prentice-Hall, 1982.

Havighurst, R. J., Neugarten, B. L., & Tobin, S. C. Disengagement and patterns of aging. In B. L. Neugarten (Ed.), *Middle age and aging*. Chicago: University of Chicago Press, 1968.

Hayflick, L. Cell aging. In A. Cherkin & C. Finch et al. (Eds.), *Physiology and cell biology of aging*. (Aging Series, Vol. 8.) New York: Raven Press, 1979.

Heath, D. *Maturity and Competence*. New York: Gardner Press, 1977.

Heckman, N. A., Bryson, R., & Bryson, J. B. Problems of professional couples: A context analysis. *Journal of Marriage and the Family*, 1977, *39*, 323–330.

Hendricks, J. (Ed.) *Being and becoming old*. Farmingdale, N.Y.: Baywood, 1981.

Hendricks, J., & Hendricks, C. D. *Aging in mass society*. Cambridge, Mass.: Winthrop, 1977.

Hendricks, J., & Hendricks, C. D. *Aging in mass society*. (2nd ed.) Cambridge, Mass.: Winthrop, 1981.

Hennig, M. M. Career development for women executives. Doctoral dissertation, Harvard University, 1970.

Henry, W. E. Engagement and disengagement: Toward a theory of adult development. In R. Kastenbaum (Ed.), *Contributions to the psychobiology of aging*. New York: Springer, 1965.

Hershey, D. *Life span and factors affecting it*. Springfield, Ill.: Charles C Thomas, 1974.

Hess, B. Amicability. Doctoral dissertation, Rutgers University, 1971.

Hess, B. B., & Waring, J. M. Parent and child in later life: Rethinking the relationship. In R. Lerner & G. Spanier (Eds.), *Child influences on marital and family interaction*. New York: Academic Press, 1978.

Hetherington, E. M., Cox, M., & Cox, R. Divorced fathers. *Psychology Today*, April 1977, pp. 42–46.

Hettlinger, R. Values on campus. In E. Morrison & V. Borosage (Eds.), *Human sexuality*. Palo Alto, Calif.: Mayfield, 1977.

Hickey, T., & Kalish, R. A. Young people's perceptions of adults. *Journal of Gerontology*, 1968, *23*, 216–219.

Hicks, M. W., & Platt, M. Marital happiness and stability. *Journal of Marriage and the Family*, 1970, *32*, 553–574.

Hill, R., Foote, N., Aldous, J., Carlson, R., & McDonald, R. *Family development in three generations*. Cambridge, Mass.: Schenkman, 1970.

Hinton, J. *Dying*. Baltimore: Penguin, 1967.

Hinton, J. Speaking of death with the dying. In E. Shneidman (Ed.), *Death: Current perspectives*. Palo Alto, Calif.: Mayfield, 1976.

Hobbs, D. F., Jr. Parenthood as crisis: A third study. *Journal of Marriage and the Family*, 1965, *27*, 367–372.

Hobbs, D. F., Jr., & Cole, S. P. Transition to parenthood: A decade of replication. *Journal of Marriage and the Family*, 1976, *38*, 723–731.

Hofer, M. A., Wolff, C. T., Friedman, S. B., & Mason, J. W. A psychoendocrine study of bereavement. *Psychosomatic Medicine*, 1972, *34*, 492–504.

Hoffman, L. W. Effects of maternal employment on the child. *Child Development*, 1961, *32*, 187–197.

Hoffman, L. W., & Manis, J. D. Influences of children on marital interaction and parental satisfactions and dissatisfactions. In R. M. Lerner & G. B. Spanier (Eds.), *Child influences on marital and family interaction*. New York: Academic Press, 1978.

Hoffman, L. W., & Nye, F. I. *Working mothers*. San Francisco: Jossey-Bass, 1974.

Hoffman, M. L. Moral development in adolescence. In J. Adelson (Ed.), *Handbook of adolescent psychology*. New York: Wiley, 1980.

Hogan, R. Dialectical aspects of moral development. *Human Development*, 1974, *17*, 107–117.

Hogshead, H. P. The art of delivering bad news. In C. Garfield (Ed.), *Psychological care of the dying person*. New York: McGraw-Hill, 1978.

Holland, J. L. *The psychology of vocational choice: A theory of personality types and model environments*. Waltham, Mass.: Blaisdell, 1966.

Holland, J. L., Sorensen, A. B., Clark, S. P., Najziger, D. H., & Blum, Z. D. Applying an occupational classification to a representative sample of work histories. *Journal of Applied Psychology*, 1973, *58*, 34–41.

Hollander, E. P., & Hunt, R. G. *Current perspectives in social psychology*. New York: Oxford University Press, 1967.

Holmes, T. H., & Rahe, R. H. The social readjustment rating scale. *Journal of Psychosomatic Research*, 1967, *11*, 213–218.

Holmstrom, L. L. *The two-career family*. Cambridge, Mass.: Schenkman, 1972.

Hooper, F. Life-span analysis of Piagetian concept tasks: The search for nontrivial qualitative change. In K. Riegel & J. Meacham (Eds.), *The developing individual in a changing world*. Chicago: Aldine, 1976.

Horn, J. L. Organization of data on life-span development of human abilities. In L. R. Goulet & P. B. Baltes (Eds.), *Life-span developmental psychology: Research and theory*. New York: Academic Press, 1970.

Horn, J. L. Human ability systems. In P. B. Baltes (Ed.), *Life-span development and behavior*. Vol. 1. New York: Academic Press, 1978.

Horn, J. L. The theory of fluid and crystallized intelligence in relation to concepts of cognitive psychology and aging in adulthood. In F. I. M. Craik & S. E. Trehub (Eds.), *The 1980 Erindale Symposium*. Beverly Hills, Calif.: Sage, 1982.

Horn, J. L., & Cattell, R. B. Some comments on whimsey and misunderstandings of Gf-Gc theory. *Psychological Bulletin*, 1982, *90*, 623–633.

Horn, J. L., Donaldson, G., & Engstrom, R. Apprehension, memory and fluid intelligence decline in adulthood. *Research on Aging*, 1981, *3*, 33–84.

Horowitz, M., & Wilner, N. Life events, stress, and coping. In L. W. Poon (Ed.), *Aging in the 1980s*. Washington, D.C.: American Psychological Association, 1980.

Houseknecht, S. K. Reference group support for voluntary childlessness: Evidence for conformity. *Journal of Marriage and the Family*, 1977, *39*, 285–291.

Howard, A., & Scott, R. A. Cultural values and attitudes toward dying. *Journal of Existentialism*, 1965, *6*, 161–174.

Howell, S. C. *Shared spaces in housing for the elderly*. Cambridge: Laboratory of Architecture and Planning, Massachusetts Institute of Technology, 1978.

Howell, S. C. Environments as hypotheses in human aging research. In L. W. Poon (Ed.), *Aging in the 1980s*. Washington, D.C.: American Psychological Association, 1980.

Huesmann, L. R. Toward a predictive model of romantic behavior. In K. S. Pope (Ed.), *On loving and being loved*. San Francisco: Jossey-Bass, 1980.

Hughes, E. C. *Men and their work*. New York: Free Press, 1958.

Hulicka, I. M. Age differences in retention as a function of interference. *Journal of Gerontology*, 1967, *22*, 180–184.

Hulicka, I. M., & Grossman, J. L. Age-group comparisons of paired-associate learning as a function of paced and self-paced association and response time. *Journal of Gerontology*, 1967, *22*, 274–280.

Hultsch, D. F. Implications of a dialectical perspective for a research methodology. *Human Development*, 1980, *23*, 217–267.

Hultsch, D. F., & Pentz, C. A. Encoding, storage and retrieval in adult memory: The role of assumptions. In L. W. Poon, J. L. Fozard, L. S. Cremak, D. Arenberg, & L. W. Thompson (Eds.), *New directions in memory and aging: Proceedings of the George Talland Memorial Conference*. Hillsdale, N.J.: Lawrence Erlbaum, 1980.

Hultsch, D. F., & Plemons, J. K. Life events and life-span development. In P. B. Baltes & O. G. Brim, Jr. (Eds.), *Life-span development and behavior*. Vol. 2. New York: Academic Press, 1979.

Hunt, M. *Sexual behavior in the 1970s*. Chicago: Playboy Press, 1974.

Hurlock, E. *Developmental psychology*. (4th ed.) New York: McGraw-Hill, 1975.

Huston, T. L. Power. In H. H. Kelley et al. (Eds.), *Close relationships*. New York: Freeman, 1983.

Huston, T. L., & Burgess, R. L. Social exchange in developing relationships: An overview. In T. L. Huston & R. L. Burgess (Eds.), *Social exchange in developing relationships*. New York: Academic Press, 1979.

Inglis, J., & Caird, W. K. Age differences in successive responses to simultaneous stimulation. *Canadian Journal of Psychology*, 1963, *17*, 98–105.

Insel, P. M., & Roth, W. T. *Health in a changing society*. Palo Alto, Calif.: Mayfield, 1976.

Insel, P., & Roth, W. T. *Core concepts in health*. (3rd ed.) Palo Alto, Calif.: Mayfield, 1982.

Israel, H. Continuing growth in the human cranial skeleton. *Archives of Oral Biology*, 1968, *13*, 133–137.

Jacobs, H., & Ritchie, R. W. Functional disorders: A follow-up study of outpatient diagnosis. *British Medical Journal*, 1961, *2*, 346–348.

Jacoby, S. The truth about two-job marriages. *McCall's*, June 1982, pp. 127–128.

Janis, I., & Wheeler, D. Thinking clearly about career choices. *Psychology Today*, May 1978, p. 75.

Janson, H. W. *History of art*. Englewood Cliffs, N.J.: Prentice-Hall, 1962.

Jeffko, W. G. Redefining death. In E. S. Shneidman (Ed.), *Death: Current perspectives*. (2nd ed.) Palo Alto, Calif.: Mayfield, 1980.

Jerome, E. A. Decay of heuristic processes in the aged. In C. Tibbitts & W. Donahue (Eds.), *Social and psychological aspects of aging*. New York: Columbia University Press, 1962.

Johnson, E. S., & Bursk, B. J. Relationships between the elderly and their adult children. *The Gerontologist*, 1977, *17*, 90–96.

Jourard, S. M., & Lasakow, P. Some factors in self-disclosure. *Journal of Abnormal and Social Psychology*, 1958, *56*, 91–98.

Jung, J. *The experimenter's dilemma*. New York: Harper & Row, 1971.

Kagan, J., & Kogan, N. Individual variation in cognitive processes. In P. H. Mussen (Ed.), *Carmichael's handbook of child psychology*. (3rd ed.) New York: Wiley, 1970.

Kahana, B. Social behavior and aging. In B. B. Wolman (Ed.), *Handbook of developmental psychology*. Englewood Cliffs, N.J.: Prentice-Hall, 1982.

Kahana, E. The humane treatment of old people in institutions. *The Gerontologist*, 1973, *13*, 282–289.

Kahana, E. A congruence model of person-environment interaction. In P. G. Windley & G. Ernst (Eds.), *Theory development in environment and aging*. Washington, D.C.: Gerontological Society, 1975.

Kahana, E., Kahana, B., & McLenigan, P. The adventurous aged: Voluntary relocation in the later years. Paper presented at the Thirty-third Annual Scientific Meeting of the Gerontological Society, San Diego, Calif., November 1980.

Kales, J. D. Aging and sleep. In R. Goldman & M. Rockstein (Eds.), *The physiology and pathology of human aging*. New York: Academic Press, 1975.

Kalish, R. An approach to the study of death attitudes. *American Behavioral Scientist*, 1963, *6*, 68–80.

Kalish, R. A. *Late adulthood: Perspectives on human development*. Monterey, Calif.: Brooks/Cole, 1975.

Kalish, R. A. Death and dying in a social context. In R. H. Binstock and E. Shanas (Eds.), *Handbook of aging and the social sciences*. New York: Van Nostrand Reinhold, 1977.

Kalish, R. A., & Knudtson, F. W. Attachment versus disengagement: A life-span conceptualization. *Human Development*, 1976, *19*, 135–182.

Kalish, R. A., & Reynolds, D. K. *Death and ethnicity: A psychocultural study*. Los Angeles: University of Southern California Press, 1976.

Kangas, J., & Bradway, K. Intelligence at middle age: A thirty-eight year follow-up. *Developmental Psychology*, 1971, *5*, 333–337.

Kanter, R. *Commitment and community, communes and utopias in sociological perspective*. Cambridge, Mass.: Harvard University Press, 1972.

Kaplan, H. B., & Pokony, A. P. Aging and self-attitude: A conditional relationship. *International Journal of Aging and Human Development*, 1970, *1*, 241–250.

Kastenbaum, R. On the meaning of time in later life. *Journal of Genetic Psychology*, 1966, *109*, 9–25.

Kastenbaum, R. Death and development through the life-span. In H. Feifel (Ed.), *New meanings of death*. New York: McGraw-Hill, 1977.

Kastenbaum, R. Symposium on the life after death experience. Paper presented at the Western Psychological Association Convention, San Francisco, April 1978.

Kastenbaum, R. *Death, society and human experience*. (2nd ed.) St. Louis: Mosby, 1981. (a).

Kastenbaum, R. Exit and existence: Alternative scenarios. In S. Wilcox & M. Sutton (Eds.), *Understanding death and dying*. (2nd ed.) Palo Alto, Calif.: Mayfield, 1981. (b).

Kastenbaum, R., & Ainsenberg, R. *The psychology of death*. New York: Springer, 1972.

Katz, R. Job enrichment: Some career considerations. In J. Van Maanen (Ed.), *Organizational careers: Some new perspectives*. New York: Wiley, 1977.

Katz, R., & Van Maanen, J. *The loci of satisfaction: Job interaction and policy*. (Sloan School of Management Working Paper 741–774) Cambridge: Massachusetts

Institute of Technology, 1974.

Kay, E. *The crisis in middle management.* New York: AMACOM, 1974.

Keating, N. C., & Cole, P. What do I do with him 24 hours a day? Changes in the housewife role after retirement. *The Gerontologist,* 1980, *20,* 84–89.

Keller, S. *The urban neighborhood: A sociological perspective.* New York: Random House, 1968.

Kelley, H. H., Berscheid, E., Christensen, A., Harvey, J. H., Huston, T. L., Levinger, G., McClintock, E., Peplau, L. A., & Peterson, D. R. (Eds.), *Close relationships.* San Francisco: Freeman, 1983.

Kessen, W. *The child.* New York: Wiley, 1965.

Keyserling, M. D. Women's stake in full employment: Their disadvantaged role in the economy—challenge to action. In A. F. Cahn (Ed.), *Women in the U.S. labor force.* New York: Praeger, 1979.

Kimmel, D. C. Gay people grow old too: Life history interviews of aging gay men. *International Journal of Aging and Human Development,* 1982, *10,* 239–248.

Kinsey, A. C., Pomeroy, W. B., & Martin, C. *Sexual behavior in the human male.* Philadelphia: Saunders, 1948.

Kitchener, R. F. Epigenesis: The role of biological models in developmental psychology. *Human Development,* 1978, *21,* 141–160.

Kitson, G. C., & Sussman, M. B. Marital complaints, demographic characteristics, and symptoms of mental distress in divorce. *Journal of Marriage and the Family,* 1982, *44,* 87–102.

Kleemeier, R. W. Behavior and organization and external environment. In J. E. Birren (Ed.), *Handbook of aging and the individual.* Chicago: University of Chicago Press, 1959.

Knapp, P. H. Emotional aspects of hearing loss. *Psychosomatic Medicine,* 1948, *10,* 203–222.

Kohlberg, L. The development of children's orientations toward a moral order: A sequence in the development of moral thought. *Vita Humana,* 1963, *6,* 11–33.

Kohlberg, L. The claim to moral adequacy of a highest stage of moral development. *Journal of Philosophy,* 1973, *70,* 630–646. (a).

Kohlberg, L. Continuities in childhood and adult moral development revisited. In P. B. Baltes & K. W. Schaie (Eds.), *Life-span developmental psychology: Personality and socialization.* New York: Academic Press, 1973. (b).

Kohn, R. R. Heart and cardiovascular system. In C. E. Finch & L. Hayflick (Eds.), *Handbook of the biology of aging.* New York: Van Nostrand Reinhold, 1977.

Komarovsky, M. Cultural contradictions and sex roles: The masculine case. *American Journal of Sociology,* 1973, *78,* 873–884.

Kosberg, J. I. Differences in proprietary institutions caring for affluent and nonaffluent elderly. *The Gerontologist,* 1973, *13* (Part 1), 299–304.

Krause, E. A. *The sociology of occupations.* Boston: Little, Brown, 1971.

Krishnan, P., & Kayani, A. F. Estimates of age-specific divorce rates for females in the United States, 1960–1969. *Journal of Marriage and the Family,* 1974, *36,* 72–76.

Kübler-Ross, E. *On death and dying.* New York: Macmillan, 1969.

Kübler-Ross, E. *Questions and answers on death and dying*. New York: Macmillan, 1974.

Kuhlen, R. G. Development changes in motivation during the adult years. In B. L. Neugarten (Ed.), *Middle age and aging*. Chicago: University of Chicago Press, 1968.

Kuhlen, R. G., & Johnson, G. H. Changes in goals with adult increasing age. *Journal of Consulting Psychology*, 1952, *16*, 1–4.

Kuhn, D., Langer, J., Kohlberg, L., & Haan, N. The development of formal operations in logical and moral judgment. *Genetic Psychology Monographs*, 1977, *95*, 97–188.

Kuypers, J. A. Ego functioning in old age: Early adult life antecedents. In J. Hendricks (Ed.), *Being and becoming old*. Farmingdale, N.Y.: Baywood, 1981.

Labouvie, E. Issues in life-span development. In B. B. Wolman (Ed.), *Handbook of developmental psychology*. Englewood Cliffs, N.J.: Prentice-Hall, 1982.

Labouvie-Vief, G., & Chandler, M. J. Cognitive development and life-span development theory: Idealistic versus contextual perspective. In P. B. Baltes (Ed.), *Life-span development and behavior*. Vol. 1. New York: Academic Press, 1978.

Labouvie-Vief, G., & Schell, D. A. Learning and memory in later life. In B. B. Wolman (Ed.), *Handbook of developmental psychology*. Englewood Cliffs, N.J.: Prentice-Hall, 1982.

Lacy, W. D., & Hendricks, J. Developmental models of adult life: Myth or reality. *International Journal of Aging and Human Development*, 1980, *11*, 89–110.

Lamb, M. C. Influence of the child on marital quality and family interaction during the prenatal, perinatal and infancy periods. In R. M. Lerner & G. B. Spanier (Eds.), *Child influences on marital and family interaction*. New York: Academic Press, 1978.

Lamb, M. E. Fathers and child development: An integrative overview. In M. E. Lamb (Ed.), *The role of the father in child development*. New York: Wiley, 1981.

Lamb, M. E., & Goldberg, W. A. The father-child relationship: A synthesis of biological, evolutionary, and social perspectives. In L. W. Hoffman, R. Gandelman, & H. R. Schiffman (Eds.), *Parenting: Its causes and consequences*. Hillsdale, N.J.: Lawrence Erlbaum, 1982.

Landis, P. *Making the most of marriage*. Englewood Cliffs, N.J.: Prentice-Hall, 1975.

Langer, J. *Theories of development*. New York: Holt, Rinehart & Winston, 1969.

La Rossa, R., & La Rossa, M. M. *Transition to parenthood: How infants change families*. Beverly Hills, Calif.: Sage, 1981.

LaRue, A., & Jarvik, L. Old age and biobehavioral changes. In B. B. Wolman (Ed.), *Handbook of developmental psychology*. Englewood Cliffs, N.J.: Prentice-Hall, 1982.

LaRue, A., & Waldbaum, A. Aging versus illness as predictors of Piagetian problem-solving in older adults. Paper presented at the tenth annual interdisciplinary international conference on Piagetian theory and the helping professions. Los Angeles, February 1982.

Lasch, C. *The culture of narcissism*. New York: Norton, 1978.

Lasswell, M., & Lobsenz, N. *Styles of loving*. Garden City, N.Y.: Doubleday, 1980.

Lawton, M. P. Ecology and aging. In L. A. Pastalan & D. H. Carson (Eds.), *The spatial behavior of older people*. Ann Arbor: Michigan Institute of Gerontology, 1970.

Lawton, M. P. *Planning and managing housing for the elderly*. New York: Wiley, 1975.

Lawton, M. P. The impact of environment on aging and behavior. In J. E. Birren & K. W. Schaie (Eds.), *Handbook of the psychology of aging*. New York: Van Nostrand Reinhold, 1977.

Lawton, M. P. *Environment and aging*. Monterey, Calif.: Brooks/Cole, 1980.

Lawton, M. P., & Cohen, J. Housing impact on older people. *Journal of Gerontology*, 1974, *29*, 194–204.

Lawton, M. P., Greenbaum, M., & Leibowitz, B. The life-span of housing environments for the aging. *The Gerontologist*, 1980, *20*, 56–64.

Lawton, M. P., & Nahemow, L. Ecology and the aging process. In C. Eisdorfer & M. P. Lawton (Eds.), *The psychology of adult development and aging*. Washington, D.C.: American Psychological Association, 1973.

Layton, B. Perceptual noise and aging. *Psychological Bulletin*, 1975, *82*, 875–883.

Lee, J. A. Styles of loving. *Psychology Today*, 1974, *8*, 43–51.

Lee, J. A. A typology of styles of loving. *Personality and Social Behavior*, 1977, *3*, 173–182.

Lehman, H. C. *Age and achievement*. Princeton, N.J.: Princeton University Press, 1953.

Lehman, H. C. The age decrement in outstanding scientific creativity. *American Psychologist*, 1960, *15*, 128–134.

Leifer, M. Psychological changes accompanying pregnancy and motherhood. *Genetic Psychology Monographs*, 1977, *95*, 55–96.

Le Masters, E. E. Parenthood as crisis. *Marriage and Family Living*, 1957, *19*, 352–355.

Lemon, B. W., Bengston, V. L., & Peterson, J. A. Activity types and life satisfaction in a retirement community. *Journal of Gerontology*, 1972, *27*, 511–523.

Lerner, R. M., & Ryff, C. D. Implementation of the life-span view of human development: The sample case of attachment. In P. B. Baltes & O. G. Brim, Jr. (Eds.), *Life-span development and behavior*. Vol. 1. New York: Academic Press, 1978.

Lerner, R. M., Skinner, E. A., & Sorell, G. Methodological implications of contextual/dialectical theories of development. In D. F. Hultsch (Ed.), *Implications of a dialectical perspective for research methodology*. *Human Development*, 1980, *23*, 225–235.

Levin, R. J. The redbook report on premarital and extramarital sex. *Redbook*, Oct. 1975, 51–58.

Levinger, G. A. A social psychological perspective on marital dissolution. In G. Levinger & O. C. Moles (Eds.), *Divorce and separation*. New York: Basic Books, 1979.

Levinger, G., & Snock, D. *Attraction in relationships: A new look at interpersonal attraction*. Morristown, N.J.: General Learning Press, 1972.

Levinson, D. J., Darrow, C. M., Klein, E. G., Levinson, M. H., & McKee, B. The psychosocial development of men in early adulthood and the midlife transition. In D. F. Ricks, A. Thomas, & M. Roff (Eds.), *Life history research in psychopathology*. Vol. 3. Minneapolis: University of Minnesota Press, 1974.

Levinson, D. J., Darrow, C. N., Klein, E. B., Levinson, M. H., & McKee, B. *Seasons of a man's life*. New York: Knopf, 1978.

Levy, S. M., Derogatis, L. R., Gallagher, D., & Gatz, M. Intervention with older adults and the evaluation of outcome. In L. W. Poon (Ed.), *Aging in the 1980s*. Washington, D.C.: American Psychological Association, 1980.

Libby, R. W. Extramarital and comarital sex: A critique of the literature. In R. W. Libby and R. N. Whitehurst (Eds.), *Marriage and alternatives: Exploring intimate relationships*. Glenview, Ill.: Scott Foresman, 1977.

Lieberman, L. R. Life satisfaction in the young and the old. *Psychological Reports*, 1970, *27*, 75–79.

Lieberman, M. A. Social and psychological determinants of adaptation. In J. Hendricks (Ed.), *Being and becoming old*. Farmingdale, N.Y.: Baywood, 1981.

Lieberman, M. A., & Coplan, A. S. Distance from death as a variable in the study of aging. *Developmental Psychology*, 1969, *2*, 71–84.

Lieberman, M. A., Prock, V. N., & Tobin, S. S. Psychological effects of institutionalization. *Journal of Gerontology*, 1968, *3*, 343–353.

Lieberman, M. A., Tobin, S. S., & Slover, D. *The effects of relocation on long-term geriatric patients*. (Final Report, Project No. 17–1328.) Chicago: Illinois Department of Health Committee on Human Development, University of Chicago, 1971.

Lifton, R. J. Witnessing survival. In R. Fulton, E. Markusen, G. Owen, & J. L. Scheiber (Eds.), *Death and dying: Challenge and change*. San Francisco: Boyd & Fraser, 1981.

Lifton, R. J., & Olson, E. *Living and dying*. New York: Praeger, 1974.

Lilly, J. *The center of the cyclone*. New York: Julian Press, 1972.

Lindeman, R. D. Changes in renal function. In R. Goldman & M. Rockstein (Eds.), *The physiology and pathology of human aging*. New York: Academic Press, 1975.

Livingston, K. R. Love as a process of reducing uncertainty-cognitive theory. In K. S. Pope (Ed.), *On loving and being loved*. San Francisco: Jossey-Bass, 1980.

Livson, F. B. Paths to psychological health in the middle years: Sex differences. In D. H. Eichorn, N. Haan, J. Clausen, M. Honzik, & P. Mussen (Eds.), *Present and past in middle life*. New York: Academic Press, 1981. (a).

Livson, F. B. Patterns of personality development in middle-aged women: A longitudinal study. In J. Hendricks (Ed.), *Being and becoming old*. Farmingdale, N.Y.: Baywood, 1981. (b).

Livson, N. Developmental dimensions of personality: A life-span formulation. In P. B. Baltes & K. W. Schaie (Eds.), *Life-span development psychology: Personality and socialization*. New York: Academic Press, 1973.

Livson, N., & Peskin, H. Psychological health at age 40: Prediction from adolescent personality. In D. H. Eichorn, N. Haan, J. Clausen, M. Honzik, & P. Mussen (Eds.), *Present and past in middle life*. New York: Academic Press, 1981.

Longfellow, C. Divorce in context: Its impact on children. In G. Levinger & O. C. Moles (Eds.), *Divorce and separation*. New York: Basic Books, 1979.

Looft, W. R. Socialization and personality throughout the life span: An examination of contemporary psychological approaches. In P. B. Baltes & K. W. Schaie

(Eds.), *Life-span developmental psychology: Personality and socialization*. New York: Academic Press, 1973.

Lopata, H. Z. *Occupation: Housewife*. New York: Oxford University Press, 1971.

Lopata, H. Z. *Widowhood in an American city*. Cambridge, Mass.: Schenkman, 1973.

Lopata, H. Z. Widowhood: Societal factors in life-span disruptions and alternatives. In N. Datan & L. Ginsberg (Eds.), *Life-span developmental psychology: Normative life crises*. New York: Academic Press, 1975.

Lowenthal, M. F. Some potentialities of a life-cycle approach to the study of retirement. In F. M. Carp (Ed.), *Retirement*. New York: Behavioral Publications, 1972.

Lowenthal, M. F. Intentionality: Toward a framework for the study of adaptation in adulthood. In J. Hendricks (Ed.), *Being and becoming old*. New York: Baywood, 1981.

Lowenthal, M. F., & Chiriboga, D. Transition to the empty nest: Crisis, change, or relief? *Archives of General Psychiatry*, 1972, *26*, 8–14.

Lowenthal, M. F., & Robinson, B. Social networks and isolation. In R. H. Binstock & E. Shanas, *Handbook of aging and the social sciences*. New York: Van Nostrand Reinhold, 1977.

Lowenthal, M. F., Thurnher, M., Chiriboga, D., & Associates. *Four stages of life*. San Francisco: Jossey-Bass, 1975.

Lowenthal, M., & Weiss, L. Intimacy and crisis in adulthood. *Counseling Psychologist*, 1976, *6*, 10–15.

Lunneborg, C. E., & Lunneborg, P. W. Factor structure of the vocational interest models of Roe and Holland. *Journal of Vocational Behavior*, 1975, *7*, 313–326.

Lunneborg, P. W. Role model influences of nontraditional professional women. *Journal of Vocational Behavior*, 1982, *20*, 276–281.

Lurie, E. E. Sex and stage differences in perceptions of marital and family relationships. *Journal of Marriage and the Family*, 1974, *36*, 260–269.

Lynn, D. B. *The father: His role in child development*. Monterey, Calif.: Brooks/Cole, 1974.

Maas, H. S., & Kuypers, J. A. *From thirty to seventy*. San Francisco: Jossey-Bass, 1974.

McCary, J. L., & McCary, S. P. *McCary's Human Sexuality*. (4th ed.) Belmont, Calif.: Wadsworth, 1982.

Macedonia, R. M. Expectation: Press and survival. Doctoral dissertation, New York University, 1969.

McFarland, R. A., Domey, R. G., Warren, A. B., & Ward, D. E. Dark adaptation as a function of age: A statistical analysis. *Journal of Gerontology*, 1960, *15*, 149–154.

McGee, J., & Wells, K. Gender typing and androgyny in later life: New direction for theory and research. *Human Development*, 1982, *25*, 116–139.

McKain, W. C. *Retirement marriage*. Storrs: University of Connecticut Press, 1969.

McKeown, F. *Pathology of the aged*. London: Butterworth, 1965.

McTavish, D. G. Perceptions of older people: A review of the research methodologies and findings. *The Gerontologist*, 1971, *11*, 90–102.

Maddox, B. Neither witch nor good fairy. *New York Times Magazine*, August 8, 1976, p. 16.

Maddox, G. L. A longitudinal multidisciplinary study of human aging: Selected methodological issues. *Proceedings of the Social Statistics Section of the Ameri-*

can Statistical Association. Washington, D.C.: American Statistical Association, 1962.

Maddox, G. L. Persistence of life style among the elderly: A longitudinal study of patterns of social activity in relation to life satisfaction. In B. L. Neugarten (Ed.), *Middle age and aging.* Chicago: University of Chicago Press, 1968.

Mant, A. K. Definition of death. In A. Toynbee, A. K. Mant, N. Smart, J. Hinton, C. Yudkin, E. Rhode, R. Heywood, & H. H. Price. *Man's concern with death.* New York: McGraw-Hill, 1968.

Marcia, J. E. Identity in adolescence. In J. Adelson (Ed.), *Handbook of adolescent psychology.* New York: Wiley, 1980.

Markus, E., Blenker, M., Bloom, M., & Downs, T. Some factors and their association with post-relocation mortality among institutionalized aged persons. *Journal of Gerontology,* 1972, *27,* 376–382.

Marlowe, R. A. Effects of environment on state hospital relocatees. Paper presented at the annual meeting of the Pacific Sociological Association, Scottsdale, Arizona, May 1973.

Marsh, G. R., & Thompson, L. W. Psychophysiology of aging. In J. E. Birren & K. W. Schaie (Eds.), *Handbook of the psychology of aging.* New York: Van Nostrand Reinhold, 1977.

Marshall, V. M. Socialization for impending death in a retirement village. *American Journal of Sociology,* 1975, *80,* 1124–1144.

Martin, T. O. Death anxiety and social desirability among nurses. *Omega,* 1982–1983, *13,* 51–58.

Marx, M. *Theories in contemporary psychology.* New York: Macmillan, 1964.

Maslow, A. *Motivation and personality.* (2nd ed.) New York: Harper & Row, 1970.

Masters, W. H., & Johnson, V. E. *Human sexual response.* Boston: Little, Brown, 1966.

Masters, W. H., & Johnson, V. E. *Human sexual inadequacy.* Boston: Little, Brown, 1970.

Masters, W. H., Johnson, V. E., & Kolodny, R. C. *Human Sexuality.* Boston: Little, Brown, 1982.

Meacham, J. A. A transactional model of remembering. In N. Datan and H. W. Reese (Eds.), *Life span developmental psychology: Dialectical perspectives on experimental research.* New York: Academic Press, 1977.

Meacham, J. A. Research on remembering: Interrogation or conversation, monologue or dialogue? In D. F. Hultsch (Ed.), *Implications of a dialectical perspective for research methodology. Human Development,* 1980, *23,* 236–245.

Mead, M. *Culture and commitment: A study of the generation gap.* Garden City, N.Y.: Doubleday, 1970.

Meir, E. K., & Ben-Yehuda, A. Inventories based on Roe and Holland yield similar results. *Journal of Vocational Behavior,* 1976, *8,* 269–274.

Melville, K. *Marriage and family today.* New York: Random House, 1977.

Miernyk, W. H. The changing life cycle of work. In N. Datan & L. Ginsberg (Eds.), *Life-span developmental psychology: Normative life crises.* New York: Academic Press, 1975.

Mileski, M., & Black, D. J. The social organization of homosexuality. *Urban Life and Culture,* 1972, *1,* 187–199.

Miller, B. C. A multivariate developmental model of marital satisfaction. *Journal of Marriage and the Family*, 1976, *36*, 643–657.

Miller, P. H. *Theories of developmental psychology*. San Francisco: Freeman, 1983.

Milne, L. J., & Milne, N. *The ages of life*. New York: Harcourt Brace Jovanovich, 1968.

Mischel, W. Continuity and change in personality. *American Psychologist*, 1969, *24*, 1012–1018.

Mitford, J. *The American way of death*. New York: Simon & Schuster, 1963.

Moment, G. The Ponce de Leon trail today. In J. Behnke, C. Finch, & G. Moment (Eds.), *The biology of aging*. New York: Plenum, 1978.

Moncrieff, R. W. *Odor preferences*. New York: Wiley, 1966.

Monge, R. H., & Garner, E. F. Education as an aid to adaptation in the adult years. In K. F. Riegel & J. A. Meacham (Eds.), *The developing individual in a changing world*. Vol. 2. *Social and environmental issues*. The Hague: Mouton, 1976.

Montgomery, R. Impact of institutional care policies on family integration. *The Gerontologist*, 1982, *22*, 54–58.

Moody, R. A. *Life after life*. New York: Bantam, 1975.

Morris, W. (Ed.) *The American heritage dictionary of the English language*. Boston: Houghton Mifflin, 1979.

Murdock, B. B., Jr. Recent developments in short-term memory. *British Journal of Psychology*, 1967, *58*, 421–433.

Murstein, B. Empirical tests of role complementarity needs and homogamy: Theories of mate selection. *Journal of Marriage and the Family*, 1967, *29*, 689–696.

Murstein, B. Stimulus-value-role: A theory of marital choice. *Journal of Marriage and the Family*, 1970, *32*, 465–481.

Murstein, B. Self-ideal-self discrepancy and the choice of marital partner. In M. E. Lasswell & T. E. Lasswell (Eds.), *Love, marriage, and family: A developmental approach*. Glenview, Ill.: Scott, Foresman, 1973.

Murstein, B. I. Marital choice. In B. B. Wolman (Ed.), *Handbook of developmental psychology*. Englewood Cliffs, N.J.: Prentice-Hall, 1982.

Murstein, B. I., Cerreto, M., and MacDonald, M. G. A theory and investigation of the effect of exchange orientation on marriage and friendship. *Journal of Marriage and the Family*, 1977, *39*, 543–548.

Nahemow, L., & Kogan, L. S. *Reduced fare for the elderly*. New York: Mayor's Office for the Aging, 1971.

National Center for Health Statistics, Department of Health, Education, and Welfare. *Health in the later years*. Washington, D.C.: U.S. Government Printing Office, 1971.

Neisser, U. *Cognition and reality: Principles and implications of cognitive psychology*. San Francisco: Freeman, 1976.

Nesselroade, J. R. Issues in studying development change in adults from a multivariate perspective. In J. E. Birren & K. W. Schaie (Eds.), *Handbook of the psychology of aging*. New York: Van Nostrand Reinhold, 1977.

Nesselroade, J. R., & Baltes, P. B. Adolescent personality development and historical change: 1970–1972. *Monographs of the Society for Research in Child Development*, 1974, *39* (entire issue no. 154).

Nettler, G. Review essay: On death and dying. In F. G. Scott & R. M. Brewer (Eds.),

Confrontations of death. Corvallis: Oregon Center for Gerontology, Continuing Education Publications, 1971.

Neugarten, B. L. A new look at menopause. *Psychology Today*, December 1967, pp. 42–45, 67–69.

Neugarten, B. L. Adult personality: Toward a psychology of the life cycle. In B. L. Neugarten (Ed.), *Middle age and aging.* Chicago: University of Chicago Press, 1968. (a)

Neugarten, B. L. The awareness of middle age. In B. L. Neugarten (Ed.), *Middle age and aging.* Chicago: University of Chicago Press, 1968. (b)

Neugarten, B. L. Continuities and discontinuities of psychological issues into adult life. *Human Development*, 1969, *12*, 121–130.

Neugarten, B. L. Personality change in later life: A developmental perspective. In C. Eisdorfer & M. P. Lawton (Eds.), *The psychology of adult development and aging.* Washington, D.C.: American Psychological Association, 1973.

Neugarten, B. L. Age groups in American society and the rise of the young old. *Annals of American Academy of Science*, September 1974, pp. 187–198. (a)

Neugarten, B. L. The roles we play. In American Medical Association, *Quality of life: The middle years.* Acton, Mass.: Publishing Sciences Group, 1974. (b)

Neugarten, B. L. Personality and aging. In J. E. Birren & K. W. Schaie (Eds.), *Handbook of the psychology of aging.* New York: Van Nostrand Reinhold, 1977.

Neugarten, B. L., & Associates. *Personality in middle and later life.* New York: Atherton Press, 1964.

Neugarten, B. L., & Datan, N. The middle years. In S. Arieti (Ed.), *American handbook of psychiatry.* Vol. 1. (2nd ed.) New York: Basic Books, 1974.

Neugarten, B. L., & Hagestad, G. O. Age and the life course. In R. H. Binstock & E. Shanas (Eds.), *Handbook of aging and the social sciences.* New York: Van Nostrand Reinhold, 1977.

Neugarten, B. L., Havighurst, R. J., & Tobin, S. S. Personality and patterns of aging. In B. L. Neugarten (Ed.), *Middle age and aging.* Chicago: University of Chicago Press, 1968.

Neugarten, B. L., Kraines, R. J., & Wood, V. Women in the middle years. Unpublished manuscript of the Committee on Human Development, University of Chicago, 1965.

Neugarten, B. L., Moore, J. W., & Lowe, J. C. Age norms, age constraints, and adult socialization. *American Journal of Sociology*, 1965, *70*, 6.

Neugarten, B. L., & Weinstein, K. K. The changing American grandparent. *Journal of Marriage and the Family*, 1964, *26*, 199–206.

Neugarten, B. L., Wood, V., Kraines, R. J., & Loomis, B. Women's attitudes toward the menopause. *Vita Humana*, 1963, *6*, 140–151.

Neulinger, J. *To leisure: An introduction.* Boston: Allyn & Bacon, 1980. (a)

Neulinger, J. Introduction. In S. E. Iso-Ahola (Ed.), *Social and Psychological perspectives on leisure and recreation.* Springfield, Ill.: Charles C Thomas, 1980. (b)

Newcomb, T. M. *The acquaintance process.* New York: Holt, Rinehart & Winston, 1961.

Newman, B. M. Midlife development. In B. B. Wolman (Ed.), *Handbook of developmental psychology.* Englewood Cliffs, N.J.: Prentice-Hall, 1982.

Newsweek. The greying of America. February 28, 1977, pp. 50–65.

Nowak, C. Does youthfulness equal attractiveness? In L. Troll, J. Israel, & K. Israel (Eds.), *Looking ahead: A woman's guide to the problems and joys of growing old*. Englewood Cliffs, N.J.: Prentice-Hall, 1977.

Nucci, L. P., & Turiel, E. Social interactions and the development of social concepts in preschool children. *Child Development*, 1978, *49*, 400–407.

Nuessel, F. H. The language of ageism. *The Gerontologist*, 1982, *22*, 273–275.

Nunnally, J. L. The study of human change: Measurement, research strategies, and methods of analysis. In B. B. Wolman (Ed.), *Handbook of developmental psychology*. Englewood Cliffs, N.J.: Prentice-Hall, 1982.

Nydegger, C., & Mittemas, L. Transitions in fatherhood. *Generations*, 1979, *4*, 14–15.

Oakley, A. *Sociology of housework*. New York: Pantheon Books, 1974.

O'Neill, N., & O'Neill, G. The maturity myth. In D. Elkind & D. Hetzel (Eds.), *Readings in human development: Contemporary perspectives*. New York: Harper & Row, 1977.

Ordy, J. M. The nervous system, behavior, and aging: An interdisciplinary life-span approach. In J. M. Ordy & K. R. Brizzie (Eds.), *Neurobiology of aging: An interdisciplinary life-span approach*. New York: Plenum, 1975.

Orgel, L. E. The maintenance of the accuracy of protein synthesis and its relevance to aging. *Proceedings of the National Academy of Sciences*, 1963, *49*, 517–521.

Orlofsky, J. L. Intimacy status: Relationship to interpersonal perception. *Journal of Youth and Adolescence*, 1976, *5*, 73–88.

Orlofsky, J. L., Marcia, J. E., & Lesser, J. M. Ego identity status and the intimacy vs. isolation crisis of young adulthood. *Journal of Personality and Social Psychology*, 1973, *27*, 211–219.

Orwell, G. The art of Donald McGill. In *A collection of essays*. New York: Harcourt, Brace, [1946], 1963.

Owens, W. A., Jr. Age and mental abilities: A second adult follow-up. *Journal of Educational Psychology*, 1966, *51*, 311–325.

Palmore, E. The effects of aging on activities and attitudes. *The Gerontologist*, 1968, *8*, 259–263.

Palmore, E. Why do people retire? *International Journal of Aging and Human Development*, 1971, *2*, 269–283.

Palmore, E. Predictors of successful aging. *The Gerontologist*, 1979, *19*, 427–431.

Palmore, E., & Luikart, C. Health and social factors related to life satisfaction. In E. Palmore (Ed.), *Normal aging II*. Durham, N.C.: Duke University Press, 1974.

Papalia-Finley, D., Blackburn, J., Davis, E., Dellman, M., & Roberts, P. Training cognitive ability in the elderly—inability to replicate previous findings. *International Journal of Aging and Human Development*, 1980–1981, *12*, 111–117.

Parker, S. R. Work and leisure: Theory and fact. In J. T. Haworth & M. A. Smith (Eds.), *Work and leisure*. Princeton, N.J.: Princeton Book Co., 1975.

Parkes, C. M. *Bereavement: Studies of grief in adult life*. New York: International Universities Press, 1972.

Parks, R. D., & Swain, D. B. The father's role in infancy: A re-evaluation. *Family Coordinator*, 1976, *25*, 365–371.

Parks, R. D., & Swain, D. B. The family in early infancy: Social interactional and attitudinal analyses. Paper presented at the Society for Research in Child Development, New Orleans, March 1977.

Parr, J. The interaction of person and living environments. In L. W. Poon (Ed.), *Aging in the 1980s*. Washington, D.C.: American Psychological Association, 1980.

Paschkis, K. E., Rakoff, A. E., Cantarow, A., & Rupp, J. J. *Clinical endocrinology*. (3rd ed.) New York: Harper & Row, 1967.

Pattison, E. M. I suppose I may die someday. Pamphlet available from Forest Lawn, Glendale, Calif., undated.

Pattison, E. M. Attitudes toward death. In E. M. Pattison (Ed.), *The experience of dying*. Englewood, N.J.: Prentice-Hall, 1977. (a).

Pattison, E. M. The dying experience—retrospective analysis. In E. M. Pattison (Ed.), *The experience of dying*. Englewood Cliffs, N.J.: Prentice-Hall, 1977. (b).

Peacock, J. C., Rush, A. C., & Milkovich, G. T. Career stages: A partial test of Levinson's model of life/career stages. *Journal of Vocational Behavior*, 1980, *16*, 347–359.

Pearlin, L. Sex roles and depression. In N. Datan & L. Ginsberg (Eds.), *Life-span developmental psychology: Normative life crises*. New York: Academic Press, 1975.

Peck, R. Psychological developments in the second half of life. In B. L. Neugarten (Ed.), *Middle age and aging*. Chicago: University of Chicago Press, 1968.

Peskin, H., & Livson, N. Uses of the past in adult psychological health. In D. H. Eichorn, N. Haan, J. Clausen, M. Honzik, and P. Mussen (Eds.), *Present and past in middle life*. New York: Academic Press, 1981.

Peterson, J. A. *Married love in the middle years*. New York: Associated Press, 1968.

Pfeiffer, E. Psychopathology and social pathology. In J. E. Birren & K. W. Schaie (Eds.), *Handbook of the psychology of aging*. New York: Van Nostrand Reinhold, 1977.

Pfeiffer, E., & Davis, G. C. The use of leisure time in middle life. In E. Palmore (Ed.), *Normal aging II*. Durham, N.C.: Duke University Press, 1974.

Phillips, S. Career exploration in adulthood. *Journal of Vocational Behavior*, 1982, *20*, 129–140. (a).

Phillips, S. The development of career choices: The relationship between patterns of commitment and career outcomes in adulthood. *Journal of Vocational Behavior*, 1982, *20*, 141–152. (b).

Phillips, S., & Strohmer, D. C. Decision-making style and vocational maturity. *Journal of Vocational Behavior*, 1982, *20*, 215–222.

Piaget, J. Piaget's theory. In P. H. Mussen (Ed.), *Carmichael's Handbook of Child Psychology*. New York: Wiley, 1970.

Piaget, J. Intellectual evolution from adolescence to adulthood. *Human Development*, 1972, *15*, 1–12.

Pine, U. R., & Phillips, D. L. The cost of dying: A sociological analysis of funeral expenditures. *Social Problems*, 1970, *17*, 405–417.

Pineo, P. C. Disenchantment in the later years of marriage. *Marriage and Family Living*, 1961, *23*, 3–11.

Piotrkowski, C. S. *Work and the family system*. New York: Free Press, 1979.

Pollack, R. H., & Atkeson, B. M. A life-span approach to perceptual development. In P. B. Baltes (Ed.), *Life-span development and behavior*. Vol. 1. New York: Academic Press, 1978.

Poon, L., & Welford, A. T. A historical perspective. In L. W. Poon (Ed.), *Aging in the 1980s*. Washington, D.C.: American Psychological Association, 1980.

Pope, K. S. Defining and studying romantic love. In K. S. Pope (Ed.), *On loving and being loved*. San Francisco: Jossey-Bass, 1980.

Price-Williams, D. Concrete and formal operations. In R. H. Munroe, R. L. Munroe, & B. B. Whiting (Eds.), *Handbook of cross-cultural human development*. New York: Garland STM Press, 1981.

Propper, A. Relationship of maternal employment to adolescent roles, activities, and parental relationships. *Journal of Marriage and the Family*, 1972, *34*, 417–421.

Quinn, J. The extent and correlates of partial retirement. *The Gerontologist*, 1981, *21*, 634–643.

Rabbitt, P. Changes in problem-solving ability in old age. In J. E. Birren & K. W. Schaie (Eds.), *Handbook of the psychology of aging*. New York: Van Nostrand Reinhold, 1977.

Rapoport, R., & Rapoport, R. The dual-career family: A variant pattern and social change. *Human Relations*, 1969, *22*, 3–30.

Rapoport, R., & Rapoport, R. *Dual career families*. Baltimore: Penguin, 1971.

Rapoport, R., Rapoport, R., & Strelitz, Z. *Fathers, mothers, and society*. New York: Basic Books, 1977.

Rappoport, L. Naderizing methodology: Discussant's comments. In D. F. Hultsch (Ed.), *Implications of a dialectical perspective for research methodology. Human Development*, 1980, *23*, 217–267.

Raschke, H., & Raschke, V. Family conflict and children's self-concept: A comparison of intact and single-parent families. *Journal of Marriage and the Family*, 1979, *41*, 367–374.

Rathus, S. *Psychology*. New York: Holt, Rinehart & Winston, 1981.

Rea, M. P., Greenspoon, S., & Spilka, B. Physicians and the terminal patient. *Omega*, 1975, *6*, 291–302.

Reedy, M. N., Birren, J. E., & Schaie, K. W. Age and sex differences in satisfying love relationships across the life-span. *Human Development*, 1982, *24*, 52–66.

Rees, W. D., & Lutkins, S. G. The morality of the bereaved. *British Medical Journal*, 1967, *4*, 13–16.

Reese, H. W. Conceptions of the active organism. *Human Development*, 1976, *19*, 108–119.

Reese, H. W., & Overton, W. F. Models of development and theories of development. In L. R. Goulet & P. B. Baltes (Eds.), *Life-span development psychology: Research and theory*. New York: Academic Press, 1970.

Reinert, G. Prolegomena to a history of life-span developmental psychology. In P. B. Baltes & O. G. Brim, Jr. (Eds.), *Life-span development and behavior*. Vol. 2. New York: Academic Press, 1979.

Reiss, I. *Family systems in America*. (3rd ed.) New York: Holt, Rinehart & Winston, 1980.

Renne, K. S. Correlates of dissatisfaction in marriage. *Journal of Marriage and the Family*, 1970, *32*, 229–237.

Reuben, D. *Everything you always wanted to know about sex.* New York: McKay, 1969.

Rice, D. G. *Dual-career marriage.* New York: Free Press, 1979.

Richards, F. A., & Commons, M. L. Systematic, metasystematic, and cross-paradigmatic reasoning: A case for stages of reasoning beyond formal operations. In M. L. Commons, F. A. Richards & S. Armon (Eds.), *Beyond formal operations: Late adolescent and adult cognitive development.* New York: Praeger, 1982.

Ridley, C. A. Exploring the impact of work satisfaction and involvement on marital interaction when both partners are employed. *Journal of Marriage and the Family*, 1973, *35*, 229–237.

Riegel, K. F. The predictors of death and longevity in longitudinal research. In E. Palmore & F. C. Jeffers (Eds.), *Prediction of life span.* Lexington, Mass.: Heath, 1971.

Riegel, K. F. Dialectic operations: The final period of cognitive development. *Human Development*, 1973, *16*, 346–370.

Riegel, K. F. Adult life crises: A dialectic interpretation of development. In N. Datan & L. H. Ginsberg (Eds.), *Life-span developmental psychology: Normative life crises.* New York: Academic Press, 1975. (a)

Riegel, K. F. From traits and equilibrium toward developmental dialectics. In W. J. Arnold & J. K. Cole (Eds.), *1974–1975 Nebraska symposium on motivation.* Lincoln: University of Nebraska Press, 1975. (b)

Riegel, K. F. History of psychological gerontology. In J. E. Birren & K. W. Schaie (Eds.), *Handbook of the psychology of aging.* New York: Van Nostrand Reinhold, 1977.

Riegel, K. F. Three paradigms of developmental psychology. In A. R. Buss (Ed.), *Psychology in social context.* New York: Irvington, 1979.

Riegel, K. F., & Riegel, R. M. A study of attitudes and interests during later years of life. *Vita Humana*, 1960, *3*, 177–206.

Riegel, K. F., & Riegel, R. M. Development, drop, and death. *Developmental Psychology*, 1972, *6*, 306–319.

Riegel, K. F., Riegel, R. M., & Meyer, G. A study of the dropout rates of longitudinal research on aging and the prediction of death. *Journal of Personality and Social Psychology*, 1967, *5*, 342–348.

Riley, M. W., & Foner, A. F. *Aging and society: An inventory of research findings.* Vol. 1. New York: Russell Sage Foundation, 1968.

Risman, B., Hill, C. T., Rubin, Z., & Peplau, L. A. Living together in college: Implications for courtship. *Journal of Marriage and the Family*, 1981, *42*, 77–117.

Ritzer, G. *Working: Conflict and change.* (2nd ed.) Englewood Cliffs, N.J.: Prentice-Hall, 1977.

Robbins, S. L. *Pathology.* (3rd ed.) Philadelphia: Saunders, 1967.

Robertson, J. F. Grandmotherhood: A study of role conceptions. *Journal of Marriage and the Family*, 1977, *39*, 165–174.

Rockstein, M. The biology of aging in humans: An overview. In R. Goldman & M. Rockstein (Eds.), *The physiology and pathology of human aging.* New York:

Academic Press, 1975.

Roe, A. *The psychology of occupations*. New York: Wiley, 1956.

Roe, A. Early determinants of vocational choice. *Journal of Counseling Psychology*, 1957, *4*, 212–217.

Roiphe, A. *Can you have everything and still want babies?* New York: Brandt and Brandt Literary Agency, 1975.

Rollins, B. C., & Feldman, H. Marital satisfaction over the life cycle. *Journal of Marriage and the Family*, 1970, *32*, 20–28.

Rollins, B. C., & Galligan, R. The developing child and marital satisfaction of parents. In R. Lerner & G. Spanier (Eds.), *Child influences on marital and family interaction*. New York: Academic Press, 1978.

Rose, C. L., & Mogey, J. M. Aging and preference for later retirement. *International Journal of Aging and Human Development*, 1972, *3*, 45–62.

Rosenberg, S. D., & Farrell, M. P. Identity and crisis in middle-aged men. *International Journal of Aging and Human Development*, 1976, *7*, 153–170.

Rosenman, R. H., Friedman, M., Straus, R., Jenkins, C. D., Zyzanski, S., Jr., Wurm, M., & Kositchek, R. Coronary heart disease in the western collaborative group study: A follow-up experience of four and one-half years. *Journal of Chronic Diseases*, 1970, *23*, 173–190.

Rosenthal, R. *Experimenter effects in behavioral research*. New York: Appleton-Century-Crofts, 1966.

Rosenthal, R. Interpersonal expectations: Effects of the experimenter's hypothesis. In R. Rosenthal and R. Rosnow (Eds.), *Artifact in behavioral research*. New York: Academic Press, 1969.

Rosow, I. *Social integration of the aged*. New York: Free Press, 1967.

Rosow, I. Institutional position of the aged. In S. H. Zarit (Ed.), *Readings in aging and death: Contemporary perspectives*. New York: Harper & Row, 1977.

Rossi, A. S. Transition to parenthood. *Journal of Marriage and the Family*, 1968, *30*, 26–39.

Rossman, I. Anatomic and body composition changes with aging. In C. E. Finch & L. Hayflick (Eds.), *Handbook of the biology of aging*. New York: Van Nostrand Reinhold, 1977.

Roy, D., & Roy, R. *Honest sex*. New York: New American Library, 1968.

Rubin, L. *Shared intimacies*. New York: Harper & Row, 1983.

Rubin, Z. *Liking and loving: An invitation to social psychology*. New York: Holt, Rinehart & Winston, 1973.

Rubin, Z., Peplau, L. A., & Hill, C. T. Becoming intimate: The development of male–female relationships. Working manuscript, 1976.

Ruch, T., & Fulton, J. (Eds.), *Medical physiology and biophysics*. Philadelphia: Saunders, 1960.

Rupp, R. R. Understanding the problems of presbycusis: An overview. *Geriatrics*, 1970, *25*, 100.

Rusin, M. J., & Siegler, I. C. Personality differences between participants and dropouts in a longitudinal aging study. Paper presented at the 28th Annual Meeting of the Gerontological Society, Louisville, Ky.: Oct., 1975.

Russell, C. S. Transition to parenthood: Problems and gratifications. *Journal of Marriage and the Family*, 1974, *36*, 294–301.

Ryder, C. F., & Ross, D. M. Terminal care: Issues and alternatives. In R. Fulton, E. Markusen, G. Owen, and J. L. Scheiber (Eds.), *Death and dying: Challenge and change*. San Francisco: Boyd & Fraser, 1981.

Ryon, R. Seniors want—some surprising things. *Los Angeles Times*, January 22, 1978, Part VIII, pp. 1, 24.

Sacher, G. A. On longevity regarded as organized behavior: The role of brain structure. In R. Kastenbaum (Ed.), *Contributions to the psychobiology of aging*. New York: Springer, 1965.

Sanders, J. L., Sterns, H. L., Smith, M., & Sanders, R. E. Modification of concept identification performance in older adults. *Developmental Psychology*, 1975, *11*, 824–829.

Sanders, R. E., Clausen, J. A., Mayes, G. J., & Sielski, K. A. Enhancement of conjunctive concept attainment in older adults. *Developmental Psychology*, 1976, *12*, 485–486.

Saunders, C. *The moment of truth: Care of the dying person*. Cleveland: Case Western University, 1969.

Saunders, C. St. Christopher's hospice. In E. Shneidman (Ed.), *Death: Contemporary perspectives*. Palo Alto, Calif.: Mayfield, 1976.

Saunders, C. Should a patient know? In R. Fulton, E. Markusen, G. Owen, & J. L. Scheiber (Eds.), *Death and dying: Challenge and change*. San Francisco: Boyd & Fraser, 1981.

Sawhill, I. On the way to full equality. In A. F. Cahn (Ed.), *Women in the U.S. labor force*. New York: Praeger, 1979.

Schaie, K. W. Age changes and age differences. *The Gerontologist*, 1967, *7*, 128–132.

Schaie, K. W. A reinterpretation of age-related changes in cognitive structure. In L. R. Goulet & P. B. Baltes (Eds.), *Life-span developmental psychology: Research and theory*. New York: Academic Press, 1970.

Schaie, K. W. Developmental processes and aging. In C. Eisdorfer & M. P. Lawton (Eds.), *The psychology of adult development and aging*. Washington, D.C.: American Psychological Association, 1973.

Schaie, K. W. Quasi-experimental research designs in the psychology of aging. In J. E. Birren & K. W. Schaie (Eds.), *Handbook of the psychology of aging*. New York: Van Nostrand Reinhold, 1977.

Schaie, K. W. The primary mental abilities in adulthood: An exploration in the development of psychometric intelligence. In P. B. Baltes & O. G. Brim, Jr. (Eds.), *Life-span development and behavior*. Vol. 2. New York: Academic Press, 1979.

Schaie, K. W., & Hertzog, C. Longitudinal methods. In B. B. Wolman (Ed.), *Handbook of developmental psychology*. Englewood Cliffs, N.J.: Prentice-Hall, 1982.

Schaie, K. W., Labouvie, G., & Buech, B. Generational and cohort-specific differences in adult cognitive functioning. *Developmental Psychology*, 1973, *9*, 151–166.

Schaie, K. W., & Parham, I. A. Stability of adult personality: Fact or fable? *Journal of*

Personality and Social Psychology, 1976, *36*, 146–158.

Schlesinger, B. One-parent families in Great Britain. *Family Coordinator*, 1977, *26*, 139–141.

Schmidt, M. G. Exchange and power in special settings for the aged. *International Journal of Aging and Human Development*, 1981–1982, *14*, 157–166.

Schmitt, R. L. Symbolic mortality in ordinary contexts: Impediments to the nuclear ear. *Omega*, 1982–1983, *13*, 95–116.

Schneider, D. J. *Social psychology*. Reading, Mass.: Addison-Wesley, 1976.

Schonfield, D. Who is stereotyping whom? *The Gerontologist*, 1982, *22*, 269–271.

Schuknecht, H. F., & Igarashi, M. Pathology of slowly progressive sensorineural deafness. *Transactions: American Academy of Ophthalmology and Otolaryngology*, 1964, *68*, 222–242.

Seiber, J. E. A social learning theory to morality. In M. Windmiller, N. Lambert, & E. Turiel (Eds.), *Moral development and socialization*. Boston: Allyn & Bacon, 1980.

Seidman, A. *Working women: A study in paid jobs*. Boulder, Colo.: Westview Press, 1978.

Self, P. The further evolution of the parental imperative. In N. Datan & L. Ginsberg (Eds.), *Life-span developmental psychology: Normative life crises*. New York: Academic Press, 1975.

Selmanowitz, O. J., Rizer, R. L., & Orentreich, N. Aging of the skin and its appendages. In C. E. Finch & L. Hayflick (Eds.), *Handbook of the biology of aging*. New York: Van Nostrand Reinhold, 1977.

Selye, H. *The stress of life*. New York: McGraw-Hill, 1976.

Selzer, S. C., & Denney, N. W. Conservation abilities among middle-aged and elderly adults. *Aging and Human Development*, 1980, *11*, 135–146.

Shaw, I. *Bread upon the waters*. New York: Delacorte, 1981.

Shanas, E. Adjustment to retirement. In F. M. Carp (Ed.), *Retirement*. New York: Behavioral Publications, 1972.

Sheehy, G. *Passages: The predictable crises of adult life*. New York: Dutton, 1976.

Sheehy, G. The mentor connection. In D. Elkind & D. C. Hetzel (Eds.), *Readings in human development: Contemporary perspectives*. New York: Harper & Row, 1977.

Sheehy, G. *Pathfinders*. New York: Dutton, 1981.

Sheppard, H. Work and retirement. In R. H. Binstock & E. Shanas (Eds.), *Handbook of aging and the social sciences*. New York: Van Nostrand Reinhold, 1977.

Sheppard, M. L. *New perspectives on older workers*. Kalamazoo, Mich.: Upjohn Institute for Employment Research, 1971.

Sherman, S. R. Leisure activities in retirement housing. *Journal of Gerontology*, 1974, *29*, 325–335.

Sherwood, S., Greer, D. S., Morris, J. N., & Sherwood, C. C. *The Highland Heights experiment*. Washington, D.C.: U.S. Department of Housing and Urban Development, 1972.

Shneidman, E. S. *Deaths of man*. New York: Quadrangle, 1973.

Shneidman, E. Post-vention and the survivor-victim. In E. Shneidman (Ed.), *Death: Current perspectives*. Palo Alto, Calif: Mayfield, 1976.

Shuttlesworth, G., Rubin, A., & Duffy, M. Families vs. institutions: Incongruent role expectations in the nursing home. *The Gerontologist*, 1982, *22*, 200–207.

Siegel, A. E. The working mother: A review. *Cognitive Development*, 1963, *34*, 513–542.

Siegler, I. C. The terminal drop hypothesis: Fact or artifact? *Experimental Aging Research*, 1975, *1*, 169.

Siegler, I. C., & Edelman, C. D. Age discrimination in employment: The implications for psychologists. Paper presented at the meeting of the Western Psychological Association, San Francisco, April 1977.

Siegler, I. C., Nowlin, J. B., & Blumenthal, J. A. Health and behavior: Methodological considerations for adult development and aging. In L. W. Poon (Ed.), *Aging in the 1980s*. Washington, D.C.: American Psychological Association, 1980.

Silverman, P. R. Widowhood and preventive intervention. In S. H. Zarit (Ed.), *Readings in aging and death: Contemporary perspectives*. New York: Harper & Row, 1977.

Sinclair, D. *Human growth after birth*. London: Oxford University Press, 1969.

Sinnott, J. D. Sex-role inconsistency, biology and successful aging. *The Gerontologist*, 1977, *17*, 459–464.

Sinnott, J. D. Correlates of sex roles of older adults. *Journal of Gerontology*, 1982, *37*, 587–594.

Sistrunk, F., & McDavid, J. W. Sex variable in conforming behavior. *Journal of Personality and Social Psychology*, 1971, *17*, 200–207.

Skinner, B. F. Some contributions of an experimental analysis of behavior to psychology as a whole. *American Psychologists*, 1953, *8*, 69–78.

Skolnick, A. *The intimate environment: Exploring marriage and family*. (2nd ed.) Boston: Little, Brown, 1978.

Skolnick, A. Married lives: Longitudinal perspectives on marriage. In D. Eichorn, N. Haan, J. Clausen, M. Honzik, & P. Mussen (Eds.), *Present and past in middle life*. New York: Academic Press, 1981.

Smart, J. C. Distinctive career orientations of Holland personality types. *Journal of Vocational Behavior*, 1976, *8*, 313–319.

Smith, A. Foreword. In D. Heath, *Maturity and competence: A Transcultural View*. New York: Halsted Press, 1977.

Smith, A. D. Age differences in encoding, storage, and retrieval. In L. W. Poon, J. L. Fozard, L. S. Cremak, D. Arenberg, & L. W. Thompson (Eds.), *New directions in memory and aging: Proceedings of the George Talland Memorial Conference*. Hillsdale, N.J.: Lawrence Erlbaum, 1980.

Smith, C. Use of drugs in the aged. *Johns Hopkins Medical Journal*, 1979, *145*, 61–64.

Snyder, E. A study of homogamy and marital selectivity. In M. E. Lasswell & T. E. Lasswell (Eds.), *Love, marriage, and family: A developmental approach*. Glenview, Ill.: Scott, Foresman, 1973.

Snyder, M., & Swann, W. B., Jr. Behavioral confirmation in social interaction. *Journal of Experimental Social Psychology*, 1978, *14*, 148–162. (a).

Snyder, M., & Swann, W. B., Jr. Hypothesis testing in social interaction. *Journal of Personality and Social Psychology*, 1978, *36*, 1202–1212. (b).

Sobel, H. Aging theory: Cellular and extracellular modalities. In R. Kastenbaum

(Ed.), *Contributions to the psychobiology of aging*. New York: Springer, 1965.

Soldo, B. J. The living arrangements of the elderly in the near future. In J. G. Marsh (Ed.), *Aging: Social change*. New York: Academic Press, 1981.

Sonnenborn, T. The origin, evolution, nature and causes of aging. In J. Behnke, C. Finch, & G. Moment (Eds.), *The biology of aging*. New York: Plenum, 1978.

Sontag, S. The double standard of aging. In L. R. Allman & D. T. Jaffe (Eds.), *Reading in adult psychology: Contemporary perspectives*. New York: Harper & Row, 1977.

Sorensen, R. C. *Adolescent sexuality in contemporary America*. New York: World, 1973.

Spock, B. *Baby and child care*. New York: Pocket Books, 1974.

Srole, L., Langner, T. S., Michael, S. T., Opler, M. K., & Rennie, T. A. C. *Mental health in the metropolis: The midtown Manhattan study*. New York: McGraw-Hill, 1962.

Stafford, R., Blackman, E., & Debona, P. The division of labor among cohabiting and married couples. *Journal of Marriage and the Family*, 1977, *39*, 43–58.

Stannard, D. E. Growing up and growing old: Dilemmas of aging in bureaucratic America. In S. F. Spicker, K. M. Woodard, & D. D. Van Tassel (Eds.), *Aging and the elderly*. Atlantic Highlands, N.J.: Humanities Press, 1978.

Stephens, W. *The family in cross-cultural perspective*. New York: Holt, Rinehart & Winston, 1963.

Stern, W. Psychologie der frühen Kindheit bis zum sechsten lebensjahr. Leipzig: Quelle & Meyer, 1914.

Stevens-Long, J. Planning a funeral. Working manuscript. Los Angeles: California State University, 1978.

Stevens-Long, J., & Cobb, N. *Adolescence and early adulthood*. Palo Alto, Calif.: Mayfield, 1983.

Stinnett, N., Carter, L. M., & Montgomery, J. E. Older persons' perceptions of their marriages. *Journal of Marriage and the Family*, 1972, *34*, 665–670.

Stinnett, N., & Walters, J. *Relationships in marriage and family*. New York: Macmillan, 1977.

Storr, C. Freud and the concept of parental guilt. In J. Miller (Ed.), *Freud: The man, his world, his influence*. Boston: Little, Brown, 1972.

Strauss, A. L., & Glaser, B. G. *Anguish: A case history of a dying trajectory*. Mill Valley, Calif.: Sociology Press, 1970.

Strehler, B. L. The future and aging research. In A. Cherkin & C. Finch et al. (Eds.), *Physiology and cell biology of aging*. (Aging Series, Vol. 8.) New York: Raven Press, 1979.

Streib, G. F., & Schneider, C. J. *Retirement in American society: Impact and progress*. Ithaca, N.Y.: Cornell University Press, 1971.

Strong, E. K., Jr. *Vocational interests of men and women*. Stanford, Calif.: Stanford University Press, 1943.

Stroud, J. G. Women's careers: Work, family and personality. In D. Eichorn, N. Haan, J. Clausen, M. Honzik, & P. Mussen (Eds.), *Present and past in middle life*. New York: Academic Press, 1981.

Struyk, R. The changing housing and neighborhood environment of the elderly: A look at the year 2000. In J. G. Marsh (Ed.), *Aging: Social change*. New York: Academic Press, 1981.

Super, D. E. *The psychology of careers*. New York: Harper & Row, 1957.

Sussman, M. An analytic model for the sociological study of retirement. In F. M. Carp (Ed.), *Retirement*. New York: Behavioral Publications, 1972.

Sussman, M. B. Family life of old people. In R. H. Binstock & E. Shanas (Eds.), *Handbook of aging and the social sciences*. New York: Van Nostrand Reinhold, 1977.

Swanson, E. A., & Bennett, T. F. Degree of closeness: Does it affect the bereaved's attitudes toward selected funeral practices? *Omega*, 1982–1983, *13*, 43–50.

Talbert, G. Aging of the reproductive system. In C. E. Finch & L. Hayflick (Eds.) *Handbook of the Biology of Aging*. New York: Van Nostrand, 1977.

Tallmer, M., & Kutner, B. Disengagement and the stresses of aging. *Journal of Gerontology*, 1969, *24*, 70–75.

Tavris, C., & Sadd, S. *The Redbook report on female sexuality*. New York: Delacorte, 1977.

Taylor, D. A. Some aspects of the development of interpersonal relations: Social penetration process. *Journal of Social Psychology*, 1968, *75*, 79–90.

Teague, M. L. Aging and leisure: A social psychological perspective. In S. E. Iso-Ahola (Ed.), *Social psychological perspectives on leisure and recreation*. Springfield, Ill.: Charles C Thomas, 1980.

Terkel, S. *Working*. New York: Pantheon Books, 1974.

Tesch, S., & Whitbourne, S. Friendship, social interaction and subjective well-being of older men in an institutional setting. *International Journal of Aging and Human Development*, 1981, *13*, 317–327.

Theorell, T., & Rahe, R. H. Psychosocial factors and myocardial infarction I: An inpatient study in Sweden. *Journal of Psychosomatic Research*, 1974, *15*, 25–31.

Thomae, H. Theory of aging and cognitive theory of personality. *Human Development*, 1970, *13*, 1–16.

Thomae, H. The concept of development and life-span developmental psychology. In P. B. Baltes & O. G. Brim, Jr. (Eds.), *Life-span development and behavior*. Vol. 2. New York: Academic Press, 1979.

Thomas, L. E. Sexuality and aging: Essential vitamin or popcorn? *The Gerontologist*, 1982, *22*, 240–243.

Till, R. E., & Walsh, D. A. Encoding and retrieval factors in adult memory for implicational sentences. *Journal of Learning and Verbal Behavior*, 1980, *19*, 1–16.

Time. How long 'till equality? July 12, 1982, pp. 20–29.

Timiras, P. S. *Developmental physiology and aging*. New York: Macmillan, 1972.

Timiras, P. S., & Meisami, E. Changes in gonadal function. In P. S. Timiras, *Developmental physiology and aging*. New York: Macmillan, 1972.

Timiras, P. S., & Vernadakis, A. Structural, biochemical, and functional aging of the nervous system. In P. S. Timiras, *Developmental physiology and aging*. New York: Macmillan, 1972.

Toffler, A. *Future shock*. New York: Random House, 1970.

Toffler, A. *The third wave*. New York: Morrow, 1980.

Tonna, E. A. Aging of skeletal-dental systems and supporting tissues. In C. E. Finch & L. Hayflick (Eds.), *Handbook of the biology of aging*. New York: Van Nostrand Reinhold, 1977.

Treat, N. J., & Reese, H. Age, pacing, and imagery in paired-associate learning. *Developmental Psychology*, 1976, *12*, 119–124.

Troll, L. E. The family in later life: A decade review. *Journal of Marriage and the Family*, 1971, *33*, 263–290.

Troll, L. E. Poor, dumb, and ugly. In L. E. Troll, J. Israel, & K. Israel (Eds.), *Looking ahead: A woman's guide to the problems and joys of growing old*. Englewood Cliffs, N.J.: Prentice-Hall, 1977.

Troll, L. E. Grandparenting. In L. W. Poon (Ed.), *Aging in the 1980s*. Washington, D.C.: American Psychological Association, 1980.

Troll, L. E., & Bengston, V. Intergenerational relations throughout the life-span. In B. B. Wolman (Ed.), *Handbook of developmental psychology*. Englewood Cliffs, N.J.: Prentice-Hall, 1982.

Troll, L. E., & Smith, J. Attachment through the life span: Some questions about dyadic bonds among adults. *Human Development*, 1976, *19*, 135–182.

Turner, B. F. Sex related differences in aging. In B. B. Wolman (Ed.), *Handbook of developmental psychology*. Englewood Cliffs, N.J.: Prentice-Hall, 1982.

Udry, J. R. Marital alternatives and marital disruption. *Journal of Marriage and the Family*, 1982, *43*, 889–899.

Uhlenberg, P. Demographic change and problems of the aged. In M. W. Riley (Ed.), *Aging from birth to death*. Boulder, Colo.: Westview Press, 1979.

Underwood, B. J., & Shaughnessy, J. S. *Experimentation in psychology*. New York: Wiley, 1975.

Updike, J. *A month of Sundays*. New York: Knopf, 1975.

Urban, H. The concept of development from a systems approach. In P. B. Baltes (Ed.), *Life-span development and behavior*. Vol. 1. New York: Academic Press, 1978.

U.S. Commission on Civil Rights. *Social indicators of equality for minorities and women*. Washington, D.C.: U.S. Government Printing Office, 1978.

U.S. Department of Commerce. *Population characteristics: Profile of the United States: 1974*. (Current Population Reports, Series P-20, No. 279.) Washington, D.C.: U.S. Government Printing Office, March 1975.

U.S. Department of Commerce, Bureau of the Census. *Characteristics of the population*. Vol. 1. Washington, D.C.: U.S. Government Printing Office, 1973.

U.S. Department of Commerce, Bureau of the Census. *Population characteristics*. (Current Population Reports, Series P-20, No. 312.) Washington, D.C.: U.S. Government Printing Office, 1977.

U.S. Department of Commerce, Bureau of the Census. *Characteristics of American children and youth: 1976*. (Current Population Reports, Series P-23, No. 66.) Washington, D.C.: U.S. Government Printing Office, 1978.

U.S. Department of Commerce, Bureau of the Census. *Population estimates and projection series*. (Current Population Reports, Series P-25, No. 889.) Washington, D.C.: U.S. Government Printing Office, 1980.

U.S. Department of Commerce, Bureau of the Census. *Population profile of the*

United States: 1980. (Current Population Reports, Series P-20, No. 350.) Washington, D.C.: U.S. Government Printing Office, 1981.

U.S. Department of Health, Education, and Welfare. *Work in America: Report of the special task force to the Secretary of Health, Education, and Welfare*. (Upjohn Institute for Employment Research.) Cambridge: Massachusetts Institute of Technology Press, 1973.

U.S. Department of Health, Education, and Welfare. *Facts about older Americans, 1976*. Washington, D.C.: U.S. Government Printing Office, 1976.

U.S. Public Health Service. *Vital statistics of the United States, 1970*. Vol. 2. *Mortality Part A*. Rockville, Md.: U.S. Department of Health, Education, and Welfare, Public Health Service, 1974.

Vaillant, G. E. *Adaptation to life*. Boston: Little, Brown, 1977.

Vaillant, G. E., & McArthur, C. C. Natural history of male psychological health: The adult life cycle from eighteen to fifty. *Seminars in Psychiatry*, 1972, *4*, 415–427.

Van den Daele, L. D. Ego development and preferential judgment in life-span perspective. In N. Datan & L. Ginsberg (Eds.), *Life-span developmental psychology: Normative life crises*. New York: Academic Press, 1975.

Van den Daele, L. D. Formal models of development. In K. F. Riegel & J. A. Meacham (Eds.), *The developing individual in a changing world*. Chicago: Aldine, 1976.

Van Maanen, J. Summary: Toward a theory of the career. In J. Van Maanen (Ed.), *Organizational careers: Some new perspectives*. New York: Wiley, 1977.

Van Maanen, J., & Schein, E. H. Career development. In J. R. Hackman & J. L. Suttle (Eds.), *Improving life at work*. Santa Monica, Calif.: Goodyear, 1977.

Veatch, R. M. Brain death. In E. Shneidman (Ed.), *Death: Current perspectives*. (3rd ed.) Palo Alto, Calif.: Mayfield, 1984.

Veevers, J. E. *Childless by choice*. Toronto: Butterworth, 1980.

Veroff, J., Douvan, E., & Kulka, R. A. *The inner American: A self-portrait from 1957–1976*. New York: Basic Books, 1981.

Vonnegut, K. *Slaughterhouse-Five*. New York: Delacorte, 1969.

Walford, R. L. Immunology and aging. In R. Kastenbaum (Ed.), *Contributions to the psychobiology of aging*. New York: Springer, 1965.

Wallerstein, J. S., & Kelly, J. B. The effects of parental divorce: The adolescent experience. In E. J. Anthony & C. Koupernik (Eds.), *The child in his family: Children at psychiatric risk*. Vol. 3. New York: Wiley, 1974.

Walsh, D. Age differences in learning and memory. In D. S. Woodruff & J. E. Birren (Eds.), *Aging: Scientific perspectives and social issues*. New York: Van Nostrand, 1975.

Walsh, D., Krauss, I., & Regnier, V. Spatial abilities, environmental knowledge and neighborhood of the elderly. In L. Leben, A. Patterson, & N. Newcombe (Eds.), *Spatial representation and behavior across the life span*. New York: Academic Press, in press.

Walster, E., Walster, G. W., & Berscheid, E. *Equity: Theory and research*. Boston: Allyn & Bacon, 1978.

Walster, E., Walster, G. W., & Traupmann, J. Equity and premarital sex. *Journal of Personality and Social Psychology*, 1978, *36*, 82–92.

Walters, J., & Stinnett, N. Parent-child relationships: A decade of research. *Journal of Marriage and the Family*, 1971, *33*, 70–118.

Wanderer, Z., & Cabot, T. *Letting go*. New York: Warner Books, 1979.

Wang, J. S., & Busse, E. W. EEG of healthy old persons. In E. Palmore (Ed.), *Normal aging II*. Durham, N.C.: Duke University Press, 1974.

Wanous, J. P. *Organizational entry*. Reading, Mass.: Addison-Wesley, 1980.

Wapner, S., Werner, H., & Comalli, P. E. Perception of part-whole relationships in middle and old age. *Journal of Gerontology*, 1960, *15*, 412–416.

Watson, J. D., & Crick, F. H. Molecular structure of nucleic acids: A structure for deoxyribose nucleic acids. *Nature*, 1953, *171*, 737–738.

Weinberg, S. Measurement of stressful events associated with the transition to parenthood. Paper presented at the convention of the American Psychological Association, New York, August 1979.

Weiner, M. F. Healthy and pathological love: A psychodynamic view. In K. S. Pope (Ed.), *On loving and being loved*. San Francisco: Jossey-Bass, 1980.

Weintraub, W., & Aronson, H. A survey of patients in classical psychoanalysis: Some vital statistics. *Journal of Nervous and Mental Disorders*, 1968, *146*, 98–102.

Weisman, A. D. *On dying and denying: A psychiatric study of terminality*. New York: Behavioral Publications, 1972.

Weiss, R. S. *Marital separation*. New York: Basic Books, 1975.

Welford, A. T. Psychomotor performance. In J. E. Birren (Ed.), *Handbook of aging and the individual*. Chicago: University of Chicago Press, 1959.

Welford, A. T. Motor performance. In J. E. Birren & K. W. Schaie (Eds.), *Handbook of the psychology of aging*. New York: Van Nostrand Reinhold, 1977.

West, S., & Borgatta, E. Retirement communities. In N. McCluskey & E. Borgatta (Eds.), *Aging and retirement*. Beverly Hills, Calif.: Sage, 1981.

Wetherick, N. E. The inferential basis of concept attainment. *British Journal of Psychology*, 1966, *5*, 61–69.

Wetherick, N. E. The psychology of aging. *Occupational Therapy*, 1969, *32*, 15–17.

Wheeler, H. Closing the generation gap. In E. Pfeiffer (Ed.), *Successful aging: A conference report*. Durham, N.C.: Duke University Center for the Study of Aging and Human Development, 1974.

Whitbourne, S. K., & Waterman, A. S. Psychosocial development during the adult years: Age and cohort comparison. *Developmental Psychology*, 1979, *15*, 373–378.

White, R. *Lives in progress: A study of the natural growth of personality*. (3rd ed.) New York: Holt, Rinehart & Winston, 1975.

Whitehurst, R. N. Adultery as an extension of normal behavior: The case of the American upper-middle-class male. Paper presented at the National Council on Family Relations, Minneapolis, October 1966.

Whyte, W. H., Jr. *The organization man*. New York: Simon & Schuster, 1956.

Willis, S. L., & Baltes, P. B. Intelligence in adulthood and aging: Contemporary issues. In L. W. Poon (Ed.), *Aging in the 1980s*. Washington, D.C.: American Psychological Association, 1980.

Winch, R. F. Complementary needs and related notions about voluntary mate selection. In R. F. Winch & G. B. Spanier (Eds.), *Selected studies in marriage and the family*. New York: Holt, Rinehart & Winston, 1974.

Windley, P. G., & Scheidt, R. J. Person-environment dialectics: Implications for competent functioning in old age. In L. W. Poon (Ed.), *Aging in the 1980s*. Washington, D.C.: American Psychological Association, 1980.

Wolf, E. Glare and age. *Archives of Ophthalmology*, 1960, *64*, 502–514.

Wolman, B. B. (Ed.) *Handbook of developmental psychology*. Englewood Cliffs, N.J.: Prentice-Hall, 1982.

Woodruff, D. Biofeedback control of the EEG alpha rhythm and its effect on reaction time in the young and old. Doctoral dissertation, University of Southern California, 1972.

Wortis, R. P. The acceptance of the concept of maternal role by behavioral scientists: Its effect on women. *American Journal of Orthopsychiatry*, 1971, *41*, 733–746.

Young, A. The high school class of 1972: More work, fewer in college. *Monthly Labor Review*, June 1973, pp. 26–32.

Zarit, S. H. (Ed.) Readings in aging and death: Contemporary perspectives. New York: Harper and Row, 1977.

Zelnick, M., & Kantner, J. F. Sexual and contraceptive experiences of young married women in the United States, 1976 and 1971. *Family Planning Perspectives*, 1977, *9*, 55–71.

Zelnick, M., & Kantner, J. F. Reasons for nonuse of contraception by sexually active women aged 15–19. *Family Planning Perspectives*, 1979, *11*, 289–296.

Zelnick, M., & Kantner, J. F. Sexual activity, contraceptive use and pregnancy among metropolitan area teenagers, 1971–1979. *Family Planning Perspectives*, 1980, *12*, 230–237.

Ziajka, A. The black youth's self-concept. In W. Looft (Ed.), *Developmental psychology: A book of readings*. Hillsdale, Ill.: Dryden Press, 1972.

Zigler, E. Metatheoretical issues in developmental psychology. In M. Marx, *Theories in contemporary psychology*. New York: Macmillan, 1964.

Ziskin, J., & Ziskin, M. *The extramarital sex contract*. Los Angeles: Nash, 1973.

Author Index

Subject Index